The Holocaust and World War II Almanac

The Holocaust and World War II Almanac

Volume 2

PEGGY SAARI
AARON MAURICE SAARI
Editors

KATHLEEN J. EDGAR
ELLICE ENGDAHL
Coordinating Editors

GALE GROUP

Detroit
New York
San Francisco
London
Boston
Woodbridge, CT

Edited by Peggy Saari and Aaron Maurice Saari

Staff

Kathleen J. Edgar, *Senior Coordinating Editor*
Ellice Engdahl, *Coordinating Editor*

Julie Carnagie, Elizabeth Des Chenes, Elizabeth Manar, Christine Slovey, *Contributing Editors*
Barbara C. Bigelow, Susan E. Edgar, George Feldman, Kelly King Howes, Lorie Jenkins McElroy, Mary Kay Rosteck, Linda Schmittroth, Christine Tomassini, *Contributing Writers*
Debra M. Kirby, *Managing Editor*
Thomas Romig, *Program Director*

Rita Wimberley, *Senior Buyer*
Dorothy Maki, *Manufacturing Manager*
Evi Seoud, *Assistant Manager, Composition Purchasing and Electronic Prepress*
Mary Beth Trimper, *Manager, Composition and Electronic Prepress*

Debra J. Freitas, *Permissions Associate*
Cynthia Baldwin, *Art Director*
Barbara J. Yarrow, *Manager, Imaging and Multimedia Content*

Marco Di Vita, Graphix Group, *Typesetting*
Laura Exner, XNR Productions, Inc., *Cartographer*
Katherine Clymer, *Indexer*

Library of Congress Cataloging-in-Publication Data

The Holocaust and World War II Almanac / editors, Peggy Saari, Aaron Maurice Saari; coordinating editors, Kathleen J. Edgar, Ellice Engdahl
   p. cm.
  Includes bibliographical references and index.
  ISBN 0-7876-5018-8 (set: hardcover)—ISBN 0-7876-5019-6 (v.1)—ISBN 0-7876-5020-X (v.2)—ISBN 0-7876-5063-3 (v.3)
  1. Holocaust, Jewish (1939-1945). 2. World War, 1939-1945. 3. Holocaust, Jewish (1939-1945)—Biography. 4. World War, 1939-1945—Biography. I. Saari, Peggy. II. Saari, Aaron Maurice.

  D804.17.H65 2000
  940.53'18—dc21

00-046647

Front cover photos reproduced by permission of Corbis Corporation [Bellevue], Hulton Getty/Liaison Agency, and AP/Wide World Photos; others from Main Commission for the Investigation of Nazi War Crimes and National Archives and Records Administration.

Printed in the United States of America
10 9 8 7 6 5 4 3 2 1

Table of Contents

Advisory Board

The editors would like to thank the following members of *The Holocaust and World War II Almanac* advisory board for their invaluable assistance.

Armando Delicato majored in history as an undergraduate at the University of Detroit and earned a Masters of Arts in twentieth-century European history at Wayne State University. After teaching history at public schools and at community colleges in Michigan, he earned a degree in library science and is currently a media specialist at North Farmington High School in Michigan.

William J. Munday is a U.S. Navy veteran who has worked or volunteered at various museums and historical sites throughout the country. A military historian, he has studied the subject for more than thirty years. He is a member of several historical and veterans societies, including the Company of Military Historians and the Great Lakes Living History Society. In his spare time, he gives talks and historical demonstrations to students and the public.

Kathy Gillespie Tomajko is Head of Reference Services at the Library and Information Center at Georgia Institute of Technology in Atlanta, Georgia. She was formerly Information Consultant for the School of History, Technology and Society at Georgia Institute of Technology. She is an active member of professional associations, including the American Library Association and Special Libraries Association, and is a past member of publisher advisory committees for the *Internet Reference Services Quarterly* journal, and for the Information Access Company (IAC).

Lynn Whitehouse is Librarian IV at the San Diego Central Library. She supervises the History/Information and Interlibrary Loan sections and is responsible for much of the cultural programming.

Reader's Guide

Between 1939 and 1945, World War II was fought among all the major powers of the world. By the end of the war, more than fifty countries had become involved in the conflict. The scope and brutality of the war greatly impacted the world—more people died during the conflict than in any previous war, and the war changed the political, social, and economic climates of the entire world. *The Holocaust and World War II Almanac* provides a comprehensive range of historical information as well as current studies on World War II and the Holocaust. The three-volume set includes extensive information about the European and Pacific theaters of war as well as the Holocaust. The work also provides biographical profiles of more than 100 men and women who played key or lesser-known roles in the war, whether as civilians or soldiers. Interspersed throughout volumes 1 and 2 are primary sources, which give the reader access to the writings or words of the actual participants in the war or the Holocaust. The primary source documents, complete with introduction and aftermath sections, can be found at the end of the chapter in which that topic is mainly discussed. Each primary source contains enough information for the reader to understand what was happening around the time of the event or topic being described in the source. Information about such events or topics is often restated in the primary source section so that the reader does not have to refer to previous material in the chapter or volume.

Volume 1 begins by exploring the events after World War I (1914–1918) and how certain actions led to the rise of Nazism in Germany, Fascism in Italy, militarism in Japan, and isolationism in the United States. The volume shows how conditions after World War I ultimately led to the Holocaust and World War II. It also details how some world leaders attempted to provoke war while others tried to avoid it; how relationships formed among the Allied countries and among the Axis powers; how Jews, Roma (Gypsies), political prisoners, and others were persecuted by the Nazis and stripped of their rights; how the Nazis were able to conquer so many European countries in a relatively short amount of time; how the war in the Pacific began; how Jews were rounded up for resettlement and sent to ghettos, then labor camps and ultimately death camps; and how the Allies joined forces to thwart the expansion of the German and Japanese empires, which had caused much death among the civilian populations in conquered countries.

Volume 2 continues the story of the war and the Holocaust. The work discusses the Allied invasion of France; life on the home front; spies, secrets, and codes; major turning points in the war, including further fighting in France and the Pacific; the defeat of Nazi Germany and the liberation of the death camps; the use of two atomic bombs and the surrender of Japan; the plight of displaced persons; the Nuremberg Trials; recovery after the war; and memorials for the dead. The volume contains four appendices: A) Jewish Victims of the Holocaust—explains that the number of reported Holocaust victims is different in various sources and discusses some of the reasons why the numbers can never be more precise. B) Nuremberg War Crime Trials—provides detailed information on many of the Nuremberg Trials and includes a chart indicating defendants' names, sentences, and the outcomes. C) Japanese War Crimes—The Tokyo Trials—describes the nature of the trials, the tribunal convened to hear the cases, and the defendants brought to stand trial and why. D) World War II and Holocaust Film Overview—presents a brief look at many of the films devoted to the World War II era, including those produced during the conflict and those being released in recent years, plus many issued in between.

Volume 3 offers the life stories of more than 100 individuals who played a role in World War II and the Holocaust. The biographees were selected in order to present a diversity of wartime experiences, from Axis and Allied leaders to death camp survivors to women on the home front. The subjects include political and military leaders, enlisted men and women, and civilians, including journalists, musicians, and diarists. The volume includes readily recognizable figures, such as U.S. President Franklin D. Roosevelt, British Prime Minister Winston Churchill, Japanese Premier Hideki Tōjō, Soviet leader Joseph Stalin, and Nazi führer Adolf Hitler. The work also features Holocaust survivors, including Renée Roth-Hano, Elie Wiesel, and Simon Wiesenthal; military leaders such as American General Dwight D. Eisenhower, German Army General Erwin Rommel, British Field Marshal Bernard Montgomery, and American Women's Army Corps Director Oveta Culp Hobby; Holocaust victims such as Jewish teenager Anne Frank and Polish photographer Mendel Grossman; journalists/artists, including Edward R. Murrow, Ernie Pyle, Margaret Bourke-White, and Bill Mauldin; Holocaust rescuers such as Miep Gies, Chiune (Sempo) Sugihara, Corrie ten Boom, and Raoul Wallenberg; and Nazi officials Adolf Eichmann, Heinrich Himmler, and others. Also profiled are lesser known people, including American pacifist Jeannette Rankin, Austrian conscientious objector Franz Jaggerstatter, and Hungarian resistance fighter Hannah Senesh (Szenes). In order to include a diversity of experiences, the editors have provided several composite biographies as well on groups of people such as the Comfort Women, Rosie the Riveter, the Navajo Code Talkers, and the Tuskegee Airmen.

Each volume begins with a research and activities section, glossary, and a timeline of events and noteworthy achievements by some of the people profiled in this set. The *Holocaust and World War II Almanac* contains some 800 images, including black-and-white photographs, maps, and illustrations. Due to the nature of this work, some of the photos depict the dead or wounded as well as acts of brutality. Please view them at your own discretion. Chapters and biographies contain sidebars of related information—some focusing on people associated with the war, others taking a closer look at pivotal events. Individual bibliographies appear after each primary source entry and after all biographies. Comprehensive bibliographies appear at the back of each volume as well, followed by a cumulative index for all three volumes.

On occasion, readers might note differences in figures reported in primary sources and the text. This occurs because scholars continue to study the Holocaust and World War II era, seeking to uncover more information about that period. Historians continue to attempt to calculate precisely the total number of losses, in terms of people, resources, and property. As such, the most recent estimates were unknown when the primary sources were written years ago. As noted in Appendix A: Jewish Victims of the Holocaust, historians are unable give an exact figure because of the nature of the war and the way the "Final Solution" was conducted. Records simply do not exist for each individual who was believed to have been killed. The same logic applies to those fighting in Resistance movements and the armed services, as well as those civilians killed while defending their homelands. Plus, not all countries used the same methods for tracking those who died. In some areas, people were buried in mass graves without identification; many of those murdered at death camps were cremated, leaving no trace of their existence. In addition, estimated losses vary significantly between authoritative sources. In this work, the editors have tried to present the most commonly accepted ranges.

Acknowledgements

The editors wish to extend their gratitude to Nancy A. Edgar and Jennifer Keirans for their invaluable assistance during the compilation of this project. Thanks are also extended to the Reader's Advisor team for its support, including Beverly Baer, Dana Ferguson, Nancy Franklin, Robert Franzino, Prindle LaBarge, Charlie Montney, and

Kathy Meek. Special thanks to the Imaging department, including Dean Dauphinais, Senior Editor; Robyn V. Young, Project Manager; Kelly A. Quin, Editor; Leitha Etheridge-Sims, Mary K. Grimes, and David G. Oblender, Image Catalogers; Pam A. Reed, Imaging Coordinator; Randy Bassett, Imaging Supervisor; Robert Duncan, Senior Imaging Specialist; Dan Newell, Imaging Specialist; and Christine O'Bryan, Graphic Specialist. Additional thanks are extended to Larry Baker and Barbara McNeil.

Comments and Suggestions

The Holocaust and World War II Almanac staff welcomes your comments and suggestions for other topics in history to consider for future projects. Please write: Editors, *The Holocaust and World War II Almanac,* Gale Group, 27500 Drake Rd., Farmington Hills, MI 48331-3535; call toll-free: 1-800-347-4253; or send email via http://www.gale group.com.

Timeline

1871 Germany is unified under the domination of the state of Prussia, and the German empire is ruled by a kaiser.

1899 Houston Stewart Chamberlain publishes *The Foundations of the Nineteenth Century,* a book that uses racial theory to explain European history.

1903 Russian anti-Semites circulate *The Protocols of the Elders of Zion,* a forgery that describes the master plan of an alleged Jewish conspiracy to dominate the world.

1914 World War I begins in Europe. At that time, it is known as the Great War.

1916 Jeannette Rankin becomes the first woman elected to the U.S. Congress; she immediately causes controversy by voting against her country's entry into World War I. About 50 other Congressmen vote against war as well, but the focus is on Rankin, the only female member of Congress.

1917 The czar is overthrown in Russia and a Communist government ascends to power after the Bolshevik Revolution. The Russian empire is eventually renamed the Union of Soviet Socialist Republics (USSR), commonly known as the Soviet Union.

1918 The German army is defeated by the Allies in World War I and revolution breaks out in Germany. The kaiser is overthrown and a republic is proclaimed on November 9. The new government agrees to an armistice, ending the war, on November 11.

1919 During the month of June, Adolf Hitler joins the small German Workers' party in Munich. The party soon changes its name to the National Socialist German Workers' party (NSDAP), more commonly known as the Nazi party.

On June 23, Germany signs the Treaty of Versailles. The treaty removes some territory from German control, severely limits the size of the nation's armed forces, and requires Germany to pay reparations and accept guilt for causing World War I. Extreme nationalist groups in Germany blame socialists, communists, and Jews for Germany's defeat.

Communist revolutions in various parts of Germany are put down with much bloodshed.

1920 The League of Nations is formed.

1922 Benito Mussolini and his Fascist party march on Rome. Mussolini is named premier of Italy and eventually establishes a dictatorship that becomes a model for Hitler's Third Reich.

1923 Hyperinflation hits Germany; German currency becomes worthless, causing severe economic distress.

During the year, Alfred Rosenberg reissues an official Nazi party version of *The Protocols of the Elders of Zion*.

In November Adolf Hitler leads a failed attempt to overthrow the German government. Police end the rebellion, called the Munich Beer-Hall Putsch, by arresting Hitler and the other leaders of the party. Sixteen Nazis are killed and others wounded.

1924 At his trial for treason and armed rebellion as a result of the Beer-Hall Putsch, Adolf Hitler gains the attention of extreme nationalists. While serving only eight months of a five-year prison sentence, Hitler dictates his book *Mein Kampf* ("My Struggle"), which outlines his racial beliefs about the superiority of the German people and the inferiority of Jews.

1926 Germany joins the League of Nations.

Anti-Semitic Catholic priest Charles Coughlin broadcasts his first radio sermon in the United States.

Hirohito becomes emperor of Japan, calling his reign "Showa" (meaning "enlightened peace").

1927 Chiang Kai-Shek establishes the Kuomintang (Nationalist) government in Nanking (Nanjing), China.

1928 The Nazi party receives about 800,000 votes—2.6 percent of the total—in national elections.

1929 The Great Depression begins; it will not end until 1939. The worldwide economic depression hits Germany especially hard.

1930 The Nazi party receives almost 6.5 million votes in national elections and becomes the second-largest party in the Reichstag, or German parliament. As part of highly organized campaign tactics, storm troopers (members of the Sturmabteilung or SA)

attack opponents, break up meetings, and intimidate Jews and political dissidents.

1931 Vidkun Quisling is one of the cofounders of the Nordic Folk Awakening movement in Norway, which advocates many of the same ideas and principles as Germany's Nazi party.

The Japanese army seizes Manchuria in a short war with China, establishing Manchuria as the "independent" country of Manchukuo, actually controlled by the Japanese.

American journalist Dorothy Thompson interviews Adolf Hitler, a rising German politician, for *Cosmopolitan* magazine.

1932 Although Adolf Hitler receives 11 million votes in July in the first round of elections for German president, and more than 13 million votes (almost 37 percent) in the second round, Paul von Hindenburg, aged military hero of World War I, is reelected president. The SA is briefly banned because of its use of increased violence during the campaign.

1933 Adolf Hitler becomes chancellor of Germany on January 30. Although much of the government at the time is composed of old-line conservatives who believe they can use the Nazis, within a few months Hitler and the Nazi party have taken control of the country.

The Reichstag building is set ablaze on February 27, and Hitler receives emergency powers from President Paul von Hindenburg. Freedoms of speech and of the press are restricted. Acting as police, storm troopers arrest 10,000 opponents of the Nazis, especially Communists.

On March 4, 1933, Franklin D. Roosevelt begins the first of four terms as president of the United States.

Joseph Goebbels is appointed Hitler's minister of enlightenment and propaganda.

Dachau, the first permanent concentration camp, is opened in a suburb of Munich in March. Communists are among the first 10,000 opponents of the Nazis who are arrested and sent to the new camps.

The new Reichstag meets without Communist members, who have been arrested or are in hiding. The Nazis and their allies win support from the Catholic parties and pass the Enabling Act, giving Adolf Hitler dictatorial powers.

In April Nazis organize a national boycott of Jewish-owned businesses. Inge Deutschkron, a young Jewish girl living Berlin, witnesses the boycott. The first anti-Jewish laws are also passed, removing almost all Jews from government jobs, including teaching positions. Further laws follow, and by the end of the year, 53,000 Jews leave Germany.

German labor unions are abolished and replaced by the German Labor Front, run by the Nazis. The Social Democratic party (the largest party before the Nazi rise to power) is outlawed; all other parties follow.

Homosexual researcher Magnus Hirschfeld's Institute for Sexual Science in Berlin is destroyed by the Nazis.

The Nazis conduct public book burnings of works written by Jews and anti-Nazis and impose censorship throughout Germany.

1934 Adolf Hitler orders the murder of SA leader Ernst Röhm and his supporters in what has become known as the Night of the Long Knives, June 30.

Upon the death of German President Paul von Hindenburg, Adolf Hitler combines the offices of chancellor and president, becoming führer, or leader, of the Third Reich, with absolute power. All army officers and soldiers swear allegiance to Hitler.

Adolf Hitler orders American journalist Dorothy Thompson out of Germany, giving her twenty-four hours to leave the country.

Harry S Truman is elected to the U.S. Senate and begins to build a reputation as an effective leader.

1935 On March 16, Germany announces the reintroduction of the military draft and a major expansion of its army, violating the Treaty of Versailles.

German film director Leni Riefenstahl's *Triumph des Willens* (*Triumph of the Will*) premieres. The documentary of a 1934 Nazi party rally at Nuremberg later gains fame as a blatant propaganda film.

Germany passes the Nuremberg Laws, drafted by Wilhelm Frick, which define Jews in racial terms, strip them of German citizenship, and ban marriages and sexual relationships between Jews and non-Jews.

Italy invades Ethiopia on October 3. On May 5, 1936, Ethiopia surrenders.

1936 On March 7, the German army enters the Rhineland, an area of western Germany that had been demilitarized by the Treaty of Versailles.

During the month of March, participation in the Hitler Youth organization becomes mandatory. All ten-year-old boys are required to register at government offices for membership.

The Spanish Civil War begins in July.

Adolf Hitler and the Nazis temporarily ease anti-Jewish actions as the Olympic Games open in Berlin, Germany.

Germany and Italy enter into agreements that develop into a political and military alliance called the Rome-Berlin Axis.

Germany and Japan sign the Anti-Comintern Treaty.

1937 In the first example of aerial bombing against a civilian population, the German air force bombs Guernica, Spain, on April 26, aiding Francisco Franco's fascist troops during the Spanish Civil War.

Neville Chamberlain becomes British prime minister.

Buchenwald concentration camp is established, July 16, 1937.

During the month of July, Japan invades China, capturing Peking (Beijing), Shanghai, Canton, and other major cities. In Nanking (Nanjing), invading Japanese troops rape, torture, and murder tens of thousands of Chinese civilians. This event became known as the "Rape of Nanking."

Karl Koch becomes commandant of the Buchenwald concentration camp, and his wife, Ilse, receives the nickname "the Beast of Buchenwald" as she begins to terrorize prisoners.

1938 Austrians vote in favor of *Anschluss,* an agreement that makes their country part of Nazi Germany. The German army moves into Austria, and crowds cheer Hitler as he enters Vienna. Anti-Semitic laws rapidly go into effect.

Jewish psychotherapist Bruno Bettelheim is arrested by the Nazis and placed in the Dachau concentration camp.

An international conference is held in Évian, France, to discuss the plight of Jewish refugees in Europe. No solutions are found to resolve the crisis.

Europe is at the brink of war as Adolf Hitler makes territorial demands on Czechoslovakia. At a conference in Munich in September, leaders of France and Great Britain agree to grant Germany a section of Czechoslovakia with a large German-speaking population. British Prime Minister Neville Chamberlain signs the Munich Pact with Adolf Hitler, who will soon break his promise not to invade Czechoslovakia.

In Paris, Herschel Grynszpan, a young Jew, shoots and kills Ernst vom Rath, a German embassy official. Grynszpan's actions spark *Kristallnacht* ("Crystal Night" or the "Night of Broken Glass")—a series of organized Nazi attacks throughout Germany in which Jews are beaten, synagogues are burned, Jewish homes and businesses are destroyed, and 30,000 Jewish men are arrested and sent to concentration camps. *New York Times* reporter Otto D. Tolischus alerts the world to Nazi aggression in his account of *Kristallnacht.*

Italian dictator Benito Mussolini adopts the anti-Jewish laws of Adolf Hitler.

First nuclear fission of uranium is produced.

1939 Eugenio Pacelli becomes Pope Pius XII.

Hitler violates the Munich agreement by taking over the remainder of Czechoslovakia by March, and implements anti-Semitic measures there.

The Spanish Civil War ends on March 31.

In accordance with the principles of the Jehovah's Witnesses, young Elisabeth Kusserow refuses to salute the Nazi flag in spring 1939 and is sent to reform school for six years.

Several hundred Jews attempt to emigrate from Germany on board the steamship *St. Louis* in May, but are forced to return to Europe.

During the course of the year, Wilhelmine Haferkamp and other fertile German women receive the Mother's Cross, a medal honoring their Aryan child-bearing accomplishments.

German-born physicist Albert Einstein, at the urging of colleague Leo Szilard, writes a letter to U.S. President Franklin D. Roosevelt, urging American development of an atomic bomb.

On August 23, Germany and the Soviet Union sign the Nazi-Soviet Pact. The two countries promise not to attack each other and secretly agree to divide Poland after it is conquered by Germany.

U.S. General George C. Marshall is sworn in as chief of staff, the highest office in the U.S. Army.

World War II officially begins when Germany invades Poland on September 1; two days later, Great Britain and France declare war on Germany. Poland surrenders to Germany on September 27.

The Nazi euthanasia program begins. In time, 70,000 mentally and physically disabled Germans, including children, are murdered by Nazi doctors and their staffs.

On September 21, Reinhard Heydrich, second in command of the SS, issues a directive to Nazi task forces ordering the "resettlement" of Jewish Poles to urban centers (specifically ghettos) near railroad lines.

In October Adolf Hitler appoints Hans Frank governor-general of certain sections of Poland that later become the "resettlement" areas for Jews and others the Nazis deem unfit for Reich citizenship.

Great Britain begins evacuating children from London to rural towns during the month of November in order to protect them from potential German air raids.

On November 23, Jews in German-occupied Poland are ordered to wear the yellow Star of David on their clothing at all times.

1940 The Lódz ghetto is created in Poland in February, and sealed in April. Jewish photographer Mendel Grossman begins to capture pictures of life there.

On April 10, Germany invades Norway and Denmark. Denmark soon surrenders, but fighting continues in Norway, where Norwegian troops are aided by British and French forces. The Norwegian government flees to Great Britain.

Heinrich Himmler, head of the SS, orders the building of a concentration camp at Auschwitz in occupied Poland.

Winston Churchill becomes prime minister of Great Britain on May 10.

Germany invades the Netherlands, Belgium, Luxembourg, and France on May 10. Luxembourg capitulates shortly after the invasion, the Netherlands surrenders on May 14, and Belgium gives in on May 28.

Italy declares war on France and Great Britain, and invades France on June 10.

French troops evacuate Paris on June 13 and German forces take the city the next day. France signs an armistice with Germany on June 22 and German troops occupy northern France, while a government friendly to Germany (Vichy France) maintains some independence in the south.

Anti-Jewish measures soon begin in western European countries controlled by Germany.

The Germans begin bombing Great Britain in a long air campaign known as the Battle of Britain. American radio journalist Edward R. Murrow broadcasts dramatic reports about the Nazi air raids over London. Defeated by the fighter pilots of the British Royal Air Force (RAF), however, Hitler eventually abandons plans to invade Great Britain.

Field Marshal Philippe Pétain is appointed head of the German-controlled Vichy government in France. He is later convicted of collaborating with the Nazis.

Japanese diplomat Chiune Sugihara, head of the Japanese embassy in Kaunas, Lithuania, disobeys orders and issues transit visas to thousands of refugees.

Italy invades Egypt on September 14.

Germany, Japan, and Italy sign a military alliance called the Tripartite Pact. Within six months, Hungary, Romania, Slovakia, and Bulgaria also join the alliance.

Benjamin O. Davis, Sr., becomes the first African American general in the U.S. Army.

Italy invades Greece.

The Warsaw ghetto in Poland is sealed and nearly 450,000 Jews, including Janina David and her family, are confined within its walls. Chaim A. Kaplan records his observations of the sealing of the ghetto in his diary, later published as *Scroll of Agony*.

American journalist Ernie Pyle arrives in London to report on the war in England.

1941 Germany sends General Erwin Rommel to North Africa in February so that his Afrika Korps can help Italy with its invasion of the area. The seesaw battle for territory will continue until May 1943, when the Germans surrender to the Allies, ending the war in Africa.

A ghetto in Kraków is decreed, established, and sealed, between March 3 and March 20.

The U.S. Congress passes the Lend-Lease Act, signed by President Franklin D. Roosevelt, on March 11. It provides war aid to Great Britain, and later to the Soviet Union and other countries.

The Nazi government orders Franziska Schwarz, a deaf German woman, to appear at a health center for sterilization on March 21. The first attempt (in 1935) had failed.

As German forces attack Yugoslavia, Josip Broz Tito calls for unified resistance to German occupation and begins to organize the Partisans.

On April 13, Japan and the Soviet Union sign a treaty promising that neither will attack the other.

Rudolf Hess makes a flight to Great Britain with the hope of persuading the British to side with Germany in World War II.

Oveta Culp Hobby is named director of the new Women's Auxiliary Army Corps (WAAC), which will eventually be made part of the U.S. Army and renamed the Women's Army Corps (WAC).

The HMS *Hood* is sunk by the German battleship *Bismarck* on May 24. Only three of the 1,400 members of the *Hood* crew survive.

On May 27, the British Royal Navy tracks down the German battleship *Bismarck*. After repeated attacks, the *Bismarck* is sunk, and more than 2,000 German sailors on board die.

American pilot Jackie Cochran flies a Hudson V bomber plane from Canada to Great Britain, becoming the first woman to fly a military aircraft over the Atlantic Ocean.

On June 22, Germany invades the Soviet Union in an offensive called Operation Barbarossa and quickly takes control of much of the country. Special murder squads known as Einsatzgruppen follow the German army into the Soviet Union to eliminate Jews, political dissidents, and others.

In July the United States bans trade with Japan.

Hermann Göring, second to Hitler in Nazi hierarchy, gives Reinhard Heydrich the authority "to carry out all necessary preparations … for a total solution of the Jewish question" throughout Nazi-controlled Europe.

After pressure from the Japanese government, the Vichy French government allows Japan to establish bases in the southern part of French Indochina (Vietnam).

British Prime Minister Winston Churchill and U.S. President Franklin D. Roosevelt meet aboard a warship off the coast of the British colony of Newfoundland (now a province of Canada) in August and issue the Atlantic Charter, in which they agree to promote peace and democracy around the world.

Rudolf Höss, commandant of the Auschwitz concentration camp, oversees the first experiments using poisonous gas for the mass extermination of humans. The first victims of gassing are 600 Soviet prisoners of war and 250 Poles.

Kiev, the capital of the Ukraine, falls to the German army on September 19. More than 33,000 Jews are murdered at Babi Yar outside Kiev on September 29 and 30.

During October, construction begins on Birkenau (Auschwitz II) in Poland.

On October 17, Hideki Tōjō becomes premier of Japan.

Avraham Tory, a Lithuanian Jew, survives an October 28 Nazi-ordered action that removes nearly 10,000 people, about half of whom are children, from the Kovno ghetto.

In Poland, the construction of an extermination camp at Belzec begins on November 1.

Gonda Redlich arrives at the ghetto in Theresienstadt, Czechoslovakia, a Nazi "model Jewish settlement," during December.

Japan bombs the U.S. naval base at Pearl Harbor, Hawaii, on December 7. The United States and Great Britain declare war on Japan the next day. Japan's allies, Germany and Italy, declare war on the United States on December 11, and the United States declares war on them in return.

Jeannette Rankin becomes the only member of the U.S. Congress to vote against American involvement in World War II.

The death camp at Chelmno, in the western part of Poland, begins operation. Jews are gassed in sealed vans.

British troops in Hong Kong surrender to the Japanese on December 25.

1942 Rationing begins in the United States. In January, rationing of rubber is announced, sugar is rationed in May, and by the end of the year, gasoline is also being rationed.

Manila, capital of the Philippines, surrenders to the Japanese on January 2.

Despite having a transit visa, Jewish psychotherapist Viktor E. Frankl remains in Vienna with his parents, who are unable to procure visas, and is sent to a concentration camp in early 1942. Before the war ends, he is transferred to other camps.

Reinhard Heydrich calls the Wannsee Conference, where the "Final Solution," a plan to eliminate all European Jews, is transmitted to various branches of the German government.

In the month of February, the U.S. Marine Corps inducts twenty-nine Navajos to begin training as "Code Talkers"; the men will use the Navajo language to provide secure communications during battles in the Pacific.

Hollywood movie director Frank Capra arrives in Washington, D.C., on February 15, to begin work on *Why We Fight*, a series of documentary films designed to educate soldiers about the causes of World War II and the reasons for American involvement.

Executive Order 9066, signed by U.S. President Franklin D. Roosevelt, directs all Japanese Americans living on the West Coast of the United States into internment camps.

Slovakian Jews become the first Jews from outside Poland to be transported to Auschwitz.

American forces surrender to the Japanese at Bataan on April 9.

American aviator James "Jimmy" Doolittle leads a U.S. Army Air Corps bombing raid on Tokyo and other Japanese cities that is credited with turning the tide of American wartime morale.

During May, some 1,000 British bombers destroy Cologne, Germany's third-largest city.

On May 6, American and Filipino troops on the island of Corregidor in Manila Bay surrender to the Japanese.

On May 7, Allied naval forces ordered to the area by Chester W. Nimitz, commander in chief of the Pacific Fleet, defeat the Japanese fleet in the Battle of the Coral Sea in the Pacific. It is the first great aircraft carrier conflict.

African American sailor Dorie Miller receives the Navy Cross on May 27 for his heroic performance during the Pearl Harbor bombing.

Reinhard Heydrich dies of his wounds on June 4, as a result of an earlier assassination attempt by Czech resistance fighters in Prague.

The U.S. Navy defeats the Japanese fleet at the Battle of Midway, June 4–7, in one of the most decisive naval engagements in history. Rear Admiral Raymond A. Spruance is given tactical responsibilities during the battle.

In June, General Dwight D. Eisenhower takes command of all U.S. forces in Europe.

Erwin Rommel becomes the youngest German officer to be named a field marshal, the highest rank in the German military, in June.

Anne Frank and her family move into a secret annex constructed in the top stories of her father's office building in Amsterdam.

Etty Hillesum secures a job as a typist for the Jewish Council in Amsterdam, the Netherlands, during the month of July, and assists new arrivals at the Westerbork transit camp, where Dutch Jews are held before deportation to death camps in Poland.

During July, British bombers attack Germany's second largest city, Hamburg, on four straight nights, causing a firestorm that kills 30,000 civilians.

The Treblinka death camp begins receiving Jews from Warsaw. It is the last of the three camps, along with Belzec and Sobibór, created to exterminate Polish Jews. The Nazis call this plan "Operation Reinhard," in honor of the assassinated Heydrich.

Judenrat official Adam Czerniaków commits suicide on July 23 after the Nazis order him to hand over 9,000 Jews from the Warsaw ghetto for deportation.

Jewish orphanage director Janusz Korczak and 200 orphans under his care are deported from the Warsaw ghetto in Poland to the Treblinka concentration camp, where they all die in the gas chambers.

On August 7, American troops land on the mid-Pacific island of Guadalcanal in the Solomon Islands in the first American offensive operation of the war in the Pacific.

Edith Stein, a Jew who converted to Catholicism and became a nun, is killed at the Auschwitz concentration camp.

On August 24, Benjamin O. Davis, Jr., officially takes command of the Tuskegee Airmen, trained at the Tuskegee Institute in Alabama, the first African American pilots to enter the U.S. Army Corps.

During the month of September, Brigadier General Leslie Groves, an American civil engineer, is named head of the Manhattan Engineering District (later called the Manhattan Project), which was formed by the U.S. government to develop nuclear weapons.

In September and October, Polish Jews Shimson and Tova Draenger join other Jewish youths in forming the Jewish Fighting Organization to work against the Nazis.

On September 13, Germany begins its attack on the Soviet city of Stalingrad.

Hirsch Grunstein and his brother go into hiding in Belgium to escape the Nazis. The boys stay with a couple that volunteers to give them shelter.

Popular orchestra leader Glenn Miller enlists in the U.S. Army on October 7 with the goal of starting the Glenn Miller Army Air Force Band, which eventually performs for troops in war zones in Europe.

In October 1942 Odette Marie Celine Hallowes, a mother and wife, parachutes into France as a spy for Great Britain; she is later confined to a concentration camp and tortured by the Nazis.

In the Battle of El Alamein in Egypt, Field Marshal Bernard Montgomery leads the British Eighth Army in an important strategic victory against Italian troops and Field Marshal Erwin Rommel's German Afrika Korps.

On November 8 the Allies launch Operation Torch, an invasion of German-occupied North Africa that ends with the Germans being chased from the region. U.S. General George S. Patton takes command of the First Armored Corps (a tank division) and leads it to victory.

Physicist Enrico Fermi achieves the first self-sustaining nuclear fission chain reaction in his laboratory at Columbia University in New York City.

Wladyslaw Bartoszewski, a Catholic Polish resister, helps form a Jewish relief committee called Zegota.

1943 Allied leaders meet at Casablanca, Morocco, in January, and Cairo, Egypt, in November of the same year, to discuss the progress of the war.

German Jewish rabbi Leo Baeck is arrested and sent to the Theresienstadt concentration camp in Czechoslovakia, where he remains until after the camp is liberated by the Soviets at the end of World War II.

On February 2, the Germans surrender to Russian troops at Stalingrad, a major turning point in the war.

Hans and Sophie Scholl are arrested on a Munich university campus for distributing pamphlets for the White Rose resistance group.

Prelude to War, the first film in the *Why We Fight* film series directed by Frank Capra, wins the Oscar for best documentary.

Small groups of Jews in the Warsaw ghetto begin attacking German troops on April 19. They continue fighting for almost one month until the Germans have killed almost all of the Jewish resisters and completely destroyed the ghetto. Jewish resistance leader Mordecai Anielewicz is one of those killed during the Warsaw Ghetto Uprising, on May 8.

U.S. General George S. Patton commands American troops in Sicily, a large island south of the Italian mainland. In July American forces, along with British and Canadian troops, begin the Allied invasion that will continue on the Italian mainland.

Italian dictator Benito Mussolini is removed from office by the Fascist Grand Council on July 25 and tries to establish a separate government in northern Italy, with the help of Adolf Hitler.

During August, Jackie Cochran becomes the director of the Women's Airforce Service Pilots (WASPs).

Austrian farmer Franz Jaggerstatter is executed for refusing to serve in Hitler's army.

The Allies invade the Italian mainland on September 3; the new Italian government surrenders to the Allies on September 8. German troops in Italy continue fighting.

German attempts to deport Danish Jews are defeated when most of the entire Jewish population of Denmark is safely transported to Sweden.

British spy Noor Inayat Khan is captured and tortured by the Nazis in occupied France.

In December U.S. General Dwight D. Eisenhower is put in command of the planned Operation Overlord.

1944 During the course of 1944, Women's Airforce Service Pilots member Ann B. Carl becomes the first woman to test-pilot a jet plane when she conducts an evaluation flight of the turbojet-powered Bell YP-59A.

The Allies land at Anzio, Italy, on January 22.

After abandoning his university studies in order to fight racism, young Italian Jew Primo Levi is sent to Auschwitz in February, having been arrested two months earlier.

Dutch resistance worker Corrie ten Boom, along with several of her family members, is arrested by the Gestapo for hiding Jews in her Amsterdam home. She and her sister are later sent to the Vught concentration camp.

Hannah Senesh (also transliterated as Szenes), a Jew living in Palestine, parachutes behind enemy lines in Yugoslavia as part of a British-sponsored rescue mission to reach Jews and other resisters.

The Germans occupy Hungary on March 19, 1944, and begin large-scale deportations of Hungarian Jews; by July, more than 400,000 Jews have been sent to Auschwitz.

The United States Army enters Rome, the capital of Italy, on June 4.

On June 6, now known as D-Day, Allied forces land in Normandy in northern France during the largest sea invasion in history, called Operation Overlord. After heavy fighting, the Allies break out of Normandy and sweep eastward across France. By the end of August, France is liberated.

The United States passes the "GI Bill" on June 22, making a college education available to almost all veterans of the U.S. armed services.

On the third anniversary of the German invasion of the Soviet Union, June 22, the Soviets launch a massive offensive called Operation Bagration along an 800-mile front in White Russia (Belarus). The Soviets inflict immense losses on the German army and drive them back almost 400 miles within one month.

Young Swedish businessman Raoul Wallenberg arrives in Budapest, Hungary, to help save the surviving Jews trapped in the city.

On July 20, a small group of German army officers, eager to end the war, unsuccessfully attempts to assassinate Adolf Hitler. Many of the conspirators, along with their families, are tortured and executed.

The Soviet army enters Lublin in eastern Poland in late July and liberates the nearby Majdanek death camp. The Soviets confiscate numerous Nazi documents before they can be destroyed.

On August 4, after living undetected for twenty-five months, Anne Frank, her family, and the four others hiding in the secret annex are reported to the Nazis. The annex dwellers are all sent to the Auschwitz concentration camp.

Paris is liberated by Free French and American forces on August 23.

On September 15, U.S. Marines land on Peleliu island, one of the Palau Islands in the western Pacific Ocean.

During the course of October 1944, industrialist Oskar Schindler is granted permission by the Nazis to establish a munitions factory in Czechoslovakia. This allows Schindler to spare Jewish prisoners from death by employing them there.

Concentration camp prisoner Róza Robota participates in the inmates' revolt at Auschwitz, which leads to the destruction of one of the crematoria.

German army commander Erwin Rommel is suspected of being involved in the July 20 failed attempt to assassinate Adolf Hitler and is forced to commit suicide on October 14.

U.S. General Douglas MacArthur returns to liberate the Philippines from Japanese control, just as he had promised three years earlier he would.

The largest naval battle in history, the Battle of Leyte Gulf in the Philippines (October 23–26), ends in almost total destruction of the Japanese fleet.

On October 26, SS chief Heinrich Himmler orders the destruction of the concentration camps and their inmates.

The 761st Battalion, an African American tank unit, arrives in France to take part in the Allied drive toward Germany.

Franklin D. Roosevelt is elected to a fourth term as president of the United States.

The Germans launch a major counteroffensive on December 16 against the Americans in the Ardennes Forest region of Belgium and France. The conflict becomes known as the Battle of the Bulge. After some initial success, the Germans are defeated.

1945   On January 12, the Soviets launch an offensive along the entire Polish front, entering Warsaw on January 17 and Lódz two days later. By February 1, they are within 100 miles of the German capital of Berlin.

As Soviet troops approach, the Nazis begin the evacuation of the Auschwitz death camp on January 18, forcing about 66,000 surviving prisoners on a death march. Soviet troops reach the camp on January 27.

On January 31, U.S. Army Private Eddie Slovik becomes the only American soldier executed for desertion during World War II; in fact, he becomes the only U.S. soldier executed for desertion since 1864.

In February, Allied leaders British Prime Minister Winston Churchill, U.S. President Franklin D. Roosevelt, and Soviet dictator Joseph Stalin meet in Yalta in the Soviet Union to discuss strategies for ending the war and to plan future forms of government for Germany and other parts of Europe. They also schedule the first United Nations conference.

On February 14, Allied raids on Dresden result in firestorms as the city is crammed with German refugees from the fighting farther east.

American marines land on Iwo Jima in the Pacific on February 19.

On March 7, American troops cross the Rhine River in Germany, the last natural obstacle between the Allied forces and Berlin.

American troops land on Okinawa on April 1, beginning the largest land battle of the Pacific war. Japanese forces are defeated by June.

Pastor Christian Reger is freed from Dachau on April 2 after spending five years at the camp for defying the state-sponsored religion known as the German Faith Movement.

On April 4, Kim Malthe-Bruun, a Danish resister, writes a letter to his mother from prison, informing her that he is to be executed by the Nazis.

German Protestant minister Dietrich Bonhoeffer is executed on April 9 for his participation in the plot to assassinate Adolf Hitler.

U.S. General George S. Patton and his Third Army liberate the Buchenwald concentration camp in Germany on April 11, 1945. American photographer Margaret Bourke-White accompanies U.S. forces when they liberate the camp, and her photographs document the deplorable conditions found there. American reporter Edward R. Murrow broadcasts his impressions of the Buchenwald concentration camp a few days after its liberation.

U.S. President Franklin D. Roosevelt dies of a cerebral hemorrhage in Warm Springs, Georgia, on April 12; Vice President Harry S Truman takes the oath of office and becomes president.

British troops liberate the Bergen-Belsen concentration camp. French prisoner Fania Fénelon is among those freed.

While reporting on the Allied invasion of Okinawa, Ernie Pyle is killed by a Japanese sniper on the island of Ie Shima on April 18.

American cartoonist Bill Mauldin wins the Pulitzer Prize during 1945 for his Willie and

Joe cartoons, which realistically portray the experiences of average U.S. infantrymen through the eyes of two scruffy GIs.

On April 20, Soviet troops reach Berlin, Germany.

Swedish diplomat Folke Bernadotte negotiates a deal with Nazi official Heinrich Himmler that allows 10,000 women to be released from the Ravensbrück concentration camp.

On April 28, former Italian dictator Benito Mussolini is captured by resistance fighters and executed. His body is put on public display.

American troops liberate the Dachau concentration camp.

Eva Braun marries Adolf Hitler in his Berlin bunker on April 29.

With the advancement of Soviet troops into Berlin, Adolf Hitler and Eva Braun commit suicide in Hitler's underground bunker on April 30.

On May 8, V-E Day, the new German government officially surrenders unconditionally to the Allies.

Nazi leader Hermann Göring is arrested by American troops during May 1945; a year later, he commits suicide after being condemned to death for war crimes.

Heinrich Himmler, the senior Nazi official responsible for overseeing the mass murder of 6 million European Jews, is captured by the Allies on May 21. Two days later, he commits suicide.

J. Robert Oppenheimer, leader of a group of scientists working to develop an atomic bomb, oversees a successful bomb test on July 16 at the Alamogordo Bombing Range (the Trinity test site) in the New Mexican desert.

The Potsdam Conference begins on July 16. U.S. President Harry S Truman, British Prime Minister Winston Churchill, and Soviet leader Joseph Stalin confirm occupation of Germany by four Allied powers (France, Great Britain, the Soviet Union, and the United States) and issue an ultimatum to Japan demanding unconditional surrender.

The USS *Indianapolis* is sunk by Japanese forces on July 19; search and rescue efforts are delayed and many of the surviving crewmen are consumed by sharks.

On August 6, the United States releases an atomic bomb on Hiroshima, Japan. Some 70,000 people are killed initially during the blast.

The Soviet Union declares war on Japan on August 8; a large Soviet force invades Manchuria the following day.

The United States drops an atomic bomb on Nagasaki, Japan, on August 9.

On August 15, the Allies accept the unconditional surrender of Japan. Japanese leaders sign formal surrender papers aboard the USS *Missouri* in Tokyo Bay on September 2, V-J Day.

U.S. President Harry S Truman and other world leaders sign a charter establishing the United Nations as an international peacekeeping organization.

War crimes trials begin in Nuremberg, Germany, in November. Justice Robert H. Jackson of the U.S. Supreme Court gives the opening address for the United States before the International Military Tribunal at Nuremberg.

1946   The first session of the United Nations General Assembly opens in London, England.

On January 19, the International Military Tribunal for the Far East (IMTFE) is convened to begin prosecution of Japanese war crimes.

Hermann Göring, one of the highest Nazi officials to be accused and convicted of war crimes, testifies in his own defense during the Nuremberg Trials.

U.S. Brigadier General Telford Taylor becomes chief counsel for the remaining Nuremberg Trials after Justice Robert H. Jackson of the U.S. Supreme Court resigns.

1947   During the course of the year, Holocaust survivor Simon Wiesenthal forms the Jewish Historical Documentation Center in Austria to track down Nazi war criminals.

U.S. Secretary of State George C. Marshall proposes the European Recovery Act, or the Marshall Plan, an outline for helping European countries recover from the effects of the war.

India gains its independence from Great Britain.

1948 On May 14, the state of Israel is established.

The Soviets block all overland traffic between Berlin and the Allied-controlled zones of Germany between June 1948 and May 1949. Allies airlift food and fuel to West Berlin during those eleven months in more than 275,000 flights.

U.S. President Harry S Truman issues Executive Order 9981, which calls for the integration of the U.S. armed forces.

On December 23 Japanese Premier Hideki Tōjō is executed for war crimes.

1949 American radio personality Mildred Gillars ("Axis Sally") stands trial for treason in January.

On April 4, the North Atlantic Treaty Organization (NATO) is founded.

The Soviets establish East Germany as a Communist state called the German Democratic Republic (East Germany); France, Great Britain, and the United States combine their power zones into a democratic state called the Federal Republic of Germany (West Germany).

Defeated by the Communists, Chinese leader Chiang Kai-Shek flees his homeland with others loyal to his Nationalist party, taking refuge on the island of Formosa (now Taiwan) on December 10.

1952 Israel and Germany agree on restitution for damages done to Jews by the Nazis.

American General Dwight D. Eisenhower is elected president of the United States.

1953 During 1953, George C. Marshall of the United States wins the Nobel Peace Prize for his efforts to assist Europe's recovery from World War II, becoming the first member of the military to receive the prize.

On August 28, the Israeli parliament passes the Yad Vashem Law, which establishes the Martyrs' and Heroes' Remembrance Authority to commemorate the 6 million Jews killed in the Holocaust, the communities and institutions destroyed, the soldiers and resistance members who fought the Nazis, the dignity of the Jews attacked, and those who risked their lives in order to aid Jews.

1955 The Soviet Union declares an end to war with Germany.

1957 After emigrating to the United States, Gerda Weissmann Klein writes a memoir called *All but My Life.*

1958 Elie Wiesel revises and abridges a previous work, and the result is published in France as *La Nuit,* an autobiographical novel detailing Wiesel's experiences during the Holocaust. The work is published in English in 1960 as *Night.*

1959 German industrialist Alfried Krupp is made to pay reparations to former concentration camp inmates who were forced to work in Krupp's munitions factories.

1960 In May Adolf Eichmann is arrested in Argentina by the Israeli Security Service.

During 1960, former journalist William L. Shirer publishes *The Rise and Fall of the Third Reich: A History of Nazi Germany.*

1961 Jewish journalist Hannah Arendt covers the trial of Adolf Eichmann, a notorious Nazi criminal who escaped to Argentina after the war. Born in Germany, Arendt had fled her homeland during the rise of Nazism. Ultimately, Arendt writes *Eichmann in Jerusalem: A Report on the Banality of Evil.* The views she expresses about the character of Eichmann create considerable controversy.

Communists build the Berlin Wall in order to stop East Germans from fleeing to West Germany.

1962 Former Nazi official Adolf Eichmann is executed after being found guilty of war crimes for his part in the murder of hundreds of thousands of Jews.

1967 Franz Stangl, former commandant of the Sobibór death camp who oversaw the gassing of more than 100,000 people in his first two months there, is taken to Germany to stand trial for war crimes.

1970 After serving twenty years in prison, former Nazi Albert Speer publishes his autobiography, *Inside the Third Reich.*

1971 Beate and Serge Klarsfeld discover former SS officer Klaus Barbie in La Paz, Bolivia. Barbie is not extradited until 1983.

1976 Japanese American activist Michiko Weglyn publishes *Years of Infamy: The Untold Story of America's Concentration Camps,* which exposes the suffering of more than 100,000 Japanese Americans imprisoned in U.S. internment camps during World War II.

1979 A U.S. television miniseries called *Holocaust* is broadcast; it is later credited with breaking the silence about the Holocaust in Germany.

1983 Donald Carroll publishes "Escape from Vichy," an article about American writer Varian Fry, who helped rescue between 1,500 and 4,000 Jews in German-occupied France.

The judgment against Fred Korematsu, who tried in 1944 to claim that internment of Japanese Americans was unconstitutional, is overturned on October 4.

1985 Human remains found in Brazil are confirmed to be those of Nazi doctor Josef Mengele, who performed inhumane medical experiments on prisoners at Auschwitz.

1987 On July 4, former SS officer Klaus Barbie is found guilty of crimes against humanity and is sentenced to life in prison.

1988 The U.S. Congress formally apologizes to Japanese Americans for interning them in camps during World War II. Survivors are offered a one-time payment of $20,000.

1989 The Berlin Wall is destroyed on November 9. The Brandenburg Gate connecting East and West Germany opens on December 22.

1990 Gypsy Holocaust survivor and artist Karl Stojka opens an exhibit titled *The Story of Karl Stojka: A Childhood in Birkenau,* which displays more than 100 paintings depicting his life in a concentration camp.

East Germany and West Germany are reunited on October 3, 1990.

1992 Holocaust survivor Isabella (Katz) Leitner publishes *Isabella: From Auschwitz to Freedom* and *The Big Lie,* both of which describe her experiences during the Holocaust.

1993 The United States Holocaust Memorial Museum in Washington, D.C., is dedicated on April 27.

The Israeli Supreme Court overturns the death sentence of alleged former Nazi John Demjanjuk and acquits him.

1997 Riva Shefer, a seventy-five-year-old Latvian Jew who survived a Nazi labor camp, becomes the first recipient of money from a $200 million Swiss fund established to aid Holocaust survivors.

1998 Fred Korematsu is awarded the Presidential Medal of Freedom, the highest civilian honor in the United States, in January 1998.

The Vatican issues a document stating that Pope Pius XII, leader of the Catholic church during the Holocaust, did all he could to save Jews. Many historians disagree.

Maurice Papon, a former official of the French Vichy government, is sentenced to ten years in prison for helping the Germans illegally arrest and deport French Jews.

In July, German automaker Volkswagen agrees to pay reparations to slave laborers who worked in its factories during the war.

On October 11, Edith Stein becomes the first Jewish person in modern times to be declared a saint by the Roman Catholic church.

1999 Dinko Sakic, the last known living commandant of a World War II concentration camp, is tried for war crimes.

2000 During the year 2000, Germany sets aside $5 billion to provide compensation to slave laborers forced to work for the Nazis during World War II. The money is contributed equally by the German government and German industry

Pope John Paul II makes a historic visit to Israel in March and tours the Israeli Holocaust memorial Yad Vashem.

On August 9, Simon Wiesenthal is awarded the U.S. Presidential Medal of Freedom.

Glossary

Abwehr The intelligence service of the German armed forces' high command.

Afrika Korps Highly effective German troops who fought under General Erwin Rommel in the North African desert.

air raid An attack by aircraft on a target on the ground, often forcing people to take cover in air raid shelters.

Aktion (**plural,** *Aktionen*) Raid against Jews, often in ghettos, primarily to gather victims for extermination.

Allies Countries that fought against the Axis powers (Germany, Italy, and Japan) during World War II. The makeup of the Allies changed over the course of the war; the first major Allied countries were Great Britain and France. Germany defeated France in 1940, but some Free French forces continued to fight with the Allies until the end of the war. The Soviet Union and the United States joined the Allies in 1941.

Anschluss The annexation of Austria by Nazi Germany on March 13, 1938.

Anti-Comintern Pact Agreement signed in Berlin on November 25, 1936, by Germany and Japan. They were joined in 1937 by Italy, and later by Bulgaria, Hungary, Romania, Spain, and other states. The signers agreed to fight the Commu-

nist International organization (Comintern), that is, the Soviet Union.

anti-Semitism The hatred of or discrimination toward Jews.

appeasement The policy adopted by some European leaders, notably British Prime Minister Neville Chamberlain, toward Adolf Hitler prior to World War II. These leaders attempted to appease Hitler with political and economic concessions.

Ardennes Large forested area in southeastern Belgium; site of the 1944–1945 campaign known as the Battle of the Bulge.

Arrow Cross party A Fascist party in Hungary.

Aryan The name, used by the Nazis and others, of the "race" of people speaking languages thought to be derived from Sanskrit. Aryans were viewed by the Nazis as a superior race.

Aryanization The confiscation of Jewish businesses by the German authorities.

Atlantic Charter Agreement signed in 1941 by U.S. President Franklin D. Roosevelt and British Prime Minister Winston Churchill in which the two countries stated their commitment to worldwide peace and democracy.

Axis Coalition formed by Germany, Italy, and Japan to fight against the Allies during World

War II; during the course of the war, Hungary, Romania, Croatia, Slovakia, Finland, and Bulgaria also joined the Axis.

Beer Hall Putsch A failed attempt by Adolf Hitler and the Nazis to overthrow the Bavarian government on November 9, 1923. Also known as the Hitler Putsch or the Munich Putsch.

blackout Mandatory measure requiring citizens to turn off all lights in homes, businesses, and other facilities, as well as cars and other vehicles; the practice was intended to discourage enemy air raids as pilots would be unable to locate targets in the darkness.

blackshirts Fascists in Italy under the dictatorship of Benito Mussolini.

blitzkrieg "Lightning war"; the military strategy of sending troops in land vehicles to make quick, surprise strikes against the enemy while airplanes provide support from the air. This worked effectively for German troops in Poland and France.

brownshirts See **Sturmabteilung.**

Bund Jewish socialist, non-Zionist resistance group, active mainly in Poland between World War I and World War II.

Bund Deutscher Mädel (BDM) "German Girls' League"; the Nazi organization for girls; the female equivalent of the Hitlerjugend (Hitler Youth).

cavalry Originally referred to horse-mounted troops; in more recent times, refers to troops using armored vehicles, such as tanks.

Code Talkers A group of Native Americans who used the Navajo language as an effective American code in the Pacific theater during World War II.

collaboration Cooperation between citizens of a country and its occupiers.

commissar A Communist party official or Soviet government official.

communism An ideology and/or political philosophy that advocates the abolition of private property, and in which the state controls the means of production.

concentration camp *Konzentrationslager*; a place where people are held against their will without regard to the accepted forms of arrest and detention. During World War II, the Nazis used concentration camps to hold Jews, Roma (Gypsies), political dissidents, religious figures, homosexuals, and others they considered enemies of the state.

conscientious objector One who refuses to fight in a war for moral, religious, or philosophical reasons.

crematorium (plural, crematoria) An oven designed to incinerate human corpses.

D-Day Usually refers to June 6, 1944, the day Allied forces launched Operation Overlord, an invasion of German-occupied France on the beaches of Normandy; also a military term designating the date and time of an attack.

death marches Forced marches of concentration camp inmates (usually Jews) during the German retreat near the end of World War II; also refers to forced marches of Allied prisoners of war (POWs) in the Pacific (i.e., the Bataan Death March).

deportation Banishment; being sent out of a country.

displaced persons (DPs) Persons forced out of their countries of origin during war. After World War II, DPs had a difficult time finding refuge.

draft System by which a country requires a certain segment of its population to perform a term of military service; also called military conscription or selective service.

Einsatzgruppen "Special action groups"; mobile units of the Schutzstaffel (SS) and Sicherheitsdienst (SD), the military wing of the Nazi party, that followed the German army into Poland in September 1939, and into the Soviet Union in June 1941. Their official duties included the elimination of political opponents and the seizure of state documents. In the Soviet Union, in particular, they carried out mass murders, primarily of the Jewish population.

Endlösung See "Final Solution."

euthanasia Generally refers to mercy killing; the Nazis used the term to refer to the murder of those they deemed unfit to live, including the mentally or physically challenged.

Executive Order 9066 Order issued by U.S. President Franklin D. Roosevelt on February 19, 1942, directing all Japanese Americans on the West Coast to be sent to internment camps.

fascism Political system in which power rests not with citizens but with the central government, which is often run by the military and/or a dictator.

"Final Solution" In full, "Endlösung der Judenfrage in Europa," or "final solution of the Jewish problem in Europe"; Nazi code name for the physical extermination of all European Jews.

Free French Movement headed from outside France by General Charles de Gaulle that tried to organize and encourage French people to resist the German occupation.

Freikorps "Free Corps"; volunteer units consisting mostly of former members in the German army; much of the Sturmabteilung (SA), or storm troopers, was made up of Free Corps members.

führer "Leader"; Adolf Hitler's title as the head of Nazi Germany.

gas chamber A room in which people are killed by means of poisonous gas.

Geheime Staatspolizei (Gestapo) Secret state police in Nazi Germany.

Generalgouvernement General Government; the Germans' name for the administrative unit comprising those parts of occupied Poland that were not incorporated into the Reich. It included five districts: Galicia, Kraków, Lublin, Radom, and Warsaw.

gentiles Non-Jews, especially Christian non-Jews.

Gestapo See Geheime Staatspolizei.

ghettos Crowded, walled sections of cities where Jews were forced to live in substandard conditions; conditions often led to disease and/or starvation.

GI An abbreviation of "government issue"; a term for members of the U.S. armed forces.

Gyspies See Roma.

Hitlerjugend "Hitler Youth"; organization founded in 1922 that trained German boys to idolize and obey German leader Adolf Hitler, to follow Hitler's policies precisely, and to become Nazi soldiers.

Holocaust Period between 1933 and 1945 when Nazi Germany engaged in the systematic persecution and elimination of Jews and other people deemed inferior by the Nazis, such as citizens of eastern Europe and the Soviet Union, Roma (Gypsies), homosexuals, and Jehovah's Witnesses. Also called sho'ah in Hebrew.

Home Army Secret military resistance organization in Poland.

internment camps Guarded facilities usually used to hold citizens of an enemy country during wartime.

island hopping Allied strategy in the Pacific for taking islands one after another, skipping those that were deemed of little military value.

isolationism A country's policy of remaining out of other countries' affairs. Isolationism was a strong force in American politics before World War I (1914–1918) and continued to be an important factor until Japan attacked the United States in December 1941.

Judenrat (plural, Judenräte) "Jewish Council"; a committee of Jewish leaders formed in ghettos under German orders.

Junker A landed Prussian noble; Junkers controlled the German military until the end of World War I (1914–1918).

Kapo Probably from the Italian word capo, or "chief"; supervisor of inmate laborers in a concentration camp.

Kristallnacht "Night of the Broken Glass"; organized pogrom against Jews in Germany and Austria on November 9–10, 1938.

Lebensraum "Room to live"; Nazi idea that the German people, or Aryan race, needed expanded living space to survive and increase in size.

Lend-Lease Program U.S. legislation passed in 1941 (prior to the United States entering the war) that allowed the United States to send supplies needed for the war effort to countries fighting Germany, such as Great Britain and the Soviet Union. Payment was to be made after the war.

liquidation The Nazi process of destroying ghettos by sending prisoners to death camps and burning the buildings.

Luftwaffe German air force.

Maginot Line Defensive fortifications built to protect France's eastern border.

Manhattan Project Project funded by the U.S. government that secretly gathered scientists at facilities in New York City; Chicago, Illinois; Los Alamos, New Mexico; and other locations to work on the development of an atomic bomb.

Mein Kampf "*My Struggle*"; Adolf Hitler's book expounding his ideology, published in two volumes (July 1925 and December 1926).

Munich Pact Agreement signed by the leaders of France, Great Britain, Nazi Germany, and Italy in September 1938, allowing the Nazis to take over the Sudetenland, an area between Austria and Germany. The accord became famous as a symbol of the British and French policy of appeasement of Germany.

Nacht und Nebel "Night and Fog"; code name for rounding up suspected members of the anti-Nazi resistance in occupied western Europe; people were said to disappear in the "night and fog."

Nazi Abbreviated name for the Nationalsozialistische Deutsche Arbeiterpartei, or the National Socialist German Workers' party, the political organization led by Adolf Hitler, who became dictator of Germany. The Nazis controlled Germany from 1933 to 1945, promoting racist and anti-Semitic ideas and enforcing total obedience to Hitler and the party.

Nazi-Soviet Pact Mutual non-aggression treaty signed by Nazi Germany and the Communist Soviet Union in 1939, despite Adolf Hitler's hatred of communism; allowed Hitler to avoid a two-front war in Poland. Also called the Molotov-Ribbentrop Pact.

Night of the Long Knives *Nacht der langen Messer*; Nazi purge of the Sturmabteilung (SA), or storm troopers, June 30–July 1, 1934.

Nuremberg Laws Laws issued in 1935 to further the exclusion of Jews from German life. The first removed Jews' citizenship; the second defined Jews racially and prohibited them from engaging in marital and other relations with Germans. The laws were proclaimed at the annual Nazi party rally in Nuremberg on September 15, 1935, and were expanded on November 14, 1935.

Nuremberg Trial Trial of twenty-two major Nazi figures in Nuremberg in 1945 and 1946 by the International Military Tribunal. Other World War II war crimes trials are also sometimes referred to as the Nuremberg Trials.

occupation Control of a country by a foreign military power.

Operation Overlord Code name for the Normandy invasion, a massive Allied attack on German-occupied France. Also called D-Day.

Operation Reinhard Nazi plan to eliminate European Jews; named in honor of Reinhard Heydrich, chief architect of the "Final Solution."

Operation Torch British and American invasion of North Africa in November 1942.

pacifism A belief opposing war and violence as problem-solving techniques; sometimes is expressed as passivism or a refusal to bear arms.

Palestine Region in the Middle East captured by the British from the Ottoman Turks. In exchange for Jewish help capturing the region, the British promised the establishment of a Jewish national homeland in Palestine.

partisans Guerilla fighters.

Pearl Harbor Inlet on the southern coast of the island of Oahu, Hawaii, and the site of the Japanese attack on a U.S. naval base on December 7, 1941. The attack prompted the United States to enter World War II officially.

pogrom An organized massacre of or violence against a specific group of people, often Jews.

Potsdam Declaration Statement released by British Prime Minister Winston Churchill, U.S. President Harry S Truman, and Soviet leader Joseph Stalin on July 26, 1945, demanding the unconditional surrender of Japan.

prisoner of war (POW) Person captured during a war, especially by enemy forces during combat.

Prussia The largest state in the German empire from 1871 to 1918.

radar Technology using radio waves to detect objects or topographical features. Initial development of radar began in 1935; it allowed combatants in World War II to detect incoming planes. Later, the technology advanced so that radar devices could be fitted into planes, allowing pilots to locate potential bombing targets more easily.

RAF See Royal Air Force.

ration To make something available in fixed amounts; to limit access to scarce goods; the allotted amount of something.

Red Army An abbreviation for Rabochya Krestyanskaya Krasnaya Armiya, or "Workers' and Peasants' Red Army," the official name of the Soviet army until June 1945, when it was changed to Soviet Army.

Reich "Empire"; Adolf Hitler's regime as dictator of Germany was called the Third Reich. The First Reich was the Holy Roman Empire; the second was proclaimed by Otto von Bismarck.

Reichstag German parliament.

reparations Compensation required from a defeated nation for damage or injury during war.

resettlement The Nazi term for forcing Jews into ghettos and concentration camps.

resistance An organized movement in a conquered country designed to attack and subvert occupying troops and, often, native collaborators.

"Righteous among the Nations" Title given by Yad Vashem (Holocaust memorial and museum) to non-Jews who risked their lives to save Jews in Nazi-occupied Europe.

Roma (Gypsies) Dark-haired and dark-skinned, nomadic people who are believed to have originated in India.

"Rosie the Riveter" A nickname for more than 6 million women who entered the American workforce as factory workers during World War II, filling job vacancies left by men heading off to war.

Royal Air Force (RAF) The British aerial armed force.

SA See Sturmabteilung.

Schutzstaffel (SS) "Security squad"; unit that provided Adolf Hitler's personal bodyguards and concentration camp guards.

SD See Sicherheitsdienst.

segregation The forced separation of races. During World War II, African Americans and whites in the United States were segregated in many public places, including schools, and the military.

Selektion (plural, Selektionen) "Selection"; the process of selecting, from among Jewish deportees arriving at a Nazi camp, those who were to be used for forced labor and those who were to be killed immediately. The term also refers to the selecting, in ghettos, of Jews to be deported.

sho'ah The Hebrew term for "holocaust"; the mass destruction of Jews by the Nazis.

Sicherheitsdienst (SD) "Security police"; special unit that served as the intelligence service of the Schutzstaffel (SS).

Sonderkommando "Special squad"; SS or Einsatzgruppen detachment. Also refers to the Jewish units in extermination camps who removed the bodies of those gassed for cremation or burial.

SS See Schutzstaffel.

Star of David Jewish religious symbol; the Nazis forced Jews to wear a badge shaped like the Star of David for identification purposes.

Sturmabteilung (SA) "Storm troopers" (also known as Braunhemd, or brownshirts); members of a special armed and uniformed branch of the Nazi party.

swastika Ancient symbol originating in South Asia; appropriated by the Nazis as their emblem.

synagogue Jewish house of worship.

theater From a military standpoint, an area of operations during a war. The two main areas of operations during World War II were the European and Pacific theaters.

Third Reich The official name of the regime that Adolf Hitler headed as führer of Germany; means Third Empire. See also Reich.

Treaty of Versailles Restrictive agreement that Germany was forced to sign in 1919 after World War I (1914–1918). Germany was required to claim responsibility for the war and pay damages to other countries.

Tripartite Pact Agreement that established a military alliance between Germany, Italy, and Japan in 1940. Also known as the Axis or Three-Power Pact.

Tuskegee Airmen Group of African Americans who became the first black Army Air Corps pilots.

U-boat A contraction of *Unterseeboot*; a German submarine.

V-E Day Victory in Europe Day, the day on which German forces officially surrendered, May 8, 1945.

Vichy Regime set up in France in 1940, after the Germans invaded the country. Headed by Field Marshal Philippe Pétain, it was actually under German control. Its name comes from the French town where it was headquartered.

V-J Day Victory over Japan Day, the day on which Japanese forces officially surrendered, September 2, 1945.

Volksdeutsche "Ethnic Germans"; Germans living outside Germany.

WAC See Women's Army Corps.

Waffen-SS Military unit of the Schutzstaffel (SS), the Nazi security squad.

Wannsee Conference Meeting called by Reinhard Heydrich in 1941 to inform the German government of the "Final Solution," a plan to eliminate European Jews.

war crimes Violations of the laws or customs of war; the basis for trials held by the Allies after World War II.

Wartheland (Warthegau) Western Polish district annexed to the Reich after September 1939.

WASPs See Women's Airforce Service Pilots.

Weimar Republic Democratic German government in existence from 1919 to 1933, imposed upon Germany at the end of World War I (1914–1918).

Women's Airforce Service Pilots (WASPs) Organization that recruited and trained women pilots to perform non-combat flying duties.

Women's Army Corps (WAC) Organization that allowed American women to serve a variety of non-combat roles.

World War I A conflict that raged throughout Europe from 1914 to 1918. Austria-Hungary, Germany, Turkey, and Bulgaria fought against Serbia, Russia, France, Great Britain, Japan, Italy, and, later, the United States, along with twenty-one other nations.

Yad Vashem Holocaust memorial in Jerusalem.

Yiddish Language spoken by eastern European Jews.

Zionism Movement that advocated the formation of a Jewish nation in Palestine.

Zydowsk Organizacja Bojowa (ZOB) Military wing of the Jewish underground in the Warsaw ghetto.

Zyklon B Hydrogen cyanide; the brand name of a pesticide used by the Nazis in their euthanasia program and later, especially in the gas chambers of Auschwitz.

Research Ideas

The following research ideas are intended to offer suggestions for complementing social studies and history curricula, to trigger additional ideas for enhancing learning, and to suggest cross-disciplinary projects for library and classroom use.

Ration Recipes

Look in cookbooks published during the 1940s or women's magazines published during World War II and note how recipes account for rationing. What kinds of ingredient substitutions do they specify? Make one of the recipes and invite others to rate the flavor, or adapt a recipe from a modern cookbook to account for rationing.

Personal History

Interview a veteran of World War II or someone who lived during the war. Create a list of questions before the interview. Perhaps ask the interviewee where he or she was during the war, how the war changed his or her life, and what was his or her impression of the war's importance both at the time and in retrospect.

Design a Holocaust Memorial

Create a sketch or a paper model for a historic marker, public display, or building commemorating a person, place, or event in Holocaust history. Explain how and why you made your design choices, and why you felt your chosen person, place, or event was worthy of commemoration.

Atom Bomb Debate

Study the decision to drop atom bombs on Hiroshima and Nagasaki. Taking into consideration only what was known at the time about the bombs, form two teams, one in favor of dropping the bomb and the other against, and debate the issues. Then repeat the debate, taking into consideration what is currently known about the effects of atomic bombs. Discuss how the first and second debates differed.

Turning Points

On a large map of the world, use pushpins to mark the sites of battles that were important turning points during the war. For each site, create a note card explaining who fought there, who won, and why that battle was significant.

Modern Opinions from Historical Figures

Form a group of four to six people and choose a current event in world politics as the basis for a panel discussion. One person will serve as moderator for the discussion; the remaining group members should each choose a prominent individual involved in World War II. After researching both the issue and the prominent individuals, students will present the positions they think their selected historical figures would have taken on the subject.

War-Inspired Artwork

Choose a creative work related to World War II; this can be anything from a piece of architecture (like the memorial to the USS *Arizona* in Pearl Harbor, Hawaii) to a painting, song, or poem inspired by the war (such as Randall Jarrell's poem "The Death of the Ball Turret Gunner"). Explain the work's relationship to the war: is it about a battle, or an individual's experience of the war? What emotions does the piece evoke: bravery, fear, loneliness, anger?

Create a Board Game Based on Nazi Confiscation of Jewish Property

Trace the history of a painting that was taken from its original owner and ended up in a foreign museum by making a Monopoly-type game.

War Journal

Imagine that you were alive during World War II. You can choose to have lived in any country involved. Write a journal of your activities over the course of one week.

Propaganda

Rent a video of a movie created during World War II that is about the war. Some examples of films available on videocassette include Frank Capra's *Why We Fight* documentary series, *Casablanca,* and *Mrs. Miniver.* Write an essay discussing whether the film has a particular political message and what that message is.

Battlefield Tour

Create an itinerary for a World War II battlefield tour. You could choose to focus the tour on sites in the Pacific, sites throughout Europe or North Africa, or on one specific country. List the sites you'll be visiting on the tour, giving the name of the battles fought, codenames for the operations (if any), key events of the battles, the commanders involved, the victors, and why the battles were important.

D-Day Newspaper Article

Write an article about the June 6, 1944, invasion of France from the viewpoint of either an American or a German war correspondent.

Rescuers

Research individuals who saved or helped save Jewish lives during the Holocaust. Be sure to include less well-known people as well as more famous figures. Write their names and a brief description of the rescue(s) they made on slips of paper that can be pinned to a map in the appropriate places.

Trials

Imagine that you were a guard at a Nazi concentration camp. After the war, you are tried at Nuremberg for war crimes. Explain the reasons for your actions. Or, imagine that you are one of the prosecutors at the Nuremberg trials. Explain the types of questions you would ask and what criteria you would use to determine guilt or innocence.

16

Life in Europe During the War

World War II had a lasting effect not only on soldiers and prisoners but also on private citizens, especially in German-occupied territories. From 1940 to mid-1944, Germany controlled much of Europe and carried out policies that involved the intentional killing of millions of people, especially in eastern Europe. Even in western and northern Europe, where occupied countries received relatively mild treatment in the beginning, the Germans used the economic resources of those countries for the war effort. The impact on local populations was lower wages, less food, worse health, and sometimes forced labor in Germany. In other places, especially eastern and southeastern Europe, German economic policy was to seize available resources and leave as little as possible for citizens, who were essentially treated as slaves.

Yet the promise of economic gain was not the only reason Germany occupied countries. Nazi actions in the Soviet Union, for instance, amounted to looting and smashing of anything of value. This produced fewer benefits for Germany than it attained from smaller and less-populous France. In fact, Germany had received more farm products and other goods by purchasing them from the Soviet Union before it invaded. The Germans' long-term goal in eastern Europe was the permanent destruction of the nations it conquered. This did not mean simply dominating their governments, as in France, but instead eradicating the very concept of a country separate from German control.

German leaders sometimes described their goal as the creation of a slave empire, a goal that was tied closely to Nazi racial theories. The Nazis believed that Germans were a master race, which gave them full rein to attack, conquer, and enslave allegedly weaker races. Germany would conquer foreign countries in eastern Europe in order to provide *Lebensraum,* or "room to live." According to this plan, Poles, Russians, Ukrainians, White Russians, and others would serve German overlords as sources of cheap labor. People who resisted would be killed, and millions of others would die from lack of adequate food, shelter, and medicine. The Jews living in those areas were considered subhuman, and would be completely eradicated.

The treatment of Soviet soldiers captured by the Germans is an example of how Nazi ideas about race led to inhumane actions unrelated to economic goals. Beginning in June 1941, more than 5.5 million Soviet troops were captured, over 3 million of them in the first few months of the German invasion. An estimated 1 million of these died before they reached prison camps, often shot by the German troops to whom they surrendered. An additional 2 million died in German camps, where they were crowded together with no shelter and often no food; in some camps there were reports of cannibalism. Approximately 250,000 prisoners died as the Germans moved them from one place to another, sometimes forcing the captives to march until they died.

One of the first places the Nazis tested their conquering and assimilating plan on a large scale was Poland, which they gained control of in September 1939. Desirable parts of western Poland were annexed and made part of Germany. The Nazi plan was to force all Poles out of this area so that *Volksdeutsche,* or people living outside Germany who had German ancestry, could occupy this *Lebensraum.* Two million Poles, including 600,000 Jews, were forced hurriedly out of their homes, usually against their will, and out of the area. The part of Poland that had not been annexed was known as the *Generalgouvernement,* or General Government. The Nazis never intended to make the *Generalgouvernement* part of Germany; instead, they planned to exploit it for the good of Germany. Everything of value was sent back to Germany. Businesses and factories that were not stripped were run by Germans.

The economic plunder in Poland was only one step in the Nazis' destruction of Poland. In order to keep the country fragmented, they tried to eliminate anyone who might be a potential leader. This included all educated Poles as well as many political leaders, nobles, and priests. In order to prevent a rebirth of the educated class, the Germans shut down schools in Poland. In the city of Vilna in 1943, for example, there was only one primary school for a Polish population of 104,000. In response, the Poles created secret schools, including a university with 2,500 students. They also developed underground resistance organizations, such as the *Armia Krajowa,* or Home Army, which eventually had 300,000 members. The Polish underground published more than 1,000 newspapers and magazines, 300 of which came out regularly during the occupation.

In contrast to the brutal tactics the Germans used in occupying Poland and other parts of eastern Europe, they developed more sophisticated ways of taking over property in western Europe. The Nazis implemented a policy whereby a conquered country was forced to pay the cost of the occupation. These costs were calculated not in relation to the actual expenses of the German army in that country, but according to the wealth of the country, so Germany actually made a profit from occupying countries. For instance, France, the wealthiest and largest conquered nation, paid mil-

lions of dollars a day, more than half of all such payments collected by the Germans. The Germans also set the value of the German mark at a high rate compared with local currency, thus allowing German companies and the German government to buy local products at artificially lowered prices. Throughout western Europe, German companies were soon buying local businesses and an increasing portion of occupied countries' economies fell into German hands. Germany even used similar methods with its allies, such as Hungary and Romania. These deals were almost impossible to refuse, because behind German economic demands always lay the threat of military force.

Rationing and Food Shortages

One of Germany's main goals was to ensure that it could send home a steady supply of farm products, which caused food shortages in the occupied countries. Shortages were worsened by Allied bombing of railroad and road systems, which made it more difficult to transport food from farms to cities. Food and other products were rationed everywhere, which was supposed to ensure that everyone received an equal share. In fact, the shortages led to high prices and illegal trade on the black market. People with enough money could buy more than their share illegally, while others might not have enough to eat. Rationing varied from country to country, but Germany consistently received the majority of food and other products. In most occupied countries, people generally ate only about one-half to two-thirds as much food as they had before the war. In France, the official ration supplied around 1,200 calories a day, but even this amount was not always available outside the black market. In 1941 the official price of butter in Paris was forty francs per kilogram (two and one-fifth pounds), and by 1943, it was sixty-one francs. The actual price that citizens had to pay to acquire the butter in 1943, however, was 800 francs. In the same way, products such as wine and tobacco cost ten or twelve times more than the "official" price. A meal in a factory lunchroom, where prices were supposed to be kept low, cost workers a full day's pay. Throughout the war, some foods, like meat, were especially scarce. Often meat could not be bought in Paris for an entire month. During winter 1941–1942, adult citizens in Athens, Greece, were receiving only 600 to 800 calories per day; the result was widespread malnutrition, illness, and death. In the parts of the Netherlands that were still occupied by Germany during winter 1944–1945—known as the "hunger winter"—people consumed approximately 500 calories a day and many starved.

Food was not the only product that was expensive during the occupation. In 1943 in France, a pair of shoes cost what an average person earned in six weeks; a man's suit in Paris cost about four months' pay. Coal was so expensive that most people could not afford enough to cook their meals. As both clothing and fuel for heating became increasingly expensive and difficult to locate, each winter brought terrible suffering in northern areas that was worsened by rampant malnutrition. A general decline in health resulted in outbreaks, and sometimes epidemics, of tuberculosis, diphtheria, typhus, typhoid, and cholera. At the end of the war, 1.5 million people had tuberculosis in Poland—6 percent of the surviving population. Shortages of medicine also made it difficult to control diseases. For instance, in France, where reliable statistics are available, there was a serious increase in death rates, particularly among infants. Death could also come more suddenly. Although people in occupied Europe welcomed the sight of British and American planes on their way to bomb Germany, the raids were aimed not at military targets but at factories in occupied countries. The first successful large-scale British bombing raid in Europe was made on the Renault factory complex in a Paris suburb in March 1942, resulting in a large number of civilian deaths.

As hunger grew, there was an increase in crime, especially theft and prostitution, even though the local police had greater power to stop people and make arrests. There were virtually no private cars; train travel was restricted; citizens were usually subjected to a curfew; and no one was allowed to visit or move to another city without permission. Each person had to have an identity card, which the police could check at any time. Attendance at sports events and movies increased, however, as people sought entertainment to help them forget the realities of the war.

Censorship

Censorship in occupied countries meant people had to be extremely careful about expressing their opinions. Criticizing the Germans or the governments that cooperated with them could result in a jail sentence or deportation to a concentration camp. Police often read and censored mail. Prewar newspapers were either shut down or were allowed to print only news approved by the Germans, and fewer people wanted to read them.

Resistance papers began to appear very early in the occupation. Some of the first ones were produced on typewriters with about a half dozen copies passed from hand to hand. Later, these publications became more professional, sometimes secretly using the same printing presses as the legal newspapers. Eventually, there were about 1,000 resistance newspapers in France and 300 in Belgium, with 12,000 people working on them. In Denmark, 315 papers were distributed among a population of only 4 million people. In the Netherlands, 120 newspapers were being published as early as 1941; there were another 150 within two years.

The official radio was also controlled, but most people listened to either Swiss radio or the BBC (the British Broadcasting Corporation), which informed Europeans that Germany was losing battles and could be defeated. The Germans made every effort to prevent citizens from learning the truth—the goal was to keep people demoralized and unwilling to risk both their lives and their families' lives for a cause that seemed hopeless. The Germans levied heavy penalties on anyone caught listening to BBC, and in 1943, they even banned the ownership of private radios in the Netherlands altogether. Nevertheless, many people simply hid their radios and continued to listen in secret. To make up for the loss of radio news, the main Dutch resistance newspapers began publishing three times a week. The five largest papers had a combined circulation of 450,000 copies.

Forced Labor

German policy intentionally made jobs difficult to find in occupied areas in an attempt to divert laborers to Germany. From the first days of the occupation, people in eastern Europe were sent to Germany and forced to work on farms and in factories. In parts of Poland, children as young as twelve were subjected to forced labor. In western Europe, however, the Germans initially tried to persuade people to volunteer to work in Germany, promising high wages and good conditions. They also made sure that some workers would have little choice except to volunteer. An unemployed person who refused to work in Germany, for example, would not receive unemployment insurance and could even lose his or her ration card, which might mean starvation.

A group of Maquis, French resistance fighters, training in the forest. (Reproduced by permission of AP/Wide World Photos)

In France, the Germans promised to release French prisoners of war captured in 1940 in exchange for Frenchmen who volunteered to work. For every six voluntary workers, the Germans released one prisoner of war, often the least healthy individuals. By May 1941, about 45,000 French workers had gone to Germany, 33,000 of them from Paris, where unemployment was especially high. There were still not enough volunteers, however, and the numbers plunged even lower when rumors circulated that foreign workers in Germany were treated badly and were not making the amount of money promised by the Nazis. The Germans began drafting young men from western Europe to work in Germany. By the second half of 1942, 250,000 Frenchmen had been sent to Germany by the Service de Travaille Obligatoire (compulsory labor service), or STO. Altogether, the STO drafted 641,000 French workers, the largest number from any western European country. The earlier volunteer workers and the STO draftees were now both treated as prisoners. In 1943 there were 1.7 million French workers (including prisoners of war) in German industry.

The STO and similar programs in other occupied countries had a result not anticipated by the Germans. While most people in western Europe hated the Nazis and wanted an end to German occupation, many (probably the great majority) were not ready to risk their freedom and their lives to oppose the seemingly all-powerful German army. They were waiting, hoping that Germany would lose the war and they would be freed. With forced labor programs, though, young men faced a simple choice: either report for forced labor in Germany or go into hiding. In France, thousands of men left home and hid in the forests and hills, where they joined existing bands of resistance fighters. In the Netherlands, where the flat, treeless geography was not suited for guerrilla warfare, young men and women who hid in order to avoid compulsory labor service were called *onderduikers,* or "ones who dive under." By the end of the war, there were an estimated 300,000 *onderduikers.*

German Retaliation

The growth of armed resistance as a result of the STO also led to an increase in civilian deaths as people were shot by the Germans in revenge for acts of resistance. The high command of the German armed forces ordered all officers to follow this policy, feeling that ordinary citizens might blame the resistance for these deaths, and consequently withdraw their support from the underground. In general, the ploy did not work. People in occupied

Young German Rebels

For years, the Nazis pressured young people in Germany to join official Nazi organizations like the Hitlerjugend, the Hitler Youth movement, or the Bund Deutscher Mädel, the League of German Girls. By 1936, membership was legally required. These groups sponsored sporting events and similar social activities, but also taught young Germans Nazi philosophy and inculcated them into such Nazi activities as marching and wearing uniforms. Older boys received military training, and many entered the army. In 1944 an entire armored division, called the Hitler Youth Division, was formed entirely from recent graduates of the Hitler Youth program.

Not all young Germans, however, wanted to participate in official Nazi groups, despite the law, and some rebelled against the Reich government. In a number of large cities, especially in the Rhineland in western Germany, loose groups of unskilled workers formed, usually made up of teenagers between fourteen and eighteen. The best-known groups were the Edelweiss Pirates, named after edelweiss, a white flower that grows in the Alps in western Europe. The Pirates would often wear edelweiss, or sometimes a white pin, hidden under the left lapel of their coats.

Originally, the Edelweiss Pirates simply wanted to pursue activities such as hiking and camping without fear of Nazi interference. Soon, however, they began mocking Hitler and the Nazis in songs and in graffiti scrawled on walls. They attacked members of the Hitler Youth on the streets, engaged in industrial sabotage, and even attempted assassinations of local Nazi officials. The Nazi government considered the Pirates to be street gangs, and in some ways this was an accurate conclusion. The activities of the Pirates, however, made their anti-Nazi feelings crystal clear, and they were hunted by the Gestapo. Although twelve Pirates were publicly hanged, without trial, in Cologne in 1944, the Gestapo never succeeded in completely destroying the organization.

countries seem to have blamed the Germans, not the resistance, for the murders of innocent civilians by Nazis. The policy did, however, put many resistance organizations in the difficult position of causing the deaths of their fellow citizens. In some countries, most resistance organizations decided not to attack German occupying forces as a result of the policy.

German retaliation was often intentionally far more severe than the action of the resistance. In May 1942, a team of British-trained Czechoslovakian resistance fighters parachuted back into their country and fatally wounded high-ranking Nazi leader Reinhard Heydrich, who died in early June. The Germans immediately took revenge by killing at least 1,500 Czechs. A few days later, they surrounded the coal-mining village of Lidice, shot all 172 males over the age of sixteen, then sent all the women and most children to concentration camps.

A few of the children who "looked German" were taken from their mothers and sent to German families instead of the camps. (The policy of seizing young children and "Germanizing" them without their parents' consent was also carried out in Poland and other parts of eastern Europe.) After killing or deporting all the people of Lidice, the Germans burned every building in the town, which they had picked at random—it had no apparent connection to the assassination of Heydrich. Lidice soon became famous, and towns throughout the world were symbolically renamed after it in order to show that the Nazis could never destroy it.

Similar massacres were perpetrated by the Germans throughout occupied Europe. In April 1942 they burned down 300 houses in the Norwegian town of Televaag, deported seventy-five people to concentration camps, and arrested another 260. In retaliation for an attack that wounded one Ger-

The Origins of Sabotage

Of French origin, "sabotage" is derived from the word "sabot" meaning wooden shoes. According to popular myth, the word came into being when French factory workers threw their sabots into the machinery to shut down production during the French Revolution. Other sources say the word entered the French language around 1910 when railway workers ripped up the wooden braces (sabot) around the rails during a strike.

man, the Dutch town of Putten was burned down and all its male citizens were sent to concentration camps, where most of them died. In Paris, people who were caught outside after the official curfew were arrested, held overnight, and usually released in the morning. The deaths of German soldiers during the night, however, often resulted in reprisal deaths of curfew violators. In October 1941 the Nazis shot fifty French civilians in the western city of Nantes in retaliation for the killing of one German officer. The Germans announced they would shoot fifty more hostages if the killers were not turned over to them within two days. The next day, after another German officer was killed in the southwestern city of Bordeaux, the Nazis arrested 100 people. Fifty of these were shot immediately, and the other fifty were held hostage. These actions increased French hostility and triggered an outcry around the world. The Germans decided not to shoot the fifty hostages in each city, but their general policy remained the same. By the end of the war, they had executed 30,000 French hostages. In Greece, which had a much smaller population than France, the number of murdered hostages may have been as high as 45,000. In one Greek town, Klisura, 250 women and children were burned to death by the Nazis.

Captured resistance fighters, as opposed to civilian hostages, were often tortured to extract information before they were hanged or shot. The Germans adopted a policy, especially in western Europe, called *Nacht und Nebel* ("Night and Fog"), under which they secretly took political opponents to concentration camps in Germany, where they disappeared into the "night and fog." There were no trials, no letters, no contact with the outside world, and families and friends never found out the location or fate of the prisoner. (In fact, a small number of *Nacht und Nebel* deportees did survive the war in concentration camps.)

The Beginning of Resistance

Resistance to German occupation often began early, but usually had nonviolent roots. For instance, people in the Netherlands waiting to cross the street would raise their hats when the light turned orange, which is the Dutch national color. Danish students wore knit caps in blue, white, and red, the colors of the insignia on the planes of Britain's Royal Air Force. In many cities, conversation would cease whenever a German soldier entered a shop, and no one would say a word until he left.

From these gestures, which were not overly dangerous or threatening, some people moved on to larger, more organized anti-German activities. Writing and distributing newspapers were among the most significant efforts, but people also found other ways to injure the Germans. Some workers making products for Germany purposely did their jobs poorly, assuring that parts did not fit properly or that they would break after being used once. Clerks mislabeled shipments so that they were sent to the wrong place, causing delays. Even tardiness became a form of protest.

More serious forms of sabotage and protest also became widespread. On October 28, 1939, less than two months after the war broke out, university students in the Czech capital of Prague led public demonstrations in honor of the Czechoslovakian national holiday. As the demonstrations escalated into battles with police, the Germans retaliated by shutting down all Czech universities for the remainder of the war. In the Netherlands, university students staged a series of protests and strikes in reaction to the German order to remove all Jewish professors. In February 1941, another Dutch challenge to German anti-Jewish policy became one of the largest protests in occupied Europe. After an acid attack on German police in a Jewish-owned store, the Nazis arrested 400 Jews off the streets of Amsterdam, the largest Dutch city, and sent them to a concentration camp. In protest, thousands of Dutch workers went on strike, shutting down public services, transportation, large factories, and the

Adolf Hitler confers with Slovakian Premier, Father Josef Tiso. (Reproduced by permission of AP/Wide World Photos)

port of Amsterdam. As the strike spread to two nearby cities, the Germans declared martial law and sent large numbers of troops into the city to force people back to work. Strikers faced arrest, deportation to a concentration camp, or even execution on the spot. In 1943 a wave of strikes protesting German restrictions occurred in Denmark. At that point, the Germans had treated Denmark less harshly than any other occupied country. The Nazis retaliated by declaring martial law and disbanding the Danish government and army, both of which had been allowed to remain in existence until then. In 1943 some of the most significant strikes occurred in Italy, which was technically still an ally of Germany. Beginning in the Fiat auto factories in the northern city of Turin, strikes spread to other industries in the region. Demanding lower prices and better working conditions, the workers also called for Italy to withdraw from the war.

Armed Resistance

Armed resistance emerged in almost every country occupied by Germany. In a few places, such as Denmark and the Netherlands, geographic conditions confined the movements to small organizations in towns and cities. The Nazis sometimes succeeded in destroying much of an armed resis-

tance movement, as in Czechoslovakia after the assassination of Heydrich in 1942. From that time until the last days of the war, the Czech resistance consisted of small groups that organized work slowdowns in factories and engaged in mostly low-scale sabotage. In countries with deep forests or mountains, however, bands of resistance fighters, sometimes supplied with arms by parachute drops from Allied planes, staged hit-and-run attacks against the occupiers. In most cases, the actions were aimed not only at the Germans but also at fellow citizens who supported the Germans during the occupation. European resistance movements therefore often involved civil war.

Internal conflict occurred even in the German puppet state of Slovakia, a country the Germans had created when they took over Czechoslovakia in March 1939. The Slovakian government was a dictatorship under the leadership of Father Josef Tiso, a Catholic priest who introduced Nazi-like policies. The nation's army had attacked the Soviet Union alongside the Germans. By 1944, however, an underground guerilla army was operating in the countryside. Many Slovakian soldiers fighting in the Soviet Union had deserted and joined the Soviet army; some of them parachuted back into Slovakia with other Soviet agents to help lead the partisans. In August 1944 much of the Slovakian army stationed at home was joined by the partisans in a rebellion against Tiso and the Germans, which became known as the Slovak National Rising. Tiso's forces could not defeat the rebels, who soon controlled much of the country. The Soviets parachuted in arms and supplies, and the Soviet army attempted to break through German lines to reach Slovakia, but was stopped by the German army. Strong German reinforcements then rushed into Slovakia to crush the National Rising and, after heavy fighting, defeated the rebels by the end of October. Tiso and the Germans then engaged in large-scale and bloody reprisals.

Another country in which armed resistance led to civil war was France. The Germans swept into France in 1940 and divided the country into two parts. The German army occupied the northern half and all of the Atlantic coast, while the southern half was controlled by a new French government under the leadership of Marshal Philippe Pétain, an eighty-four-year-old World War I (1914–1918) hero. Pétain's government, which was given dictatorial powers, made its capital in Vichy, a small city in central France, and became known as the Vichy government. At first, most French citizens waited: They did not approve of Nazi Germany, but they respected Pétain and wanted to keep their everyday lives as unchanged as possible. As time went on, however, some French began to believe that Pétain and his Vichy supporters were becoming too collaborative with the Germans. The Germans demanded money from the French government, control of French companies, and bargain prices on French goods. When the Vichy government gave in to yet another demand—that Vichy draft young men for forced labor in Germany—many of those targeted by the action became active members of the resistance. In response, Vichy created special pro-Nazi units of French volunteers, called the *Milice* ("Militia"), that worked with the Nazi SS. Before long, the *Milice* and the resistance were fighting an open civil war. The French resistance also aided the Allies when they landed in France in 1944 and played an important role in liberating Paris.

Soviet Partisans

The largest armed resistance movement was the partisans of the Soviet Union. When German tanks swept into the Soviet Union in June 1941, they raced past large formations of Soviet troops. The advancing German infantry later captured

many of these units, but others remained free, regrouping in heavy forests and marshy areas that had few roads. Some of these free units were still commanded by their regular officers and were prepared to continue fighting. Others consisted mainly of men who wanted only to reach home, but this was often impossible to do without being captured, and word soon spread that the Germans were killing most Soviet soldiers who surrendered. Trapped far behind the German army, the free Soviet units became the core of a guerrilla army that operated in groups of 300 to 2,000 fighters. By the end of 1941, some 30,000 fighters were undertaking thousands of small actions that interfered with the German invasion. Partisans cut telephone wires and blew up railroad tracks. They seized or burned German supplies, forcing the Germans to guard them more heavily. They also executed civilians who cooperated with the German occupiers.

The Soviet government immediately saw the value in partisan activity and, by autumn 1941, began training officers in guerrilla warfare. Graduates of the guerilla schools then parachuted behind German lines to join existing partisan units or establish new ones. By summer 1942, there were 150,000 organized partisans; a year later, there were at least 200,000. Not all partisans were Soviet soldiers trapped behind German lines; many were local villagers who had joined the resistance. When the Germans first invaded the Soviet Union, they were welcomed by some citizens, especially in the Ukraine and the Baltic states of Estonia, Latvia, and Lithuania. Citizens in these countries thought the Germans would free them from the domination of the Russians who generally controlled the Soviet Union. Soviet dictator Joseph Stalin and his communist government had treated these conquered peoples harshly. During the 1930s in the Ukraine, Stalin's secret police had executed thousands of farmers as they fought to keep their land from being confiscated by the government. Hundreds of thousands of people had died in famines created by Soviet policies. Other opponents of the communists were arrested and sent to Siberia, a frigid area in the north of the country.

Soon, though, the Germans' policies caused most Soviet citizens to turn against the Nazis. The Germans treated the locals with contempt, and seized everything of value to be sent home. Tens of thousands of people were taken away to work as semi-slaves in Germany. The people left behind were treated just as severely: The Germans seized their crops and left them without enough to feed

Yugoslavia and neighboring countries, 1941.

their families. Before long, support for the partisans grew dramatically and large numbers of local people, including thousands of women, joined the partisans in the forests. Many thousands more cooperated with the partisans and provided them with information. Although it is impossible to know how many German troops the Soviet partisans put out of action, and it is now clear that the claims made at the time were exaggerated, 35,000 is probably a fair estimate. The military value of the partisans' efforts, however, went beyond wounding or killing German soldiers. Russian partisans had a major advantage over other European resistance movements in that they worked closely with a regular army that was near enough to sup-

port them, and so could coordinate their activities with those of the Soviet army. For example, at the beginning of major Soviet offensives, the partisans destroyed rail lines, limiting the German army's ability to transfer units by train from one area of the battlefront to another.

Civil War and Resistance in Yugoslavia

Aside from the Soviet Union, the most effective armed resistance movement in Europe was in Yugoslavia. As in France, the battle against the Germans was also partly a civil war between different groups inside the occupied country. The invasion of Yugoslavia had been one of the German army's easiest victories. The million-man Yugoslav army surrendered in less than two weeks, and the Axis powers quickly divided the country. The rapid success meant that many Yugoslav army units were still intact when the country surrendered, and some officers immediately led their units into the hills to continue fighting. Draža Mihajlović, who had been deputy chief of staff of the Yugoslav Second Army, led a band that originally consisted of only fifty soldiers. As the movement grew, its members became known as Četniki, or Chetniks, a name used by Serbs who had fought against invading Turks in previous centuries and against Austro-Hungarians and Germans in World War I. Mihajlović and most top Yugoslav army officers were Serbs, members of the largest ethnic group, who had dominated Yugoslavia. The Chetniks were loyal to the Yugoslav king, who came from the Serbian royal family.

Other ethnic groups in Yugoslavia had long resented Serbian control. The most prominent among these were the Croatians. Various Croatian political parties had struggled for greater Croatian rights throughout the 1930s, and some even demanded complete independence. The most extreme of these groups was the Ustaše ("insurgents"), who engaged in terrorist activities, including the assassination of the Yugoslavian king while he was visiting France in 1934. Receiving funds from the Fascist Italian regime of Benito Mussolini, the Ustaše modeled themselves on both the Fascists and the German Nazis—militaristic organizations that brutalized their enemies. Meanwhile, most Serbian political parties refused to give in to Croatian demands and tried to maintain Serbian domination of Yugoslavia. During the Axis invasion of the country, the Ustaše declared Croatian independence. The new, independent Croatia was then protected by German and Italian occupation forces, and became an ally of Germany. The Ustaše government was one of the most vicious and murderous in all of Nazi-controlled Europe. Its troops engaged in massacres of ethnic Serbs, Roma (Gypsies), Muslims from Bosnia (another part of Yugoslavia), and Jews. In at least a few cases, even the Nazi SS complained about Ustaše brutality. At least 200,000 people, including Croatian opponents of the Ustaše, died at the Jasenovac concentration camp, where torture was common.

The German military government in Serbia was also among the most brutal in Europe. Although there was a puppet Serbian government, it was unimportant because, unlike the Ustaše government in Croatia, the Germans ran Serbia directly. The harshness of the occupation led to a rapid increase in the strength of Mihajlović's Chetniks. Yet the Chetniks had two key disadvantages. They wanted to return Yugoslavia to its pre-war status, which meant maintaining Serbian control of the entire country. This made it virtually impossible to attract anti-Ustaše Croatians, Slovenians, Bosnians, Montenegrins, or other ethnic groups. The other drawback was that they wanted to avoid fighting the Germans immediately, preferring to gain more strength and wait until Allied armies were nearby before beginning a national uprising. One of the reasons for this policy was to avoid the reprisals against civilians that the Germans inflicted whenever there was armed resistance.

Another movement soon developed in Yugoslavia that did not have these disadvantages. The Partisans were led by Josip Broz, a Croatian known as Tito, who had been a leader of the Yugoslav Communist party before the war. This organization claimed to be campaigning for a new Yugoslavia in which each national group would be treated equally and have control of its own area. Unlike the Chetniks, Partisan leaders included non-Serbs such as Tito, and they had no plan to retain aspects of the old Yugoslavia, in which the great majority of people had lived in poverty. For Tito, the war against the Axis occupiers was also a revolution against the old system.

The Partisans consisted of about 100,000 armed soldiers who were fighting the Axis in major operations. In a series of offensives, the Germans chased the Partisans from the mountains of Bosnia into Montenegro and back again, but were unable to destroy them. During these campaigns, 20,000 Partisans were killed or wounded. The Germans also slaughtered local villagers, even if they had not helped the Partisans. Up to thirty Axis divisions, more than 300,000 men, were needed in Yugoslavia because of the Partisans' activities. Most of these Axis troops were Italian, with only a dozen German divisions, and few were first-rate combat units. The Partisans, conversely, received a tremendous amount of arms and equipment from Italian troops in Croatia and other parts of Yugoslavia when Italy surrendered to the Allies in September 1943.

The Allies also provided arms and supplies for the Partisans. The British Special Operations Executive (SOE) and the American Office of Strategic Services (OSS) were in charge of gathering information, instigating sabotage in occupied Europe,

A 90 mm gun crew shoots at Luftwaffe planes in France, keeping German pilots from reaching their intended targets. (Reproduced by permission of AP/Wide World Photos)

and aiding resistance movements. At first, the SOE and OSS favored the Chetniks because Mihajlović was the official representative of the pre-war Yugoslav government, but his reluctance to fight damaged his reputation with the British and Americans. Their opinion of him lessened even more when they began to believe that Mihajlović was more interested in destroying Tito and the Partisans than in fighting the Nazis and Fascists. Indeed, the Chetniks even cooperated with Axis forces in hunting down Partisans. Soon, the British and Americans were supporting Tito, and by 1944, the British Balkan Air Force, based in Italy, was dropping large quantities of American arms and even sometimes supplying air support to the Partisans. Despite the fact that the British and Americans generally distrusted communist resistance movements, the Partisans were obviously willing and able to fight Axis troops, while the Chetniks were not. After the war, it was learned that Tito sometimes offered temporary truces to the Germans so that the Partisans could fight the Chetniks, a fact not well-known at the time.

The Chetniks and the Partisans knew they were engaged in a civil war at the same time they were opposing the Germans; the presence of the Ustaše in Croatia made it a three-way civil war. Rugged mountains made Yugoslavia well suited to guerrilla

warfare. All of these factors, plus the cruelty of the German occupation, ensured that the conflict in Yugoslavia was among the most savage of the war. Approximately 1.4 million people, or about 10 percent of the total population, lost their lives.

German Air Raids Ravage Europe

Victory in World War II was primarily contingent upon supplying armies with huge quantities of industrial products. Modern weapons were needed, including planes, bombs, tanks, submarines, aircraft carriers, and machine guns. Ships, railroads, and trucks were needed to transport supplies. Soldiers needed sufficient quantities of boots, uniforms, and helmets. Countries depended on scientists and engineers to develop new weapons, and also writers and filmmakers to wage psychological warfare through propaganda. These needs made civilian populations crucial to war efforts in World War II. This allowed governments to request major sacrifices from citizens to advance the war effort, but also meant that civilian populations became targets for the enemy.

Air attacks brought the war home to civilian populations. The German Luftwaffe heavily bombed Warsaw, Poland, in the initial stages of the war, and also destroyed the center of the Dutch port of Rotter-

RAF gunners in full kit with oxygen masks, parachutes, and guns. (Reproduced by permission of the Corbis Corporation [Bellevue])

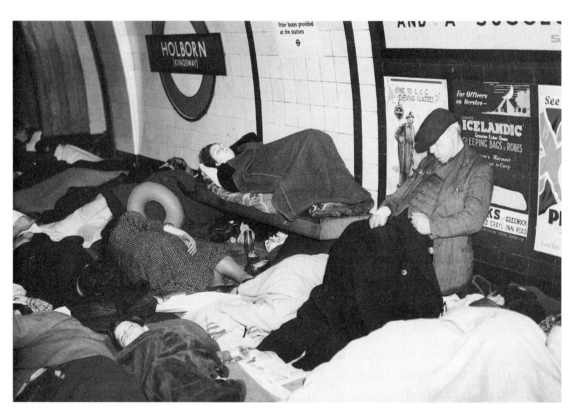

Londoners take shelter from an air raid in a subway station. (Reproduced by permission of the Corbis Corporation [Bellevue])

The Staple Inn in London, dating from the sixteenth century, was destroyed during a German bombing raid. (Reproduced by permission of the Corbis Corporation [Bellevue])

dam in May 1940. Both attacks caused many deaths and injuries, and inflicted massive damage to non-military structures such as homes, schools, and hospitals. When the Germans invaded Belgium and France, Luftwaffe planes would sometimes target the large numbers of civilians who were clogging the roads trying to escape. This machine gun strafing was designed to increase the panic of the refugees and to block the movement of Allied armies. Although the air attacks caused civilian deaths, they were closely connected to efforts by German ground troops to either capture the cities they were bombing or to cut off enemy forces. The Luftwaffe had been fashioned to work closely with the tanks and foot soldiers of the army. It had no four-engine heavy bombers that could travel long distances while carrying heavy loads of bombs. The Germans based their military planning on the belief that the war would be short; therefore they did not think they would need the Luftwaffe to operate independently of German ground troops.

Britain's RAF Plans Air Strategies

German military strategy stood in sharp contrast to that of Britain's Royal Air Force (RAF).

Formed in 1918 at the end of World War I, the RAF was the first air force that was independent of the army and navy. (The American air force was part of the army until after World War II.) The RAF developed the idea of the strategic air offensive: a direct, long-term bombing attack on the enemy's homeland to destroy the enemy's means or will to continue the war. Bomber attacks on factories, steel mills, coal mines, dams (needed to provide electric power to factories), and oil refineries (needed to provide fuel for planes and tanks) would be attacks on the enemy's weapons supply. Supporters of a strategic air offensive believed it might single-handedly bring victory, or, at the very least, would cause Germany to collapse much sooner and minimize the loss of British lives.

British planners had a wildly exaggerated estimate of the amount of damage that could be caused by German bombs in Britain. A secret study predicted that the Luftwaffe could drop an average of 700 tons of explosives on Britain every day, and expected that each ton would kill or injure fifty people—this estimates that 35,000 people would lose their lives daily, and 2 million would perish in the first two months of the war, a rate

Britain could not endure. The study expected that three-quarters of the 7 million citizens of London would have to be evacuated, while an estimated 3 to 4 million people in Britain would suffer mental breakdowns because of the bombing in the first six months. Fortunately for Britain, devastation never took place on this scale. The actual number of British people killed or injured by German bombs in the entire war was about the number predicted for the first week. Though 60,000 civilians perished, this was nowhere near enough to destroy British morale and cause citizens to give up.

The RAF's predictions about the effects of bombing were also partly based on the belief that it was impossible to defend against bombing. The idea that bombers could not be stopped was first proved wrong by the RAF itself during the Battle of Britain. Although not designed for strategic bombing, the Luftwaffe had an ongoing mission to fight and destroy the RAF's fighter planes in order to allow a German invasion of England. The Germans soon came to regard the second purpose of the air raids as psychological warfare, calculating that they could make the British people feel that Great Britain had no chance to win the war. In this way, they could force a peace, with no German invasion required. Fears of British retaliation against German cities made the Luftwaffe limit its first attacks to military or semimilitary targets. The first German attack on London was an accident, and did not come until August 24, six weeks after the beginning of the campaign. When the British retaliated by bombing German cities, the Luftwaffe launched massive attacks on London, beginning on September 7, 1940. Although these attacks were aimed at military targets, such as the docks along the Thames River, there was heavy damage and loss of life in residential and commercial neighborhoods.

Night Raids and Strategic Bombings

The fighter pilots of the RAF shot down so many German planes that by the middle of September, it became clear that Germany had lost the Battle of Britain and would therefore be unable to invade England. Shifting to night raids on London and other British cities in October and November 1940, the Luftwaffe continued the assaults for months. Because night bombing was so inaccurate at the time, these raids were not really attempts to hit military targets or factories—they were meant to cause as much damage and loss of life as possible.

Strategic bombing, even when it was accurate, caused many deaths (generally workers in the targeted factories and mines). In fact, though, the strategic bombing methods used made it very inaccurate—many bombs aimed at factories or shipyards hit the residential areas surrounding them. Strategic bombing was inaccurate during World War II because there were no computers to measure factors like speed, direction, altitude, or wind velocity, all of which were needed to precisely release the bombs. Pilots and bombardiers had to calculate these factors, use their eyes, and rely on their experience to try to time the release accurately. Clouds and smoke made targeting even more complicated. The bombers also had to fly at high altitudes to avoid antiaircraft fire from the ground, and dodging enemy ground fire and fighter planes made it difficult to keep a steady course.

The number of planes lost in bombing raids was high, especially at first. To attack cities in Germany, the RAF had to fly long distances over German-controlled Europe, where they were subject to Luftwaffe attacks on both legs of the trip. The more deeply into German territory they penetrated, the heavier losses they sustained. British fighter planes did not have the fuel capacity to fly as far as the bombers, and the bombers therefore could not be escorted all the way to their targets. In a raid on Berlin in November 1941, about 12.5 percent of the bombers were shot down. At that rate, a bomber and its crew would last an average of only eight missions. Any losses over 5 percent meant that the Luftwaffe would eventually wipe out the British bomber force. The fighter pilots of the Luftwaffe, like RAF pilots in the Battle of Britain, proved that bombers could be stopped.

As a result of these factors, the British soon stopped daylight bombing missions. After the first few months of the war, the RAF flew strategic bombing missions only at night. Cities required that all lights, streetlights, car lights, and even flashlights could not be used after dark. People had to put heavy black curtains on their windows so that light would not show outside the house, resulting in a condition known as a blackout. Especially in the first years of the war, this meant bombs were released blind, because pilots and navigators could not see any electric lights from their target cities. They relied on navigational charts, moonlight, or fires caused by earlier bombs. Crews would then report on how successful they thought they had been, reports that RAF photographs of bomb damage consistently proved

Scrutinizing the wing of a downed German Messerschmitt, British soldiers swarm around the remains of the plane. (Reproduced by permission of © Hulton Getty/Liaison Agency)

An RAF crew checks in after returning safely from a bombing raid. Air raids into Germany generally suffered heavy losses. (Reproduced by permission of the Corbis Corporation [Bellevue])

The British, who were heavily bombed by the Germans in the early part of the war, later gave Americans some instruction on how to conduct themselves in blackout situations. Here, a woman holds up a British poster describing important steps to follow. (Reproduced by permission of AP/Wide World Photos)

to be unreliable. At one point, a British study found that only 10 percent of the planes dropped their bombs within five miles of the intended target. Even when technical developments such as new versions of radar significantly increased accuracy, only a small proportion of bombs landed closer than 200 to 300 yards from their targets.

RAF chiefs realized that the only target they could count on hitting was an entire town. If the strategic air offensive were to continue, it would need a justification beyond the destruction of factories. On February 14, 1942, Bomber Command, the RAF branch in charge of strategic bombing, issued a directive that the main goal of the campaign was to destroy the fighting spirit "of the enemy civilian population and in particular of industrial workers." The head of the RAF explained that the target was residential areas, "not, for instance, the dockyards or aircraft factories." The aim was to kill people who worked in the factories, along with their families, and to destroy their homes. Of the 600,000 German civilians killed in bombing raids during the war, about 120,000 were children. The tactic was called "area bombing," but leading British military historian B. H. Liddell Hart described it as a policy of "terrorization."

RAF Attacks German Cities

In March 1942, the RAF attacked Lübeck and Rostock, two small cities on the Baltic seacoast of northern Germany. The centers of both historic cities, dating from the Middle Ages, were completely destroyed by incendiary bombs, but the factory areas outside the central districts suffered little damage. The Luftwaffe retaliated by bombing historic and militarily unimportant towns in England, including Bath and Canterbury. In May 1942 the RAF launched the first of its "1,000" raids, with the initial target being Cologne, Germany's third largest city. Involving 1,000 bombers, the raid caused fires that destroyed 600 acres in the middle of the city, and only forty bombers were shot down. From March to July 1942, the RAF dropped 58,000 tons of bombs in a series of attacks on cities in the Ruhr, Germany's most important industrial area, in a campaign the RAF called the Battle of the Ruhr.

In late July a large RAF force attacked the seaport of Hamburg, Germany's second-largest city, with incendiary bombs on four straight nights. For a combination of reasons—including the weather, the way Hamburg was built, and the fact that the raids destroyed the city's water pipes—these attacks resulted in a new event: a firestorm. Hamburg

Arthur "Bomber" Harris

A week after the RAF adopted the strategic air offensive directive, Air Marshal Arthur Harris, soon known as "Bomber" Harris, became head of Bomber Command. A firm believer in the new policy, he argued that long-term bombing attacks to destroy the enemy's industrial resources and demoralize its population were the only correct use of bombers, and he opposed the deployment of bombers in any other operations. Harris attempted to prevent the temporary interruption of the strategic air offensive in spring 1944, when the British transferred the bombers to France, where they were needed to attack railroads and bridges before the Allies invaded Normandy. With bombed-out roads, the Germans would be prevented from bringing reinforcements to the invasion beaches. Harris claimed that bombers were not suited for this job, and General Dwight D. Eisenhower, the supreme Allied commander, had to threaten to resign before Harris would give in. Military experts and historians agree that the campaign Harris opposed so strongly was probably the most successful air campaign of the war and perhaps the bombers' most important contribution to the Allied victory in Europe.

Air Marshal Arthur Harris, known as "Bomber" Harris. (Reproduced by permission of the Corbis Corporation [Bellevue])

burned continuously from July 24 to July 30, until 62,000 acres were destroyed. The fire created winds reaching tornado speeds, and in the center of the fire area, temperatures rose to 1,500 degrees Fahrenheit. Anything that could burn burst into flames—including people. Those in underground bomb shelters suffocated as the fire drew in all the oxygen, and 80 percent of the buildings in the city were damaged or destroyed. At least 30,000 people died, including about 6,000 children. Similar firestorms were created in several other cities. In some smaller cities like Magdeburg, where 9,000 people died, the proportion of deaths was much higher than in Hamburg.

The RAF launched sixteen major raids on Berlin from November 1943 to March 1944. Until then, despite four years of war, life in Berlin had gone on normally, although 1 million of its 4.5 million inhabitants had been evacuated as a precaution. A more modern city than Hamburg, Berlin featured solidly built buildings and wide avenues and open plazas that prevented fires from spreading. Consequently there were no firestorms. An extensive system of well-designed bomb shelters kept the number of deaths down, but the physical destruction was still vast. Approximately 1.5 million people were made homeless by the raids.

In February 1945, the RAF and the American air force attacked the city of Dresden in three short raids. Considered one of the most beautiful cities in Europe, Dresden had been almost undamaged until

The great cathedral is almost the only undamaged building in the center of Cologne following an attack by 1,000 British bombers in May 1942. The fact that the cathedral survived was probably just luck. (Reproduced by permission of AP/Wide World Photos)

Destruction in Hamburg after an RAF attack. (Reproduced by permission of the Corbis Corporation [Bellevue])

Considered one of the most beautiful cities in Europe, Dresden was almost undamaged until the Allies attacked it in February 1945. (Reproduced by permission of the Corbis Corporation [Bellevue])

then because it had little military importance. This meant it was almost undefended by the Luftwaffe or antiaircraft guns, and it was also jammed with German refugees trying to escape the advancing Soviet armies farther east. A total of 1,223 Allied planes caused a firestorm, like the one in Hamburg, that wiped out the city and killed a large number of civilians. Because so many people had recently arrived in the city, it is impossible to know the exact number of deaths, but estimates range from 30,000 to 135,000.

The Question of Morality and Effectiveness

The Dresden raid, coming as it did at a time when it was certain that the Allies would win the war, made even many of those who had supported

area bombing uneasy, including Winston Churchill. Even before Dresden, critics had argued that area bombing amounted to the intentional slaughter of civilians and should not be an Allied tactic, even if it was a Nazi one. In addition, the effectiveness of area bombing was doubtful. The amount of bombs dropped on Germany rose from 48,000 tons in 1942 to more than 210,000 the following year, and more than 900,000 in 1944. Nevertheless, Germany produced 28,000 fighter planes in 1944, more than five times as many as in 1942, and three times as many tanks. The Germans had begun scattering their factories by breaking up large plants and relocating them to other areas; the factories were often disguised as something else, and sometimes built underground. Even after the great Hamburg

As new recruits for the U.S. Women's Army Auxiliary Corps (WAAC) go through basic training in Daytona Beach, Florida, they don gas masks as they are taught how to survive in poisonous gas attacks. (Reproduced by permission of AP/Wide World Photos)

firestorm, industrial production in the city returned to about 80 percent of its pre-raid level within a few months. There is no indication that the people of Hamburg, or any other German city, were driven to rebel against the Nazi government—one of the stated objectives of area bombing. The Nazis, in fact, used area bombing to help convince average Germans that the British were barbarians who made war against defenseless children.

The military cost of area bombing was also high. In the campaign against Germany, Bomber Command lost 55,000 men, most of them highly trained pilots, navigators, and bombardiers. Many more were shot down and became prisoners of war. These men, and the resources used to build the planes they flew and the bombs they dropped, might have made more of a difference if used in other ways. The strategic air offensive was initially popular with the British and people living in German-occupied countries because it was the only way Britain could strike at Germany. The raids forced the Germans to use about 2 million people who could have been used elsewhere as part of the antiaircraft effort on the ground. Conducting an air war also forced the Luftwaffe to devote many of its fighter planes to defending German cities rather than using them to fight the Soviet armies. Some

historians believe this was the major contribution of Allied area bombing to the war. Still, many historians continue to question if that end justified the deaths of so many civilians.

Poison Gas?

When the war began, one of the greatest fears of governments and ordinary people was that the enemy would use poison gas like it had in World War I (1914—1918). Both sides had used this weapon on the battlefield, killing thousands of soldiers and causing many others to suffer painful and sometimes deadly aftereffects. Hitler himself had been injured in a gas attack while fighting in the German army in 1918. Fearing that German planes would drop poison gas bombs on cities in air raids, the British issued millions of gas masks (including specially designed masks for infants) to civilians.

Germany, however, did not drop poison gas on London or any other target, and did not fire gas-filled artillery shells on the battlefield. No nation used poison gas because each was afraid that the other side would then do the same. (The Allies publicly announced that they would use poison gas against Germany if the Germans used it first.) Yet

Prisoners of war were confined in Nazi concentration camps. Here, men move International Red Cross supplies sent by Canadians and destined for the Stalag VIIIB prison camp. (Reproduced by permission of AP/Wide World Photos)

there were some close calls. Each of the major countries produced poison gas weaponry and sometimes even shipped it to the battlefront to be prepared in case the enemy used it first. In December 1943, some 1,000 Allied soldiers and Italian civilians were killed when a German air raid blew up an American ship carrying poison gas bombs in the port of Bari in southern Italy. The Germans actually tested poison gas, including new forms of deadly nerve gas, using captured Soviet soldiers and concentration camp prisoners as guinea pigs. Japan used poison gas in China before World War II and continued testing it on prisoners once the war began.

In summer 1940, when everyone thought Germany would soon invade England, Churchill approved a plan to use poison gas against German attackers who got beyond the beaches. Four years later, when Germany began attacking Britain with V-1 "flying bombs" and V-2 rockets, Churchill wanted to use gas on Germany in retaliation. He dropped the idea because his generals opposed it, as did U.S. President Franklin D. Roosevelt. American military men wanted to use poison gas on the battlefield at one point to force Japanese soldiers out of their underground hiding places during the battle of Iwo Jima, but Roosevelt refused to give his approval.

British Children Evacuate Cities

British children were impacted by the war in a dramatic way. At the outbreak of the fighting, British experts believed that German air raids on London and other English cities would kill hundreds of thousands of people each week. They also expected the Germans to drop bombs containing poisonous gas. As a result of these fears, in September 1939 more than 800,000 children were evacuated without their parents from London and other large cities and sent to small towns or villages in the countryside. Half a million mothers and their preschool children were also evacuated.

Most evacuees returned within a few months, during the period known as the phony war, when there were no German attacks on Britain. When German air raids resumed, many again left London. The same thing happened in 1944 when the V-weapon attacks began. Apart from physical dangers and shortages, one of the most dramatic effects of the war on children in Britain and the United States was the disruption of normal adolescent experiences. An English child who was eight years old when the war began was fourteen when it concluded, and probably could not remember the

American airmen also flew raids over Germany. From a base in England, the *Memphis Belle* was among the first B-17s to complete 25 combat missions against the Third Reich. Today, the Flying Fortress is displayed on Mud Island Airfield in Memphis, Tennessee. (Library of Congress)

American pilots often decorated their airplanes with wing and nose art. While some aviators painted women on their planes, others used cartoon characters. Today, this piece is part of the collection at the Museum of the Pacific War (Chester Nimitz Museum), Fredericksburg, TX, Texas Parks and Wildlife. (Reproduced by permission of Kathleen J. Edgar)

American Bombing of Germany

The American strategic bombing campaign against Germany generally avoided area bombing (though the United States did use area bombing against Japan). The American air force instead concentrated on hitting specific industrial targets, chosen after economic experts analyzed which factories were most needed and most difficult to replace. In one such raid, for example, the Americans attacked a plant that was one of Germany's few sources of ball bearings, which were needed in all motor vehicles. Sites such as these, however, were strongly defended and American daylight raids suffered heavy losses, just as Air Marshal Arthur Harris and the Royal Air Force predicted.

The most important goal for the Americans became the interruption of Germany's production of gasoline and aviation fuel. Germany had few sources of petroleum and increasingly relied on synthetic fuel made from coal and other sources. The plants that produced fuel could not be broken up into smaller units and were difficult to hide. The campaign against synthetic oil plants eventually became highly successful, but only after the introduction of a new American plane, the P-51 Mustang. It was the first fighter that had the fuel capacity to accompany the bombers all the way to their targets and protect them against German attack. The shortage of fuel, especially aviation fuel, was a key factor in the final collapse of the German armies.

Another major American target was the German transportation system, which became increasingly important as the Germans continued to scatter their major factories. The collapse of German industry in 1945 was probably caused by the destruction of the transportation system, not because the industries themselves had been bombed. By the time this collapse occurred, however, Allied ground troops were pouring through Germany. It is therefore impossible to know what part bombing played in the Allied victory.

The American Eighth Air Force Flying Fortress planes unload bombs in Axis-occupied Europe. (Reproduced by permission of Corbis-Bettmann)

Although many children were evacuated from London during the war, some stayed. This child was wounded during the German Blitz. (Reproduced by permission of AP/Wide World Photos)

In order to raise money to send to England, the relief organization Bundles for Britain published the "British Children's Prayer." (Reproduced by permission of AP/Wide World Photos)

A Child's View of the War

In 1940, when she was five years old, Ann Stalcup watched German bombers on their way to attack the city of Bristol in western England, less than twenty miles from her home in the small town of Lydney. She heard the explosions and saw the flames' reflection on the river that passed her town. In 1943 German prisoners of war were put to work on some farms near Lydney. Stalcup remembers that when they first arrived, they had only bloody rags to wear until the local people found old clothes for them. Even at the age of eight, Stalcup later remembered, she knew no one blamed the German soldiers—the war was the sole responsibility of Hitler.

London children waiting to be evacuated. Most returned to their families in London after a few months. (Reproduced by permission of the Corbis Corporation [Bellevue])

time before the war. Some soldiers might be separated from their families for years, and no one was sure whether or not they would ever come back. Every child knew a friend whose father, older brother, or uncle was killed in the war.

Children under Nazi Control

Children in countries conquered by the Nazis suffered much more. Even before the war, Jewish children in Germany suffered constant discrimination, were expelled from schools, and were attacked by Nazi thugs. Many Jewish families left Germany, but escaping the Third Reich became increasingly difficult. In the last ten months before the war began, German Jewish parents who were unable to leave themselves sent approximately 9,000 children to Britain. The children traveled through Europe on special trains called *kindertransporte* ("children's transports"). Although separated from their parents, friends, and homeland, these children were the lucky ones. The overwhelming majority of Jewish children in German-controlled Europe, perhaps 85 percent, were murdered during the war—a much higher rate than adults. In extermination camps such as Auschwitz, which were designed to kill thousands of people each day, healthy adults might be spared and used as slave labor, but children were killed immediately. Starvation was rampant in the ghettos and epidemics of diseases were caused by malnutrition, exhaustion, and inadequate sanitation. Children, especially very young children, were more likely to die from these diseases than adults. Children were also less likely to survive hiding in forests or escaping over mountains. An estimated 1.5 million Jewish children died in the Holocaust. Thousands of Jewish children managed to survive the war, usually by being hidden by non-Jewish families or by Christian churches, even though their parents had died. There were 1 million orphans in Poland at the end of the war and tens of thousands in France. One of every eight children in Greece was without parents. In 1945, when Germany surrendered, more than 10 million children in Europe had, at least temporarily, been abandoned or lost by their parents.

Heading back to war, a soldier leans out a window for one last farewell. (Reproduced by permission of © Hulton Getty/Liaison Agency)

PRIMARY SOURCE

Hannah Senesh

Excerpt from *Hannah Senesh: Her Life & Diary*, written between 1934 and 1944

This edition published in 1986

After the Nazis seized control of the German government and outlawed all political opposition, few people in Germany could safely disagree with Nazi policies. As Germany invaded one European country after another, the Nazis instituted a similar pattern of suppression and domination. The party restricted civil rights, demanded loyalty to its regime, and brutally punished those who resisted. Anti-Jewish measures stripped Jews of their citizenship rights, jobs, and assets and segregated all people of Jewish ancestry into restricted areas known as ghettos. Although the Nazis first imposed a strict program

of forced emigration and imprisonment on the Jewish people, by 1941 the Reich had turned to mass murder as a way of solving the "Jewish problem."

The following year Hitler and other top-level Nazi leaders formally approved a plan—code named the *Endlösung* or "Final Solution"—for the annihilation of all European Jews. By the summer of 1942, reports of the systematic extermination of Jews began to leak to the free world. When news of Nazi atrocities reached Jewish settlers living in British-occupied Palestine, many decided to attempt rescue missions. After

Heinrich Himmler (1900–1945)

Heinrich Himmler was the senior Nazi official responsible for carrying out the "Final Solution," the code name for the mass extermination of European Jews. Himmler—the second most powerful man in wartime Germany—was born near Munich, Germany, to devout Catholic parents. He received a gymnasium (high school) education before joining the Bavarian army as a cadet-clerk in World War I. After the war, Himmler earned a diploma in agriculture from a technical college and worked as a sales consultant for a fertilizer manufacturer.

In 1923, Himmler joined the Nazi party and participated in an attempted overthrow of the German government, an action now known as the Beer Hall Putsch. From 1926 to 1930 he served as the acting propaganda leader of the party. After marrying Margarete Boden, Himmler tried his hand at poultry farming, but was unsuccessful. Then, in January 1929, Hitler selected Himmler to head his personal bodyguard detail, known as the Schutzstaffel, or SS. This appointment became the foundation of Himmler's rise to power within the Third Reich. Himmler expanded the SS, also known as the Black Guard, from 300 to 50,000 men in four years.

Himmler was appointed chief of police in Munich in 1933 and was later made head of the Gestapo organization. Acting in his role as police chief, he set up the first concentration camp at Dachau to house "enemies" of the Nazi party. By 1936, Himmler had gained control over the entire political and criminal police system of the Third Reich, becoming Reichsführer of the SS and head of the German police.

When World War II broke out in 1939, Himmler mobilized his SS forces to follow the regular army into occupied territories. Under his command, SS forces captured civilians and brutally killed them. Millions of so-called "racial degenerates" were either displaced from their homes or murdered. While witnessing a mass execution staged especially for him, Himmler reportedly grew faint from the bloodbath and hastened the construction of death camps with gas chambers to allow for "a more humane means" of execution.

In late 1944, when the tides of the war turned against Germany, Himmler tried to cover traces of his mass murder apparatus by ordering the death camps closed and crematoria and gas chambers destroyed. Himmler proposed that Germany should surrender to then-U.S. General Dwight D. Eisenhower and the Western Allies, while continuing to fight the Soviets in the East. Hitler regarded Himmler's suggestion as treasonous, became enraged, and stripped him of all his offices and responsibilities. When Germany finally surrendered, Himmler assumed a false identity and attempted to escape Germany. He was arrested by British troops and committed suicide by swallowing cyanide on May 23, 1945.

considerable debate, the British agreed to train volunteers as parachutist agents; these agents would then be dropped behind enemy lines in order to carry out specific missions. Because many of the volunteers were natives of the target countries, they had the necessary linguistic skills and familiarity with the terrain to blend in with the citizenry and perform the desired duties. Some 250 men and women volunteered; 110 received training. However, due to operational and technical difficulties, only thirty-two of the volunteers actually parachuted in missions between 1943 and 1945. Twelve were captured; seven were executed.

Hannah Senesh was one of the Palestinian Jews who parachuted into occupied Europe as an emissary, or agent, to aid Jews living under Nazi oppression. Originally from Budapest, Hungary, Senesh had immigrated to Palestine in 1939 when she was nineteen years old. A talented writer and poet, she lived on the Kibbutz Sedot Yam near Caesarea. After learning of the fate of fellow Jews trapped in Europe, she became determined to attempt the rescue of Jews stranded in Hungary and neighboring countries. Senesh volunteered in 1943 and received training in Egypt. Like the other men and women who offered their services to the resistance effort, Senesh was willing to place herself in tremendous danger by parachuting behind Nazi lines. She believed that even if she and her comrades did not succeed in rescuing their Jewish brothers and sisters, their courage and sacrifice would inspire Jews throughout Europe. Of the thirty-two parachutists, Senesh was one of five who was able to penetrate into her target country. She parachuted into Yugoslavia on March 13, 1944, determined to cross into Hungary.

In the first diary entry that follows, Senesh mentions that she had become a Zionist. As a teenager growing up in Budapest, Hungary, she was exposed to many different factions within the Zionist movement. Members of this worldwide initiative were committed to the creation of a Jewish homeland in Palestine. Due to the nature of her mission, Senesh wrote a letter to her brother George in case she did not return alive. However, when George arrived in Palestine before she left for Cairo, Egypt, she allowed him to see the letter. Written on December 25, 1943, it contains an apology for undertaking a deed that would perhaps cost Senesh her life. Senesh wrote the last two letters cited in this primary source on the day she parachuted into Yugoslavia. Also included here is the last poem written by Senesh, which she composed while in prison in Budapest, when she was not yet twenty-three years old.

Hannah Senesh: Her Life & Diary

October 27, 1938

I don't know whether I've already mentioned that I've become a Zionist. This word stands for a tremendous number of things. To me it means, in short, that I now consciously and strongly feel I am a Jew, and am proud of it. My primary aim is to go to Palestine, to work for it. Of course this did not develop from one day to the next; it was a somewhat gradual development. There was first talk of it about three years ago, and at that time I vehemently attacked the Zionist Movement. Since then people, events, times, have all brought me closer to the idea, and I am immeasurably happy that I've found this ideal, that I now feel firm ground under my feet, and can see a definite goal towards which it is really worth striving. I am going to start learning Hebrew, and I'll attend one of the youth groups. In short, I'm really going to knuckle down properly. I've become a different person, and it's a very good feeling.

One needs something to believe in, something for which one can have whole-hearted enthusiasm. One needs to feel that one's life has meaning, that one is needed in this world. Zionism fulfills all this for me. One hears a good many arguments against the

Movement, but this doesn't matter. I believe in it, and that's the important thing.

I'm convinced Zionism is Jewry's solution to its problems, and that the outstanding work being done in Palestine is not in vain.

*Caesarea
February 22, 1943*

How strangely things work out. On January 8, I wrote a few words about the sudden idea that struck me. A few days ago a man from Kibbutz Ma'agan, a member of the Palmach, visited the kibbutz and we chatted awhile. In the course of the conversation he told me that a Palmach unit was being organized to do—exactly what I felt then I wanted to do. I was truly astounded. The identical idea!

My answer, of course, was that I'm absolutely ready. It's still only in the planning stage, but he promised to bring the matter up before the enlistment committee since he considers me admirably suited for the mission.

I see the hand of destiny in this just as I did at the time of my Aliyah. I wasn't master of my fate then either. I was enthralled by one idea, and it gave me

A group of Jewish parachutists waits to leave Palestine for Cairo in May 1944. (USHMM Photo Archives)

Hannah Senesh and her brother, George, in Palestine. (Photograph by Beit Hannah Senesh/USHMM Photo Archives)

no rest. I knew I would emigrate, despite the many obstacles in my path. Now I again sense the excitement of something important and vital ahead, and the feeling of inevitability connected with a decisive and urgent step. The entire plan may miscarry, and I may receive a brief notification informing me the matter will be postponed, or that I don't qualify. But I think I have the capabilities necessary for just this assignment, and I'll fight for it with all my might.

I can't sleep at night because of the scenes I envisage: how I'll conduct myself in this or that situation … how I'll notify Mother of my arrival … how I'll organize the Jewish Youth. Everything is still indefinite. We'll see what the future brings.…

January 11, 1944

This week I leave for Egypt. I'm a soldier. Concerning the circumstances of my enlistment, and my feelings in connection with it, and with all that led up to it, I don't want to write.

I want to believe that what I've done, and will do, are right. Time will tell the rest.

Haifa
December 25, 1943

Darling George!

Sometimes one writes letters one does not intend sending. Letters one must write without asking oneself, 'I wonder whether this will ever reach its destination.'

Day after tomorrow I am starting something new. Perhaps it's madness. Perhaps it's fantastic. Perhaps it is dangerous. Perhaps one in a hundred—or one in a thousand—pays with his life. Perhaps with less than his life, perhaps with more. Don't ask questions. You'll eventually know what it's about.

George, I must explain something to you. I must exonerate myself. I must prepare myself for that moment when you arrive inside the frontiers of the Land, waiting for that moment when, after six years, we will meet again, and you will ask, 'Where is she?' and they'll abruptly answer, 'She's not here.'

I wonder, will you understand? I wonder, will you believe that it is more than a childish wish for adventure, more than youthful romanticism that attracted me? I wonder, will you feel that I could not do otherwise, that this was something I had to do?

There are events without which one's life becomes unimportant, a worthless toy; and there are

times when one is commanded to do something, even at the price of one's life.

I'm afraid, George, that feelings turn into empty phrases even though they are so impassioned before they turn into words. I don't know whether you'll sense the doubts, the conflicts, and after every struggle the renewed decision.

It is difficult because I am alone. If I had someone with whom I could talk freely, uninhibitedly—if only the entire burden were not mine, if only I could talk to you. If there is anyone who would understand me, I think you would be that one. But who knows … six years is a long time.

But enough about myself. Perhaps I have already said too much. I would like to tell you a few things about the new life, the new home, as I see them. I don't want to influence you. You'll see for yourself what the country is. But I want to tell you how I see it.

First of all—I love it. I love its hundred faces, its hundred climates, its many-faceted life. I love the old and the new in it; I love it because it is ours. No, not ours, but because we can make ourselves believe it is ours.

And I respect it. Not everything. I respect the people who believe in something, respect their idealistic struggle with the daily realities. I respect those who don't live just for the moment, or for money. And I think there are more such people here than anywhere else on earth. And finally, I think that this is the only solution for us, and for this reason I don't doubt its future, though I think it will be very difficult and combative.

As far as the kibbutz is concerned, I don't think it is perfect, and it will probably pass through many phases. But in today's circumstances it best suits our aims, and is the closest to our concept of a way of life—about this I have absolutely no doubt.

We have need of one thing: people who are brave and without prejudices, who are not robots, who want to think for themselves and not accept outmoded ideas. It is easy to place laws in the hands of man, to tell him to live by them. It is more difficult to follow those laws. But most difficult of all is to impose laws upon oneself, while being constantly self-analytical and self-vigilant. I think this is the highest form of law enforcement, and at the same time the only just form. And this form of law can only build a new, contented life.

I often ask myself what the fate of the kibbutz will be when the magic and novelty of construction and

Hannah Senesh (1921-1944)

Hannah Senesh (pronounced SZENES) was born in Budapest, Hungary. She came from a distinguished family of poets, writers, and musicians. At the age of thirteen, she began keeping a diary, displaying remarkable talent as a writer and poet. Senesh became a Zionist at the age of seventeen, immigrated to Palestine two years later, and joined the Kibbutz Sedot Yam near Caesarea.

In 1943, Senesh volunteered to participate in a secret parachute mission organized by the British military and intelligence service. She parachuted into Yugoslavia in March of 1944 and was captured three months later in Nazi-occupied Hungary. After five months of captivity and torture in a prison in Budapest, she was brought to trial and convicted of treason against Hungary. Senesh was executed shortly before the city of Budapest fell to the advancing Russian army.

creation wear off, when the struggle for existence assumes reality and—according to plan—becomes an organized, abundant communal life. What will the incentive of the people be, what will fill their lives? I don't know the answer. But that day is so far in the future that it is best to think of existing matters.

Don't think I see everything through rose-coloured glasses. My faith is a subjective matter, and not the result of outer conditions. I see the difficulties clearly,

both inside and out. But I see the good side, and above all, as I said before, I think this is the only way.

I did not write about something that constantly preoccupies my thoughts: Mother. I can't.

Enough of this letter. I hope you will never receive it. But if you do, only after we have met.

And if it should be otherwise, George dear, I embrace you with everlasting love.

Your sister.

P.S. I wrote the letter at the beginning of the parachute training course.

March 13, 1944

Dearest Comrades:

On sea, land, in the air, in war and in peace, we are all advancing towards the same goal. Each of us will stand at his post. There is no difference between my task and that of another. I will be thinking of all of you a great deal. That's what gives me strength.

Warmest comradely greetings.

March 13, 1944

Mother Darling,

In a few days I'll be so close to you—and yet so far. Forgive me, and try to understand. With a million hugs.

One–Two–Three*

One—two—three …
        eight feet long,
Two strides across, the rest is dark …
Life hangs over me like a question mark.
One—two—three …
        maybe another week,
Or next month may still find me here,
But death, I feel, is very near.
I could have been
        twenty-three next July;
I gambled on what mattered most,
The dice were cast. I lost.

Budapest 1944
[*Her last poem, written in prison;
translated from the Hungarian by Peter Hay.]
(Senesh, pp. 63, 127, 131-34, 167, 257)

Aftermath

After parachuting into Yugoslavia in March 1944, Senesh and her team spent several months traveling throughout the countryside working with numerous resistance groups. They witnessed first-hand the destruction caused by German forces; entire villages and towns were burned and pillaged. Dressed as British officers, the four parachutists received the cooperation of numerous partisans engaged in guerrilla tactics against the Nazis. Because of her gender and charisma, Senesh impressed civilians and partisans everywhere she went. She was fearless, perceptive, inspirational, and completely devoted to the cause of saving Jews and fighting the Nazis. When Senesh and her comrades met one particular group of Jewish partisans, they revealed their true identities and connections to Palestine. This chance meeting inspired Senesh to write the poem "Ashrei ha-Gafrur" ("Blessed Is the Match") in May 1944, a month before her capture by the Nazis. Like a match that is consumed by its use, Senesh believed her life was worth sacrificing for a higher cause. "Blessed Is the Match" later became famous throughout Israel. Senesh gave the poem to her fellow parachutist Reuven Dafni just before her departure into Hungary.

In June 1944, Senesh crossed into Nazi-occupied Hungary and was immediately captured. She spent five months in a prison in Budapest, where she was tortured by the Gestapo. The Nazis attempted to force Senesh to reveal the secret codes for her transmitter radio. Even when Gestapo officers threatened to kill her mother, Senesh maintained her resolve. On October 28, 1944, she appeared before a military tribunal and was convicted of treason against Hungary. Senesh's eloquent and forceful defense affected the judges, who decided to postpone her sentencing for over a week. Amidst heavy bombing by Allied air forces and the approach of the Russian army, the judges who had tried Senesh fled Budapest. She was executed by firing squad on November 7, a month before the Soviets completely encircled Budapest.

In 1950 Senesh's remains were taken to Israel and buried alongside six other parachutists in the national military cemetery at Mount Herzl in Jerusalem. An outline of a parachute is carved on each headstone, and their graves form the shape of V. Today, Senesh is considered a national heroine in Israel, where her legacy symbolizes courage and moral strength. In Israel, more than thirty streets bear Senesh's name, as do two farming settlements, a forest, and a ship. Her story has been the subject of numerous plays, books, and a motion picture. Most modern Israelis can recite from memory "Blessed Is the Match."

Sources

Books

Atkinson, Linda, *In Kindling Flame: The Story of Hannah Senesh,* Lee & Shepard (New York), 1985.

Kertyesz, Imre, *Fateless,* Northwestern University Press (Evanston, IL), 1992.

Senesh, Hannah, *Hannah Senesh: Her Life & Diary,* first English edition, Nigel Marsh, 1971, Schocken Books (New York), 1972, reprinted, Hakibbutz Hameuchad Publishing House Ltd., 1986.

Other

Holocaust Education–Women of Valor, http://www.interlog.com/~mighty/valor/kath_f.htm (May 16, 2000).

Jewish Partisans, http://www.ushmm.org/outreach/jpart.htm (May 16, 2000).

Schindler's List
Excerpt from the book by Thomas Keneally

First published in 1982

After invading Poland in September 1939, the Nazi party divided the country according to the goals of the Third Reich. To gain additional *Lebensraum,* or "room to live," they annexed a part of Poland and called this new territory Wartheland. As part of their plan to reorganize the races of Europe, the Nazis ordered the evacuation of all Poles and Jews from Warthegau to the southeastern portion of Poland. Only Polish people who resembled the Aryan ideal (tall, blond, blue-eyed, chiseled features) and who were not Jewish were allowed to remain in Warthegau. Hitler and other Nazi chiefs envisioned the Third Reich area cleansed of Jews and Poles so that racially pure Germans could establish colonies on the vacated land. Those Polish people who resembled the Aryan ideal were allowed to stay in segregated areas and undergo a "re-Germanization" program.

In the southeastern portion of Poland, the Nazis set up a civil administration called the *Generalgouvernement,* or the General Government. Under the supervision of Governor-General Hans Frank, this area became the designated holding place for Polish Jews and all others deemed unfit for Reich citizenship. Of the 22 million people in German-occupied Poland, more than 2 million were Jews. About 600,000 Jews lived in the Warthegau area and 1.5 million in the *Generalgouvernement.* In accordance with a directive issued by Nazi leader Reinhard Heydrich, local Nazi officials began forcing Polish Jews into ghettos in the larger cities within the *Generalgouvernement.* Heydrich's written orders stipulated that these cities should be situated along railroad lines. (The Nazi leaders had plans to deport the Jews by train to death camps in the future.)

In addition to forced displacement, the German authorities subjected German Poles to violence and discrimination. They humiliated and assaulted Jews wearing traditional religious garb, drove them away from food lines, and randomly seized them off the streets for forced labor assignments. Many Jews lost their jobs without receiving compensation or the prospect of securing a new position. In addition, the

Oskar Schindler at his Emalia enamelware factory in Kraków, Poland. (Courtesy of Prof. Leoppold Pfeffergerg-Page/USHMM Photo Archives)

Nazis issued numerous anti-Jewish decrees, including the requirement that Jews wear arm bands depicting the Star of David. They banned Jews from owning radios and from traveling by train. But the most damaging orders were the ones that forbade Jews from participating in economic activities and ordered the confiscation of Jewish property.

Chaos ensued as large groups of people, both Poles and Jews, left their homes and possessions behind and traveled across Poland. As a result of this massive upheaval, many businesses closed because they lacked both workers and employers. These abandoned businesses provided entrepreneurs with an ideal opportunity: Aryan businesspeople could take over a deserted factory, start a business in support of the German war effort, and pay practically nothing for the plant or the labor to run it. Inhabitants of the Jewish ghettos served as virtual slave laborers in such factories. Jews who obtained the designation "skilled laborer"—meaning they were employable in factories essential to war production—were assured some level of protection from Nazi *Aktions* within the ghetto.

When the Nazi government began to prepare for the Soviet invasion, its planning organization (known as the Main Armaments Board) asked businesses in occupied Poland to produce supplies for German troops. One business owner who responded to their request was Oskar Schindler, who had been born in 1908 in Zwittau, Austria, which was located in a region known as the Sudetenland or Moravia. Inhabitants of this area between Austria and Germany were considered ideal Aryans by the Nazis. When Schindler was born, the territory was part of the Austrian Empire, then under the rule of Emperor Franz Josef. Schindler's family groomed him to inherit the family farm equipment business. This background in machinery combined with fierce aggressiveness led the young Schindler to competitive motorcycle racing. He served briefly in the Czech army, but did not enjoy life in the service. During the Great Depression, Schindler found employment by relying on his natural charisma and selling skills.

His contact with Abwehr ("Defense"), the German intelligence division, which he joined in order to avoid military service, allowed him to follow the German advance into Poland in 1939. His involvement with Abwehr and his natural sales ability helped him establish important connections within both the Polish business community and the German military. Through these influential relationships, Schindler acquired a contract to supply kitchenware to the military, and he took over a bankrupt factory outside Kraków. To operate the factory, Schindler began to rely on the Jewish population interned in the local ghetto, and later, the labor camp.

At some point, Schindler ceased being an ordinary employer and began functioning more as a rescuer to his employees. He urged the SS to prohibit random acts of terror against "his Jews," claiming they were essential to the German war effort. When the Nazis began the final liquidation of Polish Jews, Schindler invented a scheme to move his workers to a remote location away from enemy lines. To ensure that the Nazis would grant his request to relocate the Jews, he promised to open a munitions company that would supply much-needed weaponry to the beleaguered German forces. Schindler was an

Schindler's Story Becomes Popular Film

Producer-director Steven Spielberg adapted Keneally's book *Schindler's List* into the enormously successful motion picture of the same name. Starring Liam Neeson in the title role, the film won seven Academy Awards in 1993.

unlikely hero, as nothing in his past suggested or predicted that he would one day risk his life to save others. During the course of the war, however, he fulfilled a promise he made to his Jewish employees: He said he would treat them well and that they would survive the war. Schindler saved the lives of some 1,100 Jews.

Schindler's ghetto employees in Poland identified him as a Jewish sympathizer and put him in touch with a secret Jewish relief organization in Hungary. The excerpt from *Schindler's List* that follows begins with a description of a meeting in the capital city of Budapest between Schindler and two Hungarian Jewish resistance agents, Dr. Rezso Kastner and Samu Springmann. While rumors about Nazi atrocities had reached their country, the two Hungarians hoped to obtain from Schindler an actual firsthand account of the treatment of Jews detained in Polish ghettos. As Russian forces closed in on eastern Poland in 1944, and the Germans began the final liquidation of the Jewish ghetto in Kraków and the local Plaszów labor camp, Schindler sought to move his Jewish workers to Brinnlitz, and create a munitions factory. He prepared a list containing the names of all the Jewish prisoners he knew; hence the name "Schindler's List."

Schindler's List by Thomas Keneally is regarded as a combination of documentary and dramatization. While it is impossible to recreate Schindler's entire story, all people and events cited were real, and all conversations were reconstructed based on eyewitness reports and available records. Still, readers of the following excerpt should bear in mind that gaps in the story, which was written decades after the actual events it depicts, may have been filled in with conjecture.

Schindler's List

Dr. Sedlacek [Schindler's initial contact person with the Jewish underground] had promised an uncomfortable journey, and so it was. Oskar traveled in a good overcoat with a suitcase and a bag full of various comforts which he badly needed by the end of the trip. Though he had the appropriate travel documents, he did not want to have to use them. It was considered better if he did not have to present them at the border. He could always then deny that he had been to Hungary that December.

He rode in a freight van filled with bundles of the Party newspaper, Völkischer Beobachter, for sale in Hungary. Closeted with the redolence of printer's ink and among the heavy Gothic print of Germany's official newspaper, he was rocked south over the winter-sharp mountains of Slovakia, across the Hungarian border, and down to the valley of the Danube.

A reservation had been made for him at the Pannonia, near the University, and on the afternoon of his arrival, little Samu Springmann and an associate of his, Dr. Rezso Kastner, came to see him. The two men who rose to Schindler's floor in the elevator had heard fragments of news from refugees. But refugees could give you little but threads. The fact that they had avoided the threat meant that they knew little of its geography, its intimate functioning, the numbers it ran to. Kastner and Springmann were full of anticipation, since—if Sedlacek could be believed—the Sudeten [one descended from those living in the Sudentenland area of Czechoslovakia] German upstairs could give them the whole cloth, the first full-bodied report on the Polish havoc.

In the room the introductions were brief, for Springmann and Kastner had come to listen and they could tell that Schindler was anxious to talk. There was no effort, in this city obsessed with coffee, to formalize the event by calling Room Service for coffee and cakes. Kastner and Springmann, after shaking the enormous German by the hand, sat down. But Schindler paced. It seemed that far from Cracow [Kraków] and the realities of Aktion [organized roundup of ghetto inmates] and ghetto, his knowledge disturbed him more than it had when he'd briefly informed Sedlacek. He rampaged across the carpet. They would have heard his steps in the room below—their chandelier would have shaken when he stamped his foot, miming the action of the SS man in the execution squad in Krakusa, the one who'd pinned his victim's head down with a boot in full sight of [a] child at the tail of the departing column.

He began with personal images of the cruel parishes of Cracow, what he had beheld in the streets or heard from either side of the wall, from Jews and from the SS. In that connection, he said, he was carrying letters from members of the ghetto, from the physician Chaim Hilfstein, from Dr. Leon Salpeter, from Itzhak Stern. Dr. Hilfstein's letter, said Schindler, was a report on hunger. "Once the body fat's gone," said Oskar, "it starts to work on the brain."

The ghettos were being wound down, Oskar told them. It was true equally of Warsaw as of Lodz and of Cracow. The population of the Warsaw ghetto had been reduced by four-fifths, Lodz by two-thirds, Cracow by half. Where were the people who had been transferred? Some were in work camps; the gentlemen here this afternoon had to accept that at least three-fifths of them had disappeared into camps that used the new scientific methods. Such camps were not exceptional. They had an official SS name— "Vernichtungslager": Extermination Camp.

In the past few weeks, said Oskar, some 2,000 Cracow ghetto dwellers had been rounded up and sent not to the chambers of Belzec, but to labor camps near the city. One was at Wieliczka, one at Prokocim, both of these being railway stations on the Ostbahn line which ran toward the Russian front. From Wieliczka and Prokocim, these prisoners were being marched every day to a site at the village of Plaszow, on the edge of the city, where the foundations for a vast labor camp were being laid. Their life in such a labor camp, said Schindler, would be no holiday—the barracks of Wieliczka and Prokocim were under the command of an SS NCO named Horst Pilarzik who had earned a reputation last June when he had helped clear from the ghetto some 7,000 people, of whom only one, a chemist, had returned. The proposed camp at Plaszow would be under a man of the same caliber. What was in favor of the labor camps was that they lacked the technical apparatus for methodical slaughter. There was a different rationale behind them. They had economic reasons for existing....

The forced-labor camps would be run by men appointed for their severity and efficiency in clearing the ghettos. There would be sporadic murders and

A portrait of some of the Emalia factory office staff. (Courtesy of Prof. Leopold Pfeffergerg-Page/USHMM Photo Archives)

beatings, and there would certainly be corruption involving food and therefore short rations for the prisoners. But that was preferable to the assured death of the Vernichtungslagers. People in the labor camps could get access to extra comforts, and individuals could be taken out and smuggled to Hungary.

These SS men are as corruptible as any other police force, then? the gentleman of the Budapest rescue committee asked Oskar. "In my experience," growled Oskar, "there isn't one of them who isn't."…

At some point in any discussion of Schindler, the surviving friends of the Herr Direktor will blink and shake their heads and begin the almost mathematical business of finding the sum of his motives. For one of the commonest sentiments of Schindler Jews is still "I don't know why he did it." It can be said to begin with that Oskar was a gambler, was a sentimentalist who loved the transparency, the simplicity of doing good; that Oskar was by temperament an anarchist who loved to ridicule the system; and that beneath the hearty sensuality lay a capacity to be outraged by human savagery, to react to it and not to be overwhelmed. But none of this, jotted down, added up, explains the doggedness with which, in the autumn of 1944, he prepared a final haven for the graduates of Emalia [a name used to refer to Schindler's kitchenware factory].

And not only for them. In early September he drove to Podgorze and visited [Julius] Madritsch, who at that point employed more than 3,000 prisoners in his uniform factory. This plant would now be disbanded. Madritsch would get his sewing machines back, and his workers would vanish. If we made a combined approach, said Oskar, we could get more than four thousand out. Mine and yours as well. We could relocate them in something like safety. Down in Moravia.

Madritsch would always and justly be revered by his surviving prisoners. The bread and chickens smuggled into his factory were paid for from his pocket and at continuous risk. He would have been considered a more stable man than Oskar. Not as flamboyant, and not as subject to obsession. He had not suffered arrest. But he had been much more humane than was safe and, without wit and energy, would have ended in Auschwitz.

Now Oskar presented to him a vision of a Madritsch-Schindler camp somewhere in the High Jeseniks; some smoky, safe little industrial hamlet.

Madritsch was attracted by the idea but did not rush to say yes. He could tell that though the war was lost, the SS system had become more instead of less implacable. He was correct in believing that, unhappily, the prisoners of Plaszow would—in coming months—be consumed in death camps to the west. For if Oskar was stubborn and possessed, so were the SS Main Office and their prize field operatives, the commandants of the Concentration Camps.

He did not say no, however. He needed time to think about it. Though he couldn't say it to Oskar, it is likely he was afraid of sharing factory premises with a rash, demonic fellow like Herr Schindler.

Without any clear word from Madritsch, Oskar took to the road. He went to Berlin and bought dinner for Colonel Erich Lange. I can go completely over to the manufacture of shells, Oskar told Lange. I can transfer the heavy machinery.

Lange was crucial. He could guarantee contracts; he could write the hearty recommendations Oskar needed for the Evacuation Board and the German officials in Moravia.

Later, Oskar would say of this shadowy staff officer that he had given consistent help. Lange was still in that state of exalted desperation and moral disgust characteristic of many who had worked inside the system but not always for it. We can do it, said Lange, but it will take some money. Not for me. For others....

[Oskar] had drawn up what he called a preparatory list and delivered it to the Administration Building. There were more than a thousand names on it—the names of all the prisoners of the backyard prison camp of Emalia, as well as new names. Helen Hirsch's name was freshly on the list, and Amon was not there to argue about it.

And the list would expand if Madritsch agreed to go to Moravia with Oskar. So Oskar kept working on Titsch, his ally at Julius Madritsch's ear. Those Madritsch prisoners who were closest to Titsch knew the list was under compilation, that they could have access to it. Titsch told them without any ambiguity: You must get on it. In all the reams of Plaszow paperwork, Oskar's dozen pages of names were the only pages with access to the future.

But Madritsch still could not decide whether he wanted an alliance with Oskar, whether he would add his 3,000 to the total.

There is again a haziness suitable to a legend about the precise chronology of Oskar's list. The haziness doesn't attach to the existence of the list—a copy can be seen today in the archives of the Yad Vashem. There is no uncertainty as we shall see about the names remembered by Oskar and Titsch at the last minute and attached to the end of the official

paper. The names on the list are definite. But the circumstances encourage legends. The problem is that the list is remembered with an intensity which, by its very heat, blurs. The list is an absolute good. The list is life. All around its cramped margins lies the gulf.

Some of those whose names appeared on the list say that there was a party at [Amon] Goeth's villa, a reunion of SS men and entrepreneurs to celebrate the times they'd had there. Some even believe that Goeth was there, but since the SS did not release on bail, that is impossible. Others believe that the party was held at Oskar's own apartment above his factory. Oskar had for more than two years given excellent parties there. One Emalia prisoner remembers the early hours of 1944 when he was on night watch duty and Oskar had wandered down from his apartment at one o'clock, escaping the noise upstairs and bringing with him two cakes, two hundred cigarettes, and a bottle for his friend the watchman.

At the Plaszow graduation party, wherever it took place, the guests included Dr. Blancke, Franz Bosch, and, by some reports, Oberführer Julian Scherner, on vacation from his partisan-hunting. Madritsch was there too, and Titsch. Titsch would later say that at it Madritsch informed Oskar for the first time that he would not be going to Moravia with him. "I've done everything I can for the Jews," Madritsch told him. It was a reasonable claim: he would not be persuaded although he said Titsch had been at him for days.

Madritsch was a just man. Later he would be honored as such. He simply did not believe that Moravia would work. If he had, the indications are that he would have attempted it.

What else is known about the party is that an urgency operated there, because the Schindler list had to be handed in that evening. This is an element in all the versions of the story survivors tell. The survivors could tell and expand upon it only if they had heard it in the first place from Oskar, a man with a taste for embellishing a story. But in the early 1960's Titsch himself attested to the substantial truth of this one. Perhaps the new and temporary Commandant of Plaszow, a Hauptsturmführer Büscher, had said to Oskar, "Enough fooling around, Oskar! We have to finalize the paperwork and the transportation." Perhaps there was some other form of deadline imposed by the Ostbahn, by the availability of transport.

At the end of Oskar's list, therefore, Titsch now typed in, above the official signatures, the names of Madritsch prisoners. Almost seventy names were *added, written in by Titsch from his own and Oskar's memories. Among them were those of the Feigenbaum family—the adolescent daughter who suffered from incurable bone cancer; the teen-age son Lutek with his shaky expertise in repairing sewing machines. Now they were all transformed, as Titsch scribbled, into skilled munitions workers. There was singing in the apartment, loud talk and laughter, a fog of cigarette smoke, and, in a corner, Oskar and Titsch quizzing each other over people's names, straining for a clue to the spelling of Polish patronyms.*

In the end, Oskar had to put his hand on Titsch's wrist. We're over the limit, he said. They'll balk at the number we already have. Titsch continued to strain for names, and tomorrow morning would wake damning himself because one had come to him too late. But now he was at the limit, wrung out by this work. It was blasphemously close to creating people anew just by thinking of them. He did not begrudge doing it. It was what it said of the world—that was what made the heavy air of Schindler's apartment so hard for Titsch to breathe. (Keneally, pp. 153–291)

Aftermath

With the permission of the German government, Schindler and his Jewish workers left Poland to relocate in the Sudetenland region. They opened an armaments factory in the town of Brinnlitz. Officially, Schindler managed to classify his workers as skilled craftsmen who were essential to the war effort, an accomplishment that saved them from the Auschwitz gas chambers. When the Nazis mistakenly routed a trainload of his Jewish female workers to Auschwitz, Schindler personally intervened and bribed the death camp authorities. He fought to persuade them that returning the Jewish prisoners would be for the good of the war effort. As the officials considered the plea, they housed his employees in a separate area in Auschwitz. While most prisoners transported to death camps died within hours, Schindler's workers managed to survive. After arriving by boxcar in Brinnlitz, however, many of the women were starving and in poor health. Schindler made sure that those who died were given a proper Jewish burial, which was an unusual event since Jews under Nazi rule were banned from practicing their religion in public.

The local Brinnlitz labor camp, like the one in Poland, was run by the Nazi SS, but once again, the conditions within the armaments factory were considerably better than those in the labor camp. Schindler insisted that the SS not disturb his workers at the factory, arguing that the assembly of secret weapons required intense concentration. He fearlessly prohibited guards from entering the factory. At his own expense, he provided Jewish employees with a life-sustaining diet, unlike the starvation-level rations mandated by the Nazis. Production at the Brinnlitz plant can only be described as a farce: Schindler no longer attempted to fulfill his contracts with quality goods, and only wanted to keep the hoax up long enough to survive the war. The Jewish workers deliberately and skillfully rigged factory equipment so that it passed Nazi inspection and yet continually produced defective ammunition. To save Jews from other labor camps, Schindler demanded that the Nazis direct more laborers to his ammunition plant. When the SS questioned him regarding his use of child labor, Schindler argued that their long, small fingers were necessary to polish the inside of specially constructed antitank shells. Since the few shells produced at Brinnlitz failed all inspection criteria, they were not sent to the fighting fields. This greatly relieved Schindler, who did not wish unsuspecting German soldiers to die as a result of his deliberately inferior products.

Schindler's "confidence game" continued until the end of the war. As a final act of courage, he convinced the SS guard brigade to lay down their weapons and refrain from exterminating their prisoners when Soviet troops began approaching the Brinnlitz factory and labor camp. The constant need for capital to pay bribes and the lack of successful production at Brinnlitz left Schindler with little hard currency or gems with which to barter at the end of the war. He used his few remaining resources to pay for transport to the American front.

After World War II, Schindler could never repeat his wartime business successes. He and his wife emigrated to Argentina, where they tried their hand, unsuccessfully, at farming. Schindler returned to Germany and opened a cement company in Frankfurt in 1961; this venture also failed. The Jews he had helped save, who came to be called "Schindler Jews," provided him with financial support as he grew older, some even donating one day's pay each year toward his income. During the last decade of his life, Schindler split his time between Israel and Frankfurt.

Yad Vashem bestowed upon Schindler the "Righteous Among the Nations" honor in recognition of his efforts to save 1,200 Jews in Kraków and Brinnlitz. Even after receiving the Yad Vashem honor, however, Schindler met with harassment and abuse in Germany. While people around the world praised his courageousness, workmen jeered at him on the streets of Frankfurt. He once ended up in a local court for punching a man who had called him a "Jew Kisser." After Schindler died in Frankfurt on October 9, 1974, his body was flown to Jerusalem for burial in accordance with his wishes.

SOURCES

Books

Adelson, Alan, *Lodz Ghetto*, Viking (New York), 1989.

Keneally, Thomas, *Schindler's List*, Simon and Schuster (New York), 1982.

Kuper, Jack, *Child of the Holocaust*, Berkley Books (New York), 1993.

Stadtler, Bea, *The Holocaust: A History of Courage and Resistance*, Behrman House (West Orange, NJ), 1973.

PRIMARY SOURCE

Hirsch Grunstein
Excerpt from *Hiding to Survive: Stories of Jewish Children Rescued from the Holocaust*
Written by Maxine Rosenberg
Published in 1994

During the Nazis' reign, the fate of each European country's Jews depended greatly on those countries' wartime relationships with Germany. Wherever German rule was total and uncontested, the Jews faced almost certain annihilation. About 90 percent of Jews living in Germany, Austria, Poland, the Baltic counties (Lithuania, Latvia, and Estonia), and the Protectorate of Bohemia and Moravia perished in the Holocaust. Better odds for survival favored Jews living in countries that had remained neutral before German invasion and occupation. In spring 1940, German armies invaded several neutral countries in Europe—Norway, Denmark, Belgium, Luxembourg, and the Netherlands—all of which quickly gave in to Nazi control. Each of these countries was eventually forced to implement anti-Jewish measures.

German armies attacked Belgium in May 1940. The Nazi government incorporated several districts into the Reich and placed the majority of the country under military rule. Six months after the Belgian occupation began, the Nazi regime issued the first anti-Jewish decrees, which barred certain Jewish religious practices, defined Jews according to German racial standards, and excluded them from positions in civil service, education, law, and the media. Other decrees required Jews to register with the authorities and to surrender their assets and businesses in a process called "Aryanization." In fall 1941, the Nazis began isolating the Jews from other Belgians, requiring them to live in certain cities and to abide by nightly curfews. In Antwerp, Jews were prohibited from using public parks or walking on the streets. Eventually, laws expelled Jewish children from public schools, instituted forced labor, and required all Jews to wear Star of David arm bands. In summer 1942, the Nazis began deporting Jews from Belgium to the Auschwitz-Birkenau death camp via transit camps.

At the time of the German invasion, 90,000 Jews lived in Belgium, most of them refugees or immigrants. Some 25,000 Jews quickly fled to

France. With the help of sympathetic, non-Jewish Belgians and the organized underground resistance, about 20,000 Jews went into hiding. One group to do so was the Grunstein family, who had emigrated to Belgium from Poland in 1930 and went into hiding about the time the deportations began. In 1942 fourteen-year-old Hirsch and his brother Salomon were sent to live in a small village with a couple named Adrienne and Gaston, whom they did not know.

During the next two years, these strangers became more like family members as they risked their lives to protect the two brothers. They faced punishment and even death if they were caught. During the two years he lived with Adrienne and Gaston, Hirsch stayed inside their house by day to hide from villagers. His younger brother, Salomon, could pass as a non-Jew, and so he went to school and played with neighborhood children. In an attempt to become assimilated, the brothers

A Resistance Action in Belgium

In April 1943 armed Jewish resisters intercepted a deportation train carrying Jews from a transit camp in Belgium to the Auschwitz death camp. This operation is the only recorded instance of an armed attack against a train taking Jews to their death.

changed their names: Hirsch became "Henri" and Salomon became "Sylvain." Hirsch's story, included in Maxine Rosenberg's *Hiding to Survive*, documents the plight of Jews in Poland and Belgium during Hitler's reign.

Hiding to Survive: Stories of Jewish Children Rescued from the Holocaust

For the first two years of my life I lived in Poland. Then my family moved to Antwerp, Belgium, where my father was in the diamond business. Although I went to a state high school and was called "Henri" there, my family was very religious. We didn't travel or turn on lights on the Sabbath, and I always kept my head covered.

As I was growing up, my parents talked about why we had left Poland. They said it was dangerous for us there, because the police did not protect the Jews. Yet my parents didn't seem to mind that in Belgium there were signs saying JEWS DON'T APPLY HERE FOR APARTMENTS. They felt this country was safe. Then in 1940 the Germans invaded. I was twelve at the time, and my brother Salomon was six and a half.

Within two years Jews weren't allowed on the street, and there was a rumor that Jews were being sent back to their country of origin. When my mother heard this, she cried, "Go back to Poland? We might as well throw ourselves into the river."

That's when she and my father decided to hide my brother and me. She spoke to a friend whose two

young sons were already with the Van Dammes, a Gentile couple in a small village. The couple's daughter, Alice, had made the arrangements and had now convinced her brother, Gaston, and his wife, Adrienne, to hide Jewish children too.

Gaston and Adrienne were in their twenties and were hoping to get very young children. When Adrienne came with Alice to meet us, she was disappointed to see how old we were. Yet she and Gaston decided to take us in anyhow, thinking the war would be over soon and our stay would be short.

Meanwhile my father was saying that maybe our family should escape to Switzerland. He told Adrienne that if we came to live with her, we'd arrive unannounced on a Saturday, the day Belgians dressed up and visited one another.

By the end of the week my father had contacted my former schoolteacher, René Govaerts, who was helping to hide Jews. He asked René to take us to Adrienne and Gaston's house on the Friday night of Rosh Hashanah, the Jewish New Year, when we'd ordinarily never travel. My father said that if we

A First Communion portrait of Janina Nebe, a Jewish child who was hidden from the Nazis for three years. (Courtesy of Janina Zimnowodzki/USHMM Photo Archives)

were going to play Aryan, we might as well do it all the way. He even told my brother and me not to cover our heads anymore. And he changed our last name to "Govaerts" to sound Gentile, while Salomon became "Sylvain," and I kept "Henri."

My father packed one tiny suitcase for both of us so we wouldn't attract attention. In mine he put a little prayer book and the Book of Psalms. "If Mama and I don't survive, I want you to teach your brother about Judaism," he said. He also made me memorize the address of my uncle in America in case I needed to get in touch with him after the war....

At ten the next morning we arrived at Adrienne's house and surprised her as she was busily scrubbing her patio. Later Gaston came home and was happy to see us. He and Adrienne gave us their room with the big bed, while they moved into a smaller one. They wanted us to be comfortable and did whatever they could to cheer us up, even staging wrestling matches on the kitchen floor. But Salomon and I were very sad. We missed our parents.

From the beginning I felt responsible for reminding Salomon he was a Jew and insisted that he pray every day. But he wanted to play with the village kids, while I read books and took long walks. Soon he was speaking the local Flemish dialect and wearing wooden shoes and peasant clothing like a native.

Two weeks after we arrived, my parents suddenly appeared. They were going to be staying close by, with Adrienne's parents. At first I was thrilled to have them near, but then I realized this wasn't a good arrangement. Because they had heavy Polish accents, they couldn't move about freely, so visiting them was like seeing people in jail. Also, Salomon and I were running to Adrienne's parents' house too often, and Adrienne was afraid the villagers might become suspicious. So my parents went to live with her sister in another town.

By the middle of October, it was obvious the war was not ending quickly. As city kids supposedly on a short vacation, Salomon and I should have been returning home, especially since the local children my age were already in school or taking up a trade. When I asked Gaston if I could help him and his father in their blacksmith shop, he said he didn't want me around the glowing hot irons.

Meanwhile he and Adrienne had already told the villagers that Salomon was staying with them longer because he was sickly and needed fresh country air. But they couldn't think of an excuse for my being there. So they said I should stay indoors and keep out of sight.

Now that Salomon and I were going to be around for a while, Adrienne and Gaston reclaimed their bedroom. Since I had to be inside, they let me use it during the day because it was large and had a window. If I stood in the shadows, I could watch the people on the street.

Other than that there wasn't much for me to do. After I said my morning prayers, read the newspaper, and ate the meals that Adrienne brought up for me, I was very bored. I knew that all my Gentile friends in Antwerp had started their third year of Latin and algebra and thought maybe I should teach myself those subjects. When Govaerts came to visit Adrienne and Gaston (they had become friends), I asked him to bring me some textbooks. But as soon as I took one look at the books, I put them aside for another day, thinking I had plenty of time to study....

In the late spring, it was even harder for me. Through the open bedroom window I sometimes heard music and saw people going to the cafes or for a walk. I had just turned fifteen, and I too wanted to be free to come and go. Instead I was in my own private prison. Other than the cat, there was no one to keep me company. Sometimes Salomon came up, but he was five and a half years younger than I, and we didn't share the same interests.

Each day I became more and more furious. I'd read the ritual prayers, wanting to hear about a God who would sock it to the Nazis, but that wasn't the kind I was finding. Although I knew that there were periods in history when Jews suffered, I wondered, Why is this happening to me? Sometimes I'd remember Bible passages with the phrase "because of your sins" and think maybe I was being punished for having torn paper on the Sabbath. For spite, I'd rip up paper to see what might occur.

Then one day I opened the Hebrew Book of Psalms that my father had slipped into my suitcase. I wasn't even sure what I was looking for. Suddenly I came upon phrases like "smite the enemy" and "shatter them to pieces." The words startled me. They had been written thousands of years ago, and yet they seemed to be directed at the Germans. For the first time in months, I was excited. I felt a connection in time and space to the Jewish people.

I couldn't wait to read more of the Psalms and made them my reward for the day. I'd rush through my morning prayers, do my exercise, and read the newspaper, building up energy toward the Psalms. The words were so gripping, I felt as though I was being transported to another world....

Around this time Gaston gave me a book titled Automobile Course, written by an engineer. As a blacksmith, Gaston knew that the days of the horse and wagon were numbered, and he thought I would be interested in what the future might bring. Although the book was very thin, it carefully detailed how a car worked, starting with the very first raw explosion within the engine to the car's being thrust into motion. I was fascinated. Then and there in my isolated room I decided to become an engineer and an inventor....

Occasionally on a holiday or a Sunday Adrienne and Gaston told people that I had come for a short

European Jewish Children Hidden from Nazis

Between 10,000 and 50,000 children throughout Europe were hidden from the Nazis during the war. More precise estimates are impossible because of the absence of records.

visit, having arrived from the city on the night train....

On some of these "visits," Adrienne took Salomon and me to see our parents. Although I was happy being with them, the get-togethers were always sad. Instead of the four of us sitting down to dinner like a real family, I felt more like a guest who had to leave at a certain hour.

Meanwhile Salomon had learned how to move among the villagers without arousing the slightest suspicion. Whenever he got into a fight with another child, he was the first to throw the insult, "You Jew!"

One time he was on the road when the priest came by, leading a procession through the village. Salomon saw the people go down on one knee and cross themselves, and he did the same. Later he came home all excited and proudly told Adrienne what had happened. From my room upstairs I overheard Adrienne say, "You did just fine...."

One day in April of 1944 they captured a courier from the underground and found him with a list of Jewish children being hidden. From the list, the Germans learned about the two young boys who were staying with Gaston's parents and came to get them. Gaston, who had been in the house, ran for the fields under a hail of bullets.

The Germans then came looking for him at our house. When Adrienne said she didn't know where he was, they arrested her and me. Salomon, who had been watching all this from the street, hid in the field until dark, and then he went to Adrienne's mother's house.

The Germans took all of us on the list to a temporary shelter for children until we could be deported. They didn't know that the Belgian underground *was helping us there, making sure we had enough food while they planned for our escape. Oddly, at the shelter I felt more free than at Adrienne and Gaston's house. At least I was with Jewish kids my age. Still, I was petrified that at any moment the German police would surround the place and take us away.*

Four months later, just two days before the Germans were to deport us, the Belgian underground got us out of the shelter and brought us to a little village. Soon after, Belgium was liberated, and within a few days my parents found me. We returned to Antwerp and waited to hear news about Adrienne. The day she was let out of the concentration camp, I went to visit her. (Grunstein in Rosenberg, pp. 95–103)

Aftermath

As a result of the efforts of resistance members and non-Jewish citizens, about 25,000 Jews in Belgium managed to live through the war. Yad Vashem in Jerusalem has awarded the "Righteous Among the Nations" medal to dozens of non-Jewish Belgians for helping to save Jews during the war. Hirsch Grunstein and his family were among 8,000 Polish Jews who survived.

About 40,000 of the Jews living in Belgium perished—60 percent of the nation's Jewish population. Memorials honoring the perished Jews of Belgium were unveiled at Anderlecht in 1970 and at Yad Vashem in 1987. Memorial marches take place annually to the Dossin transit camp at Mechelen, the place where thousands of Jews departed for the extermination camps.

Hirsch Grunstein immigrated to the United States in 1958 and works as an engineer in data communications. Both Hirsch and his brother Salomon have remained close to their wartime protectors, Adrienne and Gaston—when the couple had a son, they even named him after Salomon's alias "Sylvain." In 1993 the Grunsteins helped Adrienne and Gaston celebrate their joint eightieth birthday. Le Consistorie Central Israelite de Belgique awarded the couple, along with Gaston's sister Alice, a medal and certificate on behalf of the entire Jewish Belgian community.

SOURCES

Books

Kuper, Jack, *Child of the Holocaust,* Berkley Books (New York), 1993.

Reiss, Johanna, *The Upstairs Room,* G. K. Hall (Boston), 1973.

Rosenberg, Maxine B., *Hiding to Survive: Stories of Jewish Children Rescued from the Holocaust,* Clarion Books (New York), 1994.

Operation Overlord

By the end of 1943, the Allies had won a series of victories that had altered the course of World War II. Yet the final defeat of Germany still seemed remote. In the Soviet Union, the Red Army had prevailed in a great tank battle around Kursk in July, and continued to drive the Germans westward. Still, powerful German armies remained in Soviet territory. Millions of Soviet soldiers had already died in battle, and the Germans had captured millions more in the early part of the war. No one could be certain that the Russians could continue to bear the major brunt of the fighting against Germany. Although the Americans and British had successfully invaded French North Africa in November 1942 and Sicily in July 1943, those victories had not taken much pressure off the Soviet armies. The invasion of Italy, which had begun soon afterward, was proceeding more slowly than expected. Italy had changed its government, ended its alliance with Germany, and had even declared war on its former ally; yet American and British armies were bogged down by strong German defensive positions along the mountainous Italian peninsula.

Throughout the struggle against the German armies, the Russians had been pressing Britain and the United States to open a second front in western Europe. American military leaders had favored an invasion of France almost from the outset of American entry into the war. After crossing France, the

British and Americans could attack Germany from the west while the Russians closed in from the east. The Allies had been planning the invasion for years, but it was consistently delayed. The British feared that launching an early invasion without proper preparation would be a tactical disaster, resulting in a greater number of casualties. They remembered their defeat at German hands in France in 1940, and also the terrible bloodshed of World War I (1914–1918), when armies attacked built-up defensive positions. Political factors also played a part in the delays. British Prime Minister Winston Churchill wanted to maintain British influence in the Mediterranean and southeastern Europe—one of the reasons the Allies had invaded Italy. Churchill wanted to send the Allied armies from Italy into Yugoslavia and toward the Austrian capital, Vienna. Many historians believe Churchill was concerned that otherwise the Russians would take control of these areas after the war. But Churchill's plan might take years: The Allied armies were still in the southern half of Italy.

By the end of 1943, the Allies agreed that a great invasion of France could be delayed no longer; they slated the attack for spring 1944. Dwight D. Eisenhower, the American general who had commanded the invasions of North Africa and Italy, was named supreme commander of Allied land, sea, and air forces for the invasion. Bernard Montgomery, the British general who had defeated

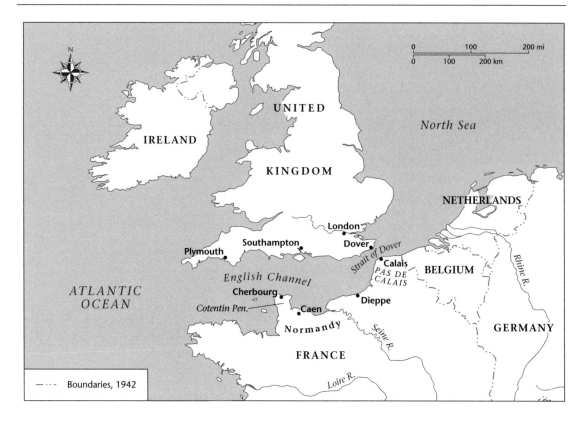

Northwestern Europe, 1942.

the German Afrika Korps at the Battle of El Alamein in Egypt and led the British troops in Sicily, was named commander of ground troops. The invasion was code-named Operation Overlord; the day of the invasion would come to be known as D-Day.

The Question of Location

The Allied planners needed to decide on the location of the invasion, which had to be within easy range of the fighter planes that would be launched from airfields in England. The planners believed that the invasion would fail unless Allied planes covered the troops in their first hours onshore. (Providing sufficient protection for the troops was so important that the American and British air forces assigned more than 5,000 fighter planes to the operation, while the Luftwaffe, the German air force, had only 169 fighters to cover a much larger area.) The closer the invasion was to the airfields, the longer the fighter planes could stay in action before they had to return to their bases to refuel. In addition, the shorter the distance, the easier it would be to transport troops, equipment, and supplies needed for the invasion.

These factors required the landings to take place on the French coast facing the English Channel, somewhere between Belgium and the tip of the Cotentin Peninsula in Normandy, France. The English Channel, which separates the island of Great Britain from France, is quite narrow, in some places only thirty miles wide. It was an easy crossing in good weather. However, the channel, which has strong currents, is sometimes overtaken by storms that develop suddenly, causing high waves. Since the troops would land in fairly small boats, not large troopships, rough seas would endanger their safety and ability to come ashore. While an invasion farther east would place the Allied armies closer to Germany, it would be too far away for the fighter planes and would require a more difficult journey on the North Sea. Any location farther west or south would mean sending the landing boats across a section of the open Atlantic, again without fighter support.

Of course, the Germans also understood these factors. Two German armies guarded the English Channel coast of France, and the Germans had lined the coast with high-quality artillery units, including coastal artillery that could fire on invading ships, as well as antiaircraft and antitank guns.

Germany's system of fortifications, obstacles, and mines called the Atlantic Wall protected the coast of France. (Reproduced by permission of AP/Wide World Photos)

Concrete blockhouses often protected the weapons while other fortifications shielded the troops. Networks of barbed wire would make it difficult to attack German machine gunners firing on the invading Allies. In some places, concrete tunnels connected machine gun and artillery positions. The Germans had dug ditches and placed large metal obstacles in the open fields behind the coast, making it difficult for planes or gliders carrying troops to land and for tanks to cross. They purposely flooded some of the fields so that parachute troops landing there might drown. They placed other obstacles underwater near the beaches to tear out the bottoms of landing boats as they approached the shore. By the time of the invasion, 250,000 of these obstacles were in place. The water obstacles were often rigged with explosive mines. Other mines were placed in the water and on the beaches. By May 1944, some 4 million mines were set along the French coast. This system of fortifications, obstacles, and mines was called the Atlantic Wall. The Germans worked frantically to strength-en it, and by the time of the invasion, it was a very powerful defensive position. Still, there were numerous gaps along the coast that were manned by second-rate troops.

The Germans could not guard the entire length of the coast equally. Most of their best troops were fighting in Russia, and others were needed to block Allied armies moving up through Italy. The Germans therefore did not have enough material or manpower to fortify every section of the hundreds of miles of coastline where a potential invasion could take place. They had to guess where the Allies would land—and they guessed wrong. The Germans expected that the invasion site would be one of the large ports on the Channel. Ideally, the Allies wanted to capture a major port in the invasion, which would have allowed them to bring supplies across the English Channel (or even directly from America) on large ships to unload on the docks. Having a port would also make it much easier, in the days after the first troops had landed, to

The USS *Texas,* which saw action in both World War I and World War II, was one of the ships used to fire upon Nazi fortifications during the Normandy invasion. Today it rests in the waters near Houston, Texas, in honor of those who served. (Reproduced by permission of Kathleen J. Edgar)

bring in tanks, trucks, and artillery, as well as vast quantities of gasoline to supply them. They could also bring in ammunition and food for the troops, and an ever increasing number of soldiers.

Contrary to the Germans' belief, however, the Allies were selecting a site for the invasion on the basis of their failed attempts to capture the French port of Dieppe in August 1942. At that time, the war had been overwhelmingly dominated by the Axis, and the Allies were in need of a victory to bolster the spirits of their people and their soldiers. Though Dieppe was not designed to be a real military victory—the Allies knew they could not hold the port for long—they wanted to capture it temporarily and then evacuate their troops back to England. This would also show the people of Europe, suffering under German rule, that the Allies were planning to return to Europe, and that Germany's power would not last forever. Unlike the small raids launched by British commandos, the invasion of Dieppe was not aimed at destroying any specific target, and involved many more troops—it was essentially a rehearsal for the great invasion that would be launched later. The Allies wanted to assess the difficulty of capturing a port.

The rehearsal in Dieppe made them believe that taking a port was impossible. The Canadian troops who attacked Dieppe outnumbered German defenders by about twelve to one. The German troops guarding the port were not special elite units: They were the same kind of troops the Allies would meet wherever they landed. But the Germans did not need reinforcements. They were dug in and protected from the Canadians' fire. The Germans had carefully placed German machine guns and artillery to cover the attack area. Many Canadians were killed before they could leave their landing craft, and the rest were trapped on the beach. In one section, where three waves of Canadian soldiers landed, it took only three hours for the Germans to either kill or capture every soldier. Almost 5,000 Canadian soldiers landed at Dieppe; only 2,110 returned to England, 378 of them wounded. More than 1,000 were killed and another 1,800 were captured, including 500 who were wounded. Almost 40 percent of the troops were killed or wounded in only a few hours of fighting. All twenty-nine Allied tanks used in the attack were destroyed, most by German artillery. The Allies chose not to bombard Dieppe from the air largely because of the fear of civilian

In the raid on Dieppe in 1942, a Canadian tank makes its way through the city. (Reproduced by permission of © Hulton Getty/Liaison Agency)

casualities. This left the Canadian soldiers helpless before the dug-in German defenders. The raid was a disaster. The Allied generals were determined that they would not make the same mistake for the big invasion.

The Allies were convinced that it would be impossible to land troops at a major port. German defenses at ports were too powerful—at ports, the Germans had positioned the most cannons and had built the strongest fortifications against Allied air attacks. Allied losses at Dieppe had also demonstrated that a small number of well-fortified defenders could destroy a much larger attacking force. Even if an invading force succeeded in mov-

ing beyond the beach into a port city, every house would become a German stronghold, hiding machine guns and riflemen. Allied troops would have to fight their way through the town street by street and house by house. While the Allies struggled to take the city, the Germans would have time to bring in reinforcements from other parts of France. This would happen quickly, since ports were always on roads and railway lines. If the Germans could bring in enough soldiers and tanks before the Allies were able to reinforce their troops, the invasion would fail. Finally, attacking a port would also greatly increase the number of French civilians who were killed or wounded, another lesson the Allies had learned at Dieppe.

Mulberries

To compensate for not capturing a port in the invasion, the Allies decided to build two artificial harbors, called Mulberries, near the invasion beaches. Two million tons of steel and concrete were used to build more than 600 separate sections of the harbors. Tugboats towed the sections across the English Channel in the days immediately following the Normandy landings. The harbors included more than 200 concrete structures that were sixty feet tall, which the Allies sank in thirty feet of water to create a seawall that protected Allied supply ships from the wind and waves of the Channel. They also sank old freighters, built a floating pier inside the protected water, and constructed roadways from the pier to the beaches. Large ships would unload at the floating piers, and trucks, jeeps, and tanks could be driven directly onto the shore.

The Mulberries were a massive engineering and construction feat: One Mulberry was capable of holding 500 vessels at a time. Despite the size of the project, it was accomplished with amazing speed. The first ship unloaded at one of the Mulberries only ten days after the first troops landed. Just three days later, however, one of the worst June storms in decades hit the English Channel. For three days, heavy winds and high waves tore at the piers, smashing them into one another. The Mulberry used by the Americans was completely destroyed, and the British Mulberry was severely damaged. Within a few days, the British, using parts from the wrecked American harbor, were again unloading ships. Although the Americans were unable to rebuild their Mulberry, they still managed to land sufficient supplies on the beaches without it.

The British Mulberry helped make up for the fact that the Allies could not capture a port on the coast of France. Supplies were unloaded from the prefabricated harbor. (Reproduced by permission of the Corbis Corporation [Bellevue])

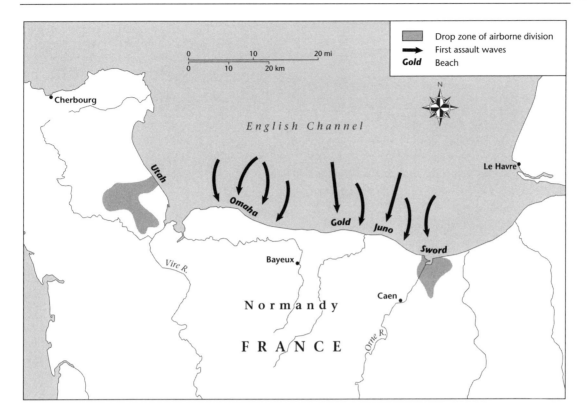

The Normandy invasion area, including the five beaches and the drop zones of the three airborne divisions.

The Allies also decided that, prior to the landing of troops, they would blast the invasion site with giant guns on warships and bombs from planes. This tactical maneuver would kill many German soldiers and destroy some of their tanks, artillery, and fortifications. The Allied planners hoped the assault would also make it harder for surviving German soldiers to fight when Allied troops landed because they would be stunned and confused by the naval and aerial bombardment. Some would have been deafened by the noise, and others would be afraid, possibly fleeing or surrendering when the Allies came ashore. For all these reasons, the Allies decided that the invasion force would land on beaches and capture a port at the first available opportunity after landing. In the meantime, although it would be more difficult, they would land supplies and reinforcements on the beaches they had captured at the beginning of the invasion.

Eventually, the location of the invasion came down to two choices. The planners had ruled out sites where the beaches were not wide enough or were faced by high cliffs that Allied troops would have to climb while the Germans were firing down on them. They also rejected landing locations that were too far away from good ports. One of the remaining options was the eastern end of the English Channel coast, a department of France called Pas-de-Calais, which was on the narrowest part of the Channel—a short distance from the English port of Dover. Besides being near England, this area was also relatively close to Germany, especially the industrial areas where weapons were manufactured for the German army. A successful invasion at Pas-de-Calais would put Allied armies in an excellent position to drive into Germany and end the war quickly. The Germans also knew this was a prime location for an attack, however, and were concentrating on defending the area.

The Allies decided that the invasion force would land instead on the beaches of Normandy, located west of the town of Caen. The landing would be on five separate beaches, stretching along fifty miles of coast. Each beach was given a code name, which has since become famous, and was assigned to various parts of the Allied armies. From east to west, the beaches were called Sword, Juno, Gold, Omaha, and Utah. The British would attack Sword and Gold, the Canadians would land at Juno, and Americans would take Omaha and Utah. Five infantry divisions would land from the sea,

Two Messages

Around noon on June 6, 1944, British radio broadcast a simple message to the people of England and the world: "Under the command of General Eisenhower, Allied naval forces supported by strong air forces began landing armies this morning on the coast of France."

In Eisenhower's wallet, however, was a slip of paper on which he had written a different message—one that he never needed to use. "Our landings in the Cherbourg-Havre area have failed to gain a satisfactory foothold and I have withdrawn the troops," he wrote. "My decision to attack at this time and place [was] based on the best information available. The troops, the air and Navy did all that bravery and devotion to duty could do. If any blame or fault attaches to the attempt it is mine alone."

one at each beach. A British airborne division, which included parachute troops and glider-carried soldiers, would land east of the five beaches to prevent the Germans from attacking the invasion force from that side. Two American parachute divisions would land on the west side of the invasion area, inland from Utah Beach, to protect that area.

Further Planning and the Weather

The plan was that the soldiers would win control of the beaches and push inland several miles. Meanwhile, reinforcements would be landing constantly. The five separate forces, plus the airborne troops, would link up, so that the Allies would control an area fifty miles wide and several miles deep. Then part of the invasion force would turn north to capture the port of Cherbourg, located on the Cotentin Peninsula. The invasion was scheduled for June 5, 1944. On that day and the following two days, the right combination of tides and moonlight would exist. Moonlight was needed so that the

parachute troops could see where they were landing when they were dropped into France the night before the invasion. The tides had to be at the right stage so that the obstacles and mines placed by the Germans would not be hidden underwater when the landing craft reached the beaches at dawn. If the invasion did not take place on one of these three days, it would have to be delayed two weeks until conditions were ideal again.

On the evening of June 4, the weather in England was stormy, as heavy winds blew rain almost parallel to the ground. Bomber pilots would have a difficult time seeing their targets, and glider pilots might be unable to locate their landing zones. Pilots would also have trouble delivering parachute troops over the correct drop zone, and the wind would scatter the soldiers, making it almost impossible for them to land in large groups. Small landing craft, not designed for rough seas, might sink and drown soldiers before they could even reach the beaches. Furthermore, bad weather and heavy clouds immediately after the invasion would allow German tanks and troop-carrying trucks to travel toward Normandy without being detected—and attacked—by Allied planes.

The German commanders knew that the invasion would need good weather. They were sure the Allies would not land in the storm, and many of them took the opportunity to relax. General Erwin Rommel, commander of German forces on the coast, went home to Germany for a few days to celebrate his wife's birthday. Allied weather forecasters, however, predicted that the winds would die down just long enough to launch the invasion. An accurate weather forecast was essential to the success of the mission, but no one could be certain the Allies' predictions were correct.

Once the invasion was set in motion, it would be difficult to stop. The soldiers were packed tightly on the ships that would later transfer them to landing boats. Many of the soldiers—who would soon have to fight a major battle—were becoming seasick, and could not be left waiting on the ships much longer. To maintain secrecy, they had not been allowed to communicate with anyone. If they were unloaded, however, and returned to their bases, it would be impossible to prevent the Germans from learning which ports were being used—and that would tell them that the invasion was heading for Normandy, not Pas-de-Calais. In addition, new soldiers were filling the bases that the Normandy troops had left in England. Sending

General Dwight D. Eisenhower visits paratroopers of the American 101st Airborne Division just before they leave for Normandy. (National Archives and Records Administration)

them back would create a transportation nightmare. Also, for days, the Allies had been bombing railroads and roads in northern France to prevent them from being used to bring German reinforcements to Normandy. If the invasion were delayed, the Germans could repair some of the damage. In addition, the bombing had not yet focused on Normandy itself, to keep the location of the invasion a secret. Just before the invasion, the bombers would concentrate entirely on Normandy. Premature bombardment might reveal the location and allow the Germans to be waiting when the Allies did land.

Sometime after midnight on the morning of June 5, while the wind and rain continued over England, the Channel, and Normandy, General Eisenhower made his final decision. The landings would begin at dawn on June 6, 1944, with parachute landings starting several hours earlier. The invasion was on.

The Airborne Attack

The three airborne divisions began landing east and west of the invasion beaches during the night. At the eastern edge of the area, British troops, many landing by glider, captured several important bridges over rivers and canals that German reinforcements would have to cross. The

lightly armed airborne troops were to hold these positions until the main invasion force, equipped with more powerful weapons and tanks, fought its way to them from the beaches. At the western end, the wind and poor light prevented American paratroopers of the 101st and 82nd Airborne Divisions from landing in large groups as planned. Many fell miles away from their drop zones and were scattered over the countryside. A number of paratroopers drowned in the flooded fields. Others were shot by the Germans while they hung helpless above the ground, their parachutes tangled in trees. Combat units that had been trained to fight as teams found themselves separated from the other soldiers in their squads. Each unit had been assigned specific targets to attack, but in most cases, this was now impossible. For hours—and in some cases, for days—small groups of paratroopers from different units searched for others, formed a larger group, and attacked a crossroad or a bridge or an artillery position. Gradually, the groups became larger and better organized, and began to launch attacks on their assigned targets. Although the confusion cost the lives of many paratroopers, some military historians believe it actually may have contributed to the success of the invasion. The Germans were not sure what was happening; they had no idea how many paratroopers had landed or what their targets were. In fact,

Lieutenant-General Joseph Lawton Collins

One of the Allied leaders at Normandy was Lt.-Gen. J. Lawton Collins. Born in New Orleans, Louisiana, in 1896, he later served as commander of the 25th Infantry Division on Guadalcanal. His nickname, "Lightnin' Joe," derived from the lightning-bolt insignia of the 25th. In January 1943, he and his men participated in the bloody fighting that succeeded in clearing Japanese forces from Guadalcanal. Collins's leadership in the Pacific and on Guadalcanal cemented his reputation as an aggressive fighting commander.

Later in 1943, Collins was transferred to the European theater, and led the VII U.S. Corps in the Normandy landing in June 1944. On June 26, after four days of hard fighting, he led his men to capture the French city of Cherbourg. The victory was a crucial one, for the Allies' supply lines were long and thin, and the need for port cities was great. Unfortunately, the port at Cherbourg could not be used for some time, as the retreating Germans had mined the harbor. Collins took part in the operation to clear the harbor of explosives, scuttled ships, and reefs of discarded equipment. By November 1944, Cherbourg had become the most important port in the Allies' supply network.

After Cherbourg, Collins and the VII Corps turned south to battle across the hedgerows of Normandy and take the cross-roads town of Coutances. This was part of the Allied strategy to break away from the Normandy beachhead and strike inland.

In December 1944 Hitler's forces launched the massive counterattack that came to be known as the Battle of the Bulge. Collins and the VII Corps again distinguished themselves in the Allied push to recapture the heavily forested and highly defensible Ardennes forest region.

After the war, Collins served as army chief of staff until his retirement in 1953. He died in 1963.

(Reproduced by permission of AP/Wide World Photos)

for a long time the Germans remained uncertain whether this was simply another commando raid or part of an invasion.

At 3 a.m. more than 1,000 bombers of the British Royal Air Force began their attack on German defenses at Sword, Juno, and Gold. The assault continued for two hours, during which time the RAF dropped more than 10 million pounds of bombs. In the meantime, American bombers did the same at Utah and Omaha Beaches. At 5 a.m. the bombing stopped and the big guns of the navy warships opened fire from off the coast. The ships (including seven battleships, twenty-three cruisers, and more than 100 destroyers) fired shells—some as heavy as automobiles—into the German fortifications. Many Allied soldiers waiting aboard incoming landing ships claimed they could actually see the shells flying over their heads toward the beaches. Every witness, Allied and German, who later described the bombardment mentioned the incredible noise. No one had ever heard such noise or seen so much firepower focused on such a small area. Some American soldiers, waiting to land, later remembered thinking that no single German could have survived the onslaught.

The Beach Landings

Behind the smoke of the bombardment were about 5,000-6,000 ships, including landing craft—the largest fleet ever assembled. Between 6 and 7:30 a.m. (depending on the tides at each of the five beaches), the troops began to land. On the rough sea, many small landing boats were filling with water, and some soldiers had to use their helmets to bail out the water. Others were not so lucky: Their boats sank, and the soldiers, wearing combat boots and carrying heavy backpacks and other equipment, often drowned. Other boats hit mines and exploded; sometimes boats struck sandbars and were forced to let the soldiers out too far from shore. Then the troops charged into water over their heads, trying desperately to run toward the beach as the Germans fired on them. Despite these setbacks, landings at four of the five beaches progressed well. At Sword, Juno, and Gold, the boats deposited tanks right onto the beaches, where they could give immediate protection to troops. The three attacking divisions of British and Canadian forces overwhelmed the single, poor-quality German division that opposed them. By 10 a.m., the invaders had landed 30,000 men, 3,000 cannons, and 700 armored vehicles, including tanks. Soon, the British troops who had landed on Sword Beach, the easternmost part of the landing areas, linked up with the paratroopers and glider-borne soldiers of the British airborne division. German resistance was somewhat stronger at Gold Beach, but by the end of the day, the British had pushed several miles inland.

At Utah Beach, the American 4th Infantry Division completely surprised another poor-quality German division, whose members were stunned by the bombardment and felt surrounded by the landing forces in front of them and American paratroopers behind them. After relatively little resistance, most of the Germans surrendered. A total of 23,000 American troops landed on Utah Beach on D-Day, with only a dozen Americans killed and fewer than 200 wounded. The mission at Utah Beach was a resounding success, and even the mishaps of the operation aided the Americans. For example, strong currents had carried many boats away from their intended landing areas, but although they were initially confused and unsure where to go, the troops eventually came ashore in an area that was almost undefended.

At Omaha Beach, however, everything went wrong. Much of the beach led to steep banks, some 200 feet high, that allowed the German defenders to fire down on the Americans. In addition, at each end of Omaha were high cliffs topped with German cannons that had probably been spared by cloud cover from the huge air and sea bombardment. (Elite American units called Rangers, similar to the British commandos, attacked on D-Day by using ropes to climb the cliffs in the face of German fire.) This was exactly the type of beach that the planners of Operation Overlord had wanted to avoid. However, Omaha was in the center of the invasion area. It provided the link between Utah Beach and American paratroopers on the west and the British and Canadians on the east.

Other factors weighed heavily against the success of Allied forces at Omaha. The area was defended by the best German troops in the region—tough combat veterans who had recently been sent to Normandy for more training. The Allied landing boats were blasted by German fire long before they reached the beaches, and many soldiers lost their lives in the boats or in the water before they could reach shore. The specially designed amphibious tanks were launched too far from shore, and most of them sank, often drowning their crews. (These tanks had canvas covers that were filled with air. When the tanks reached land, the covers were removed.) Many combat engineers, whose job was to clear the beach of obstacles, also died, and their specialized equipment was lost in the water.

The first wave of soldiers at Omaha had neither tank support nor any means of clearing the beach of obstacles placed by the Germans. They were pinned down by German artillery, machine gun, and rifle fire. Some soldiers clung to the half-submerged obstacles, trying to get any cover they could from the barrage of enemy fire. As the bodies of their dead comrades floated in the water and the wounded lay screaming on the beaches, moving forward seemed impossible. Staying at the edge of the water was equally impossible. Finally, little by little, one or two soldiers at a time, then in small

Supplies and reinforcements move inland from Omaha Beach some days after the invasion, while more ships wait their turn. (Reproduced by permission of AP/Wide World Photos)

An aerial view of Normandy fields surrounded by hedgerows. (Reproduced by permission of the Corbis Corporation [Bellevue])

groups, they began to advance toward the Germans. One of their officers (no one is certain who) summed up the situation in words that became famous: "Two kinds of people are staying on this beach," he shouted. "The dead, and those about to die. Now let's get the hell out of here." By the end of D-Day, some 2,500 Americans had been killed or wounded at Omaha Beach; yet the Germans were unable to drive them back into the sea. As night fell on June 6, 1944, the Allied armies had gained five footholds on the coast of France.

The Battle of Normandy

The Germans were slow to send reinforcements to the battle, fearing another invasion would be launched at Pas-de-Calais. In addition, Allied bombing and sabotage by the French resistance made it difficult for the Germans to move their armored divisions, the best in the German army, to the battlefield. Only German tanks could now defeat the Allies, but the scattered German divisions arrived one at a time, and too late. By

American soldiers help wounded comrades make it to the shore on the Normandy coast. (Reproduced by permission of AP/Wide World Photos)

June 12, the Allies had connected their troops into a continuous front, and by June 18, they had landed more than 600,000 soldiers at Normandy. On that day, American troops who had cut across the neck of the Cotentin Peninsula reached the Atlantic coast. They captured the port of Cherbourg eight days later, on June 26, but the Germans had heavily damaged the harbor and the Allies could not use it for several weeks. It took months before the port became an important unloading point. Even so, Allied reinforcements kept pouring into the battle area until the Americans and British had more troops, tanks, artillery, and—as was the case throughout the fighting—air power than the Germans.

The German army was under increasing Allied pressure, but could not bring reinforcements from Russia. The Soviets had promised the British and Americans that its army would begin a massive offensive, which it implemented on June 22. Within a week, almost 200,000 German troops had been killed, wounded, or captured, and the entire German army in the Soviet Union was in danger.

Heavy fighting continued at Normandy for more than two months. The British failed several times to capture the town of Caen, which they had almost reached on D-Day. The fighting was made especially difficult by the Normandy countryside. Each farm was surrounded by tall mounds of earth covered with thick plant growths. These hedgerows, as they are called, made it impossible for Allied tanks to cross the fields. Instead, they were forced to creep along the narrow roads between the hedgerows, where they made easy targets for the Germans. Allied foot soldiers had to take each field under fire from the Germans, who used the hedgerows as cover.

On July 25, Americans at the west end of the Normandy front attacked German defenders near the town of Saint-Lô. The Germans had fought with tremendous determination since D-Day, but were now exhausted. The units in this area began to retreat and then to fall apart as many of the soldiers surrendered. The American armored divisions of General George S. Patton's Third Army broke through a gap in the German lines toward

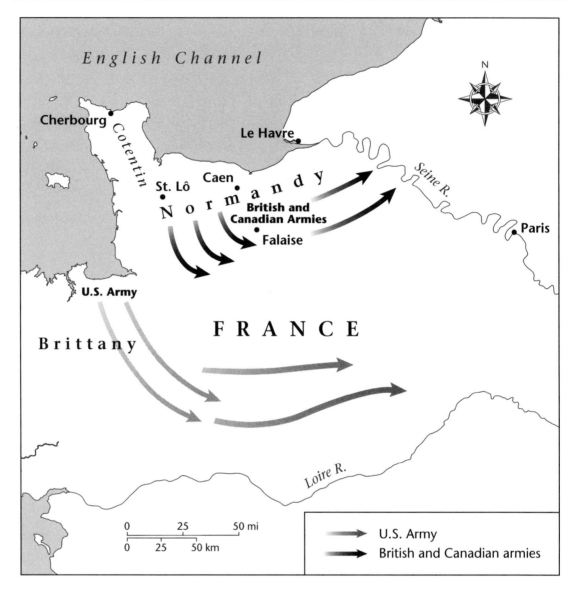

After the landing at Normandy, Allied armies moved east and south through France. General George S. Patton's Third Army advanced south and east and British and Canadian troops drove east from the Caen area.

the south, then swung east, while British and Canadian troops attacked from the north. Much of the German army in Normandy was trapped between these two forces near the town of Falaise.

On Adolf Hitler's direct orders, the Germans attempted a counterattack on August 7, hoping to cut off Patton's Third Army from its supplies. The strategy was quickly defeated. The Germans had committed their last tank forces to the assault and now they too were trapped, under constant bombardment from Allied air forces, with Allied ground troops closing the circle around them. Only a narrow gap separated the advancing Allied troops. The Germans managed to remove 300,000 soldiers and

25,000 vehicles through this gap before it closed on August 20. They retreated east, trying to establish a new defensive line closer to the German border, but 50,000 soldiers were dead and 200,000 had surrendered. Two German armies, along with their tanks and artillery, had been destroyed.

The Battle of Normandy had ended. German defenses had collapsed, and Patton's tanks, almost unopposed, raced east across France, as the British chased the retreating Germans through the northern part of the country. At one point, they advanced more than 100 miles in two days. Within two weeks, they had entered Belgium, freeing the capital city of Brussels on September 4, 1944.

U.S. Army medical corpsmen try to comfort a young French girl who was wounded during the Battle of Normandy. (Reproduced by permission of AP/Wide World Photos)

Meanwhile, on August 15, the American Seventh Army landed eight divisions, five of them French, on the Mediterranean coast of France, between Nice and the port of Marseilles. These divisions had previously been fighting in Italy. The second invasion, code-named Operation Anvil, had finally begun—at the other end of the country from Pas-de-Calais, where the Germans had expected it. Allied forces overwhelmed the German troops, capturing Marseilles and racing north from the Mediterranean deep into France. The German army retreating from Normandy was now in danger of being cut off and surrounded if it tried to make a stand too far west. This was one of the reasons that the Germans moved so far east so quickly.

The French Free Paris

On August 17, 1944, Patton's troops had reached the river Seine, northwest and southeast of Paris. The Allies were not planning to capture Paris

immediately, however, because they wanted to avoid a battle that might destroy the famous monuments, historic buildings, and artistic treasures of the city. They also did not want to risk the lives of the people of Paris. Perhaps most of all, they did not want to have to supply the city with food and fuel, as all available trucks were being used to supply the armored divisions trying to destroy the retreating German army. But Paris was not simply a great city; it was the symbol of France. Liberating Paris from the Germans had political as well as military importance, and General Eisenhower had long since promised that the first Allied troops to enter Paris would be French.

Although the different French resistance organizations and movements were supposed to be united under the authority of General Charles de Gaulle, the leader of the Free French, there were many conflicts among them. One of the most important resistance organizations was dominated by the French Communist party, which did not

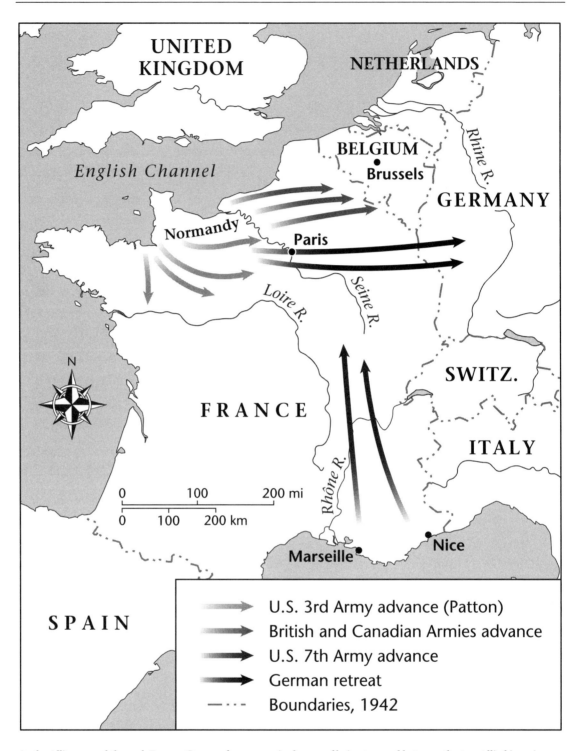

As the Allies moved through France, German forces were in danger of being trapped between the two Allied invasion forces unless they retreated far enough east. The Allied code name for the second invasion was Operation Anvil, because the German army would be smashed down on it by the "hammer" of the Allied troops coming from Normandy.

After the Allied invasion of Normandy in June of 1944, French resistance fighters found the support they needed to force the Axis powers out of France. Shown here, resistance fighters share a meal with American soldiers as they discuss strategies. (Reproduced by permission of AP/Wide World Photos)

trust de Gaulle's plans for postwar France. De Gaulle reciprocated their distrust. The Communists wanted the people of Paris to rise up and liberate themselves from the Germans, not wait for the American army to free them. De Gaulle's supporters were afraid that such an action would lead to a bloodbath if it failed; they were also afraid that a successful uprising would result in Communist control of the city. Yet they still wanted to fight the Germans and regain the honor France had lost in the surrender of 1940.

As tensions mounted in Paris and Allied armies began to break out of Normandy, the Germans ordered the French police in Paris to disarm to prevent their weapons from being used by the resistance. Instead of surrendering their firearms, however, the police went on strike. Other workers were also on strike, defying the Germans. On August 17, 1944, the police took over the main headquarters in central Paris, barricaded themselves inside, and raised the French flag above the building—the first time it had flown over Paris since June 1940. Soon

other barricades appeared on the streets. Young men and women, armed with rifles, pistols, and Molotov cocktails, attacked German patrols. Resistance groups began taking over official buildings. Some of the buildings were now empty; heavy fighting against the Germans took place in others. Similar small actions occurred throughout the city. By the standards of the great battles in Russia and Normandy, these did not amount to a major military action. Nevertheless, about 1,500 French resistance fighters died in the next few days, and another 3,000 were wounded—more than the number of American soldiers who had been killed or wounded on Omaha Beach on D-Day.

For the next several days, the fighting spread across Paris. After a short truce, arranged by the representative of neutral Sweden, hostilities broke out again. On August 22 Hitler ordered the Germans to destroy Paris rather than surrender, and told German military commander Dietrich von Choltitz that only a "field of ruins" should be left. Von Choltitz, however, did not want to be remem-

General Courtney H. Hodges

One of the Americans who led the campaign to liberate France was Courtney H. "Hicks" Hodges. Born in Perry, Georgia, in 1887, he attended West Point but failed his exams, and enlisted in the army as a private in 1906. He received his commission in 1909 and distinguished himself during World War I (1914–1918). Between the wars, he served as chief of the Infantry School at Fort Benning.

In 1944 he participated in the Normandy landing and in the crucial Cobra operation, led by General Omar Bradley, that led to the Allies' breakout from the Normandy beachhead. After this victory, General Bradley took over the U.S. Twelfth Army group, and appointed Hodges commander of the U.S. First Army.

Hodges led the U.S. First Army with great distinction throughout the campaign to liberate France. In August 1944 the French resistance began an insurrection in the German-occupied capital of Paris. The Allies had not planned to liberate Paris, but when the resistance pleaded for aid, General Dwight D. Eisenhower dispatched General Jacques Philippe Leclerc's French 2nd Division to aid the rebels. Since he mistrusted the French commander's ability to take orders, Hodges was appointed to supervise the operation. On August 25 Leclerc and Hodges succeeded in liberating Paris.

In October Hodges succeeded capturing the city of Aachen, Germany, a city which, as the former capital of the Holy Roman Empire, held special significance for the Third Reich. It was the first capture of a major German city by the Allies, but as the city lay in ruins, the victory was an empty one. Through November 1944, Hodges's First Army pushed eastward. Like most Allied commanders, Hodges was entirely taken by surprise by the massive German counteroffensive that began the Battle of the Bulge on December 16. His First Army held the northern flank through the battle.

Hodges was known as a soft-spoken fighting commander. He was promoted to full general in April 1945 and commanded the First Army until his retirement in 1949.

(Library of Congress)

As the Allied troops continued to retake cities and towns in France, Canadian troops re-entered Dieppe as victors on September 3, 1944, as French residents lined the streets. (Reproduced by permission of AP/Wide World Photos)

bered as the man who had destroyed Paris, no matter what Hitler ordered. The destruction of landmarks such as the Eiffel Tower or the Louvre Museum, as opposed to tactical locations like bridges, went beyond the scope of military duty and violated von Choltitz's sense of honor. But von Choltitz's honor also would not allow him to surrender without putting up a fight. Moreover, he felt he could not surrender his command to a group of armed civilians, only to officers of a regular army. In addition, on July 20 there had been an attempt by some German military officers to kill Hitler, and von Choltitz knew any sign of disobedience would put him under suspicion of being part of the plot and would endanger his family back home in Germany.

As news of the uprising reached Allied commanders, the French Second Armored Division, which had been among the best Allied forces in the recent battle around Falaise, received new orders to move immediately to Paris, 120 miles away. The next day, August 23, the division sped toward the city, avoiding the Germans as much as possible. On

August 24, as they reached the suburbs, they were held up several times by German antitank defenses. Their advance was also slowed by crowds and celebrations that broke out along the route. One American general accused them of "dancing to Paris." Afraid that American troops would be ordered to take the city, French commander General Jacques Philippe Leclerc decided to send a small force into Paris that night. One platoon of soldiers (about thirty men) and three tanks headed into the city, turning down side streets and circumventing defended German positions. At 9:30 p.m. they reached city hall, near the city center. Even though the force was small, church bells rang throughout Paris, as the fighting between the resistance and the Germans continued.

At 7 a.m. on August 25, 1944, Leclerc's main force entered the city from the south, as huge crowds, sometimes twenty deep, cheered them. At first, the Parisians thought American troops had arrived because the tanks, jeeps, and even the uniforms were American. The celebrations were even more joyful when it became clear that the soldiers were French. The crowds passed them food and drink and flowers, and opened bottles of champagne that had been hidden away for more than four years in anticipation of this day. Women embraced and kissed the liberating troops, many of whom were Paris natives. The soldiers passed notes to people in the crowd, asking them to phone their families with the news they had come home. The premature celebration caused many to forget that the Germans were still fighting in Paris, however, and some of the French soldiers were killed before they could see their families. As Leclerc's men

approached the center of Paris, many German positions held out fiercely. At about 2:30 p.m. on August 25, 1944, some of the French troops reached the German headquarters, fought their way inside, and captured General von Choltitz. They drove him to police headquarters, where Leclerc was waiting, and the two generals signed the terms of the German surrender of Paris. A short while later, one of the leaders of the resistance added his name to the agreement. The people of Paris and the French army had freed Paris together.

PRIMARY SOURCE

Veterans of D-Day
Excerpt from *Voices of D-Day: The Story of the Allied Invasion Told by Those Who Were There*
Edited by Ronald J. Drez
Published in 1994

The Allied invasion of the beach of Normandy, on the northwestern coast of France, remains the largest and most difficult wartime invasion ever planned. France was heavily fortified by the German military, and had to be conquered before the Allies could advance into Germany. The beaches of Normandy were chosen as the site for a massive amphibious invasion of the European continent by British and American forces. It was code-named Operation Overlord and was set to begin on June 6, 1944—now known as D-Day. German forces in France were led by Field Marshal Erwin Rommel, the "Desert Fox," under whose command German tank divisions in Africa had repeatedly defeated the British. In France, Rommel oversaw the construction of an elaborate defense system, known as the Atlantic Wall, to guard the Normandy shore. The coast was lined with barbed wire, mines, armed concrete bunkers, huge wooden posts rigged with explosives, and an underwater network of sharp steel barriers.

By 1944, the Germans were feeling the effects of Allied air assaults on their factories, airfields, and oil refineries. Prior to the invasion at Normandy,

the British Royal Air Force (RAF) and U.S. Army Air Force crippled the Luftwaffe, leaving the Germans more vulnerable to an invasion. Although the German army had conquered most of Europe, it was already reeling from months of unsuccessful fighting in Italy and the Soviet Union. German military leaders knew the Allies were organizing an invasion of German-occupied France, but did not know when or where the attack would take place. Rumor spread that U.S. General George S. Patton had assembled troops and was planning to cross the English Channel at Dover and go ashore at the French seaport of Calais, in the department of Pas-de-Calais. The Germans increased their forces at Calais, falling into the Allies' trap; the actual landing spot would be farther to the southwest, along the Caen area in Normandy.

Nevertheless, the planners of the Allied invasion had to adapt their strategy to the weather. The English Channel is well known for its unpredictable nature. In spite of stormy weather, General Dwight D. Eisenhower, supreme commander of the Allied invasion force, ordered the launch of Operation Overlord on June 5, 1944. Forecasters predicted a short break in the stormy conditions for June

Dwight David Eisenhower

Dwight David "Ike" Eisenhower was born October 14, 1890, in Denison, Texas. The Eisenhower family moved to Abilene, Kansas, when Eisenhower was an infant. Money was tight, but deep religious faith and strong family ties kept the family going. Young Eisenhower and his five brothers worked together to help their mother with the household chores, including laundry, gardening, and cooking. In school, Eisenhower excelled at competitive sports. He also developed a keen interest in war history and mathematics. After graduating from the U.S. Military Academy at West Point in 1915, Eisenhower served as a second lieu-

As supreme commander of the Allied forces in Europe, U.S. General Dwight D. Eisenhower launched Operation Overlord, which took place on June 6, 1944. (National Archives and Records Administration)

tenant at Fort Sam Houston in Texas. He married Mamie Doud the next year.

During the final phase of World War I (1914–1918), Eisenhower instructed American troops in tank warfare. World War II erupted in Europe in 1939. As tensions escalated worldwide, the United States began gearing up for military involvement in the conflict. Eisenhower was promoted to the rank of brigadier general in 1941, directed Operation Torch (the invasion of North Africa) in 1942 and 1943, and oversaw the assault on Italy. As supreme commander of the Allied forces in Europe, he launched Operation Overlord, the invasion of Normandy, France, in 1944. Eisenhower accepted Germany's surrender on May 8, 1945.

Three years later, Eisenhower retired from the U.S. Army as a five-star general. While serving for a few years as president of New York's Columbia University, he began thinking about running for the office of U.S. president, an election he won in 1952. As a two-term president, Eisenhower served through a tumultuous time in U.S. history: The Korean War (1950–1953) was in full swing, anti-Communist sentiment was strong in the United States, an arms race between the Soviet Union and the United States was escalating, and the civil rights movement was born.

In 1961 Eisenhower and his wife retired to a farm near Gettysburg, Pennsylvania. Eisenhower wrote several books and attempted to stay out of the political limelight, favoring the role of avid golfer to that of political consultant. He died March 28, 1969, in Washington, D.C.

6, 1944, and those predictions determined the exact date of the D-Day invasion. A contingent of Allied paratroopers landed in France the night of June 5, charged with scouting the terrain and guiding the later landings of airborne divisions from Great Britain, Canada, and the United States. Heavy fire from the Germans on the ground forced the initial groups of paratroopers off course, but the multinational Allied invasion went on as scheduled. Some 900 planes flew over Normandy, dropping an estimated 13,000 paratroopers inland from the beaches. Their mission was to stall the Germans by destroying bridges, blocking roads, and disrupting communications. They also served as backup for the main invasion forces that would land on the beaches the morning of June 6, 1944, D-Day.

The invasion took place over a fifty-mile area divided into five beaches with the code names Sword, Juno, Gold, Omaha, and Utah. Sword and Juno were attacked by British regiments, Gold was taken by the Canadian infantry, and Omaha and Utah were in the American sector. American, British, Canadian, and French soldiers (a total of 155,000 troops) who would fight on those beaches were crammed into about 5,000-6,000 Allied ships, with 10,000 accompanying aircraft. Americans of the 29th Division landed at Omaha and met the heaviest resistance from Germans stationed on the cliffs above the beach. The Germans showered the landing force with shells and machine-gun fire. Some troops never made it out of the landing craft, while others drowned in the turbulent waters of the English Channel. By the end of D-Day, there were some 2,500 Allied casualties on Omaha Beach alone.

Voices of D-Day: The Story of the Allied Invasion Told by Those Who Were There describes the Normandy landing in vivid detail. The personal accounts of soldiers who took part in the invasion were collected by editor Ronald J. Drez for a special D-Day Project of the University of New Orleans' Eisenhower Center. The accounts of Warner Hamlett and Harold Baumgarten appear in the chapter titled "The 116th at Omaha Beach." Robert H. Miller and Warren Rulien's stories are taken from "Easy Red and the First Division." (Easy Red was a subsection of Omaha Beach.) The following excerpts reveal the young soldiers' fear and bravery amid the chaos and confusion of the Normandy landing.

Excerpt from *Voices of D-Day*

WARNER HAMLETT (Sergeant, Company F):... *"After we jumped into the water, it was every man for himself. I waded parallel to the beach with my squad because the heavy fire was directed towards the boats. As I was going straight towards the beach, I saw Lieutenant Hilscher go down on his knees as a shell exploded. He fell into the hole caused by the explosion. He died there on the beach....*

"When I finally reached the edge of the water, I started to run towards the seawall under a deafening roar of explosions and bullets. I saw a hole about seventy-five feet away, so I ran and jumped in, landing on top of O. T. Grimes. As soon as I caught my breath, I dashed forward again, but had to stop between the obstacles in order to rest. The weight of wet clothes, sand, and equipment made it difficult to run. One ... soldier ... had run straight to the seawall and was motioning for us to come on. At the same time, he was yelling, 'Get off the beach!' Our only chance was to get off the beach as quick as possible, because there we were sitting ducks. While resting in between the obstacles, Private Gillingham fell beside me, white with fear. He seemed to be begging for help with his eyes. His look was that of a child asking what to do. I said, 'Gillingham, let's stay separated as much as we can, because the Germans will fire at two quicker than one.' He remained silent and then I heard a shell coming and dove into the sand face down. Shrapnel rose over my head and hit all around me. It took Gillingham's chin off, including the bone, except for a small piece of flesh. He tried to hold his chin in place as he ran towards the seawall. He made it to the wall, where Will Hawks and I gave him his morphine shot. He stayed with me for approximately thirty minutes until he died. The entire time, he remained conscious and aware that he was dying.*

"We were supposed to wait at the seawall until wire cutters could cut the tremendous web of wire

A landing craft loaded with soldiers heads for the Normandy coast. Many soldiers got seasick from the rough ride across the English Channel. (Reproduced by permission of Corbis/The Mariner's Museum)

that the Germans had placed on top of it. During this time, Lieutenant Wise of F Company was directing his team behind the seawall, when a bullet hit him in the forehead. He continued to instruct his men until he sat down and held his head in the palm of his hand before falling over dead.

"We waited at the seawall until [it was] time to cross over the path cleared by the wire cutters. As we crossed the seawall, Germans in pillboxes [roofed concrete compartments for machine guns and anti-tank weapons] fired upon each man as he dashed forward. After we crossed, the ground provided more protection, with small bushes and gullies. We took time to reorganize and planned to knock out the pill-box. First we tried direct attack using TNT on the end of long poles, but this was impossible because the Germans could shoot the men down as soon as they saw them coming through the barbed wire strung in front of the pillboxes. We then decided to run between the pillboxes and enter the trenches that connected them. These trenches had been dug by the Germans and gave them mobility and a means of escape. We entered the trenches, slipped behind the pillboxes, and threw grenades into them. After the explosion, we ran into the boxes to kill any that survived the grenade. Rows of pillboxes stood between us

and the top of the cliff. Slowly, one by one, we advanced...."

HAROLD BAUMGARTEN (Company B): "....Shells were continually landing all about me, in a definite pattern, and when I raised my head up to curse the Germans in the pillbox on our right flank ... one of the shell fragments from an 88 [an 88-millimeter shell] exploded twenty yards in front of me and hit me in my left cheek. It felt like being hit with a baseball bat, only the results were much worse. My upper jaw was shattered; the left cheek was blown open, and my upper lip was cut in half. The roof of my mouth was cut up, and teeth and gums were laying all over inside. Blood poured freely from the gaping wound. The same 88–millimeter shell that hit me in the left side of my face hit Sergeant Hoback, of Company A, flush in the face, and he went under. I washed my face out in the six-inch cold, dirty [English] Channel water, and managed somehow not to pass out. I got rid of most of my equipment.

"The water was rising about an inch a minute, as the tide was coming in, so I had to get moving or drown. I had to reach a fifteen-foot seawall, which appeared to be two hundred yards in front of me, and I crawled forward, trying to take cover behind

After the initial landings on French beaches in June of 1944, Allied invaders dig into foxholes in the sand. From their fortified positions, the soldiers watch for enemy movement as new Allied troops and supplies are unloaded. (Reproduced by permission of © Hulton Getty/Liaison Agency)

American soldiers leaving the ramp of a coast guard landing boat during the invasion of Normandy. (Photograph by Robert F. Sergeant/National Archives and Records Administration)

bodies and water obstacles made of steel. I got another rifle along the way as the Germans were zeroing in on me. I continued forward in a dead-man's float with each wave of the incoming tide.

"Finally, I came to dry sand, and there was another hundred yards to go, and I started across the sand, crawling very fast.... I reached the stone wall without further injury....

"At the wall, I met a fellow from Company B from my boat team named Dominick Surrow, a boy from Georgia about my age, a rugged fellow, who looked at my face and said, 'Stay here, I'm going to run down the beach and get help.' He got killed.

"I watched him being washed around by the incoming water, and I saw the bodies of my buddies who had tried in vain to clear the beach. It looked like the beach was littered with the refuse of a wrecked ship that were the dead bodies of what once was the proud, tough ... well-trained combat infantrymen of the 1st Battalion of the 116th Infantry."

ROBERT H. MILLER (Corporal, 149th Engineer Combat Battalion): "I was in Company B. Our Beach was the Easy Red Beach, which was situated right in front of Saint-Laurent-sur-Mer [a beach that lies along the Bay of Seine, part of the English Channel].

"A jeep was the first off the craft, and it went down and dropped clear underwater but made it in, since it was waterproofed and the exhaust pipe was extended well above the jeep itself, up above the waterline. The trucks came off and they made it in as well. The men started unloading at that point, and I jumped off the end of the ramp and went underwater completely, over my head. I ejected all of my equipment underwater and jumped as well as I could underwater and finally reached the waterline.... [I] got my head above water and started swimming in. That was a tough swim. The wet, heavy clothes were weighing me down.... My body felt like it weighed five hundred pounds, and I was very tired.

"I heard a number of screams behind me and many of the men drowned trying to make their way in to the beach.... I got about ten feet up the beach when I saw just a big white ball of nothingness, and the next thing I knew I was flat on my back looking up at the sky. My first thought was that my legs were blown off because I had tried to move them and nothing happened.... For some reason I just couldn't move....

"Shortly, the medics came down behind a half-track [a military vehicle with wheels in front and

Saving Private Ryan

The 1998 motion picture *Saving Private Ryan* won five Academy Awards that year, including Best Director. It contains a half-hour sequence set during the Allied landing at Omaha Beach. Many of the actors who portrayed the Omaha soldiers, however, including Tom Hanks, were much older than the men they were depicting. Many of the Americans who landed at Omaha Beach were in their late teens and early twenties.

tank-like tracks in the rear] and picked me up, and it was there that they gave me a shot of morphine. I woke up at the first-aid station on the beach, and the doctors were going over me and the nurse cutting off clothing and that sort of thing. I passed out shortly again. The next time I woke up I was loaded on an LST [landing ship, tank; an amphibious ship that can drive onto a beach to unload cargo] and the navy aide was talking to me and asking what he could do for me ... and I could hear ack-ack guns, the antiaircraft guns, going off up on deck.

"I passed out again and woke up on an LCVP [landing craft, vehicle and personnel] and we were headed toward the dock of some town in England. A colonel was next to me with a head wound, and he was just screaming terribly, and there were wounded laying all over the LCVP. The consequences of my injury was that I became a paraplegic and lost the use of my legs entirely."

WARREN RULIEN (16th Infantry): "Eight rope nets had been hung over the side of the ship and we began climbing down into the landing crafts. This wasn't an easy thing to do with all the equipment you had on and the rifle. Waves from the English Channel would separate the landing craft from the side of the ship and then it would crash back against the hull. I got down near the bottom of the net and had to time my jump into the landing craft.

"I felt so rotten from the seasickness that I was half enthusiastic about hitting the shore just to get off that landing craft. As we got nearer to the shore, bul-

Soldiers trying to get ashore at Omaha Beach. The posts seen sticking out of the water were part of the German fortifications. (Reproduced by permission of the Corbis Corporation [Bellevue])

lets began hitting the sides but could not penetrate as we ducked down low. It wasn't long after we stopped when the front of the landing craft was lowered. For a few seconds, everything seemed quiet and nobody moved. The image that flashed through my mind was 'They can shoot us through the front of the craft.'

"Someone shouted, 'Let's go!' We began pouring out of the craft, and as I stepped off of the ramp, I dropped into water up to my chest and I lost my rifle and began wading in to shore.

"On both sides of me were many soldiers coming from other landing crafts, all wading in to shore. In front of me were steel rails driven into the bottom of the sea, which extended six feet out of the water, and on top were mines. By the time I got to the steel rails, the water was up to my waist. There were many dead soldiers floating around in the water, and bullets began hitting only a few feet in front of me, so I stepped behind one of the steel rails and squatted down. A young replacement about nineteen years old that was from my platoon shouted at me, 'Hey, Rulien, here I go!' and began running toward shore. He stepped onto the sandbar, and machine—gun fire opened up, and he dropped into the water on the other side.

"I took one of the bodies that was floating in the water and pushed it in front of me toward the shore. I had only gone a short distance when three or four

soldiers began lining up behind me. I stood up and shouted, 'Don't bunch up!' and walked off, leaving them with the body. I got down as low as I could in the water until I reached the sandbar, and then I crossed it on my belly and kept moving forward until I reached the beach, where soldiers were bunched-up behind a sandbank.

"Lying beside me, on his back, was a soldier who had been shot in the stomach. He held his hand over his stomach, moaning, but only for a short time; then he died. I picked up his rifle, threw back the bolt, and looked down the barrel to make sure that sand hadn't been jammed into the barrel. I put a clip of ammunition in and looked up the hill and saw German soldiers running along the crest. At that distance, they looked about two inches high and I began firing at them. On the shore, there were officers sitting there, stunned. Nobody was taking command. Landing crafts were continuing to bring waves of soldiers in, and they were bunching up on the beach.

"Finally, out on the water, coming towards the shore, walking straight up with a staff of officers with him, I recognized Colonel Taylor, regimental commander. He stepped across the sandbar and bullets began hitting the water around him. He laid down on his stomach and started crawling towards shore, and when he got in, I heard him say to the officers, 'If *we're going to die, let's die up there.' It seemed to take effect, because the officers began moving their men* *from that two yards of beach to reach their objective."* (Drez, pp. 208–209, 216–217, 237–238, 253–254)

Aftermath

In all, 10,000 aircraft, about 5,000-6,000 ships, and 155,000 soldiers landed at Normandy. Even though the losses at Omaha beach were extremely heavy, the Allied invasion of Normandy was considered a success. Having established a foothold in France, the Allies began their march eastward toward Germany. A huge tank still sits on the sand of Normandy beach as a reminder of D-Day.

SOURCES

Books

Ambrose, Stephen E., *D-Day, June 6, 1944,* Simon and Schuster (New York), 1994.

Dolan, Edward F., *America in World War II: 1944,* Millbrook Press (Brookfield, CT), 1993.

Drez, Ronald J., editor, *Voices of D-Day: The Story of the Allied Invasion Told by Those Who Were There,* Louisiana State University Press (Baton Rouge, LA), 1994.

Eisenhower, Dwight D., *At Ease: Stories I Tell to Friends,* Doubleday (Garden City, NY), 1967.

Eisenhower, Dwight D., *Crusade in Europe,* Doubleday (Garden City, NY), 1948.

Hargrove, Jim, *Dwight D. Eisenhower: Thirty-Fourth President of the United States,* Encyclopedia of Presidents Series, Children's Press (Chicago), 1987.

Hastings, Max, *Overlord: D-Day and the Battle for Normandy,* Simon & Schuster (New York), 1985.

Ryan, Cornelius, *The Longest Day,* Touchstone/Simon & Schuster (New York), 1994.

Sandberg, Peter Lars, *World Leaders Past and Present: Dwight D. Eisenhower,* Chelsea House (New York), 1986.

Stein, R. Conrad, *Cornerstones of Freedom: D-Day,* Children's Press (Chicago), 1977.

Sweeney, James B., *Army Leaders of World War II,* F. Watts (New York), 1984.

Webster, David Kenyon, *Parachute Infantry: An American Paratrooper's Memoir of D-Day and the Fall of the Third Reich,* Louisiana State University Press (Baton Rouge, LA), 1994.

Periodicals

Newsweek, March 8, 1999, pp. 48–49.

Other

Britannica.com Presents Normandy 1944, http://www.normandy.eb.com/normandy/ (May 16, 2000).

D-Day, The Normandy Invasion (video), International Video Entertainment, Inc., 1988.

D-Day Remembered (video), Direct Cinema Limited, 1994.

Normandy: The Great Crusade (video), Discovery Communications, Inc., 1994.

The Normandy Invasion, http://www.army.mil/cmh-pg/reference/normandy/normandy.htm (May 16, 2000).

Saving Private Ryan (movie), 1998.

18

Spies and Scientists

Of primary importance to both the Allied and Axis powers during World War II was determining the strengths, weaknesses, and tactical plans of the enemy. Intelligence, the gathering of such information, and counterintelligence, preventing the enemy from obtaining that information, were used by each side to advance its strategies and to prevent the other from gaining an advantage. Both the Axis and the Allies, like most countries at war, tried to develop technology and weaponry that superseded those of its enemy. Scientists played a major role in advancing this technology by enhancing already extant equipment and by creating everything from new drugs to heal wounded soldiers to stronger and more accurate bombs to drop on the enemy.

Deceptions

During wartime, one of the most carefully guarded military secrets is the time and location of a planned attack. The Axis and Allied powers used various methods to protect such information. For example, when the Japanese fleet set sail for the surprise attack on the U.S. naval installation at Pearl Harbor, Hawaii, in December 1941, its orders were hand-delivered by courier. At sea, Japanese ships did not use their radios to communicate with one another or with bases in Japan. This radio silence prevented the Americans from knowing where the

Japanese ships were—or even that they had sailed. The fleet also took advantage of natural conditions to conceal its movements by sailing on the edge of an advancing weather front; heavy clouds and constant rain minimized chances that the ships would be detected by U.S. reconnaissance planes.

Similarly, in December 1944, the Germans imposed radio silence and took cover under fog in heavily wooded terrain in the Ardennes Forest in southwestern Belgium to prevent Allied planes from seeing their preparations for the Battle of the Bulge. Despite these precautions, however, the Allies received strong hints that there might be a major attack in the Ardennes. For instance, they knew that the Germans were moving tough armored divisions into the area. Nevertheless, top American generals were convinced that the German army was too weak to launch an attack, and that even if an assault took place, it would not be in the Ardennes. Allied officials explained away the German presence there, concluding that those divisions were simply resting in a quiet sector of the battlefront. This was a fatal error in judgment. The Battle of the Bulge would become the costliest engagement of the war for the Americans.

An even more effective strategy than concealing an offensive is tricking the enemy into believing that an offensive will take place in another location. This occurred in the Allied invasion of Sicily, Italy, in July 1943. The Allies had successfully driven Ger-

The Man Who Never Was

In 1943 British official Ewen Montagu headed the successful scheme that tricked the Germans into believing the Allies would invade Greece and Sardinia instead of Sicily. Disguising a corpse as a British marine captain on a mission to North Africa, Montagu and his colleagues planted fake documents that convinced the Germans they should divert elite tank and infantry divisions to Greece and Sardinia rather than Sicily. In 1954 Montagu published *The Man Who Never Was* (J. B. Lippincott: New York) a book that gave step-by-step details of the clever ruse. A motion picture by the same title was released the following year.

man and Italian troops from North Africa, so nearby Sicily was the obvious next target, or so it seemed. Allied officials decided to concoct a ruse to convince the Germans that the attack would take place in Greece and on the Italian island of Sardinia, not in Sicily. British intelligence agents in England found the body of a man who had died of pneumonia, which can appear to be death by drowning, and dressed the corpse in the uniform of a British officer. They placed various fake documents in his wallet and in a briefcase chained to his waist. The papers identified the man as a captain in the British marines and an expert on landing craft who was on his way to North Africa to join the staff of the British commanding general there.

The man also carried personal items that confirmed his identity. Most important, he carried a top-secret personal letter from one British general to another, revealing that the next Allied invasion was planned for Greece and Sardinia. The letter also stated that the British should continue to try to make the Germans think Sicily was the target, and included some negative comments about other top generals, thus explaining why the communication was being hand delivered instead of transmitted through official (and coded) radio messages. The agents then took the body by sub-

marine to the coast of Spain and released it where it would float to shore. The plan was to make the Germans believe the "officer" had drowned after his plane crashed into the sea. The British chose Spain for a specific reason: Although Spain was officially neutral in the war, the government was unofficially pro-German. The ruse worked: The body attracted the attention of German agents in Spain, who were unsure whether the documents in the wallet and briefcase were authentic; the letter from a top British general explaining invasion plans seemed especially suspect—too good to be true. Nevertheless, probably on personal orders from Adolf Hitler, the Germans sent reinforcements to Greece and Sardinia. Consequently, one of Germany's best armored divisions and a mechanized infantry division were not in Sicily when the Allies launched their attack.

The Allies used a more complex deception to divert German resources from the Allied invasion of Normandy in 1944. Code-named Operation Fortitude, it was by far the most successful counterintelligence operation conducted by any country during World War II. The Germans knew the invasion of Europe was imminent and felt the most likely site would be the department of Pas-de-Calais in northeastern France, the closest part of Europe to England. The Germans had placed many of their best troops nearby, with armored divisions ready to rush to the coast and drive the invaders back into the sea. The Allies developed an elaborate plan to convince the Germans that the invasion force would indeed land at Pas-de-Calais. Furthermore, they wanted to keep German generals guessing as to whether the invasion would actually take place at Pas-de-Calais even after Allied troops were already landing in Normandy on D-Day. If German leaders believed Normandy was the decoy and that the real invasion would begin in Pas-de-Calais, they would be reluctant to send their tanks and best troops into Normandy. Allied officials hoped they could fool the Germans, even for a few days, so that German tanks and reinforcements might arrive in Normandy too late to defeat the Allies.

In an effort to outwit the Germans, the Allies created an imaginary army, the First United States Army Group (FUSAG). FUSAG was commanded by a real American general, George S. Patton, whom the Germans knew as one of the best American tank commanders. The Germans fell for the Allied bait, believing that Patton would be commanding ground troops in the invasion of France. Patton had a headquarters, as did the various army divisions and army corps that were supposedly part of FUSAG. Radio messages were constantly being transmitted among these different groups, and also between FUSAG and other Allied military commands. Although the Germans could not understand the encoded messages, they concluded that such frequent radio communication meant that FUSAG must be a large force. FUSAG headquarters was in southeastern England, across from Pas-de-Calais. German planes took aerial photographs that showed tanks, trucks, jeeps, and tents; German spies in England confirmed the evidence. FUSAG was, of course, a fake: The tents were empty, and the tanks were made of cardboard. The Allies purposely allowed the Germans to hear the radio messages; they also let German planes fly over the area and escape back into German-held France, while they shot down planes that came near actual Allied bases.

The German spies who confirmed the aerial reconnaissance were also fake—they were working for the Allies. The British Double-Cross System involved agents who had started out as spies for Germany, but had been arrested. Those who agreed to work for the Allies had been released. For years, the British had carefully allowed the spies to report certain information back to Germany in order to ensure that the Germans believed the spies were still loyal to them, but that information, although accurate, was always unimportant or too dated to be of any real value. Now the spies sent false information to Germany, helping to convince the German high command that FUSAG was an authentic invasion army poised to strike at Pas-de-Calais.

The deception continued until the invasion of Normandy on June 6, 1944. The Allies successfully jammed nearly all of the ninety-two German radar stations on the coast with electronic interference, but purposely allowed the eighteen installations around Pas-de-Calais to keep operating. As the great Allied invasion fleet approached the Normandy beaches, a smaller group of Allied ships sailed toward Pas-de-Calais. Each boat towed balloons that dangled specially shaped strips of aluminum. Consistent with Allied plans, German radar at Pas-de-Calais detected a huge invasion fleet approaching. Operation Fortitude helped keep the German tanks far from Normandy until it was too late for them to resist the invasion. Even as many tens of thousands of American and British troops swarmed onto the beaches on June 6, 1944—now known as D-Day—Hitler refused to allow the German armored divisions from Pas-de-Calais to go to

Noor Inayat Khan

Noor Inayat Khan was born in Russia but raised in France, the daughter of an Indian father and an American mother. After escaping to England when Germany conquered France, she volunteered to be an SOE agent. She parachuted back into France in June 1943 and became a radio operator for an intelligence network in Paris. The network was destroyed by a Gestapo raid just after Khan arrived, and she was the only member not captured. She chose to stay in Paris instead of escaping to England. For the next three months, she handled nearly all the radio work from Paris to England, barely eluding capture on several occasions. In one instance, a German soldier inspected the radio transmitter she was carrying in a suitcase on the subway, but Khan convinced him it was part of a movie projector. In October an informer betrayed her to the Gestapo; she was arrested and tortured, but refused to reveal any information. After an escape attempt, Khan was kept in solitary confinement, chained to a wall, for ten months. Eventually, she was transferred to the concentration camp at Dachau in southern Germany, where she was executed at the age of thirty.

the rescue. Instead, they waited for the "real" invasion. Meanwhile, back at Normandy, Allied forces established footholds on the beaches by the end of D-Day. By June 12, those forces formed a continuous front, and by June 18, the Allies had landed more than 600,000 soldiers at Normandy.

Double Agents

Spies can provide valuable information about an enemy, but, as the British Double-Cross System showed, intelligence agents can also be turned into

German journalist Richard Sorge provided crucial information to the Soviets during the war. (Reproduced by permission of AP/Wide World Photos)

double agents and used to report false information. Both the Germans and the Allies succeeded in turning spies several times during the war. For instance, one major spy network in the Netherlands gave the British information that was in fact created by the Gestapo. Yet even reliable spies rarely have a complete picture of military secrets because they are usually privy to only a small piece of information, which by itself may be misleading. Agents who had access to important military or political leaders in enemy countries were rare during World War II. The more common way to obtain enemy intelligence was to employ a number of spies, each of whom relayed small bits of information. When all the pieces were put together and analyzed, accurate pictures unfolded.

During World War II, one source of information might have affected not only a battle but even the war itself. At various times, Allied intelligence agents had secret contacts with Admiral Wilhelm Canaris, head of the German military intelligence agency, Abwehr. Due to the nature of Canaris's job, he knew most German military plans and secrets. Eventually executed for his part in the plot to assassinate Hitler, Canaris apparently quietly opposed Hitler's war plans from the beginning, but was playing complicated political games inside

the German military. In fact, historians are still not sure of Canaris's goals, or even his actions. He and other Abwehr agents seem to have given away some (but certainly not all) of Germany's military secrets for years. In fact, a ring of anti-Hitler spies was active inside Abwehr. Abwehr agents, possibly with Canaris's knowledge, apparently warned the Dutch about Germany's plan to invade the Netherlands in 1940. The Dutch ignored the information, however, because they had no reason to trust its source. Abwehr may also have been the origin of the Oslo Report, a document given to the British in Norway in 1940, which listed all secret weapons being developed by Germany. The British doubted the accuracy of the document, thinking it might be a bluff intended to intimidate them.

The spy who may have had the greatest effect during World War II was Richard Sorge, a German journalist in Tokyo who was also a spy for the Soviet Union. He became a trusted friend of important Japanese officials and German diplomats in Japan. Like most Soviet spies in World War II, Sorge was a Communist who was secretly loyal to the Soviet Union because it was the first Communist country. Sorge and his small ring of cohorts, who included Japanese Communists, passed a great deal of information to the Soviet Union, but he is best remembered for two reports: one that was not believed, and one that was taken as fact. In spring 1941 Sorge warned that Germany was preparing to invade the Soviet Union, even providing the exact date, June 22, on which the Germans would mount the attack. This information, however, had no impact on Soviet military plans because Joseph Stalin, the Soviet dictator, simply did not want to believe that Germany was planning a war against his country. A few months later, Sorge told the Soviets that Japan would not invade the Soviet Union, as the Soviets feared. Instead, Japan would attack the United States and Britain. The Soviets believed this information, confirmed by their own observations of Japanese troop movements. It allowed the Soviet army to transfer a large number of troops, including some of the best soldiers in the Soviet army, from the border between the Soviet Union and Japanese-occupied northern China, sending them west to repulse the German invasion. This was a crucial moment in the war, because the German army had almost reached Moscow, the Soviet capital. Helping to stop the German advance, the reinforcements played a major role in the Soviet counterattack. By the time of the Soviet victory near

Moscow, however, the Japanese secret police had arrested Sorge. After being held prisoner for nearly three years, he was executed in July 1944.

Resistance Movements Spy for Allies

Unlike Canaris and Sorge, most spies are not in a position to learn top-level secrets. Nevertheless, having many spies who can each gather small pieces of information can reveal the enemy's military situation. The Allies had an advantage in this kind of intelligence gathering. Throughout Europe, thousands of people were willing to risk their lives to defeat the Germans who occupied their countries. They secretly formed resistance movements, which engaged in a wide variety of anti-German activities, from secretly publishing newspapers to blowing up railroad lines. They also spied on the Germans and sent information to the Allies. Even small pieces of information, seemingly unimportant, revealed a great deal when analyzed. For example, a member of a resistance organization might note the insignia worn by German soldiers entering a town café; the insignia would show which units were stationed in the area. If one unit left or a new armored division arrived, it was almost always known to local resistance groups, who then sent the information to England by radio. Radio communication was extremely dangerous, however, because the Germans had detecting devices to locate transmitters. Radio sets were therefore carefully hidden, often in suitcases, and sometimes moved from one attic hideout to another, taken out only for short transmissions. Sometimes intelligence agents reached England aboard a plane that landed at night in a field, guided by resistance flashlights.

Resistance movements often provided the Allies with valuable details about German weapons and defensive measures. For instance, members of the Polish resistance recovered key parts of a secret German V-1 flying bomb that crashed during tests, and smuggled the parts to England. Information from resistance networks also helped ensure the success of the Normandy invasion. The Atlantic Wall was a system of fortifications, obstacles, and mines along the coast of Europe designed to provide protection against Allied invasion. French resistance groups learned every detail about the construction in each area and passed that data on to Britain. These details helped the Allies choose landing sites for the invasion. In addition, the resistance built scale models of the landing beaches, showing the location of the German fortifications. With the help of these mod-

els, Allied troops could practice attacking German positions, knowing where enemy troops were located, how well they were protected, and the kind of equipment they had.

Spy Networks

In addition to the resistance groups that engaged in espionage, the Allies set up their own intelligence networks. In July 1940, less than a month after France surrendered to the Germans, Britain started an organization called the Special Operations Executive, known as the SOE. In charge of both intelligence activities and sabotage in Europe, the SOE had sections responsible for each occupied country. The agency recruited spies from among the thousands of foreign refugees who fled to Britain and still wanted to fight the Germans; they also enlisted the services of English people who spoke other European languages. The SOE established training centers in the English countryside, usually in large houses, where newly recruited agents were taught Morse code, which was used to transmit messages. They were also taught how to assemble and operate secret radio transmitters, and

American OSS agent Allen Dulles had secret contacts with German military intelligence officer Admiral Wilhelm Canaris. (Reproduced by permission of the Corbis Corporation [Bellevue])

Pianists and Communists

The Red Orchestra received its name from the Gestapo. The secret radio transmitters used during World War II resembled old-fashioned telegraph machines, with keys on which people tapped out messages. The women and men who sent these messages were known as "pianists" because they "played the keys." The radio sets themselves were called "pianos." The Gestapo therefore called a network of spies an "orchestra." Resembling actual pianists, each radio operator had a distinct touch, like a signature, and an experienced listener could recognize a sender from his or her touch. The word "red" in the Red Orchestra's name came from the fact that the network reported to the Communist Soviet Union, which had a brilliant red flag.

even how to use invisible ink. Sergeants from the British army gave them lessons in hand-to-hand combat and showed them how to kill an enemy silently. The SOE then sent the agents into Europe by parachute, or sometimes by submarine.

The American Office of Strategic Services (OSS) had the same mission as the British SOE: intelligence and sabotage. The OSS was run by Colonel William J. Donovan, a millionaire lawyer who had received the nickname "Wild Bill" while serving in World War I (1914–1918). OSS agents such as Allen Dulles (later the longtime director of the Central Intelligence Agency), working in neutral Switzerland, had important secret contacts with men such as Canaris in Germany. Later, OSS agents helped armed resistance groups fighting the Germans. Still, most of the spying networks in western Europe were already in existence when the OSS was created. Especially in France, the largest and most important country in the area, the spy network reported to the British SOE.

One of the main groups working with the SOE was the Alliance, which the Gestapo called Noah's Ark, because each agent took the code name of an animal. The Alliance leader was Marie-Madeleine

Fourcade, code-named Hedgehog. Though the Alliance received most of its funds and equipment from the SOE, and in turn reported its findings back to the SOE, all the members and leaders of the group were French. The Alliance organized a network of spies in every part of France, including people from all levels of French society—military officers who were supposedly working for the pro-German government, naval engineers, and salesmen. One of the most valued agents was a young woman who worked as a seamstress in the French port of Brest, where she sewed damaged life vests for German submarine crews. By listening to the crewmen's conversations, she learned which submarines were scheduled to leave port, and on exactly what date. This meant British warships would often be waiting for the submarines.

Although France was the SOE's most important area of operation, there were also 35 networks in Belgium with a total of 10,000 people, including about 300 who had parachuted in. Networks in the Netherlands, Belgium, and France cooperated in setting up escape routes for Allied air crews who had been shot down.

The largest spy network, and one of the most successful, was probably the Red Orchestra. Many of its most important members already had experience in secret activity because they were communists, and Communist parties had often been illegal in prewar Europe. The Red Orchestra did not report to the British SOE but instead sent its information to the Soviet Union. In some ways, the Red Orchestra resembled other resistance networks. It distributed anti-Nazi pamphlets and posters, helped fugitives escape from the Gestapo, and even engaged in small-scale sabotage of war industry. The group stationed agents in France, Belgium, and the Netherlands. What made it unique was that it also had a substantial network in Germany itself, where it pursued the aforementioned activities. The Red Orchestra is remembered today primarily for its main work—intelligence activities. It focused mainly on giving the Soviet Union an accurate, day-to-day assessment of German forces. Between 1940 and 1943, members of the Red Orchestra sent about 1,500 radio messages to the Soviet Union. For a time, one of its sources was an intelligence officer in the German air force. In August 1942 the Gestapo arrested about 100 Red Orchestra members and tortured them to make them reveal information about the network. Germany then tried and executed many of them, a result that was guaranteed by the fact that Hitler took a personal interest in the proceedings.

The Navajo Code Talkers

One of the most successful codes in World War II was also one of the simplest. Beginning at the Battle of Guadalcanal and continuing through many campaigns in the Pacific, some battlefield messages were transmitted by Native American soldiers speaking the Navajo language. The Navajo language is quite complex and it was estimated that at the time fewer than thirty non-native speakers could understand the language. A relatively simple code was created using Navajo words. Since the code relied more on translation than on coding and decoding, orders could be sent and understood more quickly, but remained as secure as if encrypted with an elaborate code.

Two Navajo Code Talkers use the radio to relay orders in the Pacific Theater. (Reproduced by permission of © Corbis-Bettmann)

Codes and Code-Breaking

The most important and dependable source of intelligence in World War II, both in Europe and the Pacific, was not spies but the interception of secret messages sent by the enemy. In 1940, even before the United States went to war, American experts broke the Purple Code, which was used by the Japanese government to communicate with its ambassadors and other diplomats around the world. Japan never discovered that the code had been broken and continued to use it, as the Ameri-

The Germans used the infamous code machine, "The Enigma," to transmit messages during the war. The Allies succeeded in capturing a few of the machines, without the Germans' knowledge, which enabled them to break the code. (Photo reprinted with permission from Debra M. Kirby.)

cans continued to intercept it, until 1945. These diplomatic messages provided a general picture of Japanese intentions, but did not cover Japanese military or naval plans. Nevertheless, the Purple Code allowed the Allies to learn German military secrets. Japanese diplomats in Germany used the Purple Code to send reports home to the Japanese government that included information about new German weapons and the effectiveness of Allied bombing in Germany.

By spring 1942, the United States could read many of the most important Japanese navy codes; a year later, the Americans were beginning to break the codes used by the Japanese army. The United States gave the name Magic to their system for breaking and reading Japanese military and naval codes. Magic influenced the outcome of the war in the Pacific—for instance, the Japanese probably lost hundreds of ships because Magic intercepts (intercepted and decoded messages) were used to send American submarines to sink them. The most significant use of Magic occurred in June 1942 at the Battle of Midway, the turning point of the Pacific war. Partly because Magic revealed the

Japanese attack plan, the outnumbered American aircraft carriers won a decisive victory. Magic proved effective again in April 1943. Admiral Isoroku Yamamoto, one of Japan's most prominent naval commanders and the planner of the attack on Pearl Harbor, was flying to the island of Bougainville in the South Pacific. The Japanese transmitted, in code, the exact route and time of his flight. A squadron of American fighter planes, specially outfitted with extra gas tanks for this mission, waited for Yamamoto's plane and shot it down; Yamamoto was killed.

The vast size of the Pacific Ocean meant that both the Americans and Japanese relied on radio messages, which could be intercepted by the enemy. In Europe, the Germans could communicate by telephone and telegraph, land lines, which at the time were more difficult to intercept than radio messages. They also could use messengers traveling by train or car. Even in Europe, however, orders to ships or submarines had to be transmitted by radio. As the war continued, sabotage of land lines and the bombing of railroads increased German reliance on radio messages. Unbeknownst to the Germans, however, land lines and messengers were the only sure ways of keeping their communications secret.

Germany developed its code long before the war, and military intelligence agents from Poland, France, and Britain had been working to break the code since before the outbreak of hostilities. An anti-Nazi German helped the Allies break the code by turning over key information to the French. The organization that decoded, evaluated, and distributed German messages was called Ultra, and was headquartered at the Government Code and Cipher School at Bletchley Park in the English countryside. The Bletchley Park staff included mathematicians from nearby Oxford and Cambridge Universities. Among them was Max Norman, who designed the world's first electronic computer, built at Bletchley Park specifically to help break German codes. The Germans used an encoding machine called Enigma, which looked like a typewriter. Using information from intelligence agents, the code breakers at Bletchley reconstructed a version of an Enigma machine, but this alone did not break the German codes. Special gears inside the Enigma allowed trillions of possible code combinations, and the decoders had to figure out which combination was being used for each message—and they had to perform the operation quickly enough for the result to be useful. The person sending a message from the

Enigma machine had to let the recipient know how to decode it. Therefore, at the start of each message was a key, which established a pattern that the mathematicians at Bletchley could use in breaking the code. Also crucial to breaking the code were successful Allied efforts to capture Enigma coding machines without the Germans' knowledge. If the Germans suspected that the Allies could translate the code, they were likely to abandon the Enigma for another method. As such, it was crucial for the Allies to keep silent about their success obtaining the infamous coding machines.

For most of the war, the Allies could decode many German radio transmissions. Eventually, they could decipher messages so rapidly that Allied generals knew the contents of the communications as quickly as the German generals who received them. Consequently, the Americans and the British often learned precise details of German military plans. Probably the most important incident where this occurred was during the last stages of the Battle of Normandy, in August 1944. Hitler ordered a surprise counteroffensive centered on the town of Mortain, committing all available armored divisions to the attack. The Allies, however, already knew the German plan, and so positioned their own armored divisions to halt the German offensive. The defeat of the German army at Mortain opened the way for the Allies to sweep from Normandy across France to the German border. The Germans never knew that Enigma messages could be read, and the Allies took extraordinary precautions to prevent them from finding out. Sometimes the Allies did not act on secret information because it would have alerted the Germans that their code had been broken. When the British warned the Soviet Union that Germany was about to invade, they did not tell the Soviets that this information had come from reading top-secret German messages. Like Richard Sorge's similar warning, it was distrusted by the Soviets.

The Germans were also successful at breaking Allied codes. During parts of the Battle of the Atlantic, the German navy was reading decoded British naval messages being used to direct convoys of cargo ships from America to Great Britain. The Germans sent packs of submarines to intercept and destroy the ships. The American Black Code, which was used by military attachés in U.S. embassies and named for the color of its binder, was stolen by the Germans in August 1941, before American entry into the war. Knowledge of the Black Code gave the Germans a strategic advantage in the battles of North Africa. For many months, General Erwin Rommel, the famous German "Desert Fox," was fully informed about British military plans, because they had been discussed with the American military attaché in the Egyptian capital of Cairo. The Americans changed the code after the British captured documents in July 1942 that revealed the source of the German knowledge.

Technological Advances: Radar and Jets

The Bletchley computer was only one example of the role played by scientists in World War II. Perhaps the most important technological advancement was radar, originated by the British. Secret development of radar began in 1935; the first radar station was built two years later. By 1940, when the Germans launched massive bombing raids in the Battle of Britain, a chain of fifty radar stations was operating on the coasts of England, providing the British with vital early warnings about the number, direction, speed, and altitude of attacking German planes. This information allowed the outnumbered British to send planes from other areas to defend each day's targets. Yet scientists elsewhere were also working on the same concept, and the Germans were soon operating their own radar systems. The technology kept improving throughout the war: At first, radar required large sensing devices (dishes) mounted on towers, but eventually the instruments were made small enough to fit into aircraft, thus guiding bombers to unseen targets and enabling fighter pilots to find and attack bombers at night. Special British planes were also equipped with radar that spotted submarines thirty miles away.

Another development, based on the same principle as radar, was the proximity fuse for artillery shells. The fuse caused antiaircraft shells to explode when they came near their target, destroying planes that had not been directly hit. The British were using the proximity fuse to shoot down V-1s in August 1944. The Germans did not develop this technology.

The German air force did, however, develop jet-powered planes for combat. Jet engines allowed planes to fly at much faster speeds and at much higher altitudes than propeller-driven aircraft. The test flight of the first German jet took place in 1939, just prior to World War II. Yet the project was not considered high priority, probably because Hitler and most German generals were convinced the war would be short, and long-term projects

A V-2 rocket in flight. (Reproduced by permission of AP/Wide World Photos)

would not be timely enough. Later, it seemed more important to devote Germany's limited resources to producing more tanks and submarines. In summer 1944, however, jet-powered German fighters began to appear in air battles over France. By this time, the Allies had complete control of the skies, and the German jets were vastly outnumbered by Allied planes. Since jets require longer runways, the Allies could easily find their bases and attack the jets on the ground. Also, Germany had a severe shortage of aviation fuel. For this reason, about half of the 2,000 jets Germany built by the end of the war never flew. The fuel shortage also made it impossible to properly train pilots to fly the aircraft. British and American jets were beginning to fly, and would soon have become available, if needed, to challenge the Germans.

German Bombs: The V-1 and V-2

During World War II, Germany developed two new weapons. "V-1" and "V-2" were not the official German designations for the bombs; instead, they were nicknames used in German radio broadcasts meant to encourage German civilians and frighten the Allies. "V" stood for the German word *Vergeltung,* which means "retribution" or "revenge." The idea was that these weapons would

pay back the Allies for the devastation their bombers had caused in Germany. The V-1 and V-2 might have been ready earlier and used more extensively in the war if the British had not learned of the German projects from spies. The two bombs were secretly developed, built, and tested by the German air force at opposite ends of the island of Peenemünde, in the Baltic Sea. In August 1943 330 British bombers attacked the small island, causing severe damage to the weapons projects, especially the V-2. Several hundred technicians were killed, and construction of the weapons had to be shifted to other locations. The debuts of both the V-1 and the V-2 were delayed by at least several months.

On June 12, 1944, a few days after the Allied invasion of Normandy, Germany launched the first V-1s against England, catapulting them from portable ramps on the coast of France. The V-1 was a pilotless jet plane that could travel a maximum distance of about 250 miles, reaching speeds of 375 miles an hour, about the same as the fastest regular fighter planes of that era. Since the V-1 made a buzzing sound, Londoners called it the buzz bomb. The buzzing stopped when a V-1 ran out of fuel; the bomb then fell to earth and detonated the nearly one ton of explosives it carried. The V-1s inflicted greater damage than regular bombs because the angle at which they fell caused the greatest force of the explosion to remain near the surface instead of underground.

V-1s were not accurate enough to be aimed against specific targets, so the Germans randomly directed them toward the city of London. The Germans produced a total of 35,000 V-1s, and fired more than 9,000 at London. About one-third of these bombs were defective, however, and never reached their targets, or were shot down by British fighter planes and antiaircraft guns. Because the V-1s still exploded when they hit the ground, it was paramount that they be destroyed over the countryside before they reached the city. Before long, Allied armies in northern France pushed the Germans away from the coast and the V-1s could no longer reach London. About 10,000 were fired at the Belgian port of Antwerp after the Allies captured it in September 1944. Altogether, about 2,500 V-1s exploded in Antwerp, and the same number hit London.

The V-2 bomb was a fifty-foot-long rocket powered by liquid fuel that was launched straight

The Allies captured a V-2 factory in Nordhausen that was mainly staffed by forced laborers. American troops found some 4,000 civilians living in the underground factory, seeking shelter during the Allied bombing attack. (Reproduced by permission of AP/Wide World Photos)

up and then flew at more than 2,000 miles per hour, faster than the speed of sound—so people on the ground could not hear the missile coming before it landed. The lack of warning made the V-2 bomb especially frightening.

The Germans fired the first V-2s at England in early September 1944. Because development of the bombs had been so rushed, many were defective; up to 25 percent crashed immediately after being launched. More than half of the remaining bombs disintegrated as they came to earth, but the explosives they carried still exploded. Although some radio-controlled course correction was possible for V-2s, the bomb was hardly more accurate than the V-1. About 3,200 V-2s were launched during the war, more than half at Antwerp. They killed a total of about 15,000 people, about 2,500 of them in London, and injured perhaps 50,000. The V-2s also blinded many people because shattered window glass flew into their eyes before they could raise their arms to protect their faces. The Allies finally captured the Germans' last launching sites in March 1945. Both the V-1 and V-2 caused extensive damage to homes and other buildings, but because of their lack of accuracy, they had limited value as military weapons. The Germans meant them to terrorize civilians.

The Atomic Bomb

The largest scientific project of World War II—and the most secret—was the building of the atomic bomb. It is also the military development that has had the greatest impact on the world since the war. Yet this weapon of mass destruction was completed only at the very end of World War II. By that time, Germany had surrendered, and the Allies dropped the bomb on an almost-defeated Japan. It is somewhat ironic that the bomb was used against Japan, since the main reason the Allies mounted an intensive effort to build it was because they feared Germany would produce a bomb first. Many of the scientists who built the bomb were German refugees who hated and feared the Nazis and believed Germany's outstanding scientists would give them a head start.

By the beginning of World War II, every top physicist in the world knew the theory of atomic weapons, but no one was sure that a bomb could actually be built. Even if it were possible, the process might be so expensive and time-consuming that it was not worth the effort. The German scientists who explored the viability of developing an atomic bomb—including Werner Heisenberg, one of the most prominent physicists of the twen-

Refugees Play Key Roles in Creating Atomic Bomb

The reason Otto Frisch and Rudolf Peierls were working on atomic theory in early 1940 was that the British did not trust enemy scientists, even those who had fled Germany to escape the Nazis, to work on military projects like radar. Eventually, however, the British altered this position. Many of the scientists responsible for the atomic bomb were originally from countries fighting the Allies, including Germany, Hungary, and Italy. A large number were Jews who had been forced to leave Europe by Nazi hatred and persecution. In fact, the first steps in the American project to build the bomb were prompted by a letter President Franklin D. Roosevelt received in October 1939 from Albert Einstein, a German Jewish refugee and the most famous scientist in the world. In the letter, Einstein warned Roosevelt that Nazi Germany might be building atomic weapons and he urged the United States to study the issue. When the Manhattan Project got under way, foreign scientists played a crucial part. Enrico Fermi, who had won a Nobel Prize for his work on radioactivity in Italy before the war, led the team that produced the first self-sustaining nuclear chain reaction in Chicago in December 1942. Hans Bethe from Germany and Leo Szilard from Hungary were among the most important of the many anti-Hitler Europeans working on the atom bomb.

tieth century—made vital errors in their theoretical calculations. These errors led them to believe that constructing a bomb would be more difficult and expensive than was actually the case. Consequently, the Germans never considered the project a top priority. There was no single agency to ensure that people, equipment, and funds were committed to developing a bomb. When Germany surrendered in May 1945, its atomic weapons program was only at about the same stage the Allies had reached in 1940, before the American bomb program had even started.

The reaction that makes an atomic bomb feasible begins when a certain kind of uranium, uranium-235 (or U-235), is bombarded with neutrons (one of the particles that makes up the atom). Its nucleus, or center, then splits in two, releasing energy. It also frees other neutrons, which in turn collide with nearby uranium atoms, causing them to split. If there is enough uranium "fuel," the process continues until all the uranium atoms have been split, which takes only a fraction of a second. The result is a nuclear chain reaction that releases previously unimaginable amounts of energy, which can take the form of an explosive blast. U-235 exists only in tiny quantities in uranium ore dug from the earth. Separating U-235 from the rest of the uranium is a complicated and expensive process. In fact, in 1940 no one was sure how to do it in large quantities. The German scientists miscalculated how much U-235 would be needed, surmising that a chain reaction, and therefore a bomb, would require about two tons of U-235. This meant that building an atomic bomb, if it were possible at all, would take many years and be exorbitantly expensive. Since Germany's political and military leaders expected the war to be brief, they concluded that even an all-out effort to build an atomic weapon would not succeed in time to make a difference.

Otto Frisch and Rudolf Peierls, two refugees from Nazi Germany, were studying the same problem at the University of Birmingham in England at the beginning of the war, in April 1940. They calculated that a much smaller amount of U-235 was needed for a chain reaction: not two tons, as the German scientists had erroneously concluded, but less than one pound. Frisch and Peierls then sent a letter to the British government's leading scientific adviser, explaining that "a radioactive superbomb" could be produced. Although, like the Germans, the British first thought such a project would probably take too many resources, they appointed a committee of scientists to recommend action. After studying the problem for more than a year, the group came to the conclusion that a bomb could be built in two years and that work should begin immediately. Late in 1941, Britain launched the Directorate of Tube Alloys, purposely giving the project a name that suggested scientists were studying new and better metals to make pipes.

Trinity: The Nuclear Test Site

The first atomic bomb, also called the "Gadget" by its developers, was tested in the Jornado del Muerto desert near Alamagordo, New Mexico. The site was called "Trinity" by Dr. J. Robert Oppenheimer, who headed the project under the direction of Brigadier General Leslie Groves. Oppenheimer chose the name based on a poem by John Donne. The plutonium core of the bomb, which was about the size of an orange, was assembled at the McDonald Ranch near the Trinity test site. The core weighed 13.5 pounds.

The bomb was detonated from a 100-foot steel tower. The exact location of the tower was called "Ground Zero." The designers were not sure the bomb would actually work, or if it did, how much damage it would cause. The authorities were prepared to evacuate the area and even the state if necessary. When the bomb was detonated, it created a blast equal to 21,000 tons of TNT and provided a successful test of the first atomic weapon. According to the web site of the Los Alamos National Laboratory, witness General Thomas Farrell described the scene: "It was golden, purple, violet, gray and blue. It lighted every peak, crevasse and ridge of the nearby mountain range.... Seconds after the explosion came first the air blast pressing hard against the people, to be followed almost immediately by the strong, sustained awesome roar that warned of doomsday...." After the test, Farrell remarked to Groves that the war would soon be over.

Trinity is now part of the White Sands Missile Range. People can tour the site twice a year on the first Saturday of April and October. A plaque marks the spot of the first atomic bomb test. For more information see the Los Alamos National Laboratory web site at http://www.lanl.gov/worldview/welcome/history.html.

At first, the British made greater progress than the United States on building an atom bomb and—although no one knew it—much greater progress than the Germans. But in June 1942, six months after the United States entered the war, President Franklin D. Roosevelt gave approval for a full-scale American atomic project. The Americans soon caught up with and then surpassed the British. The organization that controlled all aspects of research, construction, and testing had the deceptive name the Manhattan District of the Army Corps of Engineers, and became known as the Manhattan Project. The project cost $2.5 billion, an enormous sum, and eventually involved 120,000 people. The Americans built secret factories in Oak Ridge, Tennessee, to work on separating U-235 from uranium. Since no one was sure which of three possible methods would prove the most effective, scientists decided to attempt all three despite the expense. Another huge facility was built in Hanford, Washington, to produce plutonium, a second element that scientists correctly thought could be used as fuel for an atomic bomb. In both places, workers and their families lived in newly built housing, surrounded by fences and armed guards to keep the work secret.

The heart of the Manhattan Project, however, was located at Los Alamos, New Mexico, where 4,000 experts—physicists, mathematicians, chemists, engineers, skilled metalworkers—gathered to design and build the new weapon. The head of the project was J. Robert Oppenheimer, himself a brilliant young physicist, who managed to keep all the different personalities working together. Brigadier General Leslie Groves supervised the project. On July 16, 1945, in the desert near Alamogordo, New Mexico, the first atomic explosion in history sent a blinding light through the predawn darkness. As Oppenheimer watched the test, he thought of words from the Bhagavad-Gita, a Hindu holy book: "I am become Death, the destroyer of worlds." In August, the United States dropped two atomic bombs on Japan, killing 120,000 people and obliterating the cities of Hiroshima and Nagasaki.

J. Robert Oppenheimer, with characteristic pork-pie hat, and Brigadier General Leslie Groves inspect twisted metal, the remains of an atomic bomb test, July 1945. (Reproduced by permission of Archive Photos, Inc.)

Harry S Truman

Excerpt of Truman's comments on the Manhattan Project from *Memoirs by Harry S. Truman, Volume 1, Year of Decisions*

Published in 1955

In the late 1930s Austrian and German physicists made major breakthroughs in the field of nuclear energy—the energy released during nuclear reactions. The term "nuclear" refers to the nucleus, or core, of an atom. Nuclear energy research in the early World War II era centered on experiments with uranium atoms. Firing just one neutron at the nucleus of a uranium atom caused the release of three new neutrons and a large amount of energy. Physicists believed that bombarding a larger sample of uranium with neutrons would trigger a powerful chain reaction: An enormous release of energy would accompany the splitting of the uranium atoms. Scientists in Germany and the United States were soon thinking about how to harness this overwhelming burst of energy in a military weapon.

Serious research on atomic weapon development began in the United States in late 1941, around the time of Japan's surprise attack on the American naval base at Pearl Harbor. Italian-born physicist Enrico Fermi was a professor at Columbia University in New York City who had settled in the United States because his wife was Jewish and Jews in Europe were facing severe persecution. In 1942 Fermi created the first nuclear reactor, a controlled environment for energy released from splitting atoms, in the United States. Fermi played a leading role in the burgeoning field of atomic weaponry. Because background work on the development of the atomic bomb took place in New York, the venture became known as the Manhattan Project. U.S. Army Brigadier General Leslie R. Groves supervised the project, and chose Dr. J. Robert Oppenheimer, a young nuclear physicist, to direct the team of scientists that would be working in the remote desert region of Los Alamos, New Mexico. Uranium and another element called plutonium—the key ingredients in bomb research—were being processed in plants in Ten-

Harry S Truman, who was famous for saying of his job as U.S. president "The buck stops here," had to make the final decision whether to drop atomic bombs on Japan. (Reproduced by permission of AP/Wide World Photos, Inc.)

nessee and Washington, respectively. Only a special type of uranium, uranium-235 (or U-235), would split easily enough to fuel a nuclear chain reaction. Scientists had discovered that for every 1,000 atoms in a sample of uranium, only about seven turned out to be uranium-235. Special production plants were built to separate and gather uranium-235 atoms.

Final assembly of the first nuclear bombs was conducted at the Los Alamos headquarters. The uranium bomb was known as "Little Boy," and the plutonium-powered bomb, which weighed about

Letters from Albert Einstein to Franklin Roosevelt

In the late 1930s Hungarian-born physicist Leo Szilard immigrated to the United States and began working with Enrico Fermi on atom-splitting research and experimentation. Szilard was particularly worried that the Germans would develop and use an atomic bomb to achieve world domination. Even before the United States entered World War II, Szilard believed that President Franklin Roosevelt should be informed about the potential uses of nuclear power. He convinced German-born physicist Albert Einstein, the most famous scientist in the world at the time, to become involved. When the two men met on Long Island, New York, in summer 1939, Einstein agreed to warn Roosevelt about Germany's alleged work on the bomb. After discussing the points that should be included in the initial letter, Einstein dictated his thoughts, which Szilard later translated from German; Einstein then added his signature. (Some sources suggest that Szilard was the actual author of the letters.)

The first of four letters, dated August 2, 1939, reached Roosevelt in October. It begins: "Some recent work by E. Fermi and L. Szilard … leads me to expect that the element uranium may be turned into a new and important source of energy in the immediate future." The letter goes on to suggest that (1) this energy could power a new kind of bomb for use in warfare; (2)

the U.S. government should stay current on the latest developments in nuclear energy; and (3) the United States should fund nuclear experiments. America's commitment to nuclear research did not begin in earnest, however, until December 1942. Later in life, Einstein is said to have regretted his role in promoting the development of nuclear weapons.

Albert Einstein warned Franklin Roosevelt that the Germans were working on an atomic bomb, encouraging the president to start research on atomic energy. (Reproduced by permission of the Granger Collection)

9,000 pounds, was nicknamed "Fat Man." The first atomic bomb ever tested—a "Fat Man"—was set off near Alamogordo, New Mexico, on July 16, 1945. The site is called Trinity. The explosion rocked the test site with a force equal to the power of 20,000 tons (40 million pounds) of TNT, scorching the earth for miles around.

The war in Europe had ended just over two months earlier with Germany's surrender on May 8, 1945, but fighting in the Pacific against the Japanese raged on. In July 1945, U.S. President Harry S Truman set out for Potsdam, a Soviet-occupied city in Germany, where he and other Allied leaders (British Prime Minister Winston

The first atomic bombs were nicknamed "Fat Man" (back) and "Little Boy" (front). (Library of Congress)

Churchill and Soviet leader Joseph Stalin) would discuss the structure of Germany's new government. On the first day of the Potsdam Conference, Truman received word that the first atomic bomb had been tested near Alamogordo, and that the Manhattan Project had reached its goal: The test was a success. The project had cost $2 billion, took nearly three years to complete, and required the combined efforts of a 100,000-person workforce.

At the time of the Potsdam Conference, the U.S. military was focusing all its strength on defeating Japan. The battle for the island of Iwo Jima in February 1945 had proved costly to both the Japanese and Americans. When the U.S. Marine invasion ended, more than 20,000 Japanese soldiers had been killed; nearly 7,000 Americans died and another 20,000 were wounded. Even more intensive

fighting began on the island of Okinawa in April. The three-month-long air and land battle was marked by streams of kamikaze attacks—Japanese pilots who purposely crashed their planes into Allied ships, knowing that the planes would explode in the attack. More than 110,000 Japanese died defending Okinawa; about 12,000 Americans were killed and 60,000 were injured.

In summer 1945 preparations were also under way for a land invasion of the Japanese home islands. After fighting the long and bloody battles for Iwo Jima and Okinawa, U.S. officials dreaded the prospect of the home island invasion, thinking it would mean another year of fighting and an estimated 500,000 more American soldiers wounded or killed. As long as they were alive, Japanese soldiers would continue fighting, for their commitment to honor in battle drove many of them to choose death over surrender. Even after B-29 bombing raids had destroyed half of Tokyo, the Japanese military would not give in. Truman had to weigh all of these factors in deciding whether to drop an atomic bomb on Japan. The following excerpt from his memoirs explicates some of his actions and the reasoning behind them.

Excerpt from
Memoirs by Harry S. Truman

The historic message of the first explosion of an atomic bomb was flashed to me in a message from Secretary of War [Henry] Stimson on the morning of July 16 [1945]. The most secret and the most daring enterprise of the war had succeeded. We were now in possession of a weapon that would not only revolutionize war but could alter the course of history and civilization. This news reached me at Potsdam [Germany] the day after I had arrived for the conference of the Big Three [the heads of the three leading Allied nations at war with Germany—U.S. President Harry S Truman, British Prime Minister Winston Churchill, and Soviet leader Joseph Stalin].

Preparations were being rushed for the test atomic explosion at Alamogordo, New Mexico, at the time I had to leave for Europe, and on the voyage over I had been anxiously awaiting word on the results. I had been told of many predictions by the scientists, but no one was certain of the outcome of this full-scale atomic explosion. As I read the message from Stimson, I realized that the test not only met the most optimistic expectation of the scientists but that the United States had in its possession an explosive force of unparalleled power.

Stimson flew ... to Potsdam the next day to see me and brought with him the full details of the test.... [W]e did not know as yet what effect the new weapon might have, physically or psychologically, when used against the enemy. For that reason the military advised that we go ahead with the existing military plans for the invasion of the Japanese home islands....

If the test of the bomb was successful, I wanted to afford Japan a clear chance to end the fighting before we made use of this newly gained power. If the test should fail, then it would be even more important to us to bring about a surrender before we had to make a physical conquest of Japan. [Chief of staff of the U.S. Army] General [George C.] Marshall told me

that it might cost half a million American lives to force the enemy's surrender on his home grounds.

But the test was now successful. The entire development of the atomic bomb had been dictated by military considerations. The idea of the atomic bomb had been suggested to President [Franklin D.] Roosevelt by the famous and brilliant Dr. Albert Einstein, and its development turned out to be a vast undertaking. It was the achievement of the combined efforts of science, industry, labor, and the military, and it had no parallel in history....

Only a handful of the thousands of men who worked in these plants knew what they were producing. So strict was the secrecy imposed that even some of the highest-ranking officials in Washington had not the slightest idea of what was going on. I did not. Before 1939 it had been generally agreed among scientists that it was theoretically possible to release energy from the atom. In 1940 we had begun to pool with Great Britain all scientific knowledge useful to war, although Britain was at war at that time and we were not.... [W]e learned that the Germans were at work on a method to harness atomic energy for use as a weapon of war. This, we understood, was to be added to the V-1 and V-2 rockets with which they hoped to conquer the world. They failed, of course, and for this we can thank Providence. But now a race was on to make the atomic bomb—a race that became "the battle of the laboratories."...

We could hope for a miracle, but the daily tragedy of a bitter war crowded in on us. We labored to construct a weapon of such overpowering force that the enemy could be forced to yield swiftly once we could resort to it. This was the primary aim of our secret and vast effort....

The task of creating the atomic bomb had been entrusted to a special unit of the Army Corps of Engineers, the so-called Manhattan District, headed

Harry S Truman

Harry S Truman, the eldest of three children, was born in Lamar, Missouri, on May 8, 1884. (His middle initial, S, is unpunctuated because it does not stand for a specific middle name—rather, it was added to Truman's name as a tribute to his grandfathers, Anderson Shippe Truman and Solomon Young.) At the age of eight, he contracted a serious case of diphtheria and nearly died. He also had poor eyesight. Because he had to wear expensive eyeglasses, he was not allowed to play sports, so he spent a lot of time reading. After graduating from high school, Truman was unable to afford college tuition, so he went to work as an accountant and a bank clerk in Kansas City. In 1906 he took over the Young family farm, which had previously been run by his aging grandmother and his Uncle Harrison. Over the next ten years, he successfully managed the large farm, doing much of the farm work himself. During the last two years of World War I (1914–1918), Truman served as a soldier in the U.S. Army. After returning from the war, he married Bess Wallace, his childhood playmate, school companion, and longtime sweetheart. In the early 1920s Truman embarked on a political career, beginning as a Missouri county judge in 1922 and becoming the Democratic senator from Missouri in 1934. During his ten years in the Senate, he gained a reputation as a plainspoken, honest, and efficient representative.

For the 1944 presidential election, Truman reluctantly accepted President Franklin D. Roosevelt's invitation to be his running mate. (Truman liked his job in the Senate and wanted to stay there, but could not refuse Roosevelt's request.) They won the election, but President Roosevelt died less than three months later; Truman was sworn into the presidency on April 13, 1945. He found himself in the most challenging role of his life. After Germany's surrender on May 8, 1945, he was left with the monumental task of reorganizing postwar Europe. He met with British Prime Minister Winston Churchill and Soviet leader Joseph Stalin in Potsdam, Germany, to discuss bringing an end to the long years of fighting. While Truman was in Potsdam in July 1945, America's first successful atomic bomb test took place. On Truman's order, U.S. forces dropped an atomic bomb on the Japanese city of Hiroshima on August 6; Nagasaki was bombed three days later. Japan surrendered to the Allies on September 2, 1945.

Foreign policy problems continued throughout the post–World War II years in America. Truman was committed to involving the United States in world affairs, and was especially concerned with controlling the spread of communism. The Soviet Union was a strong Communist country that sought to expand its influence throughout Eastern Europe and farther south into Greece and Turkey after World War II. Truman's opposition to communism was probably best reflected in the Truman Doctrine, a policy that provided military and financial aid to countries being threatened by the Communist Soviet Union in the late 1940s.

After winning a surprise victory over Republican candidate Thomas Dewey in the 1948 presidential election, Truman embarked on another term marked by international turmoil. In 1950 the Korean War (1950–1953) erupted. Forces from Communist North Korea invaded South Korea on June 24, 1950. Within hours, Truman sent American troops to South Korea to put down the invasion. The United Nations backed his decision and sent forces to the war-ravaged nation, but the bloody conflict would not end until 1953, the year after Truman left office. At the end of his second term, Truman retired to his home in Independence, Missouri, with Bess and wrote his memoirs. He died on December 26, 1972, in Kansas City.

by Major General Leslie R. Groves. The primary effort, however, had come from British and American scientists working in laboratories and offices scattered throughout the nation.

Dr. J. Robert Oppenheimer, the distinguished physicist from the University of California, had set up the key establishment in the whole process at Los Alamos, New Mexico. More than any other one man, Oppenheimer is to be credited with the achievement of the completed bomb.

My own knowledge of these developments had come about only after I became President, when Secretary Stimson had given me the full story. He had told me at that time that the project was nearing completion and that a bomb could be expected within another four months. It was at his suggestion, too, that I had then set up a committee of top men and had asked them to study with great care the implications the new weapon might have for us....

This committee was assisted by a group of scientists ... [that included] Dr. Oppenheimer, Dr. Arthur H. Compton, Dr. E. O. Lawrence, and the Italian-born Dr. Enrico Fermi....

It was their recommendation that the bomb be used against the enemy as soon as it could be done. They recommended further that it should be used without specific warning and against a target that would clearly show its devastating strength.... It was their conclusion that no technical demonstration they might propose, such as over a deserted island, would be likely to bring the war to an end....

The final decision of where and when to use the atomic bomb was up to me. Let there be no mistake about it. I regarded the bomb as a military weapon and never had any doubt that it should be used. The top military advisors to the President recommended its use, and when I talked to Churchill he unhesitatingly told me that he favored the use of the atomic bomb if it might aid to end the war.

Colonel Paul Tibbets, commander of the *Enola Gay*, the plane that dropped the atomic bomb on Hiroshima. (Reproduced by permission of Corbis/Bettmann)

In deciding to use this bomb I wanted to make sure that it would be used as a weapon of war in the manner prescribed by the laws of war. That meant that I wanted it dropped on a military target. I had told Stimson that the bomb should be dropped as nearly as possible upon a war production center of prime military importance....

Four cities were finally recommended as targets: Hiroshima, Kokura, Niigata, and Nagasaki. They were listed in that order as targets for the first attack....

On July 28 Radio Tokyo announced that the Japanese government would continue to fight.... There was no alternative now. The bomb was scheduled to be dropped after August 3 unless Japan surrendered before that day.

On August 6, the fourth day of the journey home from Potsdam, came the historic news that shook the world.... (Truman, Memoirs, pp. 415–421)

Aftermath

On July 26, 1945, the Allies issued the Potsdam Declaration, which gave the Japanese a choice of unconditional surrender or "prompt and utter destruction." No specific mention was made of America's plan to use an atomic weapon in the war against Japan; the Japanese refused to surrender. On August 6, 1945, at 8:16 a.m., the United States bombed the city of Hiroshima. Two days later, the Soviet Union declared war on Japan. By this time, it was clear that the Japanese had lost the war, but still they refused to give up the fight. On August 9 a "Fat Man" bomb, twice as powerful as "Little Boy," was dropped on Nagasaki. A few days later, Japan surrendered, ending World War II. In *Where the Buck Stops,* a collection of his writings, Truman noted: "I gave the final order, saying I had no qualms 'if millions of lives could be saved.' I meant both American and Japanese lives.... I did what I thought was right."

SOURCES

Books

Beyer, Don E., *The Manhattan Project: America Makes the First Atomic Bomb,* F. Watts (New York), 1991.

Black, Wallace B., and Jean F. Blashfield, *Hiroshima and the Atomic Bomb,* World War II 50th Anniversary Series, Crestwood House (New York), 1993.

Dolan, Edward F., *America in World War II: 1945,* Millbrook Press (Brookfield, CT), 1994.

Leavell, J. Perry, Jr., *World Leaders Past and Present: Harry S. Truman,* Chelsea House (New York), 1988.

Miller, Merle, *Plain Speaking: An Oral Biography of Harry S. Truman,* Berkley Publishing (New York), 1974.

Seddon, Tom, *Atom Bomb,* W. H. Freeman (New York), 1995.

Truman, Harry S., *The Autobiography of Harry S. Truman,* edited by Robert H. Ferrell, Colorado Associated University Press (Boulder), 1980.

Truman, Harry S., *Memoirs by Harry S. Truman,* Volume 1, *Year of Decisions,* Doubleday (Garden City, NY), 1955.

Truman, Harry S., *Where the Buck Stops: The Personal and Private Writings of Harry S. Truman,* edited by Margaret Truman, Warner (New York), 1989.

Wheeler, Keith, and the editors of Time-Life Books, *The Fall of Japan,* Time-Life Books World War II Series, Time-Life Books (Alexandria, VA), 1983.

Periodicals

Newsweek, Special Report: "Hiroshima: August 6, 1945," July 24, 1995.

Other

Hiroshima and Nagasaki: Was Truman's Decision to Use the Bomb Justified? (video), Zengar Video, 1989.

19

The Home Front

When World War II erupted in Europe in 1939, the United States had not fully recovered from the Great Depression, which had begun in fall 1929. Although the economy had reached its lowest point in 1932, some 8 million people were still unemployed in 1940, and American industry was not producing as much as it had ten years earlier. As many as 40 percent of American families, both urban and rural, were living in poverty. In many ways, the 1930s were a decade of turmoil and division in the United States. Workers trying to organize labor unions clashed with armed company guards and police in many cities. In 1937 a wave of "sit-down strikes" were staged, in which more than 400,000 workers took over their workplaces and refused to leave. That spring, Chicago police fired on a crowd of strikers outside a steel mill, killing ten and injuring eighty, in what became known as the Memorial Day Massacre.

War Transforms U.S. Economy

The onset of World War II altered America in two closely connected ways: It ended the Depression by creating millions of new jobs and also produced a sense of unity in the country. Economic changes came even before the United States entered the war in 1941. France and Britain ordered war planes and other weapons from the United States, and soon factories and farms were sending products to Great Britain in record quantities. When it became apparent that Britain might not be able to pay for further purchases, the U.S. government, through the Lend-Lease law, in effect loaned Britain money to buy more U.S. goods. Although the law was enacted to assist Britain's struggle against the Nazis, it would also help the U.S. economy.

By the time Japan attacked Pearl Harbor in December 1941 and the United States declared war, America had become the "Arsenal of Democracy," a phrase made popular by President Franklin D. Roosevelt. Production had grown tremendously, creating more jobs. In addition, the United States had established its first peacetime military draft, so hundreds of thousands of young men who might have been unemployed were now in the army. After Pearl Harbor, the American economy reached levels unparalleled by any other country. Before the Pearl Harbor attack, factories had not been working at full capacity because production had exceeded demand. Now, military orders were outpacing production, which forced new factories to be built.

In 1939 the average American factory had been in operation forty hours per week; in six years, that figure more than doubled to ninety hours. On New Year's Day in 1942, a newly formed government agency, the Office of Production Manage-

In order to track war production goals, some factories used scoreboards like this. When each goal was reached, a blank square was turned over, ultimately revealing the picture of Hitler hanging from a noose. (Reproduced by permission of AP/Wide World Photos)

ment, banned the sale of new private cars or trucks, so that automobile plants could assemble tanks, jeeps, and trucks. U.S. industry was manufacturing vehicles and weapons for the British and the Soviets as well as the American armed forces. Factories turned out 2.4 million trucks, 86,000 tanks, 6,500 ships, 15 million rifles and machine guns, 44 billion bullets, 400,000 cannons, and 47 million tons of shells. Prior to the war, the aircraft industry employed 46,000 people, but by 1945, there were fifty times that number of workers in

the field, and the industry turned out 300,000 planes. The total value of industrial goods produced in the United States doubled during the four years of war.

The war also resulted in the creation of entirely new industries, such as the production of synthetic rubber. A single B-17 bomber required half a ton of rubber, but natural rubber came mainly from areas conquered by the Japanese. By 1944, some 800,000 tons of synthetic rubber had been produced.

In 1945 the United States was providing one-half of the world's coal supply and two-thirds of its crude oil. The United States Steel Corporation singlehandedly made more steel than Germany and Japan combined; the Ford Motor Company alone produced 8,600 bombers, 278,000 jeeps, and 57,000 aircraft engines. Maintaining peak production levels was more important to the army and navy than efficiency or cost. The government therefore paid manufacturers on a cost-plus basis—a promise to reimburse the production cost plus a certain percentage as a profit—which meant that companies were guaranteed to make money. Profits increased dramatically despite the fact that a large share of defense contracts were awarded to only a few dozen large companies. Average weekly wages for workers doubled from $25 to $50. Overtime work was common, and often mandatory, in defense industries, resulting in additional income. Total farm income went up 250 percent, even though there were 800,000 fewer agricultural workers. The income of the poorest one-fifth of the population rose 68 percent, a higher increase than for those who were better off, leading to greater economic equality by the end of the war.

The federal government spent an estimated $360 billion on the war. Although taxes rose, that revenue accounted for only half this amount, and the government borrowed money to pay for the rest. The solution was to issue war bonds, which would be repaid later with interest. Banks and other financial institutions bought most bonds, but $36 billion worth were sold in small units to the general public. Bond drives, often featuring Hollywood stars, urged people to show their patriotism by buying war bonds. Every week, schoolchildren bought "Defense Stamps," a nickel or a dime's worth at a time. Not only were these campaigns important economically, but they also made citizens feel they were participating in the war and provided a greater sense of unity.

Social Change and Rationing

Instead of widespread unemployment, there was soon a labor shortage, and new sources of workers had to be found. People from poverty-stricken farm regions, especially in the South, moved to great industrial cities such as Detroit. Among them were large numbers of African Americans seeking a new life. Aircraft plants in Los Angeles and naval facilities in San Diego attracted so many new residents that southern California soon became the fastest-growing area of the country. More than 15 million Americans moved during the war, either to find work in war industries or to follow a family member to a new army base. As millions of men entered the armed services, 6 million women worked outside the home for the first time.

These rapid changes brought new problems and new tensions, but the nation was also revitalized by a sense of excitement and purpose—and, most of all, a sense of unity. Soon after Pearl Harbor, the leaders of America's major unions promised not to strike for the duration of the war. Few Americans doubted that the war was necessary, that the United States was fighting for freedom, and that sacrifices, disruptions, and inconveniences were worth the effort. It seemed obvious: The United States had been attacked, and Japan and Germany were trying to conquer the world. Only by defending freedom everywhere could the American people preserve their own liberty. Many Americans who lived through World War II always thought of it as "the good war," as author Studs Terkel called it.

With industrial power directed toward winning the war, however, there were domestic shortages of many products that had once been taken for granted. There was also a danger that shortages would cause prices to rise rapidly, canceling out the higher pay Americans were enjoying. The federal government created new agencies with new responsibilities and powers to prevent economic disruptions from interfering with the war effort. The Office of Price Administration and Civilian Supply (OPA) was created in April 1941, a few months after the attack on Pearl Harbor. The OPA announced the rationing of rubber, leading to an 80 percent decline in civilian use. Within a month, the OPA was given authority to set prices on all nonagricultural products. In April 1942 the agency responded to one of the most serious shortages of the war, a lack of adequate housing, especially near new defense plants, with a program of rent stabilization to prevent dramatic rent increases.

War bond drives helped raise money to keep the Allied troops fighting a successful war. (National Archives and Records Administration)

In May 1942 sugar was rationed, and, on the east coast, gasoline. The following December, gasoline rationing was implemented nationwide. A ration sticker had to be displayed on the windshield of every car. An "A" sticker indicated that a car was used for pleasure only, thus entitling the driver to only three gallons of gas per week. "B" designated a car that was driven to work; "C" was placed on vehicles used on the job. Emergency vehicles were assigned an "E," which entitled them to unlimited purchases of gasoline. Gasoline rationing soon became unpopular among Americans, who loved cars; people were also suspicious of anyone who received a sticker other than an "A." As was true of other rationed products, gasoline was available on the black market for those who were willing to pay higher prices to buy it illegally.

In July 1942 the government introduced a coupon system for rationing. Every family received coupon books containing tiny stamps worth a certain number of points. Stamps would then be turned in when buying rationed products, each of which was assigned points depending on the scarcity of the item. The list of products grew increasing-

Rationing Fashion

During the war, shortages and rationing had an impact on fashion. For instance, the price of women's silk stockings skyrocketed, and they soon became impossible to find. Most silk had come from Japan, and whatever was still available was used to make parachutes. Although nylon stockings had been recently introduced and had become popular, the government soon took the entire production of nylon for items like tents, airplane tires, and parachutes. Many women began painting black lines on the backs of their legs to look like the seams of stockings.

Leather was also in short supply, so beginning in February 1943, each person was limited to three pairs of shoes per year. Wool, cotton, and other materials were needed for uniforms, so the government restricted the fashion industry's designs. Only one and three-quarters yards of fabric could be used to make a woman's dress. Men's suits could not be double-breasted and could not have vests or cuffs, because such features required more fabric.

ly longer. Coffee was rationed in November 1942. Even though most of the coffee came from Latin America, an area unaffected by the war, the ships that transported coffee to the United States were needed elsewhere. Long-distance telephone calls were limited to five minutes. Beginning March 1, 1943, canned goods were rationed, and meat, butter, and cheese were rationed later that month. Meat was limited to twenty-eight ounces per person per week, and butter to four ounces each week. People were encouraged to grow "victory gardens" in backyards and vacant lots, a campaign that produced 40 percent of all vegetables consumed in the United States in 1942. Victory gardens also created a sense of involvement in the war effort and a feeling of national unity.

Despite these restrictions, a greater quantity (and probably, a better quality) of food was available to Americans than at any previous time. This stood in contrast to the situation in Britain, where people ate less. In most of Europe, in fact, hunger and even starvation were common during the war. The main reason for the disparity between European and American food supplies was the increased income of the poorest Americans—a direct result of war jobs.

While there was a growing sense of unity in the country, many Americans began to resent what they perceived as an inequality in sacrifices. Anger at the rich and a low opinion of big business had become common during the Great Depression. Although many people were now earning more money than ever before, they worked long hours, lived in substandard and overcrowded housing, and could buy only a limited number of products. In the meantime, they saw companies making record profits and watched the wealthy, who could obtain apparently anything they wanted by paying high prices on the black market. Workers in many industries felt that companies were taking advantage of the war to make money, while ignoring such issues as workplace safety and fair promotions. In many cases, they could not even leave their jobs; in April 1943 the government declared 27 million workers "essential," forbidding them to quit.

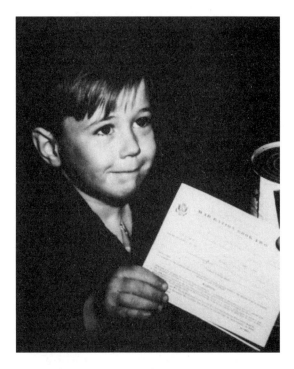

A young boy using a ration slip at a grocery store. (National Archives and Records Administration)

Civilians were encouraged to grow their own fruits and vegetables in victory gardens to ease the strain of rationing. (Reproduced by permission of AP/Wide World Photos)

In Great Britain, homemakers wait in lines to turn in their ration coupons. During the war, this butcher shop sold horse flesh, which was "passed as fit for human consumption." (Reproduced by permission of AP/Wide World Photos)

Men lining up for gas ration coupons in 1942. (Reproduced by permission of Corbis/Bettmann)

The push for production led to accidents that caused 17,000 workplace deaths a year and the permanent disabling of 250,000 workers during the war. Another 4.5 million were less seriously injured. Despite the unions' no-strike pledge, workers in many industries staged protest strikes over safety and other issues. Most were walkouts that occurred against the wishes of union leaders and lasted only a few hours or a couple of days, but some were more substantial, and some had serious consequences. In December 1943 the government took over the railroads to prevent a major strike. The president of the coal miners' union, John L. Lewis, called for a series of strikes that same year. Other union leaders accused Lewis of being a traitor, despite his earlier national popularity.

Civilian Defense

As the United States geared up for war, citizens realized the need to provide civilian defense programs. With so many men away fighting the war in Europe and the Pacific, civilians on the home front rallied together to ensure that basic services—such as fire fighting, road repair, medical, emergency, and rescue services—would continue to remain effective. Also, civilians were concerned about planning to counter the threat of enemy bombings and invasions.

In Washington, D.C., the Office of Civilian Defense was established, and was headed for a time by Eleanor Roosevelt, wife of President Franklin D. Roosevelt. Efforts were made to coordinate activities

British Rationing, Recycling, and Fellowship

Rationing and recycling were facts of life in Britain during World War II. Nothing was wasted, and anything that could be recycled was recycled: even potato peels were saved to use as animal feed. The government limited the clothing styles that could be manufactured. To save material, men's pants could not have cuffs, and women's skirts were made shorter. Clothing was severely rationed, and people could rarely buy new apparel. Children wore hand-me-downs. New shoes for civilians, including children, were unavailable: Leather was reserved for soldiers' boots. People were allowed to buy new furniture only if their house had been bombed. Only one pattern of dishware was produced.

Tea and fresh eggs were difficult to obtain. Oranges and other imported fresh fruit almost disappeared, as did chocolate. Even staples like butter and meat were rationed. People ate less and had less variety in their diets.

There were other inconveniences, too. The blackout made it hard to go anywhere after dark. In many places, street signs and road names were removed to delay the Germans if they invaded, but this confused residents.

Although the shortages and rationing were inconvenient, many of the British viewed the wartime atmosphere in a positive way, enjoying the feeling that the whole country was working together for a common goal. Everyone seemed to belong to one of the numerous volunteer organizations. Many were air raid wardens, who made sure people got into shelters during raids. (Many families built shelters in their backyards, and in London, thousands of people used subway stations as shelters.) Posters everywhere urged people not to repeat any information they learned because German spies were supposedly rampant. "Loose Lips Sink Ships" was the most famous slogan. Other posters showed Prime Minister Winston Churchill with a defiant look on his face. Many people later remembered a sense of English camaraderie during the war. There were fewer trains, so they were more crowded—but strangers traveling together spoke to each other rather than reading newspapers. In the cities, bustling air raid shelters became neighborhood meeting places.

with neighboring Canada. Throughout the United States, local and state civilian defense groups formed. Pamphlets and posters were prepared to encourage participation; training sessions were held to explain the latest techniques; drills were conducted so that the nation would be ready to counter emergencies, natural disasters, and enemy threats; and people were chosen to head up certain aspects of the program, including service as air raid wardens.

Participation in civilian defense was widespread as people wanted to do their part to ensure a safe America. Civilian defense groups conducted air raid drills so that people knew where to go in the event of enemy bombing attacks on the United States. They also created plans in case a city or town needed to conduct a blackout during an air raid. Citizens were given specific instructions on what to

do in a blackout situation if they were on the road or in their homes. In various towns, workers experimented with street lights, turning some off, leaving others on, and painting the sides of others so that they only directed light downward. Civilian defense instructors visited factories engaged in war production work. They trained plant staff on how to respond to emergencies, including fires, accidents, bombs, and sabotage. Factory managers were also instructed in how to camouflage their buildings and create air raid shelters for workers.

In civilian defense, as in other aspects of life on the home front, workers were needed to replace the men who had gone off to war, and women answered the call. Some women became fire fighters and went through training to learn how to combat blazes, including basic techniques needed

In an air raid situation, citizens had to observe blackout conditions. This poster shows the city of New York before and during a trial blackout. (Library of Congress)

With so many men off fighting the war, women served in the Civilian Defense Corps as firefighters. Showing aptitude for the work, they form a "V" for victory with their hose lines. (Reproduced by permission of AP/Wide World Photos)

An example of American propaganda, this poster drove home the message that the enemy could be listening to any conversation. A similar slogan that appeared on other posters was "Loose lips sink ships." (Library of Congress)

the organization known as the Civil Air Patrol was born on December 1, 1941, less than a week before the Japanese military bombed the U.S. naval base at Pearl Harbor, Hawaii. As the United States entered the war, the CAP quickly organized. Eventually, its rolls would include 150,000 men and women who often flew their own yellow and red planes.

The CAP provided valuable services. As the U.S. military began its extensive buildup of troops and supplies to send overseas, there were not as

Women aided the war effort in many ways. Here, two women (called "spotters") scan Virginia's skies, looking for approaching enemy aircraft. (Reproduced by permission of AP/Wide World Photos)

to work hoses and other fire equipment. Other women served as air raid wardens, volunteered in hospitals and other care centers, and joined the ranks of munitions workers. Some women volunteered to work as "spotters." With binoculars in hand, they climbed to observation posts on high to watch for (or "spot") approaching enemy aircraft. Men and women worked as spotters from rooftops, observation decks, and the like.

Many groups became involved in civilian defense, including the American Red Cross and scouting groups. Others, such as the Civil Air Patrol (CAP), were established because of the war. Talk of the CAP actually began in the late 1930s, when some Americans suspected that the country would eventually enter World War II. Aviation editor for the *New York Herald Tribune* and pilot Gill Robb Wilson conceived the idea to organize a group of civilian aviators to help protect American shores. Wilson succeeded in getting General Henry "Hap" Arnold's approval, and

After bombing Pearl Harbor, the Japanese threatened the continental United States in June 1942. A Japanese submarine launched torpedoes at the coast of Oregon, near the town of Seaside. Defense workers checked for shell fragments, but found no serious damage. (Reproduced by permission of AP/Wide World Photos)

many servicemen available to defend the nation's borders. CAP pilots took to the skies searching for enemy submarines, planes, and ships. They also performed search and rescue missions, as well as transported supplies to service personnel. Comparing CAP aviators to citizen patriots of the American Revolutionary War, people began calling Civil Air Patrol members "Flying Minutemen." They rescued hundreds of people and reported numerous enemy craft patrolling American shores.

In the early years of American participation in World War II, patrolling the U.S. coast was a necessity, as enemy submarines were seen off both the Atlantic and Pacific shores. In fact, on the West Coast in June 1942, a Japanese submarine launched torpedoes near the town of Seaside, Oregon. Defense workers made an extensive check of the area and found no serious damage. On the east coast, citizens were alarmed to find out that an enemy submarine had surfaced in outer New York Harbor. People were concerned that enemy subs

could fire torpedoes to the shore or the crafts could surface and use weaponry from their decks. CAP pilots greatly aided in the country's attempts to dissuade enemy forces from entering American waters. Guarding the skies, they helped oil tankers bring much needed fuel to the country. Some attacked submarines, even sinking two. Other planes were unarmed but pretended to have weaponry onboard if they spotted an enemy craft. On many occasions, the pilots would dive at the submarine, faking a bombing run, and the vessel would hurriedly leave the area. CAP aviators devoted their time and equipment to keeping the country safe from invasion or enemy bombing. Although the government paid them about $8 per day when they flew, CAP pilots often dug into their own pockets to fund their civilian defense activities. On occasion, defense efforts were supplemented with money donated by organizations like the "Sink-a-Sub Club."

During the war, sixty-four CAP pilots died. However, the efforts of the CAP proved highly suc-

African American soldiers stand at attention while an officer reviews the troops. The U.S. armed forces remained segregated throughout the war. (National Archives and Records Administration)

cessful when, in early 1943, the Germans stopped sending U-boats to American waters. In his book, *Flying Minute Men: The Story of the Civil Air Patrol* (1948), Robert E. Neprud writes that a German naval officer explained why. The German said "It was because of those damned little red and yellow planes!" He was referring to the pilots of the CAP. Throughout the war, the CAP flew millions of miles, logging about 500,000 hours, in the effort to protect the United States.

African Americans and the War

Although the war in Europe began to create an economic boom in the United States, African Americans received few of the new jobs. In January 1941, A. Philip Randolph, the organizer and president of the Brotherhood of Sleeping Car Porters, a union of African American railroad workers, organized the March on Washington Movement. The organization planned to take thousands of African Americans to a massive demonstration in Washington, D.C. They sought to demand that the government stop awarding defense contracts to companies that discriminated; that the government itself end discrimination in the hiring of federal employees; and that the armed forces be integrated. A week before the scheduled march, Roosevelt issued Executive Order 8802, which stated that discrimination "because of race, creed, color, or national origin" would not be tolerated "in defense industries or government." Roosevelt also formed the federal Fair Employment Practices Commission (FEPC), which would receive complaints about discrimination and take "appropriate steps." For the first time since Abraham Lincoln's presidency, a U.S. president had taken executive action against racial discrimination. Randolph canceled the march but kept the organization together to apply further pressure to the government. Although the FEPC's enforcement powers turned out to be quite limited, defense industries hired significant numbers of African Americans. In general, however, they received mainly the dirtiest, lowest-paying jobs. The armed forces remained completely segregated.

Prior to the attack on Pearl Harbor, some segments of the African American community were less pro-British than many American whites. Great Britain was a great colonial power, and hundreds of millions of nonwhite people lived in Asian and African countries that Great Britain controlled. Some African Americans considered the struggles of these countries, such as India, to achieve independence to be similar to their own struggle for equal rights in America. (Great Britain's colonial history also made other groups, such as Irish Americans, less pro-British before the bombing of Pearl Harbor.) Once the United States entered the war, however, the African American community strongly supported the war effort. Many African Americans thought that the fight against Nazi racism in Europe should be combined with the fight against racism and discrimination in America. This was symbolized by the "Double-V" campaign started in 1942 by the *Pittsburgh Courier,* an African American newspaper. The "V for Victory" sign was doubled to signify that African Americans were fighting for democracy both overseas and at home.

Although the Selective Service Act banned discrimination, both the Navy Department and the army's War Department ignored the legislation. (After World War II, these two departments merged to form the Department of Defense.) The War Department claimed that allowing African Americans to serve equally would lower the morale of white soldiers. Both Secretary of War Henry Stimson and Army Chief of Staff General George C. Marshall believed that white soldiers might refuse to fight alongside blacks. Many top military officials also believed, without any supporting evidence, that African Americans were not brave and disciplined enough to serve in combat units, even segregated from whites.

The predraft U.S. Army was overwhelmingly white. Only 5,000 black soldiers and a few dozen black officers were serving in an army of about 100,000 men; the U.S. Marine Corps and the U.S. Army Air Corps did not accept any African Americans. The army did not encourage African Americans to join until after Pearl Harbor, when there was an increased need for men. Even then, African Americans were almost never placed in combat, infantry, armored, or artillery units. Instead, they were concentrated in service units, where they unloaded supplies, maintained vehicles, built barracks on army bases, and performed other manual labor. By the end of 1944, there were 700,000 African Americans in the army (about 9 percent of the total force), and about 5,000 African American officers. Although a majority served overseas, they were still generally limited to service units.

There were, however, three segregated black combat divisions—the Ninety-Second and Ninety-Third Infantry Divisions and the Second Cavalry Division. (Cavalry divisions were now "mounted" on jeeps and other vehicles, not on horses.) Although all the soldiers, corporals, and sergeants were African American, the top officers were white. The Second Cavalry was disbanded, and the Ninety-Third Division served in the Pacific but saw little combat. The Ninety-Second Division fought in Italy, seeing much more action; 600 men were killed and another 2,000 wounded. Its commander, however, was a white general who openly distrusted the ability of African American troops, who in return had no confidence in their officers. As a result, the unit developed a poor reputation. The 761st Tank Battalion, on the other hand, was a segregated armored unit that fought mainly in France and Germany as part of General George S. Patton's Third Army. From the time it entered combat in November 1944 until Germany's surrender the following May, the unit fought for 183 consecutive days. While it played an important role in defeating the last German counteroffensive, the Battle of the Bulge, the 761st did not receive a Presidential Unit Citation until 1978.

Discrimination was even worse in the navy, where African Americans had traditionally been allowed to work only in ships' kitchens and to serve food in officers' dining areas. During World War II, 95 percent of African American sailors onboard ships were still limited to these jobs.

African American soldiers serving during World War II were completely segregated from white troops and most received noncombat assignments. (National Archives and Records Administration)

Onshore, large numbers of African American sailors were used as laborers, to load ships and transport material. The WAVES, the women's naval corps, did not accept any African American women until 1944, the same year the navy allowed African American seamen to serve on twenty-five "white" ships. At that time, 165,000 African Americans were in the navy and about 17,000 were in the Marine Corps.

The U.S. Army Air Corps created some all-black squadrons under orders, but most were used to maintain airfields. The first African American airmen to see action were members of the Ninety-Ninth Fighter Squadron, which flew in Italy beginning in April 1943. Commanded by Benjamin O. Davis, Jr., who was later the first African American general in the air corps, this unit became famous as the Tuskegee Airmen (named after the Alabama town where they were trained). Yet the unit was an exception. Only three other African American squadrons were allowed in combat.

The military's discriminatory policies made it more difficult to convince African Americans that the war was being fought for freedom. In one

well-known incident, a restaurant in a small Kansas town served lunch to German prisoners of war but refused to serve African American soldiers. African American troops returning from overseas on leave were sent to different, and inferior, hotels. With the cooperation of the American Red Cross, the army even separated blood supplied by whites and blacks. There were often tensions between African American and white units, especially on bases in the segregated South, which resulted in several small-scale riots. The army attempted to keep its own facilities, including officers' clubs, racially segregated, even on bases in northern states where segregation was against the law. In fact, fights broke out when white soldiers tried to introduce segregated facilities near American bases in England.

African Americans also continued to experience discrimination in civilian life. During the war, 700,000 African Americans, many from the South, moved to industrial cities—approximately 60,000 moved to Detroit alone. Nationwide, 1.2 million were working in industrial jobs. Some whites, many of them also recent arrivals from the South, resented working with African Americans and would

U.S. Urges African American Enlistment

In spite of racial discrimination, the United States government urged African Americans to participate in the war effort. Posters featured heavyweight boxing champion Joe "the Brown Bomber" Louis, a private in the army, who was tremendously popular among African Americans. The image of Dorie Miller was also used in an attempt to increase African American enlistment. Miller was an African American sailor who had been a mess steward, or kitchen worker, aboard the battleship USS *Arizona,* which was sunk at Pearl Harbor. He shot down two attacking Japanese planes with a machine gun and received the Navy Cross, the navy's second-highest medal (after the Congressional Medal of Honor). Miller was killed two years later when the Japanese sank the escort carrier USS *Liscome Bay.*

During his service in the U.S. military during World War II, heavyweight boxer Joe Louis was awarded the Legion of Merit by Major General Clarence H. Kells. (Reproduced by permission of © Hulton Getty/Liaison Agency)

occasionally walk off the job to protest promotions of African Americans. Tensions over crowded housing in industrial cities added to the strain. In June 1943 a series of fights between blacks and whites at a city park in Detroit grew into a major riot when nearby white sailors joined in. That night, groups of African Americans attacked stores and streetcars. Two whites were beaten to death. The next day, mobs of whites began randomly attacking African Americans. Troops were called in

Riots in Detroit in June 1943 were quieted by the arrival of the military. (Reproduced by permission of AP/Wide World Photos)

to end the chaos, but a total of thirty-four people, twenty-five of them African Americans, were killed, and 700 were injured. A smaller riot occurred in the Harlem neighborhood of New York City, in August 1943, when a false rumor spread that a white police officer had shot and killed an African American soldier. When the riot ended, five people had been killed and nearly 400 injured.

Japanese Americans Interned in Camps

At the beginning of the war, 127,000 Americans of Japanese descent (less than one-tenth of 1 percent of the population) lived in the United States. Among them were 80,000 nisei, who had been born in the country and were American citizens, but the remainder, the parents of the nisei, were called issei and had been born in Japan. The issei had lived in America for years. A 1924 law had halted nearly all new Japanese immigration into the United States. The same law also prevented the issei from becoming American citizens. All but 15,000 Japanese Americans lived on the West Coast, especially in California, and had long been the victims of discrimination. Laws made it illegal for them to marry whites and barred them from some public places, such as swimming pools. Some state laws did not allow Japanese Americans to own land and prevented nisei from voting. Partly as a result of this discrimination, the issei were less integrated into

mainstream American society than some other immigrant groups, especially those from Europe. They still spoke mainly Japanese, ate Japanese food, and observed Japanese holidays. This was also true, although to a lesser extent, of the nisei.

Most Japanese Americans worked the land. Some were small farmers, usually renting their land, who raised crops such as lettuce and green beans that were sold locally. These farmers became an important part of the California economy. Other Japanese Americans were fishermen or owned small stores; very few were in other businesses. A few were professionals like lawyers or doctors; some worked in factories. In many ways, therefore, Japanese Americans were isolated from other Americans. Discrimination against them further ensured that they would have few allies and that they would be regarded as outsiders.

This isolation and intense anti-Asian racism in the United States contributed to the events that followed Pearl Harbor. American outrage at the "sneak attack" merged with racist ideas that portrayed the Japanese as shifty and treacherous people of low intelligence. They were depicted as cruel savages, and their facial features were exaggerated in cartoons to make them look like monkeys. It did not take long to extend these racist ideas from the Japanese to Japanese Americans, as newspapers and local politicians whipped up hysteria against them.

The Zoot Suit Riots

For several days in June 1943, hundreds of cars and taxis, filled mostly with white sailors, drove through the Mexican American neighborhoods of Los Angeles. There the passengers attacked young men dressed in "zoot suits," which featured extra-long jackets with shoulder pads. The pants were baggy at the knee and tapered to the ankle. Large hats and pocket watches on long chains completed the outfit. The zoot suit was a stark contrast to the trim military uniform. According to some experts, this was the reason for its popularity among young Mexican Americans in Los Angeles. The sailors' assaults were triggered by rumors that zoot-suiters had attacked servicemen. The sailors beat up "zooters" and other Mexican Americans, cut their hair, and ripped off their clothes. The Los Angeles police stood by, watching the beatings, and then often ended up arresting the zoot-suiters. The newspapers blamed the zooters for the riots and the city council made it a criminal offense to wear a zoot suit in public.

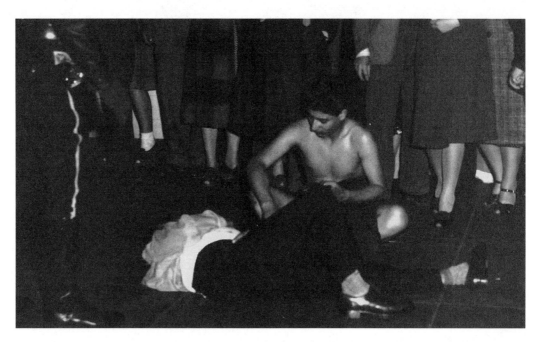

During the zoot suit riots in Los Angeles, servicemen roamed the streets looking for young men wearing fancy zoot suits. The servicemen beat some of the zoot-suiters and ripped off their clothes. (Reproduced by permission of AP/Wide World Photos)

For instance, the governor of Idaho claimed that "Japs live like rats, breed like rats, and act like rats."

The main anti-Japanese argument was that Japanese Americans could not be trusted, that some of them would help Japan by spying on or sabotaging American military facilities. Local politicians demanded the removal of all 112,000 Japanese Americans from the West Coast, even though there had been no known case of spying or sabotage. Some military leaders realized this was nonsense. If there had been a real danger of Japanese American disloyalty, the place it would have caused a serious problem was Hawaii, where one-

This window display features a caricature of a Japanese soldier, common during the war. Japanese Americans faced the same racism and stereotyping as the Japanese. (Reproduced by permission of the Corbis Corporation [Bellevue])

third of the population was of Japanese descent. The threat of further Japanese attacks in Hawaii was far more realistic than an invasion of California. In fact, Hawaii was placed under martial law, but there were no extra restrictions on people of Japanese ancestry in the area. Other military authorities, however, agreed with the newspapers that there was no difference between the Japanese in Japan and American citizens of Japanese descent. "A Jap's a Jap," said General John L. DeWitt, military commander for the West Coast.

On February 19, 1942, President Franklin D. Roosevelt issued Executive Order 9066, which authorized the War Department to classify any region of the country as a military area, and then to bar any persons it chose from those areas. This authority was used only for the states of California, Oregon, and Washington, and the only group affected by it was Japanese Americans. On March 31 all Japanese Americans in these states were required to register at control stations and then were told when to report for relocation to an internment camp. It is fairly common to intern citizens of an enemy country in wartime, especial-

ly when those people actually live in the enemy country and are planning to return. The issei, however, were immigrants to the United States who planned to remain for the rest of their lives. Even more important, the nisei were American citizens, with the same legal and constitutional rights as all other Americans. The Japanese Americans were told they would be moved between four days and two weeks later, and that they could take only what they could carry. In that short time, they were required to sell the rest of their property for whatever amount they could get. Many people took advantage of their Japanese American neighbors by buying homes, stores, and cars at exceptionally low prices.

Armed soldiers moved Japanese American families from their homes to receiving stations, such as fairgrounds or racetracks, where they might be housed in horse stalls. From the receiving stations, they were sent to relocation camps. There were eventually ten of these camps, all but one in the Far West (the exception was in Arkansas). The camps were located in remote areas unsuitable for farming, surrounded by fences, and guarded by the army.

Italian Americans Treated Differently than Japanese Americans

The U.S. government's treatment of Italian Americans stood in sharp contrast to its policy toward Japanese Americans. Three days after the Japanese attack on Pearl Harbor, Italy declared war on the United States. At that time, 600,000 Italian immigrants who were not citizens, most of them living on the east coast, were declared enemy aliens. They could not become American citizens and were subject to some restrictions on their right to travel. Only a small percentage of those suspected of being spies were arrested. The millions of Italian Americans who were citizens were not restricted in any way, and even the relatively minor restrictions on non-citizens did not last long. Although the United States remained at war with Italy, President Franklin D. Roosevelt removed Italian Americans from the category of enemy aliens ten months after Pearl Harbor, on Columbus Day 1942.

A Japanese American family reports for relocation. (Library of Congress)

The best known was Manzanar, in the southern California desert. During the course of the war, 120,000 people lived in the camps, quartered in long wooden barracks divided into one-room apartments that held entire families. There was almost no furniture and only a bare bulb for light. Toilets, bathing facilities, and dining areas were shared by many families. Although half the nisei were under eighteen years of age when they were relocated, the government had not planned adequate schools. There was no work, and few ways to pass the time; in many ways, the camps were similar to medium-security prisons. Release from the camps was possible if someone could show that he or she was loyal to the United States and had a job waiting in a community willing to accept the applicant, but this turned out to be almost impossible. Most of the 15,000 to 20,000 Japanese Americans temporarily released from the camps in 1943 were students.

The anger of Japanese Americans at their treatment was mixed with a desire to prove themselves. When nisei were made eligible to join the armed services in 1943, many of the young men did join and fought bravely, even while their parents were still being held in camps. The 442nd Infantry Regiment, a segregated unit made up entirely of nisei, fought in Italy and won more medals than any other unit in the U.S. Army. A number of nisei, however, refused to swear allegiance to the United States, and some even renounced their American citizenship. During the war, the U.S. Supreme Court rejected legal challenges to the exclusion and internment policy. Almost all legal experts now believe that these cases represent some of the lowest moments in the court's history. The exclusion order was repealed in January 1945. In 1959 American citizenship was restored to those nisei who had renounced it, and in 1989 a federal law awarded $20,000 to each surviving victim. In 1993 a court ruled that internment had violated the constitutional rights of Japanese Americans.

American Women

More dramatic changes during the war concerned the role of women in society. As production expanded and men were drafted into the army, more women entered the workforce than ever before. Some were secretaries and clerical workers, traditional jobs for women, but for the first time, large numbers were given jobs as welders and operators of lathes and other industrial machinery. The symbol of the woman war worker in industry was "Rosie the Riveter," who

With many men off fighting the war, Chicago Cubs owner Philip Wrigley started the All American Girls Professional Baseball League in 1943 to entertain sports fans. (Reproduced by permission of ©Corbis-Bettmann)

used a rivet gun to join metal plates for airplane bodies or ships' sides. Although the jobs were often dirty and dangerous, many women found—to their surprise—that the work did not require exceptional physical size or strength. For example, relatively small women could use welding torches. Having always been told that they lacked natural mechanical aptitude, women were now quickly trained to be drafters and designers; they learned to operate complicated machinery. Despite the fact that they often did the same jobs as men, however, they were rarely given the same pay. In general, women earned only about two-thirds the amount paid to men.

During the war, the number of women working outside the home in the United States rose by more than 6 million, a 50 percent increase. By 1944, about 60 percent of American women (about 19 million), including 25 percent of married women, worked outside the home. Almost 6

American Mothers and Children

The war had a profound effect on mothers and children in the United States. Many people feared that women would become toughened by factory work and that their femininity and morality would suffer. The U.S. government reminded women that taking care of children was still their most important job, even in wartime. Many of the 16 million American men in the military had children, and almost 20 percent of families were separated during the war. About 2.75 million American women workers had children under the age of fourteen, and there was a severe shortage of day-care facilities. Children had to be cared for by grandparents or neighbors, or were often left on their own while their mothers were at work.

The war affected American children in other ways as well. The labor shortage led to a loosening of restrictions on child labor, and the higher pay encouraged them to get jobs. Many families could not survive on the low pay soldiers received, and this further encouraged both women and children to enter the workforce. By 1944, 40 percent of sixteen- and seventeen-year-old boys were employed; 20 percent of boys age fourteen and fifteen had jobs. One-third of sixteen- to eighteen-year-old girls also worked. More than one-third of both boys and girls age sixteen to eighteen dropped out of school to work full-time, reversing a longtime trend toward higher graduation rates in the United States.

Some people were concerned about changes in teenagers' behavior, worrying over increasing loss of parental control, the use of "adult language," and increasing sexual activity. Others said that what was seen as a decline in morality was essentially just greater teenage independence.

million women worked in factory jobs. The number of women working in aircraft factories rose from 143 in 1941 to around 65,000 at the end of 1942. Eventually, more than half the workers in the giant Boeing aircraft plant near Seattle were women. By the end of the war, women constituted more than one-third of the American civilian workforce. According to a government survey, 80 percent of women workers, including almost 70 percent of those who were married, wanted to continue working after the war.

The government was anxious to encourage women to enter the workplace. "Rosie the Riveter" was featured on posters and in a song. Everywhere, women were told that it was patriotic to work in a factory and that calling in sick was a betrayal of the soldiers fighting in the Pacific. Women in shipyards were "soldiers without guns," the heroines of the "Ships for Victory" program. Film star Veronica Lake cut off her much-imitated long, peekaboo-style hair because it was considered a safety hazard for women working with machines. Instead of skirts, women wore trousers or, for the first time, jeans.

American women did not just help out in civil roles, however. Several months after the United States entered the war, Congress authorized the establishment of a Women's Army Auxiliary Corps, or WAAC, on May 15, 1942. A year later, the WAAC became a full-fledged branch of the army called the Women's Army Corps, or WAC. Women's navy and marine corps were established in 1943. A total of 350,000 women were members of the U.S. armed forces during the war. As in most countries, women were not permitted to serve in combat roles, but instead freed up more men for combat by filling important noncombat jobs. About half of the women performed office work, while others were weather observers and forecasters, cryptographers, radio operators, photographers, and map analysts. Although some top officers strongly encouraged recruiting women to replace men in noncombat army jobs, others were hostile to the idea.

Traditionally, women were secretaries, nurses, and teachers. During World War II, they worked to build planes, tanks, and weapons. (National Archives and Records Administration)

Poster recruiting women to work. (Reproduced by permission of the Corbis Corporation [Bellevue])

Members of the Women's Army Auxiliary Corps (WAAC) talk with young girls who may be interested in joining the armed services one day. (Reproduced by permission of AP/Wide World Photos)

Poster encouraging women to join the armed services. (National Archives and Records Administration)

The Women's Airforce Service Pilots, or WASPs, received a great deal of publicity during the war—a movie was even made about the group. Between 1942 and 1944, more than 1,000 women served as pilots in the WASPs, flying a total of 60 million miles. One of their main jobs was flying planes from the factories where they were assembled and the airfields where they were tested to ports for overseas shipment by boat. They flew every type of American military plane, including the huge B-29 Superfortress, and even, near the end of the war, experimental jet fighters. The women were responsible for testing various aspects of the aircraft they flew, such as their ability to jam enemy radar, or to swoop low and attack ground targets with machine guns. The WASPs also towed targets that were used for practice by fighter pilots and antiaircraft gunners. Live ammunition was used in these exercises, and the planes flown by the women were often hit. Although the commander of the Army Air Corps strongly supported the WASPs, many other air corps officers resented their presence. Pilots thought of themselves as the military elite, and many found it disturbing that women could fly as well as men.

Women Work and Fight for Great Britain

In Great Britain, the number of women working outside the home grew from around 5 million

WASP director Jackie Cochran met with Captain Norman Edgar of Great Britain to learn more about the British Air Transport Auxiliary—a program similar in scope to the Women's Airforce Service Pilots. (Library of Congress)

The British Air Transport Auxiliary was an organization similar to the American Women's Airforce Service Pilots. Both groups helped ferry planes loaded with supplies and troops. (Reproduced by permission of © Hulton Getty/Liaison Agency)

in 1939 to 7.75 million in 1943, the largest percentage increase of any country in the war. Even this number disguises the real magnitude of the change, however, because many women who already had jobs in traditional women's industries, such as textile and clothing manufacturing, or as domestic servants switched to jobs in heavy industry. In addition, 2 million women worked in war industries, including shipbuilding, chemicals, and vehicle and aircraft production, four times as many as at the beginning of the war. Although patriotism and good pay motivated women to take industrial jobs, the British government also used the law to increase their numbers. Starting in March 1941, British women could legally be "directed" into war work. This law eventually applied to most women under the age of fifty, including married women, but excluded those with young children. Day care provisions were never adequate for children whose mothers chose to work in industry.

In most countries, women's roles in the armed services were limited to noncombat positions. In Great Britain, nearly half a million women served in the various women's branches of the armed forces or the nursing corps. Some 400,000 were involved in defending against German air attacks, including operating antiaircraft guns during air raids. In theory, women were not allowed to fire the guns themselves, but they did other tasks, such as operating searchlights and radar sets. Women such as Princess Elizabeth (later Queen Elizabeth II) drove trucks and ambulances. There were also more than 1 million part-time members of the Women's Voluntary Service (WAS), who did things like provide tea to soldiers passing through their towns, or darn soldiers' socks, saving valuable material. In December 1941 single British women between twenty and thirty years old became subject to the military draft, though they could choose to enter civil defense and similar work instead of the armed forces. By the end of the war, 125,000 women had been drafted into the women's branches of the armed services.

Women in the Soviet Union

World War II brought about dramatic changes for women in the Soviet Union. The most impor-

Children Contribute to War Effort

C hildren also contributed to the home front war effort. In Great Britain, for example, they helped their parents plant victory gardens in every backyard and on the edge of every village. The potatoes and vegetables they grew helped reduce Britain's need to import food past the German U-boats, or submarines, that patrolled the Atlantic Ocean. Children in both Great Britain and the United States also participated in scrap drives, going door to door to collect pots and pans, old wash-basins, and other metal objects. Iron and steel items were melted down and used to make steel for ships and weapons; copper was used for electric wire.

Soviet partisans. About 200,000 women joined the troops fighting behind German lines. (Reproduced by permission of the Corbis Corporation [Bellevue])

tant change in their roles was a huge increase in the number of women working in war industries and other heavy industry. One million women joined the paid workforce in the first six months after the German invasion. By the end of the war, women comprised 55 percent of the Soviet work-force, compared with 30 percent prior to the war. On the large factory-like farms that dominated Soviet agriculture, women comprised 80 percent of the workers.

The expanded role of Soviet women also impacted direct combat. In the first few months of the German invasion, 1 million Soviet soldiers were killed and another 3 million captured. With such a severe shortage of manpower, women were recruit-

Young boys started up Tin Can Club Number One in New York City. Like similar organizations, this group searched for scrap metal, which could be recycled for use in the war effort. (Reproduced by permission of AP/Wide World Photos)

ed not only to do things like dig antitank ditches, but also to join combat units. Although they were still the exception, Soviet women drove tanks and flew planes in combat. One all-women squadron flew outdated planes on ten missions per night to bomb German troops during the Battle of Stalingrad. The Germans called them the "night witches." The most famous woman ace of the war was Soviet fighter pilot Lily Litvak, "the rose of Stalingrad," who shot down twelve German planes before she

Russian women snipers. Soviet women served in combat during World War II, in roles that included flying fighter planes and driving tanks. (Reproduced by permission of the Corbis Corporation [Bellevue])

was killed in combat. In all, about 800,000 women served with the regular Soviet armed forces, though most did not see combat. Another 200,000 were partisans, troops operating behind German lines.

Labor Forces in Germany and Japan

Although large numbers of German women worked outside the home before the war, making up 37 percent of the workforce, Hitler did not want to encourage more women to join them. Many people think this policy reflected the Nazis' conservative attitudes toward women, whom they thought should be limited to three areas: *"Kinder, Küche, Kirche"* ("children, kitchen, church"). Another major factor discouraging women from entering the workforce was Hitler's concern about interfering with German civilian life and losing

political support. The Nazi government was considerably more cautious than its British and American counterparts about disrupting civilian life and converting the German economy into one in which industry, most resources, and the labor force were all devoted to the war effort.

Instead, Germany tried to solve its wartime labor shortage by using millions of foreign workers, most of them forced or slave laborers, such as Polish prisoners of war and German civilians who were drafted as workers. At first, these forced laborers replaced farm workers, who took factory jobs or entered the army. By the end of 1941, Poles comprised one-half of the almost 4 million foreign workers in Germany, many of whom were then working in factories. In this foreign labor force were Italians, Frenchmen, Belgians, and other western Europeans who could not find work in their home countries, which were conquered or dominated by Germany, and voluntarily went to Germany in search of work. Yet they could not change jobs or go home unless they had permission, and eventually the differences between the voluntary workers and the forced laborers almost disappeared. By spring 1943, there were more than 6 million foreign workers, and almost none of the 2 million new workers were volunteers. Although the Germans introduced mandatory labor service in France and other western European countries, the largest number of forced laborers—1.5 million—came from the conquered areas of the Soviet Union. The number of foreign workers in Germany reached 7 million—about one-fifth of the entire German labor force—in the middle of 1944. Approximately 7 million more people worked for Germany in their home countries, either toiling in Nazi-controlled factories or building military fortifications. The workforce of almost every sizable factory in Germany included forced laborers, and camps or barracks for the workers were located in almost every German city. Workers faced horrible conditions, subjected to long hours at difficult jobs without adequate food. Because their housing was often located near factories, forced laborers were frequently the victims of Allied bombings. The Germans would severely punish them for disobeying orders, and thousands were shot. A large number of women, most of them from the Soviet Union, were forcibly sterilized.

Of all the major countries involved in World War II, Japan alone did not allow women to join any branch of its armed services. The number of

Japanese women working in factories increased only slightly during the war. Japan's leaders did not want to change the traditional roles of men and women; also, many Japanese women already worked on family farms, and their labor became even more important while men were away at war. The Japanese also relied extensively on forced labor, using Allied prisoners of war to perform backbreaking work in unbearable heat with inadequate food or medical attention. Projects such as building a railroad from Thailand to Burma (now Myanmar) have been depicted in books and movies like *The Bridge on the River Kwai*. Nearly

20 percent of the 61,000 Allied prisoners working on the railroad connecting these two countries perished. Still, Allied prisoners were not the major source of Japanese forced labor. About 270,000 Asians, mostly Thai and Burmese, were forced to work on the railroad, and 90,000 of them (one out of three) died. The Japanese also forced hundreds of thousands of Koreans to work in Japan. Some Korean women, as well as women of other nationalities, were euphemistically termed "comfort women." They were forced by the Japanese government into service as prostitutes for the Japanese army.

PRIMARY SOURCE

Catherine "Renee" Young Pike
Excerpt from *Since You Went Away: World War II Letters from American Women on the Home Front*
Edited by Judy Barrett Litoff and David C. Smith
Published in 1991

World War II radically changed the lives of Americans, even those not fighting on the front lines. Many Americans worked on the home front, fueling the entire war effort. The decade before the war had been particularly bleak for most Americans because of the Great Depression, which began in 1929. By 1932, approximately 12 million Americans were unemployed. The nation's entry into World War II in December 1941, however, brought a swift end to nearly twelve years of hardship and deprivation. High unemployment disappeared as U.S. government office positions and manufacturing jobs opened up in record numbers. Between 1940 and 1944, America's industrial workforce increased by more than 35 percent. War production boosted the American economy more than any government relief program ever could, as factories began churning out ammunition, bombers, jeeps, and other war supplies. Between 1942 and 1944, American industry doubled its aircraft production from 4,800 military aircraft per year to more than 9,600 per year. American production allowed Great Britain and the Soviet Union to battle Germany's forces.

At the height of the war, the U.S. armed forces had 15 million people in their ranks. When American men were drafted or volunteered, American women stepped into the workforce in unprecedented numbers. During World War II, more than 6 million women on the American home front held war-related jobs. The number of African American women in industry increased by a little more than 11 percent, as Executive Order 8802, issued by President Franklin D. Roosevelt in 1941, banned discrimination in the government and defense industries. The fabled image of tireless airplane assembler "Rosie the Riveter" became the archetype for female defense plant workers. (After the war, however, millions of women found themselves unemployed in fall 1945, when the war ended and war industry production came to a grinding halt.)

Fighting World War II cost the United States some $300 billion. Beginning in 1941, funds for the war effort were raised through the sale of U.S. savings bonds, known as "war bonds," and through the addition of a 5 percent "victory tax" on all income taxes. To save money and resources, the U.S. Office of Price Administration (OPA) directed the

America Is Inspired to Achieve Wartime Goals

President Franklin D. Roosevelt has been credited with inspiring the United States to reach phenomenal wartime production goals. "To change a whole nation from a basis of peace time production of implements of peace to a basis of war time production of implements of war is no easy task," noted Roosevelt in his January 6, 1941, message to Congress. According to Russell Freedman in *Franklin Delano Roosevelt,* "As late as 1940, the United States was so poorly prepared for war that soldiers trained with broomsticks for rifles and pieces of cardboard marked 'Tank.' And yet the nation's factories and shipyards were swiftly converted to produce planes, tanks, ships, and weapons."

U.S. President Franklin D. Roosevelt inspired American workers to achieve higher goals.

rationing of scarce items. American shoppers were issued ration books that allowed each family member a limited share of certain products each month; goods in especially short supply were rationed more strictly. Rationing of sugar, coffee, automobile tires, gasoline, and heating oil began in 1942. Americans had to keep their thermostats at 65 degrees through the harsh winter of 1942–1943. By 1943, shoes, cheese, fats, canned goods, and meat were being rationed. A pound of scarce items like sirloin steak, pork tenderloin, cheddar cheese, or even butter could cost an entire weekly meat allotment. One measure taken to combat scarcity of foodstuffs was the "victory garden," or wartime vegetable garden. More than 20 million victory gardens were planted by Americans in 1943. That year, the food grown in those gardens produced about one-third of all vegetables consumed in the United States.

Letters from home were soldiers' only links to loved ones and the "normalcy" of life in the States. Regular mail delivery was so important to American troops overseas that mail even got through to the beachheads of islands in the Pacific. The following excerpt features letters from Catherine "Renee" Young Pike to her husband, George Pike. The letters span a two-year period between February 1943 and January 1945, when Renee was living with her parents and younger brother and sister in Esmond, Rhode Island. Renee and George were married shortly before the Japanese attacked the U.S. naval base at Pearl Harbor in December 1941. George was drafted into the army in August of 1942. Renee was pregnant with their first child at the time; "Georgie" was born in March 1943. In her letters, Renee gives glimpses into life on the home front, including rationing and shortages of certain foods.

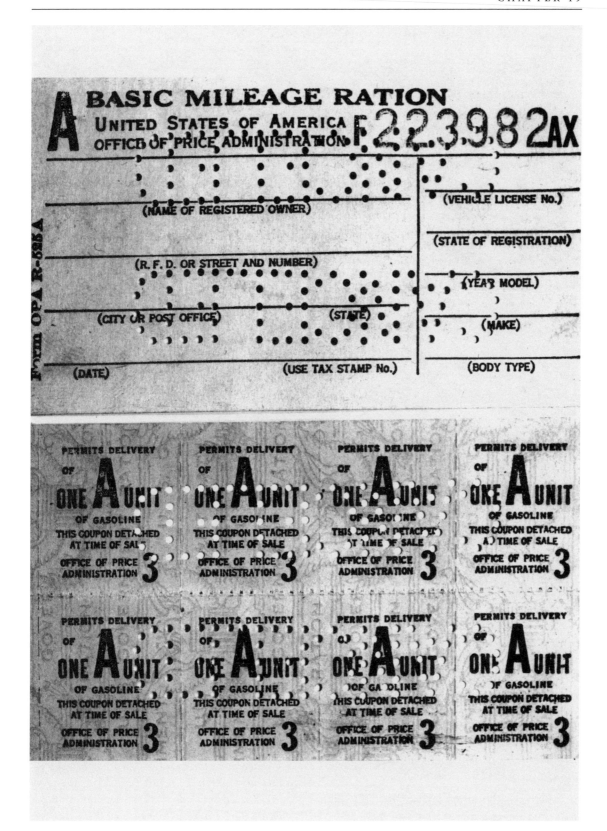

Drivers needed ration coupons, like those pictured here, to be able to purchase gasoline, which was rationed on the home front as it was needed to support the war effort. (Reproduced by permission of AP/Wide World Photos)

Women helped with the war effort in a number of ways, including sorting scrap metal to be melted down and used for war supplies. (Reproduced by permission of AP/Wide World Photos, Inc.)

Excerpt from
Since You Went Away: World War II Letters from American Women on the Home Front

Esmond, Feb. 3, 1943

My darling Husband,

Last night I had a whole mix-up of dreams. But one thing I dreamed was that I was eating banana splits one right after the other and were they good! When I awakened I thought to myself "Boy, what I wouldn't give for a nice banana." But that is just wishful thinking. I don't think anyone in America has seen a banana for over six months.

Well, George, the civilian population is certainly feeling the shortage of food-stuffs now. Last week we didn't have a scratch of butter in the house from Monday until Friday—and how I hate dry bread! It's a lot worse on we people in the country than it is on the city folks. They can go out and get some kind

of meat every day while we have plenty of meatless days up here. They can also stand in line for 2 or 3 hours for a pound of butter, but up here there are no lines as there is no butter and when there is a little butter everyone gets a 1/4 of a pound. So you can imagine how far a 1/4 of a pound goes in this family of five adults. And that's suppose to last us for a week.

Yesterday I didn't take any meat not because we didn't have any but because I'm sick of the same thing. You see, the thing that they have the most of is sausages, but people can't keep eating the same thing every day....

I received a swell letter from you yesterday. Gee, it seems that all the letters I've got from you recently have been the nicest letters.... I love you, George, more than anything in the whole, wide world.

Yours forever, Renee

Esmond, March 4, 1943

My Darling,

I've just been thinking that you'll miss getting my letters when I go the hospital, won't you?...

I'm beginning to get weary now and nervous. I want to go and get it over with. You see, Darling, I've gained 25 pounds since I first started [the pregnancy] and at the end like this you get sort of miserable. Last night after I got to bed I had what is known as "false labor." I had quite bad pains in my stomach but I didn't tell anyone and I dropped off to sleep after awhile. But it makes you think that your time has come, believe me....

Honey, whether I've had the baby or whether I haven't why don't you ask for a furlough when you're through with your schooling. Of course you know better than me if you should but let me know what you think about it. O.K.?

I want to see you so much, Honey, and I miss you something awful, especially lately. I love you with all my heart and soul and body.

Yours forever, Renee

Esmond, June 6, 1944

My Darling,

...6:45 a.m. The phone just rang about ten minutes ago. It was your mother. She told me that the Invasion [a reference to the Allied invasion of Normandy, France, on D-Day, June 6, 1944] had started. I just put on the radio and this time it's real. I don't quite know what to say, Sweetheart. It goes without saying that I feel very nervous and very afraid. I do feel though, that you weren't in this first wave. I hope and pray, Darling, that if I am right you will never have to go in. I suppose I want too much....

As I listen to the radio here I can't understand why the Germans haven't given more opposition. Either they're pretty weak or they have something up their sleeve.

Well, Darling, for all I know you may be in combat when you receive this. I pray not. But if you are, please be careful and try and take care of yourself as well as is possible in battle.

Georgie just woke up so I'll have to go get him.

With no other writing surface available, an Allied soldier steadies his message home on the hat of a fellow serviceman. (Reproduced by permission of © Hulton Getty/Liaison Agency)

I love you, Sweetheart, and I'll always love you. I miss you terribly and I'll pray for you night and day. Georgie is saying, "Da-da" as loud as he can. Come back to us, Darling.

Yours now and forever, Renee

Esmond, June 9, 1944

My Dearest,

It is a beautiful day here today. It's not too warm and not too cool. I just got through hanging out the baby's washing and as I stand in the yard looking up at the sky in the distant horizon I wondered where my Darling was and if he was all right. Three big four-motored bombers roared over about then. But you'd never know to look at this quiet calm little village that there was a terrible bloody conflict going on over there. You'd never know to look at this little village that there was a sad, heavy-hearted girl living in it, namely me.

I received two letters from you last night, Honey. They were written on Friday and Saturday, the 19th and 20th of May. I'd be very happy about it if the invasion hadn't started. I'm happy about it anyway, of course, but I wish the letter written on or before June 6th would hurry and come through....

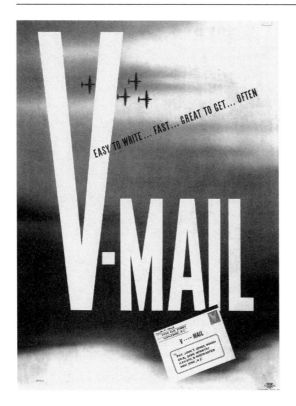

Developed by Kodak, V-Mail (or Victory Mail) was created to send letters to and from service personnel outside the United States. The letters were put on microfilm, which saved shipping space. Service personnel processed the letters, which were printed out and delivered to the recipient. (Library of Congress)

Yours now and always, Renee
P.S. Kisses and hugs from Georgie and me.

Esmond, Aug. 24, 1944

My Dearest,

…I guess when I received the letter from you last night I nearly went hysterical for a minute. I felt so terrible to think that you had been hurt and even as I read your letter I was thanking God that that was all that was the matter, bad as it is.

After I had read your letter over about three times, I called your folks and told them to come up. George, I hate to cry in front of anyone so through will-power I kept myself composed while they were here. But I didn't go to bed until 2:30 and I didn't sleep until about 4:30. I wanted to write to you but I didn't know what to say. My thoughts were all jumbled.…

Well Sweetheart, I'll write again this afternoon or tonight as the mail from Esmond goes out in half an hour and I want this to go as soon as possible.

I hope your leg takes long enough to heal so that Germany will be finished. Don't be like you always are and pretend you can walk on it … before you really can. Please don't Darling.…

So until this afternoon God bless you and keep you and speed your safe return to me.

Yours forever and always, Renee

Esmond, Nov. 25, 1944

My Darling,

It is very cold here today and a thin blanket of snow covers the ground. As I hung out Georgie's wash this a.m. my hands became so cold that I could hardly move them. It made me think about you. Gosh, Honey, how can you shoot when your hands are stiff? I wonder if you'd like me to send you a couple of pairs of gloves? You could wear them when you're not shooting maybe. I don't want to send anything that's foolish, you understand.…

Well, Darling, no mail, no lovin,' no kissin,' no nothin'—so I guess I'll close for today.…

Yours for always, Renee

Esmond, Jan. 10 [?], 1945

My Dearest,

My thoughts tonight are far-reaching. I know my thoughts of you are very tender ones. Perhaps it is the classical music on the radio, or perhaps it's just because it is Saturday night—our night that has prompted me to write tonight (my second letter to you today). Whatever the reason, I know I love you and miss you so terribly tonight.…

[My thoughts take] me back to a cold, windy night in Maryland. We were standing together in the darkness beside a building at Ft. Meade. It was almost time to say our last good-bye—almost time. You ran your fingers through my hair and said, "Whenever I feel cold, Honey, I'll think of you and I'll feel warm." I thought of how you hated to be cold, and I thought that soon you'd be leaving me, and I tried so hard not to cry and I said, "Oh no, don't ever be cold George; don't be cold, Honey." You ran your fingers through my hair again, "I'll be cold lots of times, Renee, but I'll just think of you."

I watched you until you were out of sight in the heavy fog that lay over Ft. Meade that night. There were terrible emotions fighting within me. I wanted to run after you; I wanted to call out your name, and I wanted to cry and cry and cry until I couldn't cry anymore.

Eleanor Roosevelt: In Her Own Words

Eleanor Roosevelt, the first lady of the United States from 1933 to 1945, is probably best remembered for her commitment to the improvement of human rights worldwide. Roosevelt's memoirs include thought-provoking commentary on the World War II era.

On British Prime Minister Winston Churchill: "I shall never cease to be grateful to Mr. Churchill for his leadership during the war [World War II]; his speeches were a tonic to us here in the United States as well as to his own people."

On the Japanese attack on Pearl Harbor: "I think it was steadying to know finally that the die was cast. One could no longer do anything but face the fact that this country [the United States] was in a war."

On the presidency of her husband, Franklin D. Roosevelt: "[The] President of the United States must think first of what he considers the greatest good of the people and the country.… Franklin … always gave thought to what people said, but I have never known anyone less really influenced by others."

On her own role during Roosevelt's presidency: "I think I sometimes acted as a spur, even though the spurring was not always wanted or welcome."

On Roosevelt's death: "Though this was a terrible blow, somehow you had no chance to think of it as a personal sorrow. It was the sorrow of all those to whom this man … had been a symbol of strength and fortitude."

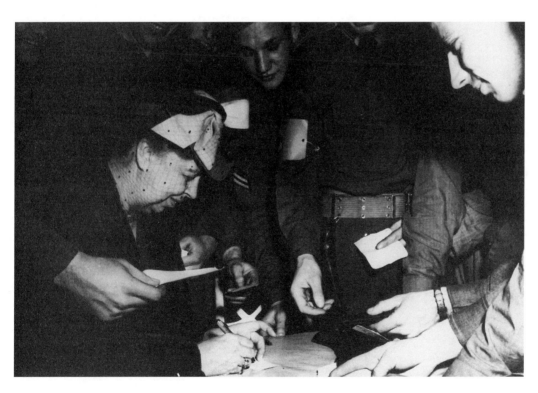

Eleanor Roosevelt signing autographs for U.S. soldiers. (Reproduced by permission of AP/Wide World Photos, Inc.)

WAC members work to sort V-Mail at the Army Post Office in New York City. (Reproduced by permission of AP/Wide World Photos)

Later, the cab driver must have sensed my feelings as he drove me to the train station. He said to me, "Is your husband going overseas?" I looked out into that deep, dense fog where you had gone, and I said, "Tonight may be the last time I will see him for a long, long time."

I hope this letter doesn't make you feel "blue," but just once I had to put my true feelings on paper. There will be more "cheery" letters tomorrow.

All my love, all my life—until that day when God brings you home safely to me.

Renee

Esmond, Jan. 31, 1945

My Darling,

I really feel terrible to think that I'm sitting here in a nice warm, cozy house and you're out in that terrible cold fighting. Yes, I know you're fighting, Darling. I figure that you must have gone into action on January 30th before dawn. Your division has been mentioned in the paper as one of them. Your division has also been mentioned on the radio as one of the "crack" divisions.... They also told about your unit receiving the Presidential Citation....

This lonesomeness for you just gnaws at my heart continually. Oceans of love, Darling, and a kiss on every wave.

God bless you and keep you and speed your safe return to me.

All my love, all my life, Cathie (Litoff and Smith, pp. 84–90)

Aftermath

The war in Europe ended in May 1945 with the surrender of Germany to the Allied forces. Fighting continued in the Pacific until shortly after the United States dropped atomic bombs on the Japanese cities of Hiroshima and Nagasaki in August 1945. Devastated by the bombings, Japan signed formal surrender papers on September 2, bringing the long and bloody war to an official close.

After George's discharge from the army, the Pikes bought a house in Greenville, Rhode Island, opened up a bakery, and had two more children.

SOURCES

Books

Bailey, Ronald H., and the editors of Time-Life Books, *The Home Front: USA,* Time-Life Books (Alexandria, VA), 1978.

Barck, Oscar Theodore, Jr., and Nelson Manfred Blake, *Since 1900: A History of the United States in Our Times,* third edition, Macmillan (New York), 1959.

Brokaw, Tom, *The Greatest Generation,* Random House (New York), 1998.

Freedman, Russell, *Franklin Delano Roosevelt,* Clarion Books (New York), 1990.

Gluck, Sherna, *Rosie the Riveter Revisited: Women, the War, and Social Change,* Twayne (New York), 1987.

Goodwin, Doris Kearns, *No Ordinary Time: Franklin and Eleanor Roosevelt: The Home Front in World War II,* Simon & Schuster (New York), 1994.

Green, Anne Bosanko, *One Woman's War,* Minnesota Historical Society (St. Paul, MN), 1989.

Harris, Mark Jonathan, Franklin Mitchell, and Steven Schechter, editors, *The Homefront:*

America during World War II, G. P. Putnam's Sons (New York), 1984.

Hoopes, Roy, editor, *Americans Remember the Home Front: An Oral Narrative,* Hawthorn Books (New York), 1977, reprinted, 1992.

Litoff, Judy Barrett, and David C. Smith, editors, *Dear Boys: World War II Letters from a Woman Back Home,* University Press of Mississippi (Jackson, MS), 1991.

Litoff, Judy Barrett, and David C. Smith, editors, *Miss You: The World War II Letters of Barbara Wooddall Taylor and Charles E. Taylor,* University of Georgia Press (Athens, GA), 1990.

Litoff, Judy Barrett, and David C. Smith, editors, *Since You Went Away: World War II Letters from American Women on the Home Front,* Oxford University Press (New York/UK), 1991.

Roosevelt, Eleanor, *The Autobiography of Eleanor Roosevelt,* Harper (New York), 1961, reprinted, Da Capo (New York), 1992.

Roosevelt, Eleanor, *This I Remember,* Harper (New York), 1949.

Roosevelt, Franklin Delano, *Nothing to Fear: The Selected Addresses of Franklin Delano Roosevelt, 1932–1945,* edited by B. D. Zevin, Houghton (New York), 1946.

Other

Fly Girls (video), PBS Video, 1999.

Homefront, http://www.homefrontmag.org (August 21, 2000).

Rosie the Riveter and Other Women World War II Heroes, http://www.u.arizona.edu/~kari/rosie.htm (August 21, 2000).

What Did You Do in the War, Grandma?, http://www.stg.brown.edu/projects/WWII_Women/WWTWref.html (August 21, 2000).

Women at War, from the Home Front to the Front Lines (video), Atlas Video, 1989.

Judith Rollins and Odette Harper Hines
"A Black Woman's Wartime Journey"
Excerpt from *All Is Never Said: The Narrative of Odette Harper Hines,* reprinted in *The Nation*

Book published in 1995; article published May 15, 1995

When the United States entered World War II in December 1941, African Americans were experiencing mixed feelings about the struggle against German Nazi racism in Europe. Their own society was segregated, and did not afford them all the rights and opportunities available to white citizens. African Americans, for example, were not benefitting from the unparalleled economic prosperity being generated by the war. Relegated to low-wage, menial jobs, they were unable to escape substandard living conditions. In January 1941 the Brotherhood of Sleeping Car Porters, a union of African American railroad workers, had pressured President Franklin D. Roosevelt into issuing Executive Order 8802. The law forbade discrimination "in defense industries or government because of race, creed, color, or national origin." Roosevelt then formed the federal Fair Employment Practices Commission (FEPC) to handle discrimination complaints. Although the FEPC had limited power to enforce the law, significant numbers of African Americans were being hired in the defense industry. Nevertheless, they were still confined to the least desirable, lowest-paying jobs.

African Americans were also discriminated against in the armed forces, which remained segregated. Racial discrimination had been banned by the Selective Service Act, yet the Navy Department and the War Department (which oversaw the U.S. Army) had ignored the legislation. Military officials claimed that giving African Americans equal status would lower the morale of white soldiers, who then might refuse to fight alongside blacks. They also questioned whether African Americans had the discipline or the bravery required to serve in combat. After the United States entered the war, however, the increasing need for men prompted the U.S. Army to open its ranks to more African Americans.

By the end of 1944, some 700,000 African Americans were serving in the army, but were generally not assigned to combat, infantry, armored, or artillery units, even when they were sent overseas. Instead, they were confined to service units, where they performed maintenance tasks and manual labor. The exceptions were three segregated black combat divisions—the Ninety-Second and Ninety-Third Infantry Divisions and the Second Cavalry Division—and the 761st Tank Battalion, a segregated armored unit. In 1945, near the end of the war, 855 African American women of the 6888th (Central Postal) Battalion of the WAC (Women's Army Corps) were assigned to the European theater, but only after considerable pressure from African American political leaders.

Discrimination was even worse in the navy, where African American sailors on ships were limited to food service jobs; sailors onshore were used as laborers. African American women were not accepted into the Women Appointed for Voluntary Emergency Service (WAVES), the women's naval corps, until 1944, the same year the navy assigned African American seamen to twenty-five "white" ships. At that time, 165,000 African Americans were in the navy. The U.S. Army Air Force created a few all-black squadrons, used primarily to maintain airfields. Nevertheless, members of the segregated Ninety-Ninth Fighter Squadron, known as the Tuskegee Airmen, began flying combat missions overseas in 1943. The unit was an exception, however, and only three other African American squadrons were allowed to enter combat. About 17,000 African Americans were in the Marine Corps in 1944.

Charles Richard Drew (1904–1950)

Charles Richard Drew was an African American surgeon, teacher, and researcher whose work on the storage and shipment of plasma resulted in the saving of hundreds of lives during World War II. The director of the first American Red Cross effort to collect and bank blood on a large scale, Drew is also credited with initiating the use of bloodmobiles.

Drew was born in Washington, D.C., the son of Richard Drew, a carpet layer, and Nora (Burrell) Drew, a schoolteacher. After graduating from Amherst College in 1926, he received a medical degree from McGill University (1933) and a doctorate from Columbia University (1940). In his doctoral dissertation, he proved that liquid plasma lasts longer than whole blood. Because of his discoveries, he was asked to become part of the World War II effort.

German warplanes were bombing British cities regularly by 1940, creating a desperate shortage of blood for treating the wounded. Unable to tend to the growing numbers of casualties on its own, the British Army sought help from the U.S. Blood Transfusion Betterment Association. Drew served as medical supervisor of the association's "Blood for Britain" campaign, which was launched in cooperation with the American Red Cross. Whole blood was found to be unsuitable for use on the battlefield because its month-long shelf life could be extended only if it was frozen and stored in blood banks. Plasma, however, has a longer shelf life, is cheaper to process, can be used by patients of all blood groups, and seldom produces serious adverse reactions in recipients. With Drew's assistance, Britain amassed a large supply of plasma.

In 1941, after the success of "Blood for Britain," Drew became director of the American Red Cross Blood Bank in New York, New York. He was also appointed professor of surgery at Howard University and chief surgeon at Freedmen's Hospital. He was asked to organize a massive blood drive, involving 100,000 donors, for the U.S. Army and Navy. When the military issued a directive to the Red Cross that blood be typed according to the race of the donor, Drew was outraged and challenged the policy as unscientific. Although the government eventually acknowledged the fact that blood types do not differ according to race, the blood donation process remained segregated.

For his contributions to blood plasma research, Drew was awarded the prestigious Spingarn Medal by the National Association for the Advancement of Colored People (NAACP) in 1944. He also received numerous honorary degrees and other awards, yet because he was African American, he was barred from membership in the American College of Surgeons and the American Medical Association. Drew died in an automobile accident in 1950. His portrait hangs in the Clinical Center of the National Institutes of Health, and in 1980 the U.S. Postal Service honored his life and career with a commemorative postage stamp.

Many African Americans became involved in the war effort through the American Red Cross. In 1942 representatives of thirteen African American organizations met with Red Cross officials to discuss ways to increase African American participation in war-related activities at home and overseas. Among the representatives were General Benjamin O. Davis, Jr., commander of the Tuskegee Airmen; Mary McLeod Bethune, founder of Bethune-Cookman College; F. D. Patterson, president of Tuskegee Institute; and Jesse O. Thomas, field secretary of the Urban League. In 1943 Thomas was named special assistant to the director of Domestic Operations of the American Red Cross. Soon,

Nurses of various races served in the American Red Cross, which recruited nurses for the U.S. army and navy during the war. The organization certified most of the 77,800 nurses who served in the war effort. (Library of Congress)

African Americans were being sent overseas to work in clubs and provide social services.

Until January 1942, the blood of African American donors had been completely refused by the U.S. military. Though this policy was rescinded, the Red Cross continued to segregate the blood supplies of whites and African Americans so that blood recipients could request blood from someone of the same race. This behavior was denounced by Charles Richard Drew, prominent African American researcher and surgeon. Drew had supervised the 1940 "Blood for Britain" campaign, the first large-scale American Red Cross blood bank effort, during German bombing raids over England. Drew charged that segregation of blood was unscientific, since there was no evidence to support the claim that blood types differ according to race. When his position was later confirmed by other scientists, the government gradually began relaxing restrictions on donors.

Odette Harper Hines was an African American woman who grew up in the New York City neighborhood of the Bronx and worked in the national office of the National Association for the Advancement of Colored People (NAACP) in the early 1940s. During World War II, she served as a Red Cross worker in Europe. By late 1944, she had been assigned to a Red Cross unit following the Ninety-Second Infantry Division with the Fifth Army in Italy. Hines recounted her experiences in Italy to Judith Rollins in "A Black Woman's Wartime Journey," an excerpt from her oral history *All Is Never Said: The Narrative of Odette Harper Hines.*

The Ninety-Second Infantry Division with which Hines traveled was composed of approximately 12,000 men, most of them African Americans. There were 200 white officers and 600 black officers; the senior commanders were white. All enlisted men were black, and the majority of them were from the South, where they had received only minimal education. For that reason, the soldiers in the division had the lowest grades in rank granted by the army. In August 1944 the first regimental unit of the Ninety-Second joined the Fifth Army, a multinational force under the command of General Mark Clark, at the front in Italy. The Italian campaign had begun on the beaches of Salerno in September 1943, as the Allies tried to drive the Axis powers from northern Italy. The Ninety-Second Division served in Italy for the duration of the war, some soldiers remaining on the front lines for as long as sixty-eight days. During this time, they were subjected to the same racism they had experienced in the United States.

In "A Black Woman's Wartime Journey," Hines tells of the harsh treatment of black soldiers by their white comrades, and describes the white GIs' bigotry toward Italians. She also gives an account of the daily hazards of wartime, which she experienced firsthand when her four-year-old adopted son, Roberto, died in an air raid. The excerpt closes with the final days of the European war in Milan, where Hines witnessed the aftermath of the shootings of deposed Fascist dictator Benito Mussolini and his mistress, Clara Petacci.

"A Black Woman's Wartime Journey"

Where I spent most of my time was in the Red Cross clubs. Beside the work being hard and emotionally difficult, racism was always an issue and often created a good deal of friction in the clubs. Everyone made use of the Red Cross clubs—no matter what the race of the Red Cross workers who ran them. They put the black women in locations where there was a large number of black troops, but the clubs were used by everyone—white Americans, East Indians, British, Brazilians, Moroccans, any Allied troops that were in the area. But, without question, the interaction was most tense between white Americans and black Americans.

The basic problem was the racism of the white American soldiers. In milder forms, it showed in their attitude toward other soldiers of color and even toward the Italians. That's why the dances we organized for the black soldiers were better attended by the local women than the dances we organized for the white soldiers. Yes, the dances were all segregated. But that wasn't my doing. It was because the Army itself was completely segregated. It worked like this: A company commander would call me and ask me to arrange a dance for "our fellows." Now, each company was either all black or all white. So you arranged the dance and you invited the young ladies of the community. So the mothers and aunts of the young ladies would ask, "soldati bianchi?" [white soldiers] or "soldati neri?" [black soldiers] And, if it was a dance for the black soldiers, we'd get an excellent turnout because the black men were so courtly and mannerly. The 92nd Division drew heavily from the South, and these Southern blacks deferred to elderly people and were very polite to all Italians. The white soldiers, on the other hand, had a terrific arrogance toward all Italians. No matter how educated and cultivated the people, many of the white American soldiers regarded them as "wops" and "guineas" and lorded it over them. Many of those whites were people who'd had to make use of outhouses back in the rural South, but they still thought they were superior to the "wops." So the Italian girls preferred to come to the black dances. If it was a bianchi dance, you just couldn't get much of a turnout of the local women.

But it was the black soldiers who got the brunt of the white soldiers' racism. There were arguments daily and fistfights regularly, often right in the Red Cross club. About absolutely anything.

For example, one morning a black soldier came into our tailor's shop and gave his jacket to the Italian tailor to have buttons replaced. Before he'd left, a white soldier brought something in to be repaired. When the Italian tailor told him he'd get to it as soon as he'd put the buttons on the black soldier's jacket, the white soldier got angry. He felt he was entitled to have his clothes done first, that the Italian should set aside the black soldier's jacket. So he grabbed the black soldier's jacket out of the tailor's hands and said, "You don't do that first! Do mine! Let the nigger wait!" And then, of course, the black soldier took issue with that: "What do you mean 'wait?'" And then it gets to be fisticuffs. That kind of thing happened all the time.

Ninety-Second Division Honored for Service

The predominantly African American Ninety-Second Infantry Division served with the U.S. Fifth Army on the front in Italy from August 1944 until the defeat of the Germans on April 30, 1945. During the Italian campaign, the men of the Ninety-Second Division received 12,096 decorations, which included two Distinguished Service Crosses, one Distinguished Service Medal, sixteen Legion of Merit awards, seven Oak-Leaf Clusters to Silver Stars, ninety-five Silver Stars, six Soldier's Medals, 723 Bronze Stars, 1,891 Purple Hearts, and 7,996 combat infantry badges. The division was also awarded 205 commendations.

This nonsense extended to the Red Cross's snack bar, where white soldiers frequently demanded preferential service. It was often, "Serve us. Let the niggers wait." The Italian employees would mutter "pazzo" under their breath, the Italian word for "crazy." And the black soldiers would be ready to fight.

Race wasn't always absent on the battlefields. Some of the black soldiers talked to us very confidentially and told of incidents where they were ordered by their white officers to move forward over an area they were certain was mined. The soldiers felt that such an order came out of the officer's animosity, his belief that black lives were not very valuable. Not only did they refuse to follow his command but they pushed him in front of them: "If anybody is going to get mined in this field, you're going to be the first!" The attitude of the black soldiers in World War II was very different, I think, from in World War I. In World War I, they were really patriotic, trying to prove themselves, getting the Croix de Guerre from the French for valor. But because nothing had improved for blacks in the States between the two wars, these black soldiers didn't have that same spirit. They were there and they were going to fight for their country but many of them didn't feel that they

had a country. And they certainly didn't have any special love for these officers.

I lost Roberto. In the middle of a bombing in Livorno, I lost him. I hadn't seen it coming. He'd been fine. He'd been playing in an office at the club and it was closing time when the bombing began. It was about 9 P.M. Livorno is a port city and our ships were out in the harbor. That's partly why the Germans bombed it so often. I grabbed Roberto and ran to the shelter. It was in the basement of a building near our office. The place was full of people, mainly local people, a few soldiers, no other Red Cross workers. We were packed in there—maybe fifty or seventy-five people. Tense, huddling. A soldier sitting near me had brought his bottle of cognac into the shelter with him. The more the bombs fell, the more he drank. He offered me some, but when I declined he said, "For God's sake, Harper, do something! Here, smoke this." And he handed me a big Cuban cigar. So that's where I smoked my first cigar. But the bombing lasted much longer than the cigar did.

I was sitting on a box with Roberto on my lap. There are the explosions, then silence. And you think that's the end. Then, all of a sudden, there are shattering noises. And you know that a building near you has been blown up. We'd been in there an hour or so when I looked down at Roberto and saw blood coming out of his mouth. He'd been fine and now he was hemorrhaging, and it was only moments until he was gone. I remember the people around me yelling in Italian, "Oh, my God!" Beyond that, I can't remember what I did or said because I was just numb. He'd been fine, I thought. He'd recovered from the T.B., I thought. And then he was dead. Roberto had become my child. And suddenly, he was gone.

The bombing stopped shortly after that. The soldiers took Roberto. I was full of tears. The soldiers took him and they buried his body. In a war, you don't have a formal funeral. You don't have any of that. If a life is over, then it's over. And my only consolation was that Roberto had a little more life than the rest of the folks that'd gotten blown up in that building in Naples.

And then there was Milan. As usual, we traveled piled into the back of a British lorry, sitting on the floor, bouncing along. Any time I was in a lorry, I thought about Roberto because he enjoyed those uncomfortable rides so much. I missed him. Really, I still miss him today. By then, we were all a little weary, but we were buoyed, too, by the progress the Army was making. Before we entered Milan, we'd heard that Mussolini had been captured and killed.

But I never expected that macabre scene I witnessed in the central square of Milan.

We walked in. I can't even remember now where we were walking from—probably some Army installation. But a group of us—some soldiers and I—decided to walk to the square because we had heard Mussolini was there. He was there? Had they put a dead man on display? Worse. They'd hung him and some of his men and his mistress up by their feet. Upside down, as a way of showing the disdain the people felt. His mistress was the only woman in this lineup of bodies and the lower part of her was completely exposed because she'd had a skirt on when she was killed and someone had deliberately torn off her panties. But I saw a local woman run up to the body and tie the skirt around the knees to cover her exposed genitals, this ultimate shame.

The square was mobbed. Thousands of people. Noisy, relieved, glad the despot was dead. They cursed and jeered at Mussolini. The Partisan guards [Fascist militia] tried to keep some kind of order but many of them were shoved out of the way by the local people, who wanted to get close to the hanging bodies. When they did, they fired shots into Mussolini's corpse. I saw one man punch Mussolini in the face. (The bodies were hanging so that their heads were just about on the same level as our heads.) And some people in the mob spit on the faces of the corpses, creating just gobs of spittle that glistened in the sunlight as it dripped off their faces. Some images you can't erase; this is one of them. I can still see glistening spittle hanging like tassels off these upside-down faces. The death of Mussolini might have been progress in the war, but I could feel no joy at this grisly scene. [See photo in Chapter 10.] It reminded me of lynching back home. I just felt sick.

This was late April 1945, and by early May the war was over. (Rollins and Hines, pp. 672–674)

Aftermath

The Ninety-Second Infantry Division fought in Italy until the campaign ended on April 30, 1945, when the Fifth U.S. Army defeated the Germans. The end of the war in Europe came on May 2, 1945, as nearly 1 million German soldiers in northern Italy and western Austria laid down their arms in unconditional surrender. By this time, the Ninety-Second Division's losses totaled 330 killed in action, 2,215 wounded, and 616 missing in action. In late 1946 only 4,000 members of the division returned to the United States, having lost nearly 8,000 of their original 12,000-man force through deaths, discharges, and transfers.

Hines also went home after the war. In 1946 she settled in a small Louisiana town, where she became active in the local civil rights movement.

SOURCES

Books

Goodman, Paul, *Fragment of Victory in Italy: The 92nd Infantry Division in World War II*, Battery Press (Nashville), 1993.

Honey, Maureen, editor, *Bitter Fruit: African American Women in World War II*, University of Missouri Press (Columbia, MO), 1999.

Moore, Brenda L., *To Serve My Country, to Serve My Race: The Story of the Only African American WACs Stationed Overseas during World War II*, New York University Press (New York), 1996.

Rollins, Judith, *All Is Never Said: The Narrative of Odette Harper Hines*, Temple University Press (Philadelphia, PA), 1995.

Periodicals

Rollins, Judith, and Odette Harper Hines, "A Black Woman's Wartime Journey," *The Nation*, May 15, 1995, pp. 672–674.

Stanley, Alessandra, "On a '44 Battlefield, a Salute for a Black Hero," *New York Times*, July 16, 2000, pp. A1, 6.

Other

African Americans—World War II, http://www.louisville.edu/library/ekstrom/govpubs/subjects/blacks/blackww2.html (July 5, 2000).

American Red Cross—African American Exhibit, http://www.redcross.org/hec/aaexhibit/ (July 5, 2000).

Emergency Assistance to Armed Services, http://www.oz.net/ThePages/charity/redcross/service.htm (July 5, 2000).

Lest We Forget.... African Americans in World War II, http://www.coax.net/people/lwf/ww2.htm (August 21, 2000).

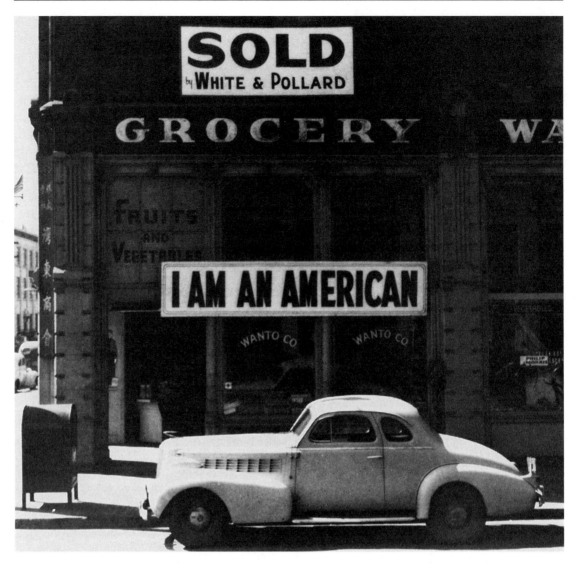

A Japanese American grocer who was forced to sell his grocery store reminds others in the community that he is an American citizen. (National Archives and Records Administration)

PRIMARY SOURCE

Jerry Stanley
Excerpt from *I Am an American: A True Story of Japanese Internment*
Published in 1994

When the American naval base at Pearl Harbor was bombed by Japanese fighter planes on December 7, 1941, there were approximately 125,000 Japanese Americans in the United States, about 95 percent of whom lived in the coastal states of Washington, Oregon, and

California. Japan's surprise attack on U.S. forces plunged the United States into World War II and, within a few months, more than 115,000 Japanese Americans—two-thirds of whom had been born in the United States—were forced to leave their West Coast homes. Americans of Japanese ancestry were easy targets of discrimination because of their distinctive Asian features. "We *looked* like the enemy," noted Japanese American author Yoshiko Uchida in her book *The Invisible Thread.* Japanese Americans were being treated like the enemy who had brought the war home to America's shores.

Fear and racism sparked a wave of hysteria that overwhelmed the nation in the wake of the Pearl Harbor attack. As Japanese forces stormed the Pacific in late 1941 and early 1942, the U.S. government feared that America's western states would be the next site for an enemy invasion. It was widely thought that Japanese Americans living on the West Coast would aid the Japanese if such an attack ever took place. Many Americans called the Japanese soldiers "Japs," but also applied the term to Japanese Americans. Throughout 1942, "No Japs Wanted" signs became familiar across the United States. Newspapers regularly reported stories of Japanese

Issei and Nisei

Some Japanese had emigrated to the United States in the early twentieth century. These immigrants, called issei, were denied U.S. citizenship because of their race. Not until 1952, with the passage of the Immigration and Nationality Act, were the issei allowed to become naturalized citizens. American-born Japanese, called nisei, were the children of the issei and held American citizenship because they were born in the United States.

restaurants being boycotted, businesses being vandalized, and other Japanese American property being destroyed. In February 1942, President Franklin D. Roosevelt signed Executive Order 9066, which allowed the U.S. Army to confine Japanese

Japanese Americans arriving at the Santa Anita Assembly Center. (National Archives and Records Administration)

Japanese Americans on the West Coast were ordered to report to internment camps. Instructions on how to proceed were nailed to trees and buildings. Today, this piece is part of the collection at the Museum of the Pacific War (Chester Nimitz Museum), Fredericksburg, TX, Texas Parks and Wildlife. (Reproduced by permission of Kathleen J. Edgar)

Americans in internment camps. In his book *The Greatest Generation,* broadcast journalist Tom Brokaw refers to the order as "one of the most shameful documents in American history" because of its racist bias. In 1942 America was also at war with Japan's allies, Italy and Germany, but Americans of European ancestry were not treated as harshly as the Asian American population. Brokaw points out: "Italian and German immigrants were picked up and questioned closely" during the frenzy that accompanied America's entry into World War II. "They may have had some uncomfortable moments during the war," he continues, "but they retained all their rights. Not so for the Japanese Americans."

Any American with a Japanese ancestor, even just one Japanese great-grandparent, was affected by Executive Order 9066. Stripped of their rights as U.S. citizens, Japanese Americans were subject to curfews, travel restrictions, illegal searches,

seizure of their property, violation of their right to privacy, and, ultimately, relocation to detention centers. Evacuation orders were issued to Japanese Americans by the U.S. Army in late winter and early spring 1942. The War Relocation Authority (WRA), established by executive order in March, directed the assembly and relocation process. The Japanese Americans had to give up their homes, property, businesses, and even pets. Families were identified by number, not by name, and packed onto buses headed for temporary holding areas called assembly centers. By fall, they were transferred to war relocation camps in Arizona, Arkansas, California, Colorado, Idaho, Oregon, Utah, Washington, and Wyoming.

In the camps, surrounded by barbed wire and armed guards, internees were expected to live in uninsulated shacks furnished only with cots and coal-burning stoves. All other furniture was made by the residents from scrap wood and other materials. Limited amounts of hot water were available in the common bathroom and laundry facilities. Interned Japanese Americans struggled to establish some sense of community by setting up schools, churches, farms, and newspapers. Many Japanese Americans even contributed to the war effort while being interned. For instance, they sent handmade blankets to the American Red Cross and purchased war bonds with the little money they were allotted by the U.S. government.

Children tried to escape the monotony of daily life by engaging in competitive sports, scouting, and arts and crafts, but the relocation process took its toll. Interned children were forced to spend their formative years in an atmosphere of tension, suspicion, and mixed messages. Instructors at camp schools tried to teach the students to be loyal Americans, but their Japanese heritage automatically brought their allegiance into question.

Author Jerry Stanley interviewed Japanese Americans Shiro and Mary Nomuri in 1986 and 1993. He used their firsthand accounts of the internment experience to write *I Am an American: A True Story of Japanese Internment.* Shiro Nomuri was the son of farmers who grew fruits and vegetables first in northern and later in southern California. His parents were issei, meaning though they lived in the United States, they had been born in Japan and were not U.S. citizens. Nomuri, nicknamed Shi, was a high school senior when he and his family were forcibly removed from their home in April 1942. A popular student and gifted athlete,

A Japanese American girl awaiting internment. (National Archives and Records Administration)

he never really thought of himself as anything but an American citizen. Shi was sent to the Manzanar Relocation Center in eastern California. Shi had been about to propose to his girlfriend, Amy Hattori, just before receiving his evacuation notice, but the internment experience altered his plans.

Excerpt from *I Am an American: A True Story of Japanese Internment*

Shi's family was evacuated to Manzanar on April 25, 1942. Earlier that month, Amy and her family had been sent to an assembly center at the Santa Anita racetrack. Built to confine the Japanese until permanent camps were constructed, the assembly centers were created in just twenty-eight days.

African Americans in the U.S. Air Force

Japanese Americans were not the only ethnic group to endure persecution during World War II. The U.S. armed forces were segregated by race, with African Americans separated from whites. African American air corps trainees received instruction at the Sixty-Sixth Air Force Flying School at Alabama's Tuskegee Institute and at Tuskegee's Army Air Field. The all-black Ninety-Ninth Squadron, later incorporated into the 332nd Fighter Group, became known as the Tuskegee Airmen. The exemplary performance of these black fighter pilots in missions over Europe and North Africa led to the slow but eventual desegregation of the U.S. military. More information on the Tuskegee Airmen is available on the following web sites: *The Tuskegee Airmen: The Sky Was the Limit*, www.afroam.org/history/tusk/tuskmain.html (August 21, 2000) and *An Unofficial Tuskegee Airmen Home Page*, www.kent.wednet.edu/KSD/SJ/TuskegeeAirmen/Tuskegee_HomePage.html (August 21, 2000).

Fashioned from fairgrounds, racetracks, and other open areas, they were enclosed by barbed wire and guarded by armed sentries in towers. In April and May 110,723 Japanese were escorted into the assembly centers, while another 6,393 were sent straight to permanent relocation camps.

With 18,000 men, women, and children, Santa Anita was the largest assembly center. The horses had been removed only four days before the Japanese started to arrive. [Some] families were housed in horse stalls heavy with manure dust....

After their baggage and clothes were searched, Amy's family moved into an open barrack, where they slept on mattresses stuffed with straw. The army had used raw lumber in hastily constructing the building. As the boards dried, gaping cracks appeared in the walls and floors. Within three weeks mushrooms were growing through the floor. Every day Amy went to the main gate where the buses unloaded, until she received word that Shi had been sent to Manzanar.

Manzanar was one of ten permanent relocation centers, or internment camps, built and supervised by the War Relocation Authority. It was located just south of the town of Independence, in Inyo County in eastern California. Two more camps were in Arizona, at Gila River and Poston. Temperatures reached 115 degrees at the latter and the Japanese poured water on their canvas cots to keep cool in what they jokingly renamed Camp Roastin'. At Minidoka, in Idaho, the average summer temperature was 110 degrees.... At Amache, in Colorado, and Heart Mountain, in Wyoming, winter temperatures fell to minus thirty degrees. In November 1942 thirty-two Nisei children were arrested for sneaking out of the Heart Mountain camp and sledding on a nearby hill. At Topaz, in Utah, an elderly Issei was shot and killed in broad daylight for walking too close to the camp's fence. An eight-foot barbed wire fence, a thousand armed soldiers, and six tanks guarded the Japanese interned at the Tule Lake camp in California. The other two camps, Rohwer and Jerome, were in the damp, swampy, lowlands of Arkansas, where the most poisonous snakes in North America lived.

Manzanar was modeled after an army base designed to house single men. It was one mile square and divided into thirty-six blocks with twenty-four barracks to a block. Each barrack was twenty feet wide and 120 feet long. Laundry and bathroom facilities were located in the center of each block, each of which had an open mess hall. There was a hospital in one corner of the camp, but the motor pool, warehouses, and administrative offices were located beyond the barbed wire perimeter. At night, searchlights scanned the brush. One of the largest internment camps, Manzanar held more than 10,000 men, women, and children guarded by eight towers with machine guns. No area within the camp was beyond the reach of a soldier's bullet.

When Shi arrived at Manzanar, he was greeted by "a great ball of dirty fog." Because of the dust storm, created by the fierce Manzanar wind, Shi did not see the guard towers with their mounted machine guns or the barbed wire fence until the next day. Visibility was near zero, he recalled. "The strong wind picked up rice-sized sand from the construction areas and pelted the buses like buckshot."

The Death of James H. Wakasa

The barracks at Manzanar. (Reproduced by permission of the Corbis/Hulton-Deutsch Collection)

In *I Am an American,* author Jerry Stanley refers briefly to "an elderly Issei ... shot and killed ... for walking too close to the camp's fence." On April 11, 1943, James H. Wakasa, a sixty-three-year-old issei who more than likely suffered some degree of hearing loss, was shot for walking too close to the barbed-wire fencing that surrounded the Topaz internment camp. Apparently, he failed to acknowledge the armed guard's calls to move away from the fence. According to Michael O. Tunnell and George W. Chilcoat in *The Children of Topaz,* the guard did not fire a warning shot before shooting Wakasa to death.

The buses rolled to a stop in the middle of a firebreak between Blocks 14 and 15....

Soldiers marched the new arrivals to a mess hall, where their numbers were recorded. Guards searched them, seizing anything they considered dangerous—kitchen knives, knitting needles, even hot plates for warming babies' milk. Each internee was issued a cot, an army blanket, and a sack to be filled with straw for a mattress; then families were assigned to a barrack according to size and number of children. Childless couples had to live in an open barrack, with only sheets hung up as partitions to separate them from strangers.... (Stanley, pp. 37–43)

Aftermath

Amy Hattori was transferred to Camp Amache in Colorado later in 1942. Thinking that he might have a chance to see her, Shi enrolled in a sixty-day program that allowed selected Manzanar internees to leave the camp and perform agricultural work in Colorado, Idaho, Utah, and Montana. (Japanese American internees could leave the camps by joining the armed forces or contributing to the war effort through work. Shi had been injured in an accident prior to internment, so was unable to join the military.) Western American farmlands were nearly ruined in the early 1940s because so many farm workers had been drafted into the military.

Interned nisei were asked to help save certain farms in the West by harvesting the remaining crops before they froze. Many agreed because they knew they would be freed from the barbed-wire camps, if only for two months. Shi was accepted into the program but was not sent to Colorado. Instead, he and the rest of his crew ended up in the icy sugar beet fields of Great Falls, Montana. In summer 1943 Shi and Amy were finally able to see each other, but the time apart had changed them both, and realizing that they would not be able to renew their relationship, they broke up. In 1945 Shi married Mary Kageyama, a singer who had gained a reputation as the "Songbird of Manzanar." He later ran his own fish market and grocery.

Japanese Americans Serve Their Country

For a little over a year after Japan attacked Pearl Harbor, nisei, or those born to Japanese immigrants in the United States, were not allowed to join the U.S. armed forces. Then, early in 1943, a segregated "all-nisei" combat unit called the 442nd Regimental Combat Team was formed. Not until January 1944 were Japanese Americans included in the draft, and even then they were forced to make an official declaration of their loyalty to the United States and forsake any allegiance to Japan.

Some of these Japanese American men who fought for their country continued to experience prejudice after they came home from the war. For instance, future U.S. senator Daniel Inouye, a decorated nisei veteran, lost his right hand fighting the Germans in Italy. Nevertheless, he was unable to get his hair cut when he returned from combat overseas. A barber in Oakland, California, told Inouye that he would not "cut Jap hair." No American of Japanese descent was ever accused of a war crime; the ten people who were accused, tried, and convicted of spying for the Japanese during World War II were all white.

Kaun Onodera, a Japanese American veteran who fought with the 442nd Infantry Regiment, holding the Bronze Star he earned in World War II. Many Japanese Americans continued to face prejudice in their home country even after demonstrating valor in combat. (Reproduced by permission of Corbis/Dean Wong)

Amy married Tatsumi Mizutani, a former Manzanar internee, in 1947.

Relocation of Japanese Americans officially ended in December 1944. Evacuees were expected to vacate the camps just as quickly as they had been rounded up and herded into them. They then faced the difficult task of reestablishing themselves in society—rebuilding their lives, their homes, and their jobs. In the postwar years, anti-Japanese sentiment continued to exist in the United States. In 1990, forty-five years after the relocation program ended, President George Bush issued letters of apology to camp survivors along with token redress payments of $20,000 per person.

SOURCES

Books

Brokaw, Tom, *The Greatest Generation,* Random House (New York), 1998.

Daniels, Roger, *Concentration Camps USA: Japanese Americans and World War II,* Holt (New York), 1972.

Davis, Daniel S., *Behind Barbed Wire: The Imprisonment of Japanese Americans during World War II,* Dutton (New York), 1982.

Fremon, David K., *Japanese-American Internment in American History,* Enslow Publishers (Springfield, NJ), 1996.

Myer, Dillon, *Uprooted Americans: The Japanese Americans and the War Relocation Authority during World War II,* University of Arizona Press (Tucson, AZ), 1971.

Stanley, Jerry, *I Am an American: A True Story of Japanese Internment,* Crown (New York), 1994.

Tunnell, Michael O., and George W. Chilcoat, *The Children of Topaz,* Holiday House (New York), 1996.

Uchida Yoshiko, *The Invisible Thread,* J. Messner (New York), 1991.

Uchida, Yoshiko, *Journey Home,* Macmillan (New York), 1978.

Uchida, Yoshiko, *Journey to Topaz,* Scribner (New York), 1971.

Weglyn, Michi, *Years of Infamy: The Untold Story of America's Concentration Camps,* Morrow (New York), 1976.

Other

Camps, http://www.geocities.com/Athens/8420/camps.html (August 21, 2000).

Children of the Camps: The Documentary (video), National Asian American Telecommunications Association, 1999.

Japanese-Americans Internment Camps During World War II, http://www.lib.utah.edu/spc/photo/9066/9066.htm (August 21, 2000).

National Japanese American Historical Society, http://www.nikkeiheritage.org/index.html (August 21, 2000).

Remembering Manzanar, http://www.qnet.com/~earthsun/remember.htm (August 21, 2000).

War Relocation Authority Camps in Arizona, 1942–1946, http://www.library.arizona.edu/images/jpamer/wraintro.html (August 21, 2000).

PRIMARY SOURCE

Constance Bowman and Clara Marie Allen
Excerpts from
Slacks and Calluses: Our Summer in a Bomber Factory
Published in 1944

As the United States prepared for war, production of weaponry, vehicles, aircraft, ships, munitions, and other war supplies increased. Many factories were converted from making consumer products to creating war necessities. Americans found themselves coming out of the Great Depression, which had been marked by high unemployment, into an era of labor shortages, increased wages, and more aggressive production goals. But as the United States entered the war and many men left to fight in the European and Pacific theaters, factory managers found themselves facing a severe labor shortage.

Factories needed to replace and train workers quickly, because the success of the war effort was linked to how well the troops could be supplied with state-of-the-art equipment. The labor crisis began to ease when women entered the work force in record numbers. In addition to performing tra-

ditional women's jobs like secretarial and clerical work, women also took a variety of roles usually held exclusively by men, as welders, lathe operators, riveters, weapons testers, machine operators, drafters, and the like. Some women joined the military or worked with relief organizations such as the American Red Cross.

Women took on their new roles quickly and effectively. In the United States alone, more than 6 million women joined the work force outside the home. That number represented a 50 percent increase. By 1944, about 25 percent of married women worked outside the home. This group was only a part of the 19 million women in the work force during that era, who made up 60 percent of all workers. Nearly 6 million women had taken jobs working in factories, where they assembled aircraft, ships, vehicles, and weapons. The U.S. government encouraged women workers with its

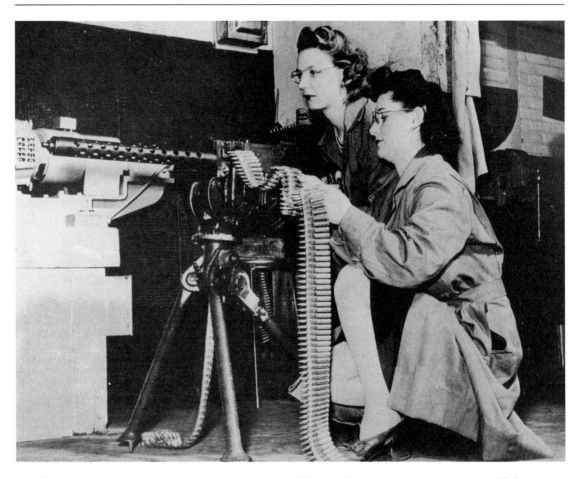

At a Remington Arms plant, two women workers test a .30 caliber machine gun in 1943. Many women filled in at munitions plants while men were off fighting overseas. (Reproduced by permission of AP/Wide World Photos)

"Rosie the Riveter" campaign, showing female factory workers in ads with sleeves pushed up, hair pulled back, and tools in hand. In order to make their jobs easier, factory women often wore trousers, which was controversial because some people believed slacks were improper attire for "ladies." Some of the workers experienced prejudice because they donned men's clothing (i.e., slacks) in order to do their jobs.

Among the many women who went to work in factories were teachers Constance Bowman and Clara Marie Allen. They decided to help the war effort by devoting their summer vacation to building bombers in San Diego, California, in 1943. They detailed their several-month stint making airplanes in *Slacks and Calluses: Our Summer in a Bomber Factory.* Bowman wrote the text while Allen provided the illustrations. They begin the book with the line: "ANYBODY can build bombers—if we could." In their book, the teachers described the hiring process, the duties of their jobs, and the discrimination they experienced when dressed in trousers. Told with a sense of humor, the book provides a unique glimpse into the female factory worker's experience.

Showing the expanded role of women during the war, this poster salutes Women Ordnance Workers. (Reproduced by permission of AP/Wide World Photos)

Slacks and Calluses:
Our Summer in a Bomber Factory

It was bad enough being tired all the time and dirty most of the time, but worst of all the first week was having to go to work in slacks—down Fourth Street where people who knew us acted as if they didn't, or down Third Street where people who didn't know us whistled as if they did.

In war-time San Diego there are just two kinds of women: the ones who go to work in skirts and the ones who go in slacks. The girls who work in slacks are sometimes cleaner and neater than the girls who work in skirts. They usually make more money than their skirted sisters behind the ribbon counter at the Five and Ten or at the controls of the elevator in the bank. But they have to wear slacks. Whether they are dust-bowl mothers buying butter and eggs for the first time, or former dime store clerks making more money than army majors, or war wives who feel they must keep them flying because their husbands are flying them, or school teachers putting in a summer vacation on a war job, they are women who work in slacks instead of skirts.

If you don't think there's a difference, just put on a Consolidated uniform and try to get service in your favorite store, make a reservation at a ticket office, or get information at the post office. Either the clerks have no conception of the position of a customer in a buying and selling economy—or they don't consider aircraft workers customers. Our prize example of such a clerk was the girl behind the counter at the café outside Gate Two, where delectable Double Decker Chocolate Ice Cream Cones were sold every afternoon. The first time we took our money up to the crowded counter, we were terrified by this clerk.

"Whaddayawant?" she snarled out of the edges of her mouth to the people ahead of us, who naturally wanted Double Decker Chocolate Ice Cream Cones too. "Shut up and wait your turn. I'll get to you when I'm good and ready!"

We melted away the first time before the wrath of this creature, who ironically bore the name of Bonnie embroidered on the sleeve of her dirty uniform. The second time we had to wait so long at the counter that we finally returned the quarter we had borrowed for the purchase and went into the plant. And the third time——! The third time we made a special effort to get to the counter in plenty of time. We even brought our own quarter with us that day. I held it up conspicuously for twenty-five minutes while Bonnie scooped up wonderful, drooly cones, four at a time, for the people ahead of us. The last one before she got to us was a special achievement, almost a triple-decker because it had an extra gob on top.

"Well, whaddayawant?" Bonnie growled as we drooled gently.

C.M. said we would like two Double Decker Chocolate Ice Cream Cones, please. The "please" she added hopefully. I held up the quarter.

"No more chocolate ice cream," Bonnie said shortly to us and to the man next to us, "Whaddayawant?" We turned away sadly.

We never did get Double Decker Chocolate Ice Cream Cones, not all summer. I think we were the only people who went through Gate Two who never went through licking beautiful spirals around Double Decker Chocolate Ice Cream Cones.

It was bad enough to have clerks ignore us, to have the members of our own sex scorn us; but what really hurt was the attitude of men. In one way, we were not women at all as far as they were concerned—if having them give us their seats on a crowded bus or stand aside to let us pass or pick up something we dropped meant that we were women. In another way, we were definitely women to them—"skirts" is the old-fashioned term, although it isn't appropriate today. Men lounging on corners looked us over in a way we didn't like, from head to toe with special focus on the "empennage" (a term for the tail assembly of an airplane with obvious implications as a slang word applied to the female form). Men grabbed us and followed us and whistled at us. They called us "Sister" in a most unbrotherly way and "Baby" in a most unfatherly way.

It was a great shock to C.M. and me to find that being a lady depended more upon our clothes than upon ourselves. We had always gone on the theory that the only girls men tried to pick up were the ones who looked as if they could be picked up. Armed in our dignified school-teacher-hood and our glasses, we were content to go unmolested with only a reassuring whistle now and then from a truck driver or a soldier in a jeep. This summer we found out that it

During World War II, women found many new job opportunities, including working on assembly lines building airplanes. (National Archives and Records Administration)

was not our innate dignity that protected us from unwelcome attentions, but our trim suits, big hats, white gloves, and spectator pumps. Clothes, we reflected sadly, make the woman—and some clothes make the man think that he can make the woman. In our dusty blue slacks we were "Sister" and "Baby;" and even our glasses … were no protection.

The Point Loma bus ran from the downtown plaza to Fort Rosecrans, past the civic center, the tuna factory, three aircraft plants, and marine base, the naval training station, the Portuguese settlement, and two residential districts. This route gave it a cosmopolitan passenger list, which included us at two o'clock in the morning.

When the Point Loma bus stopped (if it stopped at all) at Gate Two, it was usually so crowded that getting us in was like putting something you have forgotten into a weekend bag. After we squeezed ourselves in, sailors, soldiers, and marines returning from an evening in town looked up at us sleepily or drunkenly—we couldn't tell the difference. C.M. said charitably that maybe the reason they didn't offer us their seats was that they couldn't stand up, not that they wouldn't. The truth was though that the two

women in skirts who got on at the same time we did were always offered seats. One was a company nurse, all in spotless white which she tried to keep as far as possible from our dusty blue—and that wasn't very far on the Point Loma bus. She always got a seat, but that may have been a tribute to her profession and not to the fact that she wore a skirt. The other woman was an office worker. She squeaked like a talking doll and she chewed gum in a way that in the classroom would have me saying, "Put your gum in the basket, Mary." C.M. and I looked askance at her, but that was nothing to the way she looked at us. She always got a seat; and since it could not be because she was lady-like, beautiful, or intelligent, we decided it must be because she wore a skirt.…

On our first Sunday off, just to reassure ourselves that it was the slacks and not us, we put on our bright linen suits, our highest heels, our whitest gloves, and our biggest hats and went for a ride on the Point Loma bus. And when three sailors, two marines, a soldier, and even two ensigns rose to offer us their seats, we said "Thank you!" as if we were used to such attention—and we took the ensigns' seats! (Bowman and Allen, pp. 67-74)

Aftermath

When Bowman and Allen returned to their teaching jobs at San Diego High School, students were amazed to learn how the instructors had spent their summer vacations. In *Slacks and Calluses*, the teachers note that they worked at the factory out of patriotism, not for the extra income, as the pay was not substantial.

Wanting to share their experiences with others, they compiled their adventures into book form. They had difficulty finding a publisher, especially when an interested editor questioned the authenticity of their story. The editor suspected that the story was created by the factory's publicity department. Bowman and Allen verified the authenticity of their experience, and the book was published in August 1944. It was a hit.

Both Bowman and Allen continued their careers and went on to become mothers. Bowman wrote other books, mainly on the subject of mathematics.

Sources

Books

Bowman, Constance, *Slacks and Calluses: Our Summer in a Bomber Factory,* illustrated by Clara Marie Allen, Smithsonian Institution (Washington, DC), 1999.

Cohen, Stan, *V for Victory: America's Home Front during World War II,* Pictorial Histories Publishing (Missoula, MT), 1991.

Colman, Penny, *Rosie the Riveter: Women Working on the Home Front in World War II,* Crown Publishers (New York), 1995.

Frank, Miriam, Marilyn Ziebarth, and Connie Field, *The Life and Times of Rosie the Riveter: The Story of Three Million Working Women during World War II,* Clarity Educational Productions (Emeryville, CA), 1982.

Gluck, Sherna Berger, project director, *Rosie the Riveter Revisited: Women and the World War II Work Experience,* School of Social and Behavioral Sciences, California State University (Long Beach, CA), 1983.

Army nurses wade ashore in Naples, Italy. (Reproduced by permission of the Corbis/Hulton-Deutsch Collection)

World War II Nurses

Excerpt from *No Time for Fear: Voices of American Military Nurses in World War II*

Edited by Diane Burke Fessler
Published in 1996

During World War II, nearly 60,000 American nurses served in the Army Nurse Corps (ANC). Whether stationed in Europe or in the Pacific, they risked their lives daily, working on or near the front lines; on land, sea, and air transport vehicles; and in field hospitals. As caretakers of wounded soldiers fresh from the battlefield, wartime nurses dealt with every sort of injury imaginable, from gaping chest wounds and massive hemorrhages to amputations and severe burns. Soldiers were disabled by the effects of debilitating diseases, including malaria, a potentially fatal disease transmitted by infected

mosquitoes; beriberi, a serious nutritional disorder caused by inadequate intake of vitamin B_1; and dengue fever, a tropical fever also transmitted by mosquitoes. One of the most difficult aspects of a nurse's job, though, was helping soldiers handle the psychological damage brought on by brutal combat experiences.

World War II nurses, doctors, and medics remained strong in the face of death. Although vulnerable to attack by enemy forces, they shunned danger and set aside their own fears to stay with the patients who needed them. They worked in over-

Nurses served on the front lines all over the world. (Reproduced by permission of the Corbis Corporation [Bellevue])

crowded makeshift hospitals, under less-than-sanitary conditions, often without adequate supplies, and sometimes even without running water or electricity. Nurses tended to hundreds of patients each day, on their feet with little or no rest, working as many as eighty-four hours per week. Nurses treated the troops with equal measures of compassion, courage, and humor. They aided their patients by building morale and helped heal overburdened minds as well as broken bodies. Many soldiers were inspired by the example of the hardworking nurses who cared for them. If the nurses could take the daily horrors of war, then the troops felt they could do the same. Some American nurses were in charge of caring for injured enemy troops at prisoner of war (POW) camps, and had to set aside feelings of intolerance, prejudice, and anger in order to care for ailing members of the German military.

Excerpt from *No Time for Fear: Voices of American Military Nurses in World War II*

Agnes Shurr, U.S. Navy

USS *Solace*

Soon after the attack on Pearl Harbor the [hospital ship] Solace went to the South Pacific, and when we were at an island called Tongatabu [often spelled Tongatapu; an 100-square-mile island in the southwest central Pacific Ocean], an enormous number of warships appeared in the harbor. Everyone knew they were gathering for something, but we nurses were never told what. That was when the battles of the Coral Sea and Midway were being planned early in the war. We went on to Noumea, New Caledonia [capital of the New Caledonia

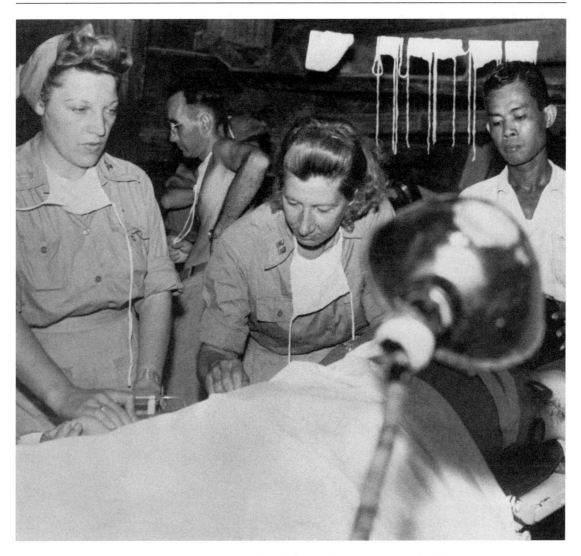

Army nurses attending a wounded soldier. Nurses often had to work in unsanitary and difficult circumstances. (Reproduced by permission of Corbis/Bettmann)

island group, located in the southwest Pacific, east of Australia].

We took on casualties from the Coral Sea battle and from Guadalcanal and that area. Casualties were terribly high. We treated them and took them to hospitals in New Zealand; we made several trips like that. Sometimes we transferred patients from our ship to another at sea.

The time I was most frightened, we were traveling "blackout" with blackout curtains and red lights inside that allowed us to see. Hospital ships usually traveled alone, and at night turned lights on. This time our commanding officer felt that if we were lighted up, the Japanese would see the warships. We were fired on in the middle of the night, and it hit not far from where I was sleeping. I woke up to the sound of the explosion and the "call to stations." Earlier that day we took on a large load of casualties. My ward had litter patients so I prepared them to abandon ship. We waited, and I was sure we were going down. How could anyone fire on us, unless they intended to sink us? After a period of time, the all-clear sounded, and we were never told what happened. In those days everything was secret, and we accepted it.

It wasn't until 1991, when a book was published by one of our hospital men, that I found out the firing was from a "friendly" ship. The book, The USS Solace Was There, states that a U.S. ship asked for identification, then fired across our bow but hit us instead. Our lights were turned on, and it was all over.

Deaths in World War II by Country

Country	Number of Deaths
Soviet Union	20,600,000
China	10,000,000
Germany	6,850,000
Poland	6,123,000
Japan	2,000,000
France	810,000
United States	500,000
Italy	410,000
Great Britain	388,000

Numbers taken from *The History Place: Statistics of World War II, Including the European and Pacific Theaters*, http://www.historyplace.com/worldwar2/timeline/statistics.htm (August 21, 2000).

Margaret Richey Raffa
U.S. Army Air Force
801st Medical Air Evacuation Squadron

We were the first flight nurse squadron to go to the Pacific, landing in New Caledonia in February 1943. We enjoyed the temperature and flowers, which are equally beautiful there all year, but conditions were very primitive. The river behind our tents was our washing machine, and we hung clothes to dry from trees. There were twenty-four nurses, and millions of mosquitoes, all living in one tent. One night during the first week, the tent blew down during a typhoon, and our foot lockers almost floated away.

C-47s [acting as medical evacuation planes] flew to the front with cargo and ammunition, and the nurses rode on top of the cargo. We often had troops going to the forward areas, which was sad for us. They would get into long discussions, feeling that they would probably never come back. The worst part is, some of them didn't.

When we went to Guadalcanal, the plane wouldn't fly directly over the island but flew along the beach, staying low to avoid being spotted by the Japanese. This was emotionally trying for us, not knowing what the landing field would be like. There were no ambulances. The most seriously wounded patients would be on litters, with other wounded in different vehicles. We took off quickly because the Japanese were strafing the field. Our casualties were still in rather bad shape, having had only first aid treatment. They had shrapnel and bullet wounds and injuries from hand grenades, often of the chest,

abdomen, or head. It presented quite a problem, since there were no doctors on board, and we had to rely on our own initiative. We always had to be alert for symptoms of shock and hemorrhage, and from the time we took off until we landed, we had our hands full with these mutilated bodies. One nurse might have twenty-four patients, most of them on litters, for a five hour flight, and in those days we didn't have the [help of] enlisted medical technicians. We felt a tremendous responsibility.

Some patients were taken to the hospital in New Hebrides [a group of islands in the southwest Pacific; now known as Vanuatu] and later evacuated back to the States, but there were general hospitals in New Caledonia where these patients received good enough care to be returned to duty. We took boys back up to the front lines a month or two after we'd brought them out wounded.

The problems were constant. For instance, after we reached [an altitude of] 8,000 feet there was a lack of oxygen, and often we climbed to 10,000 feet because of weather conditions. Then we had to give oxygen to patients continuously. Small oxygen tanks were all we had room for, and patients shared them. We did use alcohol on the tanks between patients, but it wasn't very sanitary. A lot of the planes didn't have heaters, and at 10,000 feet, even in the South Pacific, it was cold.

Sometimes we had to make forced landings because of maintenance or weather or fuel shortages, and this caused big problems for the commanding officers of the airstrips where we landed. Most of the time these fields were under attack by the Japanese, and we'd often have to head for foxholes, with the war being fought right above us. One time I was going to stand at the edge of a foxhole to watch as they went after a Japanese plane. A GI decided to head for the same place and hit my feet, knocking me over. I decided to stay down after that.

Evangeline Bakke Fairall, U.S. Army
250th Station Hospital

I didn't think I'd ever know what it was to be warm after we landed in Liverpool, England, in January 1944. It was night and pouring rain, and we marched in formation carrying our heavy packs to the train. We stood for what seemed like hours while the rain beat a tattoo on our helmets, like rain on a tin roof. The American Red Cross greeted us with doughnuts, hot coffee, and gum after we boarded the train. It was wonderful, for all we'd had to eat was breakfast that day.

These African American army nurses stationed in Australia were among the small number of black women allowed to join the Army Nurse Corps. At war's end, fewer than 500 of the nearly 60,000 nurses in the ANC were black. (Photograph by Frank Prist, Jr. Reproduced by permission of the Corbis Corporation [Bellevue].)

Blackouts were always in effect, so we had to do a lot in complete darkness, often without the aid of even a flashlight to show the way. Utter, pitch-black darkness descended about 4:30 P.M. and lasted until 8:30 A.M. Because of air raids, the blackout system was so complete that you never saw even a crack of light when a door was opened. Almost everyone had black and blue marks on their knees from bumping into signs, posts, and fences.

We soon learned to dread air alerts but had no desire to ignore them. Many a night, and often on consecutive nights, we climbed out of bed, put our trench coats over pajamas, went to the wards to be with the patients, and remained there until the "all clear" came. I remember getting patients up and putting them under each bed. It could be an hour or two hours later before we could return to our tents, cold and hungry. The tents were so cold, and heavy rains kept everything damp. We kept clothes under the pillow at night to keep them dry. The latrine and showers were up a hill, and we had to walk there out in the open, day or night.

We knew D day was coming but weren't supposed to talk about it, even among ourselves in our tents. I'll never forget the morning of D day. Very early we heard thousands of planes going overhead, toward the Continent; just thousands. As the day went on, they were coming back, and we knew fewer were returning. Everyone was quiet.

When we heard our first convoy of battle patients was coming, we were very excited, because we could finally get to do the work we had come to do. We couldn't do enough for that first group of one hundred patients. Then, as more came, the number soon jumped to over a thousand. My first battle patient had a bullet wound in the spine and was paralyzed from the neck down. I'll never forget that first patient.

This went on for several weeks, and everyone was busy. Then we were told we were to be a rehabilitation hospital, caring only for convalescent patients, getting them in shape physically and mentally to return to combat. Our spirits went down with a thud, but we gradually adjusted to the change.

About three months later our status changed again, and we received new battle casualties. We worked like beavers, never enough nurses to go around. One nurse might have responsibility for

Army nurses at a field hospital in France. (National Archives and Records Administration)

nearly two hundred very sick patients, spread over an area of approximately two city blocks. With the aid of competent wardmen, we managed to get along.

We had every type of case, and sometimes those sick, sick patients kept our morale up more than we did their's. They came to us in many ways, sometimes by plane straight from the front. Just before Christmas 1944, we were busier than ever, and I remember one patient telling me, "I was crawling out of my foxhole about 3:30 this afternoon, and here I am." It was about 7:30 in the evening when we were talking, and we were a long way from the combat area.

The number of orthopedic patients was astounding, running well over four hundred. Ward after ward was filled with fractures, almost everyone up in traction, with rarely an ambulatory patient in these wards.

One nurse who was inspecting our hospital really lifted my spirits. She had seen several of these wards with nothing but patients in traction, the nurses wearing raincoats over their uniforms for warmth, and pantlegs wet well above the knees from the heavy, drenching rain. This nurse was amazed that we could care for patients in that situation. I asked, "Have you seen the General Hospital down the

road?" It was made of brick, while we were a tent hospital. They had covered ramps between buildings, and we had to walk through the rain and mud to carry supplies and food to each tent. She said, "I've been there several times, but I like this place. You have to have what it takes to work here."

Myrtle Brethouwer Hoftiezer, U.S. Army 166th General Hospital

[Fall 1944] After training at Camp McCoy [in Wisconsin], we had more to go through at Camp Kilmer where we learned to use the gas masks, were put through an obstacle course, and more marching. I remember the GIs yelling and whistling from every barracks window as we went through the mud and did pushups.

One of my first memories of Europe was the public toilet we had to use in England. We were at the dock, waiting to cross the English Channel, and while I was seated in the "privy," a young man came in and sat next to me. When I told the other nurses about it, they asked what I did. "I passed him the paper," I told them....

It rained and rained at the beginning of our stay in France, and we often had to move the cots we slept in to higher ground to stay dry. We ate outside from our mess kits, often in the rain. Our first hot meal was Cream-of-Wheat, which tastes wonderful in a muddy field in France. We wore the ugly, olive drab underwear for a month without being able to wash it. Our bathtub was a helmet, and the latrine was a dug-out trench with a canvas screen around it, open to the sky and the pilots who flew overhead.

Everyone was excited when we were finally told to make beds and get ready for a trainload of patients. After all, we hadn't come to France to enjoy the winter climate. My strongest memory is how many times a patient would say, "Get to me when you can. He needs you more than I do." I've never taken care of patients like that since. (Fessler, pp. 29–32, 151–153, 204, 210–211)

Aftermath

Nurses from the Army Nurse Corps served in all theaters of World War II, including Asia, the Pacific, and throughout Europe. A total of 201 ANC members had died by the end of the war and sixty-seven had served time as prisoners of war. ANC nurses were also awarded 1,619 medals, citations, and commendations for their war work, including 16 awarded posthumously to nurses killed by enemy fire. In the post-World War II years, nursing increasingly came to be viewed as a serious profession. The skills the ANC nurses had absorbed, along with the G.I. Bill of Rights, which allowed them to pursue further education, gave ANC alumni a valuable head start to pursue their professional goals in the postwar years. The Army Nurse Corps continues to exist, sending nurses around the world to care for American troops.

SOURCES

Books

Ambrose, Stephen E., *Citizen Soldiers: The U.S. Army from the Normandy Beaches to the Bulge to the Surrender of Germany,* Touchstone (New York), 1998.

Archard, Theresa, *G.I. Nightingale: The Story of an American Army Nurse,* W. W. Norton (New York), 1945.

Bellafaire, Judith A., *The Army Nurse Corps: A Commemoration of World War II Service,* U.S. Army Center of Military History, 1993.

Brokaw, Tom, *The Greatest Generation,* Random House (New York), 1998.

Fessler, Diane Burke, *No Time for Fear: Voices of American Military Nurses in World War II,* Michigan State University Press (East Lansing, MI), 1996.

Goolrick, William K., Ogden Tanner, and the editors of Time-Life Books, *The Battle of the Bulge,* Time-Life Books (Alexandria, VA), 1979.

Gruhzit-Hoyt, Olga, *They Also Served: American Women in World War II,* Birch Lane Press (Secaucus, NJ), 1995.

Hardison, Irene, *A Nightingale in the Jungle,* Dorrance (Philadelphia), 1954.

Tomblin, Barbara Brooks, *G.I. Nightingales: The Army Nurse Corps in World War II,* University Press of Kentucky (Lexington, KY), 1996.

Wandry, June, *Bedpan Commando: The Story of a Combat Nurse during World War II,* Elmore Publishing (Elmore, OH), 1989.

Other

The History Place: Statistics of World War II, Including the European and Pacific Theaters, http://www.historyplace.com/worldwar2/timeline/statistics.htm (August 21, 2000).

Welcome to Army Nurse Corps History, http://www.army.mil/cmh-pg/anc/anchhome.html (August 21, 2000).

20

Art, Entertainment, and Propaganda

During World War II, the Allied and Axis nations used various methods to convince soldiers and civilians that they were engaged in a noble cause. The theory was that soldiers would perform better in battle if they thought they were protecting their countries and families against a cruel enemy, that they had been forced to go to war in order to defend themselves, and that the world would be changed for the better as a result of the conflict.

The nature of the war made it essential for governments to rally civilians around these same causes, as victory depended on devoting all resources to the conflict. The most obvious example of devoting resources concerned jobs. Millions of women in the United States and Europe worked outside the home for the first time. Both men and women engaged in labor, such as factory work, that was difficult, dirty, noisy, and often dangerous. Government officials knew, however, that workers would accept these conditions if they believed they were helping to preserve their country's freedom. The same was true for other hardships and inconveniences brought on by the war, such as crowded housing, product shortages, and separation from loved ones serving in the armed forces. In countries like Great Britain and Germany, civilians also had to endure deadly air raids. All these factors became easier to tolerate when perceived as part of a just war.

Propaganda—information usually officially communicated by a government in order to shape the opinions of large numbers of people—was a term originally applied to both true and false information. By the outbreak of World War II, however, propaganda had generally come to mean a one-sided or distorted statement, or even an outright lie. Enemy communications were always described as "propaganda," while one's own side offered "information" or "news." The governments of countries occupied by Germany did not control the information that people received. Instead, there were two opposite sets of information, one from the Germans and one from the Allies, and information came from various resistance movements as well.

The Allies reached people in occupied countries mainly by radio, especially with the programs of the BBC, or British Broadcasting Corporation, which were broadcast in twenty-three languages. Millions of Europeans listened every night even though they risked severe punishment by the Germans if they were caught. The BBC gained a reputation for broadcasting truthful information because it rarely exaggerated Allied victories or downplayed Allied losses. The propaganda aired on the BBC did not need to discuss the purpose of the war, as most of the BBC audience in German-occupied countries simply wanted to be rid of the Nazis and gain their independence. Instead, the

V for Victory

The British used the capital letter "V" as a symbol for "victory." Throughout German-occupied Europe, a hastily painted "V" on a wall was used to show defiance of the Germans and faith that the Allies would eventually win the war. People everywhere flashed the "V" sign by holding up their first two fingers, a gesture made famous by British Prime Minister Winston Churchill. The question for the BBC became how it could use the "V-for-victory" symbol on the radio in broadcasts to occupied Europe. In Morse code, the letter "V" is represented by three dots and a dash, and someone realized that the opening four notes of Beethoven's Fifth Symphony fit this pattern. Soon, these four notes were heard whenever the BBC broadcast to Europe, becoming the best-known use of classical music in the war.

BBC's message was that the war was continuing, that Germany would eventually be defeated, and that those who cooperated with the Germans would later pay for their actions.

Pro-Nazi and Anti-Allied Propaganda

At the beginning of World War II, German political and military leaders were certain that the conflict would be brief, so they did not try actively to win people in occupied countries over to their side. Instead, they simply wanted to convince them that since a German victory was inevitable, there was no point in resistance. When it became clear that the war would be lengthy, however, some Germans wished to convince citizens of occupied countries to promote the Nazi cause. Therefore, they released propaganda depicting a "New Order" and a united Europe in which Germany protected European civilization against the Communist Soviet Union. Nazi posters featured a handsome German soldier protecting a helpless child. A few people responded to these ideas, as well as to German propaganda blaming the war on the Jews, but for the most part, the Nazis' campaign came too late to have much effect. Yet even more skillful propaganda could not have overcome the reality of German occupation. Germany was seizing the wealth and natural resources of conquered countries, and no matter what was depicted on posters, hungry people blamed the Germans for their plight. They were being forced to work harder for longer hours and less pay, they could not speak freely, they were not permitted to read what they wished, and they could not vote.

Of equal importance to domestic propaganda was demoralization of the enemy. Both the Axis and Allied powers utilized radio broadcasts, leaflets dropped from planes, and other methods to convince enemy troops and civilians that their side would be defeated. Advocates of psychological warfare claimed it would make a major difference in the war, but most historians now believe such efforts had very little impact. One example was Germany's use of pro-Nazi Englishman William Joyce. For years, Joyce made broadcasts on German radio, telling British troops that they were losing the war, that they were fighting for no reason, and that their leaders were getting rich while they died. The soldiers referred to him as "Lord Haw Haw" because of his exaggerated upper-class accent. They regarded him as entertainment, and there is no evidence that anyone ever believed his broadcasts. Although Joyce failed as a propagandist, the British government tried Joyce for treason and hanged him after the war.

Similarly, American troops in Europe listened to an all-night program on German radio that played the latest jazz and swing recordings. The host of the show was Mildred Gillars, an American who had worked as an actress in prewar Germany, but American troops referred to her as "Axis Sally." Between records, Sally would talk about the loneliness the GIs must be suffering, and how their wives and girlfriends back home were probably cheating on them. Sometimes she read the serial numbers of American soldiers who had been killed or captured. In one of her programs, aimed at soldiers preparing for the Allied invasion of France, she and other actors dramatized the death and horror that awaited the GIs on the battlefield. The goal of these statements was to demoralize the listening Allied troops, yet the soldiers listened to Sally's shows for the music, and apparently ignored her anti-American messages. Nevertheless, Gillars was one of only twelve Americans convicted of treason for their actions during World War II; sentenced to ten to thirty years in prison, she was paroled after serving twelve years.

Another radio personality convicted of treason was Iva Toguri, an American-born woman whose parents were Japanese. Toguri was the most notorious of several women all known as "Tokyo Rose," who broadcast to Allied troops on Japanese radio. Like Axis Sally, Tokyo Rose mixed popular music with banter meant to demoralize soldiers; similarly, soldiers ignored her efforts in favor of the music. Toguri served six years of a seven-year prison sentence and was later pardoned.

German Propaganda in Germany: Radio and Film

Although German propaganda failed to intimidate Allied troops or people living in occupied Europe, it was much more effective when directed at Germans. Propaganda had been an important tool for the Nazis both before and after Adolf Hitler came to power in 1933, largely because of strategies created by Joseph Goebbels, Minister of Public Enlightenment and Propaganda. Expanding on the concept of the "big lie" that Hitler had introduced in *Mein Kampf*, Goebbels began repeating the same outlandish statements over and over until people believed them. He arranged mammoth spectacles that coordinated parading Nazi soldiers, banners, posters, speeches, and songs to mesmerize the German public into embracing the Nazi philosophy. In the early years of the Third Reich, Goebbels had also organized the Nazi book burnings, in which works written by Jewish authors and Nazi opponents were publicly thrown onto bonfires. Goebbels's principal contribution, however, was the use of two relatively new forms of media, radio and film, to promote Nazism. An increasingly powerful member of the government, Goebbels controlled all radio broadcasts and film production in Germany. By the beginning of the war, an estimated 70 percent of German households owned a radio. Never before had a government been able to reach such a large proportion of its country's citizens at one time.

Goebbels also understood the importance of film. Movie theaters in Germany never closed during the war, even after 1943, when the government ordered that museums, concert halls, and sports arenas be shut down. In cities where Allied bombing destroyed the available theaters, the govern-

"Axis Sally" entertaining reporters before her trial for treason. (Reproduced by permission of AP/Wide World Photos)

ment arranged special outdoor showings. Some of the films Goebbels sponsored prior to the war have remained famous. Chief among these were the films of Leni Riefenstahl, a young actress turned movie director who is best known for *Triumph of the Will*, a documentary celebrating a Nazi party rally in Nuremberg in 1934. Riefenstahl filmed Nazis marching en masse in intricate formations at torchlight ceremonies; the images in the film are so riveting that even today audiences are stirred and disturbed by them. Riefenstahl's film on the 1936 Berlin Olympic Games glorified youth, strength, and athletic excellence, as well as Hitler and the Nazis. Almost every documentary film covering sporting competitions, especially later Olympic Games, was strongly influenced by Riefenstahl.

Propaganda as Entertainment

Goebbels knew that artistic works were often the most effective propaganda, and he understood that most people did not want to be constantly reminded of the war. He therefore tried to cloak his political message in the form of entertainment. His propaganda machine achieved a major success with *Jud Süss* ("*The Jew Süss*"), an alleged-

Film director Leni Riefenstahl created *Triumph of the Will,* a documentary that celebrated the Nazi party and its leader Adolf Hitler. (Reproduced by permission of the Kobal Collection)

ly historical movie intended to stir up anti-Semitism. The film tells the story of a Jew who became an important adviser to a German duke in the early eighteenth century, and portrays Süss as a rapist who plots with fellow Jews to take over a city. The film was an apparent success, with German audiences accepting it as drama rather than propaganda. The Nazis showed *Jud Süss* throughout occupied Europe in an attempt to gain support for their anti-Jewish policies; the film was also was shown to all concentration camp guards. Another historical drama was the epic *Kolberg,* a project that Goebbels insisted on completing in the face of increasingly scarce resources. Thousands of actual German soldiers (180,000, according to the director) were used in the film, which was made in the final years of the war. Set in 1807, *Kolberg* tells the story of German townspeople who resist the army of Emperor Napoleon Bonaparte of France until the last-minute arrival of German forces saves the town. Goebbels hoped the film would inspire Germans to resist the invading Allies. *Kolberg* opened in bomb-devastat-

ed Berlin at the end of January 1945, just as the Allied armies were preparing to advance into the heart of Germany.

Other popular German films of the period were made purely for entertainment. The most successful—in fact, the most successful German film ever made up to that time—was *Die Grosse Liebe* (*"The Great Love"*), which was released in 1942 and seen by 28 million people, more than one-third of the population. *Die Grosse Liebe* portrayed the stormy romance and marriage, against a war backdrop, of a German singer, played by Swedish star Zarah Leander, and an air force fighter pilot. Leander sang "I Know Someday a Miracle Will Happen" in the film, a song which became a kind of theme for German civilians during the war years. Another popular hit movie, made in 1943, was *Baron Münchhausen,* a color film depicting the baron's fantastic adventures, such as a balloon trip to the moon.

Governments did not rely simply on films, radio, and other popular art forms to build support for the war. They also used literary and musical classics to their advantage. For instance, the Soviets distributed 500,000 copies of Leo Tolstoy's great nineteenth-century novel *War and Peace* to the starving and freezing citizens of Leningrad as the Germans surrounded the city. *War and Peace* chronicles the Russian people's resistance to and eventual defeat of Emperor Napoleon Bonaparte in 1812.

The ordeal of the people of Leningrad was also the inspiration for the best-known piece of classical music written during World War II, the Seventh Symphony, or the Leningrad Symphony, by Russian composer Dmitry Shostakovich. Composed in the German-besieged city in 1941 and first performed the following year, the work soon became the world's most widely played piece of classical music, both in concerts and on the radio. Although today the Seventh Symphony is not regarded as one of Shostakovich's better compositions, at the time it moved listeners with its dramatic and stirring melodies. For the Soviets, it was a musical tribute to the heroism of Leningrad's citizens, and in the United States, the piece was a way of showing support for, and a sense of unity with, America's Soviet ally. The Nazis also used classical music to stress patriotism, especially the operas of nineteenth-century composer Richard Wagner, who often based his plots on German folktales or the mythology of ancient Germanic tribes. For these

Documentaries, Newsreels, and Censorship

Once World War II erupted, the German government produced a series of full-length documentary films featuring the German army's early successes. Among them was *Victory in the West,* which focused on the defeat of France. The army even created propaganda companies that went into combat with regular troops and filmed each campaign. In addition, eighty "war artists" painted "combat art."

Like other countries involved in the war, Germany produced newsreels—short films about current events that were shown in theaters along with the main films. In the United States, newsreels were made by private companies, yet these films still reported only "official" government war news. Information about war zones and battles was completely controlled by the military.

Government censorship of news affected all war reporting, not just films. Stories sent to home bureaus by overseas newspaper reporters had to be read and cleared by military censors before being printed. Certain information, such as the location of Allied troops or ships, could not be revealed without endangering lives or equipment. Military censors also banned any stories that might damage the morale of soldiers or civilians. For example, during the first several years of the war, American newspapers and magazines could not publish a photograph of a dead American soldier. No one denied that Americans were dying in combat, but government officials felt that the sight of dead bodies would diminish American support for the war.

reasons, and because Wagner had been strongly prejudiced against Jews, his music was a particular favorite of Hitler.

America Produces Nonfiction Films

The American film industry was by far the biggest in the world, both before and during World War II, and in 1940 it produced more than 500 feature films. During the war, Hollywood offered free showings of all films to troops overseas and sailors aboard ships; in fact, it was the only industry that gave its products to the government. Yet this generosity did not reduce profits: Americans were going to the movies in record numbers. In 1944, when the U.S. population was approximately 130 million, nearly 100 million tickets were sold every week in the United States.

Before America entered the war, the film industry had formed the Motion Picture Committee Cooperating for National Defense to distribute and show, without charge, national defense films made by the government, which had various purposes. Recruitment films were made by different

branches of the armed services to persuade people to enlist. *Women in Defense,* which was written by first lady Eleanor Roosevelt and narrated by actress Katharine Hepburn, encouraged women to work in defense factories or to join the armed forces.

After Japan attacked Pearl Harbor in December 1941 and the United States entered the war, the government produced documentaries on various aspects of the conflict. Typical examples included *The Fighting Lady* (the "life story" of an aircraft carrier), *With the Marines at Tarawa,* and *The Liberation of Rome.* One important American documentary series was *Why We Fight.* Produced by the U.S. Army Signal Corps, the seven films were conceived by famed Hollywood director Frank Capra. Capra himself directed *Prelude to War,* the first film in the series. The goal of the series was to explain the events in Europe and Asia leading up to World War II; the types of governments the United States was fighting against; and the purposes of the conflict. Originally, its audience was supposed to be limited to members of the armed forces, but when President Franklin D. Roosevelt saw *Prelude to War* at a special White House

Claude Rains (in dark uniform), Humphrey Bogart (in trenchcoat), and Ingrid Bergman in a scene from the 1942 film *Casablanca*. (Reproduced by permission of AP/Wide World Photos)

screening, he declared that "every man, woman, and child must see this film." Despite heavy promotion, these films were not box-office favorites, though American soldiers apparently liked them more than most war films.

Hollywood and the Buildup to War

The majority of American films produced during World War II were fiction, intended purely for entertainment and profit. In 1940 about 95 percent of Hollywood films did not involve political themes or the war. This was partially due to the fact that the studios earned a significant part of their profits in foreign countries, where, like today, American movies were quite popular. Fear of offending these foreign governments, which might strike back by banning a studio's films, was one reason American movies usually did not address controversial world issues. Even so, a few films made prior to World War II dealt with the rising threat of Nazism. One of the most important was *Confessions of a Nazi Spy*, released early in 1939 and directed by German-born Anatole Litvak. A fictionalized version of the activities of a real German spy ring operating in the United States, *Confessions of a Nazi Spy* was the first

openly anti-Nazi American film. It was a major commercial success, but was banned in Germany and countries that either supported Germany or did not want to offend the Nazis. Alfred Hitchcock's *The Lady Vanishes* (1938) was somewhat more typical, and although it was a British film, it was extremely popular in the United States. It portrayed villainous characters from an undisclosed locale, apparently in Central Europe. The film's message—that ignoring evil in foreign countries will never provide safety—clearly refers to Germany.

During the more than two years between the beginning of the war and the attack on Pearl Harbor, many Hollywood films seemed to be aimed at winning support for U.S. entry into the conflict. *Sergeant York* was based on the life of Alvin York, a soldier who became America's greatest war hero fighting the Germans in 1918 during World War I. The story revolves around York's early opposition to serving in the army because of his pacifist religious beliefs. He is finally convinced that going to war is sometimes the only way to prevent more killing. An American audience seeing *Sergeant York* when it was released in 1941 understood that this message referred to World War II.

An even more obvious statement was made by *A Yank in the RAF*, which told the story of an American pilot who joined Britain's Royal Air Force to fight the Nazis. The film was made by Twentieth Century-Fox, whose top executive, Darryl F. Zanuck, strongly favored American entry into the war. *A Yank in the RAF* illustrates one of the most common themes of Hollywood films of the period: the creation of sympathy for countries fighting Germany, especially Great Britain, as a way of building support for the war. This theme continued even after the United States entered the conflict.

Perhaps the most effective, and certainly the most popular, pro-British movie was *Mrs. Miniver* (1942), which won five Academy Awards, including one for best picture. Set at the beginning of World War II, *Mrs. Miniver* tells the story of an average English middle-class family. (The family probably would have seemed somewhat wealthier than average to American audiences since they have two live-in servants.) The film shows the increasing hardships and dangers caused by the war, including German bombing of the village where the family lives. The title character, played by Academy Award–winning actress Greer Garson, displays quiet strength and determination, even capturing a downed German pilot. Each person in the village puts aside selfish concerns in an increasing sense of national unity. The final scene takes place in the badly damaged village church after a heavy air raid kills several people, including a lovable old stationmaster, a choirboy, and the beautiful young bride (played by Teresa Wright, another Academy Award winner) of the Minivers' son. The minister explains that the victims are all part of the struggle because it is a "people's war. It is our war. We *are* the fighters."

Mrs. Miniver was held up as an example by the Office of War Information (OWI), the U.S. government agency created in June 1942 to oversee American propaganda efforts. Unlike military censors, who concentrated on keeping information secret to avoid undermining military and civilian morale, the OWI was more concerned with communicating certain messages—like the one in *Mrs. Miniver*—through movies, books, and newspapers. Many American films portrayed the activities of resistance movements in Europe, often in unrealistic ways. The French resistance was a popular theme in such films as *Casablanca* (1942), which starred Humphrey Bogart and Ingrid Bergman. *Casablanca* also included one of Hollywood's favorite character types during the war—the American (Bogart)

A scene from the 1941 film *Sergeant York,* one of many Hollywood films that seemed to be aimed at winning support for U.S. entry into the war. (Reproduced by permission of the Kobal Collection)

who does not want to get involved but who soon realizes he must put aside his personal concerns and join others to fight the Nazis.

German, Japanese, and Russian Characters in U.S. Films

In the single year beginning in September 1942, Hollywood released five movies depicting the resistance in Norway. One of those films, *The Moon Is Down,* was based on a book and play by leading American writer John Steinbeck. Hollywood bought the rights to adapt the work for $300,000, a record amount at the time. Though it was expected to be a major hit, and prints were even dropped by parachute into German-occupied Norway, *The Moon Is Down* was not a blockbuster, probably because audiences had grown tired of seeing gloomy war movies. Nevertheless, it did create a controversy with the portrayal of its protagonist, a German colonel in charge of a Norwegian town, as not a violent brute but instead a complicated man partly motivated by a desire to be respected and liked. Although it was unusual to depict a German officer in this way, the "good German" was actually a common character in many American films, especially those set before the war. Such characterizations were based on the belief

Jews and Hollywood

Many film historians suggest that Hollywood's hesitation to produce anti-Nazi films may be attributed to the fact that a number of industry leaders were Jews. While this may seem surprising, in light of the Nazis' actions toward European Jews, Jews in Hollywood feared they would be accused of trying to catapult the United States into the war against Germany. Men like the Warner brothers were worried that they would be accused of putting their feelings as Jews ahead of their duties as Americans, and that this sentiment would in turn stir up anti-Jewish prejudice in America. Similar accusations were made against Darryl F. Zanuck, head of Twentieth Century-Fox, for producing *A Yank in the RAF*; unlike other important producers, however, Zanuck was not Jewish. Even when Hollywood did make anti-Nazi films—in fact, even after the United States was at war with Germany and anti-Nazi films were expected—they tended to avoid any mention of the word "Jew." Although anyone who read a newspaper knew about the Nazis' hatred of Jews, the American film industry almost always played down that angle of the conflict during the war.

that the average German was not intrinsically evil but had fallen under the spell of the Nazis. This phenomenon is not surprising, considering that many Germans, including writers, directors, and actors, had fled Hitler's regime to find work in Hollywood. One German director, Fritz Lang, had even been offered the top job in the German film industry by Goebbels in 1933, but instead chose to go to Hollywood.

The favorable portrayal of the enemy did not apply to Japanese characters in American films. Almost without exception, Japanese were depicted as sneaky, dishonest savages who enjoyed inflicting pain. Most historians believe this can be explained by anti-Japanese racism, but whether Hollywood helped create this sentiment or simply reflected the way people already felt is impossible to know.

It was not always easy to depict even an ally in an approving way. For many years before the war, the United States had been on unfriendly terms with the Soviet Union. At the beginning of World War II, the Soviet Union signed a treaty with Nazi Germany, which outraged many Americans, and then attacked neighboring Finland, which fought back bravely and won the support of most Americans. After Germany invaded the Soviet Union, however, the heaviest burden of fighting Hitler's armies was placed on the Russians. The United States sent huge amounts of supplies to the Soviets, a policy that required the support of the American public. In 1942, at President Franklin D. Roosevelt's direct request, Warner Brothers studio made a film version of Joseph E. Davies's book *Mission to Moscow*. Davies had been the American ambassador to the Soviet Union from 1936 to 1938, and both the book and the movie portray the Soviet Union and its leader, Joseph Stalin, as great champions of democracy. Stalin was in fact a brutal dictator and the film's defense of his methods became an embarrassment after the war. Some pro-Soviet films were embarrassing even at the time. For instance, *Song of Russia* uses a love story between a famous American orchestra conductor and a young Russian pianist to depict a happy country dominated by song and dance until the German invasion turns the entire population into heroic fighters for freedom. Some audiences actually laughed out loud at the movie. Other films made their point in less obvious ways. In *Action in the North Atlantic,* American merchant seamen risk their lives by sailing through submarine-infested waters to bring desperately needed supplies to Russia. By the end of the film, when Soviet planes appear overhead, the American sailors refer to them as "ours."

Hollywood after Pearl Harbor

Throughout the World War II era, Hollywood never stopped making musicals, romantic comedies, and other films that had nothing to do with the war. Some of these were far more popular than the war-related pictures, especially among soldiers, who considered most combat films unrealistic. Still, after the United States entered the war, Holly-

Bob Hope, Frances Langford, Tony Romano, and Jerry Colona performed many USO Camp Shows in the South Pacific for Allied troops. (Reproduced by permission of AP/Wide World Photos)

wood began turning out hundreds of features with war themes. A new Tarzan movie had Nazis for the enemy, and Sherlock Holmes hunted German spies in modern London. Even Donald Duck collected scrap metal for the war. The earliest combat film was *Wake Island*, released in September 1942, less than nine months after the events it portrayed. Dozens of others depicted specific battles or particular branches of the armed services. *Action in the North Atlantic* paid tribute to the bravery and sacrifice of the sailors of the merchant marine. *The Fighting Seabees* was about navy construction companies that built airfields on Pacific islands, often while fighting was still going on. *Destination Tokyo* concerned submarines, *Sahara* and *The Immortal Sergeant* depicted the desert battles of North Africa, and *The Purple Heart* and *Thirty Seconds over Tokyo* were both about Jimmy Doolittle's American bombing raid on Tokyo in April 1942. *Guadalcanal Diary,* released in late 1943, was adapted from the best-selling book of the same title by Richard Tregaskis, a twenty-six-year-old reporter who accompanied the Marines on Guadalcanal in August and September 1942. The book was based on notes Tregaskis kept for daily reports, but the film included invented scenes not found in the book. Although the military censored Tregaskis's criticisms of the navy's failure to provide adequate supplies to the marines, the book and the movie both seemed to provide a realistic picture of the day-to-day experiences of combat troops.

Entertainment Overseas: The USO

The home front was not the only arena in need of entertainment during World War II. As the United States prepared for war, citizens considered ways to keep morale high among American servicemen and servicewomen. One way was to see that troops were entertained while on leave. Through entertainment—which included dances, comedy performances, concerts, and the like—soldiers could forget, momentarily, about the grim realities of war. In an effort to create a program to provide such entertainment, President Franklin D. Roosevelt asked various organizations for help. Together, six organizations worked to form the United Service Organizations, most commonly known as the USO. The organizations that worked on the project were the National Catholic Community Service, National Jewish Welfare Board, Salvation Army, Traveler's Aid Association, Young Men's Christian Association (YMCA), and Young Women's Christian Association (YWCA).

The USO came into being in February 1941. Staffed mainly by volunteers, the organization grew quickly. By the end of the war, the USO pro-

Dressed in USO uniforms, entertainers Frank Sinatra and Phil Silvers head to their next performance. (Reproduced by permission of AP/Wide World Photos)

Helping the USO entertain the troops, comedians Bud Abbott and Lou Costello bring smiles to the faces of servicemen at the Stage Door Canteen. (Reproduced by permission of AP/Wide World Photos)

vided entertainment for soldiers on leave, at military bases, and hospitals, not only in the United States but also abroad. The overseas programs were a hit with servicemen who longed for a "touch of home." Entertainers like Bob Hope and Frances Langford ventured overseas to present "USO Camp Shows." Hope, who began his association with the USO in its early days, continued to

A group of women war correspondents near the battlefront. (Reproduced by permission of the Corbis Corporation [Bellevue])

devote time and energy to the group through the 1990s, performing for other soldiers in later wars. He even penned an account of his experiences during wartime, including visiting the wounded and sick in hospitals (*Don't Shoot, It's Only Me: Bob Hope's Comedy History of the United States,* 1990).

During World War II, other famous movie stars like Marlene Dietrich, Frank Sinatra, Phil Silvers, and the duo Bud Abbott and Lou Costello also gave their time to entertain the troops. Actress and singer Lena Horne was especially popular with African American servicemen. The USO spon-

sored whole Broadway casts to put on plays for servicemen. Opera singer Lily Pons traveled more than 100,000 miles on the USO performing circuit during the war. There were literally thousands of other individuals who volunteered to help.

Although often associated with World War II, the USO remained active in assisting military personnel after the war. A private nonprofit agency funded entirely by private donations, it is still devoted to the morale and the social and spiritual welfare of servicemen and servicewomen in all branches of the military.

Ernie Pyle working on a column. (Reproduced by permission of Archive Photos, Inc.)

War Correspondents

Many well-known journalists brought the war home to Americans by reporting on action overseas. For the first time, many of these correspondents were women, but they were not readily accepted and had to fight against the prejudices of not only top military and naval officers (whose permission was necessary to enter a war zone), but also their own editors and publishers. One of the most successful American correspondents in prewar Nazi Germany was Sigrid Schultz of the *Chicago Tribune,* who sometimes published under a false name so that the Nazis would not throw her out of the country. Her articles gave American readers an idea of the ambitions and goals of the German leaders—who were none too pleased. Hermann Göring, one of the top Nazi officials, called Schultz the "dragon lady from Chicago." Schultz continued to report from Berlin during the first year of the war, but after she left Germany for a visit home in January 1941, the Nazis refused to allow her to return. By reporting on war plans and preparations and covering war news from Berlin, Schultz had helped open the door for other women reporters, though she never traveled with armies, sailed on warships, or reported on battles as an eyewitness.

Despite opposition, many women were soon doing just those things. Helen Kirkpatrick, the London correspondent for the *Chicago Daily News,* covered the Blitz in London while riding through the city in ambulances and fire trucks. She later accompanied Allied troops in North Africa, Italy, France, and Germany. She wrote one famous eyewitness account of gunfire erupting inside Notre Dame Cathedral in Paris during a service to celebrate the liberation of the French capital. Kirkpatrick became so popular that the *Daily News* featured her in promotions, such as the placement of her picture on the sides of Chicago buses. Some women correspondents reported from areas that were more difficult to cover than the European theater. Sonia Tomara of the *New York Herald-Tribune,* for example, covered the China-Burma-India theater by flying in combat missions over the high mountains. Pictures taken by Margaret Bourke-White, one of a group of photographers for *Life* magazine, spanned many areas of the war.

She was one of the few Americans who covered the conflict in the Soviet Union.

The most famous American war correspondent was Ernie Pyle, whose reports were carried by almost 400 daily newspapers and 300 weeklies around the United States. Well respected in his profession, he won a Pulitzer Prize in 1944. Besides these achievements, Pyle was unique because he was immensely popular with, and even loved by, the troops. Whenever a GI met a reporter, the most commonly asked question was: "Do you know Ernie Pyle?" In his early forties, Pyle was significantly older than typical GIs, but he often shared their hardships. His writing was not flashy and his subjects rarely glamorous. Perhaps for these reasons, many soldiers felt that Pyle accurately captured their real war experiences. Pyle was with the troops through North Africa, Sicily, and Italy, and then in France from the Normandy beaches to the liberation of Paris. He returned home to America, but then decided to go to the Pacific to cover the war against Japan. Pyle said he was not seeking more fame or glory. "I'm going simply because there's a war on and I'm part of it," he said. "I'm going simply because I've got to, and I hate it." On April 18, 1945, Pyle was killed by Japanese gunfire on the island of Ie Shima, near Okinawa. The GIs erected a wooden sign on the island that contained Pyle's name, the date of his death, and this sentence: "At this spot, the 77th Infantry Division lost a buddy."

Another war correspondent who was extremely popular with soldiers, and who also won a Pulitzer Prize, was Bill Mauldin. Neither a writer nor a photographer, Mauldin communicated the realities of war through a cartoon about two average soldiers named Willie and Joe. Unlike Ernie Pyle, Mauldin was the same age as many of the soldiers he depicted; he had also started the war as a regular soldier who drew cartoons for his division's newspaper as a part-time assignment. After Mauldin's fame had spread to troops in other divisions, he was transferred to the staff of *Stars and Stripes,* the daily newspaper published by the U.S. Army and distributed to the troops. When Pyle wrote a column praising Mauldin, newspapers back home also began to carry his cartoons.

Like Pyle, Mauldin told the story of the GIs' war, but with humor. He presented the war through the eyes of two infantrymen named Willie and Joe, whose feet always hurt and who thought officers led

The Story of G.I. Joe

Just after the end of the war, Hollywood released a film based on Ernie Pyle's war reporting. Set in Italy and called *The Story of G.I. Joe,* the film was directed by William Wellman and starred Burgess Meredith as Pyle. Many critics think it is the best American combat film of World War II. *Time* magazine praised its authenticity and called it "the least glamorous war picture ever made." Others have additionally pointed out that the Italian civilians whom the soldiers encounter in the film seem like real people, something quite rare in war movies. General Dwight D. Eisenhower, the supreme commander of Allied forces in Europe, called *The Story of G.I. Joe* "the greatest war picture I've ever seen."

an easy life while the GIs did all the work. In Mauldin's cartoons, the soldiers were constantly unshaven, and their shirts hung outside their trousers. Willie and Joe did not have much use for army rules about neatness and slept mired in mud and misery; to them, keeping dry seemed more important than capturing Berlin. Willie and Joe were no heroes, but they did their job. They did not talk about the purpose of the war and they often expressed doubts about the way it was being run, but they never questioned the necessity of the conflict.

Some top officers did not appreciate the way Mauldin kept poking fun at them, contending that Willie and Joe set poor examples of discipline and behavior for soldiers. General George S. Patton, commander of the U.S. Third Army, threatened to ban *Stars and Stripes* from his area if Mauldin continued to publish his cartoons. General Dwight D. Eisenhower, Patton's boss, instead arranged for Patton and Mauldin to meet face-to-face and discuss the problem. Mauldin defended his cartoons, saying they made soldiers laugh at their own problems. Patton was not convinced, but *Stars and Stripes,* with Mauldin's cartoons included, continued to be read by GIs throughout Europe, including the soldiers of Patton's Third Army.

Bill Mauldin produced cartoons about Willie and Joe that were popular among GIs. (Reproduced by permission of AP/Wide World Photos)

P R I M A R Y   S O U R C E

Margaret Bourke-White
Excerpt from *Portrait of Myself*

Published in 1963

Margaret Bourke-White was a veteran photographer by the time she went to work as a war correspondent during World War II. Born in 1904 in New York City, Bourke-White received her first camera from her mother while she was attending college. Although she aspired to become a biologist, she altered her career path when she realized her love of photography. Bourke-White established her reputation in industrial photography during the 1920s in Cleveland, Ohio, where she photographed buildings, steel furnaces, and assembly lines. Bourke-White's work in Cleveland was seen by *Time* magazine's

Henry R. Luce, who hired her in 1929 as a photographer for his new venture, *Fortune*.

Through *Fortune* magazine, Bourke-White rose to the top of her profession. In the 1930s she began choosing her own assignments. During the Great Depression, she captured the devastation of flood victims in Kentucky as well as the problems affecting the disadvantaged. Many of her photographs concerned what is considered human drama. Bourke-White began working for *Life* magazine in the fall of 1936. The magazine was designed to feature many photographs that told as much—if not more—about each subject as the accompanying text. Bourke-White's first piece for *Life* concerned the Fort Peck Dam in northern Montana. In her book *Portrait of Myself*, Bourke-White notes that the photo essay was considered to be a revealing "human document of American frontier life." Bourke-White continued to present "human documents," some of which would soon be set against the backdrop of battle. As rumors of another world war brewed in Europe, Bourke-White would find herself involved in the conflict from behind the lens of a camera.

In spring 1941 Bourke-White and her new husband, author Erskine Caldwell, headed for Russia, where she was to make a comparison of Russia at that time and ten years earlier for *Life*. While the couple was in Russia, war broke out between the Soviets and the Germans. The Soviets banned the use of cameras, asserting that they would jail those who used them. Bourke-White faced a dilemma. "Here was I, facing the biggest scoop of my life: the biggest country enters the biggest war in the world and I was the only photographer on the spot, representing any publication and coming from any foreign country. I felt sure I could cope with the anti-camera law somehow."

Though warned by U.S. Embassy officials to leave Russia because of the war, Bourke-White and Caldwell remained in the Soviet Union. Bourke-White was intent on capturing images of air raids and bombing missions. She was taking photos from the roof of the American Embassy when German bombs knocked out the building's windows and toppled furniture, among other things. Bourke-White narrowly escaped serious injury, but photographed the scene for *Life*, developing the film in her makeshift darkroom, the bathroom. "Every night there was something to photograph, because whether it was a light air raid or a heavy one, the Germans managed to aim at least one bomb at the Kremlin. I remember one spectacular night when the Germans dropped eleven parachute flares like mammoth blazing parasols floating to the earth and lighting up the whole central section of the city. With flares overhead, you feel

absolutely undressed. You feel the enemy can see you wherever you are."

In time, Bourke-White was allowed to photograph Soviet leader Joseph Stalin at the Kremlin. Shortly thereafter, Bourke-White and Caldwell returned to the United States to lecture. Some of Bourke-White's photos were published in a book titled *Shooting the Russian War* (1942).

In December 1941, when the United States officially entered World War II after the Japanese bombed the U.S. naval base at Pearl Harbor, Hawaii, Bourke-White was able to get accredited to take photos of the U.S. Army Air Force. "In the late spring of 1942, when I was accredited, the first uniform for a woman war correspondent was designed for me." Other uniforms for female war correspondents were modeled after Bourke-White's. Soon, she was photographing world leaders as well as battle scenes from planes and ships. While aboard a flagship, Bourke-White learned what it was like to be on a vessel as it was torpedoed. She made her way safely to the lifeboats and was rescued from the sea.

It was not long before she ran into General Jimmy Doolittle, the American flier who had led the U.S. bombing raid on Tokyo and other Japanese cities on April 18, 1942. She asked if she could go along on a bombing mission, and her wish was granted in January 1943. Bourke-White flew on a B-17 bombing run from the El Aouina Airfield in Tunis, Tunisia. The pilot of the plane was Major Paul Tibbets, who would be called on in 1945 to drop the first atomic bomb on Hiroshima, Japan.

Eventually, Bourke-White made her way to Germany as Allied forces gained ground in the war. As she accompanied General George S. Patton's Third Army, Bourke-White saw the horrors of the Holocaust firsthand as troops liberated Buchenwald, a Nazi concentration camp outside Weimar, Germany. The following excerpt from Bourke-White's *Portrait of Myself* describes what Bourke-White saw and her reaction to the tragedy before her eyes.

Portrait of Myself
"We Didn't Know. We Didn't Know."

I left the Forgotten Front and flew by way of Paris into Germany to the exceedingly lively front on the River Rhine.

The war was racing toward its close in that crucial spring of 1945, and we correspondents were hard pressed to keep up with the march of events. It was truly a Gotterdammerung—*a twilight of the gods. No time to think about it or interpret it. Just rush to photograph it; write it; cable it. Record it now—think about it later. History will form the judgments.*

I was with General Patton's Third Army when we reached Buchenwald [a Nazi concentration camp], on the outskirts of Weimar. Patton was so incensed at what he saw that he ordered his police to get a thousand civilians to make them see with their own eyes what their leaders had done. The MPs were so enraged that they brought back two thousand. This was the first time I heard the words I was to hear repeated thousands of times: "We didn't know. We didn't know." But they did know.

I saw and photographed the piles of naked, lifeless bodies, the human skeletons in furnaces, the living skeletons who would die the next day because they had had to wait too long for deliverance, the pieces of tattooed skin for lampshades. Using the camera was almost a relief. It interposed a slight barrier between myself and the horror in front of me.

Buchenwald was more than the mind could grasp. It was as though a busy metropolis had frozen in attitudes of horror. But even Buchenwald paled before some of the smaller, more intimate atrocity camps.

I remember one we stumbled on just as our Army was in the act of capturing Leipzig: the labor camp of the Leipzig-Mochau airplane small-parts factory. The camp was a modest little square of ground

enclosed by barbed wire. The bodies were still smoldering when we got there, terribly charred but still in human form. We learned the ghastly details from one of the few survivors. The SS had made use of a simple expedient to get rid of the inmates all at once. The SS guards made pails of steaming soup, and as soon as the inmates were all inside the mess hall, the SS put blankets over the windows, threw in hand grenades and pailfuls of a blazing acetate solution. The building went up in sheets of flame. Some escaped, only to die, human torches, on the high barbed-wire fence. Even those who were successful in scaling the fence were picked off as they ran across an open field by savage youngsters of the Hitler Jugend *shooting from a tank. There had been three hundred inmates; there were eighteen who miraculously survived.*

To me, those who had died in the meadow made the most heartbreaking sight of all. To be shot down when they were so close to freedom, when the Allied armies were at the gates of the city. It was understandable that the Germans destroyed their bridges to slow up our advance. But to destroy these miserable people—what sense was there in that?

A final touch was added by the retreating Germans. On a flagpole set to one side they had run up a white surrender flag over the acre of bones.

People often ask me how it is possible to photograph such atrocities. I have to work with a veil over my mind. In photographing the murder camps, the protective veil was so tightly drawn that I hardly knew what I had taken until I saw prints of my own photographs. It was as though I was seeing these horrors for the first time. I believe many correspondents worked in the same self-imposed stupor. One has to, or it is impossible to stand it. (Bourke-White, pp. 258-260)

Aftermath

Bourke-White remained in Germany to photograph industrial centers as they were captured by the Allies. She also accompanied a group of GIs underground to look at a stash of valuables hidden in caves under the streets by the Germans. There, she saw lace, wines, flags, furs, and other treasured items. Once Germany surrendered in spring 1945, Bourke-White visited the Allied Control Commission's

U.S. Army soldiers show the remains of concentration camp victims to a group of boys in the Hitler Youth. The dead prisoners were the victims of starvation at the hands of the Nazis. (USHMM Photo Archives)

headquarters, which was set up in the Krupp Castle in Essen. The elaborate home had been confiscated from Alfried Krupp, a German industrialist who had used forced laborers during the war to make munitions. Some of his workers had been killed when they could no longer maintain a certain standard of efficiency. "[The workers] were lined up around a shell hole, their wrists tied together with telephone wire, and then shot in the back of the head so they would fall neatly into the hole. Most of the exterminating was done by a Gestapo gunman," explained Bourke-White. "But of course there was never any need for steelman Krupp to meet [the] triggerman."

While at the Krupp Castle, Bourke-White asked to photograph Krupp, who was under house arrest. She decided to ask him about the forced laborers, which he called simply "foreign workers." Bourke-White was appalled when he said they had volunteered to do the work and were not slave laborers but paid employees. "How could he think any informed person could believe he didn't know about the atrocity camps? I was reminded of a comment: 'The Germans act as though the Nazis were a strange race of Eskimos who came down from the North Pole and somehow invaded Germany.'" After Bourke-White returned home to the states, she issued a book that

contained information from her visit to Krupp. Titled *Dear Fatherland, Rest Quietly,* the work was used in the Nuremberg war crime trials, where Krupp was sentenced to twelve years imprisonment. However, he was released after less than three years, and went on to be the richest man in Europe throughout the 1950s and 1960s, with a personal worth valued at more than 1 billion dollars.

Bourke-White's photographs of Germany in World War II act as a reminder of the atrocities committed by the Nazis. In *Portrait of Myself,* Bourke-White noted that in the years following the war, people often forgot the extent of the horror. "Even the shell holes filled with dead would be conveniently forgotten, and the recollections of the concentration camps would be blurred with time and incredulity. The world would need reminders that men with hearts and hands and eyes very like our own had performed these horrors because of race prejudice and hatred." Her work continues to serve as a reminder.

SOURCES

Books

Bourke-White, Margaret, *"Dear Fatherland, Rest Quietly": A Report on the Collapse of Hitler's*

"*Thousand Years*," Simon and Schuster (New York), 1946.

Bourke-White, Margaret, *Portrait of Myself,* Simon and Schuster (New York), 1963.

Bourke-White, Margaret, *Shooting the Russian War,* Simon and Schuster (New York), 1942.

Goldberg, Vicki, *Margaret Bourke-White: A Biography,* Addison-Wesley (Reading, MA), 1987.

Hood, Robert, *Twelve at War: Great Photographers Under Fire,* Putnam (New York), 1967.

Rubin, Susan Goldman, *Margaret Bourke-White: Her Pictures Were Her Life,* Abrams (New York), 1999.

PRIMARY SOURCE

Ernie Pyle
"Notes from a Battered Country"
"The Death of Captain Waskow"
"I Thought It Was the End"
"Waiting for Tomorrow"
"On Victory in Europe"
Excerpts from *Ernie's War: The Best of Ernie Pyle's World War II Dispatches*

Written by Ernie Pyle between 1943 and 1945
Collected and published in book form, 1986

The battles of World War II spread beyond Europe and Asia to the continent of Africa when Italian forces invaded the northeast African country of Egypt in September 1940, in an attempt to expand Italian control across the Mediterranean Sea into North Africa. Italy's ally Germany landed troops in North Africa in February 1941. By 1942, the northwest African regions of Morocco, Algeria, and Tunisia had been invaded by Axis forces. In late 1942 and early 1943 the Allied powers succeeded in pushing German and Italian troops out of northern Africa.

From Africa, the Allies moved northward to the island of Sicily, which lies off the southern coast of Italy in the Mediterranean Sea. Their goal was to defeat the Italians on the island and then launch an invasion of the Italian mainland. The attack on Sicily began July 10, 1943, and lasted five weeks. After the Italians surrendered, German forces continued to defend Italy against the Allies.

Throughout September, American and British troops, joined by that time by the French, advanced into southern Italy and pushed the German forces northward. The Luftwaffe inflicted extensive damage on Allied warships at the seaports of Salerno and Bari. After intense fighting, German ground troops stopped the Allies at Cassino, a town in the mountains of central Italy that served as a key position in Germany's line of defense. By launching an invasion at Anzio, a harbor town on the Mediterranean Sea located about fifty miles south of Rome, the Allies were able to lure the Germans away from Cassino. The Battle of Anzio stretched throughout winter 1944.

Indiana-born American journalist Ernest Taylor "Ernie" Pyle witnessed the fighting at Anzio firsthand. Even before the war, he had written a daily column that appeared in about 200 U.S. newspapers, and from the end of 1940 to early 1945, his assignments took him to England, Africa,

Sicily, Italy, France, and tiny islands in the Pacific. Accompanying soldiers in combat around the globe, Pyle composed vivid, penetrating accounts of the tragedy of war as it happened. His columns brought the war home to Americans, and in 1944 he was awarded the prestigious Pulitzer Prize for reporting. Pyle's last dispatches were filed from the Pacific front in early 1945.

Capturing the islands of Iwo Jima and Okinawa was, at that time, considered crucial to an Allied victory in the Pacific, as both locations were viewed as prime launching points for air invasions of the Japanese home islands. The Japanese stationed their fighter planes on heavily fortified Iwo Jima, located 600 miles from the capital city of Tokyo on Honshu (one of Japan's four main islands). The U.S. marine invasion of Iwo Jima was scheduled for February 19, 1945. For ten straight weeks preceding the invasion, U.S. Navy warships and planes bombarded the tiny, barren island. Then, during the early morning hours of February 19, a two-mile-long stretch of beach was bombarded one last time in preparation for the 9 a.m. marine landing. Heavily armed Japanese forces fought back from concealed locations carved into the craggy rock of Mount Suribachi, situated high above the beaches. The first day of fighting left more than 500 marines dead, but the Americans continued their slow advance inland. On February 23 a small force of marines managed to climb to the top of Mount Suribachi and raise the American flag. The battle lasted nearly a month. When it was over, more than 20,000 Japanese soldiers were dead; nearly 7,000 Americans had been killed and another 20,000 were wounded.

Allied B-29 bombers attacked Tokyo in early March 1945. At the end of the month, U.S. forces began the long and bloody invasion of Okinawa (one of the Ryukyu Islands, located about 350 miles south of the Japanese main islands). By this time, the Japanese navy had been virtually shattered, causing Japanese military leaders to send out

Famed Nicknames

Bold, fiery, and controversial are just a few of the words frequently used to describe two key leaders of the Allied forces: George S. Patton of the United States and Sir Bernard Law Montgomery of Great Britain. General Patton, nicknamed "Old Blood and Guts," commanded the U.S. Seventh Army in its 1943 attack on Sicily. Field Marshal Montgomery, better known as "Monty," led forces in Sicily and Italy. Both Patton and Montgomery played important roles in the Allied invasions of French North Africa (1942) and northern France (1944).

an enormous force of kamikaze fighters—Japanese pilots who deliberately crashed their planes into Allied ships. The three-month-long air and land battle for Okinawa was the most devastating campaign carried out in the Pacific. One in three U.S. Marines who fought there was either killed or wounded, and thousands of soldiers suffered psychological as well as physical wounds. By late June 1945, when the island was finally conquered by the Allies, about 110,000 Japanese had been killed.

Ernie Pyle saw action during the war on three continents: Europe, Africa, and Asia. The dispatches he created to describe those conflicts have been noted for their sparse style, insight, and honesty. The following excerpts cover some of Pyle's experiences in Italy and the Pacific. "The Death of Captain Waskow" is generally considered his best piece. "On Victory in Europe" was found on Pyle's body after his death.

Ernie's War:
The Best of Ernie Pyle's World War II Dispatches

"Notes from a Battered Country"

IN ITALY, December 28, 1943—*The little towns of Italy that have been in the path of this war from Salerno northward are nothing more than great rubble heaps. There is hardly enough left of most of them to form a framework for rebuilding.*

When the Germans occupied the towns, we rained artillery on them for days and weeks at a time. Then after we captured a town, the Germans would shell it heavily. They got it from both sides.

Along the road for twenty or thirty miles behind the fighting front, you pass through one demolished town after another. Most of the inhabitants take to the hills after the first shelling.... Some go to live in caves; some go to relatives in the country. A few in every town refuse to leave no matter what happens, and many of them have been killed by the shelling and bombing from both sides.

A countryside is harder to disfigure than a town. You have to look closely, and study in detail, to find the carnage wrought upon the green fields and the rocky hillside. It is there, but it is temporary—like a skinned finger—and time and the rains will heal it. Another year and the countryside will cover its own scars.

If you wander on foot and look closely you will see the signs—the limb of an olive tree broken off, six swollen dead horses in the corner of a field, a straw-stack burned down, a chestnut tree blown clear out with its roots by a German bomb, ... empty gun pits, and countless foxholes, and rubbish–heap stacks of empty C-ration cans [canned food consumed by American soldiers in the field], and now and then the lone grave of a German soldier.

These are all there, clear across the country, and yet they are hard to see unless you look closely. A countryside is big, and nature helps fight for it.

"The Death of Captain Waskow"

AT THE FRONT LINES IN ITALY, January 10, 1944—*In this war I have known a lot of officers who were loved and respected by the soldiers under them. But never have I crossed the trail of any man as beloved as Capt. Henry T. Waskow of Belton, Texas.*

Capt. Waskow was a company commander in the 36th Division. He had led his company since long before it left the [United] States. He was very young, only in his middle twenties, but he carried in him a sincerity and gentleness that made people want to be guided by him.

"After my own father, he came next," a sergeant told me.

"He always looked after us," a soldier said. "He'd go to bat for us every time."...

I was at the foot of the mule trail the night they brought Capt. Waskow's body down. The moon was nearly full at the time, and you could see far up the trail, and even part way across the valley below....

Dead men had been coming down the mountain all evening, lashed onto the backs of mules. They came lying belly-down across the wooden pack-saddles, their heads hanging down on the left side of the mule, their stiffened legs sticking out awkwardly from the other side, bobbing up and down as the mule walked....

The first one came early in the morning. They slid him down from the mule and stood him on his feet for a moment, while they got a new grip. In the half light he might have been merely a sick man standing there, leaning on the others. Then they laid him on the ground in the shadow of the low stone wall alongside the road.

I don't know who that first one was. You feel small in the presence of dead men, and ashamed at being alive, and you don't ask silly questions.

We left him there beside the road, that first one, and we all went back into the cowshed and sat on water cans or lay on the straw, waiting for the next batch of mules.

Somebody said the dead soldier had been dead for four days, and then nobody said anything more about it. We talked soldier talk for an hour or more. The dead man lay all alone outside in the shadow of the low stone wall.

Then a soldier came into the cowshed and said there were some more bodies outside. We went out into

Ernie Pyle (seated second from right in front of the tank) with members of the U.S. Fifth Army in Anzio, Italy. (Reproduced by permission of the Corbis Corporation [Bellevue])

the road. Four mules stood there, in the moonlight, in the road where the trail came down off the mountain. The soldiers who led them stood there waiting. "This one is Captain Waskow," one of them said quietly.

Two men unlashed his body from the mule and lifted it off and laid it in the shadow beside the low stone wall. Other men took the other bodies off. Finally there were five lying end to end in a long row, alongside the road. You don't cover up dead men in the combat zone. They just lie there in the shadows until somebody else comes after them.

The unburdened mules moved off to their olive orchard. The men in the road seemed reluctant to leave. They stood around, and gradually one by one I could sense them moving closer to Capt. Waskow's body. Not so much to look, I think, as to say something in finality to him, and to themselves. I stood close by and I could hear.

One soldier came and looked down, and he said out loud, "God damn it." That's all he said, and then he walked away. Another one came. He said, "God damn it to hell anyway." He looked down for a few last moments, and then he turned and left.

Another man came; I think he was an officer. It was hard to tell … in the half light, for [everyone was] bearded and grimy dirty. The man looked down

American troops file down a mountainside in Sicily, an island off the southern tip of Italy. The Allied attack on Sicily began July 10, 1943, with the goal of defeating Italian forces on the island and then launching an invasion of the Italian mainland. (Reproduced by permission of AP/Wide World Photos, Inc.)

into the dead captain's face, and then he spoke directly to him, as though he were alive. He said: "I'm sorry, old man."

Then a soldier came and stood beside the officer, and bent over, and he too spoke to his dead captain, not in a whisper but awfully tenderly, and he said:

"I sure am sorry, sir."

Then the first man squatted down, and he reached down and took the dead hand, and he sat there for a full five minutes, holding the dead hand in his own and looking intently into the dead face, and he never uttered a sound all the time he sat there.

And finally he put the hand down, and then reached up and gently straightened the points of the captain's shirt collar, and then he sort of rearranged the tattered edges of his uniform around the wound. And then he got up and walked away down the road in the moonlight, all alone....

"I Thought It Was the End"

WITH THE FIFTH ARMY BEACHHEAD FORCES IN ITALY, March 20, 1944—We correspondents stay in a villa run by the 5th Army's Public Relations Section....

The house is on the waterfront. The current sometimes washes over our back steps. The house is a huge, rambling affair with four stories down on the beach and then another complete section of three stories just above it in the bluff, all connected by a series of interior stairways.

For weeks long-range artillery shells had been hitting in the water or on shore within a couple of hundred yards of us. Raiders came over nightly, yet ... this villa ... seemed to be charmed....

... [T]he part of the house down by the water [was] considered safer because it was lower down.

But I had been sleeping alone in the room in the top part because it was a lighter place to work in the daytime. We called it "Shell Alley" up there because the Anzio-bound [headed for Anzio, near Rome in central Italy] shells seemed to come in a groove right past our eaves day and night.

On this certain morning I had awakened early and was just lying there for a few minutes before getting up. It was just seven and the sun was out bright.

Suddenly the anti-aircraft guns let loose. Ordinarily I don't get out of bed during a raid, but I did get up this one morning....

I had just reached the window when a terrible blast swirled me around and threw me into the middle of my room....

The half of the window that was shut was ripped out and hurled across the room. The glass was blown into thousands of little pieces. Why the splinters or the window frame itself didn't hit me I don't know.

From the moment of the first blast until it was over probably not more than fifteen seconds passed. Those fifteen seconds were so fast and confusing that I truly can't say what took place, and the other correspondents reported the same.

There was debris flying back and forth all over the room. One gigantic explosion came after another....

I jumped into one corner of the room and squatted down and sat cowered there. I definitely thought it was the end. Outside of that I don't remember what my emotions were.

Suddenly one whole wall of my room flew in, burying the bed where I'd been a few seconds before under hundreds of pounds of brick, stone and mortar....

Then the wooden doors were ripped off their hinges and crashed into the room.... The French doors leading to the balcony blew out and one of my chairs was upended through the open door....

Finally the terrible nearby explosions ceased and gradually the ack-ack died down and at last I began to have some feeling of relief that it was over and I was still alive. But I stayed crouched in the corner until the last shot was fired.

... When our bombing was over, my room was in a shambles. It was the sort of thing you see only in the movies.

More than half the room was knee-deep with broken brick and tiles and mortar. The other half was a disarray all covered with plaster dust and broken glass. My typewriter was full of mortar and broken glass, but was not damaged.

My pants had been lying on the chair that went through the door, so I dug them out from under the debris, put them on and started down to the other half of the house.

Down below everything was a mess. The ceilings had come down upon men still in bed. Some beds were a foot deep in debris. That nobody was killed was a pure miracle....

The boys couldn't believe it when they saw me coming in. Wick Fowler of the Dallas News had thought the bombs had made direct hits on the upper part of the house. He had just said to George Tucker of the Associated Press, "Well, they got Ernie."

But after they saw I was all right they began to laugh and called me "Old Indestructible." I guess I was the luckiest man in the house, at that, although Old Dame Fortune was certainly riding with all of us that morning.

"Waiting for Tomorrow"

OFF THE OKINAWA BEACHHEAD, April 3, 1945—This is the last column before the invasion. It is written aboard a troop transport the evening before we storm onto Okinawa....

...We will take Okinawa. Nobody has any doubt about that. But we know we will have to pay for it. Some on this ship will not be alive twenty-four hours from now.

April 16, 1945—We camped one night on a little hillside that led up to a bluff overlooking a small river. The bluff dropped straight down for a long way. Up there on top of the bluff it was just like a little park.

The bluff was terraced, although it wasn't farmed. The grass on it was soft and green. And those small, straight-limbed pine trees were dotted all over it.

Looking down from the bluff, the river made a turn and across it was an old stone bridge. At the end of the bridge was a village—or what had been a village.

It was now just a jumble of ashes and sagging thatched roofs from our bombardment. In every

A wounded soldier being lifted out of the tank that brought him back from the front lines in Okinawa. The fighting there was extremely brutal, with both sides suffering heavy casualties. (Reproduced by permission of the Corbis Corporation [Bellevue])

direction little valleys led away from the turn in the river.

It was as pretty and gentle a sight as you ever saw. It had the softness of antiquity about it and the miniature charm and daintiness that we see in Japanese prints. And the sad, uncanny silence that follows the bedlam of war.

A bright sun made the morning hot and a refreshing little breeze sang through the pine trees. There wasn't a shot nor a warlike sound within hearing. I sat on the bluff for a long time, just looking. It all seemed so quiet and peaceful. I noticed a lot of the Marines sitting and just looking, too.

"On Victory in Europe"

And so it is over. The catastrophe on one side of the world has run its course. The day that it had so long seemed would never come has come at last.

I suppose emotions here in the Pacific are the same as they were among the Allies all over the world. First a shouting of the good news....

And then an unspoken sense of gigantic relief—and then a hope that the collapse in Europe [the surrender of German forces in Europe, marking the end of the war there] would hasten the end in the Pacific....

This is written on a little ship lying off the coast of the Island of Okinawa, just south of Japan, on the other side of the world from Ardennes [the forested area in southwestern Belgium that was the site of the Battle of the Bulge (1944–1945)]....

To me the European war is old, and the Pacific war is new.

... In the joyousness of high spirits it is easy for us to forget the dead....

But there are many of the living who have had burned into their brains forever the unnatural sight of cold dead men scattered over the hillsides and in the ditches along the high rows of hedge throughout the world.

Dead men by mass production—in one country after another—month after month and year after year. Dead men in winter and dead men in summer.

Dead men in such familiar promiscuity that they become monotonous.

Dead men in such monstrous infinity that you come almost to hate them.

These are the things that you at home need not even try to understand. To you at home they are columns of figures, or he is a near one who went away and just didn't come back. You didn't see him lying so grotesque and pasty beside the gravel road in France.

We saw him, saw him by the multiple thousands. That's the difference.... (Pyle, pp. 184–185, 195–197, 238–240, 402, 411, 418–419)

Aftermath

Bitter fighting continued in Italy after Pyle left in April 1944. The main goal of the American and British armies was to capture the Italian capital of Rome. Backed by French, French-African, and Polish troops, they attacked German positions from Cassino out to the Mediterranean Sea. At the same time, the Allied troops on the beaches of Anzio broke their deadlock with the Germans and managed to overpower them. With the combined strength of Britain's Royal Air Force (RAF) and the U.S. Army Air Corps paving the way, American and British ground troops were able to take Rome in June 1944 and then advance northward into the city of Bologna.

Pyle was in France the day after the Allied invasion of Normandy. He later returned to the United States for a short time, then reluctantly set out for the Pacific, fearful that he would not survive the war. "You begin to feel that you can't go on forever without being hit," he noted in one interview. "I feel that I've used up all my chances. And I hate it." Before Pyle left home for the Pacific, his wife, Jerry, begged him to reconsider. Like Pyle, she feared that he had "used up" his chances and would be killed while on assignment. He readily admitted that he wanted to stay home but felt that if he did not go he would "work up a guilty feeling that would haunt [him]." He concluded: "There's just nothing else I can do." Pyle was killed on April 18, 1945, struck in the head by a Japanese sniper's bullet while traveling with four soldiers on the tiny island of Ie Shima, located just west of Okinawa. He was buried on the island in a handmade wooden coffin. The war in Europe ended three weeks later. In 1945 *The Story of G.I. Joe*, a feature film based on Pyle's experiences with American soldiers in Italy, was released in the United States.

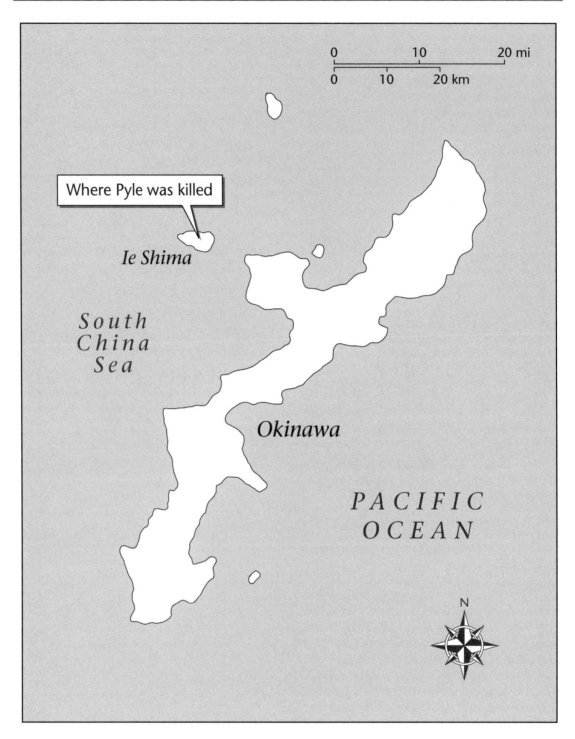

Okinawa and Ie Shima, where Ernie Pyle was killed.

Bill Mauldin
Excerpts from *Up Front*
Published in 1945

While Ernie Pyle wrote about the perils of battle and the feelings of the American soldiers sent to fight World War II, Bill Mauldin drew cartoons to bring his own wartime experiences to life. No artist conveyed the experience of the average American infantryman better than the young sergeant from New Mexico. Taking pen in hand, he created a series of cartoons that captured the essence of the situations experienced by American troops sent to fight the Axis powers in Europe.

Born in 1921, Mauldin was already a budding cartoonist when, at age eighteen, he joined his state's National Guard unit, which was quickly activated as part of the Forty-Fifth Infantry Division. He saw combat in Sicily and took part in the bloody battle at Anzio beach in Italy. Injured during the fighting, the cartoonist received the Purple Heart and continued fighting. Mauldin saw much of the war from the front lines and lived to share his experiences with others.

During the war, Mauldin quickly established a reputation for being able to capture the true feelings and experiences of American military men. Even though he poked fun at army brass, most commanding officers realized that Mauldin's musings were good for the soldiers' morale. In 1943 Mauldin landed a job as a cartoonist for *Stars and Stripes*, an army newspaper.

Using a pair of scrappy, dog-faced soldiers as his protagonists, Mauldin was able to provide social commentary on the nature of war while bringing a little levity to the tough situations that American servicemen faced day after day. Willie and Joe, the heroes of Mauldin's series, were a lovable pair of brave, unshaven, battle-weary, war-wisened men who often commented about damp European weather, wet feet, exhaustion, boredom, close calls, and many other topics. The characters were a hit with the average soldier, and Americans at home enjoyed Willie and Joe's antics, too, as the cartoons were syndicated throughout the United States.

Mauldin showed that war is a difficult experience for most, despite all the publicity back home issued to keep morale high. A soldier often does not know what the next day will bring, or who will still be around. Some of Mauldin's wartime cartoons were collected in the book *Up Front*, which eventually won the cartoonist a Pulitzer Prize. In the book, Mauldin describes some basic facts about the war according to what he saw and observed. Although cartoons are interspersed in the text, Mauldin's book provides a serious and frank account of situations faced by American soldiers. Mauldin also explains why he chose some of the topics for his cartoons. The following excerpts feature just a few of the many topics that Mauldin addresses in *Up Front*.

Up Front

Bill Mauldin on American Soldiers

Perhaps the American soldier in combat has an even tougher job than the combat soldiers of his allies. Most of his allies have lost their homes or had friends and relatives killed by the enemy. The threat to their countries and lives has been direct, immedi- *ate, and inescapable. The American has lost nothing to the Germans, so his war is being fought for more farfetched reasons.*

He didn't learn to hate the Germans until he came over here. He didn't realize the immense threat that faced his nation until he saw how powerful and

"*Now that ya mention it, Joe, it does sound like th' patter of rain on a tin roof.*"

(Reprinted by permission of Bill Mauldin and the Watkins/Loomis Agency)

cruel and ruthless the German nation was. He learned that the Nazi is simply a symbol of the German people, so his father learned that the Kaiser was only a symbol. So now he hates Germans and he fights them, but the fact still remains that his brains and not his emotions are driving him.

Many celebrities and self-appointed authorities have returned from quick tours of war zones (some of them getting within hearing distance of the shooting) and have put out their personal theories to batteries of photographers and reporters. Some say the

American soldier is the same clean-cut young man who left his home; others say morale is sky-high at the front because everybody's face is shining for the great Cause.

They are wrong. The combat man isn't the same clean-cut lad because you don't fight a kraut by Marquis of Queensberry rules. You shoot him in the back, you blow him apart with mines, you kill or maim him the quickest and most effective way you can with the least danger to yourself. He does the same to you. He tricks you and cheats you, and if you don't beat him at his own game you don't live to appreciate your own nobleness.

But you don't become a killer. No normal man who has smelled and associated with death ever wants to see any more of it. In fact, the only men who are even going to want to bloody noses in a fist fight after this war will be those who want people to think they were tough combat men, when they weren't. The surest way to become a pacifist is to join the infantry.

I don't make the infantryman look noble, because he couldn't look noble even if he tried. Still there is a certain nobility and dignity in combat soldiers and medical aid men with dirt in their ears. They are rough and their language gets coarse because they live a life stripped of convention and niceties. Their nobility and dignity come from the way they live unselfishly and risk their lives to help each other. They are normal people who have been put where they are, and whose actions and feelings have been molded by their circumstances. There are gentlemen and boors; intelligent ones and stupid ones; talented ones and inefficient ones. But when they are all together and they are fighting, despite their bitching and griping and goldbricking and mortal fear, they are facing cold steel and screaming lead and hard enemies, and they are advancing and beating the hell out of the opposition.

They wish to hell they were someplace else, and they wish to hell they would get relief. They wish to hell the mud was dry and they wish to hell their coffee was hot. They want to go home. But they stay in their wet holes and fight, and then they climb out and crawl through minefields and fight some more....

Bill Mauldin on Soldiers' Mail

The mail is by far the most important reading matter that reaches soldiers overseas. This has had so much publicity that if some people aren't writing regularly to their guys in the war, it's because they don't want to. A common excuse at home seems to be that they aren't getting much mail from the guys here. The little lady says, "Okay, if the bum is going to sightsee around Europe and not bother to write, I just won't write him." Some guys do sightsee around Europe without bothering to write. Not the doggie. He doesn't do any sightseeing, and he doesn't have many opportunities to write. If the lady could see him scrawling on a V-mail blank in a dugout, by the light of a candle stuck with its own hot grease on his knee, she would change her way of thinking.

It's very hard to write interesting letters if you are in the infantry. About the only things you can talk about are what you are doing and where you are, and that's cut out by the censor. It's very hard to compose a letter that will pass the censors when you are tired and scared and disgusted with everything that's happening.

A lot of people aren't very smart when they write to a soldier. They complain about the gasoline shortage, or worry him or anger him in a hundred different ways which directly affect his efficiency and morale. Your feelings get touchy and explosive at the front. A man feels very fine fighting a war when his girl has just written that she is thinking that perhaps they made a mistake. He might figure: What the hell, the only thing I was living for was that I knew she would wait for me. He's going to feel pretty low and he might get a little careless because of it, at a place where he can't afford to be careless.

But considerate women have done far more to help their men than they may realize. A soldier's life revolves around his mail. Like many others, I've been able to follow my kid's progress from the day he was born until now he is able to walk and talk a little, and although I have never seen him I know him very well. Jean has sent dozens of snapshots of herself and the little guy at different intervals, and it makes all the difference in the world....

Bill Mauldin on Mud

Mud, for one, is a curse which seems to save itself for war. I'm sure Europe never got this muddy during peacetime. I'm equally sure that no mud in the world is so deep or sticky or wet as European mud. It doesn't even have an honest color like ordinary mud.

I made [a] drawing about [a] jeep driver [splashing mud on] the foot infantry ... for a reason. Those guys who have had some infantry, and even those who have had to do a lot of walking in other branches, generally show it by the way they drive. If a man barrels past foot troops, splashing mud or squirting dust all over them because he doesn't bother to slow down—or if he shoots past a hitchhiker in the rain, with half his cozy truck cab empty—then he should spend a week or two learning how to use his feet, because he doesn't appreciate his job or he's just plain damned stupid.

Unfortunately, there are a lot of them in the army. I saw a big GI truck zoom past an infantry battalion in France, right after the rains began to fall. The driver spattered the troops pretty thoroughly—but they were getting used to being spattered,

"I feel like a fugitive from th' law of averages."

(Reprinted by permission of Bill Mauldin and the Watkins/Loomis Agency)

and they didn't say much. His truck bogged down half a mile up the road, and when the leading company caught up with him he had the unbelievable gall to ask them to push him out. They replied as only long-suffering infantrymen can reply. They shoved his face in the mud.

The worst thing about mud, outside of the fact that it keeps armies from advancing, is that it causes trench foot. There was a lot of it that first winter in Italy. The doggies found it difficult to keep their feet dry, and they had to stay in wet foxholes for days and weeks at a time. If they couldn't stand the pain they crawled out of their holes and stumbled and crawled (they couldn't walk) down the mountains until they reached the aid station. Their shoes were cut off, and their feet swelled like balloons. Sometimes the feet had to be amputated. But most often the men had to make their agonized way back up the mountain and crawl into their holes again because there were no replacements and the line had to be held. (Mauldin, pp. 11–16, 23–25, 36–37)

Aftermath

At times, Mauldin was criticized for making American soldiers look so disheveled, but he asserted that his work was a realistic portrayal of how men appeared after they had been on the front. He explained that after men had witnessed so much fighting and death, they aged ten or fifteen years. Ernie Pyle also defended Mauldin. In a caption for a photo of a ragged, battle-weary soldier, Pyle wrote: "So you at home think cartoonist Bill Mauldin's 'GI Joe' doesn't look that way. Well, he does, and here's proof."

Mauldin returned home from the war and finally got to meet his son face to face. Mauldin continued his popular strip after the war, showing Willie and Joe's attempts to readjust to civilian life. As Mauldin made the adjustment himself, he became an editorial cartoonist. He won a second Pulitzer Prize for his newspaper work in the late 1950s.

SOURCES

Books

Mauldin, Bill, *Back Home,* W. Sloan Associates (New York), 1947.

Mauldin, Bill, *The Brass Ring,* Norton (New York), 1971.

Mauldin, Bill, *Up Front,* Henry Holt (New York), 1945.

Wepman, Dennis, "Bill Mauldin," *The Encyclopedia of American Comics,* edited by Ron Goulart, Facts on File (New York), 1990.

The Fall of Nazi Germany

In the final year of World War II, two powerful forces closed in on Germany from the east and the west. One was the Red Army, the army of the Soviet Union, one of the Eastern Allies. The other was the combined army of the Western Allies. For a while the German army was able to shift troops and resources from one front to the other to avert potential invasions. Yet the Allied bombing of the railroad system in Germany and Nazi-controlled Europe eventually made this type of maneuvering extremely difficult. More significantly, as the war continued longer than the Nazis had expected, the Germans were overwhelmed as increasing numbers of German soldiers were killed or captured and more and more munitions and equipment were lost. Germany could no longer replace either troops or supplies. Simultaneously, internal conflict and poor military decisions were destroying the Third Reich. By May 1945 the encroaching Allied armies succeeded in crushing the last remnants of the Nazi regime.

Dual Fronts and the Liberation of White Russia

On June 6, 1944, now known as D-Day, Western Allied troops landed in Normandy, on the northwest coast of France. The Allies had been eager to begin this invasion ever since the United States entered the war in 1941, but they waited until the armies were fully prepared and had enough supplies to be fairly sure the offensive would be successful. In two weeks, the Allied force in Normandy had grown to 600,000 troops. The German army fought desperately to keep the Allies from breaking out of Normandy and moving east across France and Belgium toward Germany. At the same time, on the other side of Europe, the Germans battled the Red Army along a front that stretched 2,000 miles from north to south. For three years, since the German invasion of the Soviet Union in June 1941, the Red Army had fought massive battles against the Germans. In the largest and bloodiest campaigns of World War II, the Soviets succeeded in driving the invaders back toward the western border of their country. Soviet leaders had promised the British and American governments that the Red Army would begin a major offensive immediately after the invasion of western Europe; such an action would prevent the Germans from shifting troops, tanks, and planes from Russia to Normandy.

Just two weeks after D-Day the Soviets kept their promise. For the new offensive the Soviets chose the central part of the eastern front, an area on the western edge of Soviet territory in White Russia or Belorussia (now Belarus), that had belonged to Poland before being annexed by the Soviets in 1939. German forces in White Russia were organized as the Army Group Center, which

Finland: Germany's Only Democratic Ally

In the far north of the eastern front, the Red Army also faced the army of Finland. The Soviet Union had attacked Finland in the winter months from 1939 to 1940, fighting a brief, bitter war. While the much smaller Finnish army had won admiration throughout the world for its strong resistance to the attack, the nation had been forced to ask for peace and give up some of its territory to the Soviet Union. When Germany invaded the Soviet Union in June 1941, Finnish troops fought alongside the Germans in attempts to regain some of their land. Despite mounting German pressure, however, the Finns refused to cross the old border, claiming they would fight only on land they considered part of Finland. Although agreeing to be Germany's ally along the eastern front, Finland refused to cooperate with Germany in other ways. The nation did not declare war on Britain or the United States and chose to retain a democratic form of government, unlike any other country fighting with the Axis powers. Unlike Germany's other allies, the Finnish people were never attracted to Nazi ideas and the Finnish government successfully resisted Nazi pressure to arrest Jews and deport them to other parts of German-occupied Europe, where they would have been murdered.

On June 9, 1944, just before staging an offensive in White Russia, the Soviets advanced against the Finnish army. By the end of July, Finland was negotiating with the Soviets to withdraw from the war. The Germans no longer had enough power to prevent this move, and Finland agreed to the Soviet Union's terms early in September.

consisted of thirty-seven divisions. (A full-strength division is usually around 15,000 men, although Soviet divisions were usually smaller and many German divisions were below full strength because of losses in previous battles.) Unbeknownst to the Germans, however, the Red Army had assembled forces in White Russia that numbered 166 divisions and 2,700 tanks, far outnumbering the Germans. Waiting close by were 4,500 planes, and Soviet partisans had been targeting railroad tracks and other strategic areas for several days before the launching of the offensive.

On June 22, 1944, the third anniversary of the German invasion of the Soviet Union, the Red Army began its attack along an 800-mile section of the front. The operation was code-named Bagration, after a Russian general killed while fighting French emperor Napoleon Bonaparte's invasion of Russia in 1812. Within days the Red Army surrounded and destroyed the German Ninth Army, forcing the remainder of the German forces into a rapid retreat. In the first week of the Soviet attack, 200,000 Germans were killed, wounded, or captured, and 900 German tanks were destroyed. On July 3 the Red Army pushed the Germans west and entered Minsk, the capital of White Russia. A few days later about 60,000 men of the German Fourth Army were taken prisoner after tens of thousands of its soldiers had been killed. Northwest of Minsk, on July 10, Soviet forces freed Vilna, which had been part of Poland at the start of World War II; after Poland was defeated by the Germans in 1939, Vilna became the capital of Lithuania. The Soviets reached the Polish city of Lublin on July 23; four days later they captured Lwów (Lvov), another city that had belonged to Poland before the war. The Red Army had now won back almost all the territory that had been part of the Soviet Union when the Germans invaded, and a portion of the Soviet forces were poised on the border of East Prussia, part of Germany. In the center of the front, leading units of the Red Army reached the river Vistula in two widely separated areas; on the other side of the Vistula, between these units, was Warsaw, the capital of Poland.

At the beginning of August, the great Soviet offensive came to a halt. The Soviets had pushed the Germans 300 miles west in six weeks—in some

Legend:
- – ·· – Boundaries, 1920–1938
- **━ ━ ━** Western frontier of U.S.S.R., June 1941
- **━ ━ ━** Eastern Front (at the end of 1941)

SWEDEN

FINLAND

Lake Ladoga

N

0   100   200 mi

0   100   200 km

Baltic Sea

ESTONIA

LATVIA

LITH.

Vilna •

Danzig

East Prussia

Minsk •

Vistula R.

Belorussia (White Russia)

Warsaw •

P O L A N D

Lublin •

SLOVAKIA

Ukraine

Dnieper R.

UNION OF SOVIET SOCIALIST REPUBLICS (U.S.S.R.)

HUNGARY

ROMANIA

YUGOSLAVIA

Danube R.

Black Sea

BULGARIA

Western Soviet territory, showing 1920 to 1938 and 1941 Polish-Soviet borders.

General Wladyslaw Sikorski, head of the London Poles, was killed in a plane crash; he had the most stature among the London Poles and was the least fanatically anti-Soviet. (Reproduced by permission of AP/Wide World Photos)

places they had moved more than 400 miles. Army Group Center and thirty German divisions had been destroyed; more than 300,000 German soldiers had been killed, wounded, or captured in White Russia alone. Part of the reason for the end of the Soviet advance was that German resistance became tougher. By retreating, the Germans had a chance to pause, regroup, and establish defensive positions, such as river crossings, that gave them an advantage. In addition, German reinforcements, including three armored divisions, helped secure and hold these positions. Another possible reason for the Soviet deceleration was that their forces had moved forward so quickly that it had become difficult to supply them. A modern army depends on huge quantities of fuel, ammunition, and food. Now supplies had to be brought a longer distance, over roads and railroads that had been badly damaged or destroyed. It was a common pattern in World War II for a powerful offensive—whether Allied or German—to slow down to a halt after becoming so successful that it had outrun supply lines. Many military historians think this is exactly what happened in Operation Bagration. However, the main reason the Soviet army stopped on the Vistula is one of the most debated topics in

World War II military history. Many people believed at the time, and many still believe, that the halt was not stalled because of a lack of supplies. Instead, they posit the Soviet government purposely stopped the offensive because of political disputes with Poland. As the Red Army waited on the Vistula, the people of Warsaw rose up in armed rebellion against the Germans.

Poland's Distrust of the Soviet Union

The Germans had bombed Warsaw into surrender in September 1939, causing the city to suffer under German occupation longer than any other capital city in Europe. The Germans had treated Polish people much more harshly than they treated people of western Europe. Poland lost a higher percentage of the civilian population in the war than in any other country. A large underground movement had developed in Poland. One part of this movement was the Armai Krajowa (Home Army) or AK, which was the armed branch of the Polish underground. The Home Army was loyal to the Polish government that had escaped from Warsaw to London in 1939 and was recognized by Britain and the United States as the legal representative of the Polish people. The government-in-exile, or London Poles as they were often called, was suspicious of the Soviet Union. The most important issue between the Soviet and Polish governments concerned Poland's borders. The Soviets wanted the eastern parts of prewar Poland (the White Russian region just freed from the Germans in Operation Bagration) to remain part of the Soviet Union. Most of the people in this region were not Polish. The Soviet Union had taken this area from Poland in September 1939 as part of a deal with Nazi Germany. In effect, the Soviet Union had helped Nazi dictator Adolf Hitler eliminate Poland as an independent country. The deal between the two countries, known as the Nazi-Soviet Pact, added to the Polish anger and distrust of the Soviets. Another major difference concerned the type of government Poland would have after the war. The London Poles were strongly opposed to communism, while the Soviet Union was officially a communist country. The London Poles were afraid the Soviets would use the Red Army to impose a communist government on Poland; their fears increased at the end of July 1944, when a Polish Committee of National Liberation, dominated by Polish Communists, was created in the newly freed city of Lublin. With Soviet support, the committee soon claimed that it, and not the govern-

A group of Polish soldiers about to leave for the front is addressed by Wanda Wasilewska, chair of the Union of Polish Patriots (ZPP). (Reproduced by permission of AP/Wide World Photos)

ment represented by the London Poles, was the legitimate Polish government.

Late in July, Lublin radio called on the Polish underground to rise up against the Germans, promising that the Red Army would soon arrive. In fact, people in Warsaw could already hear the Soviet artillery across the Vistula. The London Poles came to agree that the Home Army should begin a general uprising. One reason for this decision was the fear that if the Home Army did nothing, the Soviets and the Lublin committee would accuse them of being a phony resistance movement, or, as Soviet leaders sometimes already had claimed, that the Home Army was actually pro-German. The London Poles also hoped to gain great advantages from a successful uprising. Many of the men and women in the Home Army were pleading for a chance to fight the hated Germans. If Polish forces played a major role in driving the Germans from their country, it would restore the pride of the Poles who had been severely demoralized by the Germans. Most important, such an action would establish the Home Army as a powerful military force, in control of Warsaw and inde-

pendent of the Red Army. The Home Army could then guard Poland's political and territorial interests against the Soviets.

The commander of the Home Army ordered the uprising to begin on August 1, 1944. Approximately 20,000 fighters, armed with rifles and submachine guns, took control of half of Warsaw. They carried enough ammunition for about one week of fighting. As it turned out, they had to fight for two months. At first the Germans used security troops rather than front-line combat soldiers to fight the Poles, but soon they brought in regulation army units with tanks and artillery. In slow, bloody, house-to-house fighting, the Germans recaptured large areas of the city and forced the Home Army into a few pockets. The Home Army's fighters desperately needed more arms and ammunition. Before long the fighters and the rest of the population would also need food, since the Germans had cut off all supplies into the city. British planes based in England and American bombers coming from Italy attempted to drop supplies by parachute, but many of the provisions fell into German-controlled areas. The planes could not

The First Warsaw Uprising

The Warsaw uprising of August 1944 was a separate event from the uprising of the Warsaw ghetto, which began in April 1943. The Warsaw ghetto was a walled-off section of the city where the Germans forced all of the city's Jews to live. In July 1942 the Germans started deporting the Jews of Warsaw to a secret destination. In fact, they were sending the Jews to death camps to be murdered. Small groups of Jews, especially young people, were determined to resist the Nazis. Although they had very few weapons, little military training, and no help from the rest of Warsaw, they fought fiercely against the German troops for more than a month. In the end, almost all the Jewish fighters were killed, and the Germans destroyed the ghetto. In these respects, the ghetto uprising was like a smaller version of the later uprising of the Home Army. In other ways, however, the situation of the Warsaw Jews was different from that of the non-Jewish Poles. The young leaders of the ghetto uprising did not expect to defeat the Germans or to be rescued by a friendly army; they were fighting to redeem the honor of Jewish people, since they could not save their lives. The fighters had urged their fellow Jews not to allow the Nazis to slaughter them like animals, but instead to die as human beings.

carry heavy loads because of the large amount of fuel needed to fly such long distances, which were doubled because they had to make a round trip without landing. Despite repeated British and American requests, the Soviet government, in all but one case, refused permission for the planes to land on Soviet territory to refuel.

The official Soviet response toward the uprising was negative. Soviet dictator Joseph Stalin referred to the uprising as a reckless and criminal adventure—a stunt that endangered many lives without good reason. These charges are one of the reasons that many people believe the Soviets purposely allowed the Germans to crush the Poles. On the other hand, at the end of August, Soviet forces did make serious attempts to break through to Warsaw. Polish units fighting in the Red Army led these attacks but were driven back after sustaining heavy casualties. In the middle of September the Soviets began dropping at least fifty tons of food and ammunition into Warsaw by plane. French historian Henri Michel argues in *The Second World War* (1975) that the Soviets were now willing to help the Poles because the Home Army was no longer strong enough to present a challenge to the Soviets but was still large enough to be useful against the Germans. With the Poles driven into small sections of the city by the Germans, even supply by air became impossible. On October 2 the Home Army surrendered. By that time half of its 20,000 fighters had been killed and another 7,000 wounded, but the greater loss was suffered by the city itself; more than 200,000 citizens of Warsaw died, many as a result of German revenge actions, and 90 percent of the city was destroyed.

The Plot to Kill Hitler

Crushing the Warsaw uprising could not conceal the fact that Germany had suffered a series of immense defeats in the middle of 1944. From the beginning of June to mid-September, which was a period of disaster for the German army, at least 1 million German soldiers had been killed or captured throughout Europe. In the middle of this period, on July 20, a group of anti-Hitler Germans, most of them army officers, attempted to kill Hitler, take over the government, and end the war. The leaders of the plot, which included some high-ranking generals, believed that killing Hitler was absolutely essential for taking over the government. They were certain that until he was dead, most of the army would follow his orders. It is not surprising to historians that military officers were at the center of the plot. Although they had achieved high rank and great honors under the Nazi government, Germany was a police state, with spies everywhere, and anyone found opposing the government was arrested and sent to a concentration camp. Individually, army officers were among the few Germans who still had some freedom to act as they wanted; as a group, they had the power to resist the Nazis.

Some of the officers involved in the plot had secretly opposed Hitler for a long time. Some of them had been horrified at the crimes committed by the German armed forces, such as the mass shootings of civilians. They blamed Hitler for bringing shame on both Germany and the army. Some blamed Hitler for starting the war, while others criticized him for losing it. Critics have pointed out that these plotters took action only when it was clear that Germany would lose the war. Many of them, whatever their private beliefs, continued to act with loyalty to Hitler, despite the Nazis' terrible crimes, as long as he was winning. Many of them wanted Germany to make peace without surrendering. They understood that the Allies would never agree to these terms while Hitler and the Nazis were in power. This faction hoped that a new government, headed by military men, could negotiate an end to the war. Some even hoped to make peace with the United States and Great Britain and continue the war against the Soviet Union.

The plotters had to be careful in approaching other officers to support the plan, as one word to the Gestapo could cost them their lives, and perhaps the lives of their families. Some of the people they approached, including important generals, refused to promise their support, but they did not inform the Gestapo, either. These generals seemed to take a wait-and-see approach. If Hitler were killed and it appeared the plot to end the war might succeed, they would support it. On the other hand, if the assassination failed they would not have been involved. German officers were taught that duty and honor were important. Every one of them had sworn an oath of obedience to Hitler personally. For many of them, betraying this promise constituted a loss of honor—or, at least, many claimed this was their reason for not supporting the scheme. Some also regarded an overthrow of the government while their country was at war as an act of treason. The fairly small number of officers at the center of the plot, however, believed that Hitler and the Nazis, not the Allies, were Germany's real enemies.

One of the leaders of the group was Count Claus (Schenk Graf) Von Stauffenberg, a colonel who had been badly wounded in North Africa, losing a hand, several fingers on his other hand, and an eye. He was now on the Berlin staff of the Ersazheer (Replacement Army), the organization that drafted and trained new troops to replace combat losses. Stauffenberg prepared a plan for the Ersazheer to take over emergency powers in major German cities, claiming that this action would be

Claus (Schenk Graf) Von Stauffenberg. (Reproduced by permission of © Hulton Getty/Liaison Agency)

used in the event of an uprising by the millions of forced foreign laborers. His real intention was to use the plan to take over the government after Hitler had been killed. Stauffenberg also had regular personal access to Hitler, who was concerned about finding replacements for the army's losses. On July 20, 1944, Stauffenberg was at Hitler's headquarters in East Prussia for a meeting. (Hitler had several headquarters outside Berlin during the war.) Stauffenberg entered the small wooden building, which was almost a hut, where the führer and two dozen others were gathered around an oak table, looking at maps. Stauffenberg placed his briefcase under the table, then left the building under the pretext of having to place a phone call to Berlin. Within minutes a tremendous blast shook the area, as a time bomb hidden in the briefcase exploded. The walls and roof of the building were destroyed, and fire and smoke came pouring out. During the confusion, Stauffenberg escaped in a car to an airstrip, where a plane was waiting to take off for the three-hour flight to Berlin. Believing Hitler was dead, Stauffenberg thought the second stage of the plan would have already begun.

The commander of regular army troops in Berlin, the Berlin chief of police, and some top leaders of the Ersazheer were all part of the plot. The plan had been to take over the radio station

A group of German Army officers conspired to assassinate Nazi leader Adolf Hitler in 1944 but were unsuccessful in the attempt. (National Archives and Records Administration)

radio broadcast of Hitler's voice soon convinced them to remain loyal to the government.

Some of the leaders of the plot, including Stauffenberg, were quickly arrested and shot. Like many other officers, the general who shot them had known about the plot and had taken a wait-and-see attitude. Now he wanted to cover his tracks by shooting the plotters before the Gestapo could question them. Despite his efforts, he too was later arrested by the Gestapo and killed in the same manner. The Gestapo began its investigation of the plot immediately and continued almost until the war was over. Using torture to obtain information, they hunted down officers and civilians who had participated in or had known about the plot. Approximately 5,000 people were executed and several thousand more were sent to concentration camps. A few, such as Field Marshal Erwin Rommel, Germany's most popular war hero, were given a choice between committing suicide or facing arrest and trial. To protect his family, Rommel—one of those who knew about the plot but probably had not participated—killed himself. The Nazis told the German people that Rommel died of a heart attack; he was given a hero's funeral and praised as a loyal supporter of Hitler.

Others were not treated so gently. After being tortured by the Gestapo, those leaders of the plot who had not been shot were immediately tried before a special Nazi People's Court. They were then hanged with piano wire from meat hooks to make their deaths more painful. On Hitler's orders, these trials and hangings were filmed. He would watch the films on the nights of the events. After the failure of the July plot, as it is usually called, the Nazis kept closer control over the army and its officers. To prove their loyalty, some officers participated in military Courts of Honor that expelled the plotters from the army. Then they turned them over to the People's Court to be tried and hanged as civilians. The stiff-armed Nazi salute, with its barked "Heil Hitler" ("Hail Hitler"), replaced the normal military salute. The results of July 20, 1944, also had an impact on military events. German generals were more reluctant to retreat, fearing that Hitler would see it as proof of disloyalty. Now, even more than before, Hitler distrusted the military advice of his generals. All these developments made it more likely that the German army would continue to fight even though there was no chance of victory and the only result was to increase the destruction of Germany and the suffering of the German people.

and the Gestapo headquarters, disarm SS units in the city, and arrest top Nazi leaders. The same procedures would have then taken place throughout Germany and in the rest of German-occupied Europe. With the exception of Paris, where the German military governor of France had arrested all SS and security police forces in the city, none of these things had been done. The reason for the failure of the plan was simple. Hitler was not dead. He had survived Stauffenberg's bomb with only minor injuries. It is possible that the briefcase was moved farther away from Hitler or that the heavy oak table over which he was leaning had protected most of his body from the blast. Although a member of the plot cut off communications from Hitler's headquarters for a while, contact was restored and orders from the plotters in Berlin were canceled by loyal Nazi officers. For a while army units did not know whom to obey, but a live

- - - Front line, Dec. 15, 1944
- - - Limit of German advance by Dec. 25, 1944

N

NETHERLANDS

•Antwerp

•Brussels

BELGIUM

GERMANY

Rhine R.

Meuse R.

ARDENNES

Malmédy

Bastogne•

Limit of German Advance

FRANCE

LUXEMBOURG

| 0 | 20 | 40 mi |
| 0 | 20 | 40 km |

Germany's successful offensive in the Ardennes Forest created a bulge in the Allied front line, giving this famous battle its name, the Battle of the Bulge.

The Battle of the Bulge

While the Germans were crushing the people of Warsaw, the Allies were making tremendous gains in western Europe. Breaking out of Normandy and destroying massive German forces, the Allied tanks moved quickly across France, freeing Paris in late August. On September 3 they crossed the Belgian capital of Brussels, and the next day they reached the Belgian port of Antwerp, the largest in Europe. From Switzerland almost to the North Sea, the Allied armies were approaching the borders of Ger-

Executed for Desertion: The Story of One Man

During World War II, more than 21,000 U.S. military personnel were convicted of desertion. Forty-nine were sentenced to death. Only one was executed—Private Edward Donald Slovik. After one of the shortest court-martials in military history, he was sentenced to death before a firing squad.

Eddie Slovik was born on February 18, 1920. He grew up during the Great Depression in Hamtramck, Michigan, a suburb of Detroit. Hard times hit the Polish American Slovik family, prompting 12-year-old Eddie to steal bread—the first of many scrapes with the law. As a result, he spent several years in the Michigan Reformatory School. After his release, Slovik took a job at a local drug store, where he was caught stealing chewing gum and cigarettes. Between 1932 and 1942, he was incarcerated several times for crimes ranging from car theft to disturbing the peace to violating parole.

Although originally classified as 4F (unfit for military duty) due to his prison record, Slovik received a draft notice from the U.S. Army on November 7, 1943, stating that he had been reclassified as 1A (fit for duty), due to a shortage of men on the front lines. On January 24, 1944, at the age of 21, Slovik reported for Basic Training at Fort Sheridan, on the north side of Chicago.

In June 1944, the Allies launched the D-Day invasion of Normandy on the western coast of France. After the initial inva-

sion, the Allies' ability to break out of the region was not a simple matter, as German troops offered stubborn resistance. More troops were called upon to break through enemy lines. On August 14, Slovik was sent to Scotland and given two days of instruction on fighting in a terrain similar to that of northwestern France. Then he went to Omaha Beach with Company G, 109th Infantry, 28th Division—ominously nicknamed "the jinxed division."

Faced with a real combat situation, Slovik was terrified. He later would report in a written confession that the sounds of shelling made him "so scared nervos [sic] and trembling" that he stayed in his foxhole and refused to move on with his unit. Instead, he walked to a nearby town, stayed overnight in a French hospital, and then turned himself in to a Canadian unit. Six weeks later, the Canadians turned him over to American military police, who brought him to his commander. As Slovik wrote, "I told my commanding officer my story and I said that if I had to go out their [sic] again I'd run away. He said their [sic] was nothing he could do for me if I ran away again. AND I'LL RUN AWAY AGAIN IF I HAVE TO GO OUT THEIR [sic]."

The Slovik court martial was held, significantly, on Veteran's Day—November 11, 1944. The trial lasted a mere hour and forty minutes after which the nine judges found him guilty of violating the 58th Article of War—desertion to avoid hazardous duty. He was sentenced to a dishonorable discharge, forfeiture of all pay and allowances, and death by firing squad.

In an effort to stop American troops from deserting, General Dwight D. Eisenhower,

many. The Allies now faced two major obstacles. One was a line of defensive positions built before the war and recently strengthened, called the Westwall or the Siegfried Line. Although not really a wall, this series of protected cannons, machine-gun emplacements, and tank barriers would severely

slow the Allied advance. The second obstacle was the Rhine River, which separated the Allied armies from the heart of Germany.

Supply difficulties played an even greater role in slowing down the Allies. Much of their gasoline

commander of the Allied Forces, issued the order for the execution of Private Slovik. Eisenhower hoped that by making an example of Slovik, the desertion rate would decrease. Slovik, however, was convinced that his criminal record was the reason behind his conviction and subsequent execution. He petitioned Eisenhower to pardon him for desertion, but his pleas were to no avail.

Slovik was executed on January 31, 1945, at 10:04 a.m., near Ste-Marie aux Mines, a small village in France in the Vosges Mountains. The firing squad was composed of members of the 109th Infantry—men from Slovik's own unit. Alongside Slovik, 94 other U.S. soldiers, who had been convicted of rape and murder, were hanged.

In spite of his otherwise short life, Private Eddie Slovik established a number of precedents with his death. He was the only member of the U.S. armed forces executed for desertion in World War II; in fact, he was the only American soldier executed for that offense since 1864. Like a number of other incidents from history, the Slovik trial and execution does not seem to reflect well on either side. Many historians are not satisfied with the high command's reasoning that an example needed to be made of Slovik to stop the high rate of desertion. Conversely, attempts to make Slovik a hero, a conscientious objector, or a pacifist seem misguided to some. From the facts on record, Slovik appears to have been nothing more than he claimed to be: a frightened young man who did not want to go to war.

For more information on this topic, see: Louis Snyder, *Louis L. Snyder's Historical Guide to World War II,* Greenwood (Westport, CT), 1982; David Wallechinsky and Irving Wallace, *The People's Almanac,* Doubleday (Garden City, NY), 1975; and Zena Simmons, "The Execution of Pvt. Eddie Slovik," *Detroit News* online, http://www.detroitnews.com/history/eddie/eddie.htm (August 16, 2000).

Private Eddie Slovik, the only American man executed for desertion during the war, is seen here at his wedding before he was sent off to fight. (Reproduced by permission of AP/Wide World Photos)

and other needs had to be brought all the way from Normandy by truck because the Allied air forces had destroyed the French railroad system in order to cripple Germany's defense of the Atlantic shore. The problem worsened as the armies advanced farther from Normandy. The port of Antwerp was closer to the fighting, but the Allies were unable to use it because the Germans still controlled the mouth of the river that separates Antwerp from the sea. The U.S. Army organized a system of high-speed, one-way highways, the most famous of which was called the Red Ball Express, to bring sup-

African American soldiers of the 3201st Quartermaster Service Company dig up the bodies of American soldiers massacred at Malmédy so that they can be identified and then given proper burials. (Reproduced by permission of the Corbis Corporation [Bellevue])

plies to the front from Normandy. Although the system worked better than expected, the Allied armies were still not receiving enough supplies.

The supply problem led to arguments and rivalries between General Bernard Montgomery, whose British and Canadian troops were on the northern end of the front, and General George S. Patton, whose American Third Army was farther south. Each general believed that his forces could break through into Germany and end the war quickly with more fuel and supplies. But that would require sending most of the supplies to one army and leaving the rest of the Allied forces without enough resources to resist the Germans. Dwight D. Eisenhower, the American general who was supreme commander of the Allied forces in western Europe, refused to give either Mont-

gomery or Patton all of the supplies at the expense of the other. He instead decided that the Allies would enter Germany along a broad front and would not concentrate their strength in one area. Many military historians have criticized Eisenhower for this decision, saying it was based on placating both the British and Americans. Others have defended Eisenhower, pointing out that the Germans could have attacked whichever Allied force was deprived of supplies.

The Germans soon proved that they were capable of mounting one more large offensive, which took place near the thinly defended Ardennes Forest region of Belgium and Luxembourg. The area did not have a high concentration of Allied forces (only four American divisions were stationed there) because it was widely believed that

Dead soldiers near Malmédy, Belgium. (Reproduced by permission of AP/Wide World Photos)

the Germans would not attack in this area. The Ardennes was heavily forested, with steep hills and narrow roads, and the Americans did not think it was suitable for tanks. This attitude was held despite the fact that German tanks surprised the French by smashing into France through the Ardennes in 1940, destroying the French and British armies there. The mistake was repeated four and one-half years later by the Americans.

Americans soon called the Ardennes offensive the Battle of the Bulge because the German attack created a large bulge in the American lines. The plan was Hitler's idea, not that of his generals. He sent Germany's last available tank divisions to the area against the wishes of his generals, who worried that these divisions would be needed if the Soviets attacked in the east. Further, they could see other weaknesses in the plan, such as the inability to stockpile enough gasoline to ensure that their tanks would have fuel for more than a few days. Instead, they had to rely on capturing large quantities of fuel that the Americans had collected nearby. At first Hitler's plan was successful; the narrow roads and thick forests prevented Allied airplanes from detecting the German tanks being brought

forward for the attack. In addition, the Germans purposely timed the offensive to take place in poor weather so that Allied planes, which had complete control of the skies, could not fly in heavy fog over the dense forest. When the Germans attacked through early-morning fog on December 16, 1944, they completely surprised the outnumbered Americans and made rapid progress, taking a substantial number of prisoners. Soon, however, the resistance of the GIs began to slow the German attack. The town of Bastogne, even though it was surrounded by Germans, refused to surrender.

Though these forces were able to hold the Germans back, a few miles north of Bastogne, at Malmédy, another group of American soldiers was not as fortunate. German Lieutenant Colonel Jochen Peiper, commander of the First SS Panzer Division, directed a ruthless campaign westward through the Ardennes. On the way, his division overran a less-heavily armed American unit at Malmédy, and forced an estimated 125 to 150 Americans to surrender to troops of the First SS Panzer Division. Like many German troops in the Ardennes offensive, this division was part of the Waffen-SS. These were Hitler's favorite units, and

"Who Is Betty Grable's Husband?"

One of the best-known episodes of the Battle of the Bulge had very little military importance. At the beginning of the battle a few dozen English-speaking German soldiers, wearing American uniforms and driving captured American jeeps, went behind American lines to cut telephone wires, destroy road signs, and inflict any other damage that would interfere with American defenses. Ironically, these Germans caused much greater trouble for the Americans when some of them were captured and quickly identified. The supposed size of the German operation grew as the story spread, and soon there were "reports" of thousands of German troops in American uniforms. Nervous GIs stopped other soldiers at gunpoint and questioned them to make sure they were really Americans and not Germans in disguise. General Omar Bradley, commander of the Twelfth Army Group—the second-highest American officer in Europe—was stopped at three separate crossroads and asked a series of questions. For instance, he had to identify the capital of Illinois, the names of football positions, and the husband of movie star Betty Grable. Bradley did not know the answer to the last question, but luckily he convinced the soldiers of his true identity and they did not arrest or shoot him. Incidentally, Grable was married to bandleader Harry James.

they were the best equipped and supplied because they were more "Nazified" than the regular army. Hitler trusted their officers. Rather than waste time taking the prisoners to a camp, the German troops gathered the Americans together in a field and machine-gunned them. (It remains unclear whether Peiper issued a direct order for the shooting.) The mass execution killed eighty-five captured Americans; the rest escaped into the woods or "played dead" until the Germans moved on. The same unit also murdered Belgian civilians in the same area. Soldiers from the SS unit were tried after the war and a dozen were executed for these crimes.

After some confusion on the part of the American commanders, the Allies rushed several divisions to reinforce the Ardennes area. As the weather cleared, the Allied air forces began to pound the German tanks until they slowed and then stopped. Strong Allied forces attacked the bulge from both the north and south, wearing down the Germans until they retreated to their original positions. Although the Allies could technically afford to lose men and equipment, the Germans could not. The Ardennes offensive has often been described as Hitler's last gamble. He knew that if he lost, he would use up almost all of Germany's remaining offensive ability and its best armored divisions would not be available to fight against the Soviets, even for defensive purposes. Nevertheless, a German victory in the Ardennes would not have changed the course of the war. Hitler hoped to recapture the port of Antwerp to disrupt Allied supplies and perhaps drive the British army back to the sea, as had happened after the Ardennes breakthrough in 1940. This plan was completely unrealistic because, at the end of 1944, the Germans no longer had the resources to turn success in the Ardennes into triumph in western Europe. The Battle of the Bulge may have temporarily slowed the progress of the Western Allies, but it helped ensure that when the next big Allied offensive finally came, there would be nothing to stop it.

From Warsaw to Germany

For a number of months the majority of new German divisions had gone to the western front. The German army in Poland had received few additional tanks or planes because the area had been comparatively quiet since the end of the Soviet offensive in August 1944. In their positions east of the Vistula River, however, the Soviets had prepared for their next major attack by gathering almost 2 million tons of supplies, including more than 6,000 tanks and 32,000 pieces of artillery. The attack began on January 12, 1945, along a thirty-mile section of the front where, over the next few days, Soviet forces joined the Western Allies on both sides of the sector. Soon 180 Soviet divisions were attacking along a battlefront 200 miles long.

An African American soldier stands guard over a group of German soldiers who have just surrendered. The Allies pushed into Germany to end the war. (USHMM Photo Archives)

They had twice as many troops as the Germans, four times as many tanks, seven times as much artillery, and six times as many planes. The German defenses collapsed. On January 17, the Red Army entered Warsaw, which had been occupied by the Germans for sixty-four months. Two days later the forces entered Lódz, and the next week they arrived around Breslau (Wroclaw) on the river Oder, 180 miles from where they had started. In the center of the front, the Soviet forces were commanded by Marshal Georgy Zhukov, who had defeated the Germans near Moscow in the winter of 1941 and 1942 and crushed them at Stalingrad a year later. Now Zhukov's armies drove the Germans back 220 miles in five weeks, pushing them 100 miles away from Berlin. Other Soviet units were poised only fifty miles from the suburbs of the German capital.

As the Soviet offensive swept across the German province of East Prussia, the civilian population was swept by panic. Fleeing west, 2 million people abandoned their homes in an effort to escape the Red Army. Many Germans believed the

Red Army would slaughter them in revenge for Germany's brutality in Russia. German forces had murdered millions of Russian civilians, and 3 million Soviet soldiers had been shot or had starved or had frozen to death after being captured by the Germans. The Germans' fears turned out to be accurate. Some units of the Red Army, usually carefully disciplined, turned into murderous gangs once they entered German territory. They set entire villages on fire, as the Germans had done to Russian villages, and raped thousands of German women and girls. They shot whole families, especially if the Soviet soldiers saw a Nazi symbol or a picture of Hitler in their houses. The refugees clogged the roads, and thousands of people died in the winter cold, crushed by advancing tanks, blown up by artillery shells, or machine-gunned by troops. Some units of the German army fought with great heroism to hold off the Soviets long enough for columns of refugees to escape. Apart from the terrible human toll, the Red Army's rampage in East Prussia also had military and political effects. From then until the end of the war, it was clear that the German army would fight harder in

A German Red Cross worker helps a sick Polish man who survived life in a Nazi concentration camp. (Reproduced by permission of National Archives/USHMM Photo Archives)

the east than in the west. German troops were much more willing to surrender to the Americans or British than to the Soviets.

In the middle of February 1945, the Soviet advance came to a halt. The Red Army, once again, had outrun its supplies, which were stockpiled behind the Vistula. In addition, the German retreat narrowed the front from north to south, making it easier for the remaining German troops to defend the shorter front. This area continued to shrink, signifying a definite defeat, as the Red Army was now only 400 miles from the Americans and British. During their advance, Red Army troops freed the Auschwitz concentration camp on January 27, 1945. Only about 6,000 prisoners had survived, and many were near death from disease and starvation. A week earlier the Nazi guards had forced 60,000 others on a death march, in sub-zero weather, to other concentration camps farther west. Prior to this time, more than 1 million men, women, and children, most of them Jews, had been murdered at Auschwitz.

The German Defeat in Southeastern Europe

Although the Red Army's advance had been stopped in Poland, it continued to move forward on the southern end of the eastern front. One advantage of movement in this direction was to place pressure on Germany's allies to withdraw from the war. The first to collapse was Romania, Germany's most important ally in the invasion of the Soviet Union, which sent large numbers of troops to fight alongside the Germans and participate in massacres, especially of Jews. In August 1944, after large Red Army forces entered Romania and threatened to overwhelm its army, the pro-German government was overthrown and the Romanian king arrested its leader. In response, German planes bombed Bucharest, the Romanian capital. Romania then declared war on Germany and sent its troops west to attack Hungary, Germany's remaining ally and Romania's traditional enemy. This series of events also led to the capture of 200,000 more German troops. While Romanian troops joined the Red Army's attack on Hungary, another part of the army headed toward Bulgaria. Although Bulgaria had helped Germany invade Yugoslavia and Greece, it had not joined the invasion of the Soviet Union and had never declared war on the Soviets. On September 5, 1944, the Soviet Union declared war on Bulgaria, but almost no one in Bulgaria wanted to fight the Red Army. There were mutinies in the Bulgarian army, and pro-Soviet groups took over the streets of Sofia, the Bulgarian capital. After the Soviets entered

Southeast Europe, 1942.

Sofia on September 18, Bulgaria declared war on Germany and sent 150,000 troops to fight against their former ally.

West of Romania and Bulgaria lay Yugoslavia, which had been conquered and split up by Ger-

many and its allies in April 1941. Aside from the Soviet Union, Yugoslavia had the largest partisan movement in Europe. After the Red Army entered Yugoslavia, German forces in Greece and Yugoslavia were in danger of being cut off—the Red Army could block the overland routes back to

A soldier of the U.S. Seventh Army lies dead on a bridge over the Rhine while two more soldiers crouch against the wall, attempting to cross. (Reproduced by permission of AP/Wide World Photos)

A U.S. Army tank drives through the streets in Aachen, Germany, firing at the enemy. (Reproduced by permission of AP/Wide World Photos)

Germany and the British navy could prevent evacuation by sea. The Germans began withdrawing from both countries in the middle of October. On October 20, the Yugoslav Partisans and the Red Army entered Belgrade, the capital of Yugoslavia, together. The Partisan army continued to free the rest of the country while the Soviets turned north to join the attack on Hungary. By mid-October, the Red Army was within fifty miles of the Hungarian capital of Budapest, but Hitler was determined to keep control of Hungary to prevent a Soviet advance into Austria and Germany. After two months of fighting, the Red Army surrounded Budapest on the day after Christmas, bombarding it with artillery. It took until mid-January for the Soviets to enter Budapest, and it was not until February 13, 1945, after a month of intense street fighting, that German resistance finally ended.

The Western Front: Crossing the Rhine

Back on the western front, during the months after the Battle of the Bulge, a series of Allied operations cleared German resistance from the west bank of the Rhine River, the last major obstacle in Germany. The Allies could then cross the river along the entire front, as General Eisenhower had planned. On March 8, 1945, American troops at Remagen, near Bonn, captured the only bridge over the Rhine that the Germans had not yet detonated. Soon, three American divisions had reached the other side of the river. Elsewhere, progress was more difficult; the first troops might cross the river in small boats and then hold the other shore while combat engineers, under German fire, constructed new bridges. On March 22 troops of General Patton's Third Army crossed the Rhine. The next day, farther north, British, Canadian, and American troops, commanded by General Montgomery, crossed the river in force and began their attack on the Ruhr, Germany's most important industrial region. The American Seventh Army and the French First Army reached the other side of the river quickly, their tanks striking into southern Germany.

By April 1, 1945, nine Allied armies with ninety divisions, twenty-five of them armored, were either

Western Germany, spring 1945, showing the approximate locations of Western Allied armies as they crossed the Rhine and moved into the heart of Germany.

on the other side of the Rhine or awaiting their turn to cross. There were no more natural barriers. From that day until Germany surrendered five weeks later, the Allies pushed the retreating Germans farther east. Although the Germans often fought hard, there were increasing cases of mass surrenders. As the end of the war approached, German troops sometimes took every opportunity to surrender to the British or Americans rather than be captured by the Red Army. German soldiers knew that the Nazis had murdered Soviet prisoners by the millions, and they feared the same treatment if they fell into Soviet hands.

Liberated by the U.S. Army, Ebensee camp prisoners evacuate the camp. On their way out, they pass under a banner reading "We Welcome Our Liberators." (National Archives/USHMM Photo Archives)

British and American troops soon saw examples of Nazi mass murder as well. On April 11, American soldiers liberated the Buchenwald concentration camp, and four days later the British freed Bergen-Belsen. In these and many other places, the battle-hardened soldiers and officers of the Allied armies came face to face with scenes of human cruelty beyond anything they had experienced on the battlefield. General Patton was so affected upon seeing Buchenwald that he vomited. The Nazis had continued murdering as many of their enemies as possible, especially Jews, even when the Allied armies were only a few miles away and Germany had obviously lost the war. One example of this occurred at Dachau, near Munich, the first concentration camp. When the Americans reached Dachau on April 29, only ten days prior to Germany's surrender, they found that the SS guards had evacuated the camp. By this time, however, there was no place left to transfer the prisoners and the Nazis had forced 15,000 to 20,000 people to march aimlessly around the countryside to keep American troops from freeing them. Exhausted, starving, and sick, many of them died before the GIs could find them.

Allied leaders had already decided that when Germany was defeated, they would divide the country into different occupation zones. The Soviet zone,

Toward the end of the war, young boys were recruited to fight in the German army. This boy was captured by U.S. forces in Germany. (Reproduced by permission of the Corbis Corporation [Bellevue])

The Death of Hitler

German leader Adolf Hitler lived the last three and one-half months of his life in a series of small rooms buried fifty-five feet below the center of Berlin, issuing orders to his armies by radio and telephone. His companions included some high Nazi officials, secretaries and assistants, and Eva Braun, his longtime lover, whom he married just one day before both committed suicide. At first the underground bunker was the center of the German government, but as the weeks passed, the atmosphere inside became increasingly surreal. Hitler's orders could no longer be obeyed; the armies to which he issued them no longer existed. Almost to the end, Hitler frequently believed that Germany might not lose the war. He thought the Western Allies and the Soviet Union would split apart, as he had predicted for years. When U.S. President Franklin D. Roosevelt died on April 12, 1945, some Nazi leaders were sure that his death would somehow alter the course of the war. While Hitler seemed to be awaiting a miracle that would save Germany from defeat, he also appeared determined that the war would not end until Germany was completely destroyed. He insisted that the Battle of Berlin continue, no matter what the cost. Even as Soviet troops were fighting their way into the center of Berlin, squads of SS men roamed the streets and hanged German soldiers who were trying to escape the fighting.

Hitler's own escape came on April 30, 1945, when he and Braun committed suicide. In accordance with Hitler's instructions, his men doused their bodies with gasoline and burned them in the courtyard above the bunker.

As the Red Army overtakes Berlin, a soldier hoists a Soviet flag above the Reichstag, proclaiming an Allied victory. (Reproduced by permission of Corbis)

After the announcement that Germany had surrendered, thousands of British citizens flocked to London's Trafalgar Square to celebrate V-E (Victory over Europe) Day. It would be several more months before the Allies could commemorate V-J (Victory over Japan) Day. (Library of Congress)

As they walk through town, German citizens from Gardelegen transport wooden crosses on their way to bury dead concentration camp prisoners. American soldiers had ordered the German civilians to perform the burial in an effort to show them the extent of the crimes committed by the Nazis. (Reproduced by permission of the National Archives/USHMM Photo Archives)

U.S. President Truman on German Surrender

When the war with Germany finally ended, U.S. President Harry S Truman had this to say: "This is a solemn but glorious hour. General [Dwight D.] Eisenhower informs me that the forces of Germany have surrendered to the United Nations. The flags of freedom fly all over Europe.

"For this victory, we join in offering our thanks to the Providence which has guided and sustained us through the dark days of adversity. Our rejoicing is sobered and subdued by a supreme consciousness of the terrible price we have paid to rid the world of [German leader Adolf] Hitler and his evil. Let us not forget, my fellow Americans, the sorrow and the heartache which today abide in the homes of so many of our neighbors—neighbors whose most priceless possession has been rendered as a sacrifice to redeem our liberty.

"We can repay the debt which we owe our God, to our dead, and to our children, only by work, by ceaseless devotion to the responsibilities which lie ahead of us. If I could give you a single watchword for the coming months, that word is work, work and more work. We must work to finish the war. Our victory is only half over."

For more information about Truman's life and speeches, see *Memoirs* by Harry S Truman, Volume 1, *Year of Decisions*, Doubleday (Garden City, NY), 1955.

in the east, would extend roughly to the river Elbe, which placed Berlin within the Soviet area and meant that the Red Army would make the final attack against Hitler's capital. The push began on April 16, 1945, and this last battle of the war against Germany was as massive as the other struggles on the eastern front. While 2.5 million Soviet soldiers moved against Berlin, 1 million German troops defended the city. By April 22 the fighting reached the streets of Berlin as block after block was destroyed and thousands of men died. The Germans fought ferociously. Among them were hardened veterans of countless battles, as well as men too old and boys too young to fight. Among them also were groups of foreign Nazis, who fought for Germany because they believed in Hitler and his ideas. Berlin was now a scene of suffering and destruction like those that people throughout Europe had been experiencing under the Nazi regime for years.

The remaining civilian population, short of food and water, crowded into cellars as hundreds of thousands of Soviet artillery shells exploded and fires raged throughout Berlin. Behind the Soviet front line were thousands more Soviet soldiers, many of them recently freed prisoners of war. They spread terror among the German civilians, killing, looting, and raping. More than 100,000 Berliners died in the battle. On April 30, as the Red Army reached the government buildings above him, Hitler committed suicide in his underground bunker. The next day the German military commander of Berlin asked for cease-fire terms from the Soviets. They told him they would accept only an unconditional surrender. On May 2 Berlin finally surrendered after a campaign that had killed or injured a quarter of a million Soviet soldiers. German troops still controlled sections of the country, however, and there were German forces in other parts of Europe that the Allies had bypassed in their advance. Fighting continued for several days, some of it extremely bloody. On May 8, 1945, Admiral Karl Dönitz, the man Hitler had appointed to replace him as führer of Germany, sent representatives to Eisenhower's headquarters at Reims in eastern France. There they signed an unconditional surrender. The next day representatives of the German armed forces repeated the signing at Soviet headquarters in Berlin, amidst the ruins of the war they had begun over four and one-half years earlier.

Throughout the Allied nations, thousands of joyous citizens gathered for celebrations in cities and towns, marking V-E (Victory in Europe) Day on May 8, 1945. Ticker tape parades were among the types of celebrations held as the Allies welcomed the end to the long, bloody war in Europe. Some newspapers reported scenes of celebrations where "everybody was kissing everybody."

In Great Britain, King George VI addressed the British after the German surrender. During his speech, he offered the following words: "Today we give thanks to Almighty God for a great deliverance.... Germany, the enemy who drove all Europe into war, has been finally overcome." King George VI added: "Let us remember those who will not come back, their constancy and courage in battle, their sacrifice and endurance in the face of a merciless enemy.... Then let us salute in proud gratitude the great host of the living who have brought us to victory.... Armed or unarmed, men and women, you have fought, striven, and endured to your utmost."

The scene in Germany was different. While the victors celebrated, the defeated found themselves faced with the realities of what the Nazis had done. As death camps were liberated, Allied troops often rounded up German citizens to help bury the dead. The Allies wanted the local populace to see what the Nazis had done.

Thousands come out to celebrate V-E Day (Victory in Europe Day) on May 8. This celebration at 42nd Street in New York City was one of many held throughout the country. (Reproduced by permission of AP/Wide World Photos)

PRIMARY SOURCE

Charles B. MacDonald
"Meet Company I"
Excerpt from *Company Commander*

Published in 1947
This edition published in 1999

As the Allied armies continued to sweep across Europe and advance toward the western borders of Germany, they were faced with penetrating the Siegfried Line (called the Westwall by the Germans). This line of defensive positions was built before the war and consisted of a series of protected cannons, machine-gun emplacements, and tank barriers meant to slow the Allied advance severely. The Allies also had to negotiate the Rhine River, which separated their armies from the heart of Germany. The advance was continually slowed down by supply problems, which allowed the Germans time to regroup and prepare for an attack. Despite supply problems of their own, the Germans soon proved that they could still mount one more large offensive, which came near the Ardennes Forest region of Belgium and Luxembourg. This area was thinly defended by the Allies (with only four American divisions stationed there) due to a commonly held belief that the Germans would not attack, especially with Panzer units, because the Ardennes was heavily forested, with steep hills and narrow roads. In 1940 German tanks had smashed into France through the Ardennes, destroying the French and British armies, a fact that was ignored by the Americans four and one-half years later.

Sent into this situation was a twenty-one-year-old U.S. Army company commander named Charles B. MacDonald. He was placed in command of a company at a young age and served against Germany in the Ardennes from 1944 until the end of the war in 1945. He was initially put in charge of Company I of the Twenty-third Infantry, Second Infantry Division on the Siegfried Line along the western borders of Germany. He then saw action in the Battle of the Bulge and took part in the last Allied offensives before the collapse of German forces. MacDonald wrote about these experiences in *Company Commander*, which is now considered a classic military narrative. The book was first published in 1947 and has remained almost continuously in print ever since. In this work MacDonald gives an account of the daily lives of average soldiers. He is bluntly honest about his own fears and trepidations at being placed in command of older, more experienced men. The power of *Company Commander* is that MacDonald enables the reader to see the terror and danger that confront soldiers on the front lines. In the following excerpt MacDonald describes his first command, which was defined as a "good assignment"—holding a defensive position along a quiet sector of the Siegfried Line.

Company Commander
"Meet Company I"

Dusk was approaching when the French locomotive, whistling shrilly to announce its arrival, wheezed into the station hidden sedately among the green-clad mountains along the French-Belgian border. The little moustached Frenchman who had jolted and jostled us across the whole of France jumped from his dominating perch in the engine and ran beside the train to join a cohort in chattering and gesticulating wildly. It was not too dark to read the faded black and white sign hanging above the platform—Longuyon.

I gathered my equipment and stepped from the train. Already hundreds of men in olive drab uniforms, loaded with the variety of equipment and weapons that characterizes the American soldier, were disentangling themselves from the freight cars.

I decided that the little engineer must have thought we had not played fair with his forty-and-eight cars. There was not a car in my section of the train which did not disgorge at least forty-three men, plus equipment. The equipment would more than make up for the absence of the eight horses.

"I Company over here," I shouted above the noise of the detrainment. "Column o' twos facing this way. Headquarters, first, second, third, fourth."

The milling around began to take on a semblance of unity of purpose. I signalled "forward," and the column began an accordion-like action of mov-

ing off, a man here and there making a last-minute adjustment of his pack or overcoat.

We moved through the gate in the dirty concrete fence of the station yard and out to the main street of the town. I dropped back from my position at the head of the column to survey the long line of men ... tall ones, short ones; not unlike similar companies I had commanded in the US before coming overseas. Perhaps there was something about the way these men walked—the confident swagger, perhaps. I think I would have known, even had I been one of the silent, stone-faced civilians staring at us from the open doorways and windows along the way, that underneath those stubbly growths of beard and those wisps of straw from the boxcars clinging to the unpressed uniforms lay a wealth of battlefield experience.

"Company I, 23d Infantry," I thought. "You fought your way ashore in Normandy on D plus one. You battled to the top of Hill 192 to pave the way for the St. Lô breakout. You stormed the ring of pillboxes at Brest and had your number reduced to fifty in the explosion as the Germans blew them up in your faces. And now they give you a company commander fresh from the States. They ask you to put your faith in me ... "

I felt weak and ineffectual.

I quickened my pace, regaining my place at the head of the column as we crossed a temporary US Army bridge which had replaced the demolished ancient stone structure over the gurgling mountain stream which ran through the center of the village. We approached the last houses on the edge of the town, and the road began its steep ascent to the hilltop beyond. Now a dirty little French boy came running out to yell some newly learned Yankee curse-word at us as we passed. Now a little girl bashfully thrust a bouquet of flowers into a soldier's hands and turned to disappear behind her mother's skirts in a doorway.

Our column plodded slowly up the hill, the full field packs beginning to assert their weight. Sweat formed on my body, and I wished that I had carried my heavy GI overcoat instead of wearing it. But the early evening mountain air did nip at my face and felt refreshingly cool on my hands as I took off my heavy GI woolen gloves. My nose began to run from the cold acquired on the long train ride, but I couldn't reach my handkerchief through the bundlesome overcoat and equipment.

The road made a sharp bend to the left as we reached the crest. It was light enough to see the deep valley to the right with its roving stream following the contour of the railroad track on the mountainside beyond.

"Damn," a heavily-breathing soldier in my headquarters group exclaimed between clenched teeth, "I sure hope it levels off before we reach the front. It'd be a sonofabitch to fight in this kind of country."

"We're still a helluva ways from the front," another said. "How far you reckon it is, Cap'n?"

I looked back. It was Private First Class Henry Croteau, of East Hartford, Conn. He had been the company interpreter and the company commander's runner through the campaign in France. "About twenty or thirty miles, the Colonel says," I replied.

The road continued upgrade and we walked on in silence. The cold wind felt good to my face. I was conscious of a heavy mist about us which slowly turned into a fine rain, which, coupled with the overcast that had plagued us all day, boded no good for a bivouac in the open.

A mile down the road we met the battalion commander, Lieutenant Colonel Paul V. Tuttle, of San Antonio, Texas. He was a tall, handsome young West Pointer of about twenty-eight years. His short brown hair was beginning to grey slightly at the temples, and his face had a ruddy glow from the wind as he waited for us beside the road. He motioned me to a

Pin-ups were important to many GIs, reminding them of the women back home. This private has decorated his foxhole in France with pictures of models and movie stars. (Reproduced by permission of AP/Wide World Photos)

field a few hundred yards down the road and designated a spot on the right for my company.

"We'll bivouac here for the night, Mac," he said. "There's a haystack over there. Let the men heat K-rations with the boxes but leave off the other fires. There might be some little birds around, you know."

I congratulated myself upon the good fortune that had given me such an understanding battalion commander for my first combat experience and turned off the road at the place he had designated. I directed the platoons to their respective areas in the field and noted that K, L, M and Battalion Headquarters Companies were following us in.

Our arrival seemed to be the signal for the clouds to burst. The mist that had become a drizzle now became a torrent. The men scrambled madly to get their packs undone and shelter halves spread over equipment. Then followed the rush for the haystack. The field was already a soggy mass of mud, and the downpour of rain was making it muddier by the minute.

I joined my headquarters group in heating the cans of K rations over the oblong cardboard boxes they came in. The rain and wind made it hard to get the fires started at first but the rain soon slackened. I wondered how I could force down another K-ration meal after five days of the same monotonous food aboard the train, but I found that anything edible tasted good after the hike from the station.

Colonel Tuttle sent a messenger with the message for me to report to him for instructions for the morning. My executive officer said he would fix up our tent and put my equipment in out of the rain while I was gone. He was First Lieutenant Rudolph A. (Sparky) Flaim, of Rosati, Mo., a husky young officer who had already qualified for three Purple Hearts and was on his way to flirt with the fourth. When I returned he was snoring loudly on his own side of the little pup tent, and most of the company had turned in for the night.

I walked through the disorderly rows of tents and the thick mud made sucking noises as it pulled at my overshoes. I sought out the platoon leaders. I found First Lieutenant Long H. Goffigon, of Cape Charles, Va., my 1st Platoon leader, and First Lieutenant Alfred Antey, of Evansville, Ind., my 3d Platoon leader, sleeping in the same tent. First Lieutenant Thomas D. Brock, of Plymouth, Mich., my 2d Platoon leader, and First Lieutenant Robert H. Glasgow, of Arlington, N.J., weapons platoon leader, were together. I told them the plans for the morning and walked to the end of the field where I found two guards huddled in their raincoats. I told them to pass the word on to the guards who relieved them to awaken the company at five o'clock. We would have another K-ration breakfast before loading on trucks to continue the move.

I went back to my tent and pulled off my muddy overshoes and crawled inside but I couldn't go to sleep. Sparky had pushed well over toward my side of the tent in his sleep, and a mound of dirt positioned itself squarely in the small of my back; it had seemingly escaped the softening process of the heavy rain.

My mind began to peruse the duties that were before me. In perhaps one day, and at the most, three days, I would be leading these men against a team of trained killers. I wondered how I would react. These men so deserved the best in leadership. Could I give it to them? They could boast a glorious combat record already and I knew nothing. Suddenly, all my long hours of training for just such a role as this seemed pitifully inadequate. If only there were some way I could know just what "it" was like. It seemed incredi-

ble that this group of hardened combat veterans could accept an inexperienced youth of twenty-one to lead them into battle simply because he happened to come to them wearing a set of flashy bars on his shoulders. If only I could look into their minds to see what they were thinking!

I was awakened the next morning by someone rapping on my tent and shouting that it was five o'clock. It was dark but the rain had stopped. That would make it slightly less disagreeable to roll up wet shelter-halves and damp equipment to strap to one's back. We had scarcely enough time to heat a K-ration meal before battalion headquarters sent a runner to tell us to load on the trucks.

The truck ride took us through a portion of Belgium before we crossed the border into the Duchy of Luxembourg. Civilians began to come to their doors to greet us with enthusiastic cheers and two fingers raised in the "V"-for-victory sign. In one town an effigy of Adolf Hitler hung suspended by the neck from a rope above the road. Everywhere there were spontaneous expressions of gratitude. I felt a surging feeling of pride within me that for the moment pushed my fears of the future into the background. If war but consisted of only travel and cheers from a grateful populace!

We crossed the Luxembourg border and entered Belgium once again, noticing an increase in the military traffic. As our trucks rolled into Schönberg, Belgium, numerous command post and hospital installations, the increased number of German shop signs, and the apathy of the civilians told us we could not be far from Germany.

Our convoy turned off the highway at Schönberg and wound slowly up a sandy dirt road leading into the thick fir forests beyond the town. We rode on and on, and the forest seemed of an impenetrable depth. The sandy road gave out eventually and we found ourselves on an unimproved trail that had become a morass of mud from unaccustomed heavy traffic. Our convoy came to a halt. We had reached the spot for our bivouac.

Beneath the dense covering of the fir trees our kitchens were already set up. They had arrived from France by motor the evening before. An appetizing supper of hamburgers and vegetables awaited us, but it proved too much for my stomach after the week's diet of K-rations and I suffered pains from overeating.

Darkness had fallen and the company was beginning to turn in for the night when I was called to battalion headquarters. The Colonel had set up a small command post tent in the woods. A gasoline lantern took some of the chill off the night air inside. The other company commanders were already there.

I was handed five maps, one for myself and one for each of my platoon leaders. The Colonel did not waste much time. He said, "I'd like to give you the information I have so you can get back and get some sleep."

My pulse quickened. "So this is it," I said to myself, using a phrase that every replacement uses a thousand times before he ever actually reaches combat. I would soon know if I could "take it." I would soon know if I could justify the faith of the men from Company I.

"It looks as if we've finally drawn a good assignment," Colonel Tuttle continued, and I breathed somewhat easier. Already whirling visions of attacking formidable Siegfried Line pillboxes had been flashing through my mind. "We're to relieve the 28th Division in the defense of a stretch along the Siegfried Line. It's supposed to be a quiet sector—so they tell us. There've been a few small-scale German counterattacks in the area and some artillery and SP [self-propelled gun] fire, but at least it's quieter than the attack."

There were questions and a general discussion.

"Now," the Colonel continued, "we leave in the morning at seven o'clock. Have your kitchens prepare a hot breakfast. They'll move up later under Lieutenant Koch [First Lieutenant Verner C. Koch, of San Antonio, Texas, battalion supply officer]. We'll go to a forward assembly area back of the line where you can issue more ammunition. Then we'll have time for reconnaissance, and the actual relief will take place tomorrow night."

We dispersed to our company areas. In the darkness outside the tent I noticed the flashes of artillery to the east and the deep rumble of the big guns came from the distance. A voice in my brain kept repeat-

ing, "This is it! This is it!" I stumbled blindly through the dark forest in the direction of the company.

I stopped by the first sergeant's tent where I found First Sergeant Henry D. Albin, of Houston, Texas, huddled in his tent with a raincoat over the entrance as a blackout curtain. He was a young auburn-haired, red-faced Texan who drawled pleasantly when he talked. He was preparing the company morning report by flashlight. "How does it look?" he asked.

"Not too bad," I answered. "It's the defense."

"Could be worse then, I guess," he said. "If it ain't bad it'll be the first time this outfit ever drew a good assignment."

I asked him to send for the platoon leaders to receive the information I had about the situation. They soon gathered around the tent. I was beginning to give them the information when a soldier stepped from the darkness.

"Is the first sergeant 'round?" the soldier asked.

"Right here," Sergeant Albin answered.

"I'm from the 9th Infantry, Sergeant," the soldier said. "We're bivouacked just across the way, and I got a ride over so I figured I'd stop by to see my brother. I haven't seen him in some time but he's in this company."

"What's the name?"

"Wagram [soldier's name in this instance is fictitious]," the soldier answered. "Wagram. His first name's—"

The feeble light from the flashlight inside the tent shone briefly on the soldier's face.

"Yeah. Yeah, I know," Sergeant Albin interrupted. "In the 3d Platoon. With us at Brest. Killed in action there." (MacDonald, *Company Commander*, pp. 2-7)

Aftermath

Two months later MacDonald and his division were removed from action in an attack against the Ruhr dams. They were sent to act as a blockade against the last major German offensive, known as the Battle of the Bulge but referred to as the Ardennes offensive by the Germans. MacDonald's

Second Division, assisted by the Ninety-ninth Division, formed a wall of defense under the cloak of darkness and completely dismantled the northern section of the German attack. *Company Commander* allows the reader to follow the action through the eyes of a rifle company entrenched in snow and defending themselves against the onslaught of German Tiger tanks. The account shows that even a severely weakened German army was a viable threat to the Allied soldiers serving in Europe during the last months of the war in 1945. MacDonald also wrote about the Battle of the Bulge in *The Mighty Endeavor: American Armed Forces in the European Theater in World War II* (1969), which is considered one of the most concise and accurate accounts of the conflict.

The Ardennes offensive was Hitler's idea, not a strategy developed by his generals. He had sent Germany's last available tank divisions to the area despite the protests of the generals. They were concerned that these forces would be needed if the Soviets attacked in the east, and saw the weaknesses of the plan—such as the Germans' inability to stockpile enough gasoline to ensure that the tanks would have fuel for more than a few days. Nevertheless, Hitler believed Axis troops could capture the large quantities of fuel that the Americans had collected nearby. His plan was initially successful because the narrow roads and thick forests prevented Allied airplanes from detecting the German tanks being brought forward for the attack.

The Battle of the Bulge began on December 16, 1944, when the Germans struck under a cloak of fog and completely surprised the outnumbered Americans. A substantial number of American soldiers were taken prisoner, but the success of the German offensive was short-lived. After a brief period of confusion, the Americans quickly organized and the Allies rushed several divisions to reinforce the Ardennes area. When the weather cleared, Allied air forces began to pound the German tanks until they slowed, then stopped. Strong Allied divisions attacked the bulge from both north and south, blasting the Germans until they were forced to retreat to their original positions. The Germans could not afford such a gamble, as the war had already taken a heavy toll on their industrial and military strength. Hitler's desire to recapture the port of Antwerp, as he had done in 1940, was virtually impossible, due to the heavy losses suffered by the Nazis. The Battle of the Bulge, while temporarily halting the Allied advance, did little more than ensure that the Ger-

mans would have no strength to stop the Allies from sweeping into Germany and ending the war.

After the war, MacDonald went on to a career as deputy chief historian for the U.S. Army. He wrote two of the army's official histories of the European campaign and was a co-author of a third. He also wrote books on the Battle of the Bulge and the Huertgen Forest, which were met with critical and popular acclaim. Some military historians still regard *The Mighty Endeavor* as one of the best accounts of World War II in Europe. MacDonald retired as a colonel in the army reserve, having achieved a GS-15, the government's highest civilian rank. He died in 1990.

SOURCES

Books

Ambrose, Stephen E., *Citizen Soldiers: The U.S. Army from the Normandy Beaches to the Bulge to the Surrender of Germany,* Simon & Schuster (New York), 1997.

Goldstein, Donald M., Katherine V. Dillon, and J. Michael Wenger, *Nuts! The Battle of the Bulge: The Story and Photographs,* Brassey's (Washington, DC), 1994.

MacDonald, Charles B., *Company Commander,* Burford Books (Short Hills, NJ), 1947.

MacDonald, Charles B., *The Mighty Endeavor: American Armed Forces in the European Theater in World War II,* Da Capo Press (New York), 1992.

MacDonald, Charles B., *A Time for Trumpets: The Untold Story of the Battle of the Bulge,* Bantam Books (New York), 1985.

Other

The Battle of the Bulge (video), Peter Batty Productions, 1969.

Battle of the Bulge, http://members.aol.com/_ht_a/ dadswar/bulge/ (July 14, 2000).

Battle of the Bulge Overview, http://www.ualberta. ca/~dreinbol/bulge.html (July 14, 2000).

The Last Days of World War II (video), Greystone Communications for A&E Network, 1995.

Stephen E. Ambrose
Excerpt from *Citizen Soldiers: The U.S. Army from the Normandy Beaches to the Bulge to the Surrender of Germany*
Published in 1997

The Allies broke out of Normandy, France, on July 25, 1944. Their goal was to fight their way through France and Belgium and into Germany, eventually forcing the surrender of the German armies occupying most of Europe. Allied forces made great strides throughout the summer of 1944, liberating Paris from German control on August 25. By December, however, the Allied advance was stopped in its tracks because supplies of gas, food, and ammunition were running low. The German army launched a counterattack on December 16, 1944, deploying more than 250,000 heavily armed troops to repel the Allies. They captured the Belgian city of Antwerp, the port city through which the Allied forces received their supplies. The Germans directed their attack through the dense woods of the Ardennes Forest in southeastern Belgium. The Ardennes was a weak spot in the American line, left largely unprotected by ground troops. Using blitzkrieg tactics, the Germans caught the Americans by surprise and bombarded them under the cover of thick early morning fog. The German army then pushed about forty miles into American defenses, producing a bulge in the line. Now known as the Battle of the Bulge, it would become the costliest engagement of the war for the Americans. The Battle of the Bulge is considered the last great German offensive in World War II.

In his book *Citizen Soldiers,* Stephen E. Ambrose examines the successful U.S. Army efforts to "creat[e] an army of citizen soldiers from scratch." The following excerpt describes the Ardennes at the height of the surprise attack on American troops during the Battle of the Bulge. Airborne divisions were important in the Ardennes campaign, especially the U.S. 101st, a division of General George S. Patton's Third Army whose members were veterans of combat in Normandy and Holland.

Citizen Soldiers

December 16—19, 1944

The U.S. Army in retreat was a sad spectacle. When the 101st Airborne got to Bastogne [a town in southeastern Belgium where German forces surrounded Americans in December 1944] on December 19, the columns marched down both sides of the road, toward the front. Down the middle of the road came the defeated American troops, fleeing the front in disarray, moblike. Many had thrown away their rifles, their coats, all encumbrances. Some were in a panic, staggering, exhausted....

The 101st had packed and left Mourmelon in a hurry. The troopers were short of everything, including ammunition. "Where's the ammo? We can't fight without ammo," the men were calling out as they marched through Bastogne to the sound of the guns. The retreating horde supplied some. "Got any ammo?" the paratroopers would ask those who were not victims of panic.

"Sure, buddy, glad to let you have it."

Corp. Walter Gordon noted sardonically that by giving away their ammo, the retreating men relieved themselves of any further obligation to stand and fight [originally quoted in Walter Gordon interview, Eisenhower Center, University of New Orleans]. They had long since left behind partly damaged or perfectly good artillery pieces, tanks, half-tracks, trucks, jeeps, food, rations, and more.

German soldiers take cover in a ditch beside a disabled American tank during the Battle of the Bulge. (Reproduced by permission of the Corbis Corporation [Bellevue])

Two U.S. soldiers look at dead crewmen on a snow-covered German tank. (Reproduced by permission of the Corbis Corporation [Bellevue])

Abandonment of equipment was sometimes unavoidable, but often it was inexcusable. Panic was the cause. Guns that should have been towed out of danger were not. When a convoy stalled, drivers and passengers jumped out of their vehicles and headed west on foot....

But by no means was everything abandoned. Reporter Jack Belden ... described the retreat as he saw it in the Ardennes on December 17, 1944. There were long convoys of trucks, carrying gasoline, portable bridges, and other equipment headed west, with tanks and other armed vehicles mixed in. "I noticed in myself ... the feeling of guilt that seems to come over you whenever you retreat. You don't like to look anyone in the eyes. It seems as if you have done something wrong. I perceived this feeling in others too."

Belden went on, "The road was jammed with every conceivable kind of vehicle. An enemy plane came down and bombed and strafed the column, knocking three trucks off the road, shattering trees and causing everyone to flee to ditches.... It went on all night. There must have been a buzz bomb or a piloted plane raid somewhere every five minutes" [originally quoted in Jack Belden's "Retreat in Belgium," Reporting World War II, pp. 596–599].

Belden was right in his perception that others ... fleeing the fight felt guilty.... Pvt. Kurt Vonnegut [who later became an acclaimed novelist] was a recently arrived replacement in the 106th Division. He was caught up in the retreat before he could be assigned. To his eyes, it was just rout, pure and simple.

His unit surrendered. Vonnegut decided he would take his chances and bolted into the woods, without a rifle or rations, or proper winter clothing. He hooked up with three others who wouldn't surrender and set off hoping to find American lines

An American GI captured by Germans in the Battle of the Bulge. (National Archives and Records Administration)

U.S. soldiers on their way to stop the German advance in the Ardennes. (Reproduced by permission of the Corbis Corporation [Bellevue])

[originally quoted in Kurt Vonnegut interview, Eisenhower Center, University of New Orleans].

... In May 1940, when German armor drove through the Ardennes, the French high command had thrown up its hands and surrendered.... In December 1944, when German armor drove through the Ardennes, [American General Dwight D.] Eisenhower saw his chance.

At dawn on December 19, as German tanks prepared to surround Bastogne and the 101st marched into the town, Eisenhower met with his senior commanders in a cold, damp squad room in a barracks at Verdun, the site of the greatest battle ever fought.

There was but one lone potbellied stove to ease the bitter cold. Eisenhower's lieutenants entered the room glum, depressed, embarrassed....

Eisenhower walked in, looked disapprovingly at the downcast generals, and boldly declared, "The present situation is to be regarded as one of opportunity for us and not of disaster. There will be only cheerful faces at this conference table."

[General George S.] Patton quickly picked up the theme. "Hell, let's have the guts to let the bastards go all the way to Paris," he said. "Then, we'll really cut 'em off and chew 'em up."....

Eisenhower's decisiveness and Patton's boldness were electrifying. Their mood quickly spread through the system. Dispirited men were energized. For those who most needed help, the men on the front line, help was coming....

From the Supreme Commander down to the lowliest private, men pulled up their socks and went forth to do their duty. It simplifies, but not by much, to say that here, there, everywhere, from top to bottom, the men of the U.S. Army in Northwest Europe shook themselves and made this a defining moment in their own lives, and in the history of the Army. They didn't like retreating, they didn't like getting kicked around, and as individuals, squads, and companies as well as at SHAEF [Supreme Headquarters Allied Expeditionary

Forces], they decided they were going to make the enemy pay.

That they had time to readjust and prepare to pound the Germans was thanks to a relatively small number of front-line GIs. The first days of the Battle of the Bulge were a triumph of the soldiers of democracy, marked by innumerable examples of men seizing the initiative, making decisions, leading. Captain [Charles] Roland of the 99th [U.S. Army Division] put it best: "Our accomplishments in this action were largely the result of small, virtually independent and isolated units fighting desperately for survival. They present an almost-unprecedented example of courage, resourcefulness, and tenacity...." [originally quoted in an interview with Stephen Ambrose, January 17, 1995]. (Ambrose, pp. 205–209)

Aftermath

The Allied forces rallied and fought back. Their mission was to close the forty-mile-deep bulge in the Ardennes while facing bad weather, rough terrain, and the formidable power of German "Tiger" tank warfare. Belgian citizens aided the Allied effort in small but invaluable ways, repairing blown truck tires, housing soldiers, even donating family linens for troops to drape over equipment as winter camouflage. In the struggle for the key city of Bastogne in the Ardennes, German forces sought the surrender of American General Anthony McAuliffe of the 101st Airborne Division. His response to the proposal for surrender was just one

word: "Nuts!" With the rest of General Patton's American force fighting in the south and General Bernard Montgomery's British force in the north, the Allies joined together and succeeded in driving the Germans out of Belgium by the end of December. The "bulge" in the Ardennes was eliminated by mid-January 1945. About 16,000 Americans died in the battle and another 60,000 were injured or captured. The Germans sustained even heavier losses. The First American army crossed the all-important Rhine River—Germany's largest and best natural line of defense—on March 7, 1945. Meanwhile, Soviet forces were moving in on Germany from the east. The German surrender was only two months away.

PRIMARY SOURCE

Albert Speer
Excerpt from *Inside the Third Reich*
Published in 1970

In the spring of 1945 Allied forces closed in on Germany from both the eastern and western fronts, signaling the final days of Nazi rule. As daily air raids from Allied bombers reduced cities to rubble, German citizens desperately hoped the war would end. On April 1, 1945, Adolf Hitler and his

closest aides retreated to the shelter of the bunker located beneath the Chancellery building in the capital city of Berlin. This refuge was situated fifty feet underground and held ample provisions to sustain its inhabitants during a prolonged siege. Unwilling to concede defeat, Hitler commanded his forces to fight to the last man. To repel oncoming Soviet forces, he issued the following order on April 21: "Any commander who holds his men back, will forfeit with his life within five hours." Traumatized by the impending defeat, Hitler believed his advisers and the German nation had failed him and were therefore unworthy of his genius. The following day he announced to his staff that he would stay in Berlin to the end. In a rage of tears and hysteria, he accused his advisers of telling lies and committing treason. Normally alert and sharp, Hitler appeared tired and confused.

During the final stages of the war, Hitler was in a state of extreme nervous exhaustion. Although he was only fifty-six years old, he appeared to be prematurely senile. One report claimed that he spent hours before his giant war maps, compulsively planning deployments for battalions that had long been destroyed. In those last days, the bunker in Berlin housed Hitler and the nearly fifty people who attempted to coordinate the defense of Berlin and sustain the Nazi government. Among them was Hitler's mistress, Eva Braun, whom he consented to marry in the bunker on April 29, 1945. Following the service, Hitler is said to have retired into his office to dictate his last will and political testament to his secretary. In the will he announced his plan to kill himself, disposed of his property, and explained the reasons for his marriage to Braun. In his "political testament" Hitler named Admiral Karl Dönitz to succeed him as führer and offered his personal views on the war, claiming he was compelled to engage in conflict by the forces of "International Jewry." He also expelled SS chief Heinrich Himmler and Reich marshal Hermann Göring from the Nazi party for treason. Hitler ended his testament with the following advice for future leaders of Germany: "Above all I charge the leaders of the nation and those under them to scrupulous observance of the laws of race and to merciless opposition to the universal poisoner of all peoples, International Jewry." On the following day, April 30, 1945, Hitler and Braun committed suicide. Fearing that his body would be desecrated by the Russians when they captured Berlin, he left special instructions for his bodyguards and assistants. According to his wishes, his body and that of Braun were carried into the garden at the Reich Chancellery, covered with fuel, and burned.

Albert Speer was minister of armaments and war production in the Third Reich. He participated in designing the German autobahns, or superhighways, which were used for the rapid transport of troops and armaments during the war (this system is still considered to be the finest in Europe). Speer

An early portrait of Albert Speer. (USHMM Photo)

visited the bunker under the Chancellery a few times in the month of April 1945. He observed the destruction of the city and the suffering of German citizens. He also witnessed the final days of Adolf Hitler, to whom he had dedicated twelve years of his life. The physical and emotional decline of the führer was visibly apparent. In the bunker Hitler no longer commanded the attention of his staff, but rather wandered about talking incoherently. Of the many accounts of the Nazi era and the fall of Berlin, Speer's is the most authentic, detailed, and revealing. For more than a decade he had been a close friend of Hitler and a member of the inner power circle of the Nazi leadership. Many leaders of the Nazi regime deserted Hitler at the end. Speer himself fell out of favor with Hitler by disobeying orders to launch a "scorched earth" policy, whereby all remaining German industry, communications, and transport systems would be destroyed rather than fall into the hands of the advancing Allied armies. The führer believed that if he did not survive, then all of Germany should be destroyed as well. Speer wrote *Inside the Third Reich* while serving a prison sentence after the war. The following excerpt contains what may well be the best view the world will ever have of the last days of Adolf Hitler.

Inside the Third Reich

In the last weeks of his life Hitler seemed to have broken out of the rigidity which had gradually overcome him during the preceding years. He became more accessible again and could even tolerate the expression of dissent. As late as the winter of 1944, it would have been inconceivable for him to enter into a discussion of the prospects of the war with me. Then, too, his flexibility on the question of the scorched earth policy would have been unthinkable, or the quiet way he went over my radio speech. He was once more open to arguments he would not have listened to a year ago. But this greater softness sprang not from a relaxation of tension. Rather, it was dissolution. He gave the impression of a man whose whole purpose had been destroyed, who was continuing along his established orbit only because of the kinetic energy stored within him. Actually, he had let go of the controls and was resigned to what might come.

There was actually something insubstantial about him. But this was perhaps a permanent quality he had. In retrospect I sometimes ask myself whether this intangibility, this insubstantiality, had not characterized him from early youth up to the moment of his suicide. It sometimes seems to me that his seizures of violence could come upon him all the more strongly because there were no human emotions in him to oppose them. He simply could not let anyone approach his inner being because that core was lifeless, empty.

Now, he was shriveling up like an old man. His limbs trembled; he walked stooped, with dragging footsteps. Even his voice became quavering and lost its old masterfulness. Its force had given way to a faltering, toneless manner of speaking. When he became excited, as he frequently did in a senile way, his voice would start breaking. He still had his fits of obstinacy, but they no longer reminded one of a child's temper tantrums, but of an old man's. His complexion was sallow, his face swollen; his uniform, which in the past he had kept scrupulously neat, was often neglected in this last period of life and stained by the food he had eaten with a shaking hand....

Hitler's last birthday was not actually celebrated. Formerly on this day lines of cars had driven up, the honor guard had presented arms, dignitaries of the Reich and of foreign countries had offered their congratulations. Now all was quiet. For the occasion Hitler had, it is true, moved from the bunker to the upper rooms, which in their state of neglect provided a fitting framework to his own lamentable condition. A delegation of Hitler Youth who had fought well was presented to him in the garden. Hitler spoke a few words, patted one or another of the boys. His voice was low. He broke off rather abruptly. Probably he sensed that his only convincing role now was as an object of pity. Most of his entourage avoided the embarrassment of a celebration by coming to the military situation conference as usual. No one knew quite what to say. Hitler received the expressions of good wishes coolly and almost unwillingly, in keeping with the circumstances....

Toward midnight Eva Braun sent an SS orderly to invite me to the small room in the bunker that was both her bedroom and living room. It was pleasantly furnished; she had had some of the expensive furniture which I had designed for her years ago brought from her two rooms in the upper floors of the Chancellery. Neither the proportions nor the pieces selected fitted into the gloomy surroundings. To complete the irony, one of the inlays on the doors of the chest was a four-leaf clover incorporating her initials.

We were able to talk honestly, for Hitler had withdrawn. She was the only prominent candidate for death in this bunker who displayed an admirable and superior composure. While all the others were abnormal—exaltedly heroic like Goebbels, bent on saving his skin like Bormann, exhausted like Hitler, or in total collapse like Frau Goebbels—Eva Braun radiated an almost gay serenity. "How about a bottle of champagne for our farewell? And some sweets? I'm sure you haven't eaten in a long time."

I was touched by her concern; she was the first person to think that I might be hungry after my many hours in the bunker. The orderly brought a bottle of Moet et Chandon, cake, and sweets. We remained alone. "You know, it was good that you came back once more. The Fuehrer had assumed you would be working against him. But your visit has proved the opposite to him, hasn't it?" I did not answer that question. "Anyhow, he liked what you said to him today. He has made up his mind to stay here, and I am staying with him. And you know the rest, too, of course.... He wanted to send me back to Munich. But I refused; I've come to end it here."

She was also the only person in the bunker capable of humane considerations. "Why do so many more people have to be killed?" she asked. "And it's all for nothing.… Incidentally, you almost came too late. Yesterday the situation was so terrible it seemed the Russians would quickly occupy all of Berlin. The Fuehrer was on the point of giving up. But Goebbels talked to him and persuaded him, and so we're still here."

She went on talking easily and informally with me, occasionally bursting out against Bormann, who was pursuing his intrigues up to the last. But again and again she came back to the declaration that she was happy here in the bunker.

By now it was about three o'clock in the morning. Hitler was awake again. I sent word that I wanted to bid him good-by. The day had worn me out, and I was afraid that I would not be able to control myself at our parting. Trembling, the prematurely aged man stood before me for the last time; the man to whom I had dedicated my life twelve years before. I was both moved and confused. For his part, he showed no emotion when we confronted one another. His words were as cold as his hand: "So, you're leaving? Good. Auf Wiedersehen." No regards to my family, no wishes, no thanks, no farewell. For a moment I lost my composure, said something about coming back. But he could easily see that it was a white lie, and turned his attention to something else. I was dismissed.

Ten minutes later, with hardly another word spoken to anyone, I left the Chanceller's residence. I wanted to walk once more through the neighboring Chancellery, which I had built. Since the lights were no longer functioning, I contented myself with a few farewell minutes in the Court of Honor, whose outlines could scarcely be seen against the night sky. I sensed rather than saw the architecture. There was an almost ghostly quiet about everything, like a night in the mountains. The noise of a great city, which in earlier years had penetrated to here even during the night, had totally ceased. At rather long intervals I heard the detonations of Russian shells. Such was my last visit to the Chancellery. Years ago I had built it—full of plans, prospects, and dreams for the future. Now I was leaving the ruins of my building, and of the most significant years of my life.…

That evening I returned to Hamburg. The Gauleiter offered to have my speech to the people broadcast by the Hamburg station at once, that is, even before Hitler's death. But as I thought of the drama that must be taking place during these days, these very hours, in the Berlin bunker, I realized that I had lost all urge to continue my opposition. Once

more Hitler had succeeded in paralyzing me psychically. To myself, and perhaps to others, I justified my change of mind on the grounds that it would be wrong and pointless to try to intervene now in the course of the tragedy.

I said good-by to Kaufmann and set out for Schleswig-Holstein. We moved into our trailer on Eutin Lake. Occasionally I visited Doenitz or members of the General Staff, who like me were at a standstill, awaiting further developments. Thus, I happened to be present on May 1, 1945, when Doenitz was handed the radio message significantly curtailing his rights as Hitler's successor. [Hitler had originally appointed Doenitz to succeed him as fuehrer. The new message appointed Doenitz to the lesser position of Reich president.] Hitler had appointed the cabinet for the new President of the Reich: Goebbels was Chancellor; Seyss-Inquart, Foreign Minister; and Bormann, Party Minister. Along with this message came one from Bormann announcing that he would be coming to see Doenitz shortly.

"This is utterly impossible!" Doenitz exclaimed, for this made a farce of the powers of his office. "Has anyone else seen the radio message yet?"

Except for the radioman and the admiral's adjutant, Lüdde-Neurath, who had taken the message directly to his chief, no one had. Doenitz then ordered that the radioman be sworn to silence and the message locked up and kept confidential. "What will we do if Bormann and Goebbels actually arrive here?" Doenitz asked. Then he continued resolutely: "I absolutely will not cooperate with them in any case." That evening we both agreed that Bormann and Goebbels must somehow be placed under arrest.

Thus Hitler forced Doenitz, as his first official function, to commit an act of illegality: concealing an official document. This was the last link in a chain of deceptions, betrayals, hypocrisies, and intrigues during those days and weeks. Himmler had betrayed his Fuehrer by negotiations; Bormann had carried off his last great intrigue against Goering by playing on Hitler's feelings; Goering was hoping to strike a bargain with the Allies; Kaufmann had made a deal with the British and was willing to provide me with radio facilities; Keitel was hiring out to a new master while Hitler was still alive—and I myself, finally, had in the past months deceived the man who had discovered me and furthered my career; I had even at times considered how to kill him. All of us felt forced to these acts by the system which we ourselves represented—and forced also by

Young boy operates machinery in a workshop in the Kovno ghetto. (USHMM Photo Archives)

Hitler, who for his part had betrayed us all, himself and his people.

On this note the Third Reich ended.

On the evening of that May 1, when Hitler's death was announced, I slept in a small room in Doenitz's quarters. When I unpacked my bag I found the red leather case containing Hitler's portrait. My secretary had included it in my luggage. My nerves had reached their limit. When I stood the photograph up, a fit of weeping overcame me. That was the end of my relationship to Hitler. Only now was the spell broken, the magic extinguished. What remained were images of graveyards, of shattered cities, of millions of mourners, of concentration camps. Not all

these images came into my mind at this moment, but they were there, somehow present in me. I fell into a deep, exhausted sleep.

Two weeks later, staggered by the revelations of the crimes in the concentration camps, I wrote to the chairman of the ministerial cabinet, Schwerin-Krosigk: "The previous leadership of the German nation bears a collective guilt for the fate that now hangs over the German people. Each member of that leadership must personally assume his responsibility in such a way that the guilt which might otherwise descend upon the German people is expiated.

With that, there began a segment of my life which has not ended to this day. (Speer, pp. 471–489)

Aftermath

In 1946, after the war had ended, Speer was brought before the International Military Tribunal at Nuremberg. Unlike almost all of the other Nazi leaders, Speer acknowledged his responsibility for all crimes committed by the Third Reich, even those which he claimed he had no knowledge of, such as the mass extermination of Jews. Speer was one of only two Nazi defendants to admit guilt in the crimes of the Third Reich. Speer felt that "there is a common responsibility for such horrible crimes in an authoritarian system." During the trial he recognized that he was personally responsible for the slave labor used in armament factories under his authority. By collaborating with the SS, Speer had exploited concentration camp prisoners for his war production goals. He argued, however, that his work was "technological and economic," not political. During his testimony he claimed to have rejected violence, not on humanitarian grounds, but because violence against prisoners would hinder his war production output.

The tribunal limited its judgment to Speer's involvement with the slave labor program, finding him guilty of war crimes and crimes against humanity. According to the judges, "in mitigation, it must be recognized that ... in the closing stages of the war he was one of the few men who had the courage to tell Hitler that the war was lost and to take steps to prevent the senseless destruction of production facilities." Speer was sentenced to twenty years' imprisonment, despite the Russian vote to hang him. After serving his complete sentence he was released in 1966. While at Spandau prison Speer completed the first draft of his memoirs, which became the best-selling book *Inside the Third Reich,* published in 1970. His detailed, dispassionate account gives a firsthand view of the inner workings of the Nazi hierarchy. Scholars continue to debate Speer's repeated claims that he had no knowledge of the murderous actions that took place at the extermination camps. Many contend that he knew far more than he ever admitted publicly. They argue that by ignoring the consequences of his authority and actions, he represented the typical Nazi technocrat. Through his absolute loyalty to Hitler and his remarkable talents and efficiencies, Speer—along with others like him—enabled the totalitarian German state to conduct horrendous and lawless activities for twelve years. Speer died on September 1, 1981, during a visit to London.

PRIMARY SOURCE

Edward R. Murrow
Radio Report—The Liberation of Buchenwald

Excerpt from *In Search of Light: The Broadcasts of Edward R. Murrow, 1938-1961*

Published in 1967

During its twelve years of rule (1933–1945), the German Nazi party mastered the tactics of oppression. Essential elements in their regime of terror were prisons called *Konzentrationslagers,* or concentration camps. The professed goal of concentration camps was to "reform" political opponents and to transform "anti-social" members of society into "useful" members. In Nazi Germany the rights of many citizens were altered as Adolf Hitler suspended the constitutional clause guaranteeing personal liberties and ordered the arrest of his political opponents. Thousands of Germans were taken into "protective custody" because they were members of the Communist party, the Social Democratic party, or powerful trade unions. Eventually, the Nazis detained nonpolitical prisoners who were considered "asocial elements," including habitual criminals, tramps, beggars, homosexuals, and Roma (Gypsies).

In the early years of the Third Reich, those imprisoned at concentration camps included Ger-

The End of Nazi Rule

A year before the military struggle ended in Europe, the Allies began preparing for the restoration of civilian order in soon-to-be recaptured lands. Anticipating the fall of Germany, the Allies broadcast a radio statement on September 23, 1944, announcing their intention to repeal racist Nazi laws. The Allied powers promised to restore full rights of citizenship to Jews when Nazi rule ended. Radio stations across Europe broadcast the announcement, enabling the message to reach millions of people living in Germany and German-occupied countries, where normal station operations had been banned.

The Allies explained their plan to help maintain public order after the defeat of Germany. Nazi administrative officers were instructed to remain at their posts at the end of the war to assure an orderly surrender of funds, records, and equipment. The Allies also announced their intention to take over the mail, telephone, and radio systems. All Germans, both civilian and military, would be required to hand over firearms to Allied forces. Nazi political and military organizations would be banned. This declaration, made by Allied forces nine months before Germany's surrender, provided victims with a message of hope while giving pause to Nazi criminals.

German forces formally surrendered on May 8, 1945, ending World War II in Europe. The visible destruction of European cities paled in comparison to the loss of life. Millions of people perished on the battlefields, and 6 million Jews died in the Nazi-controlled ghettos and camps. Entire Jewish communities, towns, and families disappeared at the hands of the Nazis.

man Jews belonging to outlawed political parties and organizations. However, when anti-Jewish measures escalated, so did the proportion of Jewish inmates in the camps. In the wake of the organized violent attack in 1938 known as *Kristallnacht,* or "the Night of Broken Glass," the Nazis imprisoned at least 30,000 Jews. At that point, the Nazis hoped to force Jews to emigrate from Germany and released any Jewish prisoner who could produce an emigration visa. Most German Jews who were imprisoned in concentration camps prior to 1939 managed to secure their own release, but once World War II broke out, the number of Jewish prisoners in German concentration camps rose again as victims arrived from other German-occupied countries. Then, in 1942, the Nazis ordered the Reich *judenfrei,* or "free of Jews," and most Jewish prisoners were sent to the Auschwitz camp in nearby Poland.

In the mid-1930s there were three main concentration camps in Germany—Dachau, Sachsenhausen, and Buchenwald. Other concentration camps were added as the Nazis continued to arrest anyone considered a threat to the Reich. These "enemies of the people" included Catholics, Protestants, Jehovah's Witnesses, pacifists, clergymen, monks, and even dissident Nazis. Inmates at concentration camps were tattooed with an identification number and wore a particular colored triangle on their uniform to classify their "crime." Political prisoners wore a red triangle; criminals wore green; "shiftless elements" wore black; homosexuals wore pink; Jehovah's Witnesses wore purple; and Roma wore brown. Jews wore both a yellow triangle and a classification triangle—the yellow triangle pointed up, the other pointed down, to form a Jewish Star of David. After the Reich began expanding into other countries, foreign inmates wore signifying letters, such as "P" for Poland or "F" for France.

To accommodate various political and racial goals, the Nazis established an extensive network of camps, which had differing functions. Most notorious were the extermination camps, which were specially designed for systematic mass murder. The Nazis viewed Jews, Poles, Soviets, Roma, and other groups as threats to the "purity" of German blood. By late 1941, the Nazis began to plan

On April 11, 1945, American troops from the 183rd Engineer Combat Battalion of the United States Third Army were shown a stack of corpses at Buchenwald. (USHMM Photo Archives)

the series of death camps, located in Poland, in which they could annihilate their genetic enemies. The extensive Nazi camp system also included labor camps, transit camps, and prisoner of war camps. A special division of the SS served as concentration camp guards. These units became known as SS *Totenkopfverbande,* or "Death's Head Units," named for the skeleton-head symbol they wore on the collars of their uniforms.

Concentration camps provided a ready source of forced labor, which became increasingly important to Germany as the war continued. After 1942, prisoners were systematically drafted for work in the armaments industry. Through a program coordinated by German minister of armaments Albert Speer, state-owned and private companies involved in arms production could tap into the inexpensive labor pool provided by inmates. The demand for prison labor led to some improvement in living conditions; however, the overall mortality rate remained very high. Due to the intense need for armament factory workers throughout Europe during the later stages of the war, some Jews were

diverted to concentration camps instead of being deported directly to death camps.

In spring 1945 Allied forces descended upon Germany; victory seemed near. After recapturing Poland and Hungary, the Russians marched toward the German capital of Berlin from the east, while British and American forces advanced deeper into the heart of Germany. By early April, American forces were approaching the Buchenwald concentration camp, which was situated on a mountainside near Weimar, a city in central-eastern Germany, southwest of Berlin. Buchenwald was one of the largest concentration camps in Germany, with 130 satellite camps and extension units. Established in 1937, it was also one of the oldest. As Allied forces neared the camp, the SS guards ordered the evacuation of prisoners in a frenzied attempt to hide their deeds. During the exodus, 25,500 people perished. In those last days, resistance members among the camp population sabotaged SS plans by slowing down the pace of the evacuation. By April 11, 1945, most of the SS detachment deserted the camp, and armed prisoners managed to trap the remaining guards. The American army entered Buchenwald that same day, liberating 21,000 prisoners, including 4,000 Jews and 1,000 children.

Legendary American reporter Edward R. Murrow had been providing radio coverage of the war since the early days of Hitler's rise to power. Before the advent of television, radio was the fastest way to transmit accurate news accounts around the world. As war spread across Europe, Murrow kept listeners informed with up-to-date news reports. His broadcasts from the rooftops of London, against the noise of sirens, gunfire, and falling bombs, riveted listeners around the world. He opened his narratives with the now-famous line "This is London." With an Allied victory in sight, Murrow traveled to Germany and arrived in Buchenwald on April 15, 1945, just four days after its liberation. Murrow's radio broadcast of his impressions, excerpted here, reached an American audience anxious for news. Just days before, U.S.

President Franklin D. Roosevelt had died, and listeners were hungry for information about the new administration of President Harry S Truman and about the war in Europe, which finally seemed to be nearing an end. Murrow minced no words in his firsthand account of what he had seen; in a straightforward manner he described to millions of listeners the horror he encountered when entering Buchenwald, the scenes he witnessed in the camp, and the conversations he had with survivors. Murrow's account is consistent with the reaction of other representatives of the Allied countries who entered concentration camps after liberation. Even members of the military forces who had been hardened by the war were shocked by what they encountered in the camps: the condition of the survivors, the filth, and the indescribable stench. Murrow attempted to give expression to the horrors and cruelties he witnessed. His wartime accounts and his report on the liberation of Buchenwald are among the most famous radio broadcasts in history.

Radio Report—The Liberation of Buchenwald

April 15, 1945

During the last week, I have driven more than a few hundred miles through Germany, most of it in the Third Army sector—Wiesbaden, Frankfurt, Weimar, Jena and beyond. It is impossible to keep up with this war. The traffic flows down the superhighways, trucks with German helmets tied to the radiators and belts of machine-gun ammunition draped from fender to fender. The tanks on the concrete roads sound like a huge sausage machine, grinding up sheets of corrugated iron. And when there is a gap between convoys, when the noise dies away, there is another small noise, that of wooden-soled shoes and of small iron tires grating on the concrete. The power moves forward, while the people, the slaves, walk back, pulling their small belongings on anything that has wheels.

There are cities in Germany that make Coventry and Plymouth appear to be merely damage done by a petulant child, but bombed houses have a way of looking alike, wherever you see them.

But this is no time to talk of the surface of Germany. Permit me to tell you what you would have

seen, and heard, had you been with me on Thursday. It will not be pleasant listening. If you are at lunch, or if you have no appetite to hear what Germans have done, now is a good time to switch off the radio, for I propose to tell you of Buchenwald. It is on a small hill about four miles outside Weimar, and it was one of the largest concentration camps in Germany, and it was built to last. As we approached it, we saw about a hundred men in civilian clothes with rifles advancing in open order across the fields. There were a few shops; we stopped to inquire. We were told that some of the prisoners had a couple of SS men cornered in there. We drove on, reached the main gate. The prisoners crowded up behind the wire. We entered.

And now, let me tell this in the first person, for I was the least important person there, as you shall hear. There surged around me an evil-smelling horde. Men and boys reached out to touch me; they were in rags and the remnants of uniforms. Death had already marked many of them, but they were smiling with their eyes. I looked out over that mass of men to the green fields beyond where well-fed Germans were ploughing.

General Dwight D. Eisenhower listens to survivors of Ohrdruf, a subcamp of Buchenwald, give testimony about atrocities committed in the camp. (USHMM Photo Archives)

A German, Fritz Kersheimer, came up and said, "May I show you round the camp? I've been here ten years." An Englishman stood to attention, saying, "May I introduce myself, delighted to see you, and can you tell me when some of our blokes will be along?" I told him soon and asked to see one of the barracks. It happened to be occupied by Czechoslova-kians. When I entered, men crowded around, tried to lift me to their shoulders. They were too weak. Many of them could not get out of bed. I was told that this building had once stabled eighty horses. There were twelve hundred men in it, five to a bunk. The stink was beyond all description.

When I reached the center of the barracks, a man came up and said, "You remember me. I'm Peter Zenkl, one-time mayor of Prague." I remembered him, but did not recognize him. He asked about Benes and Jan Masaryk. I asked how many men had died in that building during the last month. They called the doctor; we inspected his records. There were only names in the little black book, nothing

more—nothing of who these men were, what they had done, or hoped. Behind the names of those who had died there was a cross. I counted them. They totaled 242. Two hundred and forty-two out of twelve hundred in one month.

As I walked down to the end of the barracks, there was applause from the men too weak to get out of bed. It sounded like the hand clapping of babies; they were so weak. The doctor's name was Paul Heller. He had been there since 1938.

As we walked out into the courtyard, a man fell dead. Two others—they must have been over sixty— were crawling toward the latrine. I saw it but will not describe it.

In another part of the camp they showed me the children, hundreds of them. Some were only six. One rolled up his sleeve, showed me his number. It was tattooed on his arm. D-6030, it was. The others showed me their numbers; they will carry them till they die.

Surviving the Mauthausen camp, also known as "The Mountain of Death," women and children talk to one of the Americans who liberated the infamous camp. (USHMM Photo Archives)

Two survivors lie among corpses in the Dora-Mittelbau concentration sub-camp. (Photo by Harold M. Roberts, courtesy of National Archives/USHMM Photo Archives)

Edward R. Murrow

Egbert Roscoe Murrow was born in Greensboro, North Carolina, in 1908. His family moved to Blanchard, Washington, when he was four. While in high school, Murrow shortened his given name to Ed, and later, at Washington State College (now Washington State University) in Pullman, he took the name Edward. Throughout his college years, he participated in debates and also attended the country's first course in radio broadcasting. Murrow graduated Phi Beta Kappa in 1930. After college, Murrow traveled to Europe and throughout the United States for the National Student Federation and later as the assistant director for the International Institute of Education. He also obtained speakers for the *University of the Air* radio program of the Columbia Broadcasting System (CBS).

Murrow's travels allowed him to witness first-hand the brutal repression in Germany when the Nazis seized power in 1933. Through his associations, he helped rescue scholars from Germany. In 1935 he was appointed "director of talks" for the 100-station CBS radio network, then became

European director two years later. CBS pioneered the radio broadcasting of special events and the establishment of fully staffed foreign news bureaus. When Germany annexed Austria in 1938, Murrow broadcast to the world Hitler's arrival in Vienna. Murrow's reports of the aerial Battle of Britain and the German Blitz against London brought the realities of World War II into American homes.

In the years following the end of World War II, television began to replace radio as the most popular news medium, and Murrow took advantage of it. By 1951, Murrow again commanded huge audiences with his *See It Now* telecasts. He continued with the CBS News organization until 1961, when he accepted a position in President John F. Kennedy's administration as director of the U.S. Information Agency. Poor health forced his retirement in 1964, and he died a year later at his home in Pawling, New York.

An elderly man standing beside me said, "The children, enemies of the state." I could see their ribs through their thin shirts. The old man said, "I am Professor Charles Richer of the Sorbonne [a major university in Paris; also known as the University of Paris]." The children clung to my hands and stared. We crossed to the courtyard. Men kept coming up to speak to me and to touch me, professors from Poland, doctors from Vienna, men from all Europe. Men from the countries that made America.

We went to the hospital; it was full. The doctor told me that two hundred had died the day before. I asked the cause of death; he shrugged and said, "Tuberculosis, starvation, fatigue, and there are many who have no desire to live. It is very difficult." Dr. Heller pulled back the blankets from a man's feet to show me how swollen they were. The man was dead. Most of the patients could not move.

As we left the hospital I drew out a leather billfold, hoping that I had some money which would help those who lived to get home. Professor Richer from the Sorbonne said, "I should be careful of my wallet if I were you. You know there are criminals in this camp, too." A small man tottered up, saying. "May I feel the leather, please? You see, I used to make good things of leather in Vienna." Another man said, "My name is Walter Roeder. For many years I lived in Joliet. Came back to Germany for a visit and Hitler grabbed me."

I asked to see the kitchen; it was clean. The German in charge had been a Communist, had been at Buchenwald for nine years, had a picture of his daughter in Hamburg. He hadn't seen her for almost twelve years, and if I got to Hamburg, would I took her up? He showed me the daily ration—one piece of brown bread about as thick as your thumb, on top of it a piece of margarine as big as three sticks of chew-

U.S. Army soldiers round up guards at the Dachau concentration camp after liberation. (National Archives/USHMM Photo Archives)

ing gum. That, and a little stew, was what they received every twenty-four hours. He had a chart on the wall; very complicated it was. There were little red tabs scattered through it. He said that was to indicate each ten men who died. He had to account for the rations, and he added, "We're very efficient here."

We went again into the courtyard, and as we walked we talked. The two doctors, the Frenchman and the Czech, agreed that about six thousand had died during March. Kersheimer, the German, added that back in the winter of 1939, when the Poles began to arrive without winter clothing, they died at the rate of approximately nine hundred a day. Five different men asserted that Buchenwald was the best concentration camp in Germany; they had had some experience of the others.

Dr. Heller, the Czech, asked if I would care to see the crematorium. He said it wouldn't be very interesting because the Germans had run out of coke some days ago and had taken to dumping the bodies into a great hole nearby. Professor Richer said perhaps I would care to see the small courtyard. I said yes. He turned and told the children to stay behind. As we walked across the square I noticed that the professor had a hole in his left shoe and a toe sticking out of the right one. He followed my eyes and said, "I regret that I am so little presentable, but what can one do?" At

that point another Frenchman came up to announce that three of his fellow countrymen outside had killed three S.S. men and taken one prisoner. We proceeded to the small courtyard. The wall was about eight feet high; it adjoined what had been a stable or garage. We entered. It was floored with concrete. There were two rows of bodies stacked up like cordwood. They were thin and very white. Some of the bodies were terribly bruised, though there seemed to be little flesh to bruise. Some had been shot through the head, but they bled but little. All except two were naked. I tried to count them as best I could and arrived at the conclusion that all that was mortal of more than five hundred men and boys lay there in two neat piles.

There was a German trailer which must have contained another fifty, but it wasn't possible to count them. The clothing was piled in a heap against the wall. It appeared that most of the men and boys had died of starvation; they had not been executed. But the manner of death seemed unimportant. Murder had been done at Buchenwald. God alone knows how many men and boys have died there during the last twelve years. Thursday I was told that there were more than twenty thousand in the camp. There had been as many as sixty thousand. Where are they now?

As I left that camp, a Frenchman who used to work for Havas [French wire or news service] in Paris

A group of American editors and publishers are shown prisoners' corpses during an inspection of Dachau on May 4, 1945. (USHMM Photo Archives)

came up to me and said, "You will write something about this, perhaps?" And he added. "To write about this you must have been here at least two years, and after that—you don't want to write any more."

I pray you to believe what I have said about Buchenwald. I have reported what I saw and heard, but only part of it. For most of it I have no words. Dead men are plentiful in war, but the living dead, more than twenty thousand of them in one camp. And the country round about was pleasing to the eye, and the Germans were well fed and well dressed. American trucks were rolling toward the rear filled with prisoners. Soon they would be eating American rations, as much for a meal as the men at Buchenwald received in four days.

If I've offended you by this rather mild account of Buchenwald, I'm not in the least sorry. I was there on Thursday, and many men in many tongues blessed the name of [U.S. President Franklin D.] Roosevelt.

For long years his name had meant the full measure of their hope. These men who had kept close company with death for many years did not know that Mr. Roosevelt would, within hours, join their comrades who had laid their lives on the scales of freedom.

Back in 1941, [British Prime Minister] Mr. [Winston] Churchill said to me with tears in his eyes, "One day the world and history will recognize and acknowledge what it owes to your President." I saw and heard the first installment of that at Buchenwald on Thursday. It came from men from all over Europe. Their faces, with more flesh on them, might have been found anywhere at home. To them the name "Roosevelt" was a symbol, the code word for a lot of guys named "Joe" who are somewhere out in the blue with the armor heading east. At Buchenwald they spoke of the President just before he died. If there be a better epitaph, history does not record it. (Murrow, pp. 90–95)

The Fate of the "Witch of Buchenwald"

One of the Buchenwald camp staff sentenced to life imprisonment was Ilse Koch, an SS officer and guard at the camp who was also the wife of Karl Koch, the commandant of Buchenwald from 1937 to 1941. As commandant, Karl Koch had become a millionaire from unscrupulous racketeering and exploitation of camp labor, and in 1944 a Nazi court found him guilty of corruption. He was hanged a year later.

Ilse Koch, known as the "Witch of Buchenwald" or the "Beast of Buchenwald," used to ride horseback through the camp and viciously whip prisoners. She also collected lampshades and other household objects fashioned from the tattooed skins of dead inmates. The decision to reduce Ilse Koch's initial sentence of life imprisonment to four years aroused international protest because of its lack of severity. Koch was rearrested in 1949 and brought to trial before a West German court for killing German nationals. Due to the intense publicity surrounding the case, her name became a byword for horror. In January 1951 she was sentenced to life imprisonment for murder. Sixteen years later, at the age of sixty-one, Koch committed suicide in a Bavarian prison.

Aftermath

The Buchenwald concentration camp operated for eight years, from July 1937 to April 1945. Nearly 239,000 prisoners from 30 countries passed through the main camp and its satellite units, and some 43,000 prisoners perished there, either by execution or due to harsh conditions. After liberation, German civilians were forced, under escort by the U.S. military, to visit the Buchenwald camp and view the evidence of Nazi atrocities. In 1947 thirty-one members of the camp staff were tried for their crimes before an American military tribunal. Two were sentenced to death; four were given life sentences.

After the war, Murrow continued to broadcast via both radio and the new medium of television. Beginning with his coverage of World War II, Murrow revolutionized the broadcast industry with his on-the-scene reports. Today, all major news agencies, both radio and television, use the same innovative reporting style pioneered by Murrow.

SOURCES

Books

Forman, James, *The Survivor,* Farrar, Straus & Giroux (New York), 1976.

Gottschalk, Ellin Toona, *In Search of Coffe Mountains,* Nelson (Nashville), 1977.

Karmel-Wolfe, Henia. *Marek and Lisa: A Novel,* Dodd, Mead (New York), 1984.

Murrow, Edward R., *In Search of Light: The Broadcasts of Edward R. Murrow, 1938–1961,* edited by Edward Bliss, Jr., Knopf (New York), 1967.

Other

Edward R. Murrow Wavs & Pics, http://earthstation 1.simplenet.com/Edward_R._Murrow.html (August 24, 2000).

Gedenkstätte Buchenwald, http://www.buchenwald.de/index-e.html (August 24, 2000).

The History Place: Holocaust Timeline: Buchenwald Liberated, http://www.historyplace.com/worldwar2/holocaust/h-buch-lib.htm (August 24, 2000).

Fania Fénelon
Excerpt from *Playing for Time*
Translated by Judith Landry

Published in 1977

After France fell to the German army in June 1940, the French government offered to sign an armistice with Germany to diffuse the chaos that resulted from the early stages of World War II. Under the terms of the agreement, France agreed to disband its military and surrender three-fifths of the country to German control. France was divided into two areas—the occupied zone under German rule and the unoccupied zone under the rule of a new regime established in the town of Vichy in the south of France. The Vichy government quickly pledged cooperation with Germany and established authoritative rule by repealing civil liberties. By collaborating with Nazi Germany, the French hoped to achieve a favorable position within the "New Europe" being created by Adolf Hitler.

About 350,000 Jews lived in France in the summer of 1940, representing less than 1 percent of the population. Only 150,000 were native born; the rest were refugees from Germany, Austria, Czechoslovakia, Belgium, Holland, and eastern Europe. In the wake of the French defeat, large numbers of Jews fled to the unoccupied zone in the southern portion of the country. Persecution of Jews living in both the German-occupied zone and the Vichy zone began immediately after the armistice was signed. German and French leaders enacted harsh anti-Jewish measures that stripped Jews of their jobs and assets. Foreign Jews were particularly vulnerable and were the first to be interned at concentration camps within France or forced into labor brigades.

In the spring of 1942, the German and French police began to organize large-scale deportations of Jews from both zones. In order to assure compliance from the Jewish population, the German and Vichy leaders claimed that the Jews were going to work camps "in the East," when in reality they were being transported to the Nazi-operated death camps in Poland. In July the French police rounded up more than 12,000 Jews in Paris alone. Those individuals without families were sent immediate-

Pierre Laval, head of the government in Vichy, France. (Reproduced by permission of © Hulton Getty/Liaison Agency)

ly to Drancy, the major transit camp in France. The remaining 9,000 were crowded into the sports stadium Velodrome d'Hiver, where they spent a week without food, water, or sanitation before being sent to Auschwitz. A series of massive deportations, which continued into the fall of 1942, helped stir the first serious opposition to the Vichy government. When French Jews became the target of deportation efforts, resistance against the Germans increased. By January 1943, the French police could no longer be trusted to assemble and transport Jews. Deportations from France continued until the summer of 1944.

Allied forces landed in Normandy in June and secured the liberation of France two months later. As Vichy officials fled to Germany, French politi-

Having helped run the Nazis out of France, American troops in a tank pass by the Arc de Triomphe, a historic French landmark, in August 1944. (National Archives and Records Administration)

cian Charles de Gaulle returned from exile in Great Britain and marched triumphantly into Paris as the leader of free France. But before the Allies liberated France, between 77,000 and 90,000 Jews were killed. The Germans sent the majority of Jews to Auschwitz, the largest Nazi concentration and extermination camp, but they also sent victims to other camps—Majdanek, Sobibór, and Buchenwald. Unlike other countries occupied by Germany during World War II, the French Vichy government had retained considerable autonomy. Historians have determined that without the cooperation provided by French officials, the Germans would not have been capable of deporting such large numbers of Jewish people to their deaths. Despite widespread anti-Semitism in France, however, many French people assisted Jews during World War II. Resistance was found throughout the country, but especially among Protestants, who felt themselves to be a vulnerable minority. Perhaps the most remarkable demonstration of French resistance occurred in Le Chambon-sur-Lignon. This small Protestant village served as an underground railway, successfully smuggling several thousand Jews to safety.

One of the French Jews deported to Auschwitz was a young musician and singer named Fania Fénelon. In January 1944 Fénelon arrived at Birkenau, an extension of the main camp at Auschwitz. Nine sub-units existed at the Birkenau camp installation, including a women's section as well as gas chambers and crematoria. Upon her arrival, Fénelon survived the *Selektion* process that took place at the railway ramp, where Jewish prisoners were directed into two groups—one going immediately to the gas chambers, the other into forced labor. While in the quarantine block awaiting her labor assignment, Fénelon was recognized by another inmate who had seen her musical performances in Paris. Fénelon was selected to become a member of the Birkenau women's orchestra, which was comprised of more than forty female prisoners. The Nazis formed orchestras from prisoners in many of the large concentration and extermination camps. These orchestras were forced to play for particular events, including the *Selektion* process, the march to the gas chambers, the procession of prisoners to and from work assignments each day, and the general enjoyment of SS guards. Auschwitz had six orchestras—the largest one consisting of 100 to 120 musicians. Auschwitz camp commandant Rudolf Höss had started the orchestras to provide marching music for the work groups leaving from and returning to the camps each day. Fénelon and other members of the women's orchestra lived in separate quarters and were spared the life-threatening forced labor details assigned to other prisoners. As one of "the orchestra girls," she received adequate clothing, including an orchestra uniform comprised of a navy blue skirt, black woolen stockings, striped jacket, and a triangle of white cloth worn on top of her head similar to the headdress of German nurses.

Sensing the impending arrival of Allied forces, the Nazis began dismantling the gas chambers and crematoria at Auschwitz during November and December 1944. Special work groups of male and female prisoners were ordered to clean the crematoria pits, cover the human ashes with dirt, and plant grass to hide the murderous evidence. During this time Fénelon and other orchestra members were transferred to Bergen-Belsen, a concentration camp within northern Germany. Shortly after they arrived, tens of thousands of survivors poured in from death marches; these prisoners had been evacuated from camps

Nazis Suppress Jewish Musicians

Shortly after their rise to power in 1933, the Nazis gained control of all musical activities in Germany. They appointed composer Richard Strauss as president of the Reich Music Office and conductor Wilhelm Furtwängler as his deputy. The Nazis dismissed all Jewish professional musicians from their posts, and banned the performance of works by Jewish composers. German Jews countered by establishing the Kulturbund Deutscher Juden (Cultural Society of German Jews). The Kulturbund lasted for eight years, during which time it sponsored 500 performances.

Many Jewish musicians fled Germany, some of whom joined the Palestine Symphony Orchestra, which had been created by violinist Bronislaw Huberman with the purpose of rescuing Jewish musicians from the Nazis. This orchestra eventually became the Israeli Philharmonic.

A prisoners' orchestra performs a Sunday concert for the SS men in Auschwitz. (USHMM Photo Archives)

in the east and ordered to walk to installations farther away from encroaching forces. Camp administrators did little to care for this influx of prisoners; most received no shelter and went without food and water. Chaos broke out in the camps as conditions reached an all-time low. In early 1945 a typhus epidemic broke out, killing more than 18,000 prisoners in the month of March alone. Holocaust diarist Anne Frank was one. An estimated total of 35,000 perished from typhus between January and April 15, when the British army liberated the camp.

Fénelon was one of those infected with the deadly disease. In her autobiographical book *Playing for Time*, she describes the day British soldiers entered the Bergen-Belsen camp. As she drifted in and out of consciousness, Fénelon became aware of someone speaking English in her midst. Her orchestra friends forced her to wake up so that she could interpret for them what the soldier was saying. (Fénelon was multilingual.) The British army had liberated Bergen-Belsen only four hours before the German guards were to begin complying with orders to shoot all prisoners and burn the entire camp.

Playing for Time

"STIRB NICHT!" Don't die.

The German voice made no sense; it had no power to pull me up out of the black gulf into which I was sinking more deeply every second. For days now, I had no longer possessed the strength to keep my eyes open. I wasn't sure whether it was my urine or the fever which alternately warmed and chilled me. Typhus was emptying me of life. I was going to die.

My head felt terrible. The girls' wailing and sobbing and groanings shattered it into needle-sharp fragments, little scraps of broken mirror which sank razorlike into my brain. I ordered my hand to pull them out, but my hand was a skeleton's claw that didn't obey. The bones must have broken through the skin. Or had the hand actually come off? Impossible. I must keep my hands to play the piano. Play the piano ... those knucklebones at the end of my arm might just manage Danse macabre. The idea actually made me laugh.

I was horribly thirsty. The SS had cut off the water. It was days since we'd had anything to eat; but even longer since I'd been hungry. I had become weightless, I was floating on a cloud, I was devoured by quicksand ... no, flying in cotton wool. Odd....

A trick I'd found to cool myself was to wash in my urine. Keeping myself clean was essential to me, and there is nothing unclean about urine. I could drink it if I was thirsty—and I had done so.

I didn't know the time but I did know the date—the girls kept track of that. It was April 15. What did that matter? It was just a day like any other. But where was I exactly? I wasn't at Birkenau anymore. There, there were forty-seven of us, the "orchestra girls." Here in this windowless shed, there were a thousand of us—burgeoning corpses. What a stench. Now I remembered: Bergen-Belsen. We had arrived here on November 3, 1944.

My head was in such chaos that I was no longer sure whether it was day or night. I gave up, it was too painful.... I foundered.

Above me, over my face, I felt a breath of air, a vague smell, a delicious scent. A voice cut through the layers of fog, stilled the buzzing in my ears; "Meine kleine Sängerin."

"Little singer," that was what the SS called me.

"Stirb nicht!"

That was an order, and a hard one to obey. Anyhow, I was past caring. I opened my eyes a fraction and saw Aufseherin Irma Grese, the SS warden known as Engel, the Angel, because of her looks. The glorious fair plaits which surrounded her head like a halo, her blue eyes and dazzling complexion were floating in a fog. She shook me.

"Stirb nicht! Deine englischen Freunde sind da! ..."

"What did she say?" asked Anny and Big Irene.

I repeated the German sentence. Irritated, they insisted: "Tell us in French, translate it."

"I forget...."

"But you just said it in German."

More exhausting people; I retired from the fray, defeated.

"Come on." They were pleading. "Don't die."

That triggered it off; I repeated automatically: "Don't die. Your friends the English are here."

They were disappointed.

"Is that all?" muttered Little Irene.

Florette joined in. "The usual rubbish! We've had that with the Russians, the English, and the Yanks. They fed us that dozens of times in Auschwitz."

I heard Big Irene's calm voice: "What if it's true?"

Anny spoke dreamily: "If only one could believe it and it could all end, now, just like that...."

"I wafted off, and most of Florette's colourful rejoinder was lost on me. God, how hot I was. My tongue was a hunk of cardboard. I felt myself drifting. Then familiar voices reached me, as if from the end of a funnel: "Look Irene, you can see there's no hope. She's stopped breathing, there is no mist on my bit of glass. This really works, they even do it in hospitals."

"Try again, you never know."

I wondered who was under discussion. Me? How infuriating they were. Admittedly, I had a pretty bad case of typhus, but I hadn't yet given up the ghost. I had to know the end of the story. I would bear witness.

There were bellowings and whistle blasts around the block; a sudden surge of panic swept through the shed. By way of a full-blooded background to the tramp of boots, the sound of machine guns cut steadily through the silence of the firing range. Their rattling ate into our brains, day and night. Some of the gunners were mere children of fifteen or so.

"They surely can't be going to have us picked off by those kids?"

"They're not noted for their delicacy of feeling," sneered Florette.

"But they're just children!"

All morning the rumour had been going around that they were going to do away with us. But unlike the rumour about the liberation of the camp, this one rang true. Lunatic laughter burst from all over the shed, from the various tiers of the cojas, the name the Polish girls gave our cagelike bunks. A crazed voice asked, "What time is it? I want to know the time."

"What the hell does it matter?"

"Because they're going to shoot us at three o'clock," the voice informed us confidentially.

Outside, superficially, all seemed normal; but if one concentrated closely, one could hear new sounds: running and calling. I was completely baffled. My head was swelling until it seemed to fill the whole barracks, to hold all the din within it like a reservoir. I had no more thoughts, I was sinking into the noise, it absorbed me and digested me. I was an echo chamber, I dreamed of silence.

No, I wasn't dreaming; the silence was real. The machine guns had stopped. It was like a great calm lake, and I let myself drift upon its waters.

I must have fallen asleep again; suddenly, behind me, I heard the familiar sound of the door opening. From the remotest distance a man was speaking; what was he saying? No one was answering him. That was odd. What was going on? Strange words reached my ears—it was a language I knew. It was English!

Tumult all around, women clambering down from the cojas. It couldn't be true, I must be delirious.

The girls, those girls of whom I'd grown so fond, threw themselves at me, shaking me.

"Fania, wake up! Do you hear, the English are here. You must speak to them."

An arm was slipped under my shoulders and lifted me up: "Say something."

I was only too eager, but how could I with that leather spatula in my mouth? I opened my eyes and saw dim figures through a fog. Then suddenly one came into focus: he was wearing a funny little flat cap on his head, he was kneeling down and thumping his fist on his chest, rocking to and fro repeating, "My God, my God!" He was like a Jew at the Wailing Wall. He had blue eyes, but it wasn't a German blue. He took off his cap, revealing enchanting red hair. His face was dusted with freckles and big childlike tears rolled down his cheeks. It was both awful and funny. "Can you hear me?"

I murmured, "Yes."

The girls shrieked, "It's all right! She heard, she answered!"

Madness was unleashed around me. They were dancing, lifting their thin legs as high as they could. Some threw themselves down and kissed the ground, rolling in the filth, laughing and crying. Some were vomiting; the scene was incredible, a mixture of heaven and hell.

There was a flurry of questions: "Where have they come from?" "How did they get this far, to this hellhole?" "Did they know we were here? Ask him."

"We found you quite by luck," he answered. "We didn't know there was a concentration camp here. Coming out of Hanover, we chased the Germans through these woods and we saw some SS coming towards us with a white flag."

"Did you slaughter them?" someone chipped in.

He looked uncomprehending. I translated.

"I don't know, I'm just one of the soldiers."

Around us, the girls were clamouring. "You must kill them, you must kill them all. All."

I was upset by this outburst of hatred, deeply though I felt it; I too wanted to shout, and tried to sit up, but flopped back, too weak. For the first time now I felt myself slipping. Everything became a haze. Yet I smiled, or at least I think I did. I would have been liberated after all. Let myself drift.

Irene noticed, and shouted: "No, no, not her, it's too unfair."

The "unfair" struck me as wonderfully comical.

"Sing, Fania, sing!" someone shrieked. The order galvanized me; I opened my mouth desperately. The

Survivors wait for British Army rations at Bergen-Belsen. Some survivors of Nazi-run camps suffered ruptured stomachs when they began to eat substantial portions of food again. Their stomachs had shrunk as they were near starvation and could not handle larger meals. (USHMM Photo Archives)

After liberation, the few survivors of Bergen-Belsen begin to tidy up the camp. (USHMM Photo Archives)

soldier thought I was at my last gasp; he lifted me out of my filth, took me in his arms, showing no sign of disgust. How comfortable it was, how light I must feel (I weighed sixty-two pounds). Held firmly, head against his chest, drawing my strength from his, I started on the first verse of the Marseillaise. My voice had not died; I was alive.

The fellow staggered. Carrying me in his arms, he rushed outside towards an officer, shouting, "She's singing, she's singing."

The air hit me like a slap. I choked and was reborn. The girls ran out behind us. Technically no doubt I still had typhus, but the moment I found the strength to sing, I felt I'd recovered. The mists cleared; once more I could look around me and see what was happening. And it was well worth observing: Soldiers were arresting the SS and lining them up against the walls. We had savoured the thought of this moment so often and with such passion, and now it was a reality. Deportees were emerging from every shed. The men from whom we'd been separated for so long were coming towards us, desperately seeking out relatives and acquaintances.

Then I was in clean surroundings, in the SS block. I was bathing in a marvellous sea of khaki, and it smelled so good; their very sweat smelled sweet.

We had been liberated by the infantry, and now the motorized units were arriving. Through the window I saw the first jeep enter the camp. An officer jumped out, a Dutchman. He looked around dazedly and then began to run like a madman, arms outstretched, calling, "Margrett, Margrett!" A woman staggered towards him, her striped tatters floating like rags tied to a pole—his wife, three-quarters dead, in a frightening state of filth and decay; and he hugged her, hugged to him the smiling, living wraith.

Someone handed me a microphone.

It was strange. The process of breathing exhausted me, my heart was positively economizing on its beats, life had become a remote possibility, yet I straightened up, galvanized by joy, and I sang the Marseillaise again. This time it emerged with a violence and a strength I had never had before and which I shall probably never have again.

Clearly moved, a Belgian officer sank his hand into his pocket and handed me the most marvellous present: an old lipstick. I couldn't imagine anything lovelier, three-quarters used as it was and despite its uncertain pedigree.

The microphone holder insisted: "Please, miss, it's for the BBC [British Broadcasting Corporation]."

I sang "God Save the King," and tears filled the British soldiers' eyes.

I sang the Internationale and the Russian deportees joined in.

I sang, and in front of me, around me, from all corners of the camp, creeping along the sides of the shacks, dying shadows and skeletons stirred, rose up, grew taller. A great "Hurrah" burst forth and swept along like a breaker, carrying all before it. They had become men and women once again.

A few months later I learned that on that day, at that time, in London, my cousin heard me sing on the radio and fainted with shock: simultaneously she learned that I had been deported and that I'd just been liberated. (Fénelon, pp. 3–9)

Aftermath

When the British army liberated Bergen-Belsen on April 15, 1945, they found 60,000 prisoners in the camp, the majority of them in critical condition. The sight of thousands of unburied corpses lying around the compound sent many soldiers into a state of shock. Since the British had stumbled upon the camp, they were not prepared for the enormous rescue requirements. During the first five days after liberation, approximately 14,000 prisoners died; another 14,000 perished in the following weeks. In the fall of 1945, a British military court tried forty-eight members of the staff of Bergen-Belsen, including sixteen women. Eleven of the accused were found guilty and sentenced to death—including the commander of Bergen-Belsen, Josef Kramer. Kramer earned the reputation as the "Beast of Belsen" from the international press after the British troops who rescued the camp discovered piles of corpses and mass graves. Transferred to Bergen-Belsen from Birkenau in December 1944, he transformed what had been a camp for the privileged into a camp crowd-

Playing for Time
Adapted for TV

I n 1980 American playwright Arthur Miller adapted Fénelon's story for a made-for-television movie, starring Vanessa Redgrave as Fénelon and Jane Alexander as the leader of the women's orchestra. *Playing for Time* won several Emmy Awards, including one for outstanding drama special, one for best teleplay (Miller), one for best lead actress (Redgrave), and one for best supporting actress (Alexander).

ed with prisoners in every stage of emaciation and disease. Kramer and the other war criminals were executed on December 12, 1945. After liberation, Bergen-Belsen served as the site of a displaced persons' camp until 1951. The British army medical corps provided help in the physical rehabilitation of the former prisoners. Under the leadership of Josef Rosencraft, the camp developed an active social, cultural, and political life.

At the time of liberation, Fénelon was in her twenties. After surviving the Bergen-Belsen camp, she resumed her life's dream of singing. For twenty-five years she traveled throughout East Germany from one town to the next, performing in concert halls. In 1977, more than thirty years after World War II ended, she published *Playing for Time,* a book about her experiences at Auschwitz and Bergen-Belsen.

Dachau survivors line the wire fence as the camp is being liberated by Allied forces. (Reproduced by permission of AP/Wide World Photos)

SOURCES

Books

Fénelon, Fania, with Marcelle Routier, *Playing for Time,* translated by Judith Landry, Atheneum (New York), 1977.

Rochman, Hazel, and Darlene McCampbell, *Bearing Witness: Stories of the Holocaust,* Orchard Press (Danbury, CT), 1995.

Rubenstein, E. F., *After the Holocaust,* Archon Books (Hamden, CT), 1995.

Other

Bergen-Belsen Memorial, http://www.mznet.org/chamber/belsen.htm (May 16, 2000).

Bergen-Belsen—Simon Wiesenthal Center, http://motlc.wiesenthal.org/pages/t007/t00752.html (May 16, 2000).

The War Against Japan

By the spring of 1942, Japan had conquered a vast territory that stretched thousands of miles, from the border between Burma (present-day Myanmar) and India east to the Gilbert Islands in the middle of the Pacific Ocean. The Japanese controlled most of the immense island of New Guinea, situated south of the equator near Australia, and small Arctic islands in the Aleutians, off the coast of Alaska. Battles raged in these places from the time of the Battle of Midway in June 1942 to the final defeat of Japan in August 1945. The largest Japanese force, by far, was in China, which was the scene of large battles and great human suffering. For the most part, however, the Japanese army in China avoided major offensive actions. Likewise, the Chinese armies—almost all poorly equipped, poorly trained, and poorly led—refrained from direct confrontations with the Japanese. Despite pressure from the United States, which provided arms, supplies, and training to the best Chinese troops, Chinese leaders never seriously threatened the Japanese. Battles fought in China did not decide the outcome of World War II in Asia, and neither did the attempts to retake Burma, although troops in the British, Indian, and Japanese armies suffered heavy casualties.

The Asian War Becomes a Pacific War

The war against Japan was decided by events in the Pacific, where nearly all of the Allied forces were American. In the western Pacific, the conflict involved huge spaces—thousands of miles of open ocean dotted by groups of small islands, including the Gilberts, the Marshalls, the Carolines, and the Marianas. Farther south, nearer Australia, the islands were larger and the distances between them shorter. Month after month, from Australia northward and from Hawaii and Midway westward, the Americans pushed back the Japanese and slowly advanced on Japan. Protected by ships and airplanes, the marines and soldiers of the U.S. forces (and, in a few places, Australian soldiers) landed on island after island. After each landing, they fought to overcome the Japanese troops, who usually resisted with tremendous determination, sometimes literally to the point of suicide. When the troops had secured an island, or one region of a large island, and established airfields and facilities for warships, the war would move farther north or west to a new island. Sometimes the next target was hundreds of miles away. The Americans sometimes bypassed islands still held by the Japanese because the enemy forces there were now isolated and ineffectual. For almost three years, the Americans conquered (or reconquered) one island after another. When the war in Europe ended in the spring of 1945, American forces were engaged in the largest of these Pacific battles, located on the island of Okinawa, less than 400 miles from Japan itself.

Taking one island after another was the basic American strategy for the war against Japan. The

The Burma Road. Japan took control of this important trade route into China in May 1942. (Reproduced by permission of the Corbis Corporation [Bellevue])

The motive behind the Allied strategy was to prevent an immediate German victory in Europe. At the time the United States entered the war, in December 1941, both Great Britain and the Soviet Union were in serious danger. German submarines were winning the Battle of the Atlantic, threatening to cut off Britain's supplies, and Adolf Hitler's armies controlled most of Europe and had nearly reached Moscow, the Soviet capital. If America had concentrated on Japan initially, it might have later found itself facing Germany alone. By that time, the Soviet Union would have been conquered and destroyed by Germany, and Great Britain would have been forced to make peace.

The "Germany first" decision was the driving force behind the American approach to the war against Japan. The Pacific strategy stressed the use of American naval power. One reason was the efficient use of resources. American shipyards were building great warships in increasing numbers. These battleships, cruisers, and aircraft carriers could be spared more easily from Europe and the Atlantic than planes, tanks, and cannons. Small aircraft carriers, transporting planes designed for antisubmarine warfare, were useful in the Atlantic. But the great fleet carriers—with their fighters, bombers, and dive bombers—that were so important in the Pacific, were far less useful in Europe and the Mediterranean, where air bases on land were usually in close proximity. Due to the island-hopping strategy chosen for the Pacific war and the huge distances that the Americans crossed, a great number of warships and planes were involved in the campaign. By the end of the war, the American fleet in the Pacific was the largest in the history of warfare. The air was dominated by 3,000 planes based on aircraft carriers and thousands of others based on land. Nevertheless, the actual number of soldiers, sailors, and airmen who fought the battles in the Pacific was small compared with the size of the armies that fought in Europe.

The use of a relatively small number of combat troops was a key factor in the American Pacific strategy. The number of marines or soldiers who landed on a particular island might be fairly large, but only one or two battles were going on simultaneously. The majority of the battles in the Pacific were fought by six American army divisions and four marine divisions (a division is usually around 15,000 men). Although troops from some of the additional nineteen divisions in the area saw action, the American combat force in the Pacific essentially amounted to an army of about 150,000 soldiers.

Pacific war, in which the navy used its power to protect an invasion of an island, involved relatively few soldiers. The naval approach to the Pacific war was not the only option considered by the Americans. For example, the Allies could have sent armies to attack the large Japanese force stationed in China. Such a conflict could have been similar to the war in Europe, with masses of soldiers led by tanks, supported by artillery, and protected by planes. A land war in Asia was not a real possibility, however, because the United States had decided that the Allies should first concentrate their forces and resources on Nazi Germany. Only after Germany surrendered would they forcefully pursue the war against Japan. In the meantime the Allies would prevent the Japanese from expanding farther and, if possible, win back some of Japan's conquests.

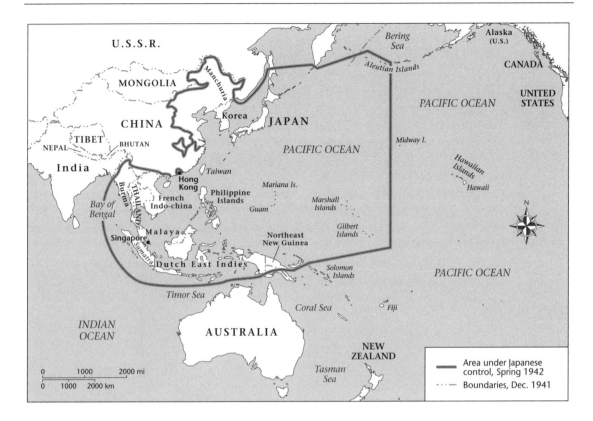

Asia and the Pacific, 1942.

In order to improve American morale, posters like this one were created to show the strength of the mighty Allied forces as they walked over Germany to crush Japan. (Library of Congress)

America's Industrial Advantage over Japan

A major reason that the "Germany first" military strategy made sense was the economic, and especially industrial, advantage the United States wielded over Japan. This advantage meant that time was on America's side. The longer the war continued, with both sides producing weapons and ships, the greater the American advantage would become. In the long run, as both American and Japanese leaders knew, Japan did not have the industrial power to defeat the United States. For example, Japan built and sent to sea a total of fourteen aircraft carriers during the years it was at war with the United States. During that same period, the United States built 104 carriers. Perhaps even more important, Japan constructed merchant ships weighing a total of 3.3 million tons during the war, and the United States built more than 50 million tons of ships. Japan built more than 28,000 planes in 1944, the most of any year, and its ally Germany built nearly 40,000. Yet the United States alone, without counting the production of its Soviet or British allies, built more than 100,000 planes that year.

The United States also produced numerous tanks for the war effort. Heading for the war, these tanks make their way via the New York Central Railroad. (Library of Congress)

A relatively small number of American combat troops, like these Marines pinned down on a beach on the island of Iwo Jima, did most of the fighting in the Pacific. (National Archives and Records Administration)

The entire Japanese army outside Japan and China was approximately the same size. In comparison, millions of soldiers were involved in the European war. In mid-1944, 300 divisions of the Soviet army were fighting the Germans in Russia, while another seventy British and American divisions fought in Western Europe. Against them, Germany and its Axis partners had about 300 divisions.

The Pacific strategy was also beneficial on the home front, as the quick successes of the island conquests gave the American people something to read about and celebrate. This was especially important after the Japanese triumphs against the United States at Pearl Harbor and the Philippines, only a few months earlier. The American strategy allowed a comparatively small number of troops to attack an island and win a clear-cut victory. In contrast, after entering the war it took almost a year for American troops to fire a shot against the Germans. (This happened during the North Africa campaign in November 1942.) Each island campaign in the Pacific meant another victory, usually within a short time, which was drastically different from the long, drawn-out fighting in Europe, where individual battles seemed to be part of a single, endless advance toward Germany.

Historians generally assert that another reason for the Pacific strategy was the rivalry between the top admirals of the U.S. Navy and the generals of the army. Admiral Ernest King, the chief of staff of the navy, and other leaders were never actually pleased with the "Germany first" decision. Throughout the war, Admiral King argued for sending more resources to the Pacific, knowing this sentiment was shared by many Americans, who wanted revenge for Pearl Harbor. Disputes about resources continued throughout the war. Probably the best-known example was the navy's reluctance to send landing craft to Europe, preferring instead to dispatch the craft to the Pacific. Some historians believe the shortage of landing craft was a major factor in delaying the D-Day invasion of France. The Normandy invasion was contingent upon naval support for the landings, but was still an overwhelmingly land-based army operation. The ships, like the soldiers and the air forces, were all under the command of army General Dwight D. Eisenhower.

It was obvious as soon as the United States entered the war that the army would play the major role in Europe. The navy was determined to serve the same function in the Pacific. If "Germany first" meant that the Pacific theater would not be allocated as many resources as Europe, then at least the

Rivalries in the Japanese Army and Navy

Rivalries between the American army and navy may have caused some problems, but they were not nearly as serious as the disputes that took place in Japan. The Japanese navy and army were like separate worlds. The top generals and admirals were each represented in the government, which they were able to control when they cooperated. When they disagreed, however, there was no one who could break the deadlock. It was almost impossible for the government to order either the army or the navy to carry out a mission that the admirals and generals did not want to undertake, which essentially allowed the separate branches of the military to act autonomously. For example, in April 1942 the Japanese navy attacked the British-controlled island of Ceylon (now the nation of Sri Lanka), off the southern tip of India, in what appeared to be the first steps of an invasion. This would have posed a serious threat to India, but the army refused to assign the two divisions needed to make a Japanese invasion of Ceylon possible.

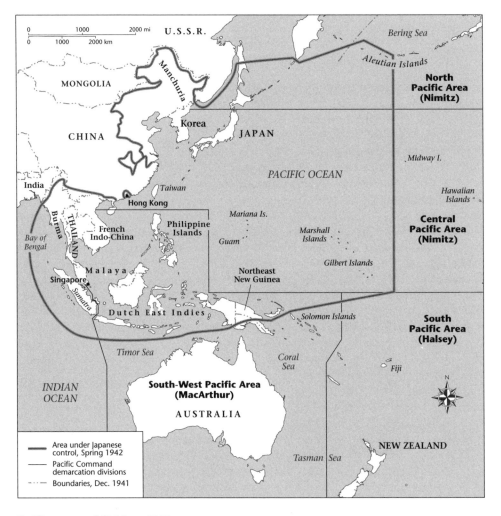

Pacific command divisions, 1942.

navy would run the operation. The island-hopping strategy proposed by the navy was based on a plan that had been drawn up long before the war, in preparation for a possible Japanese attack. It involved landings on a series of islands, some of them tiny, located in the Solomon, Gilbert, Marshall, and Mariana Islands. Ground forces, under the command of Admiral Chester Nimitz, would include army troops as well as marines, whom Nimitz preferred to use. (The U.S. Marine Corps is part of the Department of the Navy, not the army.) No army general would command any of the navy's ships. In the European theater, the commanding officer of an area, regardless of whether he was army or navy, controlled all forces in the region.

The army was frustrated with this arrangement. Especially displeased was General Douglas MacArthur, who had commanded the defense of the Philippines and was now in Australia. The heroism of American soldiers fighting in the Philippines in the early months of the war had made MacArthur popular in the United States. He and the army used his popularity to gain the advantage in disagreements with the navy. As part of a compromise between the army and navy, MacArthur was made commander of the Southwest Pacific, which included Australia, New Guinea, the Dutch East Indies, and the Philippines. Admiral Nimitz soon named Admiral William Halsey to command the South Pacific Area, east of Australia, and the rest of the Pacific was placed under Nimitz's direct command.

The division of command between MacArthur and Nimitz, and between the army and the navy, meant that the American effort against Japan would take two different forms. MacArthur's soldiers would fight the Japanese on a series of large islands north of Australia. Although often outnumbered by the Japanese, American forces defeated them through superior tactics and leadership. Nimitz and the navy would drive west across the Pacific, attacking a series of tiny islands with overwhelming naval and air forces. In one battle after another, they suffered heavy casualties, but they inflicted even greater losses on the Japanese defenders. This double strategy was originally an attempt to satisfy both the American army and navy, specifically MacArthur and Nimitz, who were both strong-willed men determined to get their way. Splitting the American attack along two routes increased the possibility of a weakened front, but in reality the opposite occurred. Each of the campaigns was powerful enough to defeat the forces Japan placed

Admiral William Halsey commanded the South Pacific Area, east of Australia. (Library of Congress)

in its path. The Japanese were never able to shift enough military and naval forces to stop one of the American advances without severely weakening their defenses against the other.

The United States Strikes Back: Guadalcanal

In August 1942, only two months after the great American naval victory at Midway, Nimitz launched the first American offensive operation of the war. A relatively small force of U.S. Marines landed on the island of Guadalcanal, in the Solomon Islands. The Americans planned the operation quickly, with little knowledge of the geography or conditions the marines would face. The island had rugged jungle terrain and was incredibly hot and humid. Outbreaks of tropical diseases, especially malaria, were common. Guadalcanal had military importance because of an airfield that could be utilized by the Americans as a base for further advances. The Americans and Japanese alike believed the fight would be short-lived, perhaps a week or two, but the battle that developed became much larger than the island's military value could justify. Japanese leaders understood that they could not defeat the United States in a long war because the United States pos-

U.S. Marine Corps tanks in the jungles of Guadalcanal; the Allied strategy in the Pacific led to deadly fighting on some of the islands. (Reproduced by permission of AP/Wide World Photos)

As they invade Guadalcanal, American marines run ashore after leaving their landing crafts. (Reproduced by permission of © Hulton Getty/Liaison Agency)

When the Americans set up a blockade around Guadalcanal, Japanese troops found their supply route cutoff. After surrendering to the Americans, these emaciated Japanese soldiers received food from their captors. (Reproduced by permission of © Hulton Getty/Liaison Agency)

sessed greater industrial power. They therefore concluded that their only chance for success was to make the cost of victory so high—in both American lives and money—that the United States would agree to a compromise peace that would leave Japan in control of much of eastern Asia. The key for Japan was to make the war so difficult and so bloody that the American people would stop supporting it.

The Battle of Guadalcanal was the first test of America's island-hopping strategy, and it was also crucial for Japan's long-term plans. Each side threw more and more resources into the fight, as winning became increasingly important. At that time, the Japanese army had not yet given up an inch of conquered territory, and American ground troops had not been involved in combat anywhere. The Americans were determined to prove that their soldiers could defeat the Japanese; the Japanese wanted to prove the opposite, so they rushed reinforcements to Guadalcanal to drive the Americans out. The Japanese, however, miscalculated the

number of landed American marines and sent too few troops. When these reinforcements could not defeat the U.S. forces, more troops arrived. For a while, Japanese warships brought small numbers of troops and supplies every night, a system the Americans called the Tokyo Express. In response, the Americans sent reinforcements of their own, eventually merging army troops with the exhausted marines. For six months, the two sides fought dozens of minor, bloody battles: for the airfield, for high ridges or narrow streams, and for a few hundred yards of jungle.

A series of five major sea battles also took place as part of the Guadalcanal campaign. Dozens of ships were lost to the guns and torpedoes of enemy warships and carrier-based planes; the Americans called the water between Guadalcanal and a nearby island "Ironbottom Sound" because so many ships had been sunk there. The ultimate result of the battles was that Japan was unable to resupply its troops on the island or defend them from the growing number of American planes and soldiers.

James J. Fahey and His *Pacific War Diary*

James J. Fahey enlisted in the U.S. Navy on October 3, 1942. Throughout the war, he served as seaman first class on the U.S.S. *Montpelier*, a light cruiser. He first tasted battle in January 1943 during the struggle for Rennell Island, south of Guadalcanal. Fahey and his machine-gun team succeeded in bringing down a Japanese plane.

Fahey was an ordinary seaman who made it through the war unscathed, but he won lasting fame by keeping a diary throughout his years on the *Montpelier*. *Pacific War Diary, 1942–1945* (Boston: Houghton Mifflin, 1963) was published later. In it, Fahey records his impressions of wartime life in the U.S. Navy: constant lack of sleep, hasty meals and bad food, grueling work, boredom and danger in turns.

Although Fahey's writing is simple and unadorned, he conveys the details of war with immediacy, as in this passage, describing the aftermath of the taking of Saipan: "After supper while we were out patrolling Saipan the fellows passed the time running from one side of the ship to the other, watching the Jap bodies float by. You could get a good look at them as they passed, because they were very close to the ship. Some were on their stomachs, others on their backs, and they floated along like rubber balls."

Fahey's diary is an invaluable record. It has earned a reputation as one of the best accounts of the experience that thousands of men shared during the war in the Pacific. Its tone is modest and devout throughout, and it concludes with Fahey's prayer of thanksgiving that he survived the war uninjured. Fahey donated all proceeds from the book to the construction of a cathedral in India.

The life of the common soldier was captured in *Pacific War Diary, 1942–1945*, written by James J. Fahey. The former serviceman holds the pages from his diary that became the basis for his well-received book. (Reproduced by permission of AP/Wide World Photos)

By January 1943 it was clear that the United States would win control of Guadalcanal.

Unlike the strategy in many later battles, the Japanese leadership in Tokyo decided to withdraw its remaining troops rather than fight to the last man. The Japanese officers on the island obeyed this order, possibly because it was personally approved by the emperor. By early February the last 13,000 Japanese soldiers boarded warships and escaped from Guadalcanal. Of the 36,000 Japanese troops who fought on the island, 14,000 had been killed and another 9,000 had died of tropical diseases. The dead included hundreds of trained pilots killed in the sea battles. Like the many experienced Japanese pilots who died at Midway, they could not be easily replaced. Almost as many Japanese soldiers had been killed on this single small island as had died conquering Japan's vast new empire in Asia less than a year earlier.

American casualties were also high, although they were much lower than the Japanese losses. This was a pattern that would be repeated throughout the Pacific war. At its height, American strength on Guadalcanal was more than 50,000 men; 1,600 were killed and 4,300 wounded; thousands more contracted malaria. The First Marine Division, the first to land on Guadalcanal, was temporarily destroyed as a fighting unit; 774 men died and nearly 2,000 were wounded. More than 5,000 men, over one-third of the entire division, became sick with malaria.

At the time of the Battle of Midway in June 1942, the Japanese had captured islands in the Aleutian chain, which was part of Alaska. The islands were quite cold, often battered by storms and high winds and covered in fog, which meant they were essentially useless as air bases. Despite these factors, Nimitz decided to retake them. In May 1943 he sent an army division and powerful naval forces, including battleships, to the island of Attu. The 2,500 Japanese troops on the island, although heavily outnumbered, strongly defended their positions, retreating slowly and inflicting serious losses on the American attackers. Yet after two weeks of fighting, the Japanese were finally at the end of their strength. Instead of surrendering, however, the Japanese commander led his troops in a bayonet charge against the Americans. Hundreds of Japanese soldiers then committed suicide rather than be captured; almost all the defenders of Attu died, with the Americans being able to capture only twenty-eight alive. The Americans, despite having to attack strong defensive positions, lost about a third as many soldiers. Two months later, Japanese warships evacuated more than 5,000 troops from the Aleutian island of Kiska under cover of fog. The waiting American invasion force of 34,000 men took the island without a fight.

The most important Japanese military and naval base in the southern Pacific was at Rabaul, on the large island of New Britain. Although driving the powerful Japanese forces from Rabaul would be extremely difficult, it became the first major goal of the combined American navy and army strategy. After the victory on Guadalcanal, the navy continued west through the remaining Solomon Islands. At the end of June 1943, troops landed on New Georgia, and on Vella Lavella in August. They skipped the island of Kolombangara, leaving the 10,000 Japanese troops there in control of the island but unable to play any part in the war because they were surrounded by American forces. This is an example of the island-hopping strategy. In November a division of marines was joined by an army division, and the collective forces landed on Bougainville, at the northwestern end of the Solomons chain. They soon built an airfield and established a powerful defensive position, which the 35,000 Japanese troops on the island were unable to penetrate. American naval and air power prevented the arrival of Japanese reinforcements. The American base on Bougainville was within striking distance of Rabaul.

Closing in on Rabaul: The Fighting in New Guinea

Meanwhile, General MacArthur's Australian and American troops were fighting on New Guinea, just north of Australia. New Guinea is the second-largest island in the world, about twice the size of France, and has high mountains, impassable rain forests, and few roads. Prior to the war it was divided between the Dutch, who controlled the western half of the island, and Australia, which controlled the eastern half, including the southeastern quarter called Papua. Japanese troops occupied the Dutch half as part of their conquest of the Dutch East Indies in early 1942. In May of that year, the Japanese attempted to land troops on the southern coast of Papua, near its capital, Port Moresby. From there, they could threaten Australia.

This attempt led to the Battle of the Coral Sea, the first great naval battle fought between aircraft carriers. With their fleet driven off in the now-famous battle, the Japanese instead landed troops on the north shore in July and attempted to attack Port Moresby by crossing the mountains along a single jungle trail—a maneuver that MacArthur and his planners had thought was impossible. Australian troops defending the trail were pushed back, and by mid-September the Japanese were only forty miles from Port Moresby. Nevertheless, they were no longer able to get enough reinforcements to replace the men they had lost because the Americans had landed on Guadalcanal. The Japanese were relying on ships to bring reinforcements and supplies there. Unlike the Allies, the Japanese did not have the resources to attack in New Guinea and Guadalcanal at the same time.

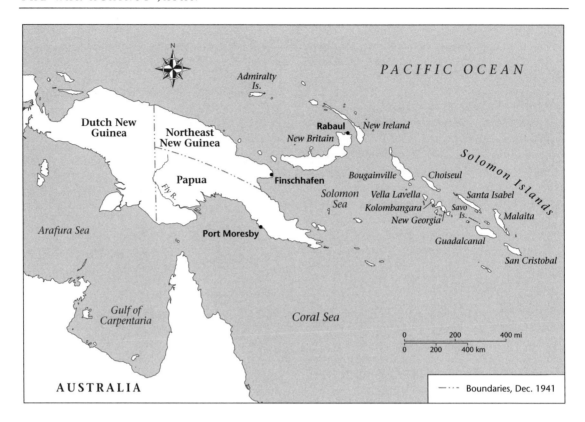

The Solomon Islands and New Guinea, 1941.

MacArthur saw Japan's weakness and went on the offensive. The Australians forced the Japanese back to the north shore of Papua. Meanwhile, American troops landed by boat at other points on the north shore. By the end of January 1943, the Allies had cleared Papua of Japanese forces. In six months of fighting, more than 12,000 Japanese soldiers died. The Allies lost almost 4,000 soldiers, more than three-quarters of them Australians, and another 7,500 Allied soldiers were wounded. In a series of battles over the next eight months, MacArthur's forces moved farther west along the New Guinea coast. In October 1943 the Allies captured Finschhafen, a port across the strait from New Britain. On the other end of New Britain was the great Japanese base at Rabaul. A month later, with the success of the American operation on Bougainville, the Allies could threaten Rabaul from New Guinea to the south and from Bougainville to the east. The attack on Rabaul might have been costly, but the 100,000 Japanese troops on New Britain and New Ireland were now isolated. They had suffered under constant American air raids, which destroyed many of their planes. American naval strength in the area was also far greater than that of the Japanese, whose forces at Rabaul did not have the air or sea power to support their troops elsewhere. The Americans therefore decided not to attack at Rabaul, confident that the Japanese forces could be contained until the end of the war.

Instead, Nimitz and MacArthur moved far beyond Rabaul. In November 1943 Nimitz's marines landed on the tiny island of Tarawa in the Gilbert Islands. Nearly the entire Japanese force of 5,000 soldiers was killed while defending the island; the troops refused to surrender even when further resistance was useless. The marines lost 1,000 men and 2,000 were wounded. In February 1944, the advance continued northwest to the Marshall Islands. Early in the month, after a tremendous naval bombardment, marine and army troops captured the island of Kwajalein in four days of fighting, suffering far fewer casualties than at Tarawa. Within two weeks, American troops landed on Eniwetok, the farthest west of the Marshall Islands, capturing it in a battle that lasted five days. The Americans bypassed the other islands between Kwajalein and Eniwetok because without a powerful navy, the Japanese soldiers stationed there presented no threat.

The next target was the Mariana Islands, which were 1,000 miles across the Pacific from Eniwetok and within striking distance of the Philippines. The new U.S. B-29 long-range bomber, known as the Superfortress, would be able to reach the cities of

Japan from the Marianas. The first island the Americans attacked was Saipan, on June 15, 1944. The date indicates how great the Allied resources were: it was barely a week after the Allies had launched the invasion of northwest Europe, landing many tens of thousands of soldiers on the beaches of Normandy. Two marine divisions and one army division attacked Saipan, which was defended by 32,000 Japanese. The Americans once again had strong naval and air support to protect their landing, and the fighting continued for three weeks. As their numbers dwindled, the remaining Japanese troops, running low on ammunition, charged the amazed Americans with bayonets before hundreds committed suicide by jumping off cliffs. The Americans quickly followed up this bloody victory with much easier victories on Tinian and then on Guam, an American island that Japan had captured in December 1941, immediately after the Pearl Harbor attack. Meanwhile, in the two-day Battle of the Philippine Sea, American carriers thoroughly defeated a Japanese fleet. The Americans lost twenty-nine planes while shooting down 243 enemy planes, almost two-thirds of the total Japanese air strength. The Americans referred to this victory as the Great Marianas Turkey Shoot. In addition, inexperienced Japanese replacement pilots were not nearly so skilled as the men who had won Japan's first great air victories. Three Japanese carriers were sunk and one was badly damaged, further confirming the United States' dominance in aircraft and radar technology.

While the battles for the Marshalls and Marianas were being fought, MacArthur's troops continued their advance northwest along the coast of New Guinea, avoiding most of the Japanese troops stationed on the island. In a series of carefully planned operations, large Allied forces landed at points along the coast, usually surprising the Japanese defenders. In each case, the American aim was to capture or build an airstrip and create a strong base that could not be eliminated by the Japanese. Planes from the new airfield would provide cover for the next operation. By July 1944 American troops had established bases in the extreme northwest corner of the giant island, the area known as Vogelkop ("bird's head" in Dutch, because of its shape), which would provide the launching point for an invasion of the Philippines.

Internment Camps in Southeast Asia

In the early 1940s, Japan began a systematic invasion of Indonesia and its surrounding area. As island after island fell to the Japanese, thousands of European and American civilians living in the region were caught up in the wake of war. Men, women, and children were forced into internment camps throughout the islands of the Philippines, Indonesia, Sumatra, Borneo, Singapore, Java, and Malaysia. As the war in the Pacific intensified, surviving soldiers and sailors from downed planes and sunken ships, as well as many troops who were forced to surrender, were held as prisoners of war (POWs) and interned in POW camps. Hundreds of thousands of POWs and civilians were held against their will, caught up in the chaos of World War II.

Many of the internment camps and POW camps were in close proximity to each other; others were not. Some camps were large—2,700 Australian and British POWs were held at Sandakan in northern Borneo. Some camps were small—twenty-one American nurses were held on the island of Banka in Indonesia. All internees shared one common experience: the harsh and brutal treatment offered by their captors. Beating, starvation, rape, murder, and even cannibalism were commonplace. Grueling marches from camp to camp in the hot, tropical sun also took a toll on the prisoners. While thousands of men, women, and children died as a result of their stay in these camps, many survived to reveal the atrocities they experienced.

One of the darkest tales of the war in the Pacific concerns the treatment of POWs, including those Allied soldiers interned at Sandakan, Borneo. Between 1942 and 1945, more than 2,700 Australian and British soldiers were held there, waiting and praying for the war to end. For all but six of the POWs, the war did not end soon enough.

On July 14, 1940, members of the 2/19th Battalion, 8th Australian Division, 2th Australian Imperial Force (AIF) left Sydney, Australia, to help repel the Japanese invasion of Malaysia. On February 14, 1942, after nearly two years of fighting, the Allied forces in Singapore, numbering 130,000, surrendered to the Japanese. Members of the 2/19th Battalion—part of that group—were taken to Sandakan, on the northeastern coast of Borneo, where the Japanese were building an airbase. The airbase was located about 10 miles outside of town. There, the Australians were placed in an internment camp, where the Japanese were already holding British prisoners of war.

The British and Australian internees were put to work constructing two airstrips and several

Showing the effects of food deprivation, these men were interned by the Japanese at the Santo Tomas Internment Camp in Manila. When the camp was liberated by American troops, these men weighed between 87 and 105 pounds. (Reproduced by permission of AP/Wide World Photos)

roads leading to the town. At first, the situation did not seem ultimately life-threatening for the POWs. They were split into work details, burning the scrub brush from the land, filling in swamps, and clearing stones from the fields. Each member of the work detail was given 10 cents per day, which could be spent at the canteen to buy extra eggs, bananas, and coconuts.

All that changed in April 1943 when Japanese guards from Formosa arrived at the camp. The new guards brought with them "the cage"—a structure used by the Japanese military to punish the POWs. The cage was made of wooden slats and was only tall enough for the prisoners to sit inside. Punishments could last anywhere from two days to several months. Private Keith Botterill of the 2/19th Battalion spent 40 days in the cage with 17 of his fellow internees. According to Botterill, the prisoners did not receive water or food for the first several days while in the cage; after seven days, he received some food. Botterill recalled (as quoted in *Laden, Fevered, Starved: The POWs of Sandakan, North Borneo, 1945,* compiled by Australia's Commonwealth Department of Veterans' Affairs in 1999):

Every evening we would get a bashing, which they used to call physical exercise.… [At

5 p.m., the cooks would] feed the dogs with swill, the kitchen rubbish. They'd pour it into this trough. We'd all hit together, the dogs and all of us, and we'd fight the dogs for the scraps.… If you've ever tried to pull a bone out of a starving dog's mouth you'll know what it was like. The dog would fasten onto your wrist to take the bone off you, and you'd still be putting the bone into your mouth.…

By September 1944, the Allied forces began air raids over Sandakan, knocking out the airstrips near the camp. In retaliation for the attacks, the Japanese guards, under the command of Captain Hoshijima Susumi, punished the Allied POWs. Rations were cut in half and the POWs were severely beaten. By January 1945, the guards cut off all rations to the POWs. Believing that the Allies would soon be landing in Borneo, the officers decided to move the internees to Ranau, about 150 miles (260 kilometers) to the west of Sandakan. The terrain between the two cities was varied. The POWs had to travel through mountainous regions, rivers and swamps, across flat land and rolling hills, and through jungles and forests to reach Ranau.

The POWs were split up into groups. The first group—455 men—began its journey from Sandakan to Ranau on January 28, 1945. The men were given four days worth of food (rice, fish, and cucumbers) for the trip, even though it would take more than 15 days to arrive at their destination. Along the route, many of the men died. In addition to the grueling march with little food, the POWs were also suffering from malaria, beriberi, malnutrition, and dysentery. If the POWs could not keep up, the Japanese officers shot them. According to Botterill: "Although I did not see the bodies of any men who had been shot in the parties that had gone before, often I could smell them."

By June 26, the first group reached Ranau. Only six survived the march—one British soldier and five Australians. The POWs that were still interned at Sandakan were not faring any better. Between February and May 1945, more than 880 died in the camp. On May 27, the Allies bombed the town. The Japanese rounded up the POWs that could walk and headed toward Ranau. Some of the prisoners, 288 of the internees, were too weak to walk. Of those, 23 were shot, while 75 escaped into the jungle—they were never seen again. The others were left, lying on the ground. As the group departed, the Japanese burned the camp to the ground. Of the 530 that attempted the trek to Ranau on the second march, only 183 made it.

When the second group arrived in Ranau on June 26, the POWs were put to work alongside the six survivors of the first march. They hauled water, rice, meat, fish, eggs, tapioca, and sweet potatoes for the officers. Each day, the POWs were given a cup of water with a few grains of rice. Each day, a few more died. By the time the Japanese surrendered on August 15, 1945, very few POWs had survived. They were shot after digging their own graves.

Private Botterill managed to escape on July 7, 1945. With the help of a local man, he and three other Australian soldiers hid in a cave on Mount Kinabalu until Allied Forces reached Ranau to liberate the camp. However, the Allied troops arrived too late for most of the POWs. In addition to Botterill's group, two other Australians escaped during the march. Out of the original 2,700 POWs, only six survived.

After hearing Botterill's account, the Australian government dispatched a group of soldiers known as the Australian War Graves unit. Between 1945 and 1947, the War Graves staff located the bodies of 2,163 POWs, either at Sandakan or Ranau, or along the way. More soldiers were known to have died;

however, their bodies were never found. Many were buried in mass graves; others were found lying in the jungle. The War Graves personnel found pay vouchers, collar tabs, hats, badges, identification disks, and used bandages throughout the route between the two camps. From these items, the searchers could identify POWs from several military units, including the Gordon Highlanders, Royal Army Medical Corps, 17th Dogras (a British unit from India), and the 2/19th Battalion.

From January to August of 1945, many POWs died during the death marches of Sandakan-Ranau—1,787 Australians and 641 British. As a result, Captain Susumi and numerous members of his staff were brought before the International Military Tribunal of the Far East on charges of war crimes. In 1946 Susumi and eight of his officers were convicted of crimes against humanity for the harsh treatment of POWs in Susumi's care, and they were executed for their crimes. Fifty-five other members of Susumi's staff were imprisoned.

Civilians Confined

Another example of the harsh treatment of prisoners by the Japanese relates to European and American civilians living in the Pacific theater during wartime. When the Japanese invaded many of the islands in the South Pacific, the civilians were rounded up and placed in camps. In many cases, they were treated as severely as were the POWs. The civilian camps, however, were divided into two types—camps for men and camps for women and children. Oftentimes, they were in close proximity to each other, operated by a single commander. Every once in a while, members of each camp were allowed to communicate with each other, allowing families to keep in touch.

Writer Agnes Newton Keith, wife of the British minister of agriculture serving in Asia, was held at the Batu Lingtang Encampment—a prison camp near Kuching, Borneo—with her two-year-old son. Prior to her internment, Keith had written a book on her time in Borneo. *Land Below the Wind,* published in 1939, had been a favorite of the internment camp's commander, Colonel Suga. Knowing that she was a writer, Suga commissioned Keith to write of her time in the camp, paying her the equivalent of $3 per month, which could be used to supply medicine, clothing, and food for the internees. For a piece titled "Captivity," Keith submitted pages occasionally to Suga for his review. Unbeknownst to Suga, Keith kept a secret diary, writing bits and pieces on scraps

Held in the Santo Tomas camp in the Philippines, this English family survived the harsh conditions and was liberated in 1945. (Reproduced by permission of © Hulton Getty/Liaison Agency)

of paper, labels from canned food, and newspapers, which she sewed into her son's clothing.

When Keith was released from the camp, she began writing of her true experiences at Batu Lingtang. In her book *Three Came Home,* published in 1946, Keith describes her living quarters: "Our barrack was regarded by non-residents as a dirty hole, a stinkhole, a pesthole, a hellhole. It was Hades let loose on a rainy day. It was the final crash of a brass band throughout feeding hours. It smelled of kids, pots, and wee-wee. The noise started at 6 a.m. and continued until 6 a.m."

She later describes atrocities imposed on POWs and interned civilians by the Japanese and their allies: "At Sandakan and Ranau and Brunei, North Borneo, batches of prisoners in fifties and sixties were marched out to dig their own graves, then shot or bayoneted and pushed into the graves, many before they were dead. All over Borneo hundreds and thousands of sick, weak, weary prisoners were marched on roads and paths until they fell from exhaustion, when their heads were beaten in

with rifle butts and shovels, and split open with swords, and they were left to rot unburied. On one march, 2,970 POWs started, and three survived." Keith and her son were eventually reunited with her husband in September 1945, when Allied troops liberated the camp.

Other internment camps were equally as life-threatening. In 1943 about 700 Dutch and British women and children were interned at a camp in Sumatra. Two women—Margaret Dryburgh and Norah Chambers—organized many of the other internees into a "vocal orchestra," performing symphony pieces. Chronicled in Helen Colijn's book *Song of Survival: Women Interned* and Bruce Beresford's film *Paradise Road,* the women sang to ease the torment of being interned for nearly three years. According to Colijn's first-hand account, the chorus performed well-known pieces, including Dvorak's "New World Symphony." Attended by internees and Japanese prison commandants alike, the singing kept their spirits lifted. The concerts continued for about a year, until there were too few internees left to sing—malaria, jaundice, dysentery, impetigo, and beriberi were all commonplace, as were beatings and other atrocities.

As the Allied forces reclaimed territory in Southeast Asia at the close of World War II, they feared that the Japanese would retaliate by harming POWs and civilian internees held in internment camps throughout the islands of the Philippines, Indonesia, and in Borneo. Often, Japanese reprisals did occur before the Allies could liberate the internees from the camps. Sometimes, the horror occurred after the prisoners were set free. A prime example of the terror resulting after the prisoners' release occurred at Los Baños during the close of the war.

During the Japanese occupation of the Philippines from 1942 to 1945, the University of the Philippines Agricultural School at Los Baños was used as an internment camp. Located about 40 miles southeast of Manila, on the island of Luzon, Los Baños held 2,122 civilians during the winter of 1945. The internees were mostly Americans living in the surrounding area when war broke out, but also included Filipinos, and other "guests" of Imperial Japan. For nearly three years, the internees lived in the university classrooms before Allied forces rescued them. In February 1945, the camp was liberated by members of the 11th Airborne Division of the U.S. Army; Hunters-ROTC Guerrillas (former cadets of the Philippine Mili-

Women internees of the Santo Tomas Internment Camp (Manila, Philippines) wash up in an old tub. (Reproduced by permission of AP/Wide World Photos)

Glenn Close leads women in song in the film *Paradise Road*, which was based on women's experiences in Sumatra. (Reproduced by permission of the Kobal Collection)

tary Academy) and former college students assist-ed in the release of the internees.

Once the 11th Airborne troops left Los Baños, Japanese hiding in the area attacked the native islanders. Homes and villages were set on fire; families were tied to housing foundations and slaughtered. U.S. Army reports estimate that the Japanese put to death nearly 1,500 Filipinos as a result of the liberation of Los Baños.

These are just a few of the many accounts of Allied prisoners of war in the Pacific forced to suf-

fer inhumane treatment by the Japanese military. Such treatment is in direct violation of the Geneva Convention (which the Japanese had refused to sign). As with Captain Susumi of Sandakan, many Japanese internment camp officers and guards were brought to trial before the International Military Tribunal of the Far East for violating international laws regarding the treatment of prisoners of war. In total, 5,700 Japanese military personnel and civilian officials were convicted of committing crimes against humanity.

PRIMARY SOURCE

E. B. Sledge
Excerpt from *With the Old Breed at Peleliu and Okinawa*
First published in 1981

On September 15, 1944, U.S. Marines invaded Peleliu, one of the Palau Islands in the western Pacific Ocean. The Palau Islands campaign was originally viewed as a crucial stepping-stone in the liberation of the Philippines from Japan. The entire area was heavily defended by Japanese troops. Peleliu was only six miles long and two miles wide, but its rugged terrain and unbearably hot climate made for a slow and miserable battle. Approximately 28,000 Americans, a combined force of marine and army divisions, participated in the brutal, bloody struggle for the island. More than 1,100 marines were killed or wounded on the first day of fighting alone. U.S. forces captured the island on October 21, 1944. The casualties suffered on both sides were staggering. When the fighting was over, more than 6,500 marines and 3,200 army soldiers were dead or wounded; about 11,000 Japanese soldiers were killed. The battle for Peleliu marked a turning point for the Japanese military. Japanese fighting tactics changed radically during this campaign. Instead of concentrating all their power on the defense of Peleliu's beaches, the soldiers spread out and fought from fortified positions in caves throughout the island. The Japanese would use and refine those methods in the fights for Iwo Jima and Okinawa.

E. B. (Eugene Bondurant) Sledge was on Peleliu during this time. His book, *With the Old*

Breed at Peleliu and Okinawa, began as a series of notes taken while he was serving in the Pacific. He later pieced together his memoir to help his family understand his World War II experiences. Sledge's wife, Jeanne, convinced him that his work should be published. Born in Mobile, Alabama, and raised in a strict household, Sledge joined the marines at the age of nineteen. By the time he was twenty-three, he had earned the nickname "Sledgehammer" and witnessed a lifetime's worth of horror.

Sledge was a member of Company K, Third Battalion, Fifth Regiment of the First Marine Division—K/3/5 for short. The Fifth Marine Regiment is known as the "Old Breed" because it fought in all of the nation's major wars in the twentieth century. In the preface to *With the Old Breed*, Sledge noted that the marines "suffered and ... did their duty so a sheltered homeland [could] enjoy the peace that was purchased at such a high cost." He describes the horrible conditions the marines were forced to endure in the Pacific, enumerating the physical and psychological stresses that reduced the men to virtual savages who found difficulty maintaining faith, decency, honor, and compassion.

Throughout *With the Old Breed*, Sledge repeatedly refers to war in general (and, in particular, fighting on the front lines) as a terrible waste: a waste of time, of effort, of human life. His account

U.S. troops make their way across a Peleliu beach. (Reproduced by permission of AP/Wide World Photos, Inc.)

of the death of Company K's commander, Captain A. A. Haldane, exemplifies this theme. For his own part, Sledge feels that he beat "the law of averages" by never getting wounded. Of the 235 marines of K/3/5 who fought on Peleliu, only eighty-five sur-

vived the battle without physical injury. The following excerpt is taken from Part I of Sledge's book, subtitled "Peleliu: A Neglected Battle" because it remains "one of the lesser known and poorly understood battles of World War II."

Excerpt from *With the Old Breed at Peleliu and Okinawa*

[Sergeant] Johnny Marmet came striding down the incline of the valley to meet us as we started up. Even before I could see his face clearly, I knew from the way he was walking that something was dreadfully amiss. He lurched up to us, nervously clutching the web strap of the submachine gun slung over his shoulder. I had never seen Johnny nervous before, even under the thickest fire, which he seemed to regard as a nuisance that interfered with his carrying out his job.…

My first thought was that the Japanese had slipped in thousands of troops from the northern Palaus and that we would never get off the island.… My imagination went wild, but none of us was prepared for what we were about to hear.

"Howdy, Johnny," someone said as he came up to us.

…"OK, you guys, OK, you guys," he repeated, obviously flustered. A couple of men exchanged quizzical glances. "The skipper is dead. Ack Ack [usually refers to machine gun fire] has been killed," Johnny finally blurted out.…

I was stunned and sickened. Throwing my ammo bag down, I turned away from the others, sat on my helmet, and sobbed quietly…

Never in my wildest imagination had I contemplated Captain [Andrew A.] Haldane's death. We had a steady stream of killed and wounded leaving

Marines on Peleliu watch as a flame thrower fires into a cave thought to be hiding Japanese soldiers. (Reproduced by permission of the Corbis Corporation [Bellevue])

us, but somehow I assumed Ack Ack was immortal. Our company commander represented stability and direction in a world of violence, death, and destruction. Now his life had been snuffed out. We felt forlorn and lost. It was the worst grief I endured during the entire war. The intervening years have not lessened it any.

... Johnny pulled himself together and said, "OK, you guys, let's move out." We picked up mortars and ammo bags. Feeling as though our crazy world had fallen apart completely, we trudged slowly and silently in single file up the rubble-strewn valley to rejoin Company K....

The Stench of Battle

Johnny led us on up through a jumble of rocks on Hill 140.... From the rim of [the hill] the rock contours dropped away in a sheer cliff to a canyon below. No one could raise his head above the rim rock without immediately drawing heavy rifle and machine-gun fire.

The fighting around the pocket was as deadly as ever, but of a different type from the early days of the campaign. The Japanese fired few artillery or mortar barrages, just a few rounds at a time when assured of inflicting maximum casualties. That they usually did, and then secured the guns to escape detection. Sometimes there was an eerie quiet. We knew they

Peleliu was only six miles long and two miles wide, but its rugged terrain and unbearably hot climate made for a slow and miserable battle. More than 1,100 marines were killed or wounded on the first day of fighting alone. (Photograph by Cpl. H. H. Clements. Reproduced by permission of the Corbis Corporation [Bellevue].)

were everywhere in the caves and pillboxes [a roofed concrete compartment for machine guns and anti-tank weapons]. But there was no firing in our area, only the sound of firing elsewhere. The silence added an element of unreality to the valleys....

The sun bore down on us like a giant heat lamp. Once I saw a misplaced phosphorous grenade explode on the coral from the sun's intense heat. We always shaded our stacked mortar shells with a piece of ammo box to prevent this.

Occasional rains that fell on the hot coral merely evaporated like steam off hot pavement. The air hung heavy and muggy. Everywhere we went on the ridges the hot humid air reeked with the stench of death. A strong wind was no relief; it simply brought the horrid odor from an adjacent area. Japanese corpses lay where they fell among the rocks and on the slopes. It was impossible to cover them. Usually there was no soil that could be spaded over them, just the hard, jagged coral. The enemy dead simply rotted where they had fallen....

It is difficult to convey to anyone who has not experienced it the ghastly horror of having your sense

of smell saturated constantly with the putrid odor of rotting human flesh day after day, night after night. This was something the men of an infantry battalion got a horrifying dose of during a long, protracted battle such as Peleliu. In the tropics the dead became bloated and gave off a terrific stench within a few hours after death....

Each time we moved into a different position I could determine the areas occupied by each rifle company.... Behind each company position lay a pile of ammo and supplies and the inevitable rows of dead under their ponchos. We could determine how bad that sector of the line was by the number of dead. To see them so always filled me with anger at the war and the realization of senseless waste. It depressed me far more than my own fear.

Added to the awful stench of the dead of both sides was the repulsive odor of human excrement everywhere. It was all but impossible to practice sim-ple, elemental field sanitation on most areas of Peleliu because of the rocky surface.... [U]nder nor-mal conditions, [each man] covered his own waste with a scoop of soil. At night when he didn't dare

Medics prepare wounded soldiers for evacuation from Peleliu. (Reproduced by permission of the Corbis Corporation [Bellevue])

As the war became more intense, the Japanese military began to use kamikaze pilots who would dive bomb into American ships and military installations. The pilot would sacrifice his life by flying his bomb-laden plane into his target, causing as much damage as possible. This wreckage of a downed Japanese bomber is on display as part of the Museum of the Pacific War (Chester Nimitz Museum), Fredericksburg, TX, Texas Parks and Wildlife. (Reproduced by permission of Kathleen J. Edgar)

venture out of his foxhole, he simply used an empty grenade canister or ration can, threw it out of his hole, and scooped dirt over it [the] next day if he wasn't under heavy enemy fire.

But on Peleliu, except along the beach areas and in the swamps, digging into the coral rock was nearly impossible. Consequently, thousands of men... fighting for weeks on an island two miles by six miles—couldn't practice basic field sanitation. This fundamental neglect caused an already putrid tropical atmosphere to become inconceivably vile....

With human corpses, ... excrement, and rotting rations scattered across Peleliu's ridges, [the blowflies on the island] were so large, so glutted, and so lazy that some could scarcely fly.... Frequently they tumbled off the side of my canteen cup into my coffee. We actually had to shake the food to dislodge the flies, and even then they sometimes refused to move. I usually had to balance my can of stew on my knee, spooning it up with my right hand while I picked the sluggish creatures off the stew with my left.... It was revolting, to say the least, to watch big fat blowflies leave a corpse and swarm into our C rations.

Even though none of us had much appetite, we still had to eat. A way to solve the fly problem was to eat after sunset or before sunrise when the insects were inactive. Chow had to be unheated then, because no sterno tablets [pellets used for heating up food] or other form of light could be used after dark. It was sure to draw enemy sniper fire....

I still see clearly the landscape around one particular position we occupied for several days. It was a scene of destruction and desolation that no fiction could invent. The area was along the southwestern border of the pocket where ferocious fighting had gone on since the second day of battle (16 September). The 1st Marines, the 7th Marines, and now the 5th Marines, all in their turn, had fought against this same section of ridges. Our exhausted battalion, 3/5, [3rd Battalion, 5th Regiment] moved into the line to relieve another slightly more exhausted battalion. It was the same old weary shuffling of one tired, depleted outfit into the line to relieve another whose sweating men trudged out of their positions, hollow-eyed, stooped, grimy, bearded zombies.

The Company K riflemen and machine gunners climbed up the steep ridge and into the crevices and holes of the company we relieved. Orders were given that no one must look over the crest of the ridge, because enemy rifle and machine-gun fire would kill instantly anyone who did.

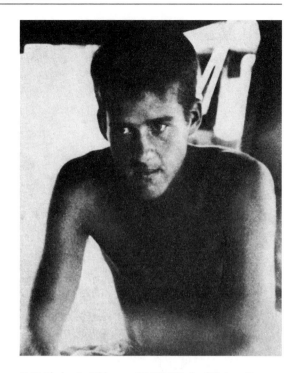

E. B. Sledge in Okinawa. (© 1990 Oxford University Press. Originally published by Presidio Press © 1981.)

As usual, the troops pulling out gave our men "the dope" on the local conditions: what type fire to expect, particular danger spots and possible infiltration routes at night.

... When ... we came closer to the gun pit to set up our mortar, I saw [that the pit's] white coral sides and bottom were spattered and smeared with the dark red blood of ... two comrades.

After we got our gun emplaced, I collected up some large scraps of cardboard from ration and ammo boxes and used them to cover the bottom of the pit as well as I could. Fat, lazy blowflies were reluctant to leave the blood-smeared rock.

I had long since become used to the sight of blood, but the idea of sitting in that bloodstained gun pit was a bit too much for me. It seemed almost like leaving our dead unburied to sit on the blood of a fellow Marine spilled out on the coral.... As I looked at the stains ... I recalled some of the eloquent phrases of politicians and newsmen about how "gallant" it is for a man to "shed his blood for his country," and "to give his life's blood as a sacrifice," and so on. The words seemed so ridiculous. Only the flies benefitted. (Sledge, pp. 140–146)

American ships and supplies pour into Okinawa after U.S. troops captured the island. (Reproduced by permission of AP/Wide World Photos, Inc.)

Aftermath

U.S. troops landed on Iwo Jima on February 19, 1945, and on Okinawa on April 1, 1945. Both islands were seen as critical locations that would serve as launching points for the Allied invasion of the Japanese home islands. Sledge and the rest of K/3/5 fought in the costly battle for Okinawa, the largest of the Ryukyu Islands, located about 350 miles south of the Japanese main islands. A combined force of about 180,000 U.S. troops engaged in eighty-two days of fighting, which was heaviest on the southern part of the island. To Sledge, Okinawa was "the most ghastly corner of hell" he had ever seen. More than 100,000 Japanese were determined to defend it to the death. U.S. naval vessels shelled a long stretch of beach on the southwestern part of the island in preparation for the landing of marine and army troops on April 1.

Japanese forces remained hidden for days before beginning their counterattack. Then, thousands of heavily armed troops emerged from their underground hiding places to fight off the advanc-

ing Americans. Kamikazes later blasted the U.S. fleet in the coastal waters. Between March 26 and June 22, 1945, approximately 1,500 kamikaze attacks were launched against American ships around Okinawa. The battle lasted for almost three months. One in three marines who fought on Okinawa died or was wounded. Nearly 7,700 men of the First Marine Division were killed, wounded, or listed as missing. Thousands of soldiers suffered psychological as well as physical wounds. The fighting continued until the third week in June, when Japanese troops began to surrender.

U.S. landings on Kyushu (one of the four main Japanese islands) were scheduled for November 1945, but the war ended in September after atomic bombs were dropped on the Japanese cities of Hiroshima and Nagasaki. When Germany surrendered to the Allies on May 8, 1945, Sledge was still on Okinawa at the time. "We were told this momentous news, but considering our own peril and misery, no one cared much," Sledge admitted in *With the Old Breed*. "Nazi Germany might as well have been on the moon." Japan followed suit, surrendering on August 15, 1945. This move, according to Sledge, made "the seizure of Peleliu … of questionable necessity." After World War II, E. B. Sledge had brief stints in the business world, but later found his niche in the fields of biology and zoology. He later became a professor of biology, with special concentration in ornithology, at the University of Montevallo in Alabama.

SOURCES

Books

Astor, Gerald, *Operation Iceberg: The Invasion and Conquest of Okinawa in World War II,* Dell (New York), 1996.

Black, Wallace B., and Jean F. Blashfield, *Iwo Jima and Okinawa,* "World War II 50th Anniversary Series," Crestwood House (New York), 1993.

Dolan, Edward F., *America in World War II: 1945,* Millbrook Press (Brookfield, CT), 1994.

Fahey, James J., *Pacific War Diary: 1942–1945,* Macmillan (New York), 1993.

Sledge, E. B., *With the Old Breed at Peleliu and Okinawa,* Presidio Press (Novato, CA), 1981, reprinted with a new introduction by Paul Fussell, Oxford University Press (New York), 1990.

Other

Okinawa (video), Columbia, 1952.

The War Chronicles: World War II, volume 6, *Air War in the Pacific* and *The Bloody Ridges of Peleliu,* volume 7, *Okinawa…The Last Battle,* produced by Lou Reda Productions (videotape), A&E Home Video Presents History Channel Video/New Video, 1995.

World War II in the Pacific, http://www.cybertours. com/~awriter/wwii.htm (September 12, 2000).

The Defeat of Japan

By the summer of 1944, the United States had secured bases in the Mariana Islands and in northwest New Guinea, both within range of the Philippines. Control of the Philippines was now the great prize of the Pacific war. If Japan lost those islands, it would be almost impossible for the resource-barren nation to import oil, tin, and other valuable products from the Dutch East Indies and Southeast Asia. In addition to the tactical advantages, the Philippines had great symbolic importance for the United States. America had controlled the islands since 1898, but gave the Philippines commonwealth status in 1938 and promised to establish the Philippines as an independent country in 1946.

The United States had a high level of support among the Filipino people, many of whom assisted the Americans in defending the islands from the Japanese invasion in December 1941. The Philippines was the only area, outside of China, conquered by Japan where a significant guerrilla movement developed. The Americans chose as a goal Leyte, a major island in the center of the Philippines. The plan was to retake Leyte and use it as a base for an attack on Luzon, the most important of the Philippine Islands. The overall commander of the operation was General Douglas MacArthur, who had led the defense of the Philippines at the beginning of the war in the Pacific. In early 1942 he had made a famous promise to the Filipino people

when, on President Franklin D. Roosevelt's orders, he had left the Philippines to avoid capture by the Japanese. MacArthur vowed: "I shall return."

As the Allied invasion force landed on the shores of Leyte Gulf on October 20, 1944, several large sections of the Japanese fleet steamed toward them. The Japanese admirals had developed a highly complicated plan involving large groups of ships coming from different directions and meeting near the American invasion beaches. The result was the Battle of Leyte Gulf, the most massive naval battle in history. Most of the other major naval battles of the Pacific war, such as Midway, were fought mainly between carrier-based planes. Although planes did play a major role at Leyte Gulf, they were not the deciding factor. In fact, the Japanese used their few remaining aircraft carriers as bait to lure away the primary American carrier force, leaving the remainder of the Japanese and American fleets to fight in relatively close proximity like sailors had done since the invention of the cannon. Warships fired their guns and torpedoes at one another, sometimes at close range. Among the vessels involved were five American battleships that the Japanese had bombed at Pearl Harbor, including two, the USS *California* and USS *West Virginia,* that had been sunk. The Americans had raised the ships from the bottom of the harbor and prepared them to return to service.

The Japanese intent was to destroy the transport ships that had brought the American forces to

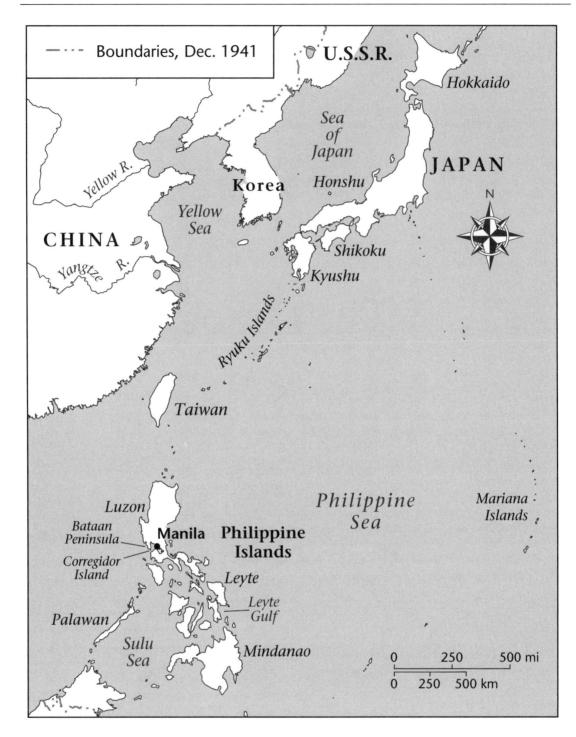

After losing the Philippines to the Japanese in 1941, the U.S. Army returned in 1944 with a plan to retake Leyte and use it as a base for an attack on Luzon.

Leyte. This would effectively cut off the American troops onshore from reinforcements and supplies, thus giving Japanese soldiers on the island a tactical advantage. The Japanese nearly succeeded in catching the transports unprotected because the most powerful part of the American fleet had sailed north in pursuit of the Japanese carriers. Yet the Japanese did not account for the tenacity of the remaining American ships.

The battle involved a series of often confused fights, with groups of ships racing from one

An Image of Triumph and of Sacrifice

Iwo Jima became one of the most famous battles fought by Americans in any war, partly because of the bloodiness of the conflict in comparison to its size. Another reason is the famous photograph of a group of marines planting the American flag atop Mount Suribachi as the fighting rages around them. The photograph, taken by Joe Rosenthal, is the model for the Marine Corps Monument in Arlington National Cemetery and has been reproduced countless times. Today the picture is associated with triumph, a tribute to fighting men who have won a great victory, but when it was first published, Americans knew what was happening while the flag was being raised. At the time, the picture was an image of sacrifice, a reminder of the price the marines had paid on Iwo Jima.

The flag-raising on Iwo Jima. This well-known photo was actually staged: During the real flag-raising, no photographs were taken, so troops later reenacted the tableau for this image. (Photograph by Joe Rosenthal, courtesy of National Archives and Records Administration)

engagement to another. It was also marked by sudden changes of direction, surprise confrontations between enemy forces, and miscommunication as leaders were misinformed about the situation. At the conclusion of the conflict, the Americans had decimated the Japanese navy. During the battle, the Americans witnessed a new threat for the first time. Japanese pilots intentionally crashed their planes,

Kamikaze pilots made suicide runs in their planes, loaded with bombs. They crashed into American warships in an effort to destroy the vessels. Yet, they sacrificed their own lives in return. (Reproduced by permission of © Hulton Getty/Liaison Agency)

loaded with bombs, into American ships. The pilots were all volunteers, although the Americans refused to believe this at the time. These suicide pilots were called kamikaze, or divine wind, a name for the sudden storm that had destroyed a Mongol invasion fleet heading for Japan hundreds of years earlier. This name implied that they were the last hope to save the Japanese from invasion, that only a miracle could protect the country from defeat.

Crucial Battles: Leyte, Luzon, Manila, and Iwo Jima

Onshore, the Japanese reinforced their troops with units brought from other parts of the Philippines, and even one division from China. Although the American army was also reinforced, it made slow progress. The fighting often resembled battles in World War I (1914–1918)—launching bloody attacks against strong defensive positions to gain only a few hundred yards. In December the Americans beat back a major Japanese counteroffensive aimed at the American airfields. Although some

Japanese units continued fighting until April 1945, the Americans controlled most of Leyte by Christmas 1944. At least 50,000 Japanese troops had already been killed. On January 8, 1945, the American army landed on Luzon, the main Philippine island, where the Philippine capital of Manila is located. Near Manila is the Bataan Peninsula and the island of Corregidor, where the Americans had held off the Japanese for several months before surrendering in the spring of 1942. On Bataan and Corregidor, more than 95,000 American and Filipino troops had been taken prisoner by the Japanese, who subjected them to brutal treatment during their years of captivity. Many American and Filipino prisoners had been killed by the Japanese. Almost three years after MacArthur promised, "I shall return," the Americans were invading the Philippines.

The large Japanese force on Luzon did not try to prevent the American landings, but instead defended carefully prepared positions and tried to hold out as long as possible. Since they had not blocked the road to Manila, American troops entered the city's suburbs by early February. To destroy Manila's harbor, the Japanese set fires, which spread through large sections of the city. In the southern part of Manila, Japanese troops went on a rampage of raping, looting, and murdering Filipino civilians; they killed tens of thousands of people, much as the Japanese army had done in China during the 1930s. At the same time, the 20,000 Japanese defenders, mostly from the navy, fought the Americans for each street and building in Manila. The battles were fought in a major city in house-to-house skirmishes with modern weapons, one of the bloodiest forms of warfare, as had been shown in European cities like Stalingrad. During the fighting in Manila, 16,000 Japanese and 12,000 Americans died; 100,000 civilians were killed either in the battle or in Japanese massacres. While the conflict in the capital was underway, the Americans cleared Japanese troops out of the area around Manila, including Bataan. On March 1 the Americans had raised the U.S. flag over Corregidor, and the conflict in Manila was over by the next day. Some difficult battles continued in Luzon and other parts of the Philippines, but the remaining Japanese forces, some of whom were still fighting when Japan finally surrendered, presented no real danger to American control of the Philippines.

The tiny island of Iwo Jima is composed of volcanic rock in the middle of the ocean, but it was a strategic position for the U.S. military. The island lies along the route that American B-29 long-range

Troops dig into foxholes on the southeast edge of Motoyama Airfield #1, near Mt. Suribachi in Iwo Jima. (Library of Congress)

Using a flame thrower, two Marines attempt to ignite Japanese defenses near Mount Suribachi on Iwo Jima. (Reproduced by permission of AP/Wide World Photos)

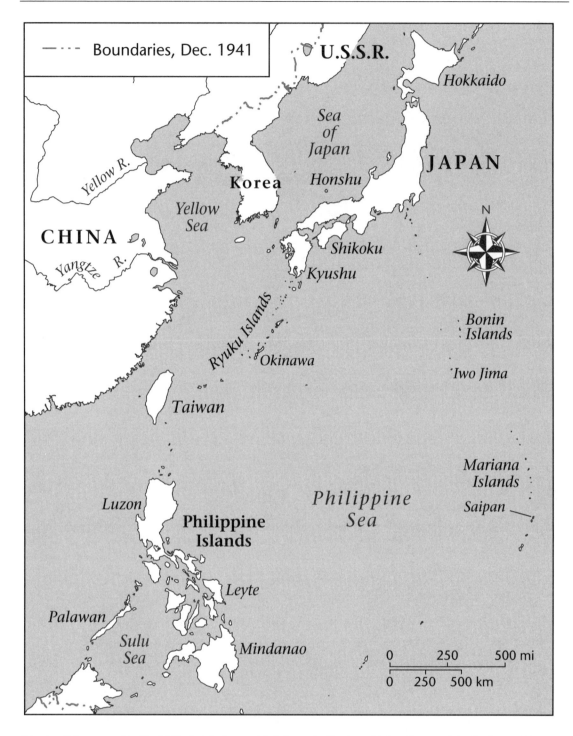

Islands of the eastern Pacific, 1941: the Marianas with Saipan, the Bonins with Iwo Jima, and the Ryukyus with Okinawa.

bombers flew from Saipan in the Marianas to bomb Japan. The B-29s had to avoid the island, thus lengthening their already long trip to Japan. The air force wanted to capture the island in order to shorten the distance; they also wanted to use it as an emergency landing field for damaged B-29s.

To gain these comparatively small advantages, however, the United States paid a high price. On February 19, 1945, three marine divisions landed on Iwo Jima and fought a nearly month-long battle, ending on March 16. The Japanese had stationed 21,000 soldiers on Iwo Jima; most of them

A Japanese prisoner, blindfolded, taken on Iwo Jima. Very few Japanese soldiers surrendered or were taken prisoner: most fought to the death. (National Archives and Records Administration)

dug into rocks, caves, and tunnels in a determination to die rather than surrender. Almost all of the Japanese forces perished in the battle; the U.S. marines lost 6,900 soldiers in the fighting and 20,000 were wounded.

The Last Pacific Island: Okinawa

The next target was Okinawa. At eighty miles long, it is the largest of the Ryukyus, a group of islands that lies approximately 400 miles from the closest of the main home islands of Japan. Despite this distance, Okinawa and the Ryukyus are often considered part of Japan itself. When the United States focused its invasion on the island, it became

the first time that Japanese troops had to defend a part of their own homeland, not territory they had taken from another country. The fight for Okinawa became the largest ground battle of the Pacific war. On the first day of the landings, 50,000 Americans came ashore; by the time the battle ended, 180,000 American troops were fighting on the island.

American ships bombarded Okinawa for a full week before the troops went ashore on April 1, 1945. There was no Japanese opposition to the landings, which was unusual. The Japanese typically attacked the Americans before the invaders even reached the beaches. This time, Japanese

Kamikaze: The Divine Wind

The word kamikaze evokes visions of Japanese pilots dive-bombing into the Pacific Fleet during World War II. However, the kamikaze first made its appearance many centuries ago in another era when Japan found itself fighting a seemingly unbeatable foe.

The term kamikaze, meaning "divine wind," dates back to the early days of Japan's history, when invaders from the mainland of China sought to conquer the small island nation. Most notable were the invasions launched by the Khans— Mongolian rulers of China during the twelfth and thirteenth centuries. At that time— and until the mid-1800s during the Meiji Restoration—Japan was a feudal state, ruled by the Shogun, a military leader, and a class of warlords. Each warlord owned a plot of land on the island nation; citizens worked the land. In return, the Shogun and his military cadre offered protection from invaders.

In 1281 Kublai Khan planned an invasion of Japan, starting with Kyushu, the southernmost island, and moving his way north throughout the rest of the island chain to seize control. His army of 120,000 men boarded sailing vessels and headed across the Sea of Japan. The emperor of Japan knew of the impending attack, but was at a loss—he knew that the Japanese could not defend Japan's coastline. They needed a miracle. He asked the Buddhist priests to help. Priests throughout Japan went to their temples to pray, asking for a miracle to deliver the nation out of harm's way. As the Chinese fleet approached Kyushu, a kamikaze (typhoon) hit the fleet, drowning most of the invaders.

Japan was spared from the attacking force by a kamikaze—divine wind.

During the final days of World War II, Emperor Hirohito and his military staff knew they needed a miracle to stop the advance of the Allied fleet, which was reclaiming territories occupied by Japan. They called on Japanese soldiers to create a "divine wind" to knock out the Allies, as had been done against Kublai Khan. Known to the world as kamikaze pilots, these young men—usually between the ages of 17 and 30—were part of the Jinrai Butai—Divine Thunderbolt Corps of the 721st Naval Task Force. They flew suicide missions, crashing their planes into vessels of the Allied forces in the Pacific.

The kamikazes flew OKHA planes, known as "Cherry Blossom Gliders." Each plane was manned by one pilot and supplied with about three-minute's worth of fuel. A 1,200-kilogram bomb was placed in each plane's nose. Several cherry blossom gliders were then attached to a larger aircraft and towed through the air until the pilots could see their final destination—the U.S. fleet. When the attack force was within striking distance, the planes were released. The pilots guided their planes, aiming for the ships. On impact, the bombs exploded, immediately killing the pilot and usually doing great damage in their wake— similar to a large torpedo.

The young men flying the suicide missions knew they would never return to their homeland—they would die an honorable death for their country, in the name of the emperor. Before they boarded their planes, they promised each other to meet again when the cherry blossoms bloomed at Yasukuni Jinja—a Buddhist Shinto shrine in Tokyo, dedicated to Japan's war dead. More than 6,000 pilots of the Jinrai Butai lost their lives in 1945—they are enshrined at Yasukuni Jinja.

Allied soldiers show their new acquisitions—captured Japanese battle flags. (Reproduced by permission of © Hulton Getty/Liaison Agency)

troops dug in and waited, putting up tremendous resistance against every yard of the Americans' advance. There was no surrender. As on Saipan, the Japanese used a suicidal strategy literally. Offshore, Japanese planes attacked the American fleet, sometimes unleashing waves of 50, 100, and even 300 kamikaze attacks at a time. It was almost impossible for U.S. antiaircraft guns and fighter planes to shoot down the Japanese bombers before they could reach the American ships.

The Japanese also sent the battleship *Yamato*, the largest and most powerful in the world, against the American fleet on a suicide mission. Japan's severe petroleum shortage contributed to this decision; the *Yamato* was loaded with only enough fuel to reach the battle. The ship sailed directly toward the American fleet, positioning its huge guns, but American planes sank the *Yamato* with torpedoes before it could cause any damage. Almost all of the 2,300 Japanese sailors died when the ship went down. The battle on Okinawa continued until the end of June. In the last days of fighting, 4,000 Japanese soldiers surrendered, bringing the total of voluntary prisoners to approximately 7,400. This number included many who were so severely wounded that they could not commit suicide. An

additional 110,000 Japanese troops lost their lives, either in combat or suicide, and not a single senior officer was taken prisoner. The Japanese lost nearly 8,000 of their remaining planes, including 1,000 on kamikaze missions. Of the 450,000 civilians on the island, somewhere between one-sixth and one-third were also dead. Many had hidden in caves to avoid the fighting, only to be killed when the Japanese troops used the caves as defensive positions and the Americans blew up the caves or fired flamethrowers into them. The Americans also sustained heavy losses—more than 7,000 U.S. soldiers and marines were killed on Okinawa, and roughly 5,000 sailors died at sea, most of them as a result of kamikaze actions.

With Okinawa as a base, the next major campaign would be against Japan itself. A limited invasion of Kyushu, the southernmost of the main Japanese islands, was scheduled for November 1, 1945. The purpose of the engagement was to provide a base for the next operation: the invasion of Honshu, the main Japanese island, which was scheduled for March 1, 1946. U.S. planners believed the invasion would require at least twenty-five divisions, a force totaling over one-third of a million men. After Germany had surrendered in

Marines on Okinawa surround a Japanese tunnel entrance. (Reproduced by permission of AP/Wide World Photos)

Kamikaze crashes into the USS *Bunker Hill* off Okinawa, May 1945. (National Archives and Records Administration)

The United States planned an invasion of Japan at the southern island of Kyushu for November 1945 and hoped to use this as a base to attack the main island Honshu in March 1946.

May 1945, a large number of the troops could be brought from Europe. The American First Army, which had landed at Normandy in June 1944 and fought its way across France and Germany, would not be sent home. Instead, those soldiers would be transferred to the Pacific to prepare for an invasion of Japan. Some 1.5 million American troops and another 500,000 British soldiers were scheduled to be sent to various parts of Asia when the European war ended, disappointing many of the soldiers and their families at home. Allied strategists anticipated that the Japanese would fight as they had in Okinawa, battling for every inch of territory, and recognized that American casualties in the inva-

sion would be high. The planners knew that several thousand kamikaze were waiting to attack American ships. If Allied forces took casualties at the same rate as on Okinawa, hundreds of thousands would be killed or wounded. Sometimes they estimated the figure at 1 million casualties, although apparently no Allied planner ever considered this a serious possibility.

Another part of the Allied plan was for the Soviet Union, which was still not at war with Japan, to participate in the fighting. The Soviets had promised they would attack Japan after Germany surrendered. According to the plan, several months

Don't Go Island Hopping During a War

When U.S. troops began invading islands in the Pacific in the war against Japan, large numbers of American soldiers were sent to secure the islands for occupation and establish communication systems. Many of the islands were not developed with the communications systems necessary to fight an effective war. Harold Ward, a young American soldier from Oklahoma, was one of the men assigned to the Pacific. During his stint with the U.S. Army, Ward performed many duties, including processing payroll, and witnessed the fighting through an average GI's eyes.

Ward decided to write a book, based on the journal he kept while in service, after hearing a comment about the World War II epic movie *Saving Private Ryan*. Apparently a college sophomore was unaware that the Germans were on the opposing side of U.S. forces. Thus, Ward put his recollections in book form and issued *Don't Go Island Hopping During a War!* (1999). In the book, Ward comments on the events in the Pacific as seen by an average soldier. He describes efforts to establish telephone and radio communications, and he reveals his feelings concerning officers, the enemy, the men who served with him, and the war in general. In the following excerpt, Ward talks about activities waged by and against the Japanese. As was common during the war, he refers to them as "Japs."

"General [Douglas MacArthur's] plan was not to try to retake every island where the Japs had taken control. Instead of taking complete control of all the islands, we would take only those where we could control the area. On some islands we had control of only a small portion, but enough that we could control the air and sea-lanes. By using this method their supplies were cut off, and they were out of food and war material. It turned out to be a very good plan and saved many lives of the Allied Forces.

"I remember one place on the coast of New Guinea ... where they never bothered to try to run the Japs out. They were completely cut off, and after months of not receiving supplies, they evidently ran out of food so they were trying to grow a garden. Every time it looked like the crops had grown enough to be close to eating, some B-25's would go in and bomb it out....

"There were small groups of Japs that had been cut off from their units and they roamed the area.... It was discovered that these guys were not only stealing food from the mess halls but also sugar. They put the sugar in the [American] planes' gas tanks and when the pilots would start their runs down the runway, the motors would be gummed up enough that they would fail and the plane would crash. Another thing we learned was to check the trees for snipers before getting in line for breakfast....

"The Kamikaze planes [came] in from one to several times each night. It was a rare occasion when they didn't.... I found out years later that the average age of these Kamikaze pilots was 18 years old at the beginning of the war and by the end of the war they were as young as 13.... We never worried about the Kamikaze or bombers harming us on the hill, but our danger came from our own anti aircraft guns. The flack from the shells would fall all around us with such force it would cut through sheet iron. The sound of the flack was as if it were ripping and tearing the air with a big whooshing sound."

Later in his book Ward comments on the firing of anti-aircraft guns after the Americans learned that a cease-fire had been called by the Japanese. The cease-fire was issued after the United States dropped a secret weapon—the atomic bomb—on Hiroshima and Nagasaki in August 1945. The soldiers were elated to hear about the cease-fire, and knew very little about the new weapon used to end the war.

"Word came to us just after dark ... about the cease-fire and a celebration broke out on Okinawa that was unbelievable. Every anti-aircraft gun on the island and on the ships was firing. All the

On Guadalcanal in the Solomon Islands, American Marines work to string telephone wire on a palm tree. The local tree will serve as a telephone pole, enabling the Allies to speed communications. (Reproduced by permission of © Hulton Getty/Liaison Agency)

searchlights were on, swinging back and forth across the sky, tracer bullets from machine guns filled the air in all directions that looked like streaks of fire. Rifles, pistols, and anything that would go boom were being fired.

"You never saw such a 4th of July fireworks display that could compare. It was great fun but the sad part was, as the old saying goes, what goes up must come down. Flack and bullets were falling all around us. Most of us got under a metal roof we had raked up and put over the mess hall. You could hear things striking the roof and some flack cut through the metal. When I went to my tent that night to go to bed, I found a bullet in some clothes I had rolled up to use as a pillow. I carried that bullet in my pocket for many years, at some point I misplaced it and never found it again.

"Several men were killed on the island that night from falling debris and the hospital was overrun with the injured. The following day there was an order that came from the area headquarters that was to be read to all troops at roll call. It stated that any man who fired a weapon when the peace treaty was signed would receive a Court Martial.

"September 2, 1945, the surrender and peace treaty was signed aboard the Battleship Missouri in Tokyo harbor.

"Not one shot was fired on Okinawa that night but we sure did holler a lot. You could not have found one man on Okinawa that would have wanted to invade the main island of Japan.

"It was finally over."

The Tragedy of the USS *Indianapolis*, Her Captain and Crew

On Sunday, July 19, 1945, around midnight, the USS *Indianapolis* was hit by Japanese torpedoes, about 600 miles off the coast of Guam, in the deep waters of the Pacific Ocean. All communications within the ship, as well as those with the outside world were cut off. Shortly thereafter, Captain Charles Butler McVay III gave the order to abandon ship. More than three hundred men went down with the ship or were killed when the torpedoes exploded. Approximately 880 men of the nearly 1,200 in the ship's crew were thrown into the shark-infested water as the ship quickly sunk—the lifeboats were never launched.

Many of the crew were asleep when the torpedoes struck the side of the *Indianapolis*—few had a chance to grab their life jackets before abandoning the ship. Many were injured from the explosion or in the ensuing chaos that followed. Captain McVay ordered the men to stay together and help the wounded sailors as best they could. All watched in despair as the ship sank in less than 15 minutes.

Several groups of men laced their life vests together, creating makeshift rafts. They placed the critically wounded on top, allowing those who were not as badly wounded to cling to the sides. Others were placed on pieces of the wreckage found floating in the water. The ocean currents pulled at the men, separating the small clusters. Some drifted off or were pulled under to drown. They waited to be rescued, but no distress call had been made.

The USS *Indianapolis* was the flagship of the U.S. Fifth Fleet. The cruiser had seen its share of combat, but had always pulled through. The ship's captain, Charles McVay, was a decorated war hero, receiving medals for bravery, including the Silver Star, Bronze Star, and the Purple Heart. Three days earlier, on July 26, the ship had completed its mission—delivering "secret" cargo to the U.S. military installation on Tinian, a small island in the Marianas island chain. Unbeknownst to the crew, the ship carried uranium for use in the atomic bombs that were soon to be dropped over Hiroshima and Nagasaki. After delivering the cargo, the *Indianapolis* was to harbor in Leyte in the Philippines and await further instructions.

Only a few high-ranking officials in Leyte knew that the *Indianapolis* was overdue in reaching its final destination. Ships were commonly overdue, so search and rescue operations were not launched. High-flying planes overhead could not see the tragedy below, as the crew was spread out over 25 miles. Meanwhile, the ship's crew was dehydrating in the salt water. Some men drank the salt water, causing them to go mad, while others were slowing starving to death. The sun scorched their faces, as their bodies went limp from expo-

before the scheduled American invasion of Japan, the Soviet army would invade Manchuria in northern China and fight the 750,000 Japanese troops stationed there. The theory was that the Japanese, having been defeated in China, would not have enough troops to defend the home island. Japanese leaders would therefore see the futility of continuing the war, thus making an invasion unnecessary. Two distinct opinions arose on the future of Allied campaigns. Most American army generals did not believe it was possible to defeat Japan without an invasion. Navy and air force leaders disagreed, contending that the combined submarine and bombing campaign might force Japan into submission. The submarine campaign was essentially a blockade of Japan, which had short supplies of food and raw materials such as oil for war industries. Many Japanese factories had shut down even before American bombers destroyed them.

American submarine warfare was extremely effective against Japan, an island country with few

sure to the ocean water. All the while, screams could be heard as the sailors were picked off one at a time by sharks patrolling the waters in search of food.

On August 3, after five days in the water, a U.S. Navy seaplane spotted what was left of the crew. The plane placed a distress call and landed on the ocean's surface. The plane was put into service as a giant life raft. The wings and fuselage were stacked with as many of the crew as possible, keeping them out of danger from the circling sharks. Several rescue ships were launched to recover the remaining crew of the *Indianapolis*. Only 316 men survived.

On December 3, 1945, several months after the Japanese surrender, Captain McVay was court-martialed for "Suffering a Vessel of the Navy to be Hazarded." He was tried for negligence because he failed to "zigzag" in hostile waters—a standard maneuver required of U.S. Navy ships sailing in waters patrolled by the enemy. The zigzag maneuver altered the ship's direction, while maintaining its course, in an effort to avoid being spotted by enemy submarines. McVay and several of his crew explained that the weather conditions made it impossible to zig and zag every 15 minutes without putting the ship and crew in peril.

Prosecutors called Mochitsura Hashimoto, commander of the Japanese submarine that launched the fatal torpedoes, to the stand at McVay's court martial. Hashimoto shocked the court, testifying that the zigzag maneuver never stopped him from sinking a ship— the Japanese knew of the trick and planned their attacks accordingly. Several high-ranking U.S. Navy officials, such as Admirals Chester Nimitz and Raymond Spruance, pleaded with the court to find McVay innocent of the charges. Never before had a ship's captain been tried for losing his ship during combat. The court found McVay guilty, but recommended clemency because of his excellent war record.

McVay returned to the navy, but never commanded a ship again. Many historians and military personnel believe he was used as a scapegoat for the naval blunders surrounding the loss of the *Indianapolis* and crew—the largest loss of life at sea in U.S. history. Search and rescue parties were never sent even though the ship was four days overdue. Also, Japanese submarines were known to be in the area of the *Indianapolis*, but because the ship's mission was of a secret nature, the captain was never informed that the ship was in danger of attack.

McVay retired from the Navy in 1949 as a Rear Admiral. He committed suicide in 1968. Surviving crew members of the USS *Indianapolis* are still trying to clear McVay's name.

natural resources that depended on shipping in materials more than any other industrialized nation. Japan also relied on ships to transport goods inside the country, which is comprised of several islands with major cities located on the coast. The poor condition of the railroads and highways compounded the problem. Japan had begun the war with approximately 6 million tons of merchant ships and had built an additional 3.3 million tons during the conflict. The Japanese navy had also seized a substantial number of British, Dutch, and other enemy merchant ships in early 1942. By the end of World War II, however, the Allies had sunk 9 million tons of Japanese shipping vessels.

Submarines, almost all of them American, sank more than half of this total. This rate increased exponentially as American submarine captains and crews became more skillful, and began operating from bases much closer to Japan. In 1944 alone, they sank 600 ships, totaling 2.7 million tons. American planes, both carrier and land-

Walter Krueger

One of the American generals who commanded forces in the Pacific during World War II was Walter Krueger. Born in 1881 in Flatlow, West Prussia (now Zlotow, Poland), he immigrated to the United States when he was eight years old. He was one of the volunteers who fought in Cuba during the Spanish American War of 1898, and in 1899 he enlisted as a private in the Regular Army. He served as an infantryman in the Philippines, and advanced through the ranks until he was commissioned second lieutenant in 1901.

Krueger graduated from the Infantry-Cavalry School in 1906 and the General Staff College in 1907. He served in the Mexican Punitive Expedition under General John J. "Black Jack" Pershing in 1916 against Mexican revolutionary Pancho Villa. In 1918 Krueger went to France to take part in the postwar occupation; that same year, he was temporarily promoted to the rank of colonel.

During the years between the world wars, Krueger continued to climb through the ranks, graduating from the Army War College in 1921 and the Naval War College in 1926. He taught at the Naval War College until 1932. Promoted to temporary brigadier general in October of 1936, he jumped to temporary major general in February 1939.

In May 1941, he was promoted to temporary lieutenant general and placed in command of the 3rd Army, a large and successful training army. In 1943, Krueger was given the command of the newly activated 6th Army, headquartered in Australia.

From 1943 to 1944, Lieutenant General Krueger and the 6th Army hopped Pacific islands, from Kiriwina and Woodlark to New Britain, to the Admiralty Islands, to New Guinea, to Morotai. In October 1944, Krueger was in command of the ground forces during the massive and long-running battles for the Philippine islands of Leyte, Mindoro, and Luzon. In July of 1945, the exhausted 6th Army in Luzon was relieved by the 8th Army.

The Joint Chiefs of Staff planned for Krueger's 6th Army to invade the Japanese island of Kyushu in November. The United States avoided this possibility by dropping atomic bombs on two Japanese cities in August 1945. After the Japanese surrendered, the 6th Army held occupation duty in Japan until its deactivation in 1946. Krueger retired in July of that year, having attained the rank of four-star general.

Krueger made his home in Pennsylvania, where he died in 1967.

(Reproduced by permission of AP/Wide World Photos)

Viewing the rubble after a bombing raid by U.S. forces, Japanese Emperor Hirohito surveys the situation. (Reproduced by permission of © Hulton Getty/Liaison Agency)

based, sank many more Japanese vessels, including those used to carry or supply Japanese troops. Large numbers of Japanese merchant ships were also hitting mines that American planes had dropped along the coast of Japan. By the end of 1944, two-thirds of Japan's available oil tankers had been destroyed, and the country was virtually unable to obtain any fuel from the Dutch East Indies. In the spring of 1945, Japan had less than 1 million tons of ships—not even enough to transport goods within its own nation.

The Bombing of Japan

While American submarines were threatening to starve Japan's cities, U.S. B-29 bombers were carrying out aerial assaults and burning them down. This was part of the Allies' strategic bombing campaign. Strategic bombing is meant to have a long-term effect on a country's ability to wage war—for example, by destroying its steel industry. In contrast, tactical bombing involves battlefield support, such as attacking trains bringing reinforcements to battle. For months, the bombers had dropped high explosives onto Japanese factories

and other targets in high-altitude daylight raids. This was the same method the United States had used to bomb Germany, yet the raids in Japan were not accurate, rarely hitting their targets.

At first the bombing did not seem to be detrimental to Japan's ability to fight, but soon the United States began to employ the methods Britain had used against Germany. On the night of March 9, 1945, 325 B-29s dropped many tons of incendiary bombs from a low altitude on Tokyo. The wood-and-paper buildings in the Japanese capital were perfect material for fire; by morning, more than 250,000 buildings had been destroyed and 1 million people had lost their homes. Nearly 90,000 people, almost all them civilians, had died in the flames and smoke. Over the next three months, similar raids devastated almost every large city in Japan, with 250,000 Japanese killed and millions of others left homeless. Combined with the sea blockade, the bombing raids had nearly devastated the Japanese economy. Malnutrition and even mass starvation were fast becoming real possibilities.

Despite the suffering of its people, the Japanese government refused to surrender. In July 1945 the

---

MAJOR CONFERENCES OF WORLD WAR II

Casablanca	January 1943	Set date for invasion of Sicily (1943) but put off invasion of France (the Normandy invasion) until 1944; announced policy of "unconditional surrender" for Axis nations.
Teheran	November 1943	Set tentative date of WesternEuropean invasion (the Normandy invasion; Operation Overlord) for May of 1944.
Yalta	February 1945	Scheduled first United Nations conference. Established postwar goals regarding future forms of government in Germany and the rest of Europe.
Potsdam	July 1945	Finalized the Potsdam Declaration and the policy on German reparations. The Soviet Union agreed to enter the war against Japan.

Allies issued a declaration at Potsdam, a city near the German capital of Berlin, where they were holding a conference to make plans for the postwar world. The declaration repeated the call for the unconditional surrender of Japan, the same demand that Germany had finally been forced to accept. Although the Potsdam Declaration made it clear that Japan would be placed under military occupation, the Japanese people were assured that they would be allowed to choose their own government eventually. The implication was that under the terms of surrender the country could keep its emperor, which was of supreme importance to the Japanese. Although emperors wielded little or no power, they were a symbol of the nation and were considered divine. While some Japanese leaders, especially military officers, wanted to continue the war regardless of the consequences, others wanted to end the slaughter. Yet even of those willing to surrender, few were willing to agree to have Emperor Hirohito removed. Some leaders in the United States strongly opposed leaving the emperor on the throne, believing him to be a symbol of the system that had started the war and committed terrible crimes—for example, those against the people of China and Allied prisoners of war. They blamed the empire system for creating blind obedience to authority and for glorifying war. Allowing the emperor to keep his title, they thought, was the same as permitting a Nazi leader to remain the official head of Germany.

Most Allied leaders took this issue less seriously, feeling that the defeated Japanese people should be allowed at some point to choose whatever government they wanted, even if they wanted an emperor. The Allies' immediate concern was ending the war, and they agreed that it would be most beneficial if the emperor were to call for surrender. Japanese military and naval officers, with large forces still undefeated in Japan, China, and elsewhere, might not obey anyone else's order to end the war. The military occupation of Japan would also be facilitated if the emperor were given a role. The Allies officially stuck to the demand that Japan surrender without *any* conditions, but they hinted strongly, in several different ways, that the Potsdam Declaration did not require removing the emperor.

Japanese political leaders who favored surrender were still afraid of ending the war without Allied guarantees that the emperor could remain on the throne. While the two sides passed hints and suggestions through various go-betweens (especially the Soviet Union, which was still at peace with Japan), American planners continued preparations for the invasion of Japan. But there would be no invasion. On August 6, 1945, the American bomber *Enola Gay* dropped an atomic bomb on the Japanese city of Hiroshima. The Americans had chosen Hiroshima because it was one of the few Japanese cities with minimal bombing damage, allowing greater ease and efficiency in evaluating the effects of the atomic attack. The impact, however, was greater than ever anticipated.

Within a few moments, a four-square-mile area at the center of Hiroshima was obliterated. The air temperature in that area reached 3,000 degrees Celsius and not one building in the central city escaped destruction. Almost all of them simply disappeared; only the skeletons of a few buildings made from reinforced concrete survived. Overall, 80 percent of the buildings in the entire city were destroyed. Thousands of people were killed instantly and thousands more died within the next few hours. This single explosion killed

---

British Prime Minister Winston Churchill, U.S. President Harry S Truman, and Soviet leader Joseph Stalin (left to right) at the Potsdam conference, July 1945. (Reproduced by permission of the Corbis Corporation [Bellevue])

The Soviet Union: A Possible Threat

On August 8, 1945, between the first and second atomic bomb attacks on Japan, the Soviet Union declared war on Japan, in accordance with its promise to the United States. (The United States had not told the Soviets of its plan to drop the bomb.) The next day, huge Soviet armies invaded Manchuria from two directions, breaking through Japanese defenses and capturing troops by the thousands. The surrender of large numbers of Japanese soldiers, instead of a fight to the death, was different from the tenacious resistance the Americans had encountered from the Japanese. In ten days the Soviets drove the remnants of the Japanese army back into the northern part of Korea.

Many historians believe that the Soviet invasion of Manchuria played as significant a role in persuading the Japanese to surrender as did the atomic bomb. Perhaps the large-scale surrender in China made the Japanese leaders less confident that their soldiers would continue to fight a hopeless war. Certainly the surrender meant that the Japanese army in China could not possibly defend Japan. If this reasoning is correct, it may indicate that Japanese leaders simply did not understand how atomic weapons differed from conventional weapons. Like many Allied leaders, when they were first informed about the bomb, the Japanese may have thought an atomic weapon simply amounted to a more powerful version of a regular bomb.

Destruction in Nagasaki after the United States dropped an atom bomb on the city. (Reproduced by permission of the Corbis Corporation [New York])

A survivor of the bombing at Hiroshima bears permanent scars from burns caused by the atomic bomb. (Reproduced by permission of the Corbis Corporation [Bellevue])

After the atomic blast at Nagasaki, the Japanese surrendered to the Allied forces to end the war in the Pacific. (Reproduced by permission of Corbis-Bettmann)

more than 70,000 people and injured about the same number. Some of the survivors were blinded by the flash of the explosion, and almost all had horrible burns that caused their skin to fall off. Many people fell victim to radiation sickness, and for years after the bomb had been dropped, they were subjected to slow, painful deaths.

On August 9, 1945, the Americans dropped a second atomic bomb, of a different and even more powerful type, on Nagasaki. Due to a combination of factors, including geographical features and the fact that the bomb missed the city center, the effects were not so devastating as at Hiroshima. At least 35,000 more people died, however, and another Japanese city was effectively wiped out almost in an instant. The United States had no more atomic bombs immediately available, but the Japanese were unaware of this fact. It appeared as though the Americans could wipe out another Japanese city every few days, or even more frequently. There was no possible defense against this weapon, and air raid shelters made little difference. Despite the deployment of the two bombs, the top Japanese military and naval leaders did not want to surrender. Arguments in the government continued, as did routine American air raids over Japan.

Emperor Hirohito finally interceded and ended the argument. On August 15 the people of Japan heard the voice of their emperor for the first time when a recording he had made the day before was broadcast over the radio. Although Hirohito never mentioned surrender, he told the Japanese people that they must prepare to "endure the unendurable."

Controversy Surrounding the Dropping of the Atomic Bomb

The reasons why the United States dropped the atomic bomb on Japan, and whether it was right to do so, are among the greatest controversies surrounding World War II. Since the bombings, this debate has not been limited to historians or military experts, but has been discussed at length by average citizens. Around the world, the anniversary of the Hiroshima bombing is observed as a day of mourning, and of reflection on the possibility of nuclear war. Even at the time of the bomb-

An Admiral's Opinion

"My own feeling was that, in being the first to use it, we had adopted an ethical standard common to the barbarians of the Dark Age. I was not taught to make war in that fashion, and wars cannot be won by destroying women and children."

—Admiral William D. Leahy, chief of staff to President Franklin D. Roosevelt and President Harry S Truman, on the use of the atomic bomb.

ing, there were disagreements in the United States, though they were not known to the public. General Dwight D. Eisenhower, supreme commander of Allied forces in Europe, did not believe the bomb should be used. According to historians, neither did General Douglas MacArthur, who was to command the invasion of Japan and found out about the bomb only shortly before it was dropped. Several of the scientists who had helped build the bomb did not favor using it against Japan.

The man who made the decision, President Harry S Truman, claimed it had been an easy one and that he never lost a single night's sleep over it. To Truman, the choice was between using the bomb and invading Japan; he believed the bomb would potentially save the lives of tens of thousands, perhaps hundreds of thousands, of American soldiers.

While stationed in Paris, France, American troops learn that the Japanese have surrendered to end World War II. As part of their V-J (Victory over Japan) Day celebration, the U.S. troops wave signs as they celebrate. (Reproduced by permission of © Hulton Getty/Liaison Agency)

Most people in the United States agreed with him at the time, and some historians have pointed out that an invasion would almost surely have caused the deaths of even more Japanese, both soldiers and civilians, than did the atomic bomb. British Prime Minister Winston Churchill was one of the few leaders who knew about the Manhattan Project; he remembered the decision to use the bomb as being a scarcely debated topic. It was assumed that atomic weapons, like any other powerful new weapon, would be used as soon as possible. Most political leaders did not fully understand the difference between the atomic bomb and previous weapons. They thought it was simply a more powerful version of a regular bomb. This may be the way Truman understood it; he had no idea of the existence of the bomb project until he became president after President Franklin D. Roosevelt's death in April 1945.

Other reasons have been suggested for the decision to drop the bomb. Developing and building the weapon was probably the most expensive, as well as the most secret, project ever undertaken by the U.S. government. People involved in the massive project naturally wanted to use the bomb in an effort to show that the project had helped win the war and that the money had not been wasted. Many historians have emphasized that by the time the bomb was dropped, serious conflicts were developing between the United States and the Soviet Union. They argue that at least part of the reason for using the bomb was to demonstrate the power of this superweapon to the Soviet Union. The deterioration of relations between the Americans and the Soviets has been offered as one explanation for the timing of the Hiroshima and Nagasaki attacks. For years, the United States had wanted the Soviet Union to declare war on Japan and invade Manchuria. When the first atomic bomb was tested in New Mexico in July 1945, however, American officials felt that they no longer needed Soviet help against Japan. They now feared that a successful Soviet invasion would enable the Russians to gain greater influence in China after the war. Although it was too late to call off the Soviet invasion, as top American military officials wanted, the sooner Japan surrendered, the less influence the Soviets would have in eastern Asia. This is one reason, according to these historians, that the United States did not wait a few more weeks or even months to see if Japan would surrender without an invasion.

In some ways, the question of timing has remained the most troubling aspect of the use of the atomic bomb. Some historians are convinced

Bomb Triggers Arms Race

The United States became involved in nuclear weapons research because of fears that Hitler's Germany would develop and use the bomb during World War II. Instead, the United States became the first country to complete development of and use a nuclear weapon, and the bombing of Hiroshima marked the beginning of the Nuclear Age. When Truman, British Prime Minister Winston Churchill, and Soviet leader Joseph Stalin met for the Potsdam Conference in July of 1945, spies for the Soviet Union had already handed over the secret plans for the atomic bomb to the Soviet government. The postwar years were marked by a feverish arms race between the United States and the Soviet Union. The Federation of American Scientists and the Atomic Energy Commission were both organized in the postwar years to promote the regulation of nuclear weaponry worldwide.

by records of secret discussions in the Japanese government that Japan would soon have accepted the terms of surrender even if Hiroshima and Nagasaki had not been bombed. American leaders had knowledge of this fact at the time because the United States had broken the secret codes used by the Japanese. In addition, critics have argued that the United States could have informed the Japanese government of the existence of the bomb, or even demonstrated it on an uninhabited island in the Pacific in the presence of Japanese observers. This idea was apparently considered but ultimately rejected because American officials feared what would happen if the bomb failed. Apart from that problem, such an approach deviated from conventional procedures between nations at war. It will never be known whether Japan would have surrendered without an atomic attack or an invasion. When Hirohito told the Japanese people that they must accept defeat, most Allies did not care about the reasons for the surrender.

Douglas MacArthur

Douglas MacArthur's signature on the Japanese agreement of surrender was significant in many ways. When the United States entered World War II in 1941, MacArthur commanded U.S. Army forces in the Far East, leading both American and Filipino soldiers in the fight for the Philippine Islands against the Japanese. In March 1942 U.S. President Franklin D. Roosevelt ordered MacArthur to leave the Philippines and establish headquarters in Australia, prompting the general to make his often-quoted promise to the Philippine people: "I shall return." As commander of the Allied forces in the Southwest Pacific, MacArthur oversaw the capture of a series of Pacific islands north of Australia for the rest of 1942 and all of 1943. He was able to go back to the Philippines in October of 1944, thus fulfilling his pledge. The Allies were victorious, and the Philippines were finally freed from Japanese control. MacArthur, by this time a five-star general, won the Congressional Medal of Honor for his role in the defense of the Philippines. The Allies were then able to begin fighting on the home islands of Japan. After years of fighting the Japanese, on September 2, 1945, on board the battleship USS *Missouri*, MacArthur accepted the surrender of the Japanese nation. MacArthur then served as supreme commander overseeing postwar Japan and its 83 million citizens.

Japanese leaders sign surrender documents aboard the USS *Missouri*, September 2, 1945. (Reproduced by permission of AP/Wide World Photos)

The End of the War

In every great city of the Allied countries, crowds cheered the news of victory. In the United States, soldiers and sailors home from Europe now knew they would not have to ship out again and face the daily threat of death. Two weeks after Hirohito's broadcast, an immense Allied fleet gathered in Tokyo Bay. Military representatives of the United States, Britain, China, the Soviet Union, and France waited aboard the American battleship USS *Missouri*. Representatives of the Japanese army and navy, and of the Japanese government, approached a small table on the *Missouri*'s deck, bent forward, and signed their names to the surrender. MacArthur signed for the Allies. The date was September 2, 1945—six years and one day after German armies had invaded Poland and started World War II. The war was over.

P R I M A R Y   S O U R C E

Rodney Barker
Excerpt from *The Hiroshima Maidens: A Story of Courage, Compassion, and Survival*
Published in 1985

In May 1945 the war in Europe came to a close, thus freeing more Allied troops for the battle against Japan. At that time, naval blockades were already strangling Japanese ports. In addition, the United States had also captured key islands in the Pacific and established air bases. Throughout the spring of 1945, air assaults were launched from these bases, crushing the Japanese military and crippling cities on the home islands (the chain of four islands making up the heart of Japan). Invasions of the main island of Kyushu, and then northward to the capital city of Tokyo on Honshu, were tentatively scheduled for late 1945 and early 1946. Yet the Allies knew that the steadfast Japanese would fight harder than ever to defend the home islands. According to most military estimates, about 500,000 American soldiers would be lost in the invasion. U.S. president Harry S Truman had repeatedly called for the "unconditional surrender" of Japan, but Japanese leaders would not agree to surrender on such terms. Their devotion to their emperor and their commitment to the honor of the Japanese nation would not allow them to unconditionally surrender.

The Potsdam Declaration, a statement released by the leaders of the Allied nations on July 26, 1945, demanded the "unconditional surrender of all Japanese armed forces." According to the declaration, failure to surrender would result in the "the prompt and utter destruction" of Japan. The Japanese did not know that a new weapon, an atomic bomb, would be used against them to hasten that surrender. Hiroshima, located on the main Japanese island of Honshu, and Nagasaki, on the island of Kyushu, were the targets of the first atomic bombs. Early on the morning of August 6, 1945, a B-29 bomber called the *Enola Gay* took off from the U.S. air base on the tiny South Pacific island of Tinian, nearly 1,500 miles southeast of Japan. Inside the bomber were the components for a ten-foot-long, 8,000-pound atomic bomb nicknamed "Little Boy." The trip from the base to Hiroshima, where the bomb was to be dropped, took five hours. The final assembly of the bomb took place after the *Enola Gay* had taken flight. This safety precaution eliminated the possibility of the bomb exploding on or over the base. Lieutenant Colonel Paul W. Tibbets piloted the *Enola Gay*, with two bombers flying behind his plane.

The people of Hiroshima were not alarmed by the sight of B-29 bombers flying over the city's business district. Since U.S. forces had established air bases on conquered islands in the Pacific, fly-overs had become a routine occurrence. No one expected the devastation that was to follow. The atomic bomb was dropped from the *Enola Gay* shortly after 8:15 a.m. and exploded less than a minute later, about 1,850 feet over Hiroshima. The bomber crew wore special glasses to protect their eyes from the burst of light that came with the explosion of the bomb. Witnesses in the air reported seeing a flash, hearing a rumble from the blast, and feeling a strong jolt. A huge fireball enveloped Hiroshima, followed by a rising mushroom cloud of smoke. On the ground, unimaginable heat and flames melted everything in sight. Thousands of buildings collapsed into heaps of rubble. Uncovered flesh was immediately charred and blistered by the high temperatures. Later, black rain fell on the city from heavy dark clouds.

The bombing of Hiroshima instantly killed more than 70,000 people. Over the next five years, thousands more people (about half the city's population) would die from the aftereffects of the bombing. The Japanese use the term *hibakusha* to refer to survivors of the atomic bombs dropped at the end of World War II. Among the survivors of the Hiroshima blast were twenty-five women known as the Hiroshima Maidens. They had all been injured in the bombing and were bonded by their common experiences. In the spring of 1955, as part of a massive humanitarian effort, the Maidens were flown to the United States for plastic surgery at Mount Sinai Hospital in New York City. While in the United States, they stayed at the homes of American host families. Rodney Barker, author of *The Hiroshima Maidens: A Story of Courage, Compassion, and Survival* and a member of one of the host families, was nine years old when two of the Maidens came to stay at his house. In 1979 Barker received a travel grant to research and write about postwar Hiroshima. His reports were published in the *Denver Post*. Background material from his visit to Japan, along with recorded interviews conducted in the United States and Japan between 1979 and 1984, provided the foundation for his book, *The Hiroshima Maidens*. The following excerpts recount the experiences of two girls, Hiroko Tasaka and Shigeko Niimoto, on the morning of August 6, 1945.

Excerpts from *The Hiroshima Maidens*

Hiroko Tasaka's Story

The sky was blue that Monday morning, but as Hiroko Tasaka dashed out the door of her grandparents' home in the suburban outskirts of Hiroshima, she could feel the humidity like a fever.… It was early, but already the streets were teeming with soldiers, laborers, students.…

This was the first day the students from the all-girls Hiroshima Commercial High School had been summoned to assist demolition crews with the house-clearing program.… Today they were to clear the debris of dismantled houses, moving stones to one spot along the street, boards to another, where they would be picked up later and carted to a dump site somewhere outside the city. Donning a white hiking cap to shade her face and white gloves to protect her hands, Hiroko began the day's work.

Perhaps fifteen minutes passed and she was struggling with a rock from the house foundation when a classmate beside her called out, "Hiroko, look. B-chan." In those days that was how they referred to B-29s, as though they were little pets.

Hiroko stopped working and looked up. She thought it made a lovely site, gleaming in the sunlight.…

"Where?" another girl asked. "I can't see it."

Hiroko raised her arm and pointed, and at that very instant the air seemed to catch fire. There was a searing white dazzle that prickled hotly and she had time only to think she had been shot before she blacked out.

When her senses returned, she was lying on her back in the middle of an unfamiliar darkness. Not a single star shone and no light could be seen. She rose shakily to her feet.… It was impossible to see more than a few feet in any direction.… In just a few steps she thought she could see more clearly, and a short distance further she broke out into the daylight. In front of her the Kyobashi River shimmered, and without hesitating she slid down the embankment and plunged into the cool current.

.…Hiroko looked around and saw that scores of other people had sought shelter in the river. The tattered remains of their uniforms identified practically all of them as schoolmates, but it was impossible to distinguish individuals because every face was

In 1955, as part of a massive humanitarian effort, the Hiroshima Maidens were flown to the United States for plastic surgery at New York's Mount Sinai Hospital. (Reproduced by permission of Corbis/Bettmann)

swollen to a piteous likeness. That led her to examine herself and she was startled to discover that her half-sleeved blouse was scorched and, even though she felt no pain, the skin on her bare arms had split open, exposing the pink tissue underneath.

No one knew what had happened. After an excited exchange, however, it was decided a bomb must have exploded directly on the work site. Just then a woman whose hair was singed, wearing rags that smoked as if they were about to burst into flames, rushed up to the riverbank crying, "The city is no longer safe. We must try to get back to school."…

As a group they scrambled out of the water, trotted across Hijiyama Bridge, and proceeded down the road that wound around the base of Hijiyama.… When the path ahead was obstructed by flames and

further progress was impossible, the group abandoned the pavement and charged the slopes of Hijiyama.… There was no path to follow and the scrub oak bushes dotting the hillside were igniting with a whoosh, so everyone went in different directions. In her quest for the safety of higher ground, Hiroko took a route that went straight up, though more than once the loose rock underfoot gave way, carrying her backward on a clattering landslide.

It took her almost an hour before she reached a clearing near the summit.… In a daze she sat down on a rock and watched others come up from below. As she saw that every single face was puffy and bloodsmeared, her hand went automatically to her own face and she wondered if hers might be the same. It was getting hard for her to keep her eyes open. In front of her a woman was working her way

Physical Effects of the Bomb on Its Victims

When uranium atoms split, the reaction is a massive exothermic release of lethal radiation waves. These waves can cause deadly radiation sickness. In Hiroshima and Nagasaki radiation poisoning affected people as far as a mile and one-half away from the explosions, and the heat and fire from the exploding bombs caused deep, painful burns on the faces and bodies of thousands of people. As their wounds healed, many victims were left severely disfigured by the formation of scar tissue. In most cases, however, the effects of radiation did not become apparent until months later. Symptoms of radiation sickness among *hibakusha* included weakness, hair loss, purplish bruise-like spots on the skin, sores in and on the mouth, bleeding gums, vomiting, diarrhea, and low resistance to infection due to low white blood cell counts. A higher than expected incidence of various cancers has also been reported among atomic bomb survivors.

Women tending a child who was wounded in the atomic bomb blast in Hiroshima. (Reproduced by permission of the Corbis Corporation [Bellevue])

up an outcropping, and when she made it over the top Hiroko called to her, "Excuse me, but would you tell me what my face looks like?"

With hardly a glance the woman responded, "We all look the same," and passed on.

....An authoritative voice call[ed] all who could still walk to proceed to the station where a rescue train was due. [Hiroko] was rapidly losing her vision and knew soon she would be blinded by the swelling.

As it was, she found the depot by clutching the clothes of those walking in front of her.

As the hours passed, direct exposure to the sun turned up the heat of her burns, and just when Hiroko was beginning to give up hope that the trains were still running, someone shouted, "Here it comes." As no one wanted to be left behind, people swarmed over the engine and climbed through the windows before the wheels rolled to a stop. Hiroko tried to stand up, but to her mortification her legs gave out each time and she was unable to crawl the last part of the way across the platform before the train pulled slowly away.

Shigeko Niimoto's Story

....Shigeko Niimoto was bent over trying to untie the air-raid hood she had left on after an earlier alarm when she heard her Middle School classmate say, "Look, Niimoto-san. Something's dropped from that plane." She stopped what she was doing and tilted her head back. Using her hands as a visor to shade the sun, she looked up just in time to witness an explosion of light, white and blinding. Screaming, she covered her face with both hands and dropped to her knees. The last thing she remembered was a violent blast of wind slamming her sideways.

....Her mind was fuzzy and everything around her blurred. As she got to her feet she peered into a thick, shifting mist through which she saw flickering fires and forms.... She was unable to make out anything distinctly until the floating mists parted to reveal a frightening procession of figures that looked

Destruction in Nagasaki after the bomb. (© Archive Photos, Inc. Reproduced by permission)

to her like cadavers making an exodus from their graves. They moved slowly, almost dreamily, without making a sound. They held their hands out in front of their chests like sleepwalkers. At first she thought they were wrapped in wisps of smoke, but as her vision increased she saw it was their skin peeling from their bodies. She drew a deep breath, holding it in. Something terrible had gone wrong and she wanted no part of it.

"Niimoto-san. Niimoto-san."

At the sound of her name being called, she turned. One of the nightmarish figures was moving toward her. Instinctively she recoiled. "Who are you?"

"Araki. Sachiko Araki."

To Shigeko's astonishment, it was her best friend. "Oh, Sachiko, what happened?"

Having seen the way she was looked at, her friend asked, "Do I look that bad?"

"No," Shigeko lied, "it's just slight." Then, noticing how Araki-san's eyes were fixed on her, she asked, "How about me?"

"Just slight too."

Without any discussion of what might have happened, Shigeko found herself pulled by the arm to a street not far away where her friend's mother was trapped under the wreckage of their completely collapsed home. The roof had come down on top of the woman and only her head stuck out. Shigeko stood dumbfounded for a moment, wondering what she was supposed to do, before joining Araki-san, who was frantically pushing splintered timbers and shattered tiles aside.

But there was a mound of debris to move and not much time. The house next door had erupted in fire and the heat grew more intense by the minute. Araki-san's mother was the first to admit it was useless. "There's nothing that can be done for mother, dear," she said in a surprisingly calm voice. "Go and find father."

When Araki-san [said that] she could not bear to desert her mother, [that] they would die together, she was ordered away. "Do as I say. Hurry. Right now."

As they backed away the house became a raging funeral pyre. "Good-bye," [Shigeko's] friend cried. "Good-bye, mother." The last they saw of Araki-san's mother [was] her face float[ing] in flames but she was still smiling. (Barker, pp. 18—25)

Aftermath

Three days after "Little Boy" was dropped on Hiroshima, a B-29 bomber named *Bock's Car* dropped the plutonium-powered "Fat Man" bomb on the city of Nagasaki, killing at least 35,000 more Japanese and injuring thousands. On September 2, 1945, V-J Day (Victory over Japan Day), the Japanese formally surrendered to the Allies and World War II came to a close. Later, the Hiroshima Peace Memorial was erected around the remains of the city's Museum of Science and Industry, a huge concrete structure left gutted but still standing after the atomic blast. The peace monument is inscribed with the words, "Repose ye in peace, for the error shall never be repeated." Each year a commemorative service is held at the site.

Yet the war was not over for the Japanese victims of the atomic blasts. "It always bothered [Hiroko]," noted Barker, "that in the American version [of the bomb story] the bomb was dropped, the war was over, and that was it, while for her and so many others that was just the beginning." The *hibakusha* had to deal with tremendous physical and psychological stresses; their injuries made them outcasts. They endured discrimination in the workplace and were not considered "marriageable" in Japan. The bottom half of Hiroko's face was badly burned and her arms were frozen at an angle, bent by scar tissue. Shigeko suffered severe burns to her face. Even after their surgeries, the girls faced rejection in Japan. Results varied, but overall the Maidens' faces did not (and never would) look the same as they had before the bombing. "They looked much better," explained Barker, "but in a number of cases the disfiguring marks were still bad enough to attract attention." Hiroko underwent twenty-seven operations—fourteen in Japan and thirteen in the States—became a dressmaker, and opened her own shop in Hiroshima. Later, she gave up her career to accept the marriage proposal of an American man who admired her bravery and inner beauty. The adjustment to her new life in the United States was difficult for Hiroko, and her marriage was, at times, troubled. Language proved to be the main barrier in the couple's path—she knew very little English, and he did not speak Japanese. After his retirement, though, Hiroko's husband agreed to go to Japan with her. Shigeko spent six months in Japan after her surgeries, then returned to the United States. She was taken in by *Saturday Review* editor and humanitarian Norman Cousins and his family. (Cousins had organized the Hiroshima Maidens

At the Atomic Bomb Dome, located in Hiroshima's Peace Memorial Park, doves fly during a remembrance ceremony on August 6, 1997. (Reproduced by permission of AP/Wide World Photos)

project.) Shigeko had a son in 1962 and later worked with the physically disabled as a home-care therapist.

SOURCES

Books

Barker, Rodney, *The Hiroshima Maidens: A Story of Courage, Compassion, and Survival,* Viking (New York), 1985.

Dolan, Edward F., *America in World War II: 1945,* Millbrook Press (Brookfield, CT), 1994.

Feinberg, Barbara Silberdick, *Hiroshima and Nagasaki,* "Cornerstones of Freedom Series," Children's Press (Chicago), 1995.

Feis, Herbert, *The Atomic Bomb and the End of World War II,* Princeton University Press (Princeton, NJ), 1966, originally published as *Japan Subdued,* 1961.

Maruki, Toshi, *Hiroshima No Pika*, Lothrop, Lee & Shepard (New York), 1982.

Morimoto, Junko, *My Hiroshima*, Viking (New York), 1990.

Seddon, Tom, *Atom Bomb*, W.H. Freeman (New York), 1995.

Sekimori, Gaynor, *Hibakusha: Survivors of Hiroshima and Nagasaki*, Charles E. Tuttle (Boston), 1986.

Periodicals

"Birth of an Atomic 'Little Boy,'" *Newsweek*, March 8, 1999, p. 50.

"Text of Statement by Truman on Development of Atomic Bomb," *New York Times*, August 7, 1945, p. 4.

Other

Hiroshima Witness (videotape), produced by the Hiroshima Peace Cultural Center and NHK (the public broadcasting company of Japan), 1986.

Voice of Hibakusha, http://www.inicom.com/hibakusha/(September 12, 2000).

P R I M A R Y   S O U R C E

Harry S Truman
Statement on the Surrender of Japan

Transcribed and published in the New York Times, *September 2, 1945*
Reprinted in Harry S Truman's Memoirs *by Harry S. Truman. Vol. 1, Year of Decisions, 1955*

After the defeat of Germany, the Allies focused their attention on Japan. By the summer of 1942, American troops were pushing the Japanese back, working their way from Australia northward and from the Hawaiian Islands westward. For three years, American troops landed on island after island in the Pacific, slowly making their way toward Japan. When the war in Europe ended in May 1945, American forces were in the middle of the largest of these island battles, on Okinawa. They captured Okinawa at the end of June and were then only 400 miles from Japan. America's next move was to invade Japan's home islands. American war planners believed the invasion would be difficult and many lives would be lost. Japanese troops had fought hard in the Pacific and would fight even harder for their home islands. If Allied forces took casualties at the same rate during an invasion of the main Japanese islands as they had on Okinawa, hundreds of thousands would be killed or wounded.

Rather than send America's troops into another vicious battle, President Harry S Truman decided to use the newly developed atomic bombs to try to force the Japanese to surrender. On August 6, 1945, the American bomber the *Enola Gay*

dropped an atomic bomb on Hiroshima, destroying the city and killing approximately 78,000 people. When the Japanese had not surrendered by August 9, the United States dropped another bomb on the Japanese city of Nagasaki. The top Japanese political and military leaders still did not want to surrender. The Japanese lived and fought by a code of honor. Members of the military considered dying in war a glorious end; they dedicated their lives, and their deaths, to their emperor, Hirohito. The Japanese government argued over the matter until August 15, when Hirohito made the difficult decision. He proclaimed that Japan was ready to stop the fighting and accept the terms of the Potsdam Declaration, provided the Allies allowed him to remain as sovereign ruler. Japan's military leaders wanted to continue the fight, but Hirohito felt that surrender was the only way to save the Japanese nation from complete destruction. In his radio broadcast to the Japanese regarding the end of the fighting, he urged his people to "unite" their "total strength to be devoted to the construction for the future." Prior to this broadcast, the citizens of Japan had never heard Hirohito's voice.

U.S. General Douglas MacArthur was appointed supreme allied commander and received the

Japanese surrender on September 2, 1945. The proceedings took place on board the battleship USS *Missouri* as it floated in Tokyo Bay. Representing the conquered nation were Mamoru Shigemitsu, the Japanese foreign minister, and Yoshijiro Umeza, the chief of the Japanese imperial staff. Both men signed the surrender documents. Then, representatives of the Allied nations added their signatures; MacArthur was the last to sign his name. Later that day President Truman addressed the American people about the unconditional surrender of Japan. His speech came less than three weeks after his controversial decision to unleash the power of a nuclear weapon on the Japanese home islands.

Truman's Statement on the Japanese Surrender, September 2, 1945

My fellow Americans ... the thoughts and hopes of all America—indeed of all the civilized world—are centered tonight on the battleship Missouri. *There on that small piece of American soil anchored in Tokyo Harbor the Japanese have just officially laid down their arms. They have signed terms of unconditional surrender.*

Four years ago the thoughts and fears of the whole civilized world were centered on another piece of American soil—Pearl Harbor. The mighty threat to civilization which began there is now laid to rest. It was a long road to Tokyo—and a bloody one.

We shall not forget Pearl Harbor.

The Japanese militarists will not forget the U.S.S. Missouri.

The evil done by the Japanese war lords can never be repaired or forgotten. But their power to destroy and kill has been taken from them. Their armies and what is left of their navy are now impotent.

To all of us there comes first a sense of gratitude to Almighty God who sustained us and our Allies in the dark days of grave danger, who made us ... grow from weakness into the strongest fighting force in history, and who now has seen us overcome the forces of tyranny that sought to destroy His civilization....

Our first thoughts, of course—thoughts of gratefulness and deep obligation—go out to those of our loved ones who have been killed or maimed in this terrible war. On land and sea and in the air, American men and women have given their lives so that this day of ultimate victory might come and assure the survival of a civilized world....

We think of those whom death in this war has hurt, taking from them husbands, sons, brothers and sisters whom they loved. No victory can bring back the faces they longed to see.

Only the knowledge that the victory, which these sacrifices made possible, will be wisely used can give them any comfort. It is our responsibility—ours, the living—to see to it that this victory shall be a monument worthy of the dead who died to win it.

We think of all the millions of men and women in our armed forces and merchant marine all over the world who, after years of sacrifice and hardship and peril, have been spared by Providence from harm.

We think of all the men and women and children who during these years have carried on at home, in lonesomeness and anxiety and fear.

Our thoughts go out to the millions of American workers and businessmen, to our farmers and miners—to all who have built up this country's fighting strength, and who have shipped to our Allies the means to resist and overcome the enemy.

Our thoughts go out to our civil servants and to the thousands of Americans who, at personal sacrifice, have come to serve in our government during these trying years; to the members of the selective service boards and ration boards; to the civilian defense and Red Cross workers; to the men and women in the USO and in the entertainment world—to all those who have helped in this cooperative struggle to preserve liberty and decency in the world.....

And our thoughts go out to our gallant Allies in this war; to those who resisted the invaders; to those who were not strong enough to hold out, but who nevertheless kept the fires of resistance alive within the souls of their people; to those who stood up against great odds and held the line, until the United

A Place of Honor

As General Douglas MacArthur signed the Japanese surrender aboard the USS *Missouri,* two men stood directly behind him in a place of honor. Both looked too thin for the uniforms they were wearing. They had lost weight in the years they had spent as prisoners of the Japanese.

One was Arthur Percival, the British general who had surrendered the island fortress of Singapore in February 1942. The other was Jonathan Wainwright, the American general who had surrendered Corregidor and the Philippines in May 1942.

General Douglas MacArthur signs the Japanese surrender documents aboard the USS *Missouri.* Jonathan Wainwright and Arthur Percival stand behind. (Reproduced by permission of UPI/Corbis-Bettmann)

GIs in a prisoner of war camp celebrate Japan's surrender. (National Archives and Records Administration)

Nations together were able to supply the arms and the men with which to overcome the forces of evil.

This is a victory of more than arms alone. This is a victory of liberty over tyranny.....

But back of it all were the will and spirit and determination of a free people—who know what

freedom is, and who know that it is worth whatever price they had to pay to preserve it.

It was the spirit of liberty which gave us our armed strength and which made our men invincible in battle. We now know that that spirit of liberty, the freedom of the individual, and the personal dignity

The famous V-J Day kiss as seen on the cover of *Life* magazine. (Photograph by Alfred Eisenstaedt, courtesy of *Life* magazine)

of man are the strongest and toughest and most enduring forces in the world.

And so on V-J Day, we take renewed faith and pride in our own way of life. We have had our day of rejoicing over this victory. We have had our day of prayer and devotion. Now let us set aside V-J Day as

one of renewed consecration to the principles which have made us the strongest nation on earth and which, in this war, we have striven so mightily to preserve.

....Liberty ... has provided more solid progress and happiness and decency for more people than any other philosophy of government in history. And this

As part of a goodwill effort to instill peaceful relations after the war, American Maj. Gen. D.B. Baker returns a captured Japanese flag to Hiroshi Saito in a ceremony in Tokyo. Family and friends had given the flag to Saito's brother, who was killed during the war. (Reproduced by permission of AP/Wide World Photos)

day has shown again that it provides the greatest strength and the greatest power which man has ever reached.

... We face the future and all its dangers with great confidence and great hope. America can build for itself a future of employment and security. Together with the United Nations, it can build a world of peace founded on justice and fair dealing and tolerance....

From this day we move forward. We move toward a new era of security at home. With the other United Nations we move toward a new and better world of peace and international goodwill and cooperation.

God's help has brought us to this day of victory. With His help we will attain that peace and prosperity for ourselves and all the world in the years ahead. (Truman, pp. 460—463)

Aftermath

After the surrender, Japan was occupied by Allied armies under the command of General MacArthur, who oversaw postwar Japan. The Japanese military was disarmed and the country received a new constitution, which was written by MacArthur's staff. Specifying that Japan would never again wage war, the constitution abolished the army and permitted only a small self-defense force. It also declared that the emperor would become a symbol of the nation rather than a god-like figurehead. The Japanese empire was dismantled: Japan lost all its colonies, Manchuria and Taiwan were returned to China, and Korea became an independent country. The Allies then put top Japanese leaders on trial in Tokyo, ultimately convicting twenty-five and sentencing seven to death for committing war crimes. Thousands of other Japanese, especially military men, were tried in territories that the Japanese army had ruled during the war. Many were charged with mistreating Allied prisoners of war, and 900 were executed. During the Allied occupation, Japan underwent profound social and economic changes, eventually becoming prosperous and developing into the second-largest economy in the world after the United States.

SOURCES

Books

Darby, Jean, *Douglas MacArthur,* Lerner Publications (Minneapolis), 1989.

Dolan, Edward F., *America in World War II: 1944,* Millbrook Press (Brookfield, CT), 1993.

Dolan, Edward F., *America in World War II: 1945,* Millbrook Press (Brookfield, CT), 1994.

Dunnahoo, Terry, *Pearl Harbor: America Enters the War,* F. Watts (New York), 1991.

Feinberg, Barbara Silberdick, *Hiroshima and Nagasaki,* "Cornerstones of Freedom Series," Children's Press (Chicago), 1995.

Feis, Herbert, *The Atomic Bomb and the End of World War II,* Princeton University Press (Princeton, NJ), 1966, originally published as *Japan Subdued,* 1961.

Freedman, Russell, *Franklin Delano Roosevelt,* Clarion Books (New York), 1990.

Mee, Charles L., Jr., *Meeting at Potsdam,* M. Evans & Company (New York), 1975.

Ross, Stewart, *World Leaders,* Thomson Learning (New York), 1993.

Sandberg, Peter Lars, *World Leaders Past and Present: Dwight D. Eisenhower,* Chelsea House (New York), 1986.

Sweeney, James B., *Army Leaders of World War II,* F. Watts (New York), 1984.

Truman, Harry S., *Memoirs by Harry S. Truman.* Vol. 1, *Year of Decisions,* Doubleday (Garden City, NY), 1955.

Wheeler, Keith, and the editors of Time-Life Books, *The Fall of Japan,* "Time-Life Books World War II Series," Time-Life Books (Alexandria, VA), 1983.

Periodicals

Newsweek, March 8, 1999, p. 53.

New York Times, May 9, 1945, pp. 1, 6; June 2, 1945, p. 4; August 15, 1945, p. 3; September 2, 1945, p. 4.

Other

The Avalon Project, *German Act of Military Surrender; May 8, 1945,* http://www.yale.edu/lawweb/avalon/wwii/gs7.htm (May 17, 2000).

MacArthur, parts I and II, narrated by David Ogden Stiers, "The American Experience" (videotape), PBS/WGBH, 1999.

The War Chronicles: World War II, volume 7, *The Return to the Philippines,* produced by Lou Reda Productions (videotape), A&E Home Video/History Channel Video/New Video, 1995.

Judgments—The Nuremberg Trials

On May 8, 1945, Nazi Germany offered an unconditional surrender to the Allied armies. After the treaty was signed, the Allies divided Germany into four zones that were occupied by American, British, French, and Soviet troops. In the waning weeks of World War II, citizens throughout the world began to learn of the inhumane actions of the Nazis. When Allied soldiers reached the concentration camps, they found the bodies or remains of thousands upon thousands of victims, with thousands more barely holding on to life. As survivors and witnesses began to speak publicly about their experiences, and as Nazi documents and records came to light, the enormity of the Nazi crimes became apparent. Questions then arose about what was to be done with those responsible for these crimes. Adolf Hitler had committed suicide. Joseph Goebbels, who had run Hitler's propaganda machine, had also ended his life, along with his wife and children. Heinrich Himmler, head of the terror machinery of the Nazi state, had tried to escape from the Allies, disguised as an ordinary soldier. When his identity was discovered, he too committed suicide. Heinrich Müller, one-time head of the Geheime Staatspolizei, or Gestapo, had disappeared. A number of others, from officials within the Nazi party to military leaders, were still alive and in custody. Should they be treated as the leaders of any other defeated country? Yet Nazi Germany was not sim-

ply a country that had lost a war. Its leaders had planned and carried out the murders of millions of civilians, including 6 million European Jews. During the war the Allies had made several public statements that the Nazis would be held responsible for their crimes and that, in fact, the punishment of these crimes was one of the aims of the war against Germany.

The First Trials

Some individuals who had committed crimes had been brought to justice before the conclusion of the war. The first trial for Nazi atrocities occurred in the Soviet Union in July 1943. In the recently recaptured city of Krasnodov, a Soviet military tribunal had tried thirteen Soviet citizens for participating in Einsatzgruppe D, one of the "special-action groups" the Nazis formed to murder Jews and others during the invasion of the Soviet Union. Einsatzgruppe D had committed more than 7,000 murders in Krasnodov, including the killing of every patient in the city hospital and the children's hospital. The Soviets had also tried members of the staff of the Majdanek extermination camp in eastern Poland a few months after their troops liberated the camp in July 1944. The Soviet army reached Majdanek before the Nazis could dismantle the facilities and transfer the survivors to other camps. The transfer of Jews became official Nazi policy in the final months of the war.

Long piles of bodies found at the Bergen-Belsen concentration camp after British forces liberated it. (Reproduced by permission of Bildarchiv Preussischer Kulturbesitz)

The Soviets captured an abundance of records the Germans did not have time to burn. The Majdanek trial produced the first evidence of the carefully organized and systematic nature of the Nazi genocidal plan.

Many people, especially in the United States and Great Britain, found the stories surrounding Nazi actions so difficult to believe, they decided that the Soviets must be exaggerating. Later the Majdanek evidence was revealed to be not only true, but also only a fraction of the widespread Nazi atrocities. As facts continued to surface, the Allies concluded that Nazi leaders must be put on trial. They wanted the world, including Germans, to comprehend the scale of Nazi crimes. In September 1945 a British military court tried Schutzstaffel (SS) guards from the Bergen-Belsen concentration camp, some of whom had also been at Auschwitz. The unsanitary and inhumane conditions at Bergen-Belsen, which the British had freed in April, shocked the world. At the next trial, forty-five defendants, including twenty-one women, were

charged; fourteen were found not guilty. The remaining eleven, including two women who had tortured prisoners, were sentenced to death and hanged. The rest received prison sentences.

The first people accused and tried were those within the camps themselves, or those involved in the mass shootings of civilians, not the officials of the Nazi party who had engineered the events. Of central importance to the Allies, and especially the United States, was a complete, systematic dismantling of the entire Nazi system. In the words of the high command of the American armed forces, "Nazism must be completely and finally removed from all aspects of German life." Holding officials accountable for the creation and execution of the Holocaust, while an important objective, was secondary to the principal goal of removing any semblance of Nazism from German society. From government to entertainment, the Allies strove to eradicate Nazi influence; thus began the denazification of Germany. Punishing war criminals was regarded as an essential step in the process.

Denazification

During the war crimes trials, the Allied administrators of defeated Germany were making other efforts to wipe out the remnants of Nazism. At the beginning of the Allied occupation, thousands of Germans were arrested and investigated by military authorities. In order to participate in public life, Germans were required to answer questions about their activities during the Nazi period. They were then classified as "major offenders," "offenders," "lesser offenders," "followers," or "non-Nazis." Depending on the category, a person might be arrested and tried, fined, or banned from activities such as holding public office. The denazification process caused resentment among many Germans. Those who had played a minor part in the government, and were truthful about their actions, were sometimes treated more harshly than those who had been fanatical Nazis but lied. The system also worked differently in the four Allied zones. The Americans tended to be more harsh, but even U.S. authorities would overlook the Nazi past of someone who was essential to the resurrection of the German economy, or who could help them in the growing conflict with the Soviet Union. (The most famous examples were German scientists who became important to the American missile and space programs. During the war, these men had worked in the German rocket program, which depended heavily on the use of slave labor.) In all three western zones, many judges, lawyers, and police officials, who had served throughout the Nazi period, continued in office. In the Soviet zone those former Nazis who cooperated with the new Communist establishment were often allowed to retain positions of authority.

The Allies created the International Military Tribunal, a multinational court with representatives from the United States, Great Britain, France, and the Soviet Union. Accused criminals who had been captured were put on trial in Nuremberg, the site where the Nazis had held their early rallies and formulated racial laws against the Jews. The first group of defendants included twenty-two men and six organizations, all charged with, among other things, having committed "crimes against peace." Although going to war was not a crime, this charge indicated that a country was justified in going to war only to defend itself or another country. The men were essentially charged with having planned and waged a war of conquest. Critics have pointed out that every nation on the tribunal could have been charged with the same crime at different times throughout history.

The second set of charges brought against the defendants involved "war crimes," or acts against "the laws and customs" of war. Included in the definition was the use of civilian populations of conquered countries as slave workers, the killing of hostages, mistreatment of prisoners of war, and the "wanton destruction of cities, towns, or villages" as well as "destruction not justified by military necessity." Many of these actions violated treaties Germany had previously signed with the occupied countries.

Nazi leaders were also charged with a third type of act, described as "crimes against humanity," which had never been considered in such trials in the past. These crimes included "murder, extermination, enslavement, deportation, and other inhumane acts committed against any civilian population, before or during the war." They also included "persecution on political, racial or religious grounds ... whether or not in violation of the domestic law of the country where perpetrated." The tribunal established that the laws formulated within the constructs of the Nazi government were not recognized by other nations, and therefore even if German law allowed the extermination of Jews, it was still a crime to carry it out. While the Nazis had never passed a law that openly allowed murder, the other forms of Jewish persecution considered legal under Nazi rule were scrutinized

The defendants being tried before the International Military Tribunal in Nuremberg. Among the defendants are Hermann Göring, Rudolf Hess, Joachim von Ribbentrop, and Wilhelm Keitel. (USHMM Photo Archives)

by the court. Laws that removed Jews from their jobs and homes, deprived them of their property, expelled them from schools and institutions, forced them into ghettos, forbade them to marry non-Jews, and forced their deportation were all considered "crimes against humanity," which led to mass murder. Although the charges against the Nazi leaders did not single out the attempted elimination of Jews, the trial that followed nevertheless often focused on the Holocaust.

The Main Nuremberg Trial

The rules of the International Military Tribunal in place for the Nuremberg trials stated that "leaders" and "organizers" who participated in formulating or executing a plan to commit crimes against humanity were "responsible for all acts performed by any person in executing such plan." The men who drafted the plan were held responsible for the actual killings. The rules created for the tribunal also rejected the idea that "following orders" was an excuse; thus lower-ranking Nazis

were prevented from pleading not guilty because the plans were made without their knowledge and that they were just doing their duty. This became especially important during the trial, as a number of men claimed they were merely following orders. If such a plea had been allowed, the number of individuals held responsible for the Holocaust would have diminished to a handful of people.

The International Military Tribunal sat from November 18, 1945, until November 1, 1946. An extraordinary amount of evidence was presented by the prosecutors from each of the four countries. (A justice of the U.S. Supreme Court, Robert Jackson, was the chief American prosecutor.) While most of the defendants denied any involvement in or knowledge of the deliberate destruction of Jews, none claimed that the events had not occurred. There were too many witnesses, including German officials such as Auschwitz commandant Rudolf Höss, and an overwhelming number of detailed documents that the Nazis had failed to destroy. Apparently realizing that denial of the events was futile, the leaders of the Nazi regime contended that the systematic attempt to destroy the Jewish people had not been their own individual responsibility. Blame was continually abdicated and shifted to another department, another person.

The following defendants at the main Nuremberg trial were found guilty and sentenced to death, and, except where noted, were hanged:

Martin Bormann was Hitler's deputy from 1941 until 1945, and was the only defendant not present at the trial, either having escaped or, more likely, having died in Berlin in 1945. He was sentenced to death but never found.

Hans Frank was one of Hitler's earliest supporters and his personal lawyer. During the war he was governor-general of occupied Poland.

Wilhelm Frick had helped the Nazis from their earliest days; he had been one of Hitler's co-defendants at his trial for treason in 1924. Eventually he became Minister of the Interior in the Nazi government and was appointed head of the police forces until he was replaced by Heinrich Himmler.

Hermann Göring was long regarded as the second most important Nazi after Hitler. He had numerous responsibilities, including serving as head of the Luftwaffe and director of economic planning. He was notorious for his vast collection of art looted from occupied Europe. Göring committed suicide with poison before he could be hanged.

Alfred Jodl was Chief of the General Staff of the Armed Forces. Although he claimed to be just a military man who carried out the orders of his superiors, Jodl supervised the shooting of hostages and was involved in planning anti-Jewish actions.

Ernst Kaltenbrunner became head of the Main Office for Reich Security (RSHA) in 1943, after the assassination of Reinhard Heydrich. The RSHA was the organization that was in charge of the Holocaust.

Wilhelm Keitel was Chief of the High Command of the Armed Forces; he issued the notorious Commissar Order, which directed the army to shoot captured Soviet officials, including prisoners of war. He signed the "Night and Fog" decree, under which captured resistance members in western Europe were made to disappear without a trace.

Joachim von Ribbentrop was Hitler's Foreign Minister from 1938 until the defeat of Germany. He pressured German allies and satellites to deport Jews to extermination camps.

Wilhelm Frick (Reproduced by permission of AP/Wide World Photos)

Alfred Rosenberg had been the Nazis' leading "philosopher" of racism and was considered one of their main "experts" on Jewish culture. From 1941 to 1943, he was in charge of a large section of captured Soviet territory, where he assisted in supervising the *Endlösung* or "Final Solution."

Fritz Sauckel was an early Nazi who became head of Germany's Labor Department in 1942. This put him in charge of a vast program of slave laborers who were forced to work in war factories in Germany.

Arthur Seyss-Inquart was an Austrian Nazi who served as Governor-General Hans Frank's deputy in Poland before being placed in charge of the occupied Netherlands, where his policies were exceptionally brutal.

Julius Streicher was the founder and editor of the newspaper *Der Stürmer,* which stood out even among Nazi papers both for the viciousness of its attacks on Jews and its semi-pornographic content. The long-time Nazi leader in Nuremberg, Streicher was responsible for storm trooper attacks against Jews and for the destruction of the Nuremberg synagogue in 1938.

The following defendants were found guilty and sentenced to prison:

The front page of *Der Stürmer,* the Nazi newspaper edited by Julius Streicher. (National Archives/USHMM Photo Archives)

Spandau Prison in Berlin, Germany, where Albert Speer, Minister of Armaments and War Production, served his term and Rudolf Hess, Adolf Hitler's deputy until 1941, was imprisoned until his suicide in 1987. (Reproduced by permission of AP/Wide World Photos)

Karl Dönitz was commander of the German navy and, after Hitler's death, served briefly as the second führer. He was acquitted of "crimes against humanity" but sentenced to ten years in prison for "crimes against peace" and for war crimes.

Walther Funk played an important role in winning business support for the Nazis before they gained power. Later he was head of the Bank of Germany, where loot taken from the victims of the Holocaust, including gold teeth, was sent. Funk was sentenced to life in prison but was released in 1957, when he was sixty-seven years old, because of ailing health.

Rudolf Hess, another early member of the Nazi party, was Hitler's deputy until 1941. In the middle of the war, and allegedly without the knowledge of the other Nazi leaders, he flew a plane to Great Britain in hopes of arranging an end to the conflict. He was denounced by Hitler as crazy, and held prisoner by the British for the remainder of the war. He was not in Germany while the Holocaust was being carried out. Hess was sentenced to life in prison and committed suicide there in 1987, at the age of ninety-three.

Konstantin von Neurath was Foreign Minister when Hitler took power. He retained the job in Hitler's government until replaced by Joachim von Ribbentrop in 1938. Later he was named "Reich Protector of Bohemia and Moravia" (present-day Czech Republic) when Germany destroyed Czechoslovakia, but was replaced in that post by Reinhard Heydrich, one of the main architects of the "Final Solution." Sentenced to fifteen years in prison, von Neurath was released after eight years, at the age of eighty-one.

Erich Raeder was commander of the German navy until replaced by Karl Dönitz in January 1943. He was sentenced to life in prison.

Baldur von Schirach had been head of the Hitler Youth and was later a Nazi party leader in Vienna. He was sentenced to twenty years imprisonment.

Albert Speer was Hitler's favorite architect and later Minister of Armaments and War Production, in which capacity he made extensive use of slave labor. Virtually the only Nazi leader who expressed a sense of regret for his actions, Speer nevertheless maintained ignorance regarding Jewish extermination. He was sentenced to twenty years in prison,

The judges' bench at the Nuremberg trials. The United States, Great Britain, France, and the Soviet Union each had one voting judge and one alternate judge. (Reproduced by permission of AP/Wide World Photos)

which he served. The book he wrote after his release, *Inside the Third Reich* (1970), is a valuable source of information.

The following defendants were found not guilty:

Hans Fritzsche was the head of German radio.

Franz von Papen was an old-line conservative politician who was Chancellor of Germany prior to Hitler and assisted Hitler in coming to power in 1933. He later served as a German ambassador.

Hjalmar Schacht was Hitler's Minister of Economics from 1934 to 1937, and was responsible for implementing policies that improved economic conditions in Germany during those years. Schacht had connections with anti-Hitler plotters in the German government and army; he was imprisoned by the Nazis near the end of the war.

Two other individuals were included in the original charges, but were not tried:

Robert Ley had been head of the Nazi "German Labor Front" that replaced the free trade unions. He committed suicide before the trial.

Gustav Krupp von Bohlen was the head of the giant Krupp steel and armaments company that had used slave labor throughout the war. He was considered too ill to stand trial.

Six organizations were also named as defendants; four of them were declared to be "criminal organizations" at the end of the trial. Individual members could be charged with crimes for simply participating in the groups. The remaining two organizations, the General Staff and High Command of the German Armed Forces and the Reich Cabinet (the highest officials of the government), were found not guilty. The organizations that were found guilty were:

Gestapo

Leadership Corps of the Nazi Party

Sturmabteilung (SA)

During the Medical trial, a victim shows her scarred leg to the court while an expert witness explains the medical experiment performed on her. The Medical trial was one of many held after the war to decide if individuals had committed crimes against humanity. (USHMM Photo Archives)

Schutzstaffel (SS), including the Sicherheitsdienst (SD)

The Later Nuremberg Trials

The first trial of top leaders within the German government, military, and Nazi party was followed by a series of twelve other Nuremberg trials. Each addressed a specific aspect of the Nazis' crimes. The first in the series, for example, focused on doctors and other medical personnel who had participated in the "selection" process at extermination camps, engaged in medical experiments on prisoners, or otherwise used their medical skills to commit crimes. The eleventh trial, the Ministries Case, involved high officials of various departments of the German government, some of whom were not Nazis but had aided the Nazis in carrying out their policy of mass murder. The twelfth trial, the High Command Case, involved high military officials.

Collectively, the evidence presented at these twelve trials demonstrated how every department of the German government, the military, and large sections of private industry were involved in crimes planned by the Nazis. While the trials were fair, with the international legal rights of each defendant being respected and maintained, they were also "show trials." The purpose was not only to punish individuals, but also to educate the public, including the Germans, about what had actually happened during the Third Reich.

As time passed, however, the political climate in Europe began to change. The Western Allies came into increasing conflict with the Soviet Union. Germany, the former enemy, was now seen as an important partner in this conflict, which soon became known as the Cold War. Trials of war criminals, and harsh punishments for those found guilty, were beginning to interfere with the goal of making Germany into a strong supporter of the West. Tensions between the Western Allies and the

The panel of judges at the I. G. Farben trial listen to testimony. (National Archives/USHMM Photo Archives)

Soviet Union eventually led to the creation of two separate Germanys. The Soviet Zone of occupation became East Germany (the German Democratic Republic), a Communist country dominated by the Soviet Union. The American, British, and French zones became West Germany (the Federal Republic of Germany), a strong ally of the West. West German political parties and churches began pressing for the end of war crime trials, and for the release of many of those who had been convicted. By the early 1950s few former Nazis remained in prison.

A Summary of the Twelve Trials at Nuremberg

1. The Medical Case began on October 25, 1946 (less than two weeks after the judgment in the original Nuremberg trial of top Nazis), and ended on August 20, 1947. Of the twenty-three defendants, seven were found not guilty. Seven were hanged, and five others received life imprisonment; these twelve sentences were all eventually reduced to either fifteen or twenty years.

2. The Milch Case ran from November 13, 1946, to April 17, 1947. It had a single defendant, Erhard Milch, who was involved in the administration of the slave labor system. He was sentenced to life in prison, but the term was reduced to fifteen years and he was released in 1954.

3. The Justice Case, which ran from January 4 to December 4, 1947, involved those who had been part of the Nazi legal system, including judges in the special courts. There were sixteen defendants, though one committed suicide and one was not tried because of his health. Four defendants were found not guilty; the others received sentences ranging from five years to life. All were released in 1950 and 1951.

4. The Pohl Case, from January 13 to November 3, 1947, included eighteen defendants who were involved in the economic aspects of the Holocaust, including the administration of slave labor and the running of companies owned by the SS. Three were acquitted and four were sentenced to death. Only one death sentence was carried out: the main defendant, Oswald Pohl, who was head of the Main Administrative Office of the SS, was hanged.

5. The Flick Case ran from February 8 to December 22, 1947. This was a trial of six people involved in the coal and steel industry. Three were found not guilty. The heaviest sentence imposed was seven years, but all the prisoners were released by 1950.

6. The I. G. Farben Case was tried from May 8, 1947, to July 30, 1948. I. G. Farben was the giant German chemical company that had built a plant at Auschwitz (known as Auschwitz III) to use slave labor. There were twenty-four defendants, one of whom did not stand trial because of poor health; ten were found not guilty and the others received prison sentences of up to eight years. Upon being released from prison, many resumed their highly successful business careers.

7. The Hostage Case, which tried German military personnel involved in executing hostages, began on May 10, 1947, and ended on February 19, 1948. Of the twelve men charged, one committed suicide, one was too ill to stand trial, and two were found not guilty. The others received sentences of up to twenty years, but all were released by 1953.

8. The RuSHA Case ran from July 1, 1947, to March 10, 1948. The RuSHA was the "Race and Resettlement Main Office" of the SS. This organization was in charge of making sure that SS members were "racially pure" and was involved in the plans of Heinrich Himmler, the head of the SS, to make the SS into the model for the future German "super race." Of the fourteen defendants, one was found not guilty. A few were given sentences of up to twenty-five years, but most were sentenced to the time they had already spent in prison before and during the trial.

9. The Einsatzgruppen Case began on July 3, 1947, and ended on April 10, 1948. (The Einsatzgruppen were the specially trained units that carried out mass shootings during the invasion of the Soviet Union.) There were twenty-four defendants, one of whom committed suicide before the trial and one of whom died shortly after the trial. Fourteen were sentenced to death, although only four were executed. The others had their sentences reduced to prison terms. At this trial the detailed testimony of Otto Ohlendorf, the commander of Einsatzgruppe D, included descriptions of mass executions, which included children. Ohlendorf was one of those who were hanged.

10. The Krupp Case was held from August 16, 1947, to July 31, 1948. The defendants were part of the management of the giant Krupp iron and steel company, which had used large numbers of slave workers during the war. The twelve defendants received sentences ranging from two to twelve years, but all were released by 1951.

11. The Ministries Case ran from November 4, 1947, to April 13, 1949. The twenty-one defendants were officials of various government departments such as the Foreign Ministry. Two were found not guilty; the others received prison terms ranging from three to twenty years. The longer terms were later reduced to ten years and most of the other defendants were released in 1950 and 1951.

12. The High Command Case was tried from November 28, 1947, to October 28, 1948. Of the fourteen high-ranking military men charged, two were acquitted and two received life in prison. One of these life sentences was reduced to eighteen years; the other defendant sentenced to life was released in 1954, as were most of the other defendants in the trial.

Trials in Other Countries

The special Nuremberg court was created to try people for crimes that had not taken place in a particular geographic location, in accordance with the Allied agreement that most war criminals should be tried in the countries in which their crimes had occurred. Poland was the country where the Nazi system of mass murder had been centered. Poland had not only been the home of the largest Jewish community in Europe, but was also the location of the extermination camps to which Jews from the rest of Europe had been sent. At the camps, 3 million Polish Jews had been killed; an additional 3 million non-Jewish Poles lost their lives at the hands of the Nazis. After the war the Polish government established a special Supreme National Court to try especially important cases involving such defendants as Rudolf Höss, the first commandant of Auschwitz, and other Auschwitz personnel. Evidence presented at this trial revealed details about the creation and operation of Auschwitz. The Polish Supreme National Court convicted Höss, along with Arthur Liebehenschel, who replaced him as Auschwitz commander; Ludwig Fischer, the German governor of Warsaw who set up the Treblinka death camp; and Amon Goeth, the commander of the Plaszów concentration camp. With few exceptions, those found guilty were sentenced to death and hanged. Other Polish courts tried additional war criminals. Among those convicted and executed were Hans Biebow, the German administrator of the Łódz

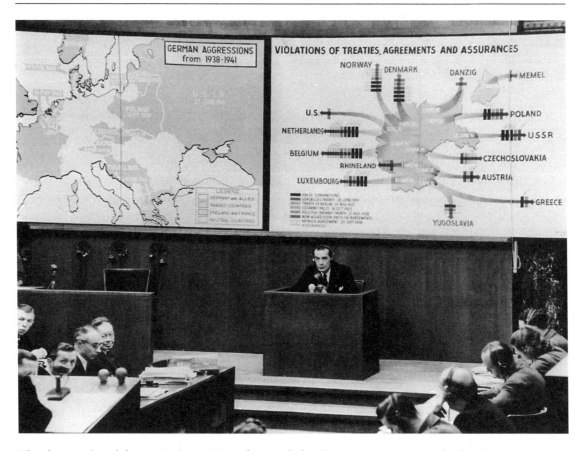

Theodore Monbostel, former Foreign Minister of Austria before the Nazi occupation, testifies for the prosecution at the Ministries trial. (USHMM Photo Archives)

ghetto, and SS General Jürgen Stroop, the commander of the forces that defeated the Warsaw ghetto uprising and destroyed the ghetto.

In many countries the principal targets of post-war trials were citizens who had helped the Germans during the occupation. (This was especially true in the first months after the defeat of the Germans.) Although the persecution and deportation of Jews were among the accusations against the defendants, it was not the main focus. Those who helped the Germans were regarded as traitors rather than war criminals. In France, for example, thousands of collaborators were shot immediately after the country's liberation; their trials often paid minimal attention to legal formalities.

In the Netherlands more than 14,000 people were convicted. Over 100 were sentenced to death, although only thirty-nine were actually executed. By 1960, only fifteen years after the war, fewer than fifty people remained in prison and all but four were released that year. In Hungary 19,000 people were convicted as war criminals and many, includ-

ing four former prime ministers, were hanged. Among them was Ferenc Szálasi, leader of the Nazi-like Arrow Cross Party, which had helped the Germans deport and kill 450,000 Hungarian Jews. The West German courts tried more than 90,000 people through 1985; relatively few were convicted and most sentences were lenient. Approximately 6,500 people received "substantial sentences."

The Eichmann Trial

The most important trial after the main Nuremberg trial occurred in 1961 and involved Adolf Eichmann, one of the most notorious Nazis. In 1960 Eichmann was found living under a false name in Argentina, where he was secretly kidnapped by Israeli agents. He was then taken to Israel, which had become a Jewish state in 1948. Members of the Israeli parliament said that when they heard Prime Minister David Ben-Gurion announce that Eichmann had been captured and was now in Israel, they were swept by feelings of joy. Eichmann was the most wanted Nazi in the world.

In his early career as a Nazi, Eichmann was appointed by Reinhard Heydrich to force Jews to leave Austria and Germany. Eichmann was then named head of the Jewish Affairs Section of the Main Office for Reich Security (RSHA). He was one of the organizers of the Wannsee Conference, where officials of the German government were informed that the Nazis had decided on the "Final Solution" to the "Jewish problem." He planned and supervised the deportation of millions of Jews from Europe, and personally directed the deportation of the Hungarian Jewish community to Auschwitz. More than any individual except Heinrich Himmler and the assassinated Reinhard Heydrich, Eichmann was responsible for carrying out the "Final Solution." He was charged with "crimes against the Jewish people." Unlike the defendants at Nuremberg who were charged with "crimes against humanity," Eichmann was specifically accused of attempting to destroy the Jews as a people. Like the Nuremberg trial, the Eichmann trial was intended to do more than punish one individual. The leaders of Israel wanted to remind the world of the crimes committed against European Jews. They wanted to educate their own people, especially the younger generation, about the complete destruction of Jewish communities. The Israeli leaders believed that the establishment of Israel, and its protection, was the only way Jews could truly be safe.

Although there were many thousands of Holocaust survivors in Israel, they rarely spoke about their experiences prior to the Eichmann trial. Many felt guilty that they had survived the Holocaust when others, often including their entire families, had died. Many simply could not bear to describe the almost unbelievable suffering they had endured. The Eichmann trial focused the attention of Israelis, and the world, on these experiences and allowed the survivors to begin to speak about their ordeal. Eichmann was questioned by Israeli investigators for eleven months and was under the constant supervision of doctors. A guard tasted all his food to ensure that no one poisoned him. A word-for-word transcript of Eichmann's statements was taken each day, and was checked for accuracy by Eichmann the next day. These transcripts totaled 3,500 pages. The trial itself lasted four months, beginning in April 1961, and was held in a 750-seat theater that had been converted for the trial. Eichmann sat in a specially constructed bullet-proof booth and was defended by a German lawyer who had represented defendants at Nuremberg. The lawyer's fee was paid by Israel.

Sympathy in South America

Nazi leader Adolf Eichmann had been a prisoner of the U.S. Army at the end of World War II, but his true identity was unknown. Upon his release he continued to live in Germany for another five years, using false papers and an assumed name. In 1950 he was able to move to Argentina, again using false papers, and was later joined by his family. Eichmann was not the only wanted Nazi to live secretly in Germany and then escape to South America. Another was Josef Mengele, the chief doctor at Auschwitz, who selected those to be gassed, performed medical experiments on twins, and subjected other prisoners (most of them children) to acts of cruelty. Another was Klaus Barbie, who was known as "The Butcher of Lyon" due to his brutal activities in Nazi-controlled France. The escape of Eichmann, Mengele, and others was made possible by a network of Nazi sympathizers in Germany and by pro-Nazi elements that had influence in some South American governments, including Paraguay and Argentina. As such, Israeli agents kidnapped Eichmann from Argentina, rather than asking the Argentine authorities to arrest him. Argentina protested the kidnaping, which was clearly an illegal act on the part of Israel. At the United Nations, Israel formally apologized to Argentina, but was allowed to keep Eichmann in custody.

The three judges who presided over the trial had been born and educated in Germany, but had moved to Palestine as young men, before the Holocaust. (Israel does not use juries.) The trial was conducted in German and the courtroom was filled with spectators throughout the duration of the 114 sessions. Reporters from around the world

Spectators in the main hall of the Eichmann trial, held from April to July 1961. (USHMM Photo Archives)

crowded into the courtroom; the trial was broadcast by Israeli radio and television, the first time in history a court case was televised. The trial was also videotaped, again the first time this had ever been done. More than 100 witnesses testified and almost 1,500 documents were presented, the most highly incriminating of which had been signed by Eichmann himself. The entire history of Nazi policy toward the Jews, from the earliest days of the Nazi government, was made public. Witnesses described what the Nazis had done in each country they had occupied; prosecutors made sure that there was at least one witness from every country in which the Nazis had attempted to carry out the "Final Solution." The ghettos, deportations, concentration camps, and death camps were described by survivors. The court sessions often became

highly emotional. One witness, who had warned the prosecutors that he did not think he would be able to relive these experiences, had a stroke while on the witness stand. On several occasions spectators began shouting and had to be removed from the courtroom by guards. Prosecutors were sometimes so overcome by the answers of the witnesses that they were unable to ask their next questions.

The Question of Resistance

One of the reasons that Holocaust survivors rarely spoke about their experiences before the Eichmann trial was a feeling that others, especially young, native-born Israelis, were ashamed of them for not fighting back. In fact, there were many examples of Jewish resistance throughout the war, such as the uprisings at Auschwitz and Treblinka and the battles in the ghettos of Warsaw, Bialystok, and Vilna. Jewish partisan units had also operated in such countries as the Soviet Union, Poland, and France. Despite these resistance efforts, the damage inflicted on the Nazis was minimal in military terms compared to the devastation caused by the Germans. The Jews of Europe had no government, no army, and in many places no organized community. They were attacked by the might of a modern, technologically advanced country that used its army and vast police forces. Usually, and especially at the beginning, the Jews could not forsee the future. The Nazis used deception tactics, and the thought that their goal was the elimination of the entire European Jewish population was almost beyond comprehension. Israeli prosecutors asked witness after witness why they had not resisted. Perhaps, one of these witnesses later said, they wanted a clear statement that resistance had been almost impossible. Most of the witnesses had difficulty describing the fear and helplessness they had felt at the time.

One answer to the question of resistance came from Abba Kovner, commander of the United Partisan Organization in the Vilna ghetto, who had led Jewish partisans in the forests. In December 1941 Kovner had called on the Jews of Vilna to resist, stating that it would be better to die fighting as free men. Kovner did not attempt to condemn the others, but he tried to explain:

> There hovers a question in the air of this courtroom. 'Why did the people not revolt?' I, as a fighting Jew, resent this question.

> Only people with a strong will may do so. And people with strong wills are not to be found among the desperate and the broken.

> But even this war, which has been called a war of despair, created people who believed, people with faith that there was a cause to die for one hour earlier, to sacrifice oneself for something that was greater than life.

> Because of this despair in which people found themselves, where their image of humanity had been taken away from them, it was not easy to accept this call to action. This is not surprising, nor is it unusual.

> On the contrary, it is a miracle that there existed a minority who believed in this call to action and did what they did during those years. The very existence of a fighting resis-

tance—that was not rational. It was an amazing achievement.

Eichmann's Defense: Following Orders

Eichmann did not claim he had no knowledge of the Holocaust throughout his tenure within the Nazi organization. He was candid about his conversation with Reinhard Heydrich, who told him: "The Führer [Hitler] has ordered the physical extermination of the Jews." He admitted that he had brought a message from Heydrich to General Odilo Globocnik, the SS commander in Lublin, Poland. "It ordered Globocnik to start liquidating a quarter of a million Polish Jews," Eichmann testified. He admitted that he had organized the transport trains that carried the Jews, a thousand at a time, to the gas chambers at Auschwitz. Eichmann's defense was that he was only a small cog in a giant machine. He asserted that he had been, for all practical purposes, a messenger with no decision-making power; others had made the decisions and carried them out. He merely passed along the orders he received. He admitted that he had joined the Nazi party knowing that it believed in the persecution of Jews. But, he said, if it had been up to him, he would have continued the policy of forcing Jews to leave Germany and Europe, not kill them. He claimed he was, in a way, a friend of the Jews, especially Zionists who wanted to establish a Jewish state. Like the Zionists, he believed the Jews should leave Europe, and he had found that the Jews were happy to leave. When a prosecutor asked whether they were happy to leave because they feared Nazi persecution, Eichmann admitted this was probably true, but he said he was not responsible for creating that fear. Rather, he claimed he had been faced with an impossible situation and he did his best to improve it.

Eichmann described himself as a soft-hearted man who frequently was unable to fulfill his duties. For instance, in Minsk in White Russia, he had watched as a group of Jews were forced to jump into a pit and then shot. He recalled: "I saw a woman hold a child of a year or two into the air, pleading." Eichmann said he was terribly upset by this scene because he had children of his own. Throughout his trial, and during his four weeks of testimony, Eichmann assumed the demeanor of a meek clerk who had no choice but to carry out jobs he was given. He was no longer the SS colonel who called himself a "bloodhound" who hunted down the Jews of Europe. He was no longer the cold-eyed killer who had offered to save a million

Eichmann in his bulletproof booth during his trial. (Reproduced by permission of Snark/Art Resource)

Jews from extermination in exchange for 10,000 trucks, in a deal he had described as "goods for blood, blood for goods." After several months of deliberations the court announced a verdict on December 11, 1961. Eichmann was found guilty of all fifteen counts in the charges against him. The court explained that each time Eichmann had organized a train carrying a thousand Jews to Auschwitz, with full knowledge that they would be killed there, he had been an accomplice in a thousand deliberate acts of murder. The court further stated that "[Even] if we had found that the accused acted out of blind obedience, as he himself argued, we would still have said that a man who took part in crimes of such magnitude, over several years, must pay the maximum penalty known to the law. This court sentences Adolf Eichmann to death." The Israeli Supreme Court confirmed the verdict and sentence the following May, and the President of Israel denied Eichmann's appeal to commute his sentence. Eichmann was hanged on June 1, 1962, the only time Israel has ever executed a criminal. Eichmann's ashes were scattered over the Mediterranean Sea.

Later Trials

Trials of Nazi war criminals continued long after the war. Sometimes, new incriminating evidence was discovered or Nazis who had been wanted for many years were finally found and arrested. One such man was Klaus Barbie, who had been head of the Gestapo in the French city of Lyon. Although wanted by the French, Barbie had worked as a secret agent for the American occupation authorities in Germany after the war. Later, probably with American help, he was able to disappear and then to move to the South American country of Bolivia. The French discovered his identity in 1972, but it took another eleven years before the Bolivian government sent him back to France for trial. Barbie, known as the "Butcher of Lyon," was especially known for two brutal events. He had organized a raid on a home for Jewish refugee children and ordered their deaths; all forty-four children were under the age of fourteen. Barbie had also tortured to death Jean Moulin, an almost legendary hero of the French resistance. In 1983 Barbie was sentenced to life imprisonment. (France had abolished the death penalty.) He died in prison in 1990.

It was not until 1989 that a Frenchman was convicted of "crimes against humanity." The defendant was Paul Touvier, head of the pro-Nazi Milice (Militia) in Lyon and co-worker of Barbie. Like Barbie, Touvier had twice been sentenced to death by French courts but had been under the protection of French people, especially elements within the French Catholic church. Convicted of ordering the shooting of seven Jewish hostages in 1944, Touvier was sentenced to life in prison, where he died in 1996. In October 1997 France began the trial of Maurice Papon. Unlike Touvier, Papon had been an important official of the French government in the city of Bordeaux during the German occupation. From 1942 to 1944, among his other duties, he was in charge of handling "Jewish questions" in the Bordeaux region. After the war he had continued his public career and was appointed to various important offices. He headed police and security in Paris for many years and was Budget Minister in the French government in the early 1980s. Since he had powerful friends, it took more than half a century after the defeat of the Germans to bring him to trial. Papon was accused of working with the Germans to deport 1,560 Jews from Bordeaux to the French transit camp at Drancy, from which they were then deported to Auschwitz to be gassed. Papon denied knowing that the Jews were being sent to their deaths, claiming that he tried to protect them from the Germans: "[I] spent the occupation fighting for the Jews, and for others." In April 1998 Papon was convicted of helping the Germans illegally arrest and deport Jews, although the court found that he did not know they were being sent to be killed. The court sentenced Papon to ten years in prison, but he remained free during appeal. During this time, Papon managed to escape to Switzerland with his granddaughter. He was arrested in Gstaad and returned to France to begin his ten-year sentence, his conviction having been upheld by the French high court in October 1999.

The trial of Papon is probably the last of its kind. Those who played a major role in the Holocaust were well into their eighties by the end of the twentieth century. Witnesses who would testify, if they were still alive, would also be elderly. Therefore a trial would have to be based on events that took place more than fifty years earlier, and the accuracy of witnesses' memories would be difficult to prove. The case of John Demjanjuk, a Ukrainian who moved to the United States after the war and became a U.S. citizen, illustrates these problems.

Records indicated that Demjanjuk had been a guard, known as "Ivan the Terrible," who served at the Treblinka death camp. After a lengthy process Demjanjuk was found to have lied about his past when he entered the United States. He was stripped of his citizenship and sent to Israel for trial.

At Demjanjuk's trial in 1986, survivors of Treblinka, by that time quite elderly, identified him as the brutal guard who had had no compassion for human suffering. Documents seemed to support the identification of Demjanjuk as the guard, but he claimed that the witnesses were mistaken and that the supporting documents were forgeries. Demjanjuk was convicted and sentenced to death, becoming the only person other than Eichmann to receive this verdict in Israel. Yet the sentence was not carried out—after a series of appeals and complicated examinations of the case in the United States, it became clear that there was insufficient evidence to convict Demjanjuk. Too many lapses in the memories of the witnesses made it impossible to identify Demjanjuk beyond a shadow of a doubt. No one could prove that Demjanjuk was really the vicious "Ivan the Terrible" at Treblinka; he was therefore acquitted of all charges and released.

PRIMARY SOURCE

Justice Robert H. Jackson
Opening Address for the United States
Delivered at the Nuremberg Trials, November 21, 1945
Text taken from *Nazi Conspiracy and Aggression*, Volume 1

While World War II still raged, the Allied powers publicly declared their intentions of prosecuting Nazi war criminals. As early as 1942 American, British, and Soviet representatives began negotiating a series of agreements concerning the standards for punishing those responsible for the Holocaust. On November 1, 1943, the Allied nations signed the Moscow Declaration, granting local authorities access to war criminals who were not tried internationally. Just months after the war ended, the Allies formally agreed to the charter of the International Military Tribunal (IMT), the court formed to prosecute major war criminals of the Axis powers. This

agreement, known as the London Agreement of August 8, 1945, was subsequently endorsed by nineteen member states of the newly established United Nations. Opening statements for the public trial of twenty-two major Nazi war criminals took place on October 18, 1945. (The term "major" refers to those military or political leaders whose crimes did not occur in a specific geographic region.) After holding the opening session in Berlin, the trial was moved to Nuremberg because of the lack of adequate accommodations in the war-ravaged German capital. One of the reasons the Allied powers chose Nuremberg was for its symbolic significance to the Nazi legacy. The for-

The press gallery at the Nuremberg Trials. (USHMM Photo Archives)

mer site of spectacular party rallies, Nuremberg was also the namesake of the Nazi racist laws that denied German Jews their citizenship status. Due to the location, these proceedings became known as the Nuremberg Trials.

The IMT represented the first time in history that countries aligned themselves to bring to justice those responsible for waging war and mistreating civilians and prisoners of war (POWs). Never before had legal proceedings been initiated against the leaders of an enemy nation. The establishment of this tribunal created controversy for several reasons: (1) The guidelines for the prosecution and the definitions of the crimes were established on August 8, 1945, three months after Germany's surrender; under the widely accepted legal principle of "ex post facto," defendants cannot be prosecuted under laws created after an act is committed. (2) Military justice often shields subordinates who carry out "superior orders" (the orders dictated by superior officers). (3) Lastly, individuals who perform actions as representatives of a state or government—a concept referred to as "act of state"—are traditionally not held personally accountable. The charter of the IMT expressly prohibited pleas of both "superior orders" and "act of state." After the extent of the crimes committed by the Nazis became apparent through testimony, legal criticism regarding these issues largely subsided.

The evidence used in the Nuremberg Trials came mostly from Nazi records. Following the defeat of Germany, the Allies found volumes of files and ledgers pertaining to every aspect of the Nazi government's workings. The invading American armies sent military investigative teams to comb through German records to secure relevant documents. One of their most important acquisitions, found behind a false wall in an old castle in eastern Bavaria, included the letters of Alfred Rosenberg, one of the party's leading supporters of anti-Jewish ideology. The IMT tried the defendants according to several major categories of crimes, including crimes against peace, war crimes, and crimes against humanity. The prosecution of "crimes against peace" upheld the principle that the only legal war was one of self-defense or against aggression. The definition of "war crimes" included the mistreatment of civilians in occupied territory and prisoners of war. Acts of persecution against civilian groups on the basis of religion, race, or politics constituted "crimes against humanity." The violence perpetrated against European Jews by the Nazis fell into the categories of war crimes and crimes against humanity. The world watched and listened as prosecutors from each of the major Allied nations presented the case against the twenty-two accused Nazi leaders. Twenty of these accused men attempted to persuade the court of their innocence.

The following address by Justice Robert H. Jackson opened the American case before the International Military Tribunal on November 21, 1945. Jackson had been appointed representative of the United States and chief of council by an executive order signed by President Harry S Truman. In his remarks that follow, Justice Jackson refers to the United Nations, the international organization that was founded on October 24, 1945, less than a month before this address.

Opening Address for the United States

May it please Your Honors,

The privilege of opening the first trial in history for crimes against the peace of the world imposes a grave responsibility. The wrongs which we seek to condemn and punish have been so calculated, so malignant and so devastating, that civilization cannot tolerate their being ignored because it cannot survive their being repeated. That four great nations, flushed with victory and stung with injury stay the hand of vengeance and voluntarily submit their captive enemies to the judgment of the law is one of the most significant tributes that Power ever has paid to Reason.

This tribunal, while it is novel and experimental, is not the product of abstract speculations nor is it created to vindicate legalistic theories. This inquest represents the practical effort of four of the most mighty of nations, with the support of seventeen more, to utilize International Law to meet the greatest menace of our times—aggressive war. The common sense of mankind demands that law shall not stop with the punishment of petty crimes by little people. It must also reach men who possess themselves of great power and make deliberate and concerted use of it to set in motion evils which leave no home in the world untouched. It is a cause of this magnitude that the United Nations will lay before Your Honors.

In the prisoners' dock sit twenty-odd broken men. Reproached by the humiliation of those they have led almost as bitterly as by the desolation of those they have attacked, their personal capacity for evil is forever past. It is hard now to perceive in these miserable men as captives the power by which as Nazi leaders they once dominated much of the world and terrified most of it. Merely as individuals, their fate is of little consequence to the world.

What makes this inquest significant is that those prisoners represent sinister influence that will lurk in the world long after their bodies have returned to dust. They are living symbols of racial hatreds, of terrorism and violence, and of the arrogance and cruelty of power. They are symbols of fierce nationalisms and militarism, of intrigue and war-making which have embroiled Europe generation after generation, crushing its manhood, destroying its homes, and impoverishing its life. They have so identified themselves with the philosophies they conceived and with the forces they directed that any tenderness to them is a victory and an encouragement to all the evils which are attached to their names. Civilization can afford no compromise with the social forces which would gain renewed strength if we deal ambiguously or indecisively with the men in whom those forces now precariously survive.

What these men stand for we will patiently and temperately disclose. We will give you undeniable proofs of incredible events. The catalogue of crimes will omit nothing that could be conceived by a pathological pride, cruelty, and lust for power. These men created in Germany, under Fuehrerprinzip, a National Socialist despotism equalled only by the dynasties of the ancient East. They took from the German people all those dignities and freedoms that we hold natural and inalienable rights in every human being. The people were compensated by inflaming and gratifying hatreds toward those who were marked as "scape-goats." Against their opponents, including Jews, Catholics, and free labor the Nazis directed such a campaign of arrogance, brutality, and annihilation as the world has not witnessed since the pre-Christian ages. They excited the German ambition to be a "master race," which of course implies serfdom for others. They led their people on a mad gamble for domination. They diverted social energies and resources to the creation of what they thought to be an invincible war machine. They overran their neighbors. To sustain the "master race" in its war making, they enslaved millions of human beings and brought them into Germany, where these hapless creatures now wander as "displaced persons." At length bestiality and bad faith reached such excess that they aroused the sleeping strength of imperiled civilization. Its united efforts have ground the German war machine to fragments. But the struggle has left Europe a liberated yet prostrate land where a demoralized society struggles to survive. These are the fruits of the sinister forces that sit with these defendants in the prisoners' dock.

In justice to the nations and the men associated in this prosecution, I must remind you of certain difficulties which may leave their mark on this case. Never before in legal history has an effort been made to bring within the scope of a single litigation the developments of a decade, covering a whole Continent, and involving a score of nations, countless individuals, and innumerable events. Despite the magnitude of the task, the world has demanded immediate action. This demand has had to be met, though perhaps at the cost of finished craftsmanship. In my country, established courts, following familiar procedures, applying well thumbed precedents, and dealing with the legal consequences of local and limited events, seldom commence a trial within a year of the event in litigation. Yet less than eight months ago today the courtroom in which you sit was an enemy fortress in the hands of German SS troops. Less than eight months ago nearly all our witnesses and documents were in enemy hands. The law had not been codified, no procedure had been established, no Tribunal was in existence, no usable courthouse stood here, none of the hundreds of tons of official German documents had been examined, no prosecuting staff had been assembled, nearly all the present defendants were at large, and the four prosecuting powers had not yet joined in common cause to try them. I should be the last to deny that the case may well suffer from incomplete researches and quite likely will not be the example of professional work which any of the prosecuting nations would normally wish to sponsor. It is, however, a completely adequate case to the judgment we shall ask you to render, and its full development we shall be obliged to leave to historians.

Before I discuss particulars of evidence, some general considerations which may affect the credit of this trial in the eyes of the world should be candidly faced. There is a dramatic disparity between the circumstances of the accusers and of the accused that might discredit our work if we should falter, in even minor matters, in being fair and temperate.

Unfortunately, the nature of these crimes is such that both prosecution and judgment must be by victor nations over vanquished foes. The worldwide scope of the aggressions carried out by these men has left but few real neutrals. Either the victors must judge the vanquished or we must leave the defeated to judge themselves. After the First World War, we learned the futility of the latter course. The former high station of these defendants, the notoriety of their acts, and the adaptability of their conduct to provoke retaliation make it hard to distinguish between the demand for a just and measured retribution, and the unthinking cry for vengeance which arises from the anguish of war. It is our task, so far as humanly possible, to draw the line between the two. We must never forget that the record on which we judge these defendants today is the record on which history will judge us tomorrow. To pass these defendants a poisoned chalice is to put it to our own lips as well. We must summon such detachment and intellectual integrity to our task that this trial will commend itself to posterity as fulfilling humanity's aspirations to do justice.

At the very outset, let us dispose of the contention that to put these men to trial is to do them an injustice entitling them to some special consideration. These defendants may be hard pressed but they are not ill used. Let us see what alternative they would have to being tried.

More than a majority of these prisoners surrendered to or were tracked down by forces of the United States. Could they expect us to make American custody a shelter for our enemies against the just wrath of our Allies? Did we spend American lives to capture them only to save them from punishment? Under the principles of the Moscow Declaration, those suspected war criminals who are not to be tried internationally must be turned over to individual governments for trial at the scene of their outrages. Many less responsible and less culpable American-held prisoners have been and will be turned over to other United Nations [members] for local trial. If these defendants should succeed, for any reason, in escaping the condemnation of this Tribunal, or if they obstruct or abort this trial, those who are American-held prisoners will be delivered up to our continental Allies. For these defendants, however, we have set up an International Tribunal and have undertaken the burden of participating in a complicated effort to give them fair and dispassionate hearings. That is the best known protection to any man with a defense worthy of being heard.

If these men are the first war leaders of a defeated nation to be prosecuted in the name of the law, they are also the first to be given a chance to plead for their lives in the name of the law. Realistically, the Charter of this Tribunal, which gives them a hearing, is also the source of their only hope. It may be that these men of troubled conscience, whose only wish is that the world forget them, do not regard a trial as a favor. But they do have a fair opportunity to defend themselves—a favor which these men, when in power, rarely extended to their fellow countrymen. Despite the fact that public opinion already condemns their acts, we agree that here they must be given a presumption of innocence, and we accept the burden of proving criminal acts and the responsibility of these defendants for their commission....

We would also make clear that we have no purpose to incriminate the whole German people. We know that the Nazi Party was not put in power by a majority of the German vote. We know it came to power by an evil alliance between the most extreme of the Nazi revolutionists, the most unrestrained of the German reactionaries, and the most aggressive of the German militarists. If the German populace had willingly accepted the Nazi program, no Stormtroopers would have been needed in the early days of the Party and there would have been no need for concentration camps or the Gestapo, both of which institutions were inaugurated as soon as the Nazis gained control of the German state. Only after these lawless innovations proved successful at home were they taken abroad....

This war did not just happen—it was planned and prepared for over a long period of time and with no small skill and cunning. The world has perhaps never seen such a concentration and stimulation of the energies of any people as that which enabled Germany twenty years after it was defeated, disarmed, and dismembered to come so near carrying out its plan to dominate Europe. Whatever else we may say of those who were the authors of this war, they did achieve a stupendous work in organization, and our first task is to examine the means by which these defendants and their fellow conspirators prepared and incited Germany to go to war....

It is my purpose to open the case, particularly under Count One of the Indictment, and to deal with the common plan or conspiracy to achieve ends possible only by resort to crimes against peace, war crimes, and crimes against humanity. My emphasis will not be on individual barbarities and perversions which may have occurred independently of any central plan. One of the dangers ever present is that this trial may be protracted by details of particular wrongs and that we will become lost in a "wilderness of single instances." Nor will I now dwell on the activity of individual defendants except as it may contribute to exposition of the common plan.

The case as presented by the United States will be concerned with the brains and authority [behind] all the crimes. These defendants were men of a station and rank which does not soil its own hands with blood. They were men who knew how to use lesser folk as tools. We want to reach the planners and designers, the inciters and leaders without whose evil architecture the world would not have been for so long scourged with the violence and lawlessness, and wracked with the agonies and convulsions, of this terrible war. (Jackson, pp. 114–120)

Aftermath

The Nuremberg Trials ended on October 1, 1946, the same date as Yom Kippur, the Jewish Day of Atonement. The entire transcript of the International Military Tribunal fills forty-two thick volumes. Most defendants either claimed that they had followed orders or that they had no knowledge of the atrocities being committed. Of the twenty-two Nazi leaders tried, twelve were sentenced to death, three received life imprisonment, four received prison terms of ten to twenty years, and three were found not guilty. Several notorious Nazi leaders escaped prosecution. Adolf Hitler committed suicide on April 30, 1945; his propaganda minister, Joseph Goebbels, followed suit several hours later, on May 1. Martin Bormann, Hitler's closest aide, is suspected to have died in the fall of Berlin at the close of the war. Chief of the SS and Interior Minister Heinrich Himmler committed suicide while in the custody of the British on May 23, 1945. And Adolf Eichmann, the Nazi leader responsible for organizing Jewish deportations to death camps, escaped from an American internment camp in 1946. (He was later tracked down in Argentina, stood trial in Israel, and was hanged in 1962.)

The term "Nuremberg Trials" is also used to refer to proceedings other than those held in 1945–1946. The city hosted trials for 177 additional criminals charged with membership in criminal organizations, including members of the Gestapo, SS, civil servants, and industrialists. A multinational tribunal also convened to examine Japanese war crimes (see Appendix C). The vast majority of war crime proceedings involved "minor" war criminals who were prosecuted in the countries where the crimes had taken place. Spandau Prison, located in West Berlin, was designated as the exclusive location for the internment of the Nazi war criminals convicted at the Nuremberg Trials. France, Great Britain, the Soviet Union, and the United States rotated guard responsibilities on a monthly basis at the prison. The last surviving defendant from the Nuremberg Trials, Rudolf Hess, died in his prison cell at Spandau on August 17, 1987. British authorities claim the ninety-three-year-old inmate hanged himself after forty-one years of imprisonment. Hess's family disputes the circumstances of his death.

SOURCES

Books

Berwick, Michael, *The Third Reich,* Putnam (New York), 1971.

Nazi Conspiracy and Aggression, volume I, office of United States Chief of Counsel for Prosecution of Axis Criminality, U.S. Government Printing Office (Washington, DC), 1946.

PRIMARY SOURCE

Hannah Arendt
Excerpt from *Eichmann in Jerusalem*

First published in 1963

Efforts to punish the criminals responsible for the Holocaust continued long after the end of World War II. Adolf Eichmann, one of the most notorious criminals of the Nazi regime, escaped prosecution by disappearing after the war. Considered a specialist in "Jewish affairs," Eichmann had played a critical role in the Nazi plot by organizing and implementing the party's anti-Jewish measures. Among his dubious accomplishments was the establishment of the ghetto system, where Jews in occupied countries were forced to live during the war years. His office also coordinated the transport of masses of people by rail to the ghettos, transit camps, and extermination centers.

In 1944, Eichmann personally supervised the rapid deportation of hundreds of thousands of Hungarian Jews. Between March and July of that year, more than 440,000 victims were rounded up and transported to labor and death camps—a staggering number in just over three months. Eichmann was responsible for altering the Theresienstadt ghetto in preparation for the International Red Cross visit in June 1944. Before allowing the Red Cross tour of the ghetto, he arranged for certain temporary improvements, including the installation of dummy stores, a cafe, a school, and

After World War II, Adolf Eichmann eluded the authorities and disappeared. Israeli agents arrested him in Argentina fifteen years later. (USHMM Photo Archives)

flower gardens. To ease conditions of overcrowding, he also authorized death camp deportations prior to the inspection team's arrival. In 1944, when Hungarian Jews were being deported, Eichmann became enraged by the rescue efforts of Swedish diplomat Raoul Wallenberg. Eichmann reportedly threatened to have Wallenberg shot, a warning that did not deter Wallenberg from his dangerous humanitarian work. Late in 1944, when the gas chambers at Auschwitz ceased functioning and the rail system became less reliable, Eichmann ordered 76,000 Jews to embark on "death marches" from Hungary to Austria.

Immediately after World War II, the Nazis used assets they had siphoned from their victims to finance an underground known as *Odessa*. This secret organization helped Nazis escape to other countries and avoid arrest by the Allies. Travel arrangements were frequently made to Buenos Aires, Argentina. Many former Nazis also fled to Canada and the United States. After the war Eichmann was arrested by Allied forces who were unaware of his key role in the Holocaust. He escaped unrecognized from a minimum security internment camp in the American zone and, aided by Odessa, went into hiding. His flight from justice ended fifteen years later, when Israeli agents seized him in Argentina, where he had been living with his family. The Israelis brought him to Jerusalem to face trial for war crimes.

Confronting a panel of three judges, Eichmann and his attorney based his defense on five arguments: (1) They contended he could not receive a fair trial in the Jewish state of Israel, before Jewish judges. (2) They claimed Eichmann was the victim of kidnapping, since he had been captured and transported against his will. (3) According to the defense, Eichmann was charged with violating laws put into effect after World War II; under the legal concept of "ex post facto," these laws should not have applied to him. (4) Since the alleged crimes occurred in Nazi Germany, the defense argued that the courts of Israel did not have jurisdiction to prosecute. (5) The defense contended that Eichmann had merely carried out "acts of state" and should not be held personally accountable for the policies of his government.

Eichmann pleaded "not guilty *in the sense* of the indictment" to each count. His unusual qualification was never questioned by the prosecution,

Hannah Arendt (1906-1975)

Hannah Arendt was born in Hanover, Germany. She was educated at the universities of Marburg, Freiburg, and Heidelberg, and left Germany for France in 1933, when the Nazis took over Germany. When France fell to Germany, Arendt fled to the United States. She worked for Jewish relief agencies until 1952, then devoted herself primarily to university teaching and writing. Arendt was a teacher, writer, and political philosopher, holding professional positions at Princeton University, the University of Chicago, and the New School for Social Research. Her writings and teachings, expressing bleak views on the human condition, have generated much controversy. Arendt's books include: *The Origins of Totalitarianism* (1951), *The Human Condition* (1958), *Eichmann in Jerusalem* (1963), *On Revolution* (1963), *On Violence* (1970), *Crises of the Republic* (1972), and *The Life of the Mind* (1977).

nor the defense attorney, nor any of the three judges. It has been assumed that Eichmann meant that he was not guilty of any crimes because he acted as a representative of the German government, obeying laws imposed by Adolf Hitler. The judges rejected all of these arguments and ordered the trial to proceed. The Eichmann trial generated worldwide publicity and was the first war crimes trial to be shown on television.

Scholar Hannah Arendt followed the trial and wrote her observations in *Eichmann in Jerusalem*. Born in Germany, Arendt herself experienced the terror of Nazism before fleeing to France. In her controversial analysis, she proposes that Eichmann demonstrated the existence of true evil in ordinary humans.

Eichmann in Jerusalem

Otto Adolf, son of Karl Adolf Eichmann and Maria née Schefferling, caught in a suburb of Buenos Aires on the evening of May 11, 1960, flown to Israel nine days later, brought to trial in the District Court in Jerusalem on April 11, 1961, stood accused on fifteen counts: "together with the others" he had committed crimes against the Jewish people, crimes against humanity, and war crimes during the whole period of the Nazi regime and especially during the period of the Second World War. The Nazis and Nazi Collaborators (Punishment) Law of 1950, under which he was tried, provides that "a person who has committed one of these ... offenses ... is liable to the death penalty." To each count Eichmann pleaded: "Not guilty in the sense of the indictment."

In what sense then did he think he was guilty? In the long cross-examination of the accused, according to him "the longest ever known," neither the defense nor the prosecution nor, finally, any of the three judges ever bothered to ask him this obvious question. His lawyer, Robert Servatius of Cologne, hired by Eichmann and paid by the Israeli government (following the precedent set at the Nuremberg Trials, where all attorneys for the defense were paid by the Tribunal of the victorious powers), answered the question in a press interview: "Eichmann feels guilty before God, not before the law," but this answer remained without confirmation from the accused himself. The defense would apparently have preferred him to plead not guilty on the grounds that under the then existing Nazi legal system he had not done anything wrong, that what he was accused of were not crimes but "acts of state," over which no other state has jurisdiction ("par in parem imperium non habet"), that it had been his duty to obey and that, in Servatius' words, he had committed acts "for which you are decorated if you win and go to the gallows if you lose." (Thus [Nazi propaganda leader Paul Joseph] Goebbels had declared in 1943: "We will go down in history as the greatest statesmen of all times or as their greatest criminals.") Outside Israel (at a meeting of the Catholic Academy in Bavaria, devoted to what the Rheinischer Merkur called the "ticklish problem" of the "possibilities and limits in the coping with historical and political guilt through criminal proceedings"), Servatius went a step farther, and declared that "the only legitimate criminal problem of the Eichmann trial lies in pro-

nouncing judgment against his Israeli captors, which so far has not been done"—a statement, incidentally, that is somewhat difficult to reconcile with his repeated and widely publicized utterances in Israel, in which he called the conduct of the trial "a great spiritual achievement," comparing it favorably with the Nuremberg Trials.

Eichmann's own attitude was different. First of all, the indictment for murder was wrong: "With the killing of Jews I had nothing to do. I never killed a Jew, or a non-Jew, for that matter—I never killed any human being. I never gave an order to kill either a Jew or a non-Jew; I just did not do it," or, as he was later to qualify this statement, "It so happened ... that I had not once to do it"—for he left no doubt that he would have killed his own father if he had received an order to that effect. Hence he repeated over and over (what he had already stated in the so-called Sassen documents, the interview that he had given in 1955 in Argentina to the Dutch journalist Sassen, a former S.S. man who was also a fugitive from justice, and that, after Eichmann's capture, had been published in part by Life in this country and by Der Stern in Germany) that he could be accused only of "aiding and abetting" the annihilation of the Jews, which he declared in Jerusalem to have been "one of the greatest crimes in the history of Humanity...."

Would he then have pleaded guilty if he had been indicted as an accessory to murder? Perhaps, but he would have made important qualifications. What he had done was a crime only in retrospect, and he had always been a law-abiding citizen, because Hitler's orders, which he had certainly executed to the best of his ability, had possessed "the force of law" in the Third Reich. (The defense could have quoted in support of Eichmann's thesis the testimony of one of the best-known experts on constitutional law in the Third Reich, Theodor Maunz, currently Minister of Education and Culture in Bavaria, who stated in 1943...: "The command of the Führer ... is the absolute center of the present legal order.") Those who today told Eichmann that he could have acted differently simply did not know, or had forgotten, how things had been. He did not want to be one of those who now pretended that "they had always been against it," whereas in fact they had been very eager to do what they were told to do. However, times *change, and he, like Professor Maunz, had "arrived at different insights." What he had done he had done, he did not want to deny it; rather, he proposed "to hang myself in public as a warning example for all anti-Semites on this earth." By this he did not mean to say that he regretted anything: "Repentance is for little children...."*

Even under considerable pressure from his lawyer, he did not change this position. In a discussion of [German Nazi leader and chief of police Heinrich] Himmler's offer in 1944 to exchange a million Jews for ten thousand trucks, and his own role in this plan, Eichmann was asked: "Mr. Witness, in the negotiations with your superiors, did you express any pity for the Jews and did you say there was room to help them?" And he replied: "I am here under oath and must speak the truth. Not out of mercy did I launch this transaction"—which would have been fine, except that it was not Eichmann who "launched" it. But he then continued, quite truthful: "My reasons I explained this morning," and they were as follows: Himmler had sent his own man to Budapest to deal with matters of Jewish emigration. (Which, incidentally, had become a flourishing business: for enormous amounts of money, Jews could buy their way out. Eichmann, however, did not mention this.) It was the fact that "here matters of emigration were dealt with by a man who did not belong to the Police Force" that made him indignant, "because I had to help and to implement deportation.... Matters of emigration, on which I considered myself an expert, were assigned to a man who was new to the unit.... I was fed up.... I decided that I had to do something to take matters of emigration into my own hands."

Throughout the trial, Eichmann tried to clarify, mostly without success, this second point in his plea of "not guilty in the sense of the indictment." The indictment implied not only that he had acted on purpose, which he did not deny, but out of base motives and in full knowledge of the criminal nature of his deeds. As for the base motives, he was perfectly sure that he was not what he called an "innerer Schweinehund," a dirty bastard in the depths of his heart; and as for his conscience, he remembered perfectly well that he would have had a bad conscience only if he had not done what he had been ordered to do—to ship millions of men, women, and children to their death with great zeal and the most meticulous care. This, admittedly, was hard to take. Half a dozen psychiatrists had certified him as "normal"—"More normal, at any rate, than I am after having examined him," one of them was said to have exclaimed, while anoth-

Journalists at the Eichmann trial, May 30, 1961. (USHMM Photo Archives)

er had found that his whole psychological outlook, his attitude toward his wife and children, mother and father, brothers, sisters, and friends, was "not only normal but most desirable"—and finally the minister who had paid regular visits to him in prison after the Supreme Court had finished hearing his appeal reassured everybody by declaring Eichmann to be "a man with very positive ideas." Behind the comedy of the soul experts lay the hard fact that his was obviously no case of moral let alone legal insanity. (Mr. Hausner's recent revelations in the Saturday Evening Post *of things he "could not bring out at the trial" have contradicted the information given informally in Jerusalem. Eichmann, we are now told, had been alleged by the psychiatrists to be "a man obsessed with a dangerous and insatiable urge to kill," "a perverted, sadistic personality." In which case he would have belonged in an insane asylum.) Worse, his was obviously also no case of insane hatred of Jews, of fanatical anti-Semitism or indoctrination of any kind. He "personally" never had anything whatever against Jews; on the contrary, he had plenty of "private reasons" for not being a Jew hater. To be sure, there were fanatic anti-Semites among his closest friends, for instance Lászlo Endre, State Secretary in Charge of Political (Jewish) Affairs in Hungary, who was hanged in Budapest in 1946; but this, according to Eichmann, was more or less in the spirit of "some of my best friends are anti-Semites."*

Alas, nobody believed him. The prosecutor did not believe him, because that was not his job. Coun-

sel for the defense paid no attention because he, unlike Eichmann, was, to all appearances, not interested in questions of conscience. And the judges did not believe him, because they were too good, and perhaps also too conscious of the very foundations of their profession, to admit that an average, "normal" person, neither feeble-minded nor indoctrinated nor cynical, could be perfectly incapable of telling right from wrong. They preferred to conclude from occasional lies that he was a liar—and missed the greatest moral and even legal challenge of the whole case. Their case rested on the assumption that the defendant, like all "normal persons," must have been aware of the criminal nature of his acts, and Eichmann was indeed normal insofar as he was "no exception within the Nazi regime." However, under the conditions of the Third Reich only "exceptions" could be expected to act "normally." This simple truth of the matter created a dilemma for the judges which they could neither resolve nor escape....

Eichmann, it will be remembered, had steadfastly insisted that he was guilty only of "aiding and abetting" in the commission of the crimes with which he was charged, that he himself had never committed an overt act. The judgment, to one's great relief, in a way recognized that the prosecution had not succeeded in proving him wrong on this point. For it was an important point; it touched upon the very essence of this crime, which was no ordinary crime, and the very nature of this criminal, who was no common criminal; by implication, it also took cognizance of the weird fact that in the death camps it was usually the inmates and the victims who had actually wielded "the fatal instrument with [their] own hands." What the judgment had to say on this point was more than correct, it was the truth: "Expressing his activities in terms of Section 23 of our Criminal Code Ordinance, we should say that they were mainly those of a person soliciting by giving counsel or advice to others and of one who enabled or aided others in [the criminal] act." But "in such an enormous and complicated crime as the one we are now considering, wherein many people participated, on various levels and in various modes of activity—the planners, the organizers, and those executing the deeds, according to their various ranks—there is not much point in using the ordinary concepts of counseling and soliciting to commit a crime. For these crimes were committed en masse, not only in regard to the number of victims, but also in regard to the numbers of those who perpetrated the crime.... The extent to which any one of the many criminals was close to or remote from the actual killer of the victim means nothing, as far as the measure of his responsibility is concerned. On the contrary, in general the degree of responsibility increases as we draw further away from the man who uses the fatal instrument with his own hands...."

What followed the reading of the judgment was routine. Once more, the prosecution rose to make a rather lengthy speech demanding the death penalty, which, in the absence of mitigating circumstances, was mandatory, and Dr. Servatius replied even more briefly than before: the accused had carried out "acts of state," what had happened to him might happen in the future to anyone, the whole civilized world faced this problem, Eichmann was "a scapegoat," whom the present German government had abandoned to the court in Jerusalem, contrary to international law, in order to clear itself of responsibility. The competence of the court, never recognized by Dr. Servatius, could be construed only as trying the accused "in a representative capacity, as representing the legal powers vested in [a German court]"—as, indeed, one German state prosecutor had formulated the task of Jerusalem. Dr. Servatius had argued earlier that the court must acquit the defendant because, according to the Argentine statute of limitations, he had ceased to be liable to criminal proceedings against him on May 7, 1960, "a very short time before the abduction"; he now argued, in the same vein, that no death penalty could be pronounced because capital punishment had been abolished unconditionally in Germany.

Then came Eichmann's last statement: His hopes for justice were disappointed; the court had not believed him, though he had always done his best to tell the truth. The court did not understand him: he had never been a Jew-hater, and he had never willed the murder of human beings. His guilt came from his obedience, and obedience is praised as a virtue. His virtue had been abused by the Nazi leaders. But he was not one of the ruling clique, he was a victim, and only the leaders deserved punishment. (He did not go quite as far as many of the other low-ranking war criminals, who complained bitterly that they had been told never to worry about "responsibilities," and that they were now unable to call those responsible to account because these had "escaped and deserted" them—by committing suicide, or by having been hanged.) "I am not the monster I am made out to be," Eichmann said. "I am the victim of a fallacy." He did not use the word "scapegoat," but he confirmed what Servatius had said: it was his "profound conviction that [he] must suffer for the acts of others." After two more days, on Friday, December 15, 1961, at nine o'clock in the morning, the death sentence was pronounced. (Arendt, pp. 21–27; 246–248)

Aftermath

Eichmann was found guilty of committing crimes against the Jewish people, crimes against humanity, and war crimes; his case was appealed to the Israeli Supreme Court. After the Supreme Court upheld the verdict of the lower court, Eichmann was hanged at midnight on May 31, 1962. His body was cremated and the ashes scattered in the Mediterranean Sea, outside the perimeter of Israeli territory. The Eichmann trial renewed worldwide interest in the atrocities committed at the hands of the Nazis. For many young adults, especially in Israel and Germany, the media coverage surrounding the trial sparked interest in the Holocaust, an event they had only heard about. "Nazi-hunter" Simon Wiesenthal, who helped track down Eichmann in Argentina, received widespread recognition, which in turn allowed him to continue and expand his searches with renewed vigor.

Arendt's book generated considerable controversy because she maintained that Eichmann was an ordinary man, not motivated by any special prejudices or hatreds. By merely following orders he acted in a manner that was socially accepted at the time. Other scholars have denounced this view, claiming Eichmann to be the personification of the inhumane Nazi ideology—someone who performed his responsibility of exterminating millions of Jewish people with enthusiasm and brutal efficiency.

SOURCES

Books

Arendt, Hannah, *Eichmann in Jerusalem*, Penguin (New York), 1994.

Ayer, Eleanor H., with Helen Waterford and Alfons Heck, *Parallel Journeys*, Atheneum (New York), 1995.

Berwick, Michael, *The Third Reich*, Putnam (New York), 1971.

PRIMARY SOURCE

Simon Wiesenthal
"The Knife"
Excerpt from *The Murderers among Us: The Simon Wiesenthal Memoirs*
Edited by Joseph Wechsberg
Published in 1967

Shortly after annexing Austria in 1938, Nazi leaders established the Mauthausen concentration camp near the town of Linz in upper Austria. During World War II the Nazis interned nearly 200,000 people at Mauthausen, where many worked as slave laborers at the nearby granite quarry. Estimates suggest about 120,000 inmates perished there—representing the highest percentage of victims among all the concentration camps in the Nazi system. On April 25, 1945, invading American and Soviet troops converged at Torgau on the Elbe River south of Berlin, effectively cutting off Mauthausen from Germany. American forces liberated the camp on May 5 and found masses of sick and dying people lying among the dead. The International Red Cross transferred thousands of the worst cases to hospitals in Germany, Switzerland, and Sweden. Despite the rescue efforts of the Red Cross and Allied forces, almost 3,000 of Mauthausen's prisoners died after liberation.

One of the prisoners liberated at Mauthausen was Simon Wiesenthal, a thirty-seven-year-old Jewish man from Buczacz, Poland. Nearly six feet tall but weighing less than 100 pounds, Wiesenthal had been assigned to the "death block," which housed prisoners who were unable to work and were therefore expected to die. He arrived at Mauthausen in February 1945, after barely surviving a long, difficult journey from the Buchenwald concentration

Simon Wiesenthal

Simon Wiesenthal was born in Buczacz, Galicia, in the Austro-Hungarian empire, then a portion of Poland and now the Ukraine. After Wiesenthal's father was killed in World War I (1914–1918), his mother took the family to Vienna, Austria, to escape anti-Jewish violence. The family returned to Buczacz later, enabling Wiesenthal to graduate from the local gymnasium (high school) in 1928. Quota restrictions for Jewish students prevented his admission to the Polytechnic Institute in Lvov, so he attended the Technical University of Prague and received a degree in architectural engineering in 1932. Wiesenthal married Cyla Mueller in 1936 and worked as an architect in Lvov, near Kraków, Poland. Shortly after taking control of Poland in 1939, the Soviets began harassing native Jews. Wiesenthal lost several family members and was forced to close his business, becoming a mechanic in a bedspring factory. Later he saved himself, his wife, and his mother from deportation by bribing a police commissar. When the Germans displaced the Russians in 1941, Wiesenthal and his wife were assigned to a forced labor camp and worked at Ostbahn Works, a railroad repair shop. Due to his wife's "Aryan" appearance, Wiesenthal was able to make a deal with the Polish underground that allowed her to escape the camp. She lived in Warsaw for two years and later worked as a forced laborer in the Rhineland under false identity papers. Wiesenthal escaped and hid successfully for nearly six months before being captured.

After being apprehended in June 1944, Wiesenthal was forced to march westward to Plaszów, then to Gross-Rosen, and on to Buchenwald. This "death march" ended in Mauthausen in upper Austria, with Wiesenthal barely alive. At the time of liberation on May 5, 1945, he weighed less than 100 pounds and could not walk.

At war's end, Wiesenthal dedicated his life to gathering and preparing evidence on Nazi criminals and the atrocities they committed. Since 1947 he and his researchers have brought more than 1,100 Nazi criminals to justice. As Wiesenthal was approaching his nineties, he continued his relentless search for war criminals. In addition to *The Murderers among Us,* Wiesenthal has published other books, including *I Hunted Eichmann.*

camp in Germany, which the Nazis had hastily evacuated to avoid the advancing Soviet Army. Of the 3,000 Buchenwald prisoners placed in open trucks for the journey from Germany to Austria, only 1,200 survived the exposure to the elements and lack of food and water. Another 180 died during the final four-mile march into the camp compound. Wiesenthal himself had fallen down during that relatively short trek due to exhaustion. One of the SS guards shot at him but missed, leaving his body in the snow to be retrieved by a collection truck sent out before the town's inhabitants awoke. During the night workers came upon Wiesenthal's seemingly lifeless body, assumed he was dead, and hoisted him on top of the corpses piled in the back of the truck. At the camp crematorium, prison workers noticed Wiesenthal was still alive and smuggled him into the barracks; he survived the three months until American forces took over the Mauthausen camp in May 1945.

During the four years he spent behind the barbed wire of various Nazi institutions, Wiesenthal promised himself that if he survived he would devote the rest of his life to being a "deputy for many people who are not alive." Shortly after his release he began working for the War Crimes section of the U.S. Army, which was stationed in Austria to track down members of the SS division of the Nazi party. Originally created as a special bodyguard unit for Adolf Hitler and other Nazi leaders, the SS became a symbol of terror as its members gained increasing power within the party. These black-shirted, black-booted men operated the extensive Nazi camp system. As an organization the SS was responsible for the deaths of eleven million people, including six million Jews, many of them children. Most perished at extermination camps but hundreds of thousands died at the concentration camps as well. Wiesenthal and others focused their efforts on finding fugitive SS members, rarely concerning themselves with the crimes committed by enlisted men in the Wehrmacht (German armed forces) or rank and file members of the Nazi party.

As a way to gather evidence against SS men after the war, Wiesenthal organized a network of correspondents at the various displaced-persons (DP) centers set up by the Western Allies to house refugees from the camps. More than 100,000 survivors lived temporarily in about 200 DP centers located in Germany and Austria. According to Wiesenthal's careful directions, correspondents gathered eyewitness reports of killings and torture, disregarding all secondhand accounts of such incidents. Wiesenthal obtained photographs of SS members and circulated copies to the refugee camps, since many inmates were never told their guards' names. He created an extensive cross-index system that allowed connections to be made between the locale of the crimes, the names of the criminals, and the names of witnesses. In 1947, after leaving the American service, Wiesenthal formed the Jewish Historical Documentation Center in Linz, Austria. His files were first used during preparations for the trials of Nazi war criminals at Nuremberg and later at an American military trial of SS men who had worked as guards at the Dachau concentration camp. In 1959, after fourteen years of investigative work, Wiesenthal helped track down Adolf Eichmann, the SS lieutenant colonel who organized the transports of Jews from all over Europe to the Nazi death camps located in Poland. After the defeat of Germany, many SS members and high-ranking Nazi officials, including Eichmann, went underground and relied on the secret organization Odessa to arrange for their escape to Buenos Aires, Argentina. Eichmann, who Wiesenthal traced to Argentina, was brought to Israel for trial, found guilty, and hanged in 1962.

After the Eichmann trial Wiesenthal accepted an offer to head a war victims' documentation center in Vienna. A year later, following disputes with the center's board, he started a separate organization called the Federation of Jewish Victims of the Nazi Regime. Wiesenthal and his wife had lost more than eighty family relatives during the Holocaust, and he remained committed to seeking justice in the cases of those who escaped punishment after World War II. In the following excerpt from *The Murderers among Us,* Wiesenthal describes the painstaking and difficult challenges involved in the conviction of war criminals. Perhaps one of the most difficult obstacles is time—as the years passed, many Jewish people simply wished to put the horrors of the Nazi regime behind them. An example is the case of Fritz Murer, who was tried in Graz, Austria, in 1963. As part of an SS detail, Murer had worked at the Vilna ghetto located in what is today Lithuania. ("Vilna" is referred to as "Wilna" in Wiesenthal's account below.) Since evidence collected immediately after the war was not allowed to be used in court, testimony against Murer had to be recollected from current sources. This requirement severely limited the prosecution's case, which could rely only on survivors' recollections of events that took place in the Vilna ghetto twenty years earlier.

The Murderers among Us:
The Simon Wiesenthal Memoirs
"The Knife"

The trial by jury against Murer opened in Graz on June 10, 1963. The indictment charged him with having committed "murder by his own hands" in fifteen specific cases; later the public prosecutor added two more cases. Over a dozen witnesses had arrived from Germany, Israel, and the United States. One of the most important witnesses for the prosecution was

Jacob Brodi, before whose own eyes Murer had shot his son Daniel at the exit of the Wilna ghetto. Brodi was now sixty-eight. After the war he had emigrated to America, and he now lived alone on a small isolated farm in New Jersey. He was a lonely man. He didn't want to see people, led a simple life, and had refused to accept the German restitution money to which he was entitled. Twenty years had gone by since the day he had seen his boy killed by Murer, but the passage of time had not helped Brodi to forget. Every day and almost every night he saw the scene at the entrance to the Wilna ghetto.

When I first wrote to ask him to come to Graz to testify, he flatly refused. He explained he couldn't bear the thought of facing the murderer. I wrote him several letters. I said we owed it to our dead to tell the living what had happened. Die Zeit, a respected German weekly, had just protested "against the new wave of distrust" and defended the new generation, "which knows Nazi crimes only from history books." The apologists were working overtime. I explained to Brodi that his silence would no longer help his boy, but it might help to save boys of Daniel Brodi's age who knew these crimes only from the history books. A courtroom with a jury, a judge, a prosecutor would make the defendant look real, not like a character out of a history book, certainly not like a hero. There was no answer. I didn't expect to hear from Brodi again. The day before the trial he sent me a cable. He would take a plane and would be there in time.

Four days later I met Jacob Brodi in his room at the Hotel Sonne in Graz, where all witnesses had been put up. He was a tired man with white hair and deep circles around his eyes. With his sunburned, wrinkled face, he looked more like an American farmer from the Middle West than like a refugee from the Wilna ghetto. I told him I was glad he had come. He would be a key witness. His testimony couldn't fail to sway the jury. The trial was not going well, from the prosecution's point of view. After four days, Murer still cynically denied everything. One witness after the other had stepped forward and identified him, but Murer said they were making a mistake; they were taking him for somebody else. He had never so much as touched a Jew. He had never seen a dead Jew. He was innocent, victim of a monstrous error.

Now Brodi said to me: "I hear that Murer's two sons sit in the front row of the courtroom with his wife and sneer at the witnesses."

I nodded. The boys thought this was a great show. They laughed and grimaced. Two foreign newspapermen who covered the trial were so shocked that they asked the presiding judge why he failed to call the boys to order. He told the correspondents that he hadn't seen the boys.

Brodi said quietly : "They'll stop sneering when I am called to the stand." He looked at me piercingly and said: "I didn't come here to testify, I came to act."

He opened his waistcoat and pulled out a long knife. Brodi spoke without emotion, a man who had made up his mind. "I was able to obtain a plan of the courtroom. I know that the witness stand is close to where Murer sits. Murer killed my child before my eyes. Now I'm going to kill him with this knife before the eyes of his wife and children."

I could see that he was deadly serious. He said he'd thought about it for the past twenty years. He no longer believed in human justice, he said. He had lost faith in God's justice. He would take justice into his own hands. He was not afraid of the consequences. His life was finished anyway. It had been finished that day in the ghetto twenty years ago.

I said: "If you try to kill Murer, you will be treated like a murderer yourself."

"Yes. But great lawyers will come to my defense."

"That's beside the point. No matter what your motives are, the world will call you a murderer. The Nazis are just waiting for such a thing to happen. They will say: 'Look at these Jews who always talk so much about justice. They accuse Murer of murder, and they are murderers themselves. So Murer killed Jews, and a Jew killed him. What's different about that?' That's the way they will argue."

Brodi gave a shrug, unconvinced.

"Think of Eichmann," I said. "He could have been executed without a trace in Argentina. But the Israelis knew it was necessary to drag him across the ocean and risk antagonizing world opinion and being accused of violating international law. Why? Because Eichmann had to be tried. The trial was more important than the defendant. Eichmann was already a dead man when he entered the courtroom. But the trial would convince millions of people—those who knew nothing, or who did not want to know, or those who knew deep in their hearts but wouldn't admit it even to themselves. All of them saw the seedy, bald man in the glass box who had engineered the 'final solution'—the killing of six million people. They heard the evidence, they read the newspapers, they saw the pictures. And at long last they knew not only that it was true but that it was much worse than anyone could imagine."

Brodi shook his head. "I am not here for the State of Israel. I am not here for the Jewish people. I came here as the father of my murdered child." He stared at me out of hard, pitiless eyes. I wished desperately that he had been able to cry. But perhaps he couldn't cry any more.

I said: "If you try to harm Murer, all our work will have become useless. We cannot achieve our purpose by using their methods.

You've read the Bible, Jacob Brodi. You know the Commandment: 'Thou shalt not kill.' I want Murer, not you, to leave the courtroom as a convicted murderer."

He shook his head.

"Words, Mr. Wiesenthal, nothing but words. It's so easy for you. Your child was not murdered. My boy was murdered. I told you I did not want to come. You said it was necessary. Well, I am here now. And you know why I came."

I turned away. I couldn't bear the expression in his eyes. I talked for a long time, although I do not remember exactly what I said. I talked about myself: Why I had decided to do what I had done for the past twenty years—because someone had to do it, for our children and for their children—but not out of hatred.

"I still cry sometimes, Mr. Brodi, when I hear what happened to children in the concentration camps," I said. "I did cry when I heard about your boy. Because he could have been my boy. Your child was also my child. Do you really believe I could go on with my work if I didn't feel that way?"

I grasped his shoulders. Suddenly Jacob Brodi put his head on my shoulder. I felt a convulsion go through his body. He cried. We stood there for a while, without saying a word. When I left his room a few minutes later, I carried his knife with me.

Jacob Brodi was called to the stand the following day. He never glanced at Murer. He told his experience in a toneless voice, as though it had happened to someone else. It was very quiet in the courtroom. Even Murer's boys sensed what this lonely man went through during his testimony. They didn't sneer at him. The defense didn't want to question Brodi. He was dismissed. After he left the courtroom, Murer got up and once more said that the witness must have been mistaken. Murer had not shot the boy. Maybe it was someone else.

The trial lasted a week. Foreign journalists sensed that the mood in the courtroom was definitely in favor of the defendant. Some jurors, dressed in the traditional green loden costumes, watched Murer with unconcealed sympathy. Some tried to follow the proceedings fairly, but they seemed to be in the minority. The leading paper in Graz supported the arguments of Murer's defense attorneys. He was said to have received many sympathetic letters from political friends.

The audience was pleased when the defense succeeded in confusing one witness. He became carried away by emotion as he told the court what had happened and mixed up a detail. Another witness was not certain about a date. He described one of Murer's crimes, and then Murer proved conclusively that he had not been in Wilna at that time. Naturally, the testimony of these people was discredited.

Among the witnesses for the defense was Martin Weiss, Murer's former assistant in the ghetto. Weiss had been brought to Graz from Straubing prison in Bavaria, where he was serving a life sentence for mass murder. When Weiss pointed out that "some Lithuanian officers wore uniforms similar to Murer's," there was a satisfied murmur among the audience.

The testimony of the witnesses for the prosecution was received with icy silence. (I was called "manhunter" by Murer's lawyer.) Israel Sebulski, now living in Munich, told the court that his fifteen-year-old son had been mercilessly beaten by Murer, and as a result had lost his mind and the use of his legs and was now in an institution. Mrs. Tova Rajzman of Tel Aviv swore that Murer had shot her sister because she had taken a piece of bread from a Polish woman. In his rage, she said, he had later killed three other women and a man who happened to be standing nearby. As Mrs. Rajzman recalled the scene, she was overcome by the memory and began to scream.

"Don't scream in the courtroom!" said Hofrat Dr. Peyer, the presiding judge.

"Forgive me, Your Honor," said Mrs. Rajzman. "But it was terrible. My sister's blood spilled over my feet."

"Couldn't it have been somebody else who did it?"

"No, Your Honor. It was Murer. I remember him from the time he first came into the ghetto. He beat me in the street. When he walked through the ghetto, everybody had to step down from the pavement, and then had to bow and take off their hats."

Dr. Schumann, the prosecutor, had prepared himself thoroughly for his task. He had studied Murer's files in Frankfurt and Munich. In his summing up speech, he pointed out that the witnesses had identified Murer beyond any doubt. He appealed to the jury to pass judgment on the defendant as they would on the murderer of their own children.

"In at least six cases there is no reasonable doubt about the defendant's guilt," said the prosecutor. "I want you to know that this trial has already badly hurt the illusion of us Austrians being a Kulturvolk."

After four hours, the jury returned a verdict of "not guilty." In Austria, the exact count of the jury votes is announced in the courtroom. The foreman of the jury said that in two of the seventeen cases there had been a tie of four to four. He had cast his ballot in favor of Murer.

I was not in Graz that day. Reporters later told me that the people in the courtroom had cheered and applauded when Murer's acquittal was announced. Some had brought in flowers while the jury was still deliberating. Now they rushed up to Murer with the bouquets.

An American diplomat who visited friends in Graz the following day and wanted to send flowers to his hostess was told in three florist shops that there was nothing left. Everything had been bought up for the trial. Murer left the courtroom a triumphant hero. He was seen being driven off in the Mercedes of Rudolph Hochreiner, a Nazi who had been indicted for the murder of nine Jews and had been acquitted.

There was a storm of indignation throughout Austria. With few exceptions, the Austrian press is anti-Nazi and democratic. Newspapers representing nearly all political groups denounced the verdict as Justizskandal, a travesty of justice. In Vienna, Catholic students pinned yellow stars on their chests and marched in protest through the streets, shouting "Murer is a murderer! Murer must be punished!" Afterward they attended a service of penitence in Michaeler Church to express remorse for the crimes committed by Christians against Jews.

The prosecutor appealed the verdict. Austria's Supreme Court has granted an appeal with respect to one charge: a case I had discovered in which Murer had been seen committing a murder by two different witnesses. The witnesses knew nothing of each other, now live in different parts of the world, but described the same scheme independently. Murer will be tried once more. Justice may still prevail.

I met Jacob Brodi in the lobby of a Vienna hotel a few days after Murer's acquittal. He looked through me as if I hadn't been there. I understood. I may have saved Murer's life. It is not a very pleasant thought, but there was nothing else I could have done. (Wiesenthal, pp. 70—77)

Aftermath

Wiesenthal has continued tracking down Nazis through painstaking investigative work. When he has evidence against a war criminal, but does not receive cooperation from the authorities, he reveals his information to the press. Experience has taught him that public outrage is a powerful weapon for bringing criminals to justice. Wiesenthal is relentless in his search. For example, some 6,000 SS men worked at Auschwitz, but only 900 are known by name. Wiesenthal determined the current names and addresses for one-third of this group. In 1963 he identified Gestapo officer Karl Silberbauer, who arrested Anne Frank and her family in Amsterdam, Holland. Silberbauer had returned to Austria after the war and resumed his post at the Vienna police department. Since 1947, when Wiesenthal began his work, he and his researchers have brought more than 1,100 Nazi war criminals to trial, often placing his own life in danger. In 1965 the neo-Nazi World Union of National Socialists offered $120,000 for his death.

Due to his neighbors' concerns for their safety, he moved the Documentation Center from his apartment in Vienna to another building a block away. Nearly two decades later a bomb planted by neo-Nazis destroyed his home in Vienna. He continued to pursue his quest for justice in spite of repeated death threats and hate mail.

Wiesenthal has received many honors and awards, including the U.S. Presidential Medal of Freedom from President Bill Clinton on August 9, 2000. Other awards include the U.S. Congressional Medal of Honor, the Dutch and Luxembourg Medals of Freedom, the United Nations Diploma of Honor, and the French Legion of Honor. He was also decorated by the Austrian and French resistance movements and nominated for the Nobel Peace Prize on two occasions. Wiesenthal lives in Vienna with his wife, where he continues to answer letters and study books and files.

In 1977 the Simon Wiesenthal Center was established in Los Angeles, California. Named in honor of Wiesenthal, the center offers a national outreach program providing education for junior and senior high school students. As part of its commitment to focus on political issues related to the Holocaust, the center campaigned to cancel the statute of limitations on war crimes in West Germany and to force South American governments to surrender Nazi criminals. The center's educational services have produced award-winning films, books, publications, and exhibitions, including the 1982 film *Genocide,* which won an Academy Award for best documentary. The Simon Wiesenthal Center has offices in Israel, France, and Canada. In the 1970s Wiesenthal was the inspiration for two popular novels, which were both adapted to film: Author Ira Levin patterned the character of Jakov Liebermann in *The Boys from Brazil* after Wiesenthal. In the 1978 movie version of Levin's novel, Sir Laurence Olivier played the role and received an Oscar nomination for his performance. Wiesenthal is also portrayed in Frederick Forsyth's novel *The Odessa File.* In the 1974 film version, Israeli actor Shmeul Rodonsky plays Wiesenthal.

SOURCE

Books

Friedman, Carl, *Nightfather: A Novel,* Persea Books (New York), 1994.

Noble, Iris, *Nazi Hunter: Simon Wiesenthal,* J. Messner (New York), 1979.

Rochman, Hazel, and Darlene McCampbell, *Bearing Witness: Stories of the Holocaust,* Orchard Books (New York), 1995.

Wiesenthal, Simon, *The Murderers among Us: The Simon Wiesenthal Memoirs,* edited by Joseph Wechsberg, McGraw Hill (New York), 1967.

Remembering the Holocaust

Much time has passed since the liberation of the Nazi death camps, yet the Holocaust has not been forgotten. Worldwide revulsion at the genocidal policies of Nazi Germany has led to the passage of international laws and regulations protecting human rights. The Holocaust has become an integral part of Western culture, as the experiences of Jews under the Nazi regime have been documented and portrayed in art, literature, music, and film. During the late twentieth century, museums and research centers were established in the United States and Europe to commemorate and promote awareness of the Holocaust.

Germany and the Past

The Holocaust had a profound impact on Germany. When West Germany was formed from the American, British, and French occupation zones after World War II, the new constitution reflected an awareness of the past. The Nazi party and Nazi flags, insignia, and uniforms were banned by law. Spreading hatred against a particular religion or nationality, either in writing or in speeches, was considered a crime. Denial of the existence of the Holocaust was also declared a crime. The laws restricted freedom of speech, a right usually protected in a democratic society, but West German leaders believed these limitations were warranted

because of Germany's Nazi history. In addition, constitutional restrictions were placed on the German army, which was banned from serving outside its own borders.

Beginning in 1953, the West German government paid reparations totaling $58 billion to Holocaust victims as acknowledgment that the nation bore responsibility for the acts perpetrated by the Nazis. People were compensated for time they spent in confinement, for injuries and damaged health, and for loss of earnings. Until 2000, the German government refused to provide similar compensation to those who were forced into slave labor during the Nazi regime. In July 2000, prompted in large part by the threat of more than fifty class action lawsuits filed in U.S. federal courts, Germany finally agreed to establish a $5 billion foundation for these victims. The funds also allow for compensation to victims of Nazi medical experiments. The foundation is funded by both the German government and German industry. The German government has continued to pay pensions and other benefits to former government workers, police, and members of the armed forces who served under the Third Reich.

Although the German government accepted responsibility for the Holocaust, a national silence generally surrounded the subject after the war. Beginning in the early 1950s and continuing for a generation, most Germans refused to discuss the

In an effort to honor those killed by the Nazis during the Holocaust, a number of U.S. cities have created memorial museums. In Houston, Texas, the design of this museum caused a stir because it resembles the smoke stack of a crematorium. (Reproduced by permission of Kathleen J. Edgar)

Hitler era. Eventually, questions began to arise about the role of individual Germans during the war. How many ordinary people had supported Hitler? Had anyone tried to oppose Nazi policies? How many soldiers had participated in rounding up Jews? After the war Germans focused their attention on strengthening the economy and rebuilding bombed-out cities. Within a few decades West Germany was one of the most prosperous countries in the world, yet the questions did not go away. When Germans finally began talking about the Holocaust, most denied that they had known about the extermination of Jews. It is possible that the general population was unaware of the *Endlösung* ("Final Solution"), which the Nazis succeeded in keeping secret as long as they could. Nevertheless, the early actions of the Nazis, such as the anti-Jewish laws, occurred openly at all levels of German society. Average citizens knew that Jews were being persecuted and fired from their jobs. People watched as Jewish shops were destroyed and Jewish children were expelled from German schools. They knew that Jews were beaten in public, arrested simply for being Jewish, and

forced to flee the country. They were aware that Nazi leaders blamed Jews for "forcing" Germany into the war, and that they publicly threatened to destroy them. For more than a decade, German citizens heard Jews referred to as "sub-human" by Nazi leaders, who also compared Jews to dangerous germs requiring extermination.

As a nation, Germany had adopted a code of silence. Consequently, the generation born after the war knew little or nothing about their parents' activities, and were told even less about the Nazi era. The silence was broken in 1979 by *The Holocaust,* an American television miniseries that was broadcast in West Germany. This fictional drama portrayed the lives of both a German Jewish family that suffered under the Nazis and non-Jews who supported Hitler. When the program was originally shown in the United States, it received generally positive reviews, although many critics labeled it a soap opera. Yet the series became tremendously popular in Germany. The whole country seemed to have watched it, and *The Holocaust* instantly became a major topic of conversation. The role of

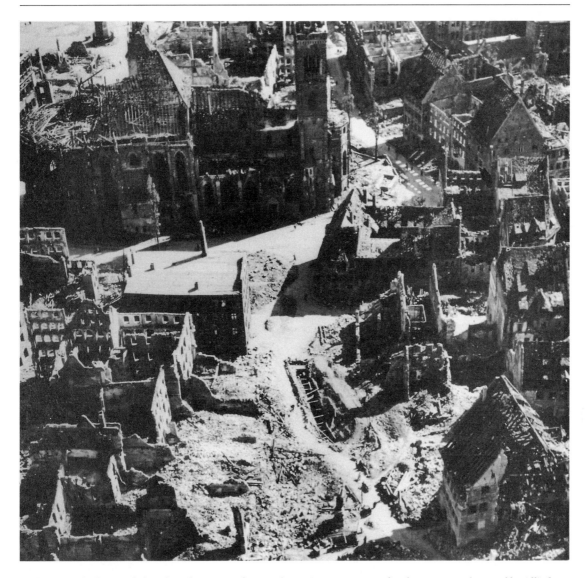

A close-up of a damaged church in the center of Nuremberg, Germany. Its roof and tower were shattered by Allied bombing during World War II. After the war, many Germans worked hard to make West Germany one of the world's most prosperous countries. (Reproduced by permission of AP/Wide World Photos)

the German nation during the Nazi era was analyzed and argued by historians and novelists, teachers and students, and political leaders. More recently, Richard von Weizäcker, the former President of Germany, spoke of the nation's shame and the need to remember the inhumanity of the country's Nazi past in order to prevent it from happening again. Von Weizäcker's views were made more relevant by his own family history. His father, Ernst von Weizäcker, although never a Nazi, had been a high-ranking diplomat under Hitler and was sentenced to five years in prison in the Ministries Case at the Nuremberg trials. Since 1996, Germany has observed January 27, the anniversary of the liberation of Auschwitz, as an official Remembrance Day.

Younger Germans remained committed to learning about their country's past, especially after the publication of *Hitler's Willing Executioners* (1996), a book by American historian Daniel Goldhagen. This highly controversial work argues that ordinary Germans willingly took part in the "Final Solution" because the nation had long subscribed to an extreme form of anti-Semitism that Goldhagen calls "eliminationist anti-Semitism." Many other historians and scholars, both in Germany and elsewhere, strongly disagree with Goldhagen. Although they do not believe that Hitler succeeded simply because most Germans shared his anti-Semitic views, they contend that the average German would not have willingly participated

Holocaust Denial

Some people, in Germany and elsewhere, claim that the Holocaust never occurred or at least that the number of victims has been greatly exaggerated. They contend there is no evidence for the existence of gas chambers and that the Nazis never planned and carried out the "Final Solution." Nonetheless, documents confiscated at the end of the war confirm the facts, as do photographs, films, and testimony from thousands of witnesses. These witnesses include survivors, Allied soldiers who liberated the death camps and concentration camps, and Germans, including many Nazis who described both the planning and the actual killing of Jews. In fact, Nazi leaders tried at Nuremberg neither denied the evidence that was presented nor questioned the validity of documents. Their defense was that they themselves were not responsible. (These trial transcripts are available.) Adolf Eichmann, at his trial in Israel, confirmed every basic fact. (Transcripts and videotapes of Eichmann's testimony also exist.) In almost all cases, the people who deny the Holocaust also accept the Nazis' ideology, especially their hatred of Jews. They maintain that all the evidence has been invented by a vast conspiracy perpetrated by the Jews. Like the Nazis, they believe that Jews control the world.

Many people fear that the constant repetition of ideas like those associated with Holocaust denial will make such beliefs more acceptable—just as Nazi leader Adolf Hitler's constantly repeated "big lies" were believed. New means of communication, such as the Internet, enable these lies to reach people who have no way of verifying their truthfulness or their source. The best defense against such lies is knowledge and education.

directly in the mass murder of Jews. As controversy swirled around *Hitler's Willing Executioners,* Goldhagen toured Germany, giving lectures and participating in debates before large audiences. Although his opponents offered convincing counter arguments, it soon became clear that Germans, especially young people, agreed with him.

Throughout the 1990s, small groups of German youths contributed to the rise of neo-Nazism. Skinheads attacked foreign-born people, especially Turks, living and working in Germany. Skinheads—so named because of their close-shaven heads—are members of white-supremacist gangs who often claim to be neo-Nazis. Many use the stiff-armed "Heil Hitler" salute, wear swastikas, and read Nazi literature. The attacks occurred with greatest frequency in what was once Communist East Germany. Reunification of East and West Germany precipitated many social problems, including unemployment, which was especially high among young people in East Germany. Some observers believed that skinheads, who wanted to demonstrate their dissatisfaction with the world, were essentially harmless and had chosen Nazi insignia and rhetoric as symbols of the most extreme rebellion then possible in Germany. Critics were more alarmed, warning that the Nazi party was also once a tiny group that was not taken seriously.

Israel and the Holocaust

The State of Israel was founded in Palestine in 1948 in accordance with the Zionists' goal to create a modern Jewish state in their ancestral homeland. Throughout the twentieth century Zionists had argued that Jews could not successfully assimilate into other societies and that they needed their own self-governing country in order to be secure and free. Until World War II, Zionism remained a minority view among European Jews, most of whom believed that they could be part of mainstream society, that prejudice against Jews was diminishing, and that in time they would be treated like anyone else. For instance, most Dutch, French, and German Jews thought of themselves as

Many Jews, like this man in a synagogue, believed that the only way for Jews to reach salvation and peace was by strictly following religious traditions. (Reproduced by permission of Bildarchiv Preussischer Kulturbesitz)

citizens of their respective countries who also happened to be Jewish. In the large communities of eastern Europe, many Jews were committed to the creation of a new society in which all people were treated equally, regardless of ethnic background. Thousands joined the Bund, the General Jewish Workers Union, and other socialist organizations. They believed that workers, both Jewish and non-Jewish, would unite to form this new society and that religion would disappear as people became more enlightened. Other eastern European Jews rejected assimilation, anti-religious socialism, and Zionism. These religious Jews wanted to lead lives centered on their own religion, in their own communities, following Jewish tradition and studying Jewish law. They felt that the safety and well-being of the Jews depended on obeying God, not on political movements. According to their view, the return of the Jewish people to Zion, or Israel, could take place only when they were worthy and God guided them to the new land.

Prior to World War II, European Jews had lived in complex, diverse communities, but that world disappeared with the Holocaust. In 1945 the surviving European Jews emerged from hiding places and from concentration camps and set about

rebuilding their lives. A few were able to return to their communities, especially in western Europe, yet hundreds of thousands had no communities. Their families, neighbors, and friends had been either killed or deported, and their synagogues destroyed. Their houses, if still standing, had often been taken over by non-Jews who remained anti-Semitic. A quarter million Jews were living in "displaced persons" camps, sometimes in the same locations where the Nazis had imprisoned them in the concentration camps. For these people, the establishment of a Jewish homeland was their only hope for a better life.

Perhaps Israel would have been created if there had been no Holocaust, but the prospect of a Jewish homeland became particularly urgent after the war. The suffering of the Jews had a powerful effect on people around the world, and non-Jews in America and throughout Europe supported the founding of Israel as a home for the survivors of the Holocaust. Even for Jews who had not been Zionists prior to the war, a separate nation was, they believed, the only way of ensuring that they would never be the victims of another Holocaust. In fact, the history of Israel has been shaped by the experience of the Holocaust. Many Israelis credit

A child lights a Hanukkah menorah during a 1945 holiday celebration in the Zeilsheim displaced persons camp in Germany. Hanukkah commemorates the rededication of the Temple of Jerusalem in 165 B.C. (Photograph by E.M. Robinson, courtesy of the Alice Lev Collection/USHMM Photo Archives)

their country for creating a new generation of Jews—people who will never allow themselves to be victims without fighting back. Especially after the trial of Adolf Eichmann in Israel in 1961, the Holocaust became a part of Israeli life. Each year, on the anniversary of the Warsaw ghetto uprising, Israel officially observes Holocaust Remembrance Day. The entire nation stops for a minute of silence, announced by sirens. Public ceremonies are held to remember the victims and to commemorate the resistance. In classrooms, schoolchildren discuss the meaning of the Holocaust, and a ceremony is held at Yad Vashem, the Holocaust memorial in Jerusalem.

France: Responsibility and Apologies

Citizens of many of countries in Europe continue to be haunted by the experience of the Nazi occupation and their role in the Holocaust. In 1995 French President Jacques Chirac acknowledged responsibility for French actions during the

Holocaust. Until that time, however, the French had maintained that the wartime Vichy government, which had cooperated with the Nazi occupiers, did not represent France. The "real France," they said, had nothing to apologize for because it was represented by the Resistance and by those who continued to fight the Germans from outside France. Then in 1989 a Frenchman named Paul Touvier was tried for his role in helping the Germans kill Jews. A decade later Maurice Papon, an official of the French government during the war, was brought to trial on similar charges, found guilty, and sentenced to ten years in prison. In 1997, shortly before Papon's trial began, the largest union representing the French police issued an apology for the significant part the police had played in rounding up Jews throughout France on behalf of the Nazis.

The role of the Catholic church during the Holocaust has been a subject of intense controversy in France. Some priests and bishops publicly opposed attacks on the Jews. For instance, Jules-

Gérard Saliège, archbishop of the city of Toulouse, told Catholics, "Jews are our brothers. No Christian dare forget that." Priests, nuns, and monks hid and protected Jews, especially the children of parents who had been deported, at great risk to themselves. The leader of the French church, Cardinal Pierre Gerlier, urged Catholics to refuse to surrender Jewish children to the Germans. For many years these events were emphasized by supporters of the church, but they represented only a portion of the truth. In September 1997 a ceremony was held at Drancy, the Paris suburb that had been the main transit point for Jews deported from France to Auschwitz. During the ceremony, Catholic officials publicly recognized the failures of the church during the Holocaust. They apologized for the "constantly repeated anti-Jewish stereotypes" that it had spread, acknowledging that these stereotypes were, at least indirectly, a factor "in the historical process that led to the Holocaust."

The Catholic church also apologized for its silence, especially the failure to protest the anti-Jewish laws passed by the French government during the war. "In the face of the persecution of Jews … silence was the rule, and words in favor of victims the exception," the statement held. "The vast majority of church officials" went along with the government's policies. They "did not realize that they had considerable power and influence." Protests from the French church might have set off many other protests, the statement continued. This public opposition could have helped create "a barrier" against the Holocaust. "Today we confess that silence was a wrong. We beg for the pardon of God and ask the Jewish people to hear our words of repentance."

Switzerland: Banks, Gold, and the Holocaust

Switzerland, which borders Germany, remained neutral throughout the duration of World War II. Although Switzerland had traditionally protected refugees escaping persecution in other countries, its record in regard to Jews fleeing the Nazis was mixed at best. Many European Jews, especially those from Germany and Austria, opened Swiss bank accounts in an attempt to protect their money from Nazi authorities. Because Switzerland was traditionally neutral, people felt confident that their money would be available even if their own country was at war. Switzerland was also a stable nation. Political turmoil that

Maurice Papon (Reproduced by permission of AP/Wide World Photos)

might threaten banks in other countries, and which was a serious concern in the first half of the twentieth century, was highly unlikely to affect Swiss banks. Moreover, Swiss bankers had a reputation for honesty, and Swiss law allowed foreigners to have secret bank accounts, often identified only by a number. This meant it would be difficult for the Nazis to trace and seize money.

After the war, many Jews who had established Swiss bank accounts were dead, their financial records oftentimes destroyed. Others, however, had escaped to non-European countries such as the United States or had survived the Holocaust and remained in Europe. In many cases the families of victims were still alive. When these people tried to obtain information concerning Swiss bank accounts that they or their relatives had opened, they rarely had any success; for years the Swiss claimed that they had found, and returned, all accounts held by Holocaust victims. These disputes continued into the 1990s. After considerable publicity and worldwide protests, the banks began a new search of their records and discovered thousands of unclaimed foreign accounts dating to the Nazi period. In 1997 the Swiss issued lists of names on these accounts, along with the banks where they were opened, which were published in newspapers throughout the world. Swiss officials said that most

A Warsaw street with Jewish shops before Germany's invasion of Poland in 1939. Warsaw and other Polish cities were centers of Jewish life in Europe before World War II. (Reproduced by permission of Bildarchiv Preussischer Kulturbesitz)

of the accounts were quite small and many clearly had no connection to Holocaust victims. Switzerland was severely criticized for not having located the accounts decades earlier and for making no effort to contact the rightful owners. (The banks were supposed to have searched for account-holders immediately after the war.) Some newspaper reporters were able to find a few of the people, or at least their closest living relatives, by using the lists to look up names in telephone directories.

Stolen Nazi gold deposited into Swiss accounts during the war also became an embarrassment to Switzerland. According to estimates, from 1933 to 1945 the Nazi government stole at least $8.5 billion worth of gold bars from the central banks of countries occupied by Germany during the war. Known as "monetary gold," some of the gold was the property of those countries, which they held to support paper currency. Nazi Germany is known to have deposited most of it in Swiss banks during the war. Sometimes the gold bars were still stamped with the name of the country from which they had been

taken, a conclusive indication that the money was stolen. Yet only a portion of the gold was returned by the Swiss banks immediately after the war. The Nazis also looted privately owned gold from homes and businesses. (It was common for Europeans to try to keep some of their assets, including jewelry, in gold because they were afraid that paper money could lose value in times of turmoil.)

Of the $8.5 billion worth of stolen gold, almost one-third is now believed to have been taken from private owners, many of whom were Jews. A 1997 study by the World Jewish Congress estimated that 85 percent of this private gold ended up in Swiss banks, often in the form of gold coins or gold bars held by businesses. Other gold came from jewelry, including wedding rings, that the Nazis confiscated from arrested or deported Jews. Some of the gold consisted of melted-down fillings taken from the teeth of the dead at Auschwitz and the other death camps. Gold bars stamped with the Nazi swastika that lay in the vaults of Swiss banks for fifty years were thus the last physical traces of murdered Jews.

Poland: Anti-Semitism Without Jews

In Poland, where Jews comprised nearly one-tenth of the population before the war, the near-total destruction of the Jewish community drastically changed Polish cultural and artistic life. The population of Warsaw had been almost one-third Jewish; Yiddish, the everyday language of Polish Jews, had been heard on its streets for centuries. Yiddish theater, Jewish shops and restaurants, community and cultural institutions, political parties, and religious schools had made Warsaw and the other cities of Poland the center of Jewish life in Europe. At the end of the war there were only 200,000 Jews left in the country, out of a pre-war population of 3.3 million. Although the Poles had cooperated less with the Nazis than any other occupied European nation, this did not mean they had been friendly to the Jews. While many Jews were saved by their non-Jewish neighbors, other Poles informed the Nazis of the whereabouts of Jews in hiding. The anti-Semitism that had existed in Poland for centuries did not disappear with the Nazi occupation or after the truth of the Holocaust became public knowledge. Even after a majority of Polish Jews fell prey to the Third Reich, anti-Semitism survived in Poland.

In July 1946, more than a year after the surrender of Germany, a Polish mob attacked Jews in the town of Kielce, committing the first post-war

A group of child survivors from the Bergen-Belsen concentration camp arrives in Tel Aviv, Israel, in 1948. After the Holocaust, many Jews believed the only way to prevent another Holocaust was to establish a Jewish nation. (USHMM Photo Archives)

pogrom. The Jews of Kielce who had managed to escape to Soviet territory during the war, thereby avoiding the Nazi cleansing of the town, had only recently returned. (Those Jews who had remained in Kielce during the war had all been killed by the Nazis.) A rumor had been spreading that Jews kidnapped Christian children to use their blood in Jewish rituals. These were the same false accusations, known as the "blood libel," that had been made against Jews since the Middle Ages. The pogrom killed forty-two people, including children. Recent investigations have indicated that the pogrom may have been deliberately stirred up as part of complicated rivalries among Polish political groups. The Kielce pogrom had a devastating

effect on Polish Jews. Since the "blood libel" rumor had been sufficient to send a mob on a murderous rampage, Jews realized there was no place for them in Poland. Approximately 100,000 left the country, many for Palestine, others for the United States.

In the next four decades, the remaining Jews in Poland continued to face periodic anti-Semitic campaigns started by different factions of the new Communist government for political purposes. Although there were no more pogroms, Jews were accused of disloyalty to Poland and forced out of jobs, causing them to either leave the country or conceal their identity. Few Jews were living in Poland after the end of the Communist regime.

In 1998 the Vatican issued a 14-page apology for maintaining its silence during the Holocaust. Pope John Paul II lived in Poland in that era. (Reproduced by permission of AP/Wide World Photos)

Political candidates of Jewish background were sometimes attacked for not being truly Polish. Near the end of the twentieth century, there was a revival of interest in the history of the Jews in Poland, as many Poles seemed to come to terms with the centuries-old history of Jewish life in Poland. Ironically there were very few Jews left in Poland to witness this focus on their contribution to Polish history.

The Holocaust and the Catholic Church

The Holocaust has led to a greater awareness of the sometimes deadly results of anti-Semitism and other forms of racism. Many countries and institutions that were not directly involved in Nazi activities have been forced to reconsider the way they have dealt with Jews throughout history. For instance, 500 years after Spain expelled Jews in 1492, the Spanish government acknowledged the wrongfulness of this action. In the 1970s the Catholic church began removing from its rituals and prayers the anti-Semitic language that helped create Christian intolerance of Jews. Pope John Paul II, who lived through the Nazi era while secretly studying to become a priest in Poland, has

often spoken of the Holocaust. In March 1998, after eleven years of preparation, the Catholic church issued a fourteen-page document titled "We Remember: A Reflection on the Shoah." ("Shoah" is the Hebrew word used to describe the Holocaust.) The document's main author, Cardinal Edward Idris Cassidy, described it as "more than an apology. This is an act of repentance." Through the document, the church states that many Christians failed to do enough to save Jews during the Holocaust, and it condemns all forms of anti-Semitism and anti-Jewish thought. The church's statement, however, does not go nearly as far as many Jews would have liked, nor as far as the statement that the French church had issued a few months earlier. For instance, the document does not state that the church, as an institution, had any responsibility for the Holocaust. It praises German Catholic clergymen who condemned Nazism, but it does not mention that the church signed an agreement with Hitler's government soon after he came to power. The statement directs attention to the gratitude expressed by Jewish leaders to Pope Pius XII, who headed the church beginning in 1939, for helping to save lives. It does not, however, mention the criticism of the pope for his failure to condemn publicly the Nazi persecutions of Jews.

In "We Remember," the church acknowledges that many Christians held anti-Jewish prejudices based on religion, but it also states that the anti-Semitism of the Nazis "had its roots outside of Christianity," and that this racial, not religious, anti-Semitism was the basis of the Holocaust. The church poses the question: "Did anti-Jewish sentiments among Christians make them less sensitive, or even indifferent, to the persecution launched against the Jews" when the Nazis came to power? The church provides no clear answer, claiming that individual decisions are influenced by various factors. Despite the importance of the issues left out of the document, many view it as a significant step. The statement is intended to be used as a teaching document in Catholic universities, as well as seminaries. One aspect of the message is clear: "The Catholic Church therefore repudiates every persecution against a people or human group anywhere, at any time. She absolutely condemns all forms of genocide, as well as the racist ideologies that give rise to them."

In another historic step, Pope John Paul II visited Israel in March 2000, stopping to mourn the victims of the Holocaust at the Yad Vashem memorial in Jerusalem. In this first papal visit to Yad Vashem, the Pope spoke of his personal sorrow

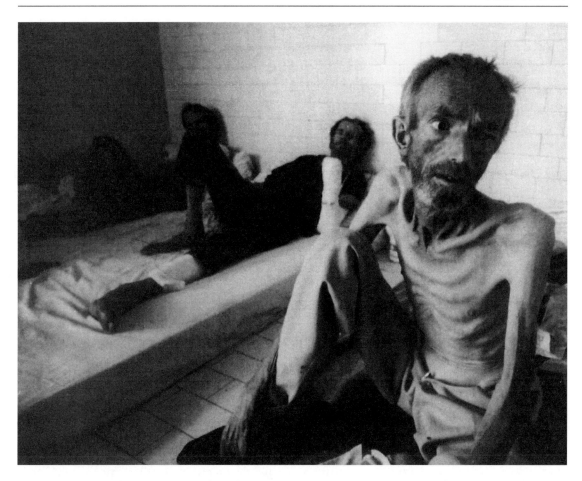

Bosnians in a Serb internment camp in the mid-1990s. The ethnic cleansing that occurred during the war in the former Yugoslavia in the 1990s recalls the genocide of the Holocaust fifty years earlier. (Reproduced by permission of AP/Wide World Photos)

and the sorrow of the church. He also talked about his memories of Jewish friends and neighbors in Poland, some of whom did not survive the Holocaust. In a meeting with Israeli President Ezer Weizman, Pope John Paul II promised that the church would do everything possible to heal the wounds of the past.

Other Echoes

In the 1990s people throughout the world were reminded of the Holocaust when they learned of the "ethnic cleansing" occurring in Yugoslavia, including Serbia, Croatia, and Bosnia. The Serbs had been driving Croatian and Bosnian Muslims from territory shared by these groups. Their method of ethnic cleansing included terrorist tactics, mass shootings of unarmed civilians, and the systematic rape of women and girls. Men were seized from towns and placed in guarded camps

where they were starved, exposed to the cold, and tortured. People acknowledged the resemblance between the Holocaust and the violence in Bosnia, and pressure was placed on the countries of Europe and the United States to send troops to stop the murders. Although it had little success by the end of the twentieth century, an international war crimes tribunal, modeled on the Nuremberg trials, was created to try war criminals from the former Yugoslavia. Similarly, a war crimes tribunal was set up after the mass murders of one ethnic group by another during the 1990s in the east African nation of Rwanda.

Arts and the Holocaust

As lawmakers, politicians, historians, and philosophers have struggled with the legacy of the Holocaust, writers, artists, composers, and filmmakers have worked to understand the event through art. Museums and memorials in many countries exhibit representations and relics of the Holocaust. Writers and lecturers detail their experiences during the Holocaust, urging the world not to forget. Noted writer Elie Wiesel has described the experiences of a concentration camp survivor. He was held in Auschwitz and Buchenwald as a teenager. In his first novel, *Night,* he describes the horrors of the Holocaust. Wiesel's attempt to find meaning in the suffering of the Holocaust has made him one of the foremost fighters against human rights abuses throughout the world. He was awarded the Nobel Peace Prize in 1986 for his human rights work. Italian Jewish writer Primo Levi was also an Auschwitz survivor and was among those still in the camp when it was freed by Soviet soldiers. Although he was a chemist before the war, Levi became a writer who turned to the theme of the Holocaust, and especially of Auschwitz, for the rest of his life. His first book, *If This Is a Man: Survival in Auschwitz* (1947), is generally considered one of the best works written on the Holocaust. Almost forty years later he used the experience of Auschwitz as a way to explore the meaning of human life in *The Drowned and the Saved.* Levi died at the age of sixty-eight in 1987.

In the first twenty-five years after the war, it was almost impossible for any Polish author to write a novel that did not depict life during the German occupation of Poland. Only a few of the many Polish works reflecting the war experience, however, are well known to Americans. One of these exceptions is Jerzy Kosinski's novel *The Painted Bird* (1966), a terrifying story possibly based on the author's own childhood experiences. Notable among German works on the Holocaust are two dramas. Rolf Hochuth's play, *The Deputy* (1964), attacks the role of Pope Pius XII in failing to condemn Nazi anti-Semitism. In 1966 Peter Weiss published the play *The Investigation,* which is closely based on the actual German trial of Auschwitz personnel. German novelist Günter Grass wrote a well-known novel depicting the war years in Germany titled *The Tin Drum* (1965). The humorous and horrifying tale traces the adventures of Oskar, a child who purposely refuses to grow and wanders through Nazi Germany as a dwarf, playing his toy drum. Oskar's adventures mockingly capture the realities of Nazism. A film version, directed by Volker Schlondorff, was released in 1979.

German poet Nelly Sachs, who fled from the Nazis to Sweden in 1940, won the Nobel Prize in literature in 1966 for her collection of poems *O the*

Chimneys. Until her death in 1970, Sachs dedicated her career to giving a voice to the victims of the Holocaust. American writer John Hersey's novel *The Wall,* which described the daily life of Jews in the Warsaw ghetto, became a bestseller when it was published in 1950. Another bestselling American novel set in the Warsaw ghetto was Leon Uris's *Mila 18* (1960). Taking its title from the address of the secret headquarters of the Jewish Fighting Organization at number 18 Mila Street, the novel tells the story of the Warsaw ghetto uprising. Through these novels American readers learned about both Nazi oppression and Jewish resistance.

Like literature, films have played an important role in bringing the subject of the Holocaust to the attention of millions of people. Few works about the Holocaust have had a greater effect than Steven Spielberg's film *Schindler's List* (1994), which won, among many other awards, an Oscar for best picture. Filmed in black and white, it tells the fact-based story of Oskar Schindler, the man the Nazis placed in charge of two Polish factories they had taken from Jewish owners in 1939. Schindler initially welcomed this as an opportunity to get rich, but in 1943 he witnessed the brutal deportations of Jews from the ghetto of Kraków, the third largest city in Poland. Most of these people, including children, were sent to the Belzec death camp, where they were murdered as soon as they arrived. Some, however, remained near Kraków in the Plaszów labor camp, which was commanded by SS Captain Amon Goeth. Schindler, who saw what was happening, used his friendship with Goeth to try to save Jews. (After the war Goeth was tried by the Polish Supreme National Court and hanged.) When the Soviet army began to drive the Germans out of Poland, Schindler moved his factory far to the west, in what had been Czechoslovakia, and insisted on taking his Jewish workers with him. He and his workers knew that anyone left behind would be killed by the Nazis. The title of the movie is based on the list of workers he intended to take with him. Schindler created this list in order to save as many lives as possible. He spent his fortune saving Jewish lives and was even able to have 300 women returned from Auschwitz. Schindler died in 1974 and was buried in Jerusalem. The movie ends by showing survivors among "Schindler's Jews," along with their children and grandchildren, placing stones on his grave in accordance with Jewish tradition.

The Holocaust has been featured in plays as well. When literature is presented in a live format, such as a stage production, it can often be altered to reflect contemporary times rather than those of its setting. One example of this relates to the stage production of *The Diary of Anne Frank,* which was first performed as a Broadway play in 1955; it was extremely successful, winning the Pulitzer Prize for drama. The film, released four years later, was similar to the play. Over the years, however, the play and movie were criticized because some felt that Frank's words had been taken out of context. The writers and producers of the Broadway play wanted to make Frank into a symbol of humanity, and it was argued that because of this desire they played down Frank's Jewish identity. The specific nature of the Holocaust, that it was an attempt to destroy the Jews, was made to seem less important, these critics said, in order to make Frank's story more appealing to a wide audience. In addition, they argued, the play portrayed Frank as a much more optimistic and hopeful person than she really was. This optimism, the critics said, improperly softened the horror of what happened to Frank, her family, and other European Jews. In 1997 a new production of *The Diary of Anne Frank* opened on Broadway. Like the first version, it was based on the words Frank actually wrote in her diary. The new play seemed to put more emphasis on Frank's anger and despair.

Some of the most effective films that deal with the Nazi period have been documentaries. An early example was *Night and Fog* (1955) by French director Alain Resnais, which deals specifically with concentration camps. Its title comes from the German order of 1941 ("*Nacht und Nebel*"), under which captured resistance fighters from western Europe were made to disappear without a trace, into "night and fog." Part of the film's impact comes from its contrasting use of black and white photographs, taken when the concentration camps were liberated, and color film of the camps taken years after they were abandoned. It is also noted for showing the massive clean up efforts at the camps, which were covered with bodies after the Third Reich fell.

French filmmaker Marcel Ophuls has made two major documentaries about the Holocaust. *The Sorrow and the Pity* (1970), which runs more than four hours, includes interviews with people who recalled the German occupation of France. The film caused a sensation in France because it emphasized that many French cooperated with the Nazis, and many others simply "went along." Ophuls's *Hotel Terminus* (1987) tells the story of

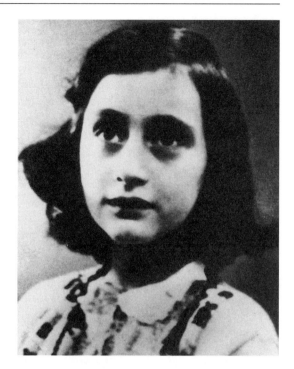

Anne Frank hid with her family for twenty-five months on the upper floors of her father's office before they were discovered by the Nazis. (Reproduced by permission of AP/Wide World Photos)

Klaus Barbie, the Geheime Staatspolizei (Gestapo) chief in Lyons during the occupation. The film won an Oscar for best documentary. Another highly acclaimed documentary is *Shoah* (1985), by French filmmaker Claude Lanzmann. In the nine and one-half hour film, Lanzmann uses interviews with witnesses, such as men who worked on the deportation trains, in the death camps, or with the Nazis. The interviews were shot especially for the film to explain the Holocaust. No pictures of the actual events are used. Slowly, detail after detail, the entire story of the Holocaust is revealed. Many of Lanzmann's subjects reveal their own psychology, and the hatreds, jealousies, and prejudices that allowed the Holocaust to happen.

A large number of fictional films also touch on Holocaust themes. American films include *Judgment at Nuremberg* (1961), directed by Stanley Kramer, which portrays one of the lesser Nuremberg trials. It includes performances by major Hollywood stars, including Spencer Tracey and Montgomery Clift. Along with Marlon Brando and Dean Martin, Clift is also one of the stars of *The Young Lions* (1958), directed by Edward Dmytryk, based on Irwin Shaw's novel of the same title. Brando plays an average, upstanding German who

Roberto Benigni, Giorgio Cantarini, and Nicoletta Braschi star in *Life Is Beautiful*, a story in which a humorous man and his family are thrust into the harsh brutality of the Nazi regime. (Reproduced by permission of the Kobal Collection)

becomes an officer in Hitler's army. Clift's character, a Jewish-American soldier, fights alongside a fellow American GI, played by Martin. The two men cross paths with Brando's character at the end of the war. A more recent American film is *Sophie's Choice* (1982), directed by Alan J. Pakula and based on William Styron's novel of the same title. The film is about a young Polish woman in New York after the war, who is destroyed by the experiences she endured in Europe. Actress Meryl Streep's portrayal of the title role won her an Oscar.

The Damned (1969) is an Italian-West German film, directed by the Italian Luchino Visconti, which tells the story of a powerful German family that becomes more and more enmeshed in Nazism. The Italian film director Vittorio De Sica made *The Garden of the Finzi-Continis* (1970), which won an Oscar as best foreign film. It recounts the lives of a wealthy and cultured Italian Jewish family who tries to ignore the ever-increasing dangers in Nazi-dominated Europe. More

recently, the Italian film *Life Is Beautiful* earned director and actor Roberto Benigni two Academy Awards, one for best foreign film and one for best actor. It portrays the fictional account of a would-be Italian bookstore owner who meets and woos his future wife as persecution of the Jews heats up in Europe. The couple and their child then find themselves rounded up and deported to concentration camps, where the father constructs an elaborate lie to help hide and ultimately save his young son from the Nazis. Both praised and criticized for its audacity in mixing comedy with the tragedy of the Holocaust, the film, most critics felt, succeeded in relaying the intended message that life is beautiful, despite its harshness.

French director Louis Malle made two films set in German-occupied France. In *Lacombe, Lucien* (1974), he tells the story of a young Frenchman who, unable to join the resistance, instead joins the pro-Nazi Milice, but then falls in love with a Jewish woman. *Au Revoir les Enfants* ("Goodbye, Chil-

Gaspard Manesse in *Au Revoir les Enfants*. (Reproduced by permission of the Kobal Collection)

dren"; 1987), one of Malle's last films, tells the story of a Jewish child hidden in a Catholic school who is eventually arrested and deported.

Memorials and Museums

Yad Vashem, the memorial located on Remembrance Hill in Jerusalem, Israel, is both a museum of the Holocaust and an institution for its study. Yad Vashem has sponsored research and published many books on various aspects of the Jewish experience in Europe. It has also recorded the oral histories of thousands of Holocaust survivors. As many of the survivors have now grown old, their accounts have been recorded for future generations to come. Yad Vashem's archives and library are among the most extensive in the world. The museum itself includes a permanent exhibit that traces the different stages of the Holocaust, beginning with Hitler's rise to power and continuing to the end of World War II. Yad Vashem also includes several areas that are specific memorials, such as the Children's Memorial Garden dedicated to the 1.5 million Jewish children killed by the Nazis. The Valley of the Destroyed Communities lists the names of 5,000 locations where Jews lived that were destroyed in the Holocaust. Also memorialized are the "Righteous Among the Nations," non-Jews such as Oskar Schindler, Raoul Wallenberg, and Jan Karski, who helped Jews at the risk of their own lives. An eternal flame burns in the Hall of Remembrance, where the names of the twenty-two largest concentration and death camps are engraved on the tile floor. Ashes from the victims of these camps lie in a vault in front of the flame.

The United States Holocaust Memorial Museum in Washington, DC, opened in 1993. The design of the building, including the use of exposed metal and brick, visible fencing and barriers, and boarded windows, evokes the environment of a concentration camp. Architecture critics were unanimous in praising the success of the design. Like Yad Vashem, the Holocaust Museum is also a research institution. Its film and photo archives, library, and oral history tapes are available to scholars. In addition, much of the material is computer accessible from the Museum's Learning Center. Among the items on display are examples of the actual railroad cars used to transport hundreds of thousands of deported Jews to the death camps of Poland.

In Amsterdam, Holland, the Anne Frank House has been preserved as a museum. The building is the actual house where Anne and her family hid for twenty-five months. Behind a movable bookcase are the stairs that lead to the "secret annex" where Frank wrote her famous diary. The postcards that Anne used to decorate the walls of her room are still there.

One of the entrances to the United States Holocaust Memorial Museum. (Reproduced by permission of AP/Wide World Photos)

In Berlin, Germany, plans are underway for three cultural projects focusing on World War II and Jewish history. The three projects, intended to tell a complete story, include the Jewish Museum, which will chronicle the 2,000 year history of Jews in Germany; the Topography of Terror, which will focus on the Nazis; and a Holocaust Memorial.

PRIMARY SOURCE

Elie Wiesel
"Why I Write"
An essay included in
From the Kingdom of Memory: Reminiscences

People who lived through the Holocaust, especially those who survived the concentration camps, can provide firsthand accounts of what happened during this murderous chapter in the history of humankind. Perhaps one of the most eloquent and forceful writers exploring the Holocaust is Elie Wiesel, who has committed his life to educating others about the Nazi atrocities. Through his work, he is trying to ensure that history is never repeated. Wiesel was raised in a religious home in Sighet Marmatiei, a small city located in present-day Romania. Under Hungarian

Elie Wiesel (second row of bunks, seventh from the left, next to the vertical beam) was an inmate of Buchenwald's "little camp." (Photograph by H. Miller, courtesy of USHMM Photo Archives)

rule from 1940 to 1944, Sighet contained a thriving Jewish community. In 1941 more than 10,000 Jews lived in the city, representing nearly 40 percent of the total population. Despite the forced deportation and massacre of "alien" Jews in 1941, the remaining Jews lived in relative stability until 1944. After the Nazis occupied Hungary in March 1944, the party immediately implemented a series of anti-Jewish measures. The situation and safety of all Hungarian Jews deteriorated rapidly in just a few short months. Jews were required to turn over their assets to German authorities, ordered to wear a yellow Star of David on their clothing, and prohibited from dining at restaurants and traveling on trains. By May the Nazis had forced the Jews from Sighet and nearby rural communities into two ghettos established within city borders. Wiesel and his family were among the nearly 13,000 Jews deported to Auschwitz between May 16 and 22, when the Nazis liquidated these ghettos.

Wiesel was not yet sixteen years old when he arrived at Birkenau, the depot area and death center of the Auschwitz compound. While still in the train cars, the Jewish captives could see the fires of the camp's furnaces where the bodies of prisoners were being burned. During the *Selektionen* (selection process), camp officials directed the deportees into two lines, separating the men from the women. Able-bodied men were "selected" for work assignments while the elderly, young children, and most of the mothers were led immediately to the gas chambers. The camp guards ordered Wiesel (who had lied about his age) and his father to join the line of prisoners leaving Birkenau and marching to the Auschwitz concentration camp. Wiesel last saw his mother and younger sister as they walked away with thousands of other women and children to their deaths. During the remainder of 1944, Wiesel and his father managed to survive the brutal conditions at Auschwitz; their emotional well-being and spirits, however, were shattered. Despite his religious upbringing, Wiesel began to question how God could allow such horrific events to take place.

All day and night, guards attacked and murdered prisoners at will. The inmates grew steadily weaker as they performed exhausting labor in twelve-hour shifts, received starvation-quota rations, and slept in filthy, overcrowded barracks. Without adequate sanitation facilities, infectious diseases ravaged the camp population. As prisoners fought for their survival, they turned against one another, even their friends and family members. After witnessing a rabbi's son forsake his father, Wiesel vowed that he would never betray his father in order to save his own life.

In January 1945, as the Soviet army advanced through Poland and toward the compound, the Nazis evacuated Auschwitz. Camp guards ordered the prisoners to march toward Buchenwald, a concentration camp located within Germany. Forced to march for days in the snow without adequate clothing and with little food or water, Wiesel's father arrived at Buchenwald ill and exhausted. When his father was no longer able to get out of bed and became ineligible to receive food, Wiesel fed him his own meager rations. Wiesel's father died after being violently attacked by a guard who was annoyed by his pleas for water. Wiesel was liberated from Buchenwald by American forces on April 11—less than three months after his father's death. After spending two weeks in the hospital on the verge of death, he was released and eventually settled in Paris, where he quickly mastered the French language and studied at the Sorbonne, the University of Paris. During the 1950s he worked as a foreign journalist and reporter for the Israeli daily newspaper *Yediot Ahronont.* His assignments as a correspondent took him to Israel and finally to the United States, where he became an American citizen in 1963.

Since 1976 Wiesel has been a professor of humanities at Boston University. In 1985 he received the Congressional Gold Medal of Achievement. The same year, former French president François Mitterand named him commander in the French Legion of Honor. Wiesel was award-

ed the Nobel Prize in 1986 for his "message" to humanity. The Nobel Committee acknowledged his fight against "blind indifference" and his push to involve people in "truth and justice, in human dignity, freedom, and atonement." Wiesel continues to give lectures, teach, and write. He lives in New York City with his Austrian-born wife, Marion, who is also a Holocaust survivor. Wiesel prefers to write in French, and Marion translates his work into English. He has written more than forty books, including works of fiction, nonfiction, and plays. In 1995 he published the first volume of his autobiography, *All Rivers Run to the Sea.* His other books include *Dawn* (1961), *The Accident* (1962), *A Beggar in Jerusalem* (1970), *The Oath* (1973), and *The Fifth Son* (1985).

Wiesel first wrote about his experiences as a concentration camp prisoner in his fictional memoir *Un di Velt Hot Geshvigen* (literally translated, "And the World Has Remained Silent"; 1958). Originally written in Yiddish, this popular work was translated into eighteen languages, appearing in English as *Night* in 1960. Though considered a novel, the book serves as Wiesel's personal testimony on the Holocaust.

In "Why I Write," an essay included in the collection *From the Kingdom of Memory: Reminiscences* and excerpted here, Wiesel describes his commitment to honor those who perished during the Holocaust, which he calls the "kingdom of night." Citing the importance of memory in the Jewish tradition, he believes that, as a survivor, he has an obligation to describe what happened to people in the camps. He is especially haunted by the million children who died. On the day he arrived at Auschwitz, he saw hundreds of children line up with their mothers to be taken to the gas chambers and killed. Wiesel says he will never forget the image of black smoke swirling into the sky as the bodies of victims—adults and children—burned in the crematoria.

"Why I Write"

Why do I write? Perhaps in order not to go mad. Or, on the contrary, to touch the bottom of madness.

Like [experimental Irish-born author who wrote primarily in French] Samuel Beckett, the survivor expresses himself "en desespoir de cause," because there is no other way.

Speaking of the solitude of the survivor, the great Yiddish and Hebrew poet and thinker Aaron Zeitlin addresses those who have left him: his dead father, his dead brother, his dead friends. "You have abandoned me," he says to them. "You are together, without me. I am here. Alone. And I make words."

So do I, just like him. I too speak words, write words, reluctantly.

There are easier occupations, far more pleasant ones. For the survivor, however, writing is not a profession, but a calling; "an honor," according to [French philosopher and author Albert] Camus. As he put it: "I entered literature through worship." Other writers have said, "Through anger; through love." As for myself, I would say, "Through silence."

It was by seeking, by probing silence that I began to discover the perils and power of the word.

I never intended to be a novelist. The only role I sought was that of witness. I believed that, having survived by chance, I was duty-bound to give meaning to my survival, to justify each moment of my life. I knew the story had to be told. Not to transmit an experience is to betray it; this is what Jewish tradition teaches us. But how to do this?

"When Israel is in exile, so is the word," says the <u>Book of Splendor</u>*. The word has deserted the meaning it was intended to convey—one can no longer make them coincide. The displacement, the shift, is irrevocable. This was never more true than right after the upheaval. We all knew that we could never say what had to be said, that we could never express in words—coherent, intelligible words—our experience of madness on an absolute scale. The walk through fiery nights, the silence before and after the selection, the toneless praying of the condemned, the Kaddish of the dying, the fear and hunger of the sick, the shame and suffering, the haunted eyes, the wild stares—I thought that I would never be able to speak of them. All words seemed inadequate, worn, foolish, lifeless, whereas I wanted them to sear.*

Where was I to discover a fresh vocabulary, a primeval language? The language of night was not human; it was primitive, almost animal—hoarse shouting, screaming, muffled moaning, savage howling, the sounds of beating.... A brute strikes wildly, a body falls; an officer raises his arm and a whole community walks toward a common grave; a soldier shrugs his shoulders and a thousand families are torn apart, to be reunited only by death. Such was the language of the concentration camp. It negated all other language and took its place. Rather than link people, it became a wall between them. Could the wall be scaled? Could the reader be brought to the other side? I knew the answer to be No, and yet I also knew that No had to become Yes. This was the wish, the last will of the dead. One had to shatter the wall encasing the darkest truth, and give it a name. One had to force man to look.

The fear of forgetting: the main obsession of all those who have passed through the universe of the damned. The enemy relied on people's disbelief and forgetfulness.

Remember, said the father to his son, and the son to his friend: gather the names, the faces, the tears. If, by a miracle, you come out of it alive, try to reveal everything, omitting nothing, forgetting nothing. Such was the oath we had all taken: "If, by some miracle, I survive, I will devote my life to testifying on behalf of all those whose shadows will be bound to mine forever."

This is why I write certain things rather than others: to remain faithful.

Of course, there are times of doubt for the survivor, times when one gives in to weakness, or longs for comfort. I hear a voice within me telling me to stop mourning the past. I too want to sing of love and its magic. I too want to celebrate the sun, and the dawn that heralds the sun. I would like to shout, and shout loudly: "Listen, listen well! I too am capable of victory, do you hear? I too am open to laughter and joy. I want to walk head high, my face unguarded." One feels like shouting, but the shout becomes a murmur. One must make a choice; one must remain faithful. This is what the survivor feels; he owes nothing to the living, but everything to the dead.

I owe the dead my memory. I am duty-bound to serve as their emissary, transmitting the history of

From the left: Harvey Meyerhoff (chairman of the United States Holocaust Memorial Council), President Bill Clinton, and Elie Wiesel light the eternal flame outside the United States Holocaust Memorial Museum in Washington, D.C. (Reproduced by permission of Archive Photos)

their disappearance, even if it disturbs, even if it brings pain. Not to do so would be to betray them, and thus myself. I simply look at them. I see them and I write.

While writing, I question them as I question myself. I write to understand as much as to be understood. Will I succeed one day? Wherever one starts from, one reaches darkness. God? He remains the God of darkness. Man? The source of darkness. The killers' sneers, their victims' tears, the onlookers' indifference, their complicity and complacency: I do not understand the divine role in all of that. A million children massacred: I will never understand.

Jewish children: they haunt my writings. I see them again and again. I shall always see them. Hounded, humiliated, bent like the old men who surround them trying to protect them, in vain. They are thirsty, the children, and there is no one to give them water. They are hungry, the children, but there is no one to give them a crust of bread. They are afraid, and there is no one to reassure them.

They walk in the middle of the road, like urchins. They are on the way to the station, and they will never return. In sealed cars, without air or food, they travel toward another world; they guess where they are going, they know it, and they keep silent. They listen to the wind, the call of death in the distance.

All these children, these old people, I see them. I never stop seeing them. I belong to them.

But they, to whom do they belong?

People imagine that a murderer weakens when facing a child. That the child might reawaken the killer's lost humanity. That the killer might be unable to kill the child before him.

Not this time. With us, it happened differently. Our Jewish children had no effect upon the killers. Nor upon the world. Nor upon God.

I think of them, I think of their childhood. Their childhood is a small Jewish town, and this town is no more. They frighten me; they reflect an image of myself, one that I pursue and run from at the same time—the image of a Jewish adolescent who knew no fear except the fear of God, whose faith was whole, comforting.

No, I do not understand. And if I write, it is to warn the reader that he will not understand either. "You will not understand, you will never understand," were the words heard everywhere in the kingdom of night. I can only echo them.

An admission of impotence and guilt? I do not know. All I know is that Treblinka and Auschwitz cannot be told. And yet I have tried. God knows I have tried.

Did I attempt too much, or not enough? Out of some thirty volumes, only three or four try to penetrate the realm of the dead. In my other books, through my other books, I try to follow other roads. For it is dangerous to linger among the dead; they hold on to you, and you run the risk of speaking only to them. And so, I forced myself to turn away from them and study other periods, explore other destinies and teach other tales; the Bible and the Talmud, Hasidism and its fervor, the shtetl and its songs, Jerusalem and its echoes; the Russian Jews and their anguish, their awakening, their courage. At times it seems to me that I am speaking of other things with the sole purpose of keeping the essential—the personal experience—unspoken. At times I wonder: And what if I was wrong? Perhaps I should have stayed in my own world with the dead.

But then, the dead never leave me. They have their rightful place even in the works about pre-Holocaust Hasidism or ancient Jerusalem. Even in my Biblical and Midrashic tales, I pursue their presence, mute and motionless…. They appear in Hasidic and Talmudic legends in which victims forever need defending against forces that would crush them. Technically, so to speak, they are of course elsewhere, in time and space, but on a deeper, truer plane, the dead are part of every story, of every scene….

After Auschwitz everything long past brings us back to Auschwitz….

I know Hasidim who never wavered in their faith; I respect their strength. I know others who chose rebellion, protest, rage; I respect their courage. For there comes a time when only those who do believe in God will cry out to him in wrath and anguish. The faith of some matters as much as the strength of others. It is not ours to judge; it is only ours to tell the tale.

But where is one to begin? Whom is one to include? One meets a Hasid in all my novels. And a

Halina Bryks was one of many displaced children whose pictures were published in newspapers in the hope that a family member would see them. (USHMM Photo Archives)

child. And an old man. And a beggar. And a madman. They are all part of my inner landscape. Why? They are pursued and persecuted by the killers; I offer them shelter. The enemy wanted to create a society purged of their presence, and I have brought some of them back. The world denied them, repudiated them: so let them live at least within the feverish dreams of my characters.

It is for them that I write.

And yet, the survivor may experience remorse. He has tried to bear witness; it was all in vain.

After the liberation, illusions shaped our hopes. We were convinced that a new world would be built upon the ruins of Europe. A new civilization would dawn. No more wars, no more hate, no more intolerance, no fanaticism anywhere. And all this because the witnesses would speak, and speak they did. Was it to no avail?

They will continue, for they cannot do otherwise. When man, in his grief, falls silent, [German poet and dramatist Johann Wolfgang von] Goethe says, then God gives him the strength to sing of his sorrows. From that moment on, he may no longer choose not to sing, whether his song is heard or not. What mat-

ters is to struggle against silence with words, or through another form of silence. What matters is to gather a smile here and there, a tear here and there, a word here and there, and thus justify the faith placed in man, a long time ago, by so many victims.

Why do I write? To wrest those victims from oblivion. To help the dead vanquish death. (Wiesel, pp. 13–21)

Aftermath

Wiesel's commitment to stirring the conscience of society earned him the Nobel Peace Prize in 1986. The citation on his award reads: "Wiesel is a messenger to mankind. His message is one of peace and atonement and human dignity. The message is in the form of a testimony, repeated and deepened through the works of a great author." In his Nobel address, Wiesel pledged to "never be silent whenever and wherever human beings endure suffering and humiliation." Silence is not an option, for "neutrality helps the oppressor, never the victim."

Between 1980 and 1986, Wiesel served as the founding chairperson of the U.S. Holocaust Memorial Council. Established by a unanimous vote of Congress in 1980, the Council represents the commitment of the American people and government to remembering the victims of the Holocaust. The council also organized the planning and funding of the United States Holocaust Memorial Museum (USHMM). During his tenure as chairperson, Wiesel helped institute Days of Remembrance of the Victims of the Holocaust, an annual commemorative program involving local ceremonies as well as a national civic ceremony held in the U.S. Capitol Rotunda. His leadership inspired the creation and introduction of Holocaust curricula into junior and senior high schools throughout the United States. Of Wiesel's forty published books of fiction and nonfiction, only a small portion deal directly with the Holocaust. His other works explore various aspects of human experience and Jewish tradition, including reflections on Hasidism, the Talmud, and French existentialism. As Holocaust survivors grow older, Wiesel urges them to write about their experiences. He hopes that "the memory of evil will serve as a shield against evil." As he remarked in a March 5, 1997 *New York Times* interview: "I believe in testimony more than anything else."

SOURCES

Books

Kuper, Jack, *Child of the Holocaust,* Berkley Books (New York), 1993.

Landau, Elaine, *We Survived the Holocaust,* F. Watts (New York), 1991.

Wiesel, Elie, *From the Kingdom of Memory: Reminiscences,* Schocken Books (New York), 1990.

Periodicals

New York Times, March 5, 1997.

Gerda Weissmann Klein
Excerpt from *All But My Life*

First published in 1957
This version, with epilogue, published in 1995

At the time of the German invasion, approximately 8,000 Jews lived in the town of Bielitz, Poland, near the Czechoslovakian border. Immediately after the war broke out, many Jews fled to either Soviet territory or to the area of Poland incorporated into greater Germany, hoping to be spared anti-Jewish persecution. By 1940 only 300 Jews remained in Bielitz. The Weissmann family, which included Gerda, her parents, and her brother Arthur, were among the few who stayed. In April 1942 Nazi authorities forced all the Jews into a ghetto near the train depot. The following month, eighteen-year-old Gerda Weissmann (later, Klein) was separated from her parents and transported to a labor camp. For the next three years she worked as a slave laborer in various work camps attached to factories involved in war production. At the end of January 1945, Klein was among some 4,000 female prisoners who were forced to march through Germany and eventually into Czechoslovakia. Death marches became especially frequent during the final stages of World War II. About 250,000 prisoners died on these marches between the summer of 1944 and the war's end in the spring of 1945. Without adequate winter clothing, many prisoners succumbed to exposure, starvation, and exhaustion. SS guards shot prisoners who fell to the ground after becoming too tired to continue. It has also been reported that guards would, at times, randomly gather small groups of victims, take them to the woods, and shoot them. Some guards even encouraged prisoners to run away, only to shoot them in the back as they fled. The guards would later collect a bonus, claiming to have stopped an attempted escape.

Klein was one of 120 women who survived the three-month death march. The ski boots her father had insisted she wear in preparation for the transports and deportations helped save her life. She was the only member of the Weissmann family to survive the Holocaust. Gerda was liberated in Volary, Czechoslovakia, on May 7, 1945, by Kurt Klein, a lieutenant with the Fifth U.S. Infantry Division.

Deathly ill and suffering from severe frostbite, she remained in an American field hospital for several months. Since Gerda Weissmann Klein had grown up in a region of Poland that had once been part of the Austro-Hungarian Empire, she knew how to speak both German and Polish. Kurt Klein, the American lieutenant who rescued her and later became her husband, was originally from Germany and spoke both German and English. The couple shared many similar sorrows: Both lost their parents at the hands of the Nazis and both knew the pain of never knowing exactly what happened to their loved ones. As the Nazis moved their victims from one place to the next, letters would be returned with the ominous stamped notice: "Moved—left no forwarding address."

In 1946, the Kleins settled in Buffalo, New York, where they eventually raised three children. Like many survivors of the Holocaust, Gerda Weissmann Klein gradually adjusted to life after the war. Grateful to be alive, she enjoyed the basic pleasures denied her for so long. After facing starvation and living in unsanitary conditions, she was keenly aware of the blessings of abundant food, clean water, and warm clothes. While life in America eventually became routine, shadows continue to haunt her. She still mourns the death of her parents, her brother, and close friends, often using "the darkness of past despair" to remind herself of "the blessings which I might otherwise take for granted."

Like many other survivors, Klein has said that living through the Holocaust was both a privilege and a burden. As she experienced the bounty of life after her war-time imprisonment, she also recalled those who were less fortunate. Klein began speaking about her Holocaust experiences and assisting children who needed help. In her memoir *All But My Life,* Klein talks about her wartime experiences and the losses she endured. The years spent in work camps under Nazi rule have taught her that "when we bring comfort to others, we reassure ourselves, and when we dispel fear, we

Concentration camp prisoners on a death march from Dachau to Wolfratshausen. (USHMM Photo Archives)

assuage our own fear as well." The following excerpt contains her recollections of her early meetings with Klein and later reflections that she recorded in 1994.

All But My Life

I don't remember the days that followed too well. The doctors and nurses spent much time over me; I was given injections and pills continuously. My body was rubbed with oil twice a day, for my skin was flaked and dry. I was weighed—sixty-eight pounds. The nurses joked about being able to circle my thigh with their fingers.

My bed seemed very high up, and the distances enormous. I did not feel like talking to anyone; I was strangely silent for the first time in my life. I noticed that many of the girls began to have visitors. I asked for Liesel several times, but was never told where she was.

Time and again I thought of the American soldier who had been so kind to me. Just before he had driven off he had said that he would see me again. With a chill, I recalled that the fighting had gone on after I had spoken to him; something might have happened to him!

A week passed. One afternoon an American came in and glanced into each bunk. My eyes met his as he approached.

"It's you I'm looking for!" he said.

I must have frowned as I recognized him. Out of his helmet and battle gear, he looked different.

"Don't you remember me?" he asked.

"Oh yes!" I said quickly, and wanted to add how worried I had been that something might have befallen him, but checked myself.

He carried a parcel under his arm. "These are for you," he said, unwrapping two magazines.

"Do you know what this means?" he asked, pointing to four bold white letters on a red background.

I gazed at the letters: L-I-F-E.

He repeated his question. "Do you know what it means? It is a fine word for you to learn. I know no better word of introduction to the English language for you."

I pronounced the word and tasted the strange sound of it.

"Say it again," he urged.

I was only too glad to try.

"That's right, that's what I wanted to see."

"To see what?" I asked.

"You smiled," he said. "I wanted to see you smile."

We talked. He told me that he had been busy with large numbers of prisoners, and that was why he had not come sooner. He said that he was stationed in a neighboring village about sixteen miles away. We talked like old friends. There was so much to ask. He seemed amazed at the limited knowledge I had about the development of the war. His German was excellent, though not fluent. At times he substituted an English word for a German one, but I nearly always knew what he meant.

The nurse came in, bringing my dinner tray, and told him that all visitors had to leave. I would have gladly foregone food if he could have stayed.

He left, and I ate my dinner, realizing that I had again forgotten to ask his name. After eating, until the light grew too poor, I studied the magazines. The pictures of the free world were exciting.

Then, unexpectedly, a voice near me said "Hello" in English. "You're not going to throw me out, are you?"

I was overjoyed to see him. It hadn't occurred to me that he might return in the evening. This time I learned his name.

"Kurt Klein," he said, laughing. "By the way, I wrote the letter to your uncle in Turkey. I hope I can bring you an answer soon."

I told Kurt about the strange sensation I felt every time I saw German soldiers under guard.

Young death camp survivors cheer as they are liberated by American forces. (USHMM Photo Archives)

"Just hurry up and get well," he said, "and I'll show you how many of them are under guard."

And he told me some of his experiences with the Germans' surprise when they heard about their concentration camps.

"It seems we fought a war against the Nazis, but I haven't met a Nazi yet," he said wryly.

And I was actually able to laugh. He could make me laugh, but I was ashamed to cry in front of him. I told him about Ilse. He seemed to understand. He didn't tell me to forget, to draw a line through the past, for he knew that I couldn't. He didn't ask questions either. He listened to what I had to tell him. He was silent when he knew that there was no answer. He joked about the present, and again and again I found myself laughing.

His daily visits continued. Although we came from different worlds, we understood each other. I did not want pity. I did not want him to like me because of what I had endured. Without knowing why, I sensed that there was something in his past that made him suffer.

A couple of days after his first visit he brought me some lilies-of-the-valley. The subtle fragrance brought back memories of my garden in May. I clutched the flowers without being able to speak. I remembered the roses in Grünberg which we had not been allowed to touch. But here were flowers that bloomed for me.

I kept my eyes downcast for quite a while, not daring to raise them and have them full of tears.

Finally Kurt asked, "Do you like them?"

My answers must have been written on my face. There was a catch in his voice when he spoke.

"I knew you would. They were my mother's favorite flowers."

"Your mother?" I asked haltingly.

Then for the first time Kurt told me about himself. He had been born in Germany. His older sister had gone to America soon after Hitler came to power, Kurt following her a year later. Finally the older brother had left for America. The parents had stayed behind. With the children safe, they waited, hoping that the Nazi regime would collapse. I remembered when Papa and Mama had talked the same way. Kurt went on to tell me how the children's combined efforts had failed to get their parents out of Germany. The Nazis had deported them to Camp de Gurs, in the south of France, in 1941. For a while letters reached them from America, then in July, 1942 a letter had been returned, stamped "Moved—left no forwarding address." Kurt fell silent. I understood so well. Impulsively I caught his hand.

"There is hope still," I said.

"Is there?" His voice was slightly ironical, but there was some concealed hope in it.

I had always felt that his understanding of my feelings had been made deeper by tragedy of his own. I was glad now that I had never given him detailed descriptions of cruelty, that I had really never told him what had happened, though he heard it from the others later. Yet the knowledge that I could shield him from pain gave me satisfaction....

[From the epilogue to All But My Life, written in 1994]

It is with trepidation that I look back at what I wrote nearly a half century ago, in the springtime of my life. A welter of emotions assails me and must be sorted out. Now that I have reached autumn, perhaps I can be more objective.

I have been asked countless times, "How and why did you go on during those unspeakable years?" And then, "How do you cope with the memory of hardships in the work camps and the pain of losing your family?" I admit I no longer remember all the answers I have given, but I am sure that they often varied and depended on my mood.

The part of my formative years over which fate cast such a large shadow imposes an enormous burden and is not fully sorted out even now. No manual for survival was ever handed to me, nor were any self-help books available. Yet somehow I made my way, grappling with feelings that would let me reconcile difficult memories with hope for the future, and balancing pain with joy, death with life, loss with gain, tragedy with happiness.

Survival is both an exalted privilege and a painful burden. I shall take a few random incidents that have become important in my life and try to make some sense of them. At the same time, I realize that it is impossible to do justice to fifty years of memory. The acuteness of those recollections often penetrates the calm of my daily life, forcing me to

confront painful truths but clarifying much through the very act of evocation. I have learned, for the most part, to deal with those truths, knowing well that a painful memory brought into focus by a current incident still hurts, but also that the pain will recede—as it has—and ultimately fade away.

When, in September 1946, the wheels of the plane bringing Kurt, my husband, and me from Paris and London touched American soil, he tightened his arms around me and said simply, "You have come home." It has been home, better than I ever dreamed it would be. I love this country as only one who has been homeless for so long can understand. I love it with a possessive fierceness that excuses its inadequacies, because I deeply want to belong. And I am still fearful of rejection, feeling I have no right to criticize, only an obligation to help correct. I marvel at my three children's total acceptance of their birthright and rejoice in their good fortune.

The establishment of the State of Israel in 1948 helped me to become a better American. The pain and loss I experienced in Poland, the country of my birth, obliterated the nostalgic thoughts of a childhood home for which I yearn. I have found the answer to that longing in the tradition of my religion and in the land of my ancient ancestors. Israel, by extending the law of return to all Jews, has become the metaphorical sepulcher of my parents as well as my spiritual childhood home.

While my love for Israel represents my love for my parents and our shared past, the United States is my country of choice, my adult home. This country represents the love I harbor for my husband, my children, and my grandchildren. One complements the other; by being mutually supportive, they enrich and heal.

I fell in love with this country from the moment I first stepped upon its soil. It felt so right, so expansive, so free, so hospitable, and I desperately wanted to become part of the American mainstream.

I had envisioned Buffalo [New York], which was to become my American home, as a utopian city beneath an ever-blue, brilliant sky, and had dismissed Paris, London, and New York, my way station to this utopia. During the drive from the grand, imposing New York Central railroad station in Buffalo, I was confronted with my new city's small wooden houses, huddled together like refugees, but my disappointment lasted only a few moments. I was ready to love the city and willing to defend it, even to myself. My affection was not misplaced. Buffalo did become a true home. It nurtured me, and later my *children played and laughed under rows of elm trees while I immersed myself in a new life.*

In time we would move from our first apartment to another part of the city, but I would occasionally drive past the familiar location that held so much of our early memories. I would remember how it had seemed to me on my first night in Buffalo, and a picture would flash through my mind. Long after Kurt had fallen asleep, I roamed through the apartment's modest rooms, stopping at the refrigerator in the tiny kitchenette that Kurt's friends had amply stocked. I had always loved fruit, so I took out an apple; but before I could catch the door, it slammed shut with a bang, and terror seized me. How many years had it been since I had lived in a home where I could take whatever I wanted with impunity? It was all mine now: the apple and the refrigerator. I opened the door, fully intending to let it slam shut. Instead, I caught it in time, closed it gently, and, grateful, went to bed.

Looking up at that third-story window of our first home, I also recalled the day which catapulted me into my life's work. I came to Buffalo in September 1946, and the following incident must have happened in late November. I loved going to grocery stores and still do. In those days I had the handy explanation that it was a great way to learn English, since I would see pictures on labels of cans that would tell me what was inside—an easy way to learn new words. The truth was different. I needed to convince myself of the abundance of available food and of its never-ending supply. I wanted the assurance of never being hungry again.

On that particular fall day, I must have dawdled in the market longer than I thought, because when I left the store, a snowstorm was gathering. I made it home, windblown, wet, and cold, and unpacked my bag on the kitchen table. Among my purchases was a loaf of bread. A whole loaf of bread, all mine! I took it into the living room and sat near the window, watching the icy gales swirling outside as I began to eat. Somehow it tasted soggy and a bit salty.

What was wrong with me? Here I was, sitting in a warm, secure place with a whole loaf of bread. Why, then, did I feel so sad, so forlorn? Slowly, the answer began to dawn. During the long years of deprivation, I had dreamed of eating my fill in a warm place, in peace, but I never thought that I would eat my bread alone. Later that evening, I told Kurt that I had been thinking of my friends still in Europe, cold and hungry. I had to do something.

Out of that need evolved my work with the local Jewish Federation, where I soon found myself putting stamps on envelopes and sealing them. I was immensely proud of having become a volunteer. When Kurt's aunt cautioned me that volunteer work was really for the wealthy, I agreed wholeheartedly. I considered myself rich now.

It didn't take long before the director of the office suggested that there were other ways to help. Could I tell some of the Buffalo Jewish community what I had seen and lived through? He waved aside protestations about my halting, faulty English. It did not matter that I was not articulate; he assured me that I would somehow manage to convey my feelings. And so, in the fall of 1946, I tried to tell my story, and I have continued to do so ever since. (Klein, pp. 219–222, 247–250)

Aftermath

Nearly half a century later Gerda Weissmann Klein returned to Volary, Czechoslovakia, the site of her liberation on May 7, 1945. Along with her husband and children, she visited the abandoned factory where she had spent her last days in Nazi captivity. They also went to the building that had housed the American field hospital, where she recuperated for several months. It was at the field hospital that she and Kurt first talked about their lives and shared hope for a brighter future. Gerda Weissmann Klein visited the graves of her friends from the labor camps who did not survive the three-month death march from Grünberg. Standing in the cemetery, she thought about the question she had asked herself many times before: Why did she survive when others did not? Through her postwar life's work, she hopes to provide a partial answer to that question.

Klein experienced another link to the past when she miraculously reacquired the complete collection of her family' photos several years after settling in Buffalo. A distant relative visited Klein's hometown of Bielitz after the war and by chance met a former neighbor of the Weissmann family. In preparing for forced departure from their home, the Weissmanns had asked the neighbor to store some precious family belongings until their return. Years later, with her entire family gone, Klein received a battered box containing some 400 family photos.

Gerda has lectured throughout the United States and has received many awards and honorary degrees. She and her husband have several grandchildren and live in Arizona. In 1996 *All But My Life* went through its thirty-eighth printing and became the subject of a film produced by Home Box Office (HBO) and the United States Holocaust Memorial Museum. The film, *One Survivor Remembers,* won

an Emmy Award and the Academy Award for documentary short subject.

Sources

Books

Auerbacher, Linda, *Beyond the Yellow Star to America,* Royal Fireworks Press (Unionville, NY), 1985.

Fluek, Toby Knobel, *Memories of My Life in a Polish Village, 1930–1949,* Random House (New York), 1990.

Klein, Gerda Weissmann, *All But My Life,* Hill & Wang (New York), 1995.

Bette Greene
Excerpt from *Summer of My German Soldier*
Published in 1973

The 1940s were a time of great upheaval as the world reeled from the effects of war and sacrifice. Throughout the world, national loyalties turned into intense patriotism. Hatred against a particular group of people resulted in one of the darkest and most tragic periods of human history. According to estimates, six million European Jews died as a result of extreme prejudice. In America, racial intolerance and other forms of discrimination were commonplace. As the world became aware of Nazi atrocities against Jews, few countries offered any real assistance to the victims. By not relaxing immigration quotas, various nations hindered the efforts of Jews to reach safety. The United States first moved to aid victims of Nazi persecution in January 1944, with the creation of the War Refugee Board. Working with Jewish organizations, neutral diplomats, and resistance groups in Europe, the board saved as many as 200,000 lives. Yet during the 1940s numerous forms of prejudice—anti-Semitism, racism, hatred of Germans and Japanese—existed in the United States. Japanese Americans endured state-sanctioned discrimination in internment camps. At the time African Americans lived in a deeply divided and segregated society with separate schools, housing, restaurants, and even water fountains.

In her first novel, *Summer of My German Soldier,* author Bette Greene explores the universal themes of bias and hatred against an American backdrop. Drawing from her own childhood experiences growing up in rural Arkansas during the 1940s, she depicts the many forms of prejudice that existed in American society. Greene's characters illustrate how hatred existed against Germans, Jews, blacks, and women, even in the idyllic setting of a rural American town. The main character, Patty Bergen, is twelve years old when German prisoners of war (POWs) from World War II are assigned to a location outside Jenkinsville, Arkansas. As a Jewish American preteen in a rural area, she lives with the assumption that everyone she meets can tell she is Jewish.

Bergen befriends a German prisoner named Anton Reiker, who speaks perfect English. After Reiker escapes from the POW camp, Bergen places herself at great risk by providing him with shelter. The story is loosely based on true historical events. Reiker's escape coincided with the actual landing of Nazi saboteurs on the beaches of the Atlantic coast. The arrival of these spy teams, who were assigned to destroy key installations on American soil, set off an intense anti-German reaction within the United

Two ovens of a crematorium remind people of the atrocities committed by the Nazis. Some Americans came to despise and fear the Germans for the Nazis' role in the Holocaust. (USHMM Photo Archives)

States. Similarly, patriotism turns to hatred in the novel, when the townspeople learn of Bergen's actions in aiding Reiker. While she is being led away by the sheriff, a riot nearly breaks out as people yell both anti-Semitic and anti-German jeers.

Summer of My German Soldier

The Germans began trying on the hats, smiling as though they were on a holiday. Reiker had pushed out from the center huddle and was exploring the broader limits of the store.

One very blond prisoner turned to my father. "Der Spiegel?"

My father shook his head. "I don't know what you're talking about."

"Wo ist der Spiegel?" said a second prisoner.

Again my father shook his head. "I don't understand your talk!"

Voices called for Reiker, and at his approach the men parted like the Red Sea for the Israelites. Again the word "Spiegel." Reiker turned to my father. "They'd like to see themselves. Have you a mirror?"

Reiker used English cleanly, easily, and with more precision than anyone I know from around these parts. And he didn't sound the least bit like a German. It was as though he had spent his life learning to speak English the way the English do.

Again Reiker left the others to walk with brisk steps across the store.

The corporal was involved in selecting off-duty socks for himself while the other guard leaned heavily against a counter and rolled himself a cigarette. Neither seemed concerned as Reiker headed unobserved towards the door. He could be gone before they even got their guns out of their holsters. Terrified that the guards' casualness was only a cover for the sharpest-shooting soldiers in anybody's army, I closed my eyes and prayed that he would make it all the way to freedom.

But I heard no door opening, no feet running, and no gun firing. By sheer force of will I opened my eyes to see Reiker calmly examining the pencils at the stationery counter.

Stationery was one of the many departments seen to by Sister Parker. But Sister Parker was busy waiting on a lady customer, and lady customers take half of forever to make up their minds. Who was going to wait on Reiker? I wanted to, but I couldn't. I didn't even have a comb. Why, in God's name, didn't I carry a purse with a fresh handkerchief and a comb like Edna Louise? I ran my fingers through my hair and patted it into place.

I took a few hurried steps and stopped short. Reiker may not wish to be disturbed, anyway not by me. The skin-and-bones girl. But I can wait on him if I want to, it's my father's store. Who does he think he is, some old Nazi?

Pushed on by adrenalin, I was at his side. "Could I help you, please?" My voice came out phony. Imitation Joan Crawford.

Reiker looked up and smiled. "Yes, please. I don't know the word for it—" Above those eyes with their specks of green were dark masculine eyebrows. "Pocket pencil sharpeners? They're quite small and work on the razor principle."

"Well," I said, reaching towards the opposite end of the counter to pick up a little red sharpener, "we sell a lot of these dime ones to the school children."

"Yes," he said. "Exactly right." He was looking at me like he saw me—like he liked what he saw.

"What color would you like?" I asked, not really thinking about pencil sharpeners. "They come in red, yellow, and green."

"I'll take the one you chose," said Reiker. He placed six yellow pencils and three stenographic pads on the counter. "And you did not tell me," he said, "what you call these pocket pencil sharpeners."

He was so nice. How could he have been one of those—those brutal, black-booted Nazis? "Well, I

Bette Greene

Bette Greene, a writer of young adult fiction, was born in a small town in Arkansas. She has also lived in Memphis, Tennessee, and Paris, France. When *Summer of My German Soldier* was published, Greene was living in Brookline, Massachusetts, with her husband and two children. The book incorporates many of Greene's own memories of growing up in wartime Arkansas. In 1973 it was named an American Library Association Notable Book and it received the Golden Kite Award. The novel was also a finalist for the prestigious National Book Award and was cited by the *New York Times* as an outstanding book of the year.

Greene has published many other books for young adults, including *Philip Hall Likes Me, I Reckon, Maybe* (1981). A more recent work, *The Drowning of Stephan Jones* (1991), received critical acclaim for its portrayal of a young gay man at the hands of his tormentors. By generating a strong emotional response from her readers, Greene seeks through her craft to call attention to the potentially devastating effects of intolerance and injustice.

don't think they actually call them much of anything, but if they were to call them by their right name they'd probably call them pocket pencil sharpeners."

Reiker laughed and for a moment, this moment, we were friends. And now I knew something more. He wasn't a bad man....

[Later in the text, Reiker has escaped.]

"I'm glad you're here." I said. "I want you to stay safe."

"I will. There's no reason why the Americans should bother with one missing prisoner. An ordinary foot soldier." [Anton] adjusted his gold ring, the

Kristy McNichol and Bruce Davison starred in the movie *Summer of My German Soldier,* based on Greene's book. (Reproduced by permission of AP/Wide World Photos)

surface of which had some sort of crest. "Also, I'm lucky. Twice I've been so close to exploding bombs that only a miracle could have saved me. And so I've had a couple of miracles."

He took a quick look out the hide-out's front and back windows. "But suppose I am recaptured. What will the Americans do? Deposit me in the nearest POW camp where I'll have to wait till the end of the war. But in the meantime this day, this month, this year belongs to me...."

"I was wondering how you managed to escape?"

"The actual mechanics of the escape are not important," he said. "The pertinent point is that I was able to create a—a kind of climate that permitted the escape. Specifically, my deception was believed because it was built on a foundation of truth. Hitler taught me that."

I heard him say it. "Hitler taught you?"

Anton smiled. "I learned it by analyzing his techniques. Hitler's first layer is an undeniable truth, such as: The German worker is poor. The second layer is divided equally between flattery and truth: The German worker deserves to be prosperous. The

third layer is total fabrication: The Jews and the Communists have stolen what is rightfully yours."

"Well, I can see how it helped him, but I don't see how it worked for you."

"Because I had a rock-bottom truth of my own," he said, striking his chest with his index finger. "My excellent English. I let it be known that I had had an English governess. And this gave me the advantage of being considered wealthy. But I didn't have a good workable plan that would capitalize on my believed riches until I saw that pin with the glass diamonds— the one you sold me."

"Yes! I couldn't for the life of me figure out why you wanted it. So gaudy and not at all like something you'd like."

"I loved it!" protested Anton. "Because those glass diamonds were going to make me a free man. One of the guards was a simple fellow with financial problems. One day I told him my father would pay five thousand dollars to the person who could get me out of prison. The guard looked too surprised to answer. But eight days later he followed me into the latrine and asked, 'What's the deal?' 'Five perfect diamonds, each diamond having been appraised in excess of one thousand dollars, will be given to the person who drives me out beyond those gates,' I told him. So he did, and I paid him with a dollar's worth of glass jewelry."

"I'm glad you made it," I said, "but that guard— he could get into an awful lot of trouble."

"I don't feel guilty." His hand rubbed across the slight indentation in the chin. "His concern was for reward; mine was for survival. But, on the other hand, I wouldn't wish to implicate him."

I nodded. "Now I'm ready to answer your question."

His teeth pressed together, giving new strength to the line of his jaw. "I'm certain you appreciate the seriousness of what you have done, aiding an escaped prisoner of war. I was wondering why you were taking these risks on my behalf. Because of your German ancestry? Perhaps your father is secretly sympathetic to the Nazi cause?"

"That's not true! My father's parents came from Russia and my mother's from Luxembourg."

Anton looked alarmed. "I'm sorry. It's just that Bergen is such a good German name."

"It's also a good Jewish name," I said, pleased by the clean symmetry of my response.

His mouth came open. "Jewish?" An index finger pointed toward me. "You're Jewish?"

I thought he knew. I guess I thought everybody knew. Does he think I tricked him? My wonderful Anton was going to change to mean. As I nodded Yes, my breathing came to a halt while my eyes clamped shut.

Suddenly, strong baritone laughter flooded the room. Both eyes popped open and I saw him standing there, shaking his head from side to side.

"It's truly extraordinary," he said. "Who would believe it? 'Jewish girl risks all for German soldier.' Tell me, Patty Bergen—" his voice became soft, but with a trace of hoarseness— "why are you doing this for me?"

It wasn't complicated. Why didn't he know? There was really only one word for it. A simple little word that in itself is reason enough.

"The reason I'm doing this for you," I started off, "is only that I wouldn't want anything bad to happen to you."

Anton turned his face from me and nodded as though he understood. Outside, a blue-gray cloud cruised like a pirate ship between sun and earth, sending the room from sunshine into shadows....

[Later, Anton is discovered and Patty is arrested.]

Pierce walked to the door of my room without entering. "All settled, Mr. Bergen. We're taking the girl into Memphis." Then he gave me a nod. "Better pack a few things."

"How long will she be gone?"

"Don't know, sir. She'd better take a few changes."

I got the smallest of the three suitcases out of the closet and began putting in some clothes like a robot who feels nothing. I wasn't even conscious anymore of wanting anything except maybe to be left alone,

and I wasn't even strong on that. Living was too big a deal and dying too much trouble....

As we came close to my father's store I saw people milling in front. Too many people for a weekday unless today is dollar day. Suddenly, the FBI men were walking at my side. "Stay close to me," whispered Pierce. There were ten, more than that, at least fifteen people and all with fixed faces. They know about me. How could they have found out so soon? Then I spotted Jenkinsville's leading gossip merchant, Mary Wren, holding onto the arm of Reverend Benn's wife.

The agents maneuvered me away from the sidewalk and into the center of Main Street. The crowd followed. A glob of liquid hit me in the back of the neck and when I saw what my hand had wiped away I gagged.

Suddenly a woman's voice called, "Nazi! Nazi!" Other voices joined in. A man's voice, one that I had heard before, shouted, "Jew Nazi—Jew Nazi—Jew Nazi!"

When we reached the car, the mob blocked the doors. "You people are obstructing justice," said Pierce. "Please move back."

"Jew Nazi-lover!" screamed the minister's wife.

Tires screeched to a stop. A car door opened and Sheriff Cauldwell shouted, "Get away from that car. What's the matter with you folks, anyway?"

People slowly moved away from the car, crowding into a huddle on the sidewalk. Sheriff Cauldwell opened the back door of the car for me, and then, whipping out a small black Bible from his shirt pocket, he pressed it into my hand. "Times when I was down this helped lift me up. God bless you."

"Thanks," I said, feeling the tears stinging at my eyes.

McFee drove in second gear all the way down Main Street before taking a right turn onto Highway 64. As we passed McDonald's dairy, I looked down the long dirt road leading to the prison camp. But I knew I wasn't going to find him there or any other place on God's earth. (Greene, pp. 41–43, 93–96, 189–192)

Aftermath

Anton successfully flees Arkansas but is killed in New York City while trying to avoid arrest. Patty is arrested and tried for aiding an escaped prisoner of war. At the end of *Summer of My German Soldier* she is in custody at a juvenile detention center for girls in Arkansas.

Regarded as a classic in young adult literature, *Summer of My German Soldier* was the basis of a 1978 television movie of the same title starring Kristy McNichol (as Patty Bergen), Bruce Davison (as Anton Reiker), and Michael Constantine. Esther Rolle won an Emmy Award for her portrayal of Ruth, Bergen's nanny and confidante. In 1978 Greene wrote a companion volume to *Summer of My German Soldier*, titled *Morning Is a Long Time Coming.*

Sources

Books

Greene, Bette, *Summer of My German Soldier*, Dial Press (New York), 1973.

Tunis, John Roberts, *His Enemy, His Friend*, William Morrow (New York), 1967.

Zaiben, Jane Breskin, *The Fortuneteller in 5B*, Henry Holt (New York), 1991.

Recovery from World War II

The world in 1945 was very different than it had been before World War II. The terror and mass murder perpetrated by Nazi Germany had been eliminated, and Japan's attempt to conquer much of Asia had been defeated. Had these events not occurred, the history of the rest of the twentieth century would have taken another direction. The end of the war brought many changes in the way people lived and the way they viewed their world. Some of those changes were a result of what the war had cost the world, the most obvious being the loss of life. The exact number of people killed during the war is not known, but the losses were staggering. Estimates indicate that 50 to 60 million people died throughout the world.

Millions Die in Europe

In Europe, only about half of the dead were military personnel; the rest were civilians. By comparison, in World War I (1914–1918) only 5 percent of war casualties were civilians. These men, women, and children died in many ways. They were crushed by the roofs and walls of their houses when air raids shattered their cities, blown up by mines on the roads as they tried to escape advancing armies, or they died while hiding in fields and forests in winter without enough food. Many thousands were hanged or shot by the Germans in

retaliation for attacks on German forces. Millions, including 6 million Jews, were deliberately murdered by the Nazis, machine-gunned and dumped into mass graves or gassed in death camps specially created for this purpose.

In some countries the proportion of civilian deaths was extremely high. For instance, the Netherlands lost 200,000 people out of a population of fewer than 9 million during the German occupation. Although the occupation was harsher in the Netherlands than in other parts of western Europe, Nazi aggression affected all occupied nations. The French lost 600,000 people, two-thirds of them civilians. Yet people in eastern and southeastern Europe were subjected to the most savage treatment. In Yugoslavia approximately 1.5 million people died, only 300,000 of them military personnel. In neighboring Greece about 250,000 died, the overwhelming majority civilians. Poland lost approximately 300,000 soldiers, many during the German invasion in 1939, yet this figure constitutes only a small percentage of Poland's overall casualties. More than one out of every five Poles—a total of 6 million, including 3 million Jews—died in World War II. If the United States lost the same proportion of its 1999 population, the figure would be more than 55 million people. The Soviet Union suffered still higher casualties; estimates range from 20 to 40 million Soviet citizens, if not more, including some 7 million soldiers. One million Russian civilians died in the city of Leningrad while it was surrounded by the Germans for two and one-half years.

British and American Losses

Britain and the United States were far less devastated by the war. Although Britain was the only nation that fought Germany for the duration of the conflict, British losses were fewer than those in occupied eastern Europe. A total of 250,000 English soldiers died, with another 100,000 troops from the countries of the British Commonwealth and British colonies also losing their lives. Among them were 37,000 from Canada, 24,000 from India, and 23,000 from Australia. German raids on England early in the war focused mainly on London and its surrounding areas. The lack of an occupation force resulted in fewer civilian losses than would otherwise have been the case. An estimated 60,000 British citizens died as a result of German bombing raids, with half of the casualties occurring in London. Although some 300,000 Americans died fighting Germany and Japan, the mainland United States never had to contend with an occupation force or a domestic attack. (Hawaii was not yet a state.)

Axis Powers Pay a High Price

The Axis powers suffered massive losses as well. Italian deaths were approximately 400,000, about half of them civilians. Hungary and Romania each lost 400,000 soldiers; the civilian death rate was especially high in Hungary. Germany paid an especially high human price during the war. Only the Soviet Union lost more soldiers; only the Soviet Union and Poland lost more civilians. More than 4 million men died fighting in Germany's armed forces, while 600,000 Germans, including 150,000 children, were killed in Allied bombing raids. An unknown number of civilians, perhaps as many as a million, died while trying to escape the Soviet Union's Red Army as it moved into Germany from the east in the last months of the war. Some died from exposure or drowned in half-frozen rivers while trying to cross to safety, but a number of the deaths can be attributed to revenge tactics used by Soviet troops in retaliation for the Nazi's brutal treatment of Russian civilians during the invasion of 1941.

In Japan, some 2 million people died, of which 800,000 were civilians. More than 70,000 were killed initially when the first atomic bomb was dropped on Hiroshima. Others died later from radiation sickness. Another 35,000 or more people died three days later when the United States dropped a second bomb on Nagasaki.

Physical and Psychological Trauma

In addition to the millions of deaths, at least as many soldiers and civilians were wounded or permanently disabled. For most countries, the number of wounded soldiers and civilians was higher than the number who died. In Germany 800,000 civilians were seriously injured in air raids. Millions of soldiers who had been held as prisoners of war endured hunger and malnutrition. In some cases they were subjected to brutal and inhumane treatment; even those who had been treated humanely were sometimes permanently weakened or suffered serious psychological effects. Concentration camp survivors would be haunted by the past for the rest of their lives. The hunger and malnutrition suffered by prisoners of war and concentration camp inmates was shared by much of the population of occupied Europe. For example, people literally starved to death in occupied Netherlands during the last winter of the war. Harsh conditions, including malnutrition, inadequate sanitation, and a lack of medical care, also increased the incidence of disease. There were 1.5 million cases of tuberculosis in Poland in 1945.

The physical destruction caused by the war mirrored the decimation of human populations. In the Soviet Union the homes of 28 million people were destroyed, 40,000 miles of railroads were wrecked, and 7 million horses and 17 million head of cattle had been taken by the Germans. Nearly 1,710 towns and cities and 70,000 villages in this vast region were seriously damaged; many lay in ruins at the end of the war. In France 1 million buildings were damaged or completely destroyed. The Germans had seized 60 percent of the country's machine tools and almost all its coal and iron supplies. Railroads, roads, bridges, and harbor facilities were extensively damaged, mainly by Allied bombing raids during the German occupation of France. Germany had been the scene of great land battles near the end of the war; the country had also been the target of the largest air attacks for the longest period. Approximately 15 percent of the country's houses had been destroyed and another 25 percent damaged; only smaller towns and villages had escaped the bomb-

A street in Berlin after an attack from the Allies in February 1945. Fifteen percent of Germany's homes were destroyed during the war. (Reproduced by permission of AP/Wide World Photos)

ing. The transportation system had collapsed, forcing factories that had survived the destruction to shut down due to inaccessibility of materials. Mass starvation was avoided only because the conquering Allied armies brought in food.

Displaced Persons

On April 15, 1945, when British tanks rolled into the concentration camp at Bergen-Belsen in northern Germany, they found more than 10,000 unburied bodies, most of them victims of starvation and typhus, and approximately 30,000 skeletal survivors, hundreds of whom did not live to enjoy liberation. Some 1,500 of the survivors were Jews, a few hundred more were Gypsies, and approximately 1,000 were Germans who had been arrested for anti-Nazi activities. The remainder were citizens of Luxembourg, the Netherlands, Yugoslavia, France, Belgium, Czechoslovakia, Greece, Poland and the Soviet Union, who had been sent to the camp for resisting Nazi occupation. All were far from their homes.

The composition of the Bergen-Belsen survivors illustrates the huge refugee problem that faced postwar Europe. Huge populations were

transported from one place to another during the course of the war. In the years after the war, all of Europe was awash in uncounted tens of millions of refugees. An army of wanderers traveled Europe's shattered roads.

German refugees numbered in the millions. Some were ethnic Germans whose ancestors had settled in other lands long before. Others had been relocated to conquered eastern European nations to establish *Lebensraum* or living-space (Hitler's plan to establish populations of Germans in conquered areas, sometimes after deporting or exterminating the people who had originally lived there). All Germans who were outside of Germany at the war's end faced violent reprisals from the people around them. The Red Army, which occupied most of eastern Europe, was authorized to wreak whatever violence it saw fit on Germans. At the Potsdam Conference in 1945, the Allies agreed that "the transfer to Germany of German populations, and of elements thereof, remaining in Poland, Czechoslovakia and Hungary ... should be effected in an orderly and humane manner." Thousands of men and women were summarily ejected from these countries, and found themselves wan-

A young displaced girl, pictured with an identification card, hopes that someone will recognize her so she can be rejoined with family members. Many children were left homeless by the war. (USHMM Museum Photo Archives)

dering the countryside, homeless and prey to the vengeance of whomever they encountered.

Approximately five million Russians were also stranded in Europe. During the war, the Nazis captured Russian prisoners of war (POWs) in astounding numbers. Slavs were regarded as a subhuman race by the Nazis, and of course many Germans bitterly hated their Russian enemies. Many of the POWs were interned in camps, where they met wholesale slaughter. Others became forced laborers in German holdings throughout Europe, and thousands more were pressed into the Wehrmacht (German armed forces). After Germany's defeat, Moscow immediately demanded the return of all Russians. Although many of the Russian POWs were terrified to return to the USSR, the Allies agreed to repatriate them and they were shipped eastward. The Allies knew that those who had fought in the Wehrmacht would be severely punished. But they did not expect that Stalin would order the imprisonment or summary execution of millions of Russian refugees who had remained loyal to the Soviet Union. As far as Stalin was concerned, any Russian who had experienced life outside the Soviet system was an enemy of the state.

The plight of many displaced eastern Europeans was a cruel one. Their countries had been seized by the Soviet Union or were being turned into communist satellite states. Approximately 30,000 Latvians, Lithuanians, and Estonians, citizens of nations annexed by the Soviet Union, succeeded in fleeing to Sweden. Many of these had joined the Wehrmacht to fight against the hated Russians, and now they threw themselves on the mercy of the Swedes. The Latvian soldiers went on a hunger strike in 1945 to win public sympathy for their plight. But in January of 1946 Sweden partially bowed to the Soviet Union's demand for repatriation and sent the soldiers to the USSR, while allowing the civilians to remain and to seek citizenship eventually. On the journey to Russia, the Baltic soldiers had to be guarded carefully by police to prevent them from committing mass suicide.

Of the 50 to 60 million refugees, approximately two million of every nationality literally had nowhere to go. The refugees included thousands of Jewish survivors of the death camps. In 1945 the United Nations set up temporary Displaced Persons camps throughout Europe to deal with this monumental problem. The camps were run by the United Nations Relief and Rehabilitation Agency (UNRRA), and were designed to place refugees as quickly as possible. Unfortunately, in all too many cases, this was an extremely slow process.

The DP camps, as they came to be called, were established in abandoned army barracks, POW camps, and concentration camps. The UN-run DP camps bore a grim resemblance to the Nazi concentration camps. Refugees were frequently brought to the camps by the thousands in packed, sweltering cattle cars. The camps were ill-equipped to deal with the vast numbers of sick, starving, traumatized refugees. They were frequently overcrowded, unsanitary, and plagued with constant food shortages. In 1945, U.S. President Harry S Truman sent Earl Harrison to tour the camps and analyze the conditions there. Harrison reported that "We appear to be treating the Jews as the Nazis treated them, except that we do not exterminate them."

Agate Nesaule was a seven-year-old Latvian girl who lived in a DP camp near Berlin for five years. In her 1995 memoir, *A Woman in Amber*, she contradicts Harrison's impression. For her, the DP camp was a haven of safety after the terrors she'd previously experienced. Nevertheless, even as a child, she was aware that it was a highly unsettled existence. "Life in the camps meant waiting," she wrote. "We

Three young refugees are helped by the American military police in Oswego, New York. (Photograph by Hikaru Iwasaki, courtesy of USHMM Photo Archives)

were all waiting. We waited for food, clothing, medication. We waited for days when we were allowed outside the gates for a few hours to walk in the surrounding woods or down the dusty roads to half-empty German villages. We waited for a chance to leave the camps, to go back to Latvia or failing that, to emigrate to another country. When opportunities to depart finally opened up, we waited again for others to decide whether we were good enough, whether we deserved to go where we wished. We were all waiting for a chance to have a real life."

The years wore on, and the hard-core DPs remained in the camps. The communities there became strangely like ordinary towns. Barbers cut hair, doctors delivered babies, homemade presses cranked out camp newspapers, and camp officials were elected. Some Jews who had lost many family members to the Nazis, started new relationships— many marriages occurred as people tried to begin their lives anew. Nesaule, who entered a camp when she was seven and left when she was twelve, wrote of the rigorous schools the DPs set up for children. "Even first graders went to school six days a week, from early morning to noon. Enough homework was assigned to keep us indoors till twilight and beyond."

The process of finding homes for the DPs was painfully slow. Few nations were willing to accept thousands of hungry, unhealthy, unskilled immigrants. England, the United States, Canada, and Australia sought immigrants on the basis of skills, although since unemployment was rampant throughout Europe, these calls for workers were extremely rare. In order to be selected to go to one

Rescue and Redemption in Palestine

Christopher Sykes was an aristocratic British traveler and writer who visited Palestine during the 1930s. In his book *Crossroads to Israel,* he wrote, "There was no more moving sight in those days than the arrival at Haifa or Jaffa of a Mediterranean ship carrying Jews from Europe: the spontaneous cries of joy at the first sight of the shore, the mass chanting of Hebrew hymns or Yiddish songs usually beginning raggedly over all the boat and sometimes swelling into a single harmony; the uncontrolled joy of these returning exiles (for so they thought of themselves); a man seizing hold of a stranger and pointing to the approaching land crying 'Zion! Zion!' and 'Jerusalem!'" Sykes continued: "Such scenes made many of those who saw them recognize as never before that the human spirit cannot be destroyed, and the Jewish inspiration is among the sublimest expressions of the unconquerable soul. Zionism showed itself at its very finest in these years. Enthusiasm went hand in hand with practical sense ... Palestine was the answer to Hitler!" Sykes added, prophetically, "The Arabs looked on with dismay. Seen through Arab eyes, this great work of rescue and redemption had nothing beautiful about it and seemed on the contrary to be a stark act of oppression against themselves."

---

of these countries, a DP had to possess the needed skill as well as endure physical and psychological examinations and a rigorous screening process to ensure that he or she was not a Nazi or Communist. The process was mired in red tape and frustrating for everyone involved. Kathryn Hulme, a UNRRA worker at the Aschaffenburg camp near Frankfurt, wrote, "The more highly educated the DP, the more absolute was his hopelessness. One Ukrainian doctor wept like a child when he was rejected from a scheme calling for hard-rock miners in Canada."

But the problem was to grow even worse. As the Soviet Union strengthened its grip on its territories, new waves of refugees fled westward toward the camps. In 1947 the UNRRA was forced to close the camps to new DPs. Refugees were turned away and were forced to make do as best they could on the wrecked streets of Germany and central Europe.

On June 28, 1948, the United States passed the Displaced Persons Act, which provided the opportunity for more than 200,000 DPs to immigrate to the United States. Additionally, in 1948 the State of Israel was created, which at last gave thousands of Jews a place to go. Nevertheless, World War II's refugees were still a problem for the United Nations into the 1950s.

The Jewish Survivors

Despite Hitler's combined quest to control Europe and exterminate all Jews, between three and six million European Jews survived. Some escaped Europe before and during the war; thousands endured the DP camps after.

Until 1939 the British administration allowed almost unlimited Jewish immigration into Palestine. Before Hitler's rise to power in Germany, most German Jews were uninterested in moving to the "Jewish national home." After the Nazi Party rose to power in 1933 and anti-Semitism was codified as law, violence against Jews became the policy of the totalitarian government. Many Jewish refugees streamed into other European countries. Few nations welcomed these refugees, and some were forced to return. The exception was British-controlled Palestine.

In 1917 the British government declared that it favored "the establishment on Palestine of a national home for the Jewish people, and will use their best endeavors to facilitate the achievement of this [objective]." The Balfour Declaration, as it was called, did not define exactly what a "national home" was; it only stipulated that it would not "prejudice the civil and religious rights of existing non-Jewish communities in Palestine."

In the first few months of 1933, more than forty thousand Jews applied for entry visas to Palestine. Surprisingly, the Nazi Party collaborated with the Zionists in Palestine to promote the emigration of thousands of Jews from Germany. In a strange win-win situation, the property of a Jewish emigrant was liquidated, heavily taxed by Germany, and then transferred to a Palestine account where the immigrant would receive the remainder in local currency. But the policy soon fell under disfavor with both the Palestinian Jewish community, who resented the fact that the Nazis were making a profit, and the Germans, who did not approve of the growing Palestinian movement for an independent Jewish state.

From 1936 to 1938, Palestine was rocked by a series of violent revolts from Palestine's Arab population. These uprisings coincided with the rising threat of war with Hitler's Germany. Britain came to the decision that further alienation of the Muslim peoples in Palestine and elsewhere in the British empire would be a strategic disaster on the eve of war. In 1939 they passed an act that sharply curtailed the number of Jewish immigrants who would be allowed into Palestine, which on the eve of the Holocaust effectively closed that means of escape for European Jews.

Countless ordinary people of every nation risked their own lives to rescue Jews from the Holocaust throughout the war. Several busy (and often highly profitable) undergrounds were established to conceal Jewish refugees and smuggle them to safety. These secret organizations brought Jews through the mountain passes into Switzerland and Spain. Danish fishermen plying the Baltic sea ferried refugees into Sweden. None of these neutral countries were pleased about the stream of Jewish refugees entering their borders and all of them were emphatic that the refugees were not to remain.

Several organizations, such as the American Jewish Joint Distribution Committee (JDC) and the American War Refugee Board (WRB), provided much-needed aid and funds to support the refugees in neutral European countries. In addition, it was through these organizations that much of the West's knowledge of the Holocaust came. They even launched an incredibly ambitious (and ultimately unsuccessful) plan to save all of Europe's Jews by bribing the Nazi hierarchy to cease their depredations. The funds for these programs came almost entirely from donations from American Jews. Due to their dependence upon American money and American law, the organizations were for the most part unable to aid in the escape of Jews from Europe.

The only truly safe haven for European Jews was Palestine, but getting there was incredibly difficult. The British administration had sharply decreased the numbers of immigrants who would

The *Sturma* Disaster

In December of 1941, a rickety river cargo boat called the *Sturma*, packed with 769 desperate Jewish refugees, left the Romanian port of Constanta. They had paid high fees for passage on the boat, and had been assured by the boat's operator that immigration certificates awaited them in Istanbul. It was a cruel hoax. The *Sturma* was dangerously unseaworthy and suffered repeated breakdowns on the several-day journey to Istanbul. There the refugees discovered that no immigration certificates had been arranged for them. The ship remained at port in Istanbul for ten weeks, during which time the refugees were not permitted to disembark. During this period, the Turks demanded that the British solve the problem of the refugees on the *Sturma*, but the British denied any involvement or responsibility. On February 23, 1942, the Turks cut the *Sturma* loose and sent it back in the direction it had come. The boat contained no food, water, or fuel, and that night it sank. All but one of the 769 Jews on board died.

The *Sturma* disaster made worldwide headlines and produced a tide of indignation among the British public. But it produced no appreciable effect in British policy toward the immigration of Jews into Palestine.

legally be accepted into Palestine. Moreover, they had to obtain permission to leave their home country and to travel through all nations in between. Finally, when the British caught illegal immigrants, they deducted their number from the legal quota of immigrants allowed, so that in some years no visas were issued at all.

None of this prevented Jewish refugees from struggling southward, through tremendous dangers, in an attempt to seek illegal asylum in Pales-

When the SS *Pan York* arrived in Haifa, it brought some 2,600 displaced persons from detention camps in Cyprus. (National Archives/USHMM Photo Archives Photo Archives)

tine. They pooled in port cities like Marseilles and Odessa, waiting for boats to take them to Palestine. The Jewish community in Palestine organized secret societies that worked feverishly to ferry as many illegal immigrants into the country as possible. Uncounted Jews were killed on the dangerous journey to Palestine. Thousands more were captured by the British before they could reach Palestine and sent to detention camps on the island of Mauritius, where they were treated with punitive cruelty. In this way the British hoped to deter further attempts to enter Palestine—but the refugees feared the Nazis far more than the British.

In spite of all this, thousands of refugees did succeed in entering Palestine, where, with the help of societies like Hagana and Mossad's Aliyah Bet (Institute for Illegal Immigration), they disappeared into Palestine's Jewish population.

At the end of the war, thousands of Jewish survivors were interned in DP camps. They were

severely malnourished, sick, weary, and desperately traumatized. They frequently faced brutal anti-Semitic violence from the other refugees in the camps. Worse, the Jews were among the DPs who languished in the camps for years. The world was aghast at the suffering they had endured, but for the most part, no one wanted them.

Many Jews attempted to return to their homes in Germany, Poland, and elsewhere. Their belief that they could somehow return to their prewar lives was quickly shattered. Hundreds of Jews were murdered in Europe in the years after the war's end. Almost all of the Jewish survivors realized that they could not go home and went to the DP camps. One UNRRA survey revealed that most Jewish DPs dreamed of going to Palestine.

In 1945, newly elected British Prime Minister Clement Atlee was under considerable pressure to ease Palestine's immigration restrictions. The Jewish Council in Jerusalem asked the British admin-

Displaced persons boarded ships like the *Exodus* in an attempt to go to Palestine illegally. When the *Exodus* was denied entry to Palestine, the refugees onboard began a hunger strike. (USHMM Photo Archives)

When Jews tried to enter Palestine illegally, many were sent to displaced persons camps in Cyprus. The camps, run by the British, functioned like POW camps. (USHMM)

istration for 100,000 entry certificates for the DPs. They were refused. The Hagana (the people's militia), led by David Ben-Gurion, began to wage an armed guerilla war against the British administration. The guerillas had the full support of both the Jewish press in Palestine and the Jewish community worldwide. U.S. President Harry Truman also urged Great Britain to allow Jewish immigration.

During this period, Jewish refugees continued to stream toward Palestine. In 1946 the British set up detention camps in Cyprus for the illegal immigrants. By 1948, some 50,000 people were housed in the Cyprus camps. These camps, surrounded by barbed wire and filled with Holocaust survivors, were a public embarrassment to the British.

Atlee stood firm until 1947, when Winston Churchill, leader of Great Britain's opposition Conservative party, declared, "If we cannot fulfill our promises to the Zionists we should, without delay, place our Mandate for Palestine at the feet of the United Nations, and give due notice of our evacuation from that country." On November 29, 1947, the UN General Assembly passed a resolution to partition Palestine into two separate states, one Jewish, one Arab. The plan was to allow open immigration of Jewish refugees on February 1, 1948. But immigration was delayed when Palestine exploded into violence as Arabs used explosives to

reject the UN's decision, and Jews responded in kind. When British forces withdrew on May 15, five independent Arab states joined the fray against the newly created State of Israel.

Israel was born, and the Jewish refugees from Cyprus and from European DP camps began to pour in. The Jews were free of the Holocaust—but their future in Israel was to be a far from peaceful one.

Economic Recovery in Europe

While the future of Israel was being decided, the economic recovery of Europe was underway. Despite the unprecedented human misery and physical destruction caused by the war, the rebuilding and economic recovery of Europe progressed rapidly. The United States provided extensive financial aid, but the most significant efforts came from the Europeans themselves. Putting aside their differences, European nations began the process of rebuilding. Even before the war was over, Belgium, Luxembourg, and the Netherlands agreed to form an economic union. Soon these three small countries and France joined two of their World War II enemies, Italy and West Germany, to establish what eventually became the Common Market. At the end of the twentieth century most western European countries were members of the Common Market.

Many Jews tried to enter Palestine illegally after the war and were caught and confined in detention camps, like the one shown here. They were provided with army rations from the Palestinian government. (Reproduced by permission of AP/Wide World Photos)

The entrance to the American zone of Berlin, Germany. (Reproduced by permission of the Corbis Corporation [Bellevue])

Germany's border in 1939 and in 1945. The four post-war power zones are indicated.

The Division of Germany

European unity came slowly, however, after many years of division. At the end of the war Allied leaders divided Germany into four zones, each occupied by the United States, Britain, France, or the Soviet Union. A decision had not yet been reached on the long-term future of Germany. Some Allied officials advocated permanent division, which would prevent a future German war effort; others wanted to return Germany to an agricultural economy, thereby disabling the industrial ability to support another modern war. Although there had always been significant disagreement between the Soviets and the Western

Allies, tensions had been put aside in the interest of defeating Germany. At the conclusion of the war, however, these issues assumed paramount importance in regard to the division of Germany.

The Soviet Union began to turn the eastern zone, which had been placed under its control, into a Communist country. In turn, the Western Allies considered the rest of Germany a valuable partner in the fight against communism. Increasingly this conflict interfered with attempts at unity among the four powers. Within a few years, the conflict escalated into the Cold War, a worldwide struggle between the United States and its supporters on one side and the Soviet Union and its

National border changes at the end of World War II led to massive deportation of Germans living in areas that no longer belonged to Germany. This map indicates areas that changed hands and the new Polish–Soviet–German borders.

allies on the other. The countries of eastern Europe, which were controlled by the Soviet army, would become Communist. The countries of western Europe would reject communism; many joined the United States in a permanent military alliance called the North Atlantic Treaty Organization (NATO). Germany would be one of the main focal points of the conflict. Despite these differences, however, the four powers collaborated at various times during the Cold War period.

Borders Restored

The violence of World War II did not end when treaties were signed and peace was declared.

As the first of the Nuremberg Trials captured the world's attention, a bloody conflict arose on Germany's borders but received comparatively little worldwide coverage. Large numbers of Germans resided in territories that the Allies had promised to return to Poland, Czechoslovakia, and other countries of eastern Europe. Many feared that the Germans living in these areas would resist the new borders and force an armed resistance. In early 1945, 2 million Germans had already fled from East Prussia, trying to escape the advancing Soviet army. The following winter, according to an Allied agreement, Germans were forced to leave their homes in eastern Europe and move to western Germany. Approximately 14 million Germans

Oppressors and Victims

In 1946 Germans were expelled from eastern Europe. With the exception of people within Germany, however, the world paid slight attention to this event. The reason is simple: at the end of the war, few Europeans and Americans were ready to sympathize with Germans being oppressed by Poles and Czechs. Germany had terrorized, brutalized, and murdered these people and other eastern Europeans for more than five years, in some cases even longer. Most Germans in the Sudetenland, for example, had apparently welcomed Adolf Hitler's dismantling of Czechoslovakia in retaliation for supposed maltreatment of Sudeten Germans. To many people, and certainly to the Czechs, it seemed that the Germans were getting what they deserved. Similarly, the brutality committed against Germans in Poland could not compare with what the Nazis had done to the Poles. Regardless of political affiliation, all people of German nationality were expelled from eastern Europe, whether they wanted to leave or not. The same argument the Nazis had given for deporting the Jews was used in the case of the Germans: They had been born into a specific nationality and therefore could never be fully loyal citizens.

were deported from Silesia in southwest Poland and Pomerania farther north, from the Sudetenland, and from other areas of Czechoslovakia. Like refugees during the war, these Germans were weak, hungry, and cold and subjected to extreme brutality. Historians estimate that 2 million people died during these expulsions.

The territorial divisions agreed upon by the Allies restored Europe to the geographic boundaries that existed in 1937. At the end of World War I (1914–1918), newly independent countries were formed, only to be crushed by the Third Reich before and during World War II. When World War II ended in 1945, these countries were restored to resemble closely their prewar locations. Austria became a separate country again, instead of being an annex of Germany. Czechoslovakia lost its eastern tip to the Soviet Union, but was returned to independence. Slovakia, a German puppet state during the war, was reunited with Czech areas that had been absorbed into Germany. Yugoslavia, which Germany, Italy, and their allies had invaded and split up, was again unified. The three small Baltic countries of Lithuania, Latvia, and Estonia did not regain the independence they had lost, first to the Soviets in 1939 to 1940 and then to the invading Germans in 1941. Instead, these countries became part of the Soviet Union and remained so until 1991. The major European border changes involved Poland and Germany. Although large parts of eastern Poland were absorbed into the Soviet Union, Poland gained territory from Germany on the west and the north, controlling half of East Prussia. The other half of East Prussia became part of the Soviet Union; the purpose of these changes was to shrink Germany and to move Polish territory 100 miles westward.

The United States at the End of the War

The United States did not experience the devastation and exhaustion of Europe. American factories, railroads, and mines had not been damaged; in fact, during the war American industry doubled its production levels. Prior to the United States' entry into the conflict, the American aircraft industry had employed 46,000 people; after 1941, 50 times as many workers were employed. American factories produced equipment and supplies for the war effort in seemingly unlimited quantities—enough to furnish the British army with most of its tanks and 86,000 jeeps. In the Soviet Union, Red Army soldiers and provisions were transported to the battlefront on American trucks. To protect the soldiers' feet during the harsh Russian winter, the United States sent millions of pairs of felt boot liners, made in American factories to Soviet specifications. In 1945 the United States produced one-half of the world's coal and two-thirds of its crude oil. The United States possessed 60 percent of the world's gold reserves. The American merchant marine was now three times the size of Britain's, which had been the largest in the world before the war. The United States had provided $30 billion in aid to its allies, including $13.5 billion to Britain and $9 billion to the Soviet Union.

A boom in new housing led to the rapid growth of suburbs like Levittown, New York, America's first mass-produced suburb. (Reproduced by permission of AP/Wide World Photos)

Unlike Europe, the United States was economically stronger at the end of the war than at the beginning. Nevertheless, World War II had an equally significant impact on the United States. The Great Depression (1929–1939) ended when the war broke out, as American factories supplying the European war effort created an unprecedented number of jobs. Contrary to the fears of economic experts, these jobs did not disappear at the end of the war. The economy was swiftly converted to peacetime conditions because Europe depended on American farms and factories to supply its needs. Product demand skyrocketed, as consumer goods that had previously been impossible to acquire became readily accessible. Millions of Americans felt they needed to make up for lost time. For example, the United States government had stopped the manufacturing of passenger cars so auto plants could build tanks and army trucks exclusively. When the war ended, many Americans wanted cars, and they had saved money to buy them.

Approximately 16 million men and women had served in the armed forces; they had been sent away from home, even if they never left the country. Upon being reunited with their loved ones, they wanted to settle into jobs and raise families. On June 22, 1944, a new law (usually called the GI Bill) made a college education available to nearly all veterans, paying their tuition and providing a stipend to help with living expenses while they were in school. Millions of veterans took advantage of the bill, drastically increasing the enrollments of universities, junior colleges, and community colleges; others finished their high school educations. The GI Bill was instrumental in raising U.S. literacy and education levels. Education also became more important to Americans because of the baby boom—a large increase in the birthrate that continued for twenty years. A veteran with a good education could generally earn a living substantial enough to support a growing family. The GI Bill also allowed veterans to buy homes without a down payment and with low-interest loans, often resulting in house payments that were lower than rent rates. By 1947, 1 million former servicemen and servicewomen had taken advantage of this provision, accounting for part of the upturn in home ownership.

A housing shortage soon developed, as most of the United States' building efforts had focused on urban areas and war industries. In 1944 only 114,000 new houses were begun in America, but the number exploded and continued to grow after

The United Nations meets in London, 1946. (Reproduced by permission of the Corbis Corporation)

the war. In 1950 construction was begun on about 1.7 million homes, creating vast suburbs and housing divisions. Communities emerged outside cities, often consisting of hundreds or even thousands of quickly built, identical houses. No industrial or commercial businesses were located near these areas, so people began commuting from their homes to work in cities. Use of private vehicles increased and elaborate highway systems were constructed, causing a decrease in public transportation. Since the new suburban areas rarely had enough existing stores for rapidly expanding populations, malls were created to accommodate shoppers. American life had undergone a dramatic transformation.

The United States was not only the largest economy in the world in 1945, but it was also the greatest military power. As tensions increased with the Soviet Union, Americans debated the proper role for the United States in world affairs. World War II had started only twenty-one years after the end of World War I. It was clear that Europe, and the world, could not afford to undergo such terrible destruction once every generation. Allied leaders, especially President Franklin D. Roosevelt, were determined to establish a protocol for dealing with future threats to peace. In Roosevelt's view, the major nations of the world needed to unite and establish an international assembly of delegates. This idea was inspired by President Woodrow Wilson's League of Nations, an organization formed in 1918 after World War I that quickly fell apart. Most historians believe one of the main reasons for the failure of the League was that the United States refused to join, even though it had been Wilson's idea. The United States' policy of isolationism was extremely popular at the beginning of World War II. Even before the Japanese attack on Pearl Harbor, an increasing number of Americans regarded the events in Europe as a potential threat to their own freedom. When the war came to an end and Americans discovered the scale of Nazi crimes, public opinion shifted toward involvement in world affairs as a defensive measure to prevent future wars and to protect U.S. interests.

Roosevelt's version of the League of Nations, called the United Nations Organization, was supported by most Americans. Roosevelt thought the downfall of the League of Nations had been caused by endless debates and the special interests of member nations. He believed that maintaining peace required that the most powerful nations agree on important matters and then work together, without the interference of smaller countries. Before World War II had even ended, the United Nations determined that the decision to use military force would not be delegated to the entire organization, but instead to a small committee that included the United States, the Soviet Union, Britain, and China. (China was included at Roosevelt's insistence, and France was later added.) According to Roosevelt, the great alliance that was fighting and winning the war would remain together and act as a police force for the world. On April 25, 1945, only two weeks after Roosevelt's death, the United Nations Conference on International Organization met in San Francisco. A charter for the new United Nations Organization was signed on June 26. A month later the U.S. Senate approved the charter by a vote of eighty-nine to two.

Distant Thunder

Difficulty in estimating World War II casualties rests on one major factor: determining who is to be included in the count. Fighting in China had been ongoing before and after the war with Japan, and disease and starvation ran rampant in many areas. When such conditions occur in wartime, it is hard to know what caused them. One example, from India rather than China, illustrates this problem. In 1943 a famine in Bengal, located in the eastern part of India, claimed the lives of 1.5 million, five times the number of American dead in World War II. These people are rarely considered victims of World War II. The Bengal famine, however, was not due to natural causes, such as a shortage of rain for crops. According to historian Gerhard Weinberg, the famine was caused by the "disruption of trade, shipping shortages, and the extraordinary incompetence of the British administration" that ruled India. British wartime needs were placed above those of the Bengalis, raising the price of food so high that poor people could not afford to buy it. Almost certainly, the famine would not have occurred if there had been no war. The Bengalis died, as suggested by the title of Satyajit Ray's film about the famine, because of "distant thunder."

The New Face of Asia

In many respects World War II had a more dramatic effect on Asia than on Europe. In Japan 2 million people died, 800,000 of them civilians. Asian cities had suffered greater physical destruction from air attacks than any other country, partly because wooden buildings were more susceptible to fires from bombs. Japan was also the first country to suffer the effects of the atomic bomb. As in Germany, the Americans were determined to destroy the Japanese militaristic system, which

they believed had caused the war. The country was placed under military occupation and run by the American commander, General Douglas MacArthur, and his staff. The major wartime leaders of Japan were put on trial in Tokyo; twenty-five were convicted and seven were sentenced to death. Thousands of other Japanese, especially military men, were tried in locations that the Japanese army had ruled during the war. Many were charged with mistreating Allied prisoners of war, and 900 were executed.

Japanese Aggression against the Chinese

Even in the nineteenth century, Japan had begun taking steps as early as 1874 to gain control over Chinese territory. In 1875 Japan seized Taiwan and portions of southern Manchuria; by 1931, Japan had occupied all of Chinese Manchuria, and other countries were beginning to protest the aggression of the Japanese and the puppet government set up by the Japanese in Manchuria. The League of Nations also voiced disapproval, so in 1933 Japan resigned from the League of Nations and continued its movements further into China and other countries.

In 1937 Japan began a full-scale war with China and conquered Beijing and Tianjing, then moved into Shanghai and the capital, Nanking. In Manchuria, and later in other cities, the Japanese were extremely brutal, killing, torturing, and raping many people. In Nanking alone, it is estimated that 140,000 to 300,000 died at the hands of the Japanese. After the destruction of Nanking, the capital was moved to Changqing, which was subjected to twenty-four-hour bombings for several months in 1940. As the Japanese rolled through China, first hundreds of thousands and then millions of Chinese civilians were killed, aside from those enlisted in the Chinese military.

The Chinese military and civilians were not only killed by machine guns, bombs, and explosives. After the end of the war, the Soviet Union found evidence that the Japanese had used medical and biological experiments to kill and torture Chinese civilians, as well as Russian, Korean, and Mongolian citizens, and Allied POWs.

The Soviet Union prosecuted some Japanese war criminals and asked for Allied help with others. There was evidence that the Japanese tested the effectiveness of tools for biological and chemical warfare on several villages in Manchuria and northern China, in direct opposition to the Geneva Convention of 1925 (which Japan had refused to sign).

The Japanese army was accused of promoting research that included infecting victims with various diseases, including bubonic plague, syphilis, anthrax, and typhoid. Poisonous and bacterial gasses were sprayed by airplane on villages, including Zhejiang and Congshan; Chinese water supplies were treated with poisonous chemicals or bacteria; and plague-carrying fleas were used to infect people. Though this research was widespread, one particular unit of the Japanese army based in Manchuria, Unit 731, was accused of developing these weapons of warfare and of conducting even more horrific experiments on its victims. The list of experiments on *marutas* ("logs of wood") includes conducting vivisections (live dissections) without anesthesia, removing limbs and reattaching them in the wrong places, submitting victims to extreme heat and cold to the point of death, and injecting animal blood, bacteria, and germs into test subjects. Most of these tests were performed on unarmed Chinese civilians, and an accurate number of those killed by these tests is unavailable. Most of those on whom tests were performed died, or if they lived, they were used in other experiments or gassed when it seemed that Japan was on the verge of surrender.

Though the United States discounted Soviet evidence of these activities at the time, new evidence supports the belief that these experiments did occur. Testimony from Chinese, Russian, and American survivors, as well as from a few Japanese who worked on the projects, documents the atrocities that were perpetrated mainly on Chinese subjects between 1931 and 1945. After the war, the American government chose to maintain ties with the Japanese in order to fight the threat of communist expansion in the Soviet Union and Russia, and so the stories of abuse went ignored in the United States for many years.

Chinese were also forced to work as slave laborers for Japanese companies against the rules of the Geneva Convention. Just as prisoners of war from other countries captured by Japan were forced to work as slave laborers in construction companies, factories, and mines, under treacherous conditions, many Chinese were taken out of their homes and placed in Japanese prisoner camps in China or Japan. The prisoners worked up to twelve hours per day, with little or no food, and many were beaten indiscriminately by Japanese guards. The mines were generally unsafe: Cave-ins and rock falls were commonplace, lung problems associated with mining were rampant due to lack of preventive measures, and medical treatment was usually nonexistent. Many of those forced into the labor camps did not return to their homes.

Women from China were forced to labor in different ways and also died in slavery. On their march through China, the Japanese raped many Chinese women and children. Some were either killed immediately or forced to work as "comfort women," or sexual slaves, for the Japanese army over extended periods of time. Many of these women contracted sexually transmitted diseases from serving the Japanese and died from lack of treatment. Others killed themselves rather than bear the shame or the conditions under which they were forced to live by the Japanese.

Though the figures for how many Chinese civilians died at the hands of the Japanese between 1937 and 1945 vary widely from source to source, all figures are more than 2 million. Most of the figures go as high as 10 million, more than the number of Jews killed during the Holocaust. The Chinese government estimates that 35 million Chinese (military and civilian) died because of the war with Japan. The Japanese debate the number of deaths caused directly by their aggression toward China. They insist that many Chinese died of starvation due to internal economic problems and that some were killed by warring forces within the Chinese government as the ruling parties fought for power. But the fact that the Japanese murdered, tortured, and treated millions of Chinese inhumanely is well-documented.

At the war crimes tribunals held after World War II, the counts on which the Japanese were convicted by the Allied nations included "mass-scale atrocities," "waging unprovoked war against China," disregarding their duties to prevent atrocities, and ordering or authorizing inhumane treatment of others. Yet few of the Japanese convicted served full terms for the crimes they committed, and several reentered high governmental positions after being paroled (within ten years of their convictions). In recent years, the American and Japanese governments have refused to address reparations issues, and though various Japanese officials have made statements expressing remorse, official apologies have not been issued. One reason is the 1951 San Francisco Peace Treaty, signed by the United States, China, and other Allied nations, which exonerated Japan from further reparations and its citizens from further prosecution under international law.

Mao Zedong was the leader of the communist movement in China. After the end of World War II, the communists took control of the country from the Nationalist Party. (Reproduced by permission of the Corbis Corporation [Bellevue])

Japan received a new constitution, written by MacArthur's staff, which declared the emperor to be a symbol of the nation rather than the godlike figure who had previously ruled Japan. Specifying that Japan would never again wage war, the constitution abolished the army; Japan would be permitted only a small self-defense force. The new laws also proclaimed equal rights for women and protected workers' rights to form labor unions. Japan lost all its colonies; Manchuria and Taiwan were returned to China, and Korea became an independent country. Over time Japan became more prosperous, eventually developing into the second-largest economy in the world after the United States. Instead of aircraft carriers, Japanese shipyards built giant oil tankers; instead of tanks, factories produced automobiles.

In a majority of the remaining Asian territories, civilian casualties had been relatively low during the war due to the remote locations (such as New Guinea and the Pacific islands) in which the

fighting had taken place. Nevertheless, there were exceptions, such as the destruction caused in Manila, the capital of the Philippines. By far the greatest exception was China. No one has a clear idea of how many Chinese were killed during the years that Japan was waging war in the country. Historians give figures ranging from 2 million to 15 million people.

The surrender of Japan did not bring peace to China. There had long been a civil war between the official Chinese government, run by the Kuomintang (Nationalist Party), and the Chinese Communist party. The internal conflict had been pushed into the background while both sides fought Japan, but tensions had never completely ended. Although attempts were made to negotiate a truce, the fighting grew worse once the war was over. By July 1946, within a year of Japan's defeat, full-scale civil war had resumed and continued until 1949, when the Communists won control of the country.

One of the most important long-term effects of World War II was the impact on the Asian colonies controlled by European countries. Three colonial powers—Great Britain, France, and the Netherlands—were so weakened by the war that they were no longer able to hold onto their empires. Japanese victories early in the war showed other Asian nations that victory against a European power was achievable. The prestige of the colonial powers, which was partly based on superior technology and military strength, had been seriously undermined.

Independence movements had emerged throughout the area before the war. The colonial powers, determined to retain their control, often declared these movements illegal and jailed their leaders. In many places Japan's defeat of the Europeans was welcomed and, in some cases, nationalist groups cooperated with the Japanese authorities. Yet pro-Japanese attitudes were usually short-lived as a result of the brutality of Japanese rule. Soon it became obvious that Japan was motivated by self interest, not by a desire to gain freedom for the other countries. Despite these complications, Japan's slogan of "Asia for the Asians" was not forgotten.

The future of European empires in Asia was also influenced by the policies of the United States. In 1941, before the United States entered the war, the United States and Great Britain issued the Atlantic Charter, which committed the Allies to opposing territorial changes that did not reflect the

The last British Viceroy of India, Lord Louis Mountbatten (seated at right of table, facing camera), meets with Indian leaders to discuss India's independence from England. To Mountbatten's right is Jawaharlal Nehru, who became the first prime minister of independent India. (Reproduced by permission of AP/Wide World Photos)

"freely expressed" desire of the people involved. The charter seemed to imply that the British, French, and Dutch should not regain their colonies unless the native peoples voted for their return. The language reflected Roosevelt's strong opposition to colonialism, an attitude shared by most Americans. Critics of this policy have often argued that the United States opposed colonies because it could influence and dominate other countries through economic power, without having to use military force or direct rule. Whether this is true, Roosevelt's attitude and American public opinion encouraged colonized people to seek independence. The language and intent of the Atlantic Charter also had an impact on Europeans. France and the Netherlands, among others, had just regained their own freedom after German domination. Reimposing French or Dutch rule in other countries seemed inconsistent with the goals of the war.

Despite these considerations, and despite their reluctance to displease the United States, on which they so heavily depended for economic aid, the colonial powers still did not want to rescind control over their colonies. In some cases they used armed force—even the defeated Japanese army—to restore power. On August 17, 1945, two days after Japan announced its surrender, the Indonesian National Party declared that the Dutch East Indies was now the independent country of Indonesia. They refused to return control of the government to Dutch officials, who were now being released from Japanese prisons. British troops soon arrived to accept the surrender of Japanese troops, disarm them, and put them in prisoner-of-war camps. When the British also tried to restore Dutch control, they found themselves greatly outnumbered by Indonesian soldiers loyal to the independence movement. The British then released the Japanese troops, rearmed them, and, with British officers in command, used them to return the Dutch to power.

A similar event occurred in the French colony of Indochina (the present-day countries of North and South Vietnam, Cambodia, and Laos). The Allies had agreed that British troops should temporarily occupy the southern part of Vietnam, the largest of the three countries of Indochina. In Vietnam, an independence movement called the Viet Minh was taking over the country from the Japanese. When a small force of British troops arrived in September 1945, they deployed released Japanese prisoners of war to control the Viet Minh. In October, French troops moved in and reestablished French control, despite the provisions of the Atlantic Charter. Before long war broke out between the Viet Minh and the French; the conflict lasted until the French were defeated in 1954.

India was considered the largest and most important European colony, the "crown jewel" of the British Empire. The Indian independence movement, led by Mohandas Gandhi and Jawaharlal Nehru, while committed to nonviolence, had used massive demonstrations to push for Great Britain to "quit India" even during the war. By the end of World War II, most British politicians realized that Great Britain could not hold onto India. Great Britain was financially exhausted, and the use of military force to crush the independence movement would be expensive and unpopular at home; it would also anger the Americans and possibly cause the Indians to abandon nonviolence. British India was split into four countries: India, Pakistan (East Pakistan is now Bangladesh), Burma (present-day Myanmar), and Ceylon (now called Sri Lanka). India became independent on August 15, 1947, exactly two years after Emperor Hirohito told the Japanese people that Japan had lost the war.

Then and Today

Although many wounds have healed, the scars of World War II and the Holocaust continue to be seen today. As war veterans and Holocaust survivors age, interest has been renewed to record their stories. Various foundations exist that are devoted to this undertaking. Among them is filmmaker Steven Spielberg's Survivors of the Shoah Visual History Foundation. The goal of the foundation is "to chronicle, before it was too late, the firsthand accounts of survivors, liberators, rescuers, and other eyewitnesses of the Holocaust." The group has recorded more than 50,000 accounts.

World War II and the Holocaust continue to make headlines and are often discussed in the classroom, political arena, and in films, books, and other art mediums. U.S. Vice President Al Gore made history by selecting Joe Lieberman, an Orthodox Jewish senator from Connecticut, as his running mate in the 2000 presidential election. Lieberman's wife, Hadassah, is the daughter of Holocaust survivors. Stories about World War II and Holocaust apologies and reparations appear with regularity.

Many people, young and old, have devoted their time and energies to recording the history of the Holocaust and the experiences of veterans and civilians during World War II. This set serves as a reminder of the diversity of experiences that marked that turbulent era.

Appendix A: Jewish Victims of the Holocaust

The number of Jews killed in the Holocaust is usually given as approximately 6 million. Although this figure was based on estimates made soon after World War II, it has turned out to be quite accurate.

As early as April 1946, the Anglo-American Committee of Inquiry Regarding the Problems of European Jewry and Palestine reached the conclusion that 5,721,500 Jews were killed by the Nazis and their accomplices. The historian Raoul Hilberg in his 1961 book, *The Destruction of the European Jews*, gave the figures of 5,397,500 based on an estimate of the number of survivors, and of 5,100,000 based on estimates of the number of victims. Lucy S. Dawidowicz in her 1975 book, *The War Against the Jews, 1933–1945*, comes to a total of 5,933,900. In his 1982 study, *A History of the Holocaust*, Yehuda Bauer cites the figure of 5,820,960. This is very close to the total given in the chart at the end of this section, although Bauer's numbers for various countries are different than the ones used in *The Holocaust and World War II Almanac*.

There are several reasons why it is impossible to give exact figures for the number of Jews killed in the Holocaust from each country. In some countries, especially in eastern Europe, it is not known how many Jews there were before World War II. Many of these countries had incomplete and inaccurate records of population figures in general, not just of Jews. In addition, there is a problem in these statistics with who was considered a Jew. The Nazis defined Jews according to "race," considering anyone with Jewish ancestors to be Jewish. But Jews who had converted to Christianity, or whose parents had converted (for example in Hungary), did not consider themselves Jews. Jews who did not practice any religion (for example in urban areas of the Soviet Union) may also not have considered themselves Jews.

A second major difficulty in trying to determine correct figures is that statistics on the number of people killed are inaccurate. Again, this is especially true with eastern Europe, and specifically the Soviet Union (Russia). Relatively few Jews in western Europe were killed in their home countries. Most were arrested and deported. Because of this, there are usually records of their arrests and arrivals at transit camps, transportation by trains, and sometimes their arrivals at the place where they were killed, such as Auschwitz.

But, in the Soviet Union, including areas that had been part of Poland, hundreds of thousands of people were shot within a few miles of their homes. Although the Einsatzgruppen, the mobile death squads that were responsible for most of these shootings, sent reports of their activities, these records are obviously not always accurate. In addition, other units—German police, army, and Waffen-SS troops, as well as Romanian and Hungarian police and soldiers—also played a major role in these killings. So did auxiliary troops of the local population in places such as Lithuania and the Ukraine. Many of the murders in the Soviet Union took place in the first weeks after the German invasion when conditions were chaotic. It is often impossible to know, in each town, how many Jews fled eastward with the retreating Soviet army and how many stayed behind and were killed by the Nazis. Part of this difficulty can be overcome by counting survivors, rather than victims. Scholars and historians have tried to do this. This is one reason why experts now agree on the approximate number of Jews killed in the Soviet-Polish area, even though the number killed in any particular place may be uncertain.

Another example of the uncertainty of the statistics is that the figure for those killed at Auschwitz was originally estimated at around 4 million while scholars now believe the number was closer to 1.25 to 1.5 million. But the vast number of people killed at the Treblinka, Sobibór, and Belzec death camps was not known after the war, and the scale of shootings by the Einsatzgruppen was underestimated.

A third major difficulty in determining the number of victims of the Holocaust involves the many border changes that occurred in Europe from 1938 through the years of the war. Hundreds of thousands of Jews, who had been Polish citizens until 1939, came under Soviet jurisdiction in that year. Many of them were killed beginning in the summer of 1941 when Germany invaded the Soviet Union. Sometimes they are counted as Polish Jews, sometimes as Soviet. In some lists, some of them have probably not been counted at all, and in other lists, some of them may have been counted twice. One example of an area with a large Jewish population may illustrate these problems. Until 1939, the city of Vilna was part of Poland. Then it became part of Lithuania, which soon became part of the Soviet Union, and then, in June 1941, was invaded and occupied by Germany. In addition, Jews from other parts of Poland fled to Vilna between 1939 and 1941 to escape the Germans. It is not always clear whether these victims have been counted as Polish, Lithuanian, or Soviet Jews.

The same problems exist in other parts of Europe. Greek and Yugoslav Jews found they were now in Bulgaria. Austria became part of the German Reich as did parts of France and Poland. A section of Czechoslovakia (the Sudetenland) became part of Germany in 1938, while other areas were given to Hungary and Poland. The next year, the remaining Czech lands (Bohemia and Moravia) became a "protectorate" of Germany, and Slovakia became a separate country. Croatia became a separate country in 1941. About 150,000 Romanian Jews, and smaller numbers of Slovakian and Yugoslav Jews, lived in areas that became part of Hungary. Large numbers of Romanian Jews lived in a territory that was part of the Soviet Union between July 1940 and July 1941. Dawidowicz treats them as Romanians, and estimates the number of Romanian Jews killed at 300,000. But Bauer includes them with Soviet Jews, and his total for Romania is 40,000. Although some of these problems do not greatly affect an accurate estimate of the total number of victims, they do affect the accuracy of the number that is listed for each country.

The same is true of refugees. For example, there were more than 500,000 Jews in Germany in 1933 when Adolf Hitler came to power. Several hundred thousand German Jews moved to other countries in Europe between 1933 and 1939. Most of these refugees were killed when the Nazis occupied their new countries. For example, around 30,000 were killed in the Netherlands alone. They are counted as Dutch Jews in most lists of victims, but this gives an unrealistic picture of the number of German Jewish victims. (In addition, thousands of German Jews were killed by the Nazis before the Holocaust. These are usually omitted from all lists.)

Keeping all these issues in mind, the following list of the number of people killed during the Holocaust cannot be perfectly accurate. However, it is based on the best recent estimates concerning each country. The numbers for Poland and the Soviet Union are the least certain. The numbers for the countries of western and northern Europe are the most exact. Except where otherwise noted, the totals refer to the September 1939 borders.

Country or Area	Number Killed
Austria	50,000
(1937 borders; does not include refugees who resettled in other countries and were later killed.)	
Belgium	29,000
Bulgaria	———
(Includes only "Old Bulgaria"; approximately 14,000 Jews killed from areas that had been part of Greece [Thrace] and Yugoslavia [Macedonia].)	
Czech lands	78,000
("Reich Protectorate of Bohemia and Moravia.")	
Denmark	100
Estonia	1,700
France	77,000
Germany	135,000
(1937 borders plus Sudetenland; does not include Austria or refugees who resettled in other countries and were later killed.)	
Greece	64,000
Hungary	550,000
(Includes territory added from Czechoslovakia, Romania, and Yugoslavia, beginning in 1938.)	
Italy	7,700
Latvia	70,000
Lithuania	140,000
Luxembourg	2,000
Netherlands	105,000
Norway	750
Poland	3,000,000
(August 1939 borders, includes territory taken by the Soviet Union in September 1939.)	
Romania	280,000
(Does not include territory that became part of Hungary, but includes territory that Romania ceded to the Soviet Union from July 1940 until it was reoccupied by Romanian troops the following summer.)	
Slovakia	70,000
Soviet Union	1,100,000
(Does not include territory added from Poland in 1939 or Estonia, Latvia, and Lithuania)	
Yugoslavia	60,000
Total for Nazi-controlled Europe	**5,820,250**

Contributor
George Feldman

SOURCES

Books

Bauer, Yehuda, with Nili Keren, *A History of the Holocaust,* F. Watts (New York), 1982, revised edition, F. Watts (New York), 2001.

Dawidowicz, Lucy S., *The War Against the Jews, 1933–1945,* Holt, Rinehart and Winston (New York), 1975, revised edition, Seth Press (Ardmore, PA), 1986.

Hilberg, Raul, *The Destruction of the European Jews,* Quadrangle Books (Chicago), 1961, revised edition, Holmes and Meier (New York), 1985.

Appendix B: Nuremberg War Crime Trials

At the end of World War II, the Allies established courts for trying German and Japanese nationals accused of war crimes. Trials of "major" war criminals—military or political leaders who committed crimes in no particular geographical location—were held by ad hoc courts according to Allied international agreement in Nuremberg and Tokyo. Although numerous and widely publicized, these trials constituted only a small percentage of the post-1945 war crimes proceedings. The overwhelming majority of trials involved "minor" war criminals, civilians or former members of enemy armed forces whose crimes were committed in specific locales, such as concentration camps. Minor war crimes trials were conducted by military courts in the British, American, French, and Soviet zones of occupied Germany; in Italy and Austria; and by other courts established for that purpose in Allied countries. New governments installed in former Axis-occupied and satellite nations also tried war criminals; German courts began prosecuting war criminals after the creation of the Federal Republic of Germany. Two defendants, Adolf Eichmann and John (Ivan) Demjanjuk, were taken to Israel, where they stood trial in 1961–1962 and 1988–1989, respectively.

The term "Nuremberg trials" is often used to describe four separate criminal proceedings. The first was the trial of twenty-four indicted "major" German and Austrian war criminals, conducted by the International Military Tribunal (IMT) from October 18, 1945, until October 1, 1946, in the city of Nuremberg. Only twenty-two of the defendants were actually tried; Robert Ley committed suicide, and Gustav Krupp von Bohlen was too ill to stand trial. Judges from Great Britain, France, the Soviet Union, and the United States presided over the IMT, which heard charges of conspiracy, crimes against peace, war crimes, and crimes against humanity. Nuremberg was also the site of twelve ensuing trials of 177 members of organizations and groups alleged to have been of a criminal nature. Former members of the Gestapo and the SS, as well as civil servants and industrialists, were among the defendants. American lawyers served as judges in these proceedings. The third type of "Nuremberg trial" was held in Tokyo (see Appendix C), where a multinational panel of eleven judges, who comprised the IMT in East Asia, heard charges against Japanese military and political leaders. The fourth type of Nuremberg proceeding involved trials of "minor" war criminals, conducted by military and national courts in Allied-occupied zones of former Axis territory, or in liberated territories, at or near the scenes of the crimes.

Krasnodar Trial

The first trial of Nazi criminals took place in the city of Krasnodar from July 14 to 17, 1943, before the Soviet military tribunal of the North Caucasian Front. The trial dealt with crimes involving 7,000 acts of murder committed by the Nazis in Krasnodar. Standing trial were thirteen Soviet citizens who had served in the auxiliary unit of Sonderkommando 10a (from Einsatzgruppe D), under the command of Dr. Kurt Christmann. They were charged with participating in murders committed by that unit, which was responsible for annihilating patients in the Krasnodar municipal hospital, in the Berezhanka convalescent home, and in the regional children's hospital. In their testimony, the accused described how they had used gas vans to commit the murders. During the four-day trial, testimony was also heard from twenty-two local witnesses, including Ivan Kotov, who survived gassing in a van by breathing through a piece of fabric soaked in urine. On July 17, 1943, eight defendants were sentenced to death by hanging, and three others to twenty years of imprisonment with forced labor. During this trial, people heard about the mass murders committed by the Einsatzgruppen and the Nazis' use of gas vans to murder people. This was the first trial to make those facts known to the world. Transcripts of the trial were printed in newspapers in the Soviet Union and the West, then later collected in booklets that were published in several languages.

Nuremberg Trial

The International Military Tribunal (IMT) had originally planned to hold the trial of major Nazi war criminals in Berlin. Although the opening session took place in Berlin on October 18, 1945, inadequate accommodations in the heavily damaged capital necessitated moving the proceedings to Nuremberg, which was selected, among other reasons, because it symbolized the stronghold of Nazi racist laws. During the war, the Allied powers had issued a series of declarations that put the world—and the criminals—on notice that perpetrators of war crimes would pay for their actions. The major Allied statements, including those that specifically mention the criminals responsible for the Holocaust, consisted of the St. James Palace Declaration of January 13, 1942; the Moscow Declaration by the Three Powers of November 1, 1943; the decision to establish the United Nations War Crimes Commission; and, especially, the London Agreement of August 8, 1945, which established the IMT charter.

The designation of the Nuremberg court as a "military tribunal" did not imply that the court had

military or political objectives in judging the vanquished countries or their populations. Instead, the purpose was to sit in judgment on the men and women who had committed crimes against humanity and peace by planning, executing, and organizing such crimes, or by ordering others to do so, during World War II. The term "international" was included in the tribunal's official designation to underline the universal validity of its judgment and importance. The IMT tried twenty-two Nazi political, military, and economic leaders: Hermann Göring, Rudolf Hess, Joachim von Ribbentrop, Wilhelm Keitel, Ernst Kaltenbrunner, Alfred Rosenberg, Hans Frank, Wilhelm Frick, Julius Streicher, Fritz Sauckel, Alfred Jodl, Martin Bormann, Franz von Papen, Arthur Seyss-Inquart, Albert Speer, Konstantin Freiherr von Neurath, Hjalmar Schacht, Walther Funk, Karl Dönitz (the commander of the navy, whom Adolf Hitler, on the eve of his suicide, appointed as his successor); Erich Raeder (the commander of the German navy prior to 1943); Baldur von Schirach (leader of the Hitlerjugend [Hitler Youth] and *Gauleiter* of Vienna); and Hans Fritzsche (in charge of radio propaganda).

The defendants were indicted under Article 6 of the charter, as follows:

Article 6. The Tribunal established by the Agreement referred to in Article I hereof for the trial and punishment of the major war criminals of the European Axis countries shall have the power to try and punish persons who, acting in the interests of the European Axis countries, whether as individuals or as members of organizations, committed any of the following crimes:

The following acts, or any of them, are crimes coming within the jurisdiction of the Tribunal for which there shall be individual responsibility:

(a) Crimes against Peace: namely, planning, preparation, initiation or waging of a war of aggression, or a war in violation of international treaties, agreements or assurances, or participation in a common plan or conspiracy for the accomplishment of any of the foregoing;

(b) War Crimes: namely, violations of the laws or customs of war. Such violations shall include, but not be limited to, murder, ill-treatment or deportation to slave labor or for any other purpose of civilian population of or in occupied territory, murder or ill-treatment of

The top row shows the photos of three Nazi officials (Alfred Rosenberg, Wilhelm Keitel, and Wilhelm Frick) during their service to the Third Reich. The bottom row reveals the subjects after their arrest for war crimes. All three were sentenced to death. (Reproduced by permission of AP/Wide World Photos)

prisoners of war or persons on the seas, killing of hostages, plunder of public or private property, wanton destruction of cities, towns or villages, or devastation not justified by military necessity;

(c) Crimes against Humanity: namely, murder, extermination, enslavement, deportation, and other inhumane acts committed against any civilian population, before or during the war, or persecutions on political, racial or religious grounds in execution of or in connection with any crime within the jurisdiction of the Tribunal, whether or not in violation of the domestic law of the country where perpetrated.

Leaders, organizers, instigators and accomplices participating in the formulation or execution of a common plan or conspiracy to commit any of the foregoing crimes are responsible for all acts performed by any person in execution of such plan.

The judgment, which was delivered on September 30 and October 1, 1946, decreed death sentences for twelve of the defendants: Göring, von Ribbentrop, Keitel, Kaltenbrunner, Rosenberg, Frank, Frick, Streicher, Sauckel, Jodl, Bormann, and Seyss-Inquart. Bormann, who was not captured, was sentenced in absentia, and Göring committed suicide; the other ten were hanged on Octo-

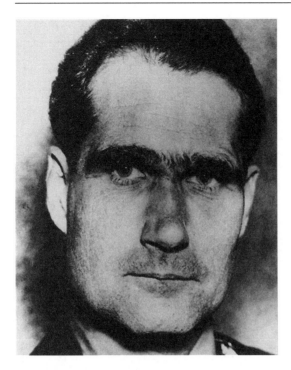

Sentenced to life imprisonment for war crimes, Rudolf Hess died in Spandau prison in 1987. (Reproduced by permission of AP/Wide World Photos)

ber 16, 1946. Hess, Funk, and Raeder were sentenced to life imprisonment; Speer, von Neurath, Dönitz, and von Schirach were given sentences ranging from ten to twenty years; and von Papen, Schacht, and Fritzsche were acquitted.

The Nuremberg Trial, the first of its kind in history, was convened to punish the leaders of a regime, a government, and an army (who were responsible for crimes committed in the framework of their policy and its implementation) by means of an independent court of law of an international character. This court would try defendants in accordance with the principles of justice and the rules of law, with the accused having every opportunity to defend themselves. The judges appointed to the tribunal were urged to follow the law and their conscience, notwithstanding the fact that they were nationals of the countries that had won the war—the United States, the Soviet Union, Great Britain, and France—and that they had been appointed by the governments of these countries. These governments also set up an investigation and prosecution team that was subject to the provisions of the tribunal's charter. Cooperating with the team, in addition to the four major powers, were representatives of countries that had been occupied by Nazi Germany, such as Poland, Nor-

way, and Belgium, and of nongovernmental international organizations, the latter in the status of *amici curiae* (friends of the court). The World Jewish Congress, as a representative of the Jewish people, was also accorded *amici curiae* status.

Both the indictment and the judgment of the IMT stressed the legal definition of a war of aggression. A formal state of war exists as soon as such a state is declared, but it is not always accompanied by an act of aggression. However, aggression, in the form of an armed attack, can be carried out without being preceded by a declaration or announcement, and without the victim putting up any resistance or having any means of defense. This was the case in Austria and Czechoslovakia, which the IMT cited as examples of states victimized by Nazi planning and preparing for wars of aggression. The IMT determined that wars of aggression, in any form, are prohibited under a great number of international treaties; it also stressed that such wars violate the dictates of conscience and of humanity, which have long been officially recognized as sources for the law of war. The tribunal, however, disregarded the parts of the indictment that charged the defendants with conspiracies to commit war crimes, instead dealing only with the defendants' common plan to prepare and conduct a war of aggression. The tribunal concluded that the other crimes were derived from crimes against peace.

Nevertheless, the IMT left no doubt that, under its charter, all leaders, organizers, inciters, and accessories to a criminal act who participated in the decision or implementation of a common plan or a conspiracy to commit crimes were guilty not only of their own acts but also of crimes carried out by any other person in the execution of the common plan or conspiracy. This crime—participation in a criminal organization—was included in the charter so that criminals would not escape justice even when their responsibility for any specific criminal act could not be proven. In adopting this rule, the IMT had in mind the members of several Nazi frameworks classified by its charter as criminal organizations. The tribunal planned to indict them, unless they could prove that despite their membership in such criminal organization or conspiracy they bore no personal responsibility for criminal acts. The basis of the decision was the fact that these were voluntary organizations whose members had joined in full knowledge of their criminal aims and methods.

The tribunal refused to accept the prosecution's demand to include the Reich government, the German General Staff, and the high command of the German armed forces among the organizations defined as criminal. The Soviet member of the tribunal, Lieutenant General Roman A. Rudenko, submitted a minority opinion on this issue. The tribunal did declare as criminal the Nazi party leadership, the SS, the Gestapo, and the SA. The prosecution excluded certain categories from the charge of criminal participation in criminal organizations, specifically, persons holding strictly administrative posts in the police and members of certain party or official bodies. The objective was to remove the slightest suspicion of trying anyone under the principle of collective responsibility. The IMT, like the courts of many countries, adhered to the principle that persons committing a criminal violation of international law should be held individually responsible, on the grounds that such crimes are the result of their own acts and not of the "state" as an abstract body.

The court also determined that holding an official position is not a basis for being absolved from punishment. Control Council Law No. 10 further established that a person being investigated or tried for any of the acts defined as criminal by the IMT charter would not be permitted to claim that the statute of limitation applied to his or her crime, insofar as the entire period of the Nazi regime, January 30, 1933, to July 1, 1945, was concerned. The charter provided that any immunity, pardon, or amnesty granted by the Nazi regime would not be regarded as an impediment to the trial and punishment of persons accused of various war crimes. In addition, the tribunal took a clear stand on the issue of responsibility for crimes carried out on orders from above, since many of the crimes had been committed in accordance with Reich policy and the decrees of its leaders, and by the official authority of those concerned. It declared that following superiors' orders was not an excuse for the perpetration of a crime.

The portion of the IMT judgment dealing with war crimes and crimes against humanity committed by the defendants in the trial and by the criminal organizations pertains, in large measure, to the persecution and murder of the Jewish people. In its analysis of these crimes, the IMT found it appropriate to single out the persecution of the Jews as a manifestation of consistent and systematic inhumanity on a huge scale. The testimony given at the Nuremberg Trial, the documents presented by the prosecution, and the entire record of the proceedings constitute an incomparable source for the study of the Holocaust, and for the determination of the measures that must be taken to prevent its recurrence in any form, with regard to any social or national group, and especially to prevent the recurrence of anti-Semitism and discrimination against foreigners. The IMT conclusions influenced the drafting of (1) the international convention for the prevention of the crimes of genocide (the Genocide Convention), adopted by the United Nations on December 9, 1948; (2) the Human Rights Declaration of December 10, 1948; (3) the Convention on the Abolition of the Statute of Limitations on War Crimes and Crimes against Humanity of November 26, 1968; and (4) the Geneva Convention on the Laws and Customs of War of 1949, and its supplementary protocols of 1977. The principle that the only legal wars are wars in self-defense or against aggressions—a fundamental rule of present-day international law—also derives from the United Nations Charter, the IMT charter, and the IMT judgment.

Subsequent British Trials

The Royal Warrant of June 14, 1945, provided the basis for jurisdiction of the British military courts for the trial of "minor" German and Japanese war criminals. Based on the Royal Prerogative, the Royal Warrant made "provision for the trial and punishment of violations of the laws and usages of war committed during any war in which … [His Majesty's Government] have been or may be engaged at any time after the second day of September, nineteen hundred and thirty-nine." The Regulations attached to the warrant governed the custody, trial, and punishment of persons charged with such violation of the laws and usages of war. All German and Japanese atrocities committed before the outbreak of World War II, and all acts that were not violations of the rules and customs of warfare—war crimes in a strict sense—were, therefore, beyond the scope of British war crimes courts. Consequently, the jurisdiction of these courts was narrower than that of the IMT. A suspected war criminal within the command area of a British court's convening officer came under the jurisdiction of that court, whether or not his or her offense had been committed before or after the promulgation of the Royal Warrant, or "within or without" the command area.

The rules of procedure applicable in a regular court-martial would be in effect, with certain modifications. Regulation 8 of the Royal Warrant introduced a relaxation of the rules of evidence otherwise applied in British court. Under this provision, affidavits or statutory declarations, which normally would not be received as evidence in a British court, were admissible before British military courts. Further, hearsay testimony was admissible as evidence in certain situations. Given the special character of the war crimes trials and the nature of Nazi criminality—crimes that left few survivors—the admission of hearsay was perhaps the most important provision in the Royal Warrant. The courts were left to judge the weight to be attached to this type of evidence. Those found guilty of war crimes could be sentenced to (1) death by hanging or shooting; (2) imprisonment for life or any other term; (3) confiscation of his or her property; or (4) payment of a fine. British military courts trying German war criminals awarded the first two penalties only. Decisions of the court could not be appealed. The accused could, however, petition the confirming officer against the finding and/or the sentence; every sentence had to be confirmed. The secretary of state for war, or any officer not below the rank of major general authorized by him, could mitigate or remit a confirmed sentence, provided that this office held a command or rank superior to that of the confirming officer.

In the British zone of occupation in Germany, two to eight military courts functioned concurrently under the Royal Warrant. Initially the war crimes trials were held where crimes had been committed. Later, the trials took place at three courts in Hamburg and at three courts in Brunswick. Under the Royal Warrant, two classes of criminals were to be tried: those who had committed breaches of the rules of war against British subjects, especially soldiers; and those who had committed war crimes against Allied nationals in British zones. In the first class of criminals were those accused of shooting parachute troops or maltreating prisoners of war (POWs). The second class of criminals were concentration camp commandants and guards. The British also included in the second class those criminals who could not be delivered to the Allies owing to multiple jurisdictional claims. When Germans had committed crimes against a non-British subject in the British zone, the British commander could order trial by a British military court or deliver the accused to the Allied authority whose national had been the victim of the crime. Most war crimes in the British zone were classified as: (1) crimes by concentration camp guards and other personnel whose victims were of various nationalities; (2) crimes against British subjects; and (3) crimes in the British zone of occupation against a specific and small number of nationals of an Allied power. German crimes against European Jews played no part in the trials of Nazi war criminals conducted by British military courts, unless the Jewish victims were also Allied nationals. German crimes against German Jews were considered acts of violence other than war crimes, and for this reason, such crimes could not be tried in British military courts. The only British trial in which Allied Jewish victims were specifically mentioned as Jews was that of Generalfeldmarschall Fritz Erich von Lewinski (called Erich von Manstein), who was tried in late 1949.

British Policy toward German War Crimes Trials

From the outbreak of World War II in September 1939 until the release of the last war criminal in British custody in June 1957, most British Foreign Office officials were skeptical of the idea of prosecuting and sentencing Nazi war criminals for atrocities committed during the war. Officials of Allied governments-in-exile did not share this skepticism. According to their view, Nazi Germany had waged a cruel and savage battle against such countries as Poland and Czechoslovakia, thereby ignoring established laws of warfare and violating international conventions—which Germany had signed—concerning the actions of victors toward inhabitants of occupied territories. Allied governments such as Great Britain and the United States, which did not experience German occupation, were less inclined to view Nazi misconduct as considerably worse than that of aggressors in past wars. British and American skepticism about the accuracy of reports of German atrocities only reinforced these doubts; moreover, the British and American governments were uncertain about what recourse, if any, would be appropriate. At first the British Foreign Office was reluctant to make any public statement about German atrocities. Foreign Office officials wished particularly to avoid commenting on German crimes against German nationals. Later, as the Polish, Czech, and other Allied governments pressured the British government to make a statement, Foreign Office officials carefully distinguished between atrocities committed against German nationals and crimes committed in occupied countries.

While publicly expressing sympathy for the victims and condemnation of the perpetrators, the

Foreign Office remembered the disastrous experience of German war crimes trials after World War I. Conducted at Leipzig by German courts, those trials resulted in such inadequate sentences that the proceedings came to be known as the "Leipzig fiasco." Hoping to prevent another disaster, the Foreign Office tried to avoid making any statement that might later be construed as an obligation to prosecute Nazi war criminals. Consequently, the Foreign Office was often one step behind the Polish, Czech, and other Allied governments, which were pressing for a British commitment to exact retribution. The Foreign Office also lagged behind British Prime Minister Winston Churchill, who made public pronouncements on German atrocities and on the need to punish Nazi war criminals.

Foreign Office efforts to maintain a detached attitude toward Nazi war crimes began to crumble with the St. James's Palace Declaration of January 13, 1942. In this document, the eight signatory Allied governments, and the French National Committee, condemned Nazi atrocities in the occupied territories. They also declared that the trial and punishment of Nazi war criminals would be one of their principal war aims. A direct result of the St. James's Declaration was that, for the first time, government officials outside the Foreign Office expressed an interest in formulating a positive policy on war crimes. Attorney General Sir Donald Somervell and Solicitor General Sir David Maxwell Fyfe sought permission to investigate British war crimes policy. British adherence to the St. James's Declaration was advocated publicly, in Parliament and, on several occasions, by representatives of the Allied governments. Reports of atrocities coming from German-occupied Europe throughout 1942 and news of Japanese brutalities against POWs aroused British public opinion and, eventually, began to erode Foreign Office skepticism. Allegations of Japanese atrocities, particularly against British subjects in occupied British territory, also undermined the noncommittal attitude of the Foreign Office.

By October 1942, the detached attitude of the Foreign Office was under fire on every front. Faced with intensifying pressure from Parliament, the public, and the Allies—including the Soviets, who openly declared that those guilty of war crimes should be put on trial—Foreign Office officials finally agreed to draw up a policy statement on Nazi war criminals. That statement was the British-American-Soviet declaration of December 17, 1942. These three governments, along with nine other Allied governments, condemned the Nazis' "bestial policy of cold-blooded extermination" of European Jews, and reaffirmed that those responsible for these crimes should not escape retribution.

As news of Nazi atrocities continued to reach London, Churchill became more involved in formulating war crimes policy. In October 1943, the Cabinet approved his recommendation that the foreign ministers of Great Britain, the United States, and the Soviet Union issue a new declaration. U.S. President Franklin D. Roosevelt and Soviet leader Joseph Stalin accepted Churchill's draft, which came to be known as the Moscow Declaration of November 1, 1943. This document pledged that those responsible for German atrocities should be returned to the countries where their crimes were committed, and then judged and punished "on the spot by the peoples whom they have outraged." The Moscow Declaration added that "most assuredly the three Allied powers will pursue [war criminals] ... to the uttermost ends of the earth and will deliver them to their accusers in order that justice may be done" (Foreign Office document 371 34378 C13682/31162). The prosecution of war criminals where they committed their crimes meant that Great Britain would not bear exclusive responsibility for the trial. Churchill feared that Great Britain would not be capable of executing criminals over an extended period, since the British had not suffered like citizens in subjugated countries. In November 1944, the Cabinet decided that military courts, established in Germany or wherever appropriate, should adjudicate war crimes against British subjects or in British territory. Foreign Secretary Anthony Eden and Lord Chancellor Viscount Simon were convinced that war crimes trials should be carried out as quickly as possible after the cessation of hostilities in order to achieve justice and restore peace in Europe.

By the end of the war, the unprecedented nature and extent of Nazi criminality had been revealed, and it became apparent that German war criminals would number in the millions. Most official British and American declarations condemning German atrocities had promised to punish both instigators and perpetrators. Yet by late 1944, many officials were voicing doubts about the practicality of large-scale retribution. Within two years, members of Parliament were pressing for an end to the British trials. Moreover, successive British military governors in Germany, and many British officials at home, were hoping for a return to normalcy in the British zone of Germany. This pressure eventually led to the cessation of British war crimes trials, thus making more difficult the extradition of war criminals, traitors, and collaborators, especially to Eastern European countries. Perhaps the most fundamental question raised by the trials pertained to assigning responsibility: To what extent were perpetrators of Nazi war crimes, acting under superior orders, responsible for their deeds? Were they more or less culpable than their instigators? This dilemma provoked considerable controversy when death sentences were commuted because instigators had, for a variety of procedural reasons, received less severe sentences.

The Trials

The trial of the commandant and staff of the Bergen-Belsen camp, which lasted from September 17 to November 17, 1945, was the first British trial of German war criminals. The last was that of Field Marshal Erich von Manstein, which began on August 23 and ended on December 19, 1949. The British conducted a total of 357 trials of German, Italian, and Austrian nationals, 314 of them involving 989 German nationals or those in German employ. The trials involved crimes against Allied civilians, including concentration camp internees, and against Allied military personnel; some German officers were tried for both types of offenses. Defendants were commandants, guards, and other staff of concentration camps, including Bergen-Belsen and Auschwitz, Gross-Rosen, Lahde-Weser, Neugraben-Tiefstak, Neuengamme, Ravensbrück, Sasel, Stocken and Ahlen, and Natzweiler-Struthof. In addition, the British tried those responsible for forced labor by civilians in work connected with military operations, for the deportation of civilians for slave labor, and for the killing of civilians as a reprisal for partisan activities. Dr. Bruno Tesch, in the Zyklon B case, and the staff of the Velpke Children's Home, were also tried.

Among the high-ranking German officers tried by British military courts were Senior General Eberhard von Mackensen; Lieutenant Generals Kurt Maeltzer and Kurt Wolff; Generals Günther von Blumentritt, Curt Gallenkamp, Max Simon, Kurt Student, and Nikolaus von Falkenhorst; and Field Marshals Albert Kesselring and Erich von Manstein. The British also tried cases involving war crimes at sea, including the illegal scuttling of U-boats and firing at life rafts carrying survivors of torpedoed ships. The British also prosecuted German military personnel who had served in POW

camps. Other cases involved the employment of POWs on prohibited and dangerous work or as human screens in the face of fire; summary executions of escapees; and the issuing of illegal orders that denied Allied POWs protection by German escorts if attacked by the local populace. The British also prosecuted cases on behalf of airmen and POWs from Great Britain, the United States, Australia, New Zealand, and Poland, as well as of civilians from France, Denmark, the Netherlands, Poland, Greece, Yugoslavia, and the Soviet Union.

British Clemency for War Criminals

In addition to establishing a number of clemency boards to review sentences of individual German war criminals, the British instituted a number of general clemency measures. The first was the September 1949 decision to allow one-third remission of sentence for good conduct in jail; the second was the February 1950 decision to commute all life sentences to twenty-one years' imprisonment; the third was the December 1951 decision to allow credit for pretrial custody; and the fourth was the April 1955 decision to reduce all twenty-one-year sentences to twenty years' imprisonment. The Wade Review, held in 1949, was the first general review of sentences of war criminals in British custody in Germany. Secretary of State for War Emanuel Shinwell, who was then responsible for granting clemency, authorized the review. In 1950 Shinwell transferred the clemency authority to Foreign Secretary Ernest Bevin, who, in turn, delegated that authority to General Brian Robertson, Great Britain's high commissioner in Germany. The Wade Review Board reduced 66 sentences out of a total of 372 considered. The Wade committee did not question the judgment; it tried instead to introduce uniformity of sentence by instituting a sentence of fifteen years for those who were accessories in the first degree to the murder of Allied POWs, and ten years for those guilty in the second degree. Sir Ivone Kirkpatrick, Robertson's successor as high commissioner, conducted a general review of sentences between 1951 and 1953. In reviewing sentences, the high commissioner exercised authority delegated to him by the foreign secretary. However, in June 1951 the Cabinet withdrew the delegation of clemency authority from the high commissioner, directing that, in the future, the monarch would grant clemency on the advice of the foreign secretary.

At the same time, Foreign Office officials were growing increasingly eager to divest themselves of responsibility for clemency and custody of war criminals. By November 1951, the Foreign Office had recommended that the three occupying powers propose the following solution of the clemency and custody problem to the West Germans: (1) the Federal Republic should accept responsibility for the custody of war criminals; (2) West Germany should be invited to appoint representatives to an advisory clemency tribunal, which would advise the three powers on clemency concerning war criminals imprisoned in the Federal Republic; and (3) this tribunal, whose unanimous decisions would be binding upon the convicting power, should be authorized to take into account all relevant circumstances, including uniformity of sentences, without, however, being competent to question the correctness of the conviction. The proposed tribunal, known as the Mixed Board, began its work in August 1955.

In the interim, clemency boards were set up in each of the three zones of Germany. In the British zone, the Mixed Consultative Board (MCB), under the chairmanship of Sir Alexander Maxwell, began work in the fall of 1953. This Anglo-German clemency board, composed of three British and two German members, carried out the third general review of sentences of war criminals passed by British military courts. When the MCB considered clemency advisable, such was recommended. Final decision lay with the secretary of state, who, if he agreed with the case for clemency, would make a submission for the approval of the monarch. Superior orders, and the degree of the accused's personal responsibility, as well as his or her age, health, rank, and mental capacity, were among the factors the Maxwell board considered in its deliberations. By March 1954, the British held only sixty-nine war criminals in the Werl prison, who were believed to be among the worst of the Nazi war criminals.

The MCB often recommended clemency on the grounds that the accused co-defendants had received much lighter sentences. Although the Foreign Office maintained that this should not be a reason for clemency, they did not challenge MCB recommendations. However, Foreign Office officials, notably Anthony Eden, occasionally rejected MCE recommendations. By the end of October 1954, the MCB had virtually finished its work. When the board began its work in the fall of 1953, the British held eighty-one war criminals in custody; by October 1954, that number had dropped to forty-one. The release rate during these twelve

months was nearly double that of the previous twelve months. For some years, the Foreign Office had been under pressure from Germans of every political persuasion to release the "honorable" German soldiers from Werl. By the fall of 1954, Chancellor Konrad Adenauer had begun to speak on behalf of the remaining prisoners. Noting the approaching end of the occupation, the establishment of West German sovereignty, and closer German cooperation with the West, Adenauer renewed his government's request for additional generous clemency measures, pointing out that the majority of those detained had been held for nearly ten years.

The Mixed Board for War Criminals (MBWC) carried out the fourth and final set of sentence reviews of "minor" German war criminals in British custody. The MBWC consisted of six members—three Germans, one British, one American, and one French. Commencing work on August 11, 1955, the board disposed of its last cases on June 4, 1958. When the MBWC convened, nineteen war criminals were in French custody, twenty-six in British custody, and forty-nine in American custody. In addition, 253 paroled criminals in American custody were still subject to the jurisdiction of the MBWC. From mid-August 1955 until the fall of 1957, the MBWC considered and acted upon clemency petitions for prisoners in British or French custody; the board also dealt with some of the American cases. By early August 1956, the MBWC had reviewed the sentences at least once of all twenty-six war criminals in British custody in the Werl prison. For various reasons unconnected with the MBWC, such as expiration of sentences, sixteen were released at that time. Toward the end of September 1956, Foreign Secretary Selwyn Lloyd ordered the release of the nine remaining prisoners by June 30, 1957, on grounds of health. During the 1950s, the West German government criticized the Foreign Office for not granting a general amnesty to Nazi war criminals, while Parliament and the British public felt that clemency had been given too freely. The Foreign Office therefore attempted to balance the Allied demand for honoring the original court decisions against the German refusal to acknowledge the convictions. This situation revealed a notable distinction between the German and Japanese postwar experiences. Under the terms of the peace treaty, Japan was obliged to recognize the validity of sentences delivered at war crimes trials, whereas West Germany was never required to accept the convictions of Nazi war criminals.

Irma Grese, also known as the "Bitch of Belsen," sits in court wearing number 9. (Reproduced by permission of AP/Wide World Photos)

Bergen-Belsen Trial

The trial of the Bergen-Belsen camp staff was held from September 17 to November 17, 1945, before a British military tribunal at Lüneburg, Germany. The accused were on trial for crimes committed in the Auschwitz and Bergen-Belsen camps. The charge sheet referred to the role of the accused in planning and conspiring to torture and murder prisoners, in committing acts of murder, and in meting out inhuman treatment and punishment with their own hands. Most of the victims was Jews, although British, Italian, and French prisoners had also been killed. Among the accused was Josef Kramer, who had been a commandant of concentration camps from 1943 onward, and before his arrival in Bergen-Belsen had been on the staff of the Auschwitz-Birkenau camp. Another defendant was Dr. Fritz Klein, who took an active role in making *Selektionen* and sending people to their deaths. Others standing trial were prisoners who collaborated with the Nazis and were given the status of agents of the camp administration, such as Stanislawa Staroska, a Polish woman known as "Stana the Flogger." Of the forty-five persons appearing before the court, twenty-one were women.

When the British liberated Bergen-Belsen in April 1945, they found hundreds of rotting corpses on the grounds and in the barracks. Many sur-

vivors were too weak to move unassisted. Hundreds of prisoners had been beaten, tortured, or starved to death, or had died of diseases such as typhus. Housing for the prisoners was intolerable; more than 1,000 people were crowded into barracks that could hardly hold 100. Hundreds of deaths were caused by the deplorable sanitary conditions, the victims having been left for many days lying on the bunks in filth and excrement.

Kramer, Klein, and nine others—among them two women, Irma Grese and EIisabeth Volkenrath, who were charged with torturing and assaulting prisoners—were sentenced to death by hanging. Erich Zoddel, the camp's Lagerdifeste (chief *Kapo*), was sentenced to life imprisonment, Staroska to ten years, and others to periods of one to three years; fourteen of the accused were acquitted.

Zyklon B Trial

In March 1946 the trial of Bruno Tesch, Joachim Drösihn, and Karl Weinbacher was held before a British military tribunal in Hamburg. The accused were owners and executives of a Hamburg factory that from January 1, 1941, to March 31, 1945, manufactured poison gas used to kill concentration camp prisoners. The gas, called Zyklon B, was manufactured by the Tesch and Stabenow

The war torn city of Nuremberg was the site for the "Trial of the Century." (Reproduced by permission of AP/Wide World Photos)

Company and was used by the SS Totenkopfverbände (Death's Head Units) stationed in Auschwitz and the other extermination camps. The defendants in the trial claimed they did not know how their product was used—a claim that was rebutted by company reports of Tesch's trips to Auschwitz. Tesch and Weinbacher (the executive manager of the "factory for means of death") were sentenced to death and executed; Drösihn, a company employee, was acquitted. The trial was conducted on the basis of Military Order 81/45, which derived its authority from a British law of June 14, 1945, that outlined the principles of the Nuremberg Trial. The Zyklon B Trial established for the first time that the manufacture of gas for killing prisoners was a war crime.

Subsequent Nuremberg Proceedings

On December 20, 1945, four weeks after the opening of the trial of major war criminals by the International Military Tribunal, the Allied Control Council issued Law No. 10. This law empowered the commanding officers of the four zones of occupation to conduct criminal trials on charges of aggression, war crimes, crimes against humanity, and membership in an organization aiming at such crimes. Under the charge of crimes against humanity, the persecution of nationals of belligerent and nonbelligerent countries on political, religious, and racial grounds was declared punishable under the principles of international law. Pursuant to Law No. 10, the Office of the United States Government for Germany (OMGUS) established six military tribunals, composed of civilian judges recruited, for the most part, from among state supreme court judges in the United States. In 1,200 sessions of twelve trials (the Subsequent Nuremberg Proceedings), held between December 1946 and April 1949, the judges heard the cases of 177 persons. The prosecution consisted of 100 attorneys, at most, with 1,600 assistants. The defense was handled by 200 attorneys, chiefly German lawyers. On trial in these cases were representatives of the leadership of the Reich ministries, the Wehrmacht, industrial concerns, the German legal and medical establishment, and the SS.

The destruction of Jews was not classified as a separate criminal offense at Nuremberg, a fact that has since been frequently deplored. In legal terms, this offense was one of several atrocities summarized as "crimes against humanity." All judgments rendered at Nuremberg claimed to enforce statutory law or international common law, and widespread petitions to administer retroactive and ad hoc special law were rejected by the courts. As a result, the "Final Solution" was classified among conventional crimes—murder, maltreatment, abduction, enslavement, and robbery—committed on racial grounds. Since the tribunals' task was to prove the criminal nature of many of the activities carried out by the pillars of the German state (the administration, the armed forces, the judiciary, and industry), each of the twelve cases dealt with a specific sphere. The destruction of Jews had not been confined to a specific sphere and was handled mainly by the regular state institutions and industrial companies. The extermination program therefore appears in the Nuremberg Proceedings not as a single entity but is split up into detailed component parts, next to and in conjunction with other criminal pursuits.

Chronologically, the stages of the persecution of the Jews are distributed among the Subsequent Nuremberg Proceedings in the following pattern:

1. Preparation of the Nuremberg Laws and their decrees of implementation. These were dealt with in count 5 of Trial 11, the Ministries Case, as a component part of the extermination program. The defendant Wilhelm Stuckart, former *Staatssekretär* (state secretary) of the Reich Ministry of the Interior, was found guilty of this and other crimes, for which he was sentenced to forty-six months' imprisonment.

2. Application of the Law for the Protection of German Blood and Honor by Rassenschande (race defilement) tribunals occurred in Trial 3, the Justice Case, in which two *Sonderrichter* (special judges) were found guilty of judicial murder and sentenced to life imprisonment.

3. Forced "Aryanization" of Jewish-owned capital. This was one of the counts in Trial 5, the Flick Case. Friedrich Flick, a coal and steel producer, and his associates were acquitted on this count, on formal as well as factual grounds. The court considered outside its jurisdiction crimes committed before the outbreak of the war, and also did not consider forced "Aryanization" a form of racial persecution.

4. Forced "Aryanization" of agricultural property. This charge came up in count 5 of Trial 11, the Ministries Case, against Richard Walther Darré, the former minister of agriculture. It was one of the charges of which he was found guilty and sentenced to seven years in prison.

5. Abduction and mass shooting of Jews in concentration camps maintained by the Wehrmacht in Serbia, in retaliation for partisan attacks. In Trial 7, the Hostage Case, the generals of the southeast front were charged with this crime. Generals Wilhelm List and Walter Kuntze were found guilty of this and other charges and were sentenced to life imprisonment and a fifteen-year term, respectively.

6. The extermination campaign by the Einsatzgruppen in the war against the Soviet Union. This was the subject of Trial 9, the Einsatzgruppen Case, which led to fourteen death sentences and prison terms ranging from three years to life.

7. Logistic support for the Einsatzgruppen, direct orders to them, and responsibility for their actions under the law of war were the charges against the army and army group commanders invested with executive power on the eastern front that were heard in Trial 12, the High Command Case. Another count was issuing orders for the so-called *Sonderbehandlung* (special treatment) of Jewish prisoners of war in the Soviet army in or near prisoner-of-war camps maintained by the Wehrmacht. Generals Georg Karl Friedrich Wilhelm von Küchler, Hermann Hoth, Hans Reinhardt, Hans von Salmuth, Karl von Roques, Hermann Reinecke, and Otto Wöhler were found guilty of these charges and sentenced to prison terms ranging from eight years to life.

8. The deportation of Jews from western Europe was addressed in Trial 8, the RuSHA Case (Rasse- und Siedlungshauptamt; Race and Resettlement Main Office). That agency, through its Ahnentafelamt (Genealogical Office), had drawn up the family trees of all Jews and descendants of Jews in the German Reich, the Netherlands, Belgium, Norway, and France, in order to determine the fate of *Mischlinge* (partial Jews). The family trees were used to compose lists for the transport of Jews. Eight defendants were found guilty of these charges, among others, and sentenced to prison terms ranging from thirty-four months to life.

9. Events relating to the deportations from Denmark, Slovakia, Croatia, Serbia, France, Italy, and Hungary were investigated in the Ministries

Case, to determine the role played by German Foreign Office diplomatic personnel. Ernst von Weizsäcker, Gustav Adolf Steengracht von Moyland, Ernst Wörmann, and Edmund Veesenmayer were found guilty and sentenced to prison terms of seven to twenty years.

10. Deportations from Greece were addressed in evidence presented by the prosecution in the Hostage Case against generals Wilhelm Speidel, Hubert Lanz, and Helmuth Felmy. They were all found guilty, but their role in the deportations was not included in the judgment.

11. Anti-Semitic indoctrination of the population and dulling of its conscience during the extermination process was one of the charges proven in the Ministries Case against Otto Dietrich, chief of the Reich press section (among other offenses). He was sentenced to seven years in prison.

12. Pillage of property left behind by Jews who were abducted from Germany was one of the charges heard in the Ministries Case. The property had been assigned to the financial offices. Former Reich minister of finance Lutz Schwerin von Krosigk was found guilty of the crime and sentenced to ten years in prison.

13. Administration of concentration camps and the *Vernichtung durch Arbeit* (annihilation through work) system in the SS-run companies Ostindustrie GBMH (Osti) and Deutsche Erd- und Steinwerke (German Earth and Stone Works; DEST) were among the counts heard in Trial 4, the Pohl Case, against Oswald Pohl and the managers of the SS Wirtschafts-Verwaltungshauptamt (Economic-Administrative Main Office; WVHA). This case ended in three acquittals, eleven sentences of prison terms ranging from ten years to life, and three death sentences.

14. The enslavement of Jews by private industry, by forcing them to work under conditions like those in concentration camps, was investigated in Trial 10, the Krupp Case, against Alfried Krupp and eleven directors of his company. The tribunals found that Krupp and ten members of his staff were implicated in the German government's forced-labor program and sentenced them to prison terms of two to twelve years. Included in the findings of the tribunals was that of maltreatment of prisoners engaged in the construction of a munitions factory at Auschwitz.

15. The government-sponsored slave economy figured in Trial 2, the Milch Case, against Field Marshal Erhard Milch, a member of the Main Planning Office, who was sentenced to life imprisonment. His sentence was later reduced to fifteen years; he was released in 1954.

16. Sale of Zyklon B (prussic acid) to the SS and construction of industrial plants in Auschwitz were among the charges heard in Trial 6, the I.G. Farben Case, in which twenty-four directors and engineers of the concern were on trial. The tribunal acquitted the defendants of the Zyklon B charge because it was not proven that they had known how the product was being used.

17. Medical experiments on human beings in concentration camps, including sterilization methods for future application to *Mischlinge* were dealt with in Trial 1, the Medical Case. One of the defendants was Wolfram Sievers, managing director of Ahnenerbe (the Ancestral Heritage Society), who was charged with establishing a collection of skeletons and skulls of Jews for anthropological research at the Reich University in Strasbourg. Seven defendants were acquitted, nine others were sentenced to prison terms ranging from ten years to life, and Sievers and six doctors and medical officials were sentenced to death.

18. Hoarding of dental gold from Auschwitz in the coffers of the Reichsbank was a charge in the Ministries Case against Reichsbank vice-chairman Emil Johann Puhl, for which he was sentenced to five years' imprisonment.

With the exception of the Reichsbahn (the national railway system) and the Reichssicherheitshauptamt (Reich Security Main Office; RSHA), the Subsequent Nuremberg Proceedings systematically exposed the principal agencies involved in the extermination of the Jews, determined the culpability of their personnel, and passed sentences on a few of their leading figures. But their achievement of laying bare the structure of the crimes committed by the bureaucracy did not play any role in later criminal trials; a precedent was not established. Both in Germany and in other countries, the courts now turned their attention predominantly to the personnel who had been directly engaged in carrying out the liquidation process in the extermination camps and the killing squads. Thus the conventional image of the barbaric Holocaust agent emerged.

Contrary to the expectations of their originator, OMGUS, the Subsequent Nuremberg Proceedings had no influence on the way the German peo-

The IG Farben firm was one of the companies that made the Zyklon B brand of poisonous gas used to kill millions in concentration camp showers. IG Farben executives were tried at Nuremberg for crimes against humanity. (National Archives/USHMM Photo Archives)

ple viewed their recent history. Germans, for the most part, felt that the sentences were arbitrary decisions made by the victorious powers, and they exerted organized pressure on U.S. High Commissioner John J. McCloy to suspend the convictions. Such demands benefitted from the growing interests of the United States in founding the North Atlantic military alliance, interests that included the indispensable territory and forces of western Germany. By 1951, primarily at the urging of German churches and political parties, a hurried pardoning policy led to the commutation to prison terms of twelve of the twenty-five death sentences and to the release of the last of the prisoners by 1958. These ex-convicts resumed their interrupted careers or retired, usually keeping entitlements to pensions for their official services. According to Article 7.1 of the Transition Agreement, one of the 1955 Paris Agreements under which the Federal Republic of Germany regained sovereignty from the Western powers, judgments passed in war

crimes trials were established as having the effectiveness of law. Later, the German federal government arrived at a different interpretation of this agreement. In its opinion, and under the federal supreme court opinion of January 9, 1959, the Nuremberg judgments lacked the power of law.

West Germany

As early as 1943, the Allies agreed that they would punish officials who were responsible for the crimes of the Nazi regime. On the basis of that agreement, after the war Allied military tribunals convicted and sentenced, according to a reliable estimate, some 60,000 Germans and Austrians of war crimes and crimes against humanity. Military tribunals of the Western Allies alone passed more than 800 death sentences (no precise information is available on the number of death sentences passed on Germans and Austrians by the Communist countries). Laws 4 and 10 (passed in 1945) of the Allied Control Council (consisting of the four powers—the United States, the Soviet Union, Great Britain, and France—who were in charge of the zones of occupation in Germany) established that German courts that had been rehabilitated after the war could try only those Nazi crimes that had been committed by Germans against Germans, or against stateless persons, and then only with the agreement of the military administration of the respective zone of occupation. This meant that the great majority of Nazi crimes—against citizens of Poland, the Soviet Union, Yugoslavia, France, and the Netherlands, and nationals of other Allied countries—were excluded from the jurisdiction of German courts.

Until late 1950, Nazi crimes that were tried in the Federal Republic of Germany dealt mainly with relatively minor transgressions, such as denunciations, physical injury, deprivation of liberty, and coercion in various degrees and at various times. The German courts also heard cases of crimes committed in the concentration camps, murders during the course of the euthanasia program, and the so-called final-phase crimes, or the murder of German soldiers and civilians who in the last few days of the war resisted the continuation of meaningless warlike action. Almost all these trials resulted from charges brought by the victims or their heirs against participants in the crimes who were known or who had been discovered by chance.

In 1950, shortly after the establishment of the Federal Republic of Germany, the restrictions imposed by the Allies at the end of the war on the jurisdiction of German courts were removed, as far as the Federal Republic was concerned. This meant that public prosecutors were now free to start a systematic investigation of Nazi crimes and to put the perpetrators on trial. Owing partly to inadequate resources and a lack of personnel and partly to lapses in communication among the prosecuting attorneys, trials did not immediately take place. The main reason, however, was that Germans were preoccupied with rehabilitating the country and restoring its economic strength.

The denazification process, which had been quite discouraging, had created a situation in which few people were interested in a renewed confrontation with the Nazi crimes and in dealing with criminal proceedings. German politicians were aware that a drive for the prosecution of Nazi crimes would not be popular with the electorate. In addition, the growing tension between East and West put pressure on both sides to embark on the rearmament of Germany; this in turn diminished the Allies' interest in punishing Nazi crimes. This tendency was clearly demonstrated by the pardons granted to Nazi criminals who had been given severe sentences by Allied military tribunals during the early postwar years. According to the statute of limitations of May 8, 1950, the operative date for Nazi crimes, as distinguished from other crimes, was the day the war ended, rather than the date on which the crime was committed, since prosecution of these crimes had not been possible during the Nazi regime. The statute thus made it possible to start a series of trials for crimes committed in the Auschwitz and Treblinka extermination camps, in the Buchenwald, Neuengamme, Gross-Rosen, Flossenbürg, and Sachsenhausen concentration camps, in the Theresienstadt camp, and in the Sajmište (Semlin) detention camp.

From 1951 to 1955 the number of trials conducted in the courts of the Federal Republic was sharply reduced because by the time the statute was issued, five years after the end of the war, offenses that bore a maximum sentence of five years could no longer be prosecuted. In most of these cases proceedings were instituted on the basis of complaints submitted by victims of crimes or their heirs, and, sometimes, against suspects of Nazi crimes who had been discovered by chance. There was still no systematic attempt to investigate and prosecute crimes that the Nazis had committed against Jews, Roma, and real or imagined political opponents.

On May 8, 1955, the statute of limitations was to go into effect for Nazi-related crimes with a maximum sentence of ten years. This meant, for all practical purposes, that henceforth only acts of premeditated murder could be prosecuted. At about the same time, on May 3, 1955, the *Überleitungsvertrag* (transition agreement) between Germany and the United States, Great Britain, and France went into effect, containing the following provision:

> Persons who have been tried for a crime by the American, British, or French authorities in their respective zones of occupation and the proceedings against them [having] terminated, will not be tried again for the same crime by the German public prosecution, regardless of the outcome of the trial under the Allied occu-

pation authorities—conviction, acquittal, or dismissal of the case because of lack of evidence; this provision also applies to cases in which new evidence has come to light against persons who have been either acquitted or have had their case dismissed.

Nevertheless, 1955 was the year that marked a change in the prosecution of Nazi crimes. It began with an investigation of a complaint concerning the murder of Jews in the German-Lithuanian border region by members of an Einsatzkommando (mobile killing subunit). In this case, contrary to previous practice, the prosecution was not confined to the specific facts in the complaint. For the first time, the prosecution pursued all leads that came to light during the investigation of other crimes committed by Einsatzgruppen and Einsatzkommandos, and added these charges to the initial complaint. The mass of information made clear that apart from a few proceedings by Allied military tribunals against top Nazi officials, some of the worst crimes committed by the Nazi regime had yet to be prosecuted.

In the fall of 1958 the ministers of justice of all the *Länder* (states) of the Federal Republic decided to establish the Ludwigsburger Zentralstelle (Central Office of the Judicial Administrations of the *Länder* for Investigation of Nazi Crimes), in Ludwigsburg. The new office was given the assignment of discovering all available sources of information on Nazi crimes and instituting criminal proceedings against responsible persons. The results were soon felt. In the first twelve months of its existence, the Ludwigsburger Zentralstelle initiated 400 investigations. The most important pertained to crimes committed by Einsatzgruppen and Einsatzkommandos in the Soviet Union and Poland; by the Sicherheitspolizei (Security Police), Ordnungspolizei ("order" police), and the so-called Volksdeutscher Selbstschutz (Ethnic Germans' Self-Defense Force) in the occupied territories; and in the Auschwitz, Belzec, Sobibór, Treblinka, and Chelmno extermination camps.

On May 8, 1960, fifteen years after the war had ended, the statute of limitations on the crimes of manslaughter, deliberate physical injury leading to death, and deprivation of liberty with lethal results went into effect. Members of the Social Democratic party had attempted to introduce a law that would block the statute, but the majority of the Bundestag (the German parliament) was in favor of the statute being applied. Henceforth, only murder could still be prosecuted by the courts. According to the law existing at the time, however, even the charge of murder would be subject to a statute of limitations unless criminal proceedings were instituted before May 8, 1960. The Ludwigsburger Zentralstelle, along with prosecuting attorneys in the German states, tried to collect all available evidence as quickly as possible and use it in time to initiate proceedings against persons known to be, or suspected of being, participants in a crime of murder under the Nazi regime.

Since most of the available evidence was held in archives of countries outside Germany, the Ludwigsburger Zentralstelle applied to Western countries for assistance. As a rule the Zentralstelle had broad access to material, especially in the United States, and was given copies of documents. Most of the relevant documents, however, were held by the Communist countries of Eastern Europe. Among these countries, Poland was the first to express a willingness to cooperate in prosecuting Nazi crimes; in the early 1960s, the Soviet Union made similar hints. For political reasons, however, the government of the Federal Republic would not approve of the Ludwigsburger Zentralstelle's establishing contact with Eastern European countries—most of which were still without diplomatic relations with the Federal Republic (the only exception being the Soviet Union). In late 1964, it became clear that the majority of Nazi acts of murder would benefit from the statute of limitations because investigations could not be completed in time. At this point, the government of the Federal Republic of Germany decided to ask foreign governments to provide all evidence in their possession on Nazi war crimes. The government also instructed the Ludwigsburger Zentralstelle to gain access to archival material held by the Communist-bloc countries. By 1965 these countries—primarily Poland, the Soviet Union, and Czechoslovakia—enabled German prosecuting attorneys and Zentralstelle officials to examine the contents of their archives and, on request, provided them with copies of hundreds of thousands of documents and protocols of interrogations and investigations. In the meantime the Bundestag, after an extremely sharp floor debate in March 1965, passed a law that postponed the date for the statute of limitations on Nazi acts of murder to December 31, 1969. It was hoped that by that time the investigation would yield judicial proceedings in all known cases and, as far as anyone could judge, there would be no more Nazi crimes left to be revealed.

After 1965, the Zentralstelle's staff was increased to a total of 121, including 48 prosecuting attorneys and judges. In addition, public prosecutors and courts for a number of years had 200 prosecuting attorneys and examining magistrates dealing exclusively with the investigation of Nazi crimes, with the assistance of more than 200 criminal-investigation officers. There were also judges sitting in the main jury trials of Nazi crimes. In many foreign countries, German consular officials were busy taking evidence from witnesses to Nazi crimes. In the Soviet Union and Czechoslovakia, but primarily in Poland and Israel, local authorities, at the request of German prosecuting attorneys, took evidence in thousands of cases from witnesses who had been among the victims. Despite greatly increased efforts, it soon became obvious that the task of completing the investigations and instituting criminal proceedings could not be carried out by the end of 1969. The Bundestag therefore—not without pressure from abroad—extended the statute of limitations for Nazi murder acts by another ten years, up to December 31, 1979. During the 1970s, the influx of documentary evidence was kept up, especially from Poland, albeit on a reduced scale. In 1978 the issue of the statute of limitations was revived all over the world. Foreign countries and multinational organizations and institutions, including the European Parliament in Strasbourg, pressed for the total abolition of the statute of limitations pertaining to war crimes and crimes against humanity.

In early 1979, the American television series *Holocaust* was broadcast in the Federal Republic and had the effect of reviving German interest, especially among young people, in the relentless prosecution of Nazi crimes. As a result, the Bundestag in July 1979 decided to abolish the statute of limitations for the crime of murder in general, thus allowing the prosecution of Nazi killers. From its inception in December 1958 until the summer of 1986, the Ludwigsburger Zentralstelle launched investigation of more than 5,000 cases, involving thousands of suspects, and on their completion submitted its findings to prosecutors in the Federal Republic. This led to the instituting of a total of 4,853 official criminal trials, which covered the entire spectrum of Nazi violence. Many proceedings involved crimes in the concentration camps, including satellite camps and Aussenkommandos (detachments); the murders by the Einsatzgruppen and Einsatzkommandos, by the mobile units of the Ordnungspolizei, and by the local police and the Gestapo offices, especially in connection with the forced *Umsiedlung* ("resettlement"; actually deportation) of the Jews—their expulsion from their homes and deportation to the ghettos and extermination camps; the murder of hospital patients and inmates of mental institutions in the euthanasia program; and the murder of Poles and Jews by members of the Volksdeutscher Selbstschutz. In addition to these spectacular mass-murder actions, the trials also involved thousands of cases of violence against individual victims or small groups.

In the majority of the cases, however, the proceedings ended without convictions. In many instances the participants in the crime could not be found, despite determined efforts; quite frequently, the evidence was not sufficient to prove the guilt of the surviving suspects. The persons presumed to have taken part in the crimes benefitted from legal principles developed by the German courts and the federal supreme court, according to which an accused person could not be convicted on the basis of membership in a unit or organization that took part in a crime. For such a person to be convicted, actual participation in the criminal act carried out by the unit or organization had to be proven. In view of the contradictions in testimony given by witnesses, and their diminishing ability to remember events that had taken place so far in the past, the courts and the prosecution often found it impossible to determine individual guilt, even when the crime was revealed down to the last detail. In the cases that did end in convictions, but in which the accused had not acted on their own initiative and had merely followed the orders of their superiors, the courts as a rule concluded that the accused had been accessories to the crime and not the actual perpetrators. This finding enabled the courts to refrain from imposing the sentence of life imprisonment that was mandatory for murder, and instead to sentence the convicted criminal to a prison term of limited duration. Considering the immense number of victims and the enormous cruelty of the murderous deeds, such leniency seemed unnecessary, even in the eyes of unbiased observers.

From the end of the war until January 1986, German courts in the Federal Republic tried 90,921 persons indicted for taking part in Nazi crimes; 6,479 persons were given substantial sentences, 12 being sentenced to death (as long as the death penalty was still in force) and 160 to life imprisonment. Another 1,300 suspects, at least, were still under investigation by the public prosecution on January 1, 1986, while the Ludwigsburger Zentralstelle was conducting preliminary probes of another 101 cases, in which the number of suspects had yet to be determined. No detailed official information has been made available regarding the efforts of the German Democratic Republic (DDR) to bring Nazi criminals to justice. What is certain, however, is that no systematic attempt was made to prosecute Nazi crimes. When a person's participation in Nazi crimes did come to light on the basis of a complaint or by chance, as a rule a stiff sentence was imposed. According to the DDR prosecutor general, a total of 12,861 persons had been convicted of "fascist war crimes and crimes against humanity" by the end of 1976.

Postwar Dispensation of Justice in Germany

In 1955 the Federal Republic of Germany added to its criminal code a paragraph (220a) adapting the provisions of the 1948 United Nations Genocide Convention and making a life sentence mandatory for murder with the intention of destroying a national group. Because genocide did not appear as a crime in the criminal code that was in force when the Nazis were in power, however, the Federal Republic does not apply paragraph 220a against Nazis found guilty of that crime. Indictments and judgments are based on the statutes that were in force when the crime was committed. Murder, physical injury, and deprivation of liberty had been illegal in the Third Reich throughout its existence. Such criminal acts, though, were not subject to prosecution in Nazi Germany when committed on official orders. After the war, the courts claimed that at the time the criminal acts were committed, they had been under duress and unable to try the offenders, but that this by no means implied that the acts in question had been legal or that the state's power to prosecute them had lapsed; and the courts in the newly created Federal Republic were empowered to try the offenders. Doubt also remained as to whether the legal officers who had served under the Nazi regime were capable of dispensing justice.

In 1949, in the course of consultations on the draft constitution of the Federal Republic, concern had been expressed over the possibility that Heinrich Himmler's police and Nazi judges would be reinstated in the civil service. This in fact did take place. On the basis of the constitutional entitlement of former government officials to be maintained by the state (article 131), nearly all the police, judges, and public prosecutors who had served under the Nazis were reinstated in their posts. Consequently, attempts to convict Nazi judges of judicial murder met with failure. During the Hitler period, judges had obeyed Nazi laws and had been blind to the illegality of their actions; this blindness carried over into the new postwar period, and proceedings instituted against these judges regularly ended in acquittals. In turn, the issues of obedience to official orders and awareness of the illegality of such orders assumed roles of central importance in the Federal Republic trials of Nazi criminals. This had not been the case in proceedings conducted by the occupying powers.

Most of the persons brought to trial in the courts of the Federal Republic had either killed with their own hands or had been in charge of killings. The higher the rank of those accused, the farther removed they had been from the actual scene of the crime, and, consequently, the more successful were their eventual efforts to invoke the protection of the popular excuse of not having been aware of the end goal, that is, extermination. Conversely, those whose awareness of the end goal was not in doubt—the actual killers—only in rare cases had acted on their own, and they thus found legal refuge in claiming that they had only been following superior orders. The court therefore spent considerable time trying to establish whether the acts of murder carried out by the defendants were indeed to be regarded as murders they had committed on their own. In this way, the judges managed to perpetuate a system in which it could not be proven that so-called desk criminals had been aware of the killings, or that the executioners had killed with intent or on their own initiative. The courts of the Federal Republic found no solution to this dilemma.

This situation did not change until the late 1950s, upon the maturity of a new generation that had not witnessed, supported, or taken part in Nazi crimes. Although the majority of the German population still called for an end to the prosecution of Nazi crimes, a minority vehemently insisted on the prosecution of the crimes involving mass extermination. This new drive primarily affected the lowest ranks in the chain of command, the subordinate echelons of the police and the SS who were charged with the physical destruction of the masses of victims delivered into their hands—the Einsatzgruppen and the personnel in the concentration camps. Prosecution of the Einsatzgruppen murders, which the Nuremberg Military Tribunals had documented as having been a joint effort of the Wehrmacht and the SS, was now confined to the SS alone. In concentration camp trials, the accused were primarily camp guards and camp commandants. Efforts to have the deportations from German cities classified as participation in murder were of no avail. This was also the outcome of efforts to convict Gerhard Peters, the managing director of DEGESCH (Deutsche Gesellschaft für Schädlingsbekämpfung mbH, or German Vermin-Combating Corporation), the sole supplier of Zyklon B hydrogen cyanide to the SS; the top officials of the Reichsbahn (the German Railways); and the participants in the Wannsee Conference.

In the German courts, the chain of command leading to the "Final Solution" was confined to the originators: Adolf Hitler, Hermann Göring, and Reinhard Heydrich, at the top level, and to the actual murder personnel at the lowest level. The responsibility of the intermediate level—the bureaucratic-military-industrial elites, which the Nuremberg Military Tribunals had exposed—was not recognized by the West German courts. Unlike the Nuremberg courts, which considered certain state organs to be criminal, the West German courts tended not to consider them as such. They based their reasoning on the idea that most Nazi crimes had resulted from the direct and conspiratorial delegation of orders from Hitler (*Führerbefehle*) to the actual murderers.

In contrast to the Nuremberg judgments, the German courts' dispensation of justice to Nazi criminals gained a degree of acceptance among the German population. The guilt of the concentration camp killers and SS firing squads was not in doubt. Yet they were given every consideration by the courts, which felt that although the accused had engaged in a mass murder operation, they were not "murderous types." The view of the courts was that since the Holocaust was carried out in obedience to orders, the executioners, for the most part, were not impelled by any murder motive of their own. Under German law, a murder motive is the intent to murder in a particularly reprehensible, compulsive, malicious, and bestial fashion, and this was not seen as fitting the discipline and speed required by the extermination operation. In the view of the judges, extermination personnel became the "murderous type" only if they were imbued with Hitlerian racist hatred, or if they performed the killing in an excessively cruel manner.

Another factor inhibiting the courts was the length of time that had elapsed between the crimes and the trials. By the time the trials were held,

decades had passed since the criminal acts had been committed, and only in a few cases was it possible to arrive at precise findings. When it came to examining the executioners' motivation, the courts, as a rule, accepted the perpetrators' own testimony of having acted in obedience to orders. Counter arguments could not be put forth easily, because the external details of the extermination operation could not be reconstructed conclusively on the evidence given by the victims. Moreover, in West German courts, the fact that a person had been a member of a murder squad or an extermination camp staff was not regarded as incriminating; it had to be proven that the suspect had personally taken part in killing or in giving orders to kill. Few witnesses had survived, and the survivors did not always remember with sufficient accuracy such particulars as dates, times of day, places, faces, and ranks. It was therefore rarely possible to give a verdict of guilty, which had to be based on many small details. The defense, for its part, diligently and skillfully tracked down inaccuracies in the evidence submitted by the survivors. The victims could often describe the overall situation, but not the minutiae of the crime, and the factory-like procedure of killing had left their memories blurred.

In general, the German courts decided that the crimes they were asked to judge did not meet the criteria of murder as required by law. If the defendants were shown to have killed, they were also generally shown to have acted as tools of the Nazi machine. This meant they were at most guilty of being accessories to murder, an offense punishable by terms in prison ranging from three years to life (as of 1975, from three to fifteen years). In most cases the judges' evaluation of the seriousness of the crimes committed in the extermination operation restricted punishment to the minimum required by law. The accused also benefitted from the fact that they were no longer considered to represent a threat to the community. The full force of the law was applied only in the rather rare cases of excessively cruel and sadistic criminals. Inflicting more pain and physical or mental torture "than was necessary" was shown to be in violation of orders the defendants had received. Federal German criminal courts regarded such behavior as indication of murderous intent, and in these cases they could therefore pass sentences of life imprisonment.

Hungary

Since the end of World War II some 40,000 suspected war criminals have been investigated and tried in Hungary, and more than 19,000 have been found guilty. As early as December 1944, the Hungarian provisional government in Debrecen began taking measures toward prosecuting suspected war criminals, and special courts for that purpose, called people's tribunals, began trying cases as soon as the war ended. By the end of 1946 most of the leading Hungarian politicians who had cooperated with Nazi Germany or had created the circumstances for Hungary's collaboration with the Nazis had been tried and punished. One of the first major cases involved former premier László Bárdossy, whose trial began on October 29, 1945. Bárdossy was accused of having violated the Hungarian constitution. Among the more specific charges against him was that of complicity in the murder of Hungarian Jews at Kamenets-Podolski and Novi Sad. Bárdossy was found guilty and was hanged on January 10, 1946.

Former premier Béla Imrédy was brought to trial on November 14, 1945. He was accused, in part, of having prepared for the later persecution of Jews by drafting the First Anti-Jewish Law in his capacity as a government minister and by signing the Second Anti-Jewish Law while serving as premier. On March 1, 1946, he was executed. The notorious anti-Semites Andor Jaross (former minister of the interior) and his undersecretaries, László Baky and László Endre, were tried between the end of December 1945 and early January 1946. All three were accused of war crimes and of having played major roles in the plundering and deportation of Hungarian Jews. On March 26, 1946, Endre and Baky were hanged; on April 11, 1946, Jaross was shot.

In the series of trials held between December 1945 and March 1946, most of the other members of the governments of Döme Sztójay and Ferenc Szálasi were tried, along with the former prime ministers themselves. Most of the former ministers were executed. Other significant trials also resulted in death sentences. Márton Zöldi and József Grassy were tried for their roles in the Novi Sad massacre. A court convicted them, but a subsequent appeal led the verdict to be overturned. Later they were extradited to Yugoslavia, the scene of the massacre, where a court again convicted them and sentenced them to death; both were executed. Emil Kovacz, an Arrow Cross party leader who was instrumental in deporting Jews from Budapest during the Szálasi regime, was also sentenced to death and executed, as were Péter Hain (Regent Miklós Horthy's personal detective, chief of the Hungarian secret police, and a German

agent) and László Ferenczy of the gendarmerie. Both Hain and Ferenczy had been instrumental in the deportation of Hungarian Jews. In 1967 former Arrow Cross men from the organization's headquarters in the Budapest suburb of Zugló were put on trial. Three of the defendants, Vilmos Kroszl, Lajos Nemeth, and Alijos Sándor, were executed. Sixteen others were sentenced to long terms of hard labor.

The Netherlands

In late 1943 the government-in-exile of the Netherlands, which had its seat in London, enacted four laws providing for the prosecution of war criminals in the Netherlands and of Dutch collaborators with the German enemy. These laws and their eventual application represented significant departures from the Netherlands' legal tradition in this area:

1. The offenses and crimes that were classified as such by the new laws were not included in the prewar code of criminal law, the retroactive force of the laws being justified by the argument that before the war the legislator had not been aware that such crimes existed.

2. A special juridical authority (including its own court of appeals) was established for war criminals and collaborators.

3. Contrary to accepted practice, these special tribunals, in addition to three professional judges, included two military men.

The special tribunals were activated in the Netherlands in late 1945 and ceased to operate in 1950. In 1944 and 1945, as the Netherlands was being liberated, regular and irregular Dutch forces arrested 450,000 suspects (some 5 percent of the country's population), of whom, however, only 200,532 had their files forwarded to the prosecution. Eventually the Dutch government freed the majority of the suspects, and by the end of 1945 the number in detention was down to 90,000.

A total of 14,562 persons were convicted and sentenced in the Netherlands, the punishment pronounced by the courts decreasing in severity as time elapsed and the impact of liberation declined. This development was a result of both the indifference manifested by the public and the policy of reconciliation with the past that was adopted by successive ministers of justice (who were all from the Catholic party). They not only based their policy on humane considerations, but also took political interests into account (most of the criminals were Catholics). Although 109 death sentences were passed, only thirty-nine were carried out, among them those of five Germans and one Jewish woman. All the other death sentences were commuted to life imprisonment.

In the course of time, prison sentences passed by the special tribunals were reduced. As a result, by early 1960 only forty-nine persons were still in prison, and they were also set free, with the exception of four who were accomplices in the murders of Jews. Attempts were made by members of parliament and cabinet ministers to have these four set free as well, but such attempts were long foiled by the violent reaction among the Dutch public. One of the four (Willi Lages) was freed for health reasons in 1966 (he died in 1971); one person died in prison; and in 1989 the last two criminals, Ferdinand aus der Fünten and Franz Fischer, were given amnesty, a decision that caused angry demonstrations in many parts of the country. Among the collaborators whom the prosecution sought to bring to trial were two heads of the Joodse Raad (Jewish Council), Abraham Asscher and Professor David Cohen. They were arrested in 1947, but a month later the minister of justice ordered their release, in the face of widespread public indignation and legal opinions arguing that their arrest had no legal foundation. In 1950 the minister of justice decided to close the files on Asscher and Cohen, on grounds of public interest, but without giving his decision the character of a rehabilitation.

Another affair that agitated public opinion in the Netherlands over many years was the conviction of Friedrich Weinreb. He was a Jew who during the war had pretended that owing to his ties with German army officers he could arrange for many Jews to emigrate. In 1948 Weinreb was tried and sentenced to six years' imprisonment on a charge of collaboration with the enemy. In the mid-1960s it was claimed that his conviction had been a miscarriage of justice; the government appointed an inquiry commission, which found that Weinreb was guilty of informing on people and that such informing had led to the arrest and subsequent death of dozens of people. The first report of the inquiry commission was submitted in 1976, and a supplementary report, in 1981. No retrial was held, since Weinreb had fled to Switzerland in the meantime.

Another famous case was that of Pieter Menten, a wealthy businessman with close connections in the Dutch administration. Habib Kenaan, an Israeli journalist, proved that Menten had been responsible for the murder of Kenaan's family and many other Jews in Galicia, and that Menten had robbed them of their possessions, which he had transferred to the Netherlands. Menten had also managed to conceal from the Dutch authorities the fact that he had served with the German administration in Poland. In 1980 Menten was brought to trial and was sentenced to ten years in prison and a fine of 100,000 gulden.

In the immediate postwar period, judicial proceedings against war criminals and collaborators were treated with indifference by the Dutch public, a fact that enabled government officials to intervene, discreetly, on behalf of influential suspects. The growing interest in the events of World War II in the 1960s, together with the findings of the inquiry commissions and the great number of published research studies, revealed to the Dutch public that grave errors had been made in the way the prosecution of Nazi criminals and their helpers had been handled.

Norway

The government of Vidkun Quisling could not prevent the emergence of a Norwegian movement of resistance to the Nazis and of aid to and rescue of their victims. Members of the resistance movement—and Jews who had not managed to escape to Sweden—who fell into the hands of the occupation authorities were brutally tortured and murdered. It was therefore natural for the Norwegian government-in-exile in London to join in the warnings and declarations issued by the Allies regarding the punishment of Nazi criminals. The trials in Norway were based on a decree issued on May 5, 1945, and a special law (Law No. 14) passed on December 13, 1946 (the text of the latter was influenced by the Nuremberg Trial). According to this legislation, punishment for crimes that had been accepted as crimes either formally or by international consensus before World War II could be enforced retroactively. Punishment for other categories of crimes, as spelled out in Law No. 14, could not be applied retroactively to World War II. The courts that tried the Nazis were also based on a resolution adopted by the Norwegian parliament on April 9, 1940. Apart from the Quisling trial, some of the most important trials of Nazis held in Norway dealt with the following war criminals:

1. Karl-Hans Klinge, a German police officer notorious for the inhuman torture of prisoners;

2. Police officer Richard Wilhelm Bruns and other police officers charged with cruel mistreatment and murder;

3. SS-Obersturmbannführer Gerhard Flesch, who, as superior officer to the commandant of the Falstad concentration camp, ordered the commandant to have shot three Jews whom Flesch had encountered by chance;

4. Hans Paul Helmut Latza, president of the Nazi Court, who bore responsibility for numerous acts of murder;

5. Hauptsturmführer Oskar Hans, charged with the murder of 312 persons, among them Jews of Norwegian and other nationalities.

In these trials, all of the accused were sentenced to death.

Poland

In view of the enormous crimes committed by the Nazis in Poland, authorities in the liberated areas of the country regarded the capture and punishment of the criminals as one of their most urgent tasks. The Polski Komitet Wyzwolenia Narodowego (Polish Committee of National Liberation), established in liberated Lublin on July 21, 1944, issued an order on August 31 of that year on the punishment of Nazi criminals found guilty of the murder and persecution of civilians and prisoners of war and of Polish traitors. The order established strict criminal responsibility for all kinds of war crimes and crimes against humanity, in the same manner in which these terms were later defined in article 6 of the Charter of the International Military Tribunal at Nuremberg. By an order dated September 12, 1944, special courts were established for the trial of Nazi criminals, with the participation of lay judges. The proceedings were of a summary nature and there was no appeal. In 1949 the special courts were abolished and subsequent trials of war crimes came before regular courts, with selected judges conducting the trials according to the general rules of procedure. On January 22, 1946, the Najwyzszy Trybunal Narodowy (Supreme National Court) was created for trials of special significance.

The special courts established in September 1944 lost no time in tackling their task. The first trial of war criminals in Poland was held from November 27 to December 2, 1944 (while the war was still in progress); the accused were staff members of the Majdanek camp who had fallen into Polish hands. The total number of Nazi war criminals tried after the war was 5,450—a tiny fraction of the total, since most of the criminals had fled with the retreating German forces. Attempts made after the war to extradite war criminals to Poland were only partially successful; the total number extradited was 1,803. In 1947 and 1948 difficulties were encountered in extraditing Nazi war criminals to Poland from the western zones of occupation in Germany, and from 1950 onward, no more extraditions were granted. This meant that another 5,600 Nazis listed as war criminals by the United Nations War Crimes Commission were not extradited. Poland's request for them was disregarded.

A mass of documentation, on a variety of subjects, was accumulated in the numerous trials of Nazi war criminals by Polish courts on the almost total extermination of the Jewish population; the selective killing of other parts of the Polish population; terror actions and persecution on grounds of ethnic origin, religion, and race; the network of extermination camps, concentration camps, and labor camps; the actions designed to restrict the natural growth of the native populations of the occupied countries; the forced-labor organization that involved moving people, against their will, out of the borders of their own country; the destruction and theft of art works and antiquities; the forced assimilation into the German nation of select groups of children and youngsters; the ruin of the economy of the occupied countries; the destruction and theft of private property; the destruction of Warsaw in 1944; and other war crimes and crimes against humanity.

The trials before the Supreme National Court were of special importance. The defendant in the first trial (June 7 to 21, 1946) was Arthur Greiser, the *Gauleiter* (district leader) of the Warthegau. Among the charges against him were those of taking part in preparing a war of aggression against Poland, organizing the killing actions against the Polish population, and participating in the creation of ghettos and in the murder of the Jewish population in the places where they lived and in the gas chambers of the Chelmno camp. Next to be tried (August 27 to September 5, 1946) was Amon Goeth, who had been the commandant of the Plaszów camp. He was charged with the murder of civilian prisoners in the camp and the final liquidation of the Kraków and Tarnów ghettos. Other trials involved Ludwig Fischer, who had been governor of the Warsaw district, and Ludwig Leist, the former governor of Warsaw, and of two Higher SS and Police Leaders, Josef Meisinger and Max Daum (December 17, 1946, to late February 1947). All the accused were found guilty of crimes against the population of Warsaw and its vicinity, including the abominable treatment of the population after the suppression of the 1944 Warsaw uprising. Fischer was also convicted on the charge of setting up the Warsaw ghetto and the Treblinka extermination camp.

The trial of Rudolf Höss, the man who set up the Auschwitz-Birkenau extermination camp and served as commandant until October 1943, was held March 11 to 29, 1947. This trial reconstructed, with great precision, the teams that had established and operated Auschwitz, making it a major element in the Nazi genocide system. These men were responsible for the fate of the 300,000 prisoners whose names were listed in the camp rolls (most of them from Poland, but also including people from other German-occupied countries, and Soviet prisoners of war) and of more than a million other prisoners, brought from various parts of Europe, who were not even registered in the camp and, on their arrival in Auschwitz, were taken straight to the gas chambers. The majority of the people murdered in Auschwitz were Jews. The first Auschwitz trial was followed by the trial of Arthur Liebehenschel (November 24 to December 16, 1947), who succeeded Höss as the commandant of Auschwitz, and thirty-nine other defendants, many of whom had held responsible posts in the camp. In the trial held from April 5 to 27, 1948, the accused was Albert Forster, who had been *Gauleiter* of Danzig and then of Danzig-East Prussia. The charges against him included participation in preparations for a war of aggression, in the murder of Jewish and Polish populations, and in the persecution and deportation of a great number of Poles.

In the last trial before the Supreme National Court (April 17 to June 5, 1948), the man in the dock was Josef Bühler, who had been deputy governor of the Generalgouvernement (that is, the deputy of Hans Frank, who was tried at the Nuremberg Trial). Bühler was charged for his role in directing the mass murder campaign against the Generalgouvernement population, which included Jews of Polish nationality, and for other crimes against "the Polish state and Polish citizens." The Nazi criminals who were tried by the Supreme National Court were all sentenced to death and executed, with the exception of Leist and some of the Auschwitz camp staff.

Of the thousands of trials held before the special courts and, later, the regular courts, the most important were those of the following persons:

1. Erich Koch (1959), who had been governor of East Prussia, to which parts of northern Poland were annexed.

2. Jürgen Stroop (1951), who in 1943, as an SS-Gruppenführer, was in charge of suppressing the Warsaw ghetto uprising.

3. Franz Konrad (1951), an SS officer charged with committing multiple murders in the Warsaw ghetto and assisting in the suppression of the ghetto uprising.

4. Herbert Buttcher (1949), SS and police leader in the Radom district, who was charged, in part, with the extermination of the Jews of Ostrowiec, Częstochowa, and Piotrków Trybunalski.

5. Hans Biebow (1947), chief of the Lódz ghetto administration.

6. Jacob Sporrenberg (1950), SS and police leader in the Lublin district, charged with, among other crimes, the mass murder of Jews, mainly in Aktion "Erntefest."

7. Paul Otto Geibel (1954), SS and police leader in Warsaw, charged with the role he played in the destruction of the Polish capital in 1944, among other crimes.

Also brought to trial were several dozen persons who had served on the staffs of the Auschwitz, Majdanek, and Stutthof camps. The Polish courts regarded the administrative institutions of the concentration camps—the camp command, administrative officers, and personnel—as criminal organizations, under the definition of that term by the Nuremberg International Military Tribunal. Also declared to be criminal organizations were the Generalgouvernement administration; the paramilitary Selbstschutz, a self-defense organization made up of *Volksdeutsche* (ethnic Germans) in Poland; and the Ukrainska Povstanska Armyia (Ukrainian Insurgent Army).

The trials of Nazi criminals in Poland were conducted in accordance with established legal procedure, with the accused having the rights of defense. The accused were tried for acts and crimes in violation not only of state law, but also of international law, mainly the Fourth Hague Convention.

Romania

Punishment of Romanian war criminals was not universally accepted. Proceedings were carried out against the background of a political struggle between the Communist party, supported by the Soviet occupying force, and the traditional forces, which included the parties in opposition to the regime of Ion Antonescu and to the king and his followers. The trials of Nazi war criminals in Romania can be divided into three periods: (1) from the overthrow of the Antonescu regime on August 23, 1944, until the rise of a majority Communist government on March 6, 1945; (2) the transitional period, from the establishment of a partially Communist regime on March 6, 1945, until the establishment of a completely Communist regime on December 30, 1947; and (3) from December 30, 1947, to 1955.

In the first period, Romania had to fulfill the conditions of the cease-fire agreement signed in Moscow on September 12, 1944, according to which it had undertaken to arrest war criminals, to immediately dissolve pro-Nazi organizations, and to prevent the establishment of such organizations in the future. The Romanian government also undertook to imprison German and Hungarian citizens and to extradite them to the Soviet Union. These conditions were met; Antonescu did not have an existing Fascist party apparatus, and he himself dissolved the pro-Nazi Iron Guard. Until March 6, 1945, the various Romanian governments were slow in dealing with legislation against war criminals. Only on January 20, 1945, were the first laws concerning legal steps against Nazi criminals passed, and since these regulations were prepared by the Ministry of the Interior, the organizations of Nazi war victims could do little to influence their wording. The committee that prepared the regulations was acutely split on how to define the term "war criminal" in a way that would satisfy the various political forces in the government. The two veteran Romanian parties, the Partidul National-Liberal (National Liberal Party) and the Partidul National-Taranesc (National Peasants' Party), wanted to reduce the negative responsibility, while the Communists and the Social Democrats wanted to expand it.

The compromise satisfied the Jewish public only partially. The regulations did not recognize the right of the victims to be represented in the courts, and no Jewish organization was included in the judiciary bodies or in the prosecution that pre-

pared the trials. At the same time, certain judges presiding in these trials had, under Antonescu, condemned Jews to long terms of imprisonment or had decreed death penalties for transgressions against the racial laws of the Antonescu regime. In this first period the Communist party supported the punishment of war criminals as part of their power struggle and a desire to remove members of the "old" political powers from key positions. By the second period, beginning in March 1945, some of the most important Nazi criminals involved in the extermination of the Jews of Bessarabia and Bukovina and of the Jewish deportees in Transnistria were brought to trial. To strike a "balance," some of the Jewish deportees who had collaborated with Romanian authorities in those regions were also tried. Under Soviet pressure, the first pro-Communist government, under Petru Groza, which was established on March 6, 1945, began to accelerate punishment of Nazi criminals. The Soviet Union sought to bring to a conclusion the trials of perpetrators of crimes on its territory and on the territories it had annexed from Romania— Bessarabia and northern Bukovina.

During the second period a new law was issued to purge the public administration, and another law was issued to bring to trial those responsible for the national disaster and for war crimes and to punish them. This law authorized the continuation of the local war trials, originally restricted to a period of six months, and expanded the range of criminal responsibility. In this period the heads of the fascist regime were sentenced and five, including Ion Antonescu, were executed in June 1946. In the course of 1946, with the approach of the general elections (November 19, 1946), Petru Groza's government reneged on its declarations, and ceased bringing war criminals to trial in order to prove to its opponents that it was neither pro-Jewish nor influenced by Jews. The peace treaty between the Allies and Romania, signed in Paris in 1947, again stipulated that Romania must bring war criminals to trial, but even after that time not all the war criminals known to the Jews were punished. The organizers and perpetrators of the Iasi pogroms of June 29, 1941, were brought to trial only in May 1948. This delay constituted part of the effort of Romanian foreign policy to conceal war crimes committed by Romanian soldiers and citizens against Jews with Romanian citizenship.

During the third period, 1947 to 1955, came the arrest and imprisonment of tens of thousands of opponents of the regime who had previously belonged to the now dissolved old Romanian parties or to the Iron Guard; among those arrested were thousands of war criminals. The aim was not to sentence the criminals who had oppressed, plundered, violated, and murdered the Jews, but to liquidate all opposition to the Communist regime. Nevertheless, in these trials a large proportion of the war criminals were sentenced. Many, however, evaded punishment or fled Romania.

In 1955 the punishment laws were repealed, effectively ending any further possibility of trying and sentencing Nazi war criminals. This was perhaps the reason for the nonintervention of Romanian jurists in the international debate on the law of limitation for Nazi war crimes. Romanian legal and historical studies tend to stress Hungarian crimes against the Romanians in northern Transylvania, and they virtually omit any mention of Romanian war criminals. The repeal of the punishment laws in 1955 also granted a general pardon to a large number of war criminals already serving prison sentences. All the criminals sentenced to terms of up to ten years were released, and the prison sentences of the rest were greatly reduced.

(Adapted from *Encyclopedia of the Holocaust*, edited by Israel Gutman, volume 3, Macmillan (New York), 1990, pp. 1488–1518.)

Contributors

Jean Ancel
Jörg Friedrich
Priscilla Dale Jones
Leszek Kubicki
Jozeph Michman
Marian Mushkat
Robert Rozett
Adalbert Rückerl
Shmuel Spector

Sources

Books

Anderaes, Johannes, and others, *Norway and the Second World War*, [Lillehammer, Norway], 1983.

Barrington, J. H., editor, *The Zyklon B Trial: Trial of Bruno Tesch and Two Others*, [London], 1948.

Belinfante, A. D., *In plaats van Bijltjesdag*, Van Gorcum (Assen, Netherlands), 1978.

Belsen, (in Hebew), [Tel Aviv], 1957

Best, Geoffrey, *Humanity in Warfare: The Modern History of the International Law of Armed Conflicts*, [London], 1983.

Central Committee for the Investigation of German Crimes in Poland, *German Crimes in Poland*, The Commission [Warsaw], 1947.

Conot, Robert E., *Justice at Nuremberg*, Harper and Row (New York), 1983.

Cyprian, T., and J. Sawicki, *Processy wielkich zbrodniarzy wojennych w Polsce* (Lódz), 1949.

Davidson, Eugene, *The Trial of the Germans: An Account of Twenty-Two Defendants before the International Military Tribunal at Nuremberg*, [New York], 1967.

Friedrich, J., *Die kalte Amnestie: NS-Täter in der Bundesrepublik*, [Frankfurt], 1984.

Groen, K., *Landverraad wat deden we met ze?*, [Weesp, Netherlands], 1974.

Henkys, Reinhard, *Die nationalsozialistischen Gewaltverbrechen*, [Stuttgart], 1965.

International Military Tribunal, *The Trial of the Major War Criminals before the International Military Tribunal*, Blue Series, 42 volumes, [Nuremberg], 1947–1949.

Jäger, H., *Verbrechen unter totalitärer Herrschaft*, [Freiburg], 1967.

Kubicki, Leszek, *Zbrodnie wojenne w swietle prawa polskiego*, Nauk (Warsaw), 1963.

Lichtenstein, H., *In Namen des Volkes?*, [Cologne], 1984.

Mason, Henry Lloyd, *The Purge of Dutch Quislings: Emergency Justice in the Netherlands*, Nijhoff (The Hague), 1952.

Mushkat, M., *Polish Charges against War Criminals*, [Warsaw], 1948.

The People's Verdict: A Full Report of the Proceedings at the Krasnodar and Kharkov German Atrocity Trials, Hutchinson and Company, Limited (London), 1944.

Phillips, R., editor, *Trial of Josef Kramer and Forty-Four Others (The Belsen Trial)*, [London], 1949.

Prozess in der Strafsache gegen die faschistischen deutschen Okkupanten und ihre Helfershelfer wegen ihre Bestialitäten im Gebiet der Stadt Krasnodar und des Krasnodarer Gaus während der zeitweiligen Besatzung dieses Gebietes: Verhandelt am 14–17 juli 1943, [Moscow], 1943.

Rückerl, Adalbert, *The Investigation of Nazi Crimes, 1945–1978: A Documentation,* Archon Books (Hamden, CT), 1980.

Rückerl, Adalbert, *NS-Verbrechen vor Gericht,* C. F. Muller (Heidelberg), 1982.

Smith, Bradley F., *The Road to Nuremberg,* Basic Books (New York), 1981.

Taylor, Telford, *Final Report to the Secretary of the Army on the Nuremberg War Crimes Trials under Control Council Law No. 10,* [Washington, D.C.], 1949.

Trials of War Criminals before the Nuremberg Military Tribunals under Control Council Law No. 10, Volumes 1–15, [Washington, D.C.], 1949–1952.

Tusa, Ann, and John Tusa, *The Nuremberg Trial,* Atheneum (London), 1984.

United Nations War Crimes Commission, *History of the United Nations War Crimes Commission and the Development of the Laws of War,* H. M. Stationery Office (London), 1948.

United Nations War Crimes Commission, *Law Reports of Trials of War Criminals,* Volume 1, H. M. Stationery Office (London), 1947, pp. 93–104.

United Nations War Crimes Commission, *Law Reports of Trials of War Criminals,* Volume 2, H. M. Stationery Office (London), 1947, pp. 1–56.

United Nations War Crimes Commission, *Law Reports of Trials of War Criminals,* Volumes 3, 5, 6, H. M. Stationery Office (London), 1947–1949.

Veth, D. G., and A. J. van der Leeuw, *Rapport uitgebracht door het Rijksinstuut voor Oorlogsdocumentatie inzake de activiteiten van Drs. F. Weinreb gedurende de jaren 1940–1945,* 2 volumes, [The Hague], 1976.

Webb, A. M., *The Natzweiler Trial,* Hodge (London), 1949.

Woetzel, Robert K., *The Nuremberg Trials in International Law,* Praeger (New York), 1960.

Periodicals

Hellendall, F., "Nazi Crimes before German Courts: The Immediate Post-War Era," *Wiener Library Bulletin,* summer 1970, pp. 14–20.

Leeuw, A. J. van der, "The Emigration Lists of Friedrich Weinreb," *Patterns of Jewish Leadership in Nazi Europe 1933–1945,* Proceedings of the Third Yad Vashem International Historical Conference, edited by Y. Gutman and C. J. Haft, [Jerusalem], 1981, pp. 259–265.

Levai, E., "The War Crimes Trials relating to Hungary," *Hungarian Jewish Studies,* 1969, pp. 252–296.

Levai, E., "The War Crimes Trials relating to Hungary: A Follow-Up," *Hungarian Jewish Studies,* 1973, pp. 251–290.

Mushkat, M., "The Concept of Crime against the Jewish People in the Light of International Law," *Yad Vashem Studies,* 1961, pp. 237–254.

Nuremberg Trial (International Military Tribunal)

The Indictment

The United States of America, The French Republic, The United Kingdom of Great Britain and Northern Ireland and The Union of Soviet Socialist Republics *against* Hermann Wilhelm Göring, Rudolf Hess, Joachim von Ribbentrop, Robert Ley, Wilhelm Kietle, Ernst Kaltenbrunner, Alfred Rosenberg, Hans Frank, Wilhelm Frick, Julius Streicher, Walter Funk, Hjalmar Schacht, Gustav Krupp von Bohlen und Halbach, Karl Dönitz, Erich Raeder, Baldur von Schirach, Fritz Sauckel, Alfred Jodl, Martin Bormann, Franz von Papen, Arthur Seyss-Inquart, Albert Speer, Konstantin von Neurath, and Hans Fritzsche, individually and as members of any of the following groups or organizations to which they respectively belonged, namely: Die Reichsregierung (Reich Cabinet); Das Korps der Politischen Leiter der Nationalsozialistischen Deutschen Arbeiterpartei (Leadership Corps of the Nazi Party); Die Schutzstaffeln der Nationalsozialistischen Deutschen Arbeiterpartei (commonly known as the "SS") and including Der Sicherheitsdienst (commonly known as the "SD"); Die Geheime Staatspolizei (Secret State Police, commonly known as the Gestapo); Die Sturmabteilungen der NSDAP (commonly known as the "SA"); and the General Staff and High Command in Appendix B of the Indictment. DEFENDANTS

The Accused

Name	Position	Sentence
1. Martin Bormann	Deputy Führer, Head of Chancellery	Death
2. Karl Dönitz	Supreme Commander of the Navy (1943), Chancellor (1945)	Ten years
3. Hans Frank	Governor-General of the Generalgouvernement	Death
4. Wilhelm Frick	Minister of the Interior	Death
5. Hans Fritzsche	Head of the Radio Division, Propaganda Ministry	Acquitted
6. Walther Funk	President of the Reichsbank (1939)	Life imprisonment
7. Hermann Göring	Reich Marshal and the Commander in Chief of the Luftwaffe	Death
8. Rudolf Hess	Deputy Führer (1939)	Life imprisonment
9. Ernst Kaltenbrunner	Chief of the Sicherheitspolizei and SD; Head of the RSHA	Death
10. Wilhelm Keitel	Chief of the OKW (Armed Forces High Command)	Death
11. Alfred Jodl	Chef of the OKW Operations Staff	Death
12. Konstantin von Neurath	Minister of Foreign Affairs (1932-1938); Reich Protector of Bohemia-Moravia (1939-1943)	Fifteen years
13. Franz von Papen	Chancellor (1932); Ambassador to Vienna (1934-1938), Ambassador to Turkey (1939-1944)	Acquitted
14. Erich Raeder	Supreme Commander of the Navy (1928-1943)	Life imprisonment
15. Joachim von Ribbentrop	Reich Foreign Minister	Death
16. Alfred Rosenberg	Reich Minister for the Eastern Occupied Areas	Death
17. Fritz Sauckel	Plenipotentiary General for Manpower	Death
18. Hjalmar Schacht	Minister of Economics (1933-1936); President of the Reichsbank (until 1939)	Acquitted
19. Baldur von Schirach	Leader of the Hitler Youth; Gauleiter of Vienna	Twenty years
20. Arthur Seyss-Inquart	Reich Commissioner for the Occupied Netherlands	Death
21. Albert Speer	Minister of Armaments and War Production	Twenty years
22. Julius Streicher	Founder of *Der Stürmer*; Gauleiter of Franconia	Death

Subsequent Nuremberg Proceedings

Trial 1. The Medical Case
October 25, 1946—August 20, 1947

Defendant	Verdict or Sentence	Outcome
Karl Brandt	Death by hanging	Executed 1948
Siegfried Handloser	Life imprisonment	Sentence reduced by Clemency Board to twenty years
Paul Rostock	Not guilty	Acquitted
Oskar Schröder	Life imprisonment	Sentenced reduced to fifteen years
Karl Genzken	Life imprisonment	Sentence reduced by Clemency Board to twenty years. Fined by denazification court, 1955.
Karl Gebhardt	Death by hanging	Executed 1948
Kurt Blome	Not guilty	Acquitted
Rudolf Brandt	Death by hanging	Executed 1948
Joachim Mrugowsky	Death by hanging	Executed 1948
Helmut Poppendick	Ten years' imprisonment	Released January 31, 1951
Wolfram Sievers	Death by hanging	Executed 1948
Gerhard Rose	Life imprisonment	Sentence reduced by Clemency Board to fifteen years
Siegfried Ruff	Not guilty	Since 1952 head of the Institute for Aeronautical Medicine of the German Air Navigational Experiment Center. Since 1954 professor at University of Bonn.
Hans Wolfgang Romberg	Not guilty	Acquitted
Georg August Weltz	Not guilty	Since 1952 professor at University of Munich
Konrad Schäfer	Not guilty	Acquitted
Waldemar Hoven	Death by hanging	Executed 1948
Wilhelm Beiglböck	Fifteen years' imprisonment	Sentence reduced to ten years
Adolf Pokorny	Not guilty	Acquitted
Herta Oberheuser	Twenty years' imprisonment	Released April 1952
Fritz Ernst Fischer	Life imprisonment	Sentenced reduced to fifteen years
Viktor (Victor) Brack	Death by hanging	Executed 1948
Hermann Becker-Freyseng	Twenty years' imprisonment	Sentence reduced to ten years

Trial 2. The Milch Case
November 13, 1946—April 17, 1947

Defendant	Verdict or Sentence	Outcome
Erhard Milch	Life imprisonment	Sentenced reduced by Clemency Board to fifteen years; released 1954

Trial 3. The Justice Case
January 4, 1947—December 4, 1947

Defendant	Verdict or Sentence	Outcome
Josef Alstötter	Five years' imprisonment	
Wilhelm von Ammon	Ten years' imprisonment	Sentence reduced to time served as of January 31, 1951
Paul Barnickel	Acquitted	
Hermann Cuhorst	Acquitted	
Karl Engert	Not tried owing to ill health	
Günther Joel	Ten years' imprisonment	
Herbert Klemm	Life imprisonment	Sentenced reduced by Clemency Board to twenty years
Ernst Lautz	Ten years' imprisonment	Sentenced reduced to time served as of January 31, 1951
Wolfgang Mettgenberg	Ten years' imprisonment	
Günther Nebelung	Acquitted	
Rudolf Oeschey	Life imprisonment	Sentenced reduced to twenty years
Hans Petersen	Acquitted	
Oswald Rothhaug	Life imprisonment	Sentence reduced by Clemency Board to twenty years; pensioned
Kurt Rothenberger	Seven years' imprisonment	Released August 1950; pensioned
Franz Schlegelberger	Life imprisonment	Released on medical probation after recommendation of Clemency Board, 1951
Carl Westphal	Not tried	Committed suicide before arraignment

Trial 4. The Pohl Case
January 13, 1947—November 3, 1947

Defendant	Verdict or Sentence	Outcome
Oswald Pohl	Death by hanging	Executed 1951
August Frank	Life imprisonment	Sentence reduced by Clemency Board to fifteen years
Georg Lörner	Death by hanging	Sentenced commuted by tribunal to life; reduced by Clemency Board to fifteen years. Upon release, acquitted by Bavarian Denazification Court, 1954.
Heinz Karl Fanslau	Twenty-five years' imprisonment	Sentence reduced by tribunal to twenty years; further reduced by Clemency Board to fifteen years
Hans Lörner	Ten years' imprisonment	Sentence reduced by Clemency Board to time served as of 1951
Josef Vogt	Acquitted	
Erwin Tschentscher	Ten years' imprisonment	Sentence reduced by Clemency Board to time served as of 1951
Rudolf Scheide	Acquitted	
Max Kiefer	Life imprisonment	Sentence reduced by tribunal to twenty years; further reduced by Clemency Board to time served as of 1951

Trial 4. The Pohl Case (continued)
January 13, 1947—November 3, 1947

Defendant	Verdict or Sentence	Outcome
Franz Eirenschmalz	Death by hanging	Sentence commuted by Clemency Board to nine years
Karl Sommer	Death by hanging	Sentence commuted by military governor to life; further reduced by Clemency Board to twenty years
Hermann Pook	Ten years' imprisonment	Sentence reduced by Clemency Board to time served as of 1951
Hans Heinrich Baier	Ten years' imprisonment	Released January 31, 1951
Hans Karl Hohberg	Ten years' imprisonment	Sentence reduced by Clemency Board to time served as of 1951
Leo Volk	Ten years' imprisonment	Sentence reduced by Clemency Board to eight years
Karl Mummenthey	Life imprisonment	Sentence reduced by Clemency Board to twenty years
Hans Bobernin	Twenty years' imprisonment	Sentence reduced by tribunal to fifteen years; freed by Clemency Board, 1951
Horst Klein	Acquitted	

Trial 5. The Flick Case
February 8, 1947—December 22, 1947

Defendant	Verdict or Sentence	Outcome
Friedrich Flick	Seven years' imprisonment	Released August 24, 1950
Otto Steinbrinck	Five years' imprisonment	
Odilo Burkart	Acquitted	
Konrad Kaletsch	Acquitted	
Hermann Terberger	Acquitted	
Bernhard Weiss	Two and one-half years' imprisonment	Vice president, Bundesverband Deutschen Industrie, Cologne

Trial 6. The I. G. Farben Case
May 8, 1947—July 30, 1948

Defendant	Verdict or Sentence	Outcome
Carl Krauch	Six years' imprisonment	
Hermann Schmitz	Four years' imprisonment	Chairman, Rheinische Stahlwerke, 1955
Georg von Schnitzler	Five years' imprisonment	
Fritz Gajewski	Acquitted	
Heinrich Hörlein	Acquitted	
August von Knieriem	Acquitted	
Fritz ter Meer	Seven years' imprisonment	Released 1950. Deputy chairman, T.G. Goldschmidt A.G., Essen; Board of directors, Bankverein Westdeutschland A.G., Düsseldorf; Board of directors, Düsseldorfer Waggonfabrik, 1955.

Trial 6. The I. G. Farben Case (continued)
May 8, 1947—July 30, 1948

Defendant	Verdict or Sentence	Outcome
Christian Schneider	Acquitted	
Otto Ambros	Eight years' imprisonment	Board of directors, Bergwerkge-sellschaft Hibernia; Board of directors, Süddeutsche Kalkstickstoffwerke; Board of directors, Grünzweig und Hartmann, 1955
Max Brüggemann	Not tried owing to ill health	
Ernst Bürgin	Two years' imprisonment	
Heinrich Bütefisch	Six years' imprisonment	Board of directors, Deutsche Gasolin A.G., Berlin; Board of directors, Feldmühle, Papier und Zellstoffwerke, Düsseldorf; Director, Technical Committee of Experts, International Convention of Nitrogen Industry, 1955
Paul Häfliger	Two years' imprisonment	
Max Ilgner	Three years' imprisonment	Chairman, Board of directors, Freundeskreis der Internationalen Gesellschaft für Christlichen Aufbau, 1955
Friedrich Jähne	One and one-half years' imprisonment	Decorated with the Distinguished Service Cross with Star of the Order of Merit by West German government
Hans Kühne	Acquitted	
Carl Lautenschläger	Acquitted	
Wilhelm Mann	Acquitted	
Heinrich Oster	Two years' imprisonment	
Karl Wurster	Acquitted	
Walter Dürrfeld	Eight years' imprisonment	Board of directors, Scholven-Chemie A.G. Gelsenkirchen, 1955
Heinrich Gattineau	Acquitted	
Erich von der Heyde	Acquitted	
Hans Kugler	One and one-half years' imprisonment	Member of Central Committee of the Chemical Industry

Trial 7. The Hostage Case
May 10, 1947—February 19, 1948

Defendant	Verdict or Sentence	Outcome
Wilhelm List	Life imprisonment	Released on medical parole, 1951
Maximilian von Weichs		Indicted; too ill to be tried
Lothar Rendulic	Twenty years' imprisonment	Sentence reduced by Clemency Board to ten years; released 1952
Walter Kuntze	Life imprisonment	Medical parole; released February 10, 1953
Hermann Förtsch	Acquitted	

Trial 7. The Hostage Case (continued)
May 10, 1947—February 19, 1948

Defendant	Verdict or Sentence	Outcome
Franz Böhme		Committed suicide after indictment and prior to arraignment
Helmuth Felmy	Fifteen years' imprisonment	Sentence reduced by Clemency Board to ten years; released 1952
Hubert Lanz	Twelve years' imprisonment	Sentence reduced by Clemency Board to time served as of 1951
Ernst Dehner	Seven years' imprisonment	Released January 31, 1951
Ernst von Leyser	Ten years' imprisonment	Released January 31, 1951
Wilhelm Speidel	Twenty years' imprisonment	Sentence reduced by Clemency Board to time served as of 1951
Kurt von Geitner	Acquitted	

Trial 8. The RuSHA Case
July 1, 1947—March 10, 1948

Defendant	Verdict or Sentence	Outcome
Ulrich Greifelt	Life imprisonment	Died 1949
Rudolf Creutz	Fifteen years' imprisonment	Sentence reduced to ten years
Konrad Meyer-Hetling	Given credit for time served from May 27, 1945, until sentencing, March 10, 1948	
Otto Schwarzenberger	Given credit for time served from May 2, 1945, until sentencing March 10, 1948	
Herbert Hübner	Fifteen years' imprisonment	Released January 31, 1951
Werner Lorenz	Twenty years' imprisonment	Sentence reduced by Clemency Board to fifteen years
Heinz Brükner	Fifteen years' imprisonment	Released January 31, 1951
Otto Hofmann	Twenty-five years' imprisonment	Sentence reduced by Clemency Board to fifteen years
Richard Hildebrandt	Twenty-five years' imprisonment	Reportedly free, 1955
Fritz Schwalm	Ten years' imprisonment	Released January 31, 1951
Max Sollmann	Given credit for time served from July 6, 1945, until sentencing, March 10, 1948	
Gregor Ebner	Given credit for time served from July 5, 1945, until sentencing, March 10, 1948	
Günther Tesch	Given credit for time served from May 13, 1945, until sentencing, March 10, 1948	
Inge Viermetz	Acquitted	

Trial 9. The Einsatzgruppen Case
July 3, 1947—April 10, 1948

Defendant	Verdict or Sentence	Outcome
Ernst Biberstein	Death by hanging	Sentence commuted by Clemency Board to life
Paul Blobel	Death by hanging	Executed 1951
Walter Blume	Death by hanging	Sentence commuted by Clemency Board to life
Werner Braune	Death by hanging	Executed 1951
Lothar Fendler	Ten years' imprisonment	Sentence reduced by Clemency Board to eight years
Matthias Graf	Time already served	Released
Walter Hänsch	Death by hanging	Sentence commuted by Clemency Board to fifteen years
Emil Haussman	Not tried	Committed suicide July 31, 1947
Heinz Jost	Life imprisonment	Sentence commuted by Clemency Board to ten years
Waldemar Klingelhöffer	Death by hanging	Sentence commuted by Clemency Board to life
Erich Naumann	Death by hanging	Executed 1951
Gustav Nosske	Life imprisonment	Sentence reduced by Clemency Board to ten years
Otto Ohlendorf	Death by hanging	Executed 1951
Adolf Ott	Death by hanging	Sentence commuted by Clemency Board to life
Waldemar von Radetzky	Twenty years' imprisonment	Sentence reduced by Clemency Board to time served as of 1951
Otto Rasch	Not sentenced	Died November 1, 1948
Felix Rühl	Ten years imprisonment	Sentence reduced by Clemency Board to time served
Martin Sandberger	Death by hanging	Sentence commuted by Clemency Board to life
Heinz Schubert	Death by hanging	Sentence commuted by Clemency Board to ten years
Erwin Schulz	Twenty years' imprisonment	Sentence commuted by Clemency Board to fifteen years
Willy Seibert	Death by hanging	Sentence commuted by Clemency Board to fifteen years
Franz Six	Twenty years' imprisonment	Sentence commuted by Clemency Board to ten years
Eugen Steimle	Death by hanging	Sentence commuted by Clemency Board to twenty years
Eduard Strauch	Death by hanging	Execution stayed because of defendant's insanity

Trial 10. The Krupp Case
August 16, 1947—July 31, 1948

Defendant	Verdict or Sentence	Outcome
Alfried Felix Alwyn Krupp von Bohlen und Halbach	Twelve years' imprisonment; forfeiture of all property, both real and personal	Sentence reduced by Clemency Board to time served; assets restored.
Ewald Oskar Ludwig Löser	Seven years' imprisonment	Sentence reduced by Clemency Board to time served as of 1951

Trial 10. The Krupp Case (continued)
August 16, 1947—July 31, 1948

Defendant	Verdict or Sentence	Outcome
Eduard Houdremont	Ten years' imprisonment	Sentence reduced by Clemency Board to time served as of 1951
Erich Müller	Twelve years' imprisonment	Sentence reduced by Clemency Board to time served as of 1951
Friedrich Wilhelm Janssen	Ten years' imprisonment	Sentence reduced to time served as of 1951
Karl Heinrich Pfirsch	Acquitted	
Max Otto Ihn	Nine years' imprisonment	Sentence reduced by Clemency Board to time served as of January 1951
Karl Adolf Ferdinand Eberhardt	Nine years' imprisonment	Sentence reduced to time served as of January 31, 1951
Heinrich Leo Korschan	Six years' imprisonment	Sentence reduced by Clemency Board to time served as of 1951
Friedrich von Bülow	Twelve years' imprisonment	Sentence reduced by Clemency Board to time served as of January 31, 1951
Werner Wilhelm Henrich Lehmann	Six years' imprisonment	Released August 24, 1950
Hans Albert Gustav Kupke	Two years' imprisonment	

Trial 11. The Ministries Case
November 4, 1947—April 13, 1949

Defendant	Verdict or Sentence	Outcome
Ernst von Weizsäcker	Seven years' imprisonment	Sentence reduced by tribunal to five years; released 1950. Died 1951.
Gustav Adolf Steengracht von Moyland	Seven years' imprisonment	
Wilhelm Keppler	Ten years' imprisonment	Sentence reduced by Clemency Board to time served as of 1951
Ernst Wilhelm Bohle	Five years' imprisonment	
Ernst Wörmann	Seven years' imprisonment	Sentence reduced by Tribunal to five years
Karl Ritter	Four years' imprisonment	
Otto von Erdmannsdorff	Acquitted	
Edmund Veesenmayer	Twenty years' imprisonment	Sentence reduced by Clemency Board to ten years
Hans Heinrich Lammers	Twenty years' imprisonment	Sentence reduced by Clemency Board to ten years
Wilhelm Stuckart	Three years, ten months, and twenty days, or time served (owing to ill health)	Fined 500 marks by denazification court. Killed in automobile accident, 1953.
Richard Walther Darré	Seven years' imprisonment	Released August 24, 1950
Otto Meissner	Acquitted	
Otto Dietrich	Seven years' imprisonment	Released August 24, 1950
Gottlob Berger	Twenty-five years' imprisonment	Sentence reduced by Clemency Board to ten years

Trial 11. The Ministries Case (continued)
November 4, 1947—April 13, 1949

Defendant	Verdict or Sentence	Outcome
Walter Schellenberg	Six years' imprisonment	Released before serving sentence. Died in Italy, 1952.
Lutz Schwerin von Krosigk	Ten years' imprisonment	Sentence reduced by Clemency Board to time served
Emil Johann Puhl	Five years' imprisonment	
Karl Rasche	Seven years' imprisonment	Released 1950
Paul Körner	Fifteen years' imprisonment	Sentence reduced by Clemency Board to time served as of 1951; pensioned
Paul Pleiger	Fifteen years' imprisonment	Sentence reduced by Clemency Board to nine years
Hans Kehrl	Fifteen years' imprisonment	Sentenced reduced to time served as of 1951

Trial 12. The High Command Case
November 28, 1947—October 28, 1948

Defendant	Verdict or Sentence	Outcome
Wilhelm von Leeb	Three years' imprisonment	
Hugo Sperrle	Acquitted	
Georg Karl Friedrich Wilhelm von Küchler	Twenty years' imprisonment	Sentenced reduced by Clemency Board to twelve years
Johannes Blaskowitz		Committed suicide in prison, February 5, 1948
Hermann Hoth	Fifteen years' imprisonment	Released on medical parole, April 8, 1954
Hans Reinhardt	Fifteen years' imprisonment	Released July 27, 1952
Hans von Salmuth	Twenty years' imprisonment	Sentenced reduced by Clemency Board to twelve years
Karl Hollidt	Five years' imprisonment	
Otto Schniewind	Acquitted	
Karl von Roques	Twenty years' imprisonment	Died 1949
Hermann Reinecke	Life imprisonment	Released October 1954
Walter Warlimont	Life imprisonment	Sentence reduced by Clemency Board to eighteen years
Otto Wöhler	Eight years' imprisonment	Released January 31, 1951
Rudolf Lehmann	Seven years' imprisonment	Released August 24, 1950

Subsequent British Trials

The Belsen Trial
September 17, 1945—November 17, 1945

Defendant	Verdict or Sentence	Outcome
Josef Kramer	Death by hanging	Executed December 13, 1945
Dr. Fritz Klein	Death by hanging	Executed December 13, 1945
Peter Weingartner	Death by hanging	Executed December 13, 1945

The Belsen Trial (continued)
September 17, 1945—November 17, 1945

Defendant	Verdict or Sentence	Outcome
George Kraft	Not guilty	
Franz Hössler	Death by hanging	Executed December 13, 1945
Juana Bormann	Death by hanging	Executed December 13, 1945
Elisabeth Volkenrath	Death by hanging	Executed by December 13, 1945
Herta Ehlert	Fifteen years' imprisonment	Reduced to twelve years; released May 7, 1953
Irma Grese	Death by hanging	Executed December 13, 1945
Ilse (Else) Lothe	Not guilty	
Hilde Lohbauer (Lobauer)	Ten years' imprisonment	Reduced to seven years; released July 15, 1950
Josef Klippel	Not guilty	
Nikolas Jenner (Jonner)	Unable to stand trial owing to illness	
Oscar Shmedidzt (Schmitz)	Not guilty	
Karl Flrazich (Francioh) (Franzisch)	Death by hanging	Executed December 13, 1945
Paul Steinmetz	Unable to stand trial owing to illness	
Ladislaw Gura	Took ill during proceedings and was withdrawn	
Fritz Mathes	Not guilty	
Otto Calesson (Kulessa)	Fifteen years' imprisonment	Sentence suspended; released September 10, 1954
Medislaw Burgraf	Five years' imprisonment	Released August 11, 1949
Karl Egersdorf	Not guilty	
Anchor Pinchen (Ansgar Pichen)	Death by hanging	Executed December 13, 1945
Walter Otto	Not guilty	
Walter Melcher	Unable to stand trial owing to illness	
Franz Stofel	Death by hanging	Executed December 13, 1945
Heinrich Schreirer	Fifteen years' imprisonment	Sentence suspended September 10, 1950
Wilhem Dor (Dorr)	Death by hanging	Executed December 13, 1945
Eric Barsch (Basch)	Not guilty	
Erich Zoddel	Life imprisonment	Sentenced to death by a military government court and executed for an offense committed after the liberation of Belsen
Ignatz Schlomoivicz	Not guilty	
Ilse Forster	Ten years' imprisonment	Released December 21, 1951
Ida Forster	Not guilty	
Vladislav Ostrowoski (Ostrowski)	Fifteen years' imprisonment	Sentence suspended September 10, 1954
Antoni Aurdzieg	Ten years' imprisonment	Released March 20, 1952
Klara Opitz	Not guilty	
Charlotte Klein	Not guilty	
Herta Bothe	Ten years' imprisonment	Released December 21, 1951

The Belsen Trial (continued)
September 17, 1945—November 17, 1945

Defendant	Verdict or Sentence	Outcome
Frieda Walter	Three years' imprisonment	Served; released November 16, 1948
Irene Haschke	Ten years' imprisonment	Released December 21, 1951
Gertrud Fiest	Five years' imprisonment	Released August 11, 1949
Gertrud Sauer	Ten years' imprisonment	Released December 21, 1951
Hilde Lisiewitz	One year imprisonment	Served; released November 16, 1946
Johanne Roth	Ten years' imprisonment	Released July 15, 1950
Anna Hempel	Ten years' imprisonment	Released December 21, 1951
Hildegarde Hahnel	Not guilty	
Helene Kopper	Fifteen years' imprisonment	Released February 25, 1952
Anton Polanski	Not guilty	
Stanislawa Staroska (Starostka)	Ten years' imprisonment	Suicide on May 10, 1946, or reduced to five years (Foreign Office files offer conflicting evidence, but the latter is probably correct)

The Natzweiler Trial
May 29, 1946—June 1, 1946

Defendant	Verdict or Sentence	Outcome
Wolfgang Zeuss	Not guilty	
Magnus Wochner	Ten years' imprisonment	Released May 10, 1953
Emil Meier	Not guilty	
Peter Straub	Thirteen years' imprisonment	Tried on other charges by another British court; sentenced to death; executed October 11, 1946
Fritz Hartjenstein	Life imprisonment	Reduced to twenty-one years. Tried on other charges by another British court; sentenced to death by shooting; commuted to life; reduced to ten years. Extradited to France; tried and sentenced to death; commuted to life. Tried on other charges by the French; sentenced to death; died of illness October 20, 1954.
Franz Berg	Five years' imprisonment	Tried on other charges by another British court; sentenced to death; executed October 11, 1946
Werner Rohde	Death by hanging	Executed October 11, 1946
Emil Bruttel	Four years' imprisonment	Extradited to France; returned to British zone and released March 4, 1950
Kurt aus dem Bruch	Not guilty	
Walter Herberg (Harberg)	Not guilty	

The von Falkenhorst Trial
July 29, 1946—August 2, 1946

Defendant	Verdict or Sentence	Outcome
Nikolaus von Falkenhorst	Death by shooting	Commuted to twenty years. Sentenced suspended; released July 13, 1953.

The Velpke Trial
March 20, 1946—April 3,1946

Defendant	Verdict or Sentence	Outcome
Heinrich Gerike	Death by hanging	Executed October 8, 1946
Georg Hessling	Death by hanging	Executed October 8, 1946
Werner Noth	Not guilty	
Hermann Müller	Not guilty	
Gustav Claus	Not guilty	
Richard Demmerich	Ten years' imprisonment	Reduced to seven years; released December 2, 1950
Fritz Flint	No finding, since accused died	
Valentina Bilien	Fifteen years' imprisonment	Sentence suspended; released January 23, 1954

Appendix C:
Japanese War Crimes—
The Tokyo Trials

In the aftermath of World War II, the world learned of the atrocities committed by the Nazis and Japanese. Stories of murder, rape, chemical warfare, and biological experimentation left citizens crying for justice. As a result, charges of war crimes were levied against the perpetrators. War crimes trials were held in Nuremberg, Tokyo and other cities, bringing the accused to the forefront to stand trial for crimes committed during war.

Under the direction of General Douglas MacArthur, thousands of Japanese were imprisoned while awaiting charges of war crimes. On January 19, 1946, the International Military Tribunal for the Far East (IMTFE) was convened. Judges were chosen from eleven nations, each with one representative on the tribunal—Sir William F. Webb of Australia, E. Stuart McDougall of Canada, Ju-ao Mei of China, Henri Bernard of France, Lord Patrick of Great Britain, R.M. Pal of India, Bernard Victor A. Roling of the Netherlands, Erima Harvey Northeroft of New Zealand, Delfin Jaranilla of the Philippines, I.M. Zaryanov of the Soviet Union, and John P. Higgins (replaced by Major General Myron C. Gramer) of the United States. Sir William Webb presided over the international court.

Under the direction of General Douglas MacArthur, thousands of Japanese were imprisoned, awaiting charges of war crimes. (U.S. Signal Corps)

The brutal treatment of Allied prisoners of war during the "Bataan Death March" and in internment camps factored into the verdicts at the Japanese War Crimes Trials. Despite their weakness from battle, fatigue, starvation, and beatings, these Allied soldiers created improvised litters to carry their fallen comrades. (National Archives and Records Administration)

According to the IMTFE, three types of crimes were committed:

Class A—Crimes Against Peace

These crimes consisted of the planning, preparation, and implementation of waging war. This was in violation of international law.

Class B—War Crimes

These crimes were in violation of the Rules of War mandated by previous treaties and agreements, which included the conduct of hostilities, status of combatants, and the duties of an occupying power toward the citizens of the occupied nation.

Class C—Crimes Against Humanity

These crimes were offenses of persecution, torture, murder, rape, enslavement, and extermination due to political, religious, or racial beliefs.

In total, about 5,700 Japanese were tried in more than 2,200 cases. Approximately 4,400 Japanese citizens—soldiers and civilians—were convicted, resulting in more than 900 executions. Of the total, 1,297 were acquitted or never sentenced; 984 were sentenced to death; and 930 were

executed. Nearly 3,000 were given prison sentences, 475 of which were life imprisonment.

Most of the defendants were accused of either Class B or Class C offenses. The B/C Trials (as they were called) were held at various locations within the former Japanese-occupied nations; some trials were held in Japan.

In 1946 the Allied forces rounded up 80 Class A offenders, who were taken to the prison in Sugamo, Japan, and held to await trial. Most of these men were military officers or civilian officials, including generals, admirals, cabinet ministers, foreign ambassadors, and premiers. Men like Hideki Tojo and Koichi Kido were accused of conspiring to wage war as well as allowing acts of brutality and other crimes against humanity to occur. Even though they were not accused of committing the brutal acts directly, they were held responsible for the men under their authority who did.

The accused were brought to trial on May 3, 1946, in the Japanese War Ministry building in downtown Tokyo. Lasting more than two years, the Tokyo Trials, as they were often called, ended on November 12, 1948. There were fifty-five counts to the indictment. Count one dealt with the scope of

Japan's Honored War Dead

Heroes of the Japanese Empire are honored at the Yasukuni Jinja in the Kudan district of Tokyo. First established during the Meiji Period, the Shinto shrine is dedicated to Japan's war heroes. Members of the Imperial military, considered martyrs for their country, were first memorialized in the shrine after the Sino-Japanese War (1894–1895).

Located near the Imperial Palace, the Yasukuni Jinja symbolizes peace in Japan. Meaning "peaceful country," Yasukuni was dedicated in the 1870s by Emperor Meiji, who believed that those who died for their country were due honor and respect, having given their lives for the peace and security of their homeland. Martyrs enshrined at Yasukuni include General Iwane Matsui of the China Expeditionary Force and General Hideki Tōjō, Premier of Japan during World War II. Along with Matsui and Tōjō, a dozen other Class A criminals tried at the Tokyo Trials have been enshrined along with 2.5 million soldiers, sailors, civilians, and kamikaze pilots.

Until 1945 the Shinto sect was the national religion of Japan. As part of the surrender agreement with the Allies in World War II, Emperor Hirohito banned the practice of Shinto, including the worship of ancestors and martyrs, separating church matters from government. Members of the newly formed Japanese government were no longer allowed to honor the war dead at Yasukuni Jinja. In 1985, forty years after the Japanese surrender ending the war, Japanese Prime Minister Yasukiro Nakasone made an official visit to the shrine. Critics in China and Korea were outraged, because to them it seemed that Japan was not honoring its agreement to separate church and state. In a statement to the press, Nakasone claimed that the Japanese people will honor its country's heroes. "America," he said, "has its Arlington Cemetery. The Russians and many other people have their tombs to the unknown soldier, places for people to give thanks to those who died in battle. If there is no such place [in Japan], who will be prepared to give his life for his country?"

Japanese aggression, charging that between January 1, 1928 and September 2, 1945, the accused had played active roles as "… leaders, organizers, instigators, or accomplices in the formulation or execution of a common plan or conspiracy … [and were] responsible for all acts performed by any person in execution of such plan … [to] secure the military, naval, political and economic domination of East Asia and of Pacific and Indian Oceans, and … for that purpose they conspired that Japan should alone … wage declared or undeclared war or wars of aggression, and war or wars in violation of international law, treaties, agreements and assurances, against any country or countries which might oppose that purpose."

The judgment of the IMTFE was read into the court record by presiding judge Sir William F. Webb of Australia, beginning November 4, 1948. The document comprised 1,500 pages—it took Webb seven days to read it aloud. The judgment chronicled the crimes and actions of the accused, and rendered a verdict of guilty to the accused. The lengthy verdict included:

> "These far-reaching plans for waging wars of aggression were not the work of one man. They were the work of many leaders acting in pursuance of a common plan for the achievement of a common object. That common object, that they should secure Japan's domination by preparing and waging wars of aggression, was a criminal object. Indeed no more grave crimes can be conceived of than a conspiracy to wage a war of aggression for the conspiracy threatens the security of the peoples of the world, and the waging disrupts it…. All of those who at any time were parties to the criminal conspiracy or who at any time with guilty knowledge played a part in its execution are guilty…."

As for war crimes against humanity, the tribunal concluded that:

"[F]rom the opening of the war in China until the surrender of Japan in August 1945 torture, murder, rape and other cruelties of the most inhumane and barbarous character" were "freely practiced by the Japanese Army and Navy.... Ruthless killing of prisoners by shooting, decapitation, drowning, and other methods; death marches in which prisoners including the sick were forced to march long distances under conditions which not even well-conditioned troops could stand, ... forced labor in tropical heat without protection from the sun; complete lack of housing and medical supplies ... beatings and torture ... killing without trial ... even cannibalism; these [were] some of the atrocities of which proof was made before the Tribunal." (Excerpted from the "Judgment" of the IMTFE, Part B, Chapter IV, pages 208–210.)

On Friday, November 12, beginning at 3:53 p.m., the verdicts were read. One by one, each defendant was led into the courtroom, in alphabetical order, starting with General Sadao Araki. Tōjō was the last to be sentenced—death by hanging. It took a moment for Tōjō to hear the verdict as he had to adjust the headphone receiver to his translator. As he heard the verdict, Tōjō nodded and bowed to the court.

The verdicts rendered for each of the accused were not unanimous. Several of the tribunal judges did not believe that the offenses violated international laws. Others did not believe all of the accused were part of a conspiracy in Japan's quest for world domination. Some believed Japan's leaders acted in self-defense, arguing that Asia should be for the Asians, and not ruled by Western powers with declared territories in Asia and the Pacific.

Of the Class A offenders, only 28 were brought before the IMTFE to face charges. As a result, all but three were found guilty; most were also convicted of Class B/C charges as well. The sentences were as follows:

• 7 executed

• 16 sentenced to life imprisonment

• 2 sentenced to prison terms

• 2 died during the trial

• 1 institutionalized for mental illness

Critics of the war crimes trials found fault with the way the Allies administered the trials. Their biggest criticism was that Emperor Hirohito was not brought before the IMTFE. He was not even called as a witness. Some reasoned that as Japan's figurehead, he was unaware of the conspiracy to wage aggressive wars. Others believed he was responsible, as everything—the wars, the atrocities, the sacrificed soldiers—was done in the name of the emperor.

Others believed that General MacArthur needed the emperor to hold Japan together during the chaos in the aftermath of war. At the time, MacArthur was trying to stop the spread of communism in Asia. China and Russia had already fallen into the hands of the Communists. He hoped Hirohito could prevent its spread into Japan.

Tōjō, Japanese general and Class A defendant, stated that the trial was "... saru shibai mitai no mono nan da *yo*"—"something like a monkey show." In an interview during the trial, he said that he believed everything was predetermined from the start. The trial was just a formality—a show for the world of democracy in action.

Verdicts of the Tokyo Trials

Sadao Araki (General)

Wartime Service: Minister of War (1931–1934); Supreme War Council (1934–1936); Minister of Education (1938–1939). Araki also served as an adviser to the Japanese cabinet from 1939 to 1940. He was an early spokesman for Japanese expansion; while serving as Minister of Education, Araki reorganized the school system to adopt a military style, including combat training.

Verdict: Araki was convicted for waging war against China and was sentenced to life imprisonment; he was paroled in 1955 and died in 1966.

Kenji Doihara (General)

Wartime Service: Commander of the Kwantung Army (1938–1940); Supreme War Council (1940–1943); Commander of the Army in Singapore (1944–1945). Doihara was instrumental in the army's drug trafficking operations in Manchuria. He also operated POW camps as well as internment camps in Borneo, Java, Malaya, and Sumatra.

Verdict: Doihara was convicted on several counts, including planning wars of aggression against China, the United States, Great Britain, the

Netherlands, and the Soviet Union. He was also convicted on counts that he "ordered, authorized, and permitted the inhumane treatment of Prisoners of War and others." He was sentenced to death by hanging and was executed on December 23, 1948.

Kingoro Hashimoto (Colonel)

Wartime Service: Commander of an artillery regiment during the Rape of Nanking; assisted in the Mukden Incident, resulting in war with China. He wrote books on racial propaganda and was instrumental in securing favorable public opinion for the war in the Pacific.

Verdict: Hashimoto was convicted of waging war against China and was sentenced to life imprisonment; he was paroled in 1954 and died in 1957.

Shunroku Hata (Field Marshal)

Wartime Service: Supreme War Council (1937); Commander of China Expeditionary Force (1938, 1941–1944); Minister of War (1939–1940). Hata planned the invasion of China in the 1930s and was responsible for atrocities committed against Chinese civilians.

Verdict: Hata was convicted on several counts, including waging aggressive wars against China, the United States, Great Britain, and the Netherlands. He was also convicted because he "ordered, authorized, and permitted the inhumane treatment of Prisoners of War and others." In addition, he "deliberately and recklessly" disregarded his duty to prevent atrocities. He was sentenced to life imprisonment but paroled in 1954. He died in 1962.

Kiichiro Hiranuma (Baron)

Wartime Service: Member of Privy Council (1924–1939); Premier (1938); Minister of Home Affairs (1940); Minister without Portfolio (1940–1941); President of Privy Council (1945).

Verdict: Hiranuma was convicted on several counts, including waging aggressive wars against China, the United States, Great Britain, the Netherlands, and the Soviet Union. He was sentenced to life imprisonment; he died in 1952.

Koki Hirota (Baron)

Wartime Service: Ambassador to the USSR (1928–1931); Foreign Minister (1933–1936); premier (1936–1937). Hirota was foreign minister during the Rape of Nanking. While serving as premier, he led his cabinet in planning the invasions of Southeast Asia, the Pacific Islands, and China.

Verdict: Hirota was convicted of "waging unprovoked war against China" and "deliberately and recklessly" disregarding his duty to prevent atrocities. He was sentenced to death by hanging and was executed on December 23, 1948.

Naoki Hoshino

Wartime Service: Chief of Financial Affairs in Manchuria (1932–1934); Director of General Affairs in Manchuria (1936); Cabinet Secretary (1941–1944).

Verdict: Hoshino was convicted on several counts, including waging aggressive wars against China, the United States, Great Britain, and the Netherlands. He was sentenced to life imprisonment but paroled in 1955. He died in 1978.

Seishiro Itagaki (General)

Wartime Service: Chief of Staff for Kwantung Army (1936–1937); Minister of War (1938–1939); Supreme War Council (1943); Commander in Singapore (1945). Troops in Itagaki's command committed atrocities against the Chinese, Allied POWs, and civilians. He also operated internment camps in Borneo, Java, Malaya, and Sumatra.

Verdict: Itagaki was convicted on several counts, including planning wars of aggression against China, the United States, Great Britain, the Netherlands, and the Soviet Union. He was also convicted on counts that he "ordered, authorized, and permitted the inhumane treatment of Prisoners of War and others." He was sentenced to death by hanging and was executed on December 23, 1948.

Okinori Kaya

Wartime Service: Minister of Finance (1937–1938, 1941–1944). Kaya was the president of the North China Development Company. He played an instrumental role in trafficking narcotics in China to finance the war effort.

Verdict: Kaya was convicted on several counts, including waging aggressive wars against China, the United States, Great Britain, and the Netherlands. He was sentenced to life imprisonment but paroled in 1955. He died in 1977.

Koichi Kido (Marquis)

Wartime Service: Secretary to the Lord Keeper of the Privy Seal (1930–1937); Minister of Education (1937); Minister of Welfare (1938); Minister of Home Affairs (1939); Lord Keeper of the Privy Seal (1940–1945). Kido served as adviser to

Emperor Hirohito throughout the war. Kido kept a diary containing logistics, names, and wartime atrocities committed by the Japanese. IMTFE prosecutors used the diary to convict him and the other defendants during the Tokyo Trials.

Verdict: Kido was convicted on several counts, including waging aggressive wars against China, the United States, Great Britain, and the Netherlands. He was sentenced to life imprisonment but paroled in 1955. He died in 1977.

Heitaro Kimura (General)

Wartime Service: Chief of Staff for Kwantung Army (1940–1941); Vice Minister of War (1941–1943); Supreme War Council (1943); Commander of the Army in Burma (1944–1945). Kimura was instrumental in planning the war in the Pacific. He was also the commander in Burma during the building of the Siam-Burma Railway, using POWs and civilians forced into slavery to construct the railroad. The workers were then put to death.

Verdict: Kimura was convicted on several counts, including waging aggressive wars against China, the United States, Great Britain, and the Netherlands. He was also convicted on counts that he "ordered, authorized, and permitted the inhumane treatment of Prisoners of War and others." In addition, he "deliberately and recklessly" disregarded his duty to prevent atrocities. He was sentenced to death by hanging and was executed on December 23, 1948.

Kuniaki Koiso (General)

Wartime Service: Vice Minister of War (1932); Chief of Staff of the Kwantung Army (1932–1934); Commander of the Army in Korea (1935–1938); Minister of Overseas Affairs (1939); Governor-General of Korea (1942–1944); Premier (1944–1945).

Verdict: Koiso was convicted on several counts, including waging aggressive wars against China, the United States, Great Britain, and the Netherlands. In addition, he "deliberately and recklessly" disregarded his duty to prevent atrocities while serving as premier. He was sentenced to life imprisonment; he died in 1950.

Iwane Matsui (General)

Wartime Service: Appointed to the Geneva Disarmament Conference (1932–1937) by Emperor Hirohito; Commander of the China Expeditionary Force (1937–1938). Matsui's troops were responsible for the Rape of Nanking. He retired from military service in 1938.

Verdict: Matsui was convicted for "deliberately and recklessly" disregarding his duty to prevent atrocities. He was sentenced to death by hanging and was executed on December 23, 1948. His remains were placed in Yasukuni shrine, as a martyr of his country.

Yosuke Matsuoka

Wartime Service: Delegate to the League of Nations (1932); Minister of Foreign Affairs (1940). Matsuoka led Japan's withdrawal from the League of Nations in 1932. He was an advocate for creating an alliance with Germany against the Soviet Union.

Verdict: Matsuoka died in 1946, while awaiting trial.

Jiro Minami (General)

Wartime Service: Minister of War (1931); Supreme War Council (1931–1934); Commander of the Kwantung Army (1934–1936); Governor-General of Korea (1936–1942); member of the Privy Council (1942–1945).

Verdict: Minami was convicted for waging war against China. He was sentenced to life imprisonment; he was paroled in 1954 and died the following year.

Akira Muto (General)

Wartime Service: Vice Chief of Staff for the China Expeditionary Force (1937); Military Affairs Bureau director (1939–1942); Commander of the Army in Sumatra (1942–1943); Army Chief of Staff in the Philippines (1944–1945). Muto's troops were responsible for the Rape of Nanking and the Rape of Manila.

Verdict: Muto was convicted on several counts, including waging aggressive wars against China, the United States, Great Britain, the Netherlands, and France (Indochina). He was also convicted on counts that he "ordered, authorized, and permitted the inhumane treatment of Prisoners of War and others." He was sentenced to death by hanging and was executed on December 23, 1948.

Osarni Nagano (Field Marshal)

Wartime Service: Naval Attache to U.S. Embassy (1912–1914); Minister of the Navy (1936); Chief of General Staff of the Navy (1941–1944). Nagano was instrumental in planning the attack on the U.S. Naval Base at Pearl Harbor, Hawaii, in 1941.

Verdict: Nagano died in 1947, while awaiting trial.

Takasumi Oka (Admiral)

Wartime Service: Chief of the Naval Affairs Bureau (1940–1944); Vice Minister of the Navy (1944). Oka played an instrumental role in the bombing of the U.S. Naval Base at Pearl Harbor, Hawaii, in 1941. He was also involved in forcing POWs and civilians to execute survivors of torpedoed ships.

Verdict: Oka was convicted on several counts, including waging aggressive wars against China, the United States, Great Britain, and the Netherlands. He was sentenced to life imprisonment, but was paroled in 1954. He died in 1973.

Shumei Okawa

Wartime Service: Chief of East Asian Economic Survey Bureau. Okawa had been previously imprisoned for the assassination of Premier Tsuyoshi Inukai in 1932. He was a supporter of Japanese militarism.

Verdict: Shortly after the start of the trial, Okawa was declared mentally unfit and was institutionalized. All charges were dropped.

Hiroshi Oshima (General)

Wartime Service: Military Attache to Germany (1934–1938); Ambassador to Germany (1938–1939, 1941–1945). As ambassador, Oshima was instrumental in securing the Axis Pact between Germany, Italy, and Japan during the war.

Verdict: Oshima was convicted on a single count—participating in planning wars of aggression in violation of international law. He was sentenced to life imprisonment but was paroled in 1955. He died in 1975.

Kenryo Sato (General)

Wartime Service: Chief of Military Affairs Bureau (1942–1944); Assistant Chief of Staff for the China Expeditionary Force (1944); Commander of the Army in Indochina (1945).

Verdict: Sato was convicted on several counts, including waging aggressive wars against China, the United States, Great Britain, and the Netherlands. He was sentenced to life imprisonment but was paroled in 1956. He died in 1975.

Mamoru Shigemitsu

Wartime Service: Ambassador to China (1931–1932); Vice Minister of Foreign Affairs (1933–1936); Ambassador to the Soviet Union (1936–1938); Ambassador to Great Britain (1938–1941); Foreign Minister (1943–1945). As Foreign Minister, Shigemitsu signed the terms of surrender with the Allied Forces.

Verdict: Shigemitsu was convicted on several counts, including waging aggressive wars against China, the United States, Great Britain, the Netherlands, and France (Indochina). He was sentenced to seven years in prison but was paroled in 1950. He was chosen by the newly formed Japanese government to head up its Foreign Ministry department in 1954. He died in 1957.

Shigetaro Shimada (Admiral)

Wartime Service: Vice Chief of Staff of the Navy (1935–1937); Commander of the China Fleet (1940); Minister of the Navy (1941–1944); Supreme War Council (1944). Shimada issued the order to attack the U.S. Naval Base at Pearl Harbor, Hawaii, in 1941. While serving as the naval minister, Shimada was responsible for the harsh treatment of interred civilians and POWs.

Verdict: Shimada was convicted on several counts, including waging aggressive wars against China, the United States, Great Britain, and the Netherlands. He was sentenced to life imprisonment but was paroled in 1955. He died in 1976.

Toshio Shiratori

Wartime Service: Director of the Information Bureau of the Foreign Ministry (1929–1933); Ambassador to Italy (1938–1940).

Verdict: While in the Foreign Service, Shiratori was a staunch supporter of Japanese expansionism. He was convicted for his participation in waging wars of aggression, which were in violation of international law. He was sentenced to life imprisonment; he died in 1948 (some sources say 1949).

Teiichi Suzuki (General)

Wartime Service: Chief of the China Affairs Bureau (1938–1941); cabinet member and adviser (1941–1944). Suzuki was responsible for enslaving POWs and civilians. He was involved with drug trafficking operations in China.

Verdict: Suzuki was convicted on several counts, including waging aggressive wars against China, the United States, Great Britain, and the Netherlands. He was sentenced to life imprisonment but was paroled in 1955.

Hideki Togo (General)

Wartime Service: Ambassador to Germany (1937); Ambassador to the Soviet Union (1938); Foreign Minister (1941–1942, 1945).

Verdict: Togo was convicted on several counts, including waging aggressive wars against China, the United States, Great Britain, and the Netherlands. He was sentenced to 20 years in prison; he died in 1948.

Hideki Tōjō (General)

Wartime Service: Chief of the Manchurian Secret Police (1935); councilor for Manchurian Affairs Bureau (1936); Chief of Staff for the Kwantung Army (1937–1938); Minister of War (1940–1944); Premier (1941–1944).

Verdict: Tōjō assumed responsibility for the Japanese people, their government, and its military, including all atrocities committed during the course of the war. He was convicted on numerous counts, including waging aggressive wars against China, the United States, Great Britain, the Netherlands, and France (Indochina). He was also convicted on counts that he "ordered, authorized, and permitted the inhumane treatment of Prisoners of War and others." He was sentenced to death by hanging and was executed on December 23, 1948. His remains are enshrined at Yasukuni in 1978.

Yoshijiro Umezu (General)

Wartime Service: General Staff (1931–1934); Commander of the China Expeditionary Force (1934); Vice Minister of War (1939–1941); Chief of Staff of the Army (1944–1945). As Chief of Staff, Umezu signed the terms of surrender with the Allied Forces.

Verdict: Umezu was convicted on several counts, including waging aggressive wars against China, the United States, Great Britain, and the Netherlands. He was sentenced to life imprisonment; he died in 1949.

Contributor
Susan E. Edgar

SOURCES

Books

Askin, Kelly Dawn, *War Crimes Against Women: Prosecution in International War Crimes Tribunals,* Martinus Nijhoff (The Hague), 1997.

Brackman, Arnold C., *The Other Nuremberg: The Untold Story of the Tokyo War Crimes Trials,* Morrow (New York), 1987.

Butow, Robert J.C., *Tojo and the Coming of the War,* Stanford University Press (Stanford, CT), 1969.

Chang, Iris, *The Rape of Nanking: The Forgotten Holocaust of World War II,* Basic Books (New York), 1997.

Daws, Gavan, *Prisoners of the Japanese: POWS of World War II in the Pacific,* W. Morrow (New York), 1994.

Ginn, John L., *Sugamo Prison, Tokyo: An Account of the Trial and Sentencing of Japanese War Criminals in 1948, by a U.S. Participant,* McFarland & Co. (Jefferson, NC), 1992.

Hicks, George L., *The Comfort Women: Japan's Brutal Regime of Enforced Prostitution in the Second World War,* W.W. Norton & Company (New York), 1995.

Hosoya, Chihiro, et. al., *The Tokyo War Crimes Trial: An International Symposium,* Kodansha (Tokyo, Japan), 1986.

International Military Tribunal for the Far East, R. John Pritchard, editor, *The Tokyo Major War Crimes Trial: The Records of the International Military Tribunal for the Far East with an Authoritative Commentary and Comprehensive Guide Annotated, Compiled and Edited by R. John Pritchard: A Collection in 124 volumes,* published for the Robert M.W. Kempner Collegium by Edwin Mellen Press (Lewiston, NY), 1998.

Minear, Richard H., *Victor's Justice: The Tokyo War Crimes Trial,* Princeton University Press (Princeton, NJ), 1971.

Piccigallo, Philip, *The Japanese on Trial: Allied War Crimes Operations in the East, 1945–1951,* University of Texas Press (Austin, TX), 1979.

Röling, Bernard Victor Aloysius, *The Tokyo Trial and Beyond: Reflections of a Peacemonger,* Polity Press (Cambridge, England), 1993.

Tanaka, Toshiyuki, *Hidden Horrors: Japanese War Crimes in World War II,* Westview Press (Boulder, CO), 1996.

Zhigeng, Xu, *Lest We Forget: Nanjing Massacre, 1937,* Chinese Literature Press.

Other

Scott, Bruce, editor, *Laden, Fevered, Starved: The POWs of Sandakan North Borneo, 1945,* Commonwealth Department of Veterans' Affairs

(Australia), 1999, http://www.dva.gov. au/com
mem/commac/sandakan (August 2000).

Smith, Robert Barr, "Justice Under the Sun: Japanese War Crime Trials," *World War II,* http://
www.thehistorynet.com/WorldWarII (August
2000).

Appendix D:
World War II and
Holocaust Film Overview

ovies about World War II—whether on the battlefield or the home front—have never been scarce. There are literally hundreds, perhaps thousands, of films, cartoons, documentaries, made-for-TV movies, miniseries, and even a few television series, covering the war and postwar years. This trend continued into the year 2000 with the success of the rousing (if historically inaccurate) submarine film *U-571* and Turner Network Television's cable movie *Nuremberg*, which covers the postwar Nuremberg war crime tribunals. Of course, these ventures are not restricted to Hollywood productions. Most countries involved in the worldwide conflict had their own take on how the war was fought, what they were fighting for, and the consequences of their endeavors.

Looking back, one of the earliest and most well-produced pieces of propaganda was that by German director Leni Riefenstahl, with 1934's *Triumph of the Will*, which depicted Hitler and the Sixth Nazi Party Congress rally in Nuremberg, Germany. Joseph Goebbels, the minister of public enlightenment and propaganda, was also well aware of the power of radio and film production—German movie theaters never closed down during the war and Goebbels' department sponsored many movies meant to strengthen Nazi claims. Among these were 1940's *Jud Suss* (*The Jew Suss*), which was intended to stir anti-Semitic feelings by depicting the evil influence that the Jewish Suss had over a German duke and his plots with fellow Jews. *Kolberg* (1945) was a late attempt to rally the German people to resist the Allied invasion by showing how the citizens in one German town resisted French emperor Napoleon Bonaparte's army in 1807 until the arrival of the German army saved the day.

Moviegoers continue to be interested in new World War II films like *The Thin Red Line* starring Jim Caviezel. (Reproduced by permission of the Kobal Collection)

In a scene from *U-571*, Hollywood actors recreate a mission to capture the infamous German code machine, "The Enigma." (Reproduced by permission of the Kobal Collection)

Of course, Germany wasn't the only country using film as propaganda—however disguised—to rally its people. Both the British and the Americans knew the power of the movies, and the American film industry was the largest in the world. President Franklin D. Roosevelt ordered the formation of the Bureau of Motion Pictures as a division of the Office of War Information in 1942. The Bureau reviewed screenplays, supplied technical support, and suggested story ideas. A number of Hollywood directors not only made engaging and stirring movies but compelling documentaries. These included the seven films of the *Why We Fight* series, directed by Frank Capra and Ernst Lubitsch, that provided an overview of recent history to explain the reasons behind the war as well as what was happening overseas. These films (*Prelude to War, The Nazis Strike, Divide and Conquer, The Battle of Russia, The Battle of Britain, The Battle of China*, and *The War Comes to America*) were required viewing for Americans in uniform posted overseas, and were later given theatrical distribution.

In 1942 director John Ford filmed the Oscar-winning documentary *Battle of Midway*. Ford, a Navy commander, was on Midway Island when the Japanese attacked, and he managed to place cameras on the beach to capture the action as it happened. Ford and co-director/cinematographer Gregg Toland also won an Academy Award the following year for the recreation of the attack on Pearl Harbor, *Dec. 7th*. Another inspiring documentary was William Wyler's *Memphis Belle: The Story of a Flying Fortress* (1944), which depicted an American B-17 crew's last mission from England before going home. This story was fictionalized for the 1990 film *Memphis Belle*, starring Matthew Modine and Eric Stolz.

Warner Bros. was only one of the Hollywood studios who used its cartoon characters for war propaganda. These wartime cartoons are rarely shown today since their anti-Japanese and anti-German stances are now considered racist. Among the Warner efforts are 1941's *Meet John Doughboy*, in which Porky Pig enlists in the military; 1942's *The Ducktators*, which portrays Adolf Hitler, Benito Mussolini, and Hirohito as ducks trying to take over a barnyard; the anti-Japanese propaganda of 1943's *Tokio Jokio* and 1944's *Bugs Bunny Nips the Nips*; 1944's *Plane Daffy*, a spoof of war pictures and espionage thrillers starring Daffy Duck; and 1945's *Herr Meets Hare* as a Nazi meets "Bugsenheimer" Bunny.

Tom Hanks, Matt Damon, and Ed Burns star in *Saving Private Ryan*. (Reproduced by permission of the Kobal Collection)

Among the many types of World War II pictures are battle recreations and unit pictures, espionage thrillers, wartime romances and heroics, home front hardships, comedies, biographies, concentration and internment camp films, prisoner of war (POW) and escape movies, postwar, and antiwar films. They cover not only Great Britain and the rest of Europe, but Russia, Scandinavia, North Africa, and the Pacific (including Japan and Australia), as well as the United States and Canada. All branches of the military, including the Merchant Marines, are represented in World War II films.

Numerous films focus on specific battles. Guy Hamilton's 1969 film *The Battle of Britain* depicts, from both British and German viewpoints, how the understaffed and overwhelmed British Royal Air Force managed to overcome the might of the German Luftwaffe. In 1965's *The Battle of the Bulge*, filmmakers highlighted Nazi efforts to change the course of the war on the Belgian front in 1944–1945, while 1962's *The Longest Day* focuses on June 6, 1944—D-Day and the invasion of Normandy. Omaha Beach also provided the harrowing 25-minute opening sequence for director Steven Spielberg's *Saving Private Ryan* (1998). This Academy Award-winning production is considered to have the most realistic recreation of the assault ever seen onscreen. The film itself shows how one U.S.

Army unit must go behind enemy lines to rescue a downed paratrooper as part of a military public relations campaign.

Tora! Tora! Tora! (1970) depicts the events leading up to the December 7, 1941 bombing of Pearl Harbor from both Japanese and American viewpoints. (The title translates to "Tiger! Tiger! Tiger!," the Japanese signal for a successful attack.) *In Harm's Way* (1965) deals with the reactions of two naval officers to the bombing of Pearl Harbor, while *Air Force* (1943) highlights the adventures of a Boeing B-17 bomber crew who are en-route to Hawaii the day before the bombing. They are ordered to continue flying west and eventually engage in combat over Manila and the Coral Sea. *From Here to Eternity* (1953) ends with the bombing of Pearl Harbor after it looks at the on- and off-duty lives of soldiers at a U.S. Army base in Honolulu, Hawaii. Director Michael Bay also features another recreation of this historic moment in his epic *Pearl Harbor*, due for theatrical release in 2001.

More films set in the Pacific theater include 1943's *Bataan*, a rugged look at combat in the Philippines in which a group of scrappy American soldiers must blow up a Japanese-held bridge. In *The Fighting Seabees* (1944) John Wayne portrays the larger-than-life foreman of a group of construction worker/soldiers, who battles naval regula-

John Litel, Claudette Colbert, Lynn Walker, Lorna Gray, Kitty Kelly, Helen Lund, Paulette Goddard, Mary Treen, and Dorothy Adams in *So Proudly We Hail*. (Reproduced by permission of the Kobal Collection)

Klaus Wennemann, Jurgen Prochnow, and Herbert Gronemeyer in *Das Boot*. (Reproduced by permission of the Kobal Collection)

tions as much as he does the Japanese. *Flying Leathernecks* (1951) is another film with John Wayne in the leading role, this time commanding a Marine Flying Squadron heading to Guadalcanal. And in *The Sands of Iwo Jima* (1949), Wayne is a tough Marine sergeant whose recruits are responsible for the capture of Iwo Jima from the Japanese.

Guadalcanal is also featured in the flag-waving *Guadalcanal Diary* (1943), and director Terrence Malick's *The Thin Red Line* (1998), a drawn-out saga, about a rifle company, that sacrifices plot to study the larger questions of man vs. nature and the origin of evil. *Thirty Seconds Over Tokyo* (1944) takes in the bombing attack on Tokyo and other Japanese cities, led by Jimmy Doolittle, which occurred less than six months after the Japanese bombed Pearl Harbor. *Merrill's Marauders* (1962) depicts American involvement in Burma as does the paratrooper drama *Objective, Burma!* (1945). *So Proudly We Hail* (1943) is the true story of the heroism of Red Cross Army nurses serving under fire in the Pacific theater. Even the musical *South Pacific* (1958) takes a not-always lighthearted look at life for naval personnel on a Pacific island.

Back at the European theater, *The Story of G.I. Joe* (1945) is an unsentimental look at foot soldiers—C Company, 18th Infantry—as they face battle in Tunisia, Sicily, and Italy. The story is told from the viewpoint of war correspondent Ernie Pyle, well-known for his grunt's eye view of the action. *Hell Is for Heroes* (1962) takes a realistic look at one small battle against the Germans by an outmanned infantry squad. *The Big Red One* (1980) is director Sam Fuller's semi-autobiographical account of a raw rifle squad and its grizzled sergeant as they go from fighting in North Africa to liberating a concentration camp in Czechoslovakia. In *The Immortal Battalion* (also known as *The Way Ahead*), a 1944 British film, a group of civilians are molded into a hardened battalion of fighters.

The Cruel Sea (1953) examines a Royal Navy warship pulling convoy duty in the Atlantic, while *A Yank in the R.A.F.* (1941) finds brash American Tyrone Power joining the British Royal Air Force in order to get into the war quickly. Some of the film's climatic air battles are taken from actual European combat footage. *Command Decision* (1948) and *Twelve O'Clock High* (1949) both examine the air war in Europe, while the 1981 German film *Das Boot* (*The Boat*) is a claustrophobic story about the final voyage of the U-96 submarine. *Run Silent, Run Deep* (1958) is another top-notch sub story—this time about an American sub stalking a Japanese destroyer, while *Enemy Below* (1957) features an American destroyer and a German U-boat squaring off in the South Atlantic. For comedy fans, there is *Operation Petticoat* (1959), in which a sub captain (Cary Grant) is forced to share his ship with a contingent of Navy women.

Although many World War II movies deal with victories, not all movies present successful campaigns. One example is *A Bridge Too Far* (1977), which depicts the disastrous Allied defeat at Arnhem, Holland, in 1944.

War also makes for good spy stories. *Confessions of a Nazi Spy* (1939) finds FBI agent Edward G. Robinson investigating an espionage operation in the United States, while Bette Davis and Paul Lukas play Germans involved in anti-Nazi activities who are pursued by the bad guys in Washington, D.C., in *Watch on the Rhine* (1943). In Alfred Hitchcock's *Foreign Correspondent* (1940), American reporter Joel McCrea heads to London where he uncovers a Nazi spy-ring. *Across the Pacific* (1942) finds ex-military man Humphrey Bogart sailing to China via the Panama Canal and discovering that some of his fellow passengers want to blow up the passage way. *Five Graves to Cairo* (1943) features a British soldier stranded amid spies and informers after the fall of Tobruk and before the advancing army of German Field Marshal Erwin Rommel. And who could forget the action-adventure *The Rocketeer* starring Bill Campbell, set shortly before the war during the Nazis' rise to power. In the movie, the Rocketeer works to keep scientific secrets out of the hands of the Nazis, who are aided by spy Timothy Dalton.

Spies, romance, and self-sacrifice highlight the classic *Casablanca* (1942), which is set in Nazi-occupied Morocco, while *The Eagle Has Landed* (1977) depicts a Nazi plot to assassinate British Prime Minister Winston Churchill. Another spy story with romantic elements is *Shining Through* (1992), starring Michael Douglas as the heroic agent on assignment in Berlin, with Melanie Griffith as the spunky heroine who volunteers for a dangerous mission. *Night Train to Munich* (1940) is an early adventure story about allied intelligence agents trying to retrieve secret documents, while Alfred Hitchcock's 1946 film *Notorious*, featuring Ingrid Bergman and Cary Grant, focuses on postwar Nazi sympathizers hiding out in Brazil. The setting of Brazil is also featured in the thriller *The Boys from Brazil* (1978) where the infamous Nazi,

James Cagney and Henry Fonda in *Mister Roberts*. (Reproduced by permission of the Kobal Collection)

Dr. Josef Mengele, tries to revive the Third Reich from his sanctuary.

Even during the worst of times, people need to laugh. World War II saw its share of comedies, including Charlie Chaplin's *The Great Dictator* (1940), a parody of Adolf Hitler. The comedy team of Bud Abbott and Lou Costello had their first starring roles in 1941's *Buck Privates*, about a couple of accidental Army enlistees. The same year they also wreaked havoc for other branches of the service in *In the Navy* and *Keep 'Em Flying*. More sophisticated comedy is shown in director Ernst Lubitsch's *To Be or Not to Be* (1942), which is set in wartime Poland and features an acting troupe using their talents against the invading Nazis. Mel Brooks created a version of the movie in 1983 starring himself, Anne Bancroft, Charles Durning, and Tim Matheson.

Other comedies that feature wartime or postwar settings include *Francis the Talking Mule* (1949), which finds the title character hooked up with a dim G.I. in Burma; *I Was a Male War Bride* (1949), in which Cary Grant disguises himself as a woman in order to be reunited with his WAC wife; the comedy/drama *Mister Roberts* (1955), about the crew of

a Navy cargo freighter in the South Pacific with stellar performances by James Cagney and Henry Fonda; the black comedy *Catch-22* (1970), the story of a group of fliers stationed in the Mediterranean; and Steven Spielberg's chaotic home front comedy *1941* (1979), which looks at Los Angeles in the days following the bombing of Pearl Harbor when civilians feared invasion by Japanese troops.

Also focusing on the home front are 1943's *The More the Merrier*, which finds a young woman sharing an apartment with two bachelors in war-crowded Washington, D.C.; the weepy *Since You Went Away* (1944), about how an American family copes with the war; and the romantic *The Clock* (1945), in which office worker Judy Garland falls in love with a soldier on a two-day leave. Both of the musicals *Anchors Aweigh* (1945), set in Hollywood, and New York's *On the Town* (1949) feature sailors on shore leave, while *Swing Shift* (1984) follows Goldie Hawn's character as she takes a job in a defense plant. *Bye Bye Blues* (1989) shows how a young Canadian wife, whose husband is a POW, copes by taking a job as a singer in a swing band. Also set in Canada is *For the Moment* (1994), a

Anna Friel, Catherine McCormack, and Rachel Weisz in *The Land Girls*. (Reproduced by permission of the Kobal Collection)

romance starring Russell Crowe, set amid fighter pilot training on the Canadian prairie.

Mrs. Miniver (1942) won six Academy Awards for its story of how a middle-class British family struggles to survive the war, while *The White Cliffs of Dover* (1944), starring Irene Dunne, follows a woman's sacrifice through two world wars. *Hope and Glory* (1987) is director John Boorman's autobiographical view of how a young boy in London views the war as an exciting challenge, while *The Land Girls* (1998) is based on the real life Woman's Land Army in England. There is also *Yanks* (1979), which shows what happens when a group of oversexed American soldiers are billeted in England during the war.

The unfathomable horrors of the Holocaust have also provided filmmakers with many stories. *The Wannsee Conference* (1984) is a German film depicting a historical event in 1942 when Nazi party and German government officials met to discuss the "Final Solution" to the "Jewish question." Nazis first rounded up Jews into ghettos, one of

which is depicted in the Robin Williams's film *Jakob the Liar* (1999). War profiteer-turned-hero Oscar Schindler saved more than 1,000 lives by employing Polish Jews from the ghetto in his factories—a story told in Steven Spielberg's powerful *Schindler's List* (1993), which also led to the director's establishment of the Survivors of the Shoah Visual History Foundation, to make sure survivors' experiences are recorded.

Life Is Beautiful (1998) is Italian director Roberto Benigni's comedy/drama about how a father tries to help his young son cope with their internment in a concentration camp by making it all into an elaborate game. French director Louis Malle's autobiographical 1987 film *Au Revoir les Enfants* (*Goodbye Children*) also shows the war from a youngster's point of view. At a Catholic boarding school in 1944, a young boy befriends a new student, eventually learning he is Jewish and one of three boys hiding from the Gestapo at the school.

Internment camps were not confined to Europe. Steven Spielberg's 1987 film *Empire of the Sun* finds

Christian Bale in *Empire of the Sun*. (Reproduced by permission of the Kobal Collection)

Alec Guiness in *Bridge on the River Kwai*. (Reproduced by permission of the Kobal Collection)

a British youngster, living in Shanghai, who is separated from his family and forced into a camp when the Japanese invade China. *Paradise Road* (1997) follows the plight of a group of women who are taken prisoner by the Japanese in Sumatra, while the Australian miniseries *A Town Like Alice* (1985) depicts women prisoners in Malaya. *Three Came Home* (1950) is also about how women survive in a Japanese internment camp and is notable for its even-handed portrayal of the enemy captors.

The Bridge on the River Kwai (1957) finds a battle of wills between the Japanese commander of a POW camp and a British colonel over the construction of a rail bridge, while *Merry Christmas, Mr. Lawrence* (1983) depicts another battle of wills between a Japanese commander and a British POW played by rock star David Bowie. *King Rat* (1965) is a Japanese POW story in which an American prisoner bribes his captors in order to survive. *Stalag 17* (1953), starring William Holden and Peter Graves, deals with American soldiers in a German POW camp who suspect one of their own is a spy. There were even internment camps in the United States when war hysteria

resulted in the imprisonment of Japanese emigrants and Japanese Americans, as depicted in *Come See the Paradise* (1990) and *Snow Falling on Cedars* (1999).

And there are escape stories. *The Great Escape* (1963) is one of the best, featuring Steve McQueen as a G.I. who is determined to escape from an "escape-proof" German camp even as his fellow prisoners work on a mass breakout. Both *Von Ryan's Express* and *Escape from Sobibor* (1987) depict mass escape attempts—the first from a POW camp in Italy and the latter from a Nazi death camp. *The Colditz Story* (1955) is based on the true story of the escape attempts by British and European prisoners from the supposedly impregnable Colditz castle. *The Mackenzie Break* (1970) features German captives plotting their escape from a British POW camp, and *The Brylcreem Boys* (1996) has Allied and German soldiers, confined to the same internment camp in neutral southern Ireland, planning to break out.

In war there are always resistance movements. The 1978 TV miniseries *Holocaust* follows the rise

Steven Spielberg

American filmmaker Steven Spielberg has contributed to an understanding of the events of World War II with three films, *Empire of the Sun* (1987), *Schindler's List* (1993), and *Saving Private Ryan* (1998).

Spielberg was born in Cincinnati, Ohio, the eldest of four children of Leah and Arnold Spielberg. According to Frank Sanello, the author of *Spielberg: The Man, The Movies, The Mythology* (1996), as a child Spielberg was a "reluctant Jew" who would tape his nose at bedtime in attempts to divert its growth upward and make it appear more like a gentile's. His father, who was a pioneer in the computer industry in the late 1940s and early 1950s, frequently moved the family around the country as he pursued his career. At one point during his youth, Steven became the only Jew in his high school. He later recalled that his classmates taunted him with anti-Semitic comments.

Once, Spielberg decided to appeal to his tormentor's vanity by casting the school bully in a fifteen-minute film called *Escape to Nowhere.* Spielberg was only fourteen years old at the time. The 1961 production, which cost $50, won first prize in a local film festival. By the age of twenty-eight Spielberg had made the classic thriller *Jaws* (1975) and established his career as a promising young director. He went on to score hits with other popular films such as *Raiders of the Lost Ark* (1981), starring Harrison Ford, and *Jurassic Park* (1997), featuring Sam Neill and Laura Dern.

Spielberg began addressing more serious themes in films such as *Empire of the Sun,* which is based on British writer J. G. Ballard's semi-autobiographical novel of the same title. The film chronicles the adventures of a nine-year-old British boy (played by Christian Bale), living with his upper-class family in Shanghai, China, on the eve of World War II. The boy is separated from his parents in the rush to evacuate the city when war breaks out, and he ends up in a Japanese civilian internment camp. Conditions are grim and survival a struggle. *Empire of the Sun* was met with positive critical reviews, but its dark subject matter was too intense for many viewers.

In 1993 the excitement over Spielberg's highly successful *Jurassic Park* had not yet subsided when he released *Schindler's List,* a drama based on the book of the same title by Australian writer Thomas Keneally. The film tells the real-life story of Oskar Schindler (played by Liam Neeson), a German industrialist allied with the Nazi party who saved more than 1,000 Jews from certain death in the extermination camps by employing them in his factory. Spielberg shot the movie in Europe, with some scenes actually set at Auschwitz, in black-and-white utilizing cinéma vérité techniques to achieve a documentary effect. It took just seventy-one days to shoot, cost a relatively modest

of Nazism and its effects on the German Dorf family and the Jewish Weiss family. While some members of the Weiss family wind up in concentration camps, others manage to join the resistance movement. Francois Truffaut's *The Last Metro* (1980) tells the story of a leading actor in a theater company who secretly works for the French resistance, while *The Train* (1965) finds the resistance trying to prevent the Nazis from taking art treasures loot- ed from Paris out of the country. *A Soldier of Orange* (1978) is the true story of students working for the Dutch resistance, while *The White Rose* (1983) is the fact-based story of Hans and Sophie Scholl—German students who were dissidents in Munich in 1942.

Biographies and autobiographies also describe various contributions to the war. *Patton* (1970)

$23 million, and involved more than 125 actors and 30,000 extras.

The end product was an original drama about the horrors of the Holocaust. A coda (shot in color) showed the actors and their real-life counterparts, who had survived because of Schindler, visiting the industrialist's grave. Spielberg used this technique in an effort to reinforce the reality and immediacy of the story. *Schindler's List* became one of the most talked-about films in Hollywood history and was an overwhelming commercial success. It won Spielberg an Academy Award for best director and the film was given the award for best picture of 1993. Spielberg reportedly took no salary for his work. Instead, he committed his share of the proceeds, approximately $16 million, to establishing a non-profit organization called the Survivors of the Shoah Visual History Foundation. Its purpose is to use the latest computer digital technology to record video interviews with as many Holocaust survivors as possible and to make this material available to a mass audience.

Five years after the huge success of *Schindler's List,* Spielberg released *Saving Private Ryan.* In the dramatic opening scenes of the movie, he recreated the U.S. Army landings at Omaha Beach during the Normandy invasion on D-Day, June 6, 1944. This thirty-minute sequence graphically depicts the men being killed by German fire as they try to reach the shore, thus immersing the audience in the brutal reality of war. Many of the images resemble photographs taken by Robert Capa and other photojournalists who accompa-

nied the troops at Omaha Beach. *Saving Private Ryan* goes on to tell the story of American army captain John Martin (actor Tom Hanks), who leads a group of rangers on a mission through the French countryside to find Private James Ryan (actor Matt Damon), the youngest of four brothers. The other three Ryan brothers were believed to be dead in action elsewhere during the war. The plot is partially based on the true story of Fritz Niland, one of four brothers from New York State who fought in World War II. Two of the brothers were killed on D-Day, while another was missing and presumed dead in Burma; he was later found alive. In an article in the July 27, 1998, issue of the *Washington Post,* Spielberg is quoted as saying that he grew up watching World War II movies, but he was troubled that audiences regarded the war simply as entertainment. In *Private Ryan* he was determined to show the gruesome as well as the glorious aspects of battle. The invasion scenes took a month to film on the coast of Ireland; the rest of the movie was shot on an abandoned English airfield, where a French town was built. Winner of Academy Awards for best director and best actor, *Saving Private Ryan* was praised for its faithful depiction of French locations and its realistic portrayal of confrontations between Allied and German troops.

won the Best Picture Oscar and a Best Actor Oscar for George C. Scott in the title role of Army General George S. Patton Jr. *The Gallant Hours* (1960) covers five weeks in the career of Admiral "Bull" Halsey and the South Pacific battle of Guadalcanal while *To Hell and Back* (1955) depicts the wartime career of Audie Murphy (who plays himself), the war's most-decorated American soldier. *PT-109* (1963) is a showcase for the heroics of Lt. John F. Kennedy in

the South Pacific. *The Fighting Sullivans* (1942) displays the tragic fate of five brothers who were all killed aboard the Battleship Juneau at Guadalcanal.

The affecting story of the only American soldier executed for desertion since the Civil War is told in *The Execution of Private Slovik* (1974), a made-for-TV drama starring Martin Sheen in the title role. *The Diary of Anne Frank* (1959) recalls the years

Claude Lanzmann

French journalist and filmmaker Claude Lanzmann spent eleven years creating *Shoah,* a nine-and-one-half-hour documentary about the Holocaust. In the film Lanzmann interviews numerous survivors of the mass exterminations that occurred in the Nazi death camps. He also talks with Nazi officials who supervised the extermination process and with Polish peasants who lived near the camps. The film premiered in 1985 to critical acclaim.

Lanzmann was born to Jewish parents in Paris, France, in 1925. After the Nazis invaded France in 1940, the family moved to the town of Clermont-Ferrand. Lanzmann's father required them to practice hiding techniques they would use in the event of a Nazi raid of their home. As a young man Lanzmann joined the Communist Resistance in the fight against the Nazi occupation. Because of his involvement in the group, he was forced to leave town, with the Gestapo in pursuit. After the liberation of France, Lanzmann was decorated for his resistance activities and he returned to Paris to study philosophy. He continued his schooling in Germany, where he became a journalist.

In an interview for the February 10, 1986, issue of *People* magazine, Lanzmann commented that he "wanted to see a German in plainclothes." He began writing for the French newspaper *Le Monde,* producing

Claude Lanzmann directed the nine-and-one-half-hour documentary *Shoah,* which took him 11 years to produce. (Reproduced by permission of AP/Wide World Photos)

that Anne and her family spent trying to avoid imprisonment by the Nazis. In the unbelievable, though true, story told in *Europa, Europa* (1991), Solomon Perel conceals his Jewish identity and winds up being drafted into the German army and educated at a Nazi-run academy. There are also many depictions of Adolf Hitler, including that by Alec Guinness in *Hitler: The Last Ten Days* (1973)

and Anthony Hopkins in *The Bunker* (1981), both of which cover the dictator's final hours.

Notable Holocaust documentaries include the award-winning, nine-and-one-half-hour documentary *Shoah* (1985), which features interviews with Holocaust survivors, Nazi officials, and Polish citizens who lived near the death camps. The French

a series of articles while traveling illegally through what was then East Germany. Lanzmann eventually became a close friend of French existentialist writer Jean-Paul Sartre and worked as the editor of the philosopher's left-wing periodical, *Les Temps Modernes,* of which he is now the director.

In the early 1970s Lanzmann made the film, *Israel, Why?,* which presented a majority of Israel's development history within the framework of the Holocaust. Some of his friends then suggested that his next film focus on the genocide itself. In 1974 Lanzmann began work on what would later become *Shoah.* He spent approximately three years researching the subject and locating the people he wanted to interview for the project. In the initial stages of production he decided not to use any of the historical footage that had come from the liberation of the concentration camps by the Allies. Instead, he interspersed his own filmed interviews with contemporary shots of the abandoned death camp sites. Most critics agreed that this technique ultimately made *Shoah* more powerful and affecting, requiring audience members to use their imaginations to see the disturbing events described by the subjects of the film.

Although Lanzmann had difficulty locating particular Holocaust survivors for interviews, he had even more trouble getting former Nazis to agree to appear on camera. Since Lanzmann was forthright with them from the onset of the project, many refused to speak with him. He later armed himself with a hidden camera and microphone, presenting a false name and passport as he approached various ex-Nazis, who in turn spoke freely of their involvement in the Holocaust.

On one occasion his equipment was discovered by an interviewee and he and his assistant were assaulted and forcibly removed from the premises. Lanzmann collected approximately 350 hours of film from survivors, Nazi perpetrators, and witnesses. When *Shoah* (the Hebrew word for "annihilation," "holocaust," or "catastrophe") began reaching theater audiences, the film provoked positive responses and received a statement of praise from Pope John Paul II.

Nevertheless, *Shoah* was assailed by some Polish groups, who believed that Lanzmann had gone out of his way to interview Poles who still showed signs of anti-Semitism. These critics charged that, although Lanzmann included footage of a gentile Polish resistance leader, he should have provided more balance by using interviews with Poles who hid Jews from the Nazis.

Despite the controversy, *Shoah* was shown on television in Poland. The film received numerous awards, including the New York Film Critics Award in 1985, the Los Angeles Film Critics Award in 1985, and the Peabody Award in 1987. In 1985 Lanzmann published the text of *Shoah* in book form.

documentary, *Night and Fog,* provides a haunting look at the liberation of concentration camps and the clean up involved in burying the dead.

When the big screen turned most of its focus to Vietnam, television continued to highlight World War II in miniseries, made-for-TV movies, and documentaries (including numerous shows now available on video from the History Channel and National Geographic, among other producers). Beyond the previously mentioned *Holocaust,* television also covered WWII in the miniseries *The Winds of War* (1983) and its follow-up *War and Remembrance* (1988) and *War and Remembrance: The Final Chapter* (1989). British television contributed *Danger: UXB* (1981), about the

Bob Crane and Werner Klemperer in *Hogan's Heroes*. (Reproduced by permission of AP/Wide World Photos)

Bomb Disposal Company of the Royal Engineers in London; *We'll Meet Again* (1982), about a bomber group of the U.S. 8th Air Force stationed in Suffolk, England; and *Fortunes of War* (1987), which depicts a British couple's adventures in Athens and Cairo.

The cable station Showtime presented a series of original movies under the title *The Rescuers: Stories of Courage* (1997—1998), each profiling true stories of people who risked their lives to aid Jewish refugees during the Holocaust. These include *Two Women, Two Couples* and *Two Families*. Also made for cable are *When Trumpets Fade* (1998) starring Ron Eldard, featuring the 1944 Battle of the Hurtgen Forest, and *The Tuskegee Airmen* (1995), which concerns the formation and accomplishments of the U.S. Army Air Corps' first squadron of black combat fighter pilots. *Hiroshima* (1995) recreates the circumstances surrounding the dropping of the first atomic bomb on Japan in 1945. The made-for-television movie *Enola Gay* (1980) features the true story of the airmen aboard the B-29 that released the bomb.

The Summer of My German Soldier is a 1978 TV movie, adapted from the novel by Bette Greene, about a young Jewish girl (Kristy McNichol) who befriends an escaped German POW (Bruce Davison) in a small Georgia town. The true story of British woman Mary Liddell is shown in the Hallmark Hall of Fame presentation *One Against the Wind* (1991), as Mary smuggles downed Allied pilots out of France. *Playing for Time* (1980) is an award-winning TV movie and another true story that concerns Fania Fénelon, who survives in a concentration camp by leading an inmate orchestra that plays for the Nazis. *Mutiny* (1999) is a fact-based story about 50 black sailors who were court-martialed for refusing to load munitions onto ships in San Francisco after a disaster that three weeks earlier claimed the lives of about 300 of their fellow sailors. The men cited the Navy's lack of concern for their safety as the reason for their actions.

There are also several television shows that were set during World War II or shortly afterward. *McHale's Navy* (1962–1966) starred Ernest Borgnine as PT boat commander Quinton McHale and

Orson Welles starred in Carol Reed's *The Third Man,* featuring Joseph Cotten. (Reproduced by permission of the Kobal Collection)

depicted his adventures and that of his outrageous crew (which included the zany antics of Tim Conway). The sitcom was the basis for three feature films: *McHale's Navy* (1964), *McHale's Navy Joins the Air Force* (1965), and a 1997 remake also titled *McHale's Navy* that starred Tom Arnold in the leading role. A Nazi POW camp provided comedy for the long-running *Hogan's Heroes* (1965–1971) about a group of wily prisoners, lead by Col. Robert Hogan (Bob Crane), and their incompetent Nazi guards. *The Rat Patrol* (1966–1968) was a series depicting the adventures of four Allied commandos battling General Rommel's Afrika Corps in the North African desert. *Homefront* (1991–1993) dealt with returning G.I.s, foreign war brides, and the families they left behind. It starred Kyle Chandler, Sammi Davis, and Wendy Phillips.

No discussion of World War II movies is complete without a brief look at postwar and anti-war films. *Judgment at Nuremberg* (1961) depicts the 1948 war crime trials while *The Man in the Glass Booth* (1975), another trial story, is loosely based on the Israeli capture and trial of SS officer Adolf Eichmann. Postwar Vienna is as treacherous as any battlefield in Carol Reed's nightmarish *The Third Man* (1949) while *The Big Lift* (1950) deals with G.I.s assigned to the Berlin airlift. In 1969's *Hell in the Pacific,* the futility of war is explored as two soldiers—one American, one Japanese who are stranded on a tiny island—battle each other for survival.

The Young Lions (1958) covers the experiences of two American soldiers and a disillusioned Nazi in the war's last days. *The Best Years of Our Lives* (1946) picks up the lives of three WWII vets as they struggle with civilian life—a similar plot to that of *The Miniver Story* (1950), which provides a look at postwar England and is the sequel to the more successful *Mrs. Miniver. Sophie's Choice* (1982) features Meryl Streep in the Academy Award-winning role of an Auschwitz survivor who settles in New York after the war, but is ultimately unable to overcome the horrors she experienced in the death camp. *Black Rain* (1988) is a Japanese portrait of one family five years after the Hiroshima bombing.

Japanese directors are also responsible for *Fires on the Plain* (1959) about a private unhinged by his experiences in the Philippines, and the three-film series *The Human Condition* (1958, 1959,

1961), which follows a Japanese pacifist who is forced into military service and is eventually captured by Russian troops. One controversial anti-war film from Germany is Volker Schlondorff's *The Tin Drum* (1979) in which a young German child wills himself to stop growing in response to the rise of Nazism and who expresses his anger by beating on a tin drum. Other German anti-war films include 1959's *The Bridge*, concerning the bewilderment of ill-trained and very young German recruits at the end of the war, and *The Nasty Girl* (1990), which is based on a true story about a young woman who researches her hometown's history during the Third Reich, digging up information the inhabitants would rather forget.

It seems that the "last good war" will never be forgotten, no matter how many years pass. This worldwide conflict continues to fascinate new generations of film directors as they offer their own personal visions of the men and women willing to pay the cost for freedom.

Contributor
Christine Tomassini

SOURCES

Books

Carnes, Mark C., general editor, *Past Imperfect: History According to the Movies,* Henry Holt and Company, Inc. (New York), 1995.

Connors, Martin, and James Craddock, editors, *VideoHound's Golden Movie Retriever 2000,* Visible Ink Press (Detroit), 1999.

Fraser, George MacDonald, *The Hollywood History of the World,* The Harvill Press (London), 1996.

Friedwall, Will, *The Warner Brothers Cartoons,* The Scarecrow Press, Inc. (Metuchen, NJ), 1981.

Maltin, Leonard, editor, *Leonard Maltin's Movie & Video Guide 2000,* Penguin Putnam Inc. (New York), 1999.

Mayo, Mike, *VideoHound's War Movies: Classic Conflict on Film,* Visible Ink Press (Detroit), 1999.

Further Reading

The following list of resources focuses on material appropriate for high school or college students. The list is divided into two major sections: Holocaust Bibliography and World War II Bibliography. The main sections are further subdivided into more specific topics. Please note that although some titles are applicable to more than one topic, they are listed only once. Please also note that web site addresses, though verified prior to publication, are subject to change.

Holocaust Bibliography

General Histories and Overviews of the Holocaust:

Adler, David A., *We Remember the Holocaust*, Henry Holt (New York), 1995.

Altman, Linda Jacobs, *Forever Outsiders: Jews and History from Ancient Times to August 1935*, Blackbirch Press (Woodbridge, CT), 1998.

Arad, Yithak, *The Pictorial History of the Holocaust*, Macmillan (New York), 1992.

Ayer, Eleanor H., *A Firestorm Unleashed: January 1942 to June 1943*, Blackbirch Press (Woodbridge, CT), 1998.

Ayer, Eleanor H., *Inferno: July 1943 to April 1945*, Blackbirch Press (Woodbridge, CT), 1998.

Ayer, Eleanor H., and Stephen D. Chicoine, *From the Ashes: May 1945 and After*, Blackbirch Press (Woodbridge, CT), 1998.

Bachrach, Susan D., *Tell Them We Remember: The Story of the Holocaust*, Little, Brown (Boston), 1994.

Bauer, Yehuda, and Nili Keren, *A History of the Holocaust*, Franklin Watts (New York), 1982.

Chaikin, Miriam, *A Nightmare in History: The Holocaust, 1933–1945*, Clarion Books (New York), 1987.

Cornwell, John, *Hitler's Pope: The Secret History of Pius XII*, Viking (New York), 1999.

Dawidowicz, Lucy S., *The War against the Jews, 1933–1945*, Bantam Books (New York), 1986.

Epstein, Eric Joseph, and Philip Rosen, *Dictionary of the Holocaust: Biography, Geography, and Terminology*, Greenwood Press (Westport, CT), 1997.

Feingold, Henry L., *The Politics of Rescue: The Roosevelt Administration and the Holocaust, 1938–1945*, Rutgers University Press (New Brunswick, NJ), 1970.

Friedman, Saul S., *No Haven for the Oppressed: United States Policy Toward Jewish Refugees, 1933–1945*, Wayne State University Press (Detroit), 1973.

Gilbert, Martin, *Auschwitz and the Allies*, Holt, Rinehart, and Winston (New York), 1981.

Gilbert, Martin, *The Holocaust: The History of the Jews of Europe during the Second World War,* Henry Holt (New York), 1986.

Gutman, Israel, editor, *The Encyclopedia of the Holocaust,* Macmillan (New York), 1990.

Herzstein, Robert E., *The Nazis,* Time-Life Books (Alexandria, VA), 1980.

Hilberg, Raoul, *The Destruction of the European Jews,* Holmes & Meier (New York), 1985.

Lanzmann, Claude, *Shoah: The Complete Text of the Acclaimed Holocaust Film,* Da Capo Press (New York), 1995.

Levin, Nora, *The Holocaust: The Nazi Destruction of European Jewry, 1933–1945,* Schocken (New York), 1973.

Lipstadt, Deborah E., *Beyond Belief: The American Press and the Coming of the Holocaust 1933–1945,* The Free Press (New York), 1986.

Lipstadt, Deborah E., *Denying the Holocaust: The Growing Assault on Truth and Memory,* Penguin (New York), 1993.

Mauldin, Bill, *Up Front,* Henry Holt (New York), 1945.

Meltzer, Milton, *Never to Forget,* Harper and Row (New York), 1976.

Morse, Arthur D., *While Six Million Died: A Chronicle of American Apathy,* Hart (New York), 1967.

Resnick, Abraham, *The Holocaust,* Lucent Books (San Diego), 1991.

Rogasky, Barbara, *Smoke and Ashes,* Holiday House (New York), 1988.

Rossel, Seymour, *The Holocaust: The Fire That Raged,* Franklin Watts (New York), 1989.

Sherrow, Victoria, *The Blaze Engulfs: January 1939 to December 1941,* Blackbirch Press (Woodbridge, CT), 1998.

Sherrow, Victoria, *Smoke to Flame: September 1935 to December 1938,* Blackbirch Press (Woodbridge, CT), 1998.

Shoenberner, Gerhard, *The Yellow Star: The Persecution of the Jews in Europe, 1933–1945,* Bantam Books (New York), 1979.

Shulman, William L., compiler, *Voices and Visions: A Collection of Primary Sources,* Blackbirch Press (Woodbridge, CT), 1998.

Snyder, Louis L., *Encyclopedia of the Third Reich,* McGraw-Hill, 1976.

Strahinich, Helen, *The Holocaust: Understanding and Remembering,* Enslow (Springfield, NJ), 1996.

Trunk, Isaiah, *Judenrat: The Jewish Councils in Eastern Europe Under Nazi Occupation,* Macmillan (New York), 1972.

Weinberg, Jeshajahu, and Rina Elieli, *The Holocaust Museum in Washington,* Rizzoli (New York), 1995.

Wigoder, Geoffrey, editor, *The Holocaust: A Grolier Student Library,* 4 volumes, Grolier Educational (Danbury, CT), 1997.

Yahil, Leni, *The Holocaust: The Fate of European Jewry, 1932–1945,* Oxford University Press (New York), 1991.

Zentner, Christian, Friedemann Bedürftig, and Amy Hackett, editors, *Encyclopedia of the Third Reich,* Collier Macmillan (New York), 1991.

Atlases:

Gilbert, Martin, *Atlas of the Holocaust,* Macmillan (New York), 1982.

United States Holocaust Memorial Museum, *Historical Atlas of the Holocaust,* Macmillan (New York), 1996.

German History, the Early Nazi Movement, the Nazi Government, and Policy toward the Jews before the Holocaust:

Allen, William Sheridan, *The Nazi Seizure of Power: The Experience of a Single German Town, 1930–1935,* Franklin Watts (New York), 1973.

Arendt, Hannah, *The Origins of Totalitarianism,* Harcourt, Brace (New York), 1966.

Auerbacher, Inge, *I Am a Star: Child of the Holocaust,* Prentice-Hall (Paramus, NJ), 1986.

Ayer, Eleanor, *Adolf Hitler,* Lucent (San Diego), 1996.

Bauer, Yehuda, *Jews for Sale?: Nazi-Jewish Negotiations, 1933–1945,* Yale University Press (New Haven, CT), 1994.

Berman, Russell A., *Paul von Hindenburg,* Chelsea House (New York), 1987.

Bullock, Alan, *Hitler: A Study in Tyranny,* Harper and Row (New York), 1964.

Cohn, Norman, *Warrant for Genocide: The Myth of the Jewish World Conspiracy and the Protocols of the Elders of Zion,* Harper & Row Publishers (New York), 1969.

Eimerl, Sarel, *Hitler over Europe: The Road to World War II,* Little, Brown (Boston), 1972.

Friedlander, Saul, *Pius XII and the Third Reich,* Knopf (New York), 1966.

Fuller, Barbara, *Germany,* Marshall Cavendish (New York), 1996.

Gallo, Max, *The Night of the Long Knives,* Harper and Row (New York), 1972.

Goldston, Robert C., *The Life and Death of Nazi Germany,* Bobbs-Merrill (New York), 1967.

Graff, Stewart, *The Story of World War II,* E. P. Dutton (New York), 1978.

Halperin, S. William, *Germany Tried Democracy: A Political History of the Reich from 1918 to 1933,* Norton (New York), 1965.

Josephson, Judith P., *Jesse Owens: Track and Field Legend,* Enslow Press (Springfield, NJ), 1997.

Kluger, Ruth Peggy Mann, *Secret Ship,* Doubleday (New York), 1978.

Marrin, Albert, *Hitler,* Viking (New York), 1987.

Mayer, Milton Sanford, *They Thought They Were Free: The Germans, 1933-35,* University of Chicago Press (Chicago), 1966.

The New Order, Time-Life Books (Alexandria, VA), 1989.

Niemark, Anne E., *Leo Baeck and the Holocaust,* E. P. Dutton (New York), 1986.

Patterson, Charles, *Anti-Semitism: The Road to the Holocaust and Beyond,* Walker (New York), 1989.

Read, Anthony, *Kristallnacht: The Nazi Night of Terror,* Times Books/Random House (New York), 1989.

Rubinstein, William D., *The Myth of Rescue,* Routledge (New York), 1997.

Schleunes, Karl A., *The Twisted Road to Auschwitz: Nazi Policy toward German Jews, 1933–1939,* University of Illinois Press (Urbana), 1970.

Shirer, William L., *The Rise and Fall of Adolf Hitler,* Random House (New York), 1961.

Shirer, William L., *The Rise and Fall of the Third Reich,* Simon and Schuster (New York), 1960.

Snyder, Louis L., *Hitler's Elite,* Hippocrene Books (New York), 1989.

Spence, William, *Germany Then and Now,* Franklin Watts (New York), 1994.

Start, Clarissa, *God's Man: The Story of Pastor Niemoeller,* Washburn (New York), 1959.

Stein, R. Conrad, *Hitler Youth,* Children's Press (Danbury, CT), 1985.

Stewart, Gail, *Hitler's Reich,* Lucent Books (San Diego), 1994.

Thalmann, Rita, and Emmanuel Feinermann, *Crystal Night, 9–10 November, 1938,* Holocaust Library (New York), 1974.

Thomas, Gordon, and Max M. Witts, *Voyage of the Damned,* Stein and Day (New York), 1974.

Toland, John, *Adolf Hitler,* Doubleday (New York), 1976.

Wepman, Dennis, *Adolf Hitler,* Chelsea House (New York), 1989.

Zurndorfer, Hannele, *The Ninth of November,* Quartet Books (Berrien Springs, MI), 1983.

The "Final Solution":

Aly, Gotz, *Final Solution: Nazi Population Policy and the Murder of the European Jews,* Oxford University Press (New York), 1999.

Bower, Tom, *Klaus Barbie, the "Butcher of Lyons,"* Pantheon Books (New York), 1984.

Breitman, Richard, *The Architect of Genocide: Himmler and the Final Solution,* Knopf (New York), 1991.

Browning, Christopher R., *Nazi Policy, Jewish Workers, German Killers,* Cambridge University Press (New York), 2000.

Browning, Christopher R., *Ordinary Men: Reserve Police Battalion 101 and the Final Solution in Poland,* HarperPerennial (New York), 1992.

Des Pres, Terrence, *The Survivor: An Anatomy of Life in the Death Camps,* Washington Square Press (New York), 1976.

Dobroszycki, Lucjan, editor, *The Chronicle of the Lódz Ghetto, 1941–1944,* Yale University Press (New York), 1984.

Friedlander, Henry, *The Origins of Nazi Genocide: From Euthanasia to the Final Solution,* University of North Carolina Press (Chapel Hill, NC), 1995.

Friedrich, Otto, *The Kingdom of Auschwitz,* Harper Perennial (New York), 1994.

Gilbert, Martin, *Auschwitz and the Allies,* Henry Holt (New York), 1990.

Goldhagen, Daniel J., *Hitler's Willing Executioners: Ordinary Germans and the Holocaust,* Knopf (New York), 1996.

Graf, Malvina, *The Kraków Ghetto and the Plaszów Camp Remembered,* Florida State University Press (Tallahassee, FL), 1989.

Gutman, Israel, *Anatomy of the Auschwitz Death Camp,* Indiana University Press (Bloomington, IN), 1998.

Gutman, Israel, *The Jews of Warsaw, 1939–1943,* Indiana University Press (Bloomington, IN), 1982.

Hellman, Peter, *The Auschwitz Album: A Book Based upon an Album Discovered by a Concentration Camp Survivor, Lili Meier,* Random House (New York), 1981.

Höss, Rudolf, *Death Dealer: The Memoirs of the SS Kommandant at Auschwitz,* edited by Steven Paskuly, translated by Andrew Pollinger, Prometheus Books (Buffalo, NY), 1992.

Kogon, Eugen, *The Theory and Practice of Hell: The German Concentration Camps and the System behind Them,* Octagon (Los Angeles), 1973.

Leitner, Isabella, *The Big Lie: A True Story,* Scholastic (New York), 1992.

Levi, Primo, *Survival in Auschwitz,* Macmillan (New York), 1987.

Lifton, Robert Jay, *The Nazi Doctors: Medical Killing and the Psychology of Genocide,* Basic Books (New York), 1988.

Millu, Liana, *Smoke over Birkenau,* Jewish Publication Society (Philadelphia), 1991.

Nomberg-Przuytyk, Sara, *Auschwitz: True Tales from a Grotesque Land,* University of North Carolina Press (Chapel Hill, NC), 1986.

Posner, Gerald L., *Mengele: The Complete Story,* McGraw-Hill (New York), 1986.

Reitlinger, Gerald, *The SS: Alibi of a Nation, 1922–1945,* Viking (New York), 1957.

Rubinstein, William D., *The Myth of Rescue,* Routledge (New York), 1997.

Steiner, Jean Francis, *Treblinka,* Simon and Schuster (New York), 1967.

Stern, Ellen Norman, *Elie Wiesel: Witness for Life,* Ktav Publishing House (New York), 1982.

Swiebocka, Teresa, compiler and editor, *Auschwitz: A History in Photographs,* Indiana University Press (Bloomington, IN), 1993.

Whiting, Charles, *Heydrich: Henchman of Death,* Leo Cooper (S. Yorkshire, England), 1999.

Wiesel, Elie, *The Night Trilogy: Night, Dawn, The Accident,* Hill and Wang (New York), 1960.

Willenberg, Samuel, *Surviving Treblinka,* Basil Blackwell (Maldin, MA), 1989.

Wyman, David S., *The Abandonment of the Jews: America and the Holocaust, 1941–1945,* Pantheon (New York), 1984.

Zyskind, Sara, *Struggle,* Lerner (Minneapolis, MN), 1989.

Poland:

Adelson, Alan, and Robert Lapides, editors, *Lódz Ghetto: Inside a Community Under Siege,* Viking (New York), 1989.

Bernheim, Mark, *Father of the Orphans: The Story of Janusz Korczak,* E. P. Dutton (New York), 1989.

Davies, Norman, *God's Playground,* Columbia University Press (New York), 1982.

Drucker, Malka, and Michael Halperin, *Jacob's Rescue: A Holocaust Story,* Bantam Skylark (New York), 1993.

Eichengreen, Lucille, *Rumkowski and the Orphans of Lódz,* Mercury House (San Francisco, CA), 1999.

Frister, Roman, *The Cap: The Price of a Life,* translated by Hillel Halkin, Grove Press (New York), 1999.

George, Willy, *In the Warsaw Ghetto, Summer 1941,* Aperture Foundation (New York), 1993.

Heller, Celia S., *On the Edge of Destruction: Jews of Poland between the Two World Wars,* Columbia University Press (New York), 1977.

Hoffman, Eva, *Shtetl: The Life and Death of a Small Town and the World of Polish Jews,* Houghton Mifflin Company (Boston), 1998.

Hyams, Joe, *A Field of Buttercups,* Prentice-Hall (Paramus, NJ), 1968.

Kaplan, Chaim A., *Scroll of Agony: The Warsaw Diary of Chaim A. Kaplan,* Indiana University Press (Bloomington, IN), 1999.

Keller, Ulrich, editor, *The Warsaw Ghetto in Photographs,* Dover (Mineola, NY), 1984.

Klein, Gerda Weissmann, *All but My Life,* Hill & Wang Publishers (New York), 1995.

Landau, Elaine, *The Warsaw Ghetto Uprising,* Macmillan (New York), 1992.

Lewis, Mark, and Jacob Frank, *Himmler's Jewish Tailor: The Story of Holocaust Survivor Jacob Frank,* Syracuse University Press (Syracuse, NY), 2000.

Lifton, Betty Jean, *The King of Children: The Life and Death of Janusz Korczak,* St. Martin's Griffin (New York), 1997.

Lukas, Richard C., and Norman Davies, *The Forgotten Holocaust: The Poles Under German Occupation 1939–1944,* Hippocrene Books (New York), 1997.

Nelken, Halina, *And Yet, Here I Am!* University of Massachusetts Press (Amherst, MA), 1999.

Sender, Ruth Minsky, *The Cage,* Macmillan (New York), 1986.

Sender, Ruth Minsky, *To Life,* Macmillan (New York), 1988.

Spiegelman, Art, *Maus: A Survivor's Tale: And Here My Troubles Began,* Pantheon Books (New York), 1992.

Spiegelman, Art, *Maus: A Survivor's Tale: My Father Bleeds History,* Pantheon Books (New York), 1997.

Stewart, Gail B., *Life in the Warsaw Ghetto,* Lucent Books (San Diego), 1995.

Szner, Zvi, and Alexander Sened, editors, *With a Camera in the Ghetto: Mendel Grossman,* Schocken Books (New York), 1977.

Szpilman, Wladyslaw, *The Pianist,* Picador USA (New York), 1999.

Vishniac, Roman, *A Vanished World,* Farrar, Straus, and Giroux (New York), 1983.

Watt, Richard M., *Bitter Glory: Poland & Its Fate 1918–1993,* Hippocrene Books (New York), 1998.

Ziemian, Joseph, *The Cigarette Seller of Three Crosses Square,* Lerner (Minneapolis, MN), 1975.

Other Countries:

Asscher-Pinkoff, Clara, *Star Children,* Wayne State University Press (Detroit), 1986.

Bitton-Jackson, Livia, *I Have Lived a Thousand Years: Growing up in the Holocaust,* Simon and Schuster (New York), 1997.

Denes, Magda, *Castles Burning: A Child's Life in War,* W. W. Norton (New York), 1997.

Frank, Anne, *The Diary of a Young Girl: The Definitive Edition,* edited by Otto Frank and Mirjam Pressler, Doubleday (New York), 1995.

Gies, Miep, and Alison L. Gold, *Anne Frank Remembered: The Story of the Woman Who Helped to Hide the Frank Family* Simon and Schuster (New York), 1987.

Gold, Alison L., *Memories of Anne Frank: Reflections of a Childhood Friend,* Scholastic (New York), 1997.

Handler, Andrew, and Susan Meschel, editors, *Young People Speak,* Franklin Watts (New York), 1993.

Hutok, J. B., *With Blood and with Iron: The Lidice Story,* R. Hale (London), 1957.

Isaacman, Clara, *Clara's Story,* Jewish Publication Society (Philadelphia), 1984.

Klarsfeld, Serge, *The Children of Izieu: A Human Tragedy,* Abrams (New York), 1985.

Lewy, Guenter, *The Nazi Persecution of the Gypsies,* Oxford University Press (New York), 2000.

Lindwe, Willy, *The Last Seven Months of Anne Frank,* Pantheon (New York), 1991.

Marrus, Michael R., *Vichy France and the Jews,* Basic Books (New York), 1981.

Perl, Lila, and Marian Blumenthal Lazar, *Four Perfect Pebbles: A Holocaust Story,* Greenwillow Books (New York), 1996.

Rol, Ruud van der, and Rian Verhoeven, *Anne Frank: Beyond the Diary,* Viking (New York), 1993.

Roth-Hano, Renée, *Touch Wood: A Girlhood in Occupied France,* Four Winds Press (Portland, OR), 1988.

Siegal, Avanka, *Grace in the Wilderness: After the Liberation, 1945–1948,* Farrar, Straus, Giroux (New York), 1985.

Siegal, Avanka, *Upon the Head of the Goat: A Childhood in Hungary, 1939–1944,* Farrar, Straus, Giroux (New York), 1981.

Velmans, Edith, *Edith's Story,* Soho Press (New York), 1998.

Zuccotti, Susan, *The Italians and the Holocaust: Persecution, Rescue and Survival,* Basic Books (New York), 1987.

Resistance, Survival, and Rescue:

Ainszstein, Reuben, *Jewish Resistance in Nazi-Occupied Eastern Europe: With a Historical Survey of the Jew as a Fighter and Soldier in the Diaspora,* Barnes & Noble (New York), 1975.

Aliav, Ruth, *The Last Escape: The Launching of the Largest Secret Rescue Movement of All Time,* Doubleday (Garden City, NY), 1973.

Atkinson, Linda, *In Kindling Flame: The Story of Hannah Senesh,* Lee & Shepard (New York), 1985.

Ayer, Eleanor A., *The United States Holocaust Memorial Museum,* Silver Burdett Press (Parsipanny, NJ), 1995.

Bauer, Yehuda, *They Chose Life: Jewish Resistance in the Holocaust,* American Jewish Committee (New York), 1973.

Berenbaum, Michael, *The World Must Know,* Little, Brown (Boston), 1993.

Bierman, John, *Righteous Gentile: The Story of Raoul Wallenberg,* Viking (New York), 1981.

Blatt, Thomas Toivi, *From the Ashes of Sobibor: A Story of Survival,* Northwestern University Press (Evanston, IL), 1997.

Block, Gay, and Malka Drucker, *Rescuers,* Holmes and Meier (New York), 1992.

Bosanquest, Mary, *The Life and Death of Dietrich Bonhoeffer,* Harper and Row (New York), 1968.

Chevrillon, Claire, *Code Name Christiane Clouet: A Woman in the French Resistance,* Texas A & M University (College Station, TX), 1995.

Elkins, Michael, *Forged in Fury,* Ballantine Books (New York), 1971.

Flender, Harold, *Rescue in Denmark,* Simon and Schuster (New York), 1963.

Friedman, Ina R., *Flying against the Wind: The Story of a Young Woman Who Defied the Nazis,* Lodge Pole Press (Brookline, MA), 1995.

Gelman, Charles, *Do Not Go Gentle: A Memoir of Jewish Resistance in Poland, 1941–1945,* Archon Books, (North Haven, CT), 1989.

Gilbert, Martin, *The Boys: The Untold Story of 732 Young Concentration Camp Survivors,* Henry Holt & Company (New York), 1997.

Greenfield, Howard, *The Hidden Children,* Ticknor and Fields (New York), 1993.

Gutman, Israel, *Resistance: The Warsaw Ghetto Uprising,* Houghton Mifflin (Boston), 1994.

Haas, Gerda, *These I Do Remember: Fragments from the Holocaust,* Cumberland (Brooklyn, NY), 1982.

Hallie, Philip, *Lest Innocent Blood Be Shed,* Harper & Row (New York), 1980.

Healey, Tim, *Secret Armies; Resistance Groups in World War II,* Macdonald (London), 1981.

Helmreich, William B., *Against All Odds: Holocaust Survivors and the Successful Lives They Made in America,* Simon & Schuster (New York), 1992.

Hewins, Ralph, *Count Folke Bernadotte: His Life and Work,* Hutchinson (New York), 1950.

Holocaust Education—Women of Valor, http://www.interlog.com/~mighty/valor/kath_f.htm (September 12, 2000).

Jewish Partisans, http://www.ushmm.org/outreach/jpart.htm (September 12, 2000).

Keneally, Thomas, *Schindler's List,* Simon and Schuster (New York), 1982.

Kertyesz, Imre, *Fateless,* Northwestern University Press (Evanston, IL), 1992.

Kurzman, Dan, *The Bravest Battle: The Twenty-Eight Days of the Warsaw Ghetto Uprising,* Da Capo Press (New York), 1993.

Landau, Elaine, *The Warsaw Ghetto Uprising,* Macmillan (New York), 1992.

Landau, Elaine, *We Survived the Holocaust,* Franklin Watts (New York), 1991.

Laska, Vera, editor, *Women in the Resistance and in the Holocaust: The Voices of Eyewitnesses,* Greenwood Press (Westport, CT), 1983.

Linnea, Sharon, *Raoul Wallenberg: The Man Who Stopped Death,* Jewish Publication Society (Philadelphia), 1993.

Marton, Kati, *Wallenberg,* Random House (New York), 1982.

Meltzer, Milton, *Rescue: The Story of How Gentiles Saved Jews in the Holocaust,* Harper and Row (New York), 1988.

Mochizuki, Ken, *Passage to Freedom: The Sugihara Story,* Lee and Low Books (New York), 1997.

Pettit, Jayne, *A Time to Fight Back: True Stories of Wartime Resistance,* Houghton Mifflin (Boston), 1996.

Rashke, Richard, *Escape from Sobibor,* University of Illinois Press (Urbana, IL), 1995.

Rittner, Carol, *The Courage to Care,* New York University Press (New York), 1986.

Roberts, Jack L., *Oskar Schindler,* Lucent Books (San Diego), 1996.

Rosenberg, Maxine B., *Hiding to Survive: Stories of Jewish Children Rescued from the Holocaust,* Clarion (New York), 1994.

Schul, Yuri, *They Fought Back: The Story of Jewish Resistance in Nazi Europe,* Schocken Books (New York), 1967.

Stadtler, Bea, *The Holocaust: A History of Courage and Resistance,* Behrman House (West Orange, NJ), 1994.

Stein, R. Conrad, *Resistance Movements,* Children's Press (Chicago), 1982.

Sutin, Lawrence, editor, *Jack and Rochelle: A Holocaust Story of Love and Resistance,* Graywolf Press (Saint Paul, MN), 1996.

Vinke, Hermann, *The Short Life of Sophie Scholl,* Harper and Row (New York), 1984.

Vogel, Ilse-Margaret, *Bad Times, Good Friends,* Harcourt Brace Jovanovich (New York), 1992.

Weinstein, Irving, *That Denmark Might Live; The Saga of Danish Resistance in World War II,* Macrae Smith (Philadelphia), 1967.

Werner, Harold, *Fighting Back,* Columbia University Press (New York), 1994.

Wind, Renate, *Dietrich Bonhoeffer: A Spoke in the Wheel,* Eerdmans (Grand Rapids, MI), 1992.

Wood, E. Thomas, *Karski: How One Man Tried to Stop the Holocaust,* John Wiley & Sons (New York), 1994.

Wygoda, Hermann, *In the Shadow of the Swastika,* University of Illinois Press (Urbana, IL), 1998.

Zahn, Gordon, *In Solitary Witness: The Life and Death of Franz Jaggerstatter,* Holt, Rinehart, and Winston (New York), 1964.

Zassenhaus, Hiltgunt, *Walls: Resisting the Third Reich, One Woman's Story,* Beacon Press (Boston), 1974.

Zeinert, Karen, *The Warsaw Ghetto Uprising,* Millbrook Press (Brookfield, CT), 1993.

Zuccotti, Susan, *The Italians and the Holocaust: Persecution, Rescue, and Survival,* University of Nebraska Press (Lincoln, NE), 1996.

Justice:

Arendt, Hannah, *Eichmann in Jerusalem: A Report on the Banality of Evil,* Penguin (New York), 1977.

Gilbert, G. M., *Nuremberg Diary,* New American Library (New York), 1947.

Hausner, Gideon, *Justice in Jerusalem,* Harper and Row (New York), 1966.

Jackson, Robert H., *The Nürnberg Case, As Presented by Robert H. Jackson, Chief Counsel for the United States, Together with Other Documents,* Cooper Square Publishers (New York), 1971.

Landau, Elaine, *Nazi War Criminals,* Franklin Watts (New York), 1990.

Morin, Isobel V., *Days of Judgment: The World War II War Crimes Trials,* Millbrook Press (Brookfield, CT), 1995.

Noble, Iris, *Nazi Hunter: Simon Wiesenthal,* J. Messner (New York), 1979.

Persico, Joseph E., *Nuremberg: Infamy on Trial,* Viking (New York), 1994.

Ryan, Allan A., *Quiet Neighbors: Prosecuting Nazi War Criminals in America,* Harcourt Brace Jovanovich (San Diego), 1984.

Taylor, Telford, *The Anatomy of the Nuremberg Trials: A Personal Memoir,* Knopf (New York), 1992.

Wiesenthal, Simon, *Justice Not Vengeance,* translated from German by Edward Osers, Grove Weidenfeld (London), 1989.

Wiesenthal, Simon, *The Murderers Among Us: The Simon Wiesenthal Memoirs,* edited, with a profile of the author, by Joseph Wechsberg, McGraw-Hill (New York), 1967.

Displaced Persons:

Blumenson, Martin, *Liberation,* Time-Life Books (Alexandria VA), 1983.

Botting, Douglas, *The Aftermath: Europe,* Time-Life Books (Alexandria, VA), 1983.

Gilbert, Martin *The Holocaust: A History of the Jews of Europe during the Second World War,* Holt, Rinehart and Winston (New York), 1998.

Gilbert, Martin, *Israel: A History,* William Morrow (New York), 1998.

Levi, Primo, *The Reawakening,* Collier Books (New York), 1996.

Nesaule, Agate, *A Woman in Amber: Healing the Trauma of War and Exile,* Soho Press (New York), 1995.

O'Brien, Conor Cruise, *The Siege: The Saga of Israel and Zionism,* Simon and Schuster (New York), 1986.

Sykes, Christopher, *Crossroads to Israel,* Indiana University Press (Bloomington, IN), 1973.

Yahil, Leni, *The Holocaust: The Fate of European Jewry,* Oxford University Press (Oxford), 1987.

World War II Bibliography

General Sources:

Allen, Peter, *The Origins of World War II,* Bookwright Press (New York), 1992.

The Avalon Project at the Yale Law School—World War II: Documents, http://www.yale.edu/lawweb/avalon/wwii/wwii.htm (September 8, 2000).

Bradley, Omar N., *A Soldier's Story,* Holt, Rinehart & Winston (New York), 1951.

Calvocoressi, Peter, Guy Wint, and John Pritchard, *Total War: Causes and Courses of the Second World War,* Pantheon (New York), 1987.

Churchill, Winston, *The Second World War,* Houghton (New York), 1948–1954, reprinted, 1986.

Collier, Basil, *The Second World War: A Military History,* William Morrow (New York), 1967.

Eisenhower, General Dwight D., *Crusade in Europe,* Doubleday (New York), 1948.

Ethell, Jeffrey L., and Robert T. Sand, *Air Command: Fighters and Bombers of World War II,* Motorbooks International (Osceola, WI), 1998.

Fleming, Peter, *Operation Sea Lion,* Simon and Schuster (New York), 1957.

Graff, Stewart, *The Story of World War II,* E. P. Dutton (New York), 1978.

Hills, Ken, *Wars That Changed the World: World War II,* Marshall Cavendish (New York), 1988.

Keegan, John, *The Battle for History: Re-Fighting World War II,* Vintage Books (New York), 1996.

Keegan, John, *The Second World War,* Penguin (New York), 1990.

Krull, Kathleen, *V Is for Victory,* Knopf (New York), 1995.

Lawson, Don, *Great Air Battles: World War I and II,* Lothrop, Lee & Shepard (New York), 1968.

Leckie, Robert, *Delivered from Evil: The Saga of World War II,* HarperPerennial (New York), 1987.

Leckie, Robert, *The Story of World War II,* Random House (New York), 1964.

Leutze, James R., *Bargaining for Supremacy: Anglo-American Naval Collaboration, 1937–1941,* University of North Carolina Press (Chapel Hill, NC), 1977.

MacArthur, Douglas, *Reminiscences,* Da Capo Press (New York), 1985.

MacDonald, Charles B., *Company Commander,* Burford Books (Springfield, NJ), 1999.

Marrin, Albert, *The Airmen's War: World War II in the Sky,* Atheneum (New York), 1982.

Michel, Henri, *The Second World War,* translated by Douglas Parmee, Deutsch (London), 1975.

Military History: World War II (1939–1945), http://www.cfcsc.dnd.ca/links/milhist/wwii.html (September 8, 2000).

A People at War, http://www.nara.gov/exhall/people/people.html (September 8, 2000).

Reynolds, Quentin J., *Only the Stars Are Neutral,* Random House (New York), 1942.

Roskill, Stephen W., *The Navy at War, 1939–1945,* Collins (London), 1960.

Ross, Stewart, *Propaganda,* Thomson Learning (New York), 1993.

Ross, Stewart, *World Leaders,* Thomson Learning (New York), 1993.

Snyder, Louis L., *World War II,* Franklin Watts (New York), 1981.

Wilmot, Chester, *The Struggle for Europe,* Harper & Row Publishers (New York), 1952.

World War II, http://www.awesomelibrary.org/Classroom/Social_Studies/History/World_War_II.html (September 8, 2000).

Atlases:

Freeman, Michael, and Tim Mason, editors, *Atlas of Nazi Germany,* Macmillan (New York), 1987.

Young, Peter, *Atlas of the Second World War,* Berkley Windhover (New York), 1974.

Asia and the Pacific:

Alexander, Joseph H., *Utmost Savagery: The Three Days of Tarawa,* Naval Institute Press (Annapolis, MD), 1995.

Astor, Gerald, *Operation Iceberg: The Invasion and Conquest of Okinawa in World War II*, D. I. Fine (New York), 1995.

Battling Bastards of Bataan, http://home.pacbell.net/fbaldie/Battling_Bastards_of_Bataan.html (September 26, 2000).

Blassingame, Wyatt, *The U.S. Frogmen of World War II*, Random House (New York), 1964.

Bradley, James, and Ron Powers, *Flags of Our Fathers*, Bantam (New York), 2000.

Castello, Edmund L., *Midway: Battle for the Pacific,* Random House (New York), 1968.

Chang, Iris, *The Rape of Nanking: The Forgotten Holocaust of World War II*, Basic Books (New York), 1997.

Conroy, Robert, *The Battle of Bataan: America's Greatest Defeat,* Macmillan (New York), 1969.

Daws, Gavan, *Prisoners of the Japanese: POWs of World War II in the Pacific,* W. Morrow (New York), 1994.

Dull, Paul S., *A Battle History of the Japanese Navy (1941–1945),* United States Naval Institute Press (Annapolis, MD), 1978.

Fahey, James, *Pacific War Diary: 1942–1945,* Houghton Mifflin (Boston), 1992.

Frank, Richard B., *Guadalcanal: The Definitive Account of the Landmark Battle,* Penguin (New York), 1992.

Fuchida, Mitsuo, and Masatake Okumiya, *Midway: The Battle that Doomed Japan: The Japanese Navy's Story,* Naval Institute Press (Annapolis, MD), 1992.

Gayle, Gordon D., *Bloody Beaches: The Marines at Peleliu,* U.S. Marine Corps (Washington, DC), 1996.

Grant, R. G., *Hiroshima and Nagasaki,* Raintree, Steck-Vaughn (Austin, TX), 1988.

Griffith, Samuel B., *The Battle for Guadalcanal,* University of Illinois Press (Urbana, IL), 2000.

Hallas, James H., *The Devil's Anvil: The Assault on Peleliu,* Praeger (Westport, CT), 1994.

Harris, Nathaniel, *Pearl Harbor,* Dryad Press (North Pomfret, VT), 1986.

Hirschfeld, Wolfgang, *Hirschfeld: The Story of a U-Boat NCO, 1940–1946,* as told to Geoffrey Brooks, U.S. Naval Institute (Annapolis, MD), 1996.

Hoehling, A. A., *The Lexington Goes Down: A Fighting Carrier's Last Hours in the Coral Sea,* Stackpole Books (Mechanicsburg, PA), 1993.

Hubbard, Preston John, *Apocalypse Undone: My Survival of Japanese Imprisonment during WWII,* Vanderbilt University Press (Nashville, TN), 1990.

Kessler, Lynn, editor, *Never in Doubt: Remembering Iwo Jima,* Naval Institute Press (Annapolis, MD), 1999.

Linzey, Stanford E., *God Was at Midway: The Sinking of the USS Yorktown (CV-5) and the Battles of the Coral Sea and Midway,* Black Forest Press (San Diego, CA), 1996.

Manchester, William, *American Caesar: Douglas MacArthur, 1880–1964,* Little, Brown (Boston) 1978.

Manchester, William, *Goodbye, Darkness: A Memoir of the Pacific War,* Little, Brown (Boston), 1979.

Marrin, Albert, *Victory in the Pacific,* Atheneum (New York), 1983.

Mishler, Clayton, *Sampan Sailor: A Navy Man's Adventures in WWII China,* Brassey's (Washington, DC), 1994.

Morin, Isobel V., *Days of Judgment,* Millbrook Press (Brookfield, CT), 1995.

Morison, Samuel Eliot, *History of United States Naval Operations in World War II: Coral Sea, Midway and Submarine Actions, May 1942–August 1942,* Vol. 4, Little, Brown (Boston), 1950.

Petillo, Carol Morris, *Douglas MacArthur: The Philippine Years,* Indiana University Press (Bloomington, IN), 1981.

Prange, Gordon W., Donald M. Goldstein, and Katherine V. Dillon, *At Dawn We Slept: The Untold Story of Pearl Harbor,* Viking (New York), 1991.

Prange, Gordon W., Donald M. Goldstein, and Katherine V. Dillon, *God's Samurai: Lead Pilot at Pearl Harbor,* Brassey's (Washington, DC), 1990.

Raymer, Edward C., *Descent into Darkness: Pearl Harbor, 1941: A Navy Diver's Memoir,* Presidio Press (Novato, CA), 1996.

Rice, Earle, Jr., *The Attack on Pearl Harbor,* Lucent (San Diego), 1997.

Ross, Bill D., *Iwo Jima: Legacy of Valor,* Vanguard Press (New York), 1986.

Ruhe, William J., *War in the Boats: My World War II Submarine Battles,* Brassey's (Washington, DC), 1994.

Sauvrain, Philip, *Midway,* New Discovery Books (New York), 1993.

Schaller, Michael, *Douglas MacArthur: The Far Eastern General,* Oxford University Press (New York), 1989.

Schlesinger, Arthur, Jr., and Richard H. Rovere, *The MacArthur Controversy and American Foreign Policy,* Farrar, Straus and Giroux (New York), 1965.

Shapiro, William E., *Pearl Harbor,* F. Watts (New York), 1984.

Sherrow, Victoria, *Hiroshima,* New Discovery Books (New York), 1994.

Skipper, G. C., *Battle of Leyte Gulf,* Children's Press (Chicago), 1981.

Skipper, G. C., *Submarines in the Pacific,* Children's Press (Chicago), 1980.

Sledge, Eugene B., *With the Old Breed: At Peleliu and Okinawa,* Naval Institute Press (Annapolis, MD), 1996.

Smith, Myron J., Jr., *The Battles of the Coral Sea and Midway, 1942,* Greenwood Publishing (New York), 1991.

Smith, William Ward, *Midway: Turning Point of the Pacific,* Thomas Y. Crowell Company (New York), 1966.

Smurthwaite, David, *The Pacific War Atlas: 1941–1945,* Facts on File (New York), 1995.

Spector, Ronald H., *Eagle against the Sun: The American War with Japan,* Free Press (New York), 1985.

Stafford, Edward P., *The Big E: The Story of the U.S.S. Enterprise,* Random House (New York), 1962.

Stein, R. Conrad, *The Battle of Guadalcanal,* Children's Press (Chicago), 1983.

Stein, R. Conrad, *The Battle of Okinawa,* Children's Press (Chicago), 1985.

Stein, R. Conrad, *Fall of Singapore,* Children's Press (Chicago), 1982.

Stein, R. Conrad, *Hiroshima,* Children's Press (Chicago), 1982.

Stinnett, Robert B., *Day of Deceit: The Truth about FDR and Pearl Harbor,* Free Press (New York), 2000.

Sullivan, George, *The Day Pearl Harbor Was Bombed: A Photo History of World War II,* Scholastic (New York), 1991.

Takaki, Ronald, *Hiroshima: Why America Dropped the Atomic Bomb,* Little, Brown (Boston), 1995.

Taylor, Theodore, *The Battle off Midway Island,* Avon (New York), 1981.

Thomas, Gerald W, and Roger D. Walker, editors, *Victory in World War II: The New Mexico Story,* University of New Mexico Press (Las Cruces, NM), 1994.

Tregaskis, Richard, *Guadalcanal Diary,* Modern Library (New York), 2000.

Tuleja, Thaddeus V., *Climax at Midway,* W. W. Norton (New York), 1960.

Ward, Harold, *Don't Go Island Hopping during a War!,* Harold Ward, 1999.

Webber, Bert, *Silent Siege-III: Japanese Attacks on North America in World War II: Ships Sunk, Air Raids, Bombs Dropped, Civilians Killed: Documentary,* Webb Research Group (Medford, OR), 1992.

Yahara, Hiromichi, *The Battle for Okinawa,* John Wiley and Sons (New York), 1997.

Zhigeng, Xu, *Lest We Forget: Nanjing Massacre, 1937,* Chinese Literature Press (Beijing), 1995.

Zich, Arthur, and the editors of Time-Life Books, *The Rising Sun,* Time-Life Books (Alexandria, VA), 1977.

Europe, the Atlantic, Africa, and the Soviet Union, 1939–1943:

Allen, Kenneth, *Battle of the Atlantic,* Wayland (London), 1973.

Barnett, Correlli, *The Battle of El Alamein: Decision in the Desert,* Macmillan (New York), 1964.

Blanco, Richard L., *Rommel, the Desert Warrior: The Afrika Korps in World War II,* J. Mesmer (New York), 1982.

Brook-Shepherd, Gordon, *Anschluss: The Rape of Austria,* Macmillan & Company (London), 1963.

Churchill, Winston S., *The Second World War: The Gathering Storm, Vol. 1,* Cassell (London), 1948.

Ciano, Galeazzo, conte, *The Ciano Diaries, 1939–1943*, edited by H. Gibson, Doubleday (Garden City, NY), 1946.

Collier, Basil, *The Battle of Britain*, B.T. Batsford (London), 1962.

Collier, Richard, *The Sands of Dunkirk*, E. P. Dutton (New York), 1961.

Cook, Don, *Charles de Gaulle: A Biography*, Putnam (New York), 1983.

Corti, Eugenio, *Few Returned: Twenty-Eight Days on the Russian Front, Winter 1942–1943*, University of Missouri Press (Columbia, MO), 1997.

De Gaulle, Charles, *Memoirs of Hope, 1958–62*, Simon & Schuster (New York), 1971.

Drieman, J. E., editor, *Winston Churchill: An Unbreakable Spirit*, Dillon Press (Minneapolis, MN), 1990.

FitzGibbon, Constantine, *London's Burning*, Ballantine Books (New York), 1970.

Gehl, Jürgen, *Austria, Germany, and the Anschluss, 1931–1938*, Oxford University Press (New York), 1963.

Hoobler, Dorothy, and Thomas Hoobler, *World Leaders Past and Present: Joseph Stalin*, Chelsea House (New York), 1985.

Humble, Richard, *U-Boat*, Franklin Watts (New York), 1990.

James, Robert Rhodes, editor, *Winston S. Churchill: His Complete Speeches 1897–1963*, Chelsea House (New York), 1974.

Keller, Mollie, *Winston Churchill*, F. Watts (New York), 1984.

Kronenwetter, Michael, *Cities at War: London*, New Discovery Books (New York), 1992.

Lane, Tony, *The Merchant Seamen's War*, Manchester University Press (Manchester, England), 1990.

Lewis, Jonathon, and Phillip Whitehead, *Stalin: A Time for Judgment*, Pantheon (New York), 1990.

Macintyre, Donald G. F. W., *Narvik*, W.W. Norton & Company (New York), 1960.

Manchester, William, *The Last Lion: Winston Spencer Churchill* Little, Brown (Boston), 1983–88.

Marrin, Albert, *Stalin*, Viking Kestrel (New York), 1988.

McNeal, Robert, *Stalin: Man and Ruler*, New York University Press (New York), 1988.

Medvedev, Roy, *Let History Judge: The Origins and Consequences of Stalinism*, Columbia University Press (New York), 1989.

Mellor, John, *Forgotten Heroes: The Canadians at Dieppe*, Methuen (Toronto), 1975.

Payne, Robert, *The Great Man: A Portrait of Winston Churchill*, Coward, McCann and Geoghegan (New York), 1974.

Pitt, Barrie, and the editors of Time-Life Books, *The Battle of the Atlantic*, Time-Life Books (Alexandria, VA), 1977.

Reynaud, Paul, *In the Thick of the Fight*, translated by J. D. Lambert, Simon and Schuster (New York), 1955.

Reynolds, Quentin James, *The Battle of Britain*, Random House (New York), 1953.

Rose, Norman, *Churchill: The Unruly Giant*, Free Press (New York), 1994.

Ross, Stewart, *World Leaders*, Thomson Learning (New York), 1993.

Ryan, Cornelius, *A Bridge Too Far*, Simon and Schuster (New York), 1995.

Schoenfeld, Maxwell P., *Sir Winston Churchill: His Life and Times*, second edition, R.E. Krieger (Malabar, FL), 1986.

Severance, John B., *Winston Churchill: Soldier, Statesman, Artist*, Clarion Books (New York), 1996.

Shirer, William L., *The Collapse of the Third Republic*, Simon and Schuster (New York), 1969.

Shirer, William L., *The Sinking of the Bismarck*, Random House (New York), 1962.

Simon, Yves, *The Road to Vichy, 1918–1938*, translated by James A. Corbett and George J. McMorrow, Sheed and Ward (New York), 1942.

Skipper, G. C., *The Battle of Britain*, Children's Press (Chicago), 1980.

Skipper, G. C., *Battle of Stalingrad*, Children's Press (Chicago), 1981.

Skipper, G. C., *The Battle of the Atlantic*, Children's Press (Chicago), 1981.

Skipper, G. C., *Fall of the Fox, Rommel*, Children's Press (Chicago), 1980.

Skipper, G. C., *Goering and the Luftwaffe*, Children's Press (Chicago), 1980.

Skipper, G. C., *Invasion of Sicily*, Children's Press (Chicago), 1981.

Sloan, Frank, *Bismarck!*, Franklin Watts (New York), 1991.

Snell, John L., *Illusion and Necessity*, Houghton Mifflin (Boston), 1963.

Souster, Raymond, *Jubilee of Death: The Raid on Dieppe*, Oberon Press (Ottawa, Ontario, Canada), 1984.

Stein, R. Conrad, *Dunkirk*, Children's Press (Chicago), 1982.

Stein, R. Conrad, *Invasion of Russia*, Children's Press (Chicago), 1985.

Stein, R. Conrad, *Siege of Leningrad*, Children's Press (Chicago), 1983.

Taylor, Theodore, *Battle of the Arctic Seas: The Story of Convoy PQ 17*, Crowell (New York), 1976.

Topp, Erich, *The Odyssey of a U-Boat Commander: Recollections of Erich Topp*, translated by Eric C. Rust, Praeger (Westport, CT), 1992.

Ulam, Adam, *Stalin, the Man and His Era*, Beacon Press (Boston), 1989.

Vause, Jordan, and Jurgen Oesten, *Wolf: U-Boat Commanders in World War II*, Airlife (Osceola, WI), 1997.

Warth, Robert D., *Joseph Stalin*, Twayne (New York), 1969.

Weygand, Maxime, *Recalled to Service*, William Heinemann (London), 1952.

Whitelaw, Nancy, *Joseph Stalin: From Peasant to Premier*, Dillon Press (New York), 1992.

Woodrooffe, T., *The Battle of the Atlantic*, Faber (New York), 1965.

Germany:

Allen, William Sheridan, *The Nazi Seizure of Power: The Experience of a Single German Town, 1922–1945*, Franklin Watts (New York), 1984.

Ayer, Eleanor, *Adolf Hitler*, Lucent (San Diego), 1996.

Ayer, Eleanor, *Cities at War: Berlin*, New Discovery Books (New York), 1992.

Baynes, Norman H., editor, *The Speeches of Adolf Hitler, April 1922–August 1939: An English Translation of Representative Passages*, Gordon Press (New York), 1981.

Berman, Russell A., *Paul von Hindenburg*, Chelsea House (New York), 1987.

Binion, Rudolph, *Hitler among the Germans*, Elsevier (Amsterdam), 1976.

Bracher, Karl Dietrich, *The German Dictatorship: The Origins, Structure, and Effects of National Socialism*, Praeger (New York), 1970.

Bullock, Alan, *Hitler: A Study in Tyranny*, Harper and Row (New York), 1971.

Clark, Alan, *Barbarossa: The Russian-German Conflict, 1941–1945*, William Morrow (New York), 1965.

Eimerl, Sarel, *Hitler over Europe; The Road to World War II*, Little, Brown (Boston), 1972.

Fest, Joachim C., *The Face of the Third Reich: Portraits of the Nazi Leadership*, Pantheon (New York), 1970.

Friedman, Ina R., *The Other Victims: First-Person Stories of Non-Jews Persecuted by the Nazis*, Houghton Mifflin (Boston), 1990.

Gallagher, Hugh Gregory, *By Trust Betrayed: Patients, Physicians, and the License to Kill in the Third Reich*, Holt (New York), 1990.

Gilbert, Felix, editor, *Hitler Directs His War: The Secret Records of His Daily Military Conferences*, Octagon Books (New York), 1982.

Goldston, Robert C., *The Life and Death of Nazi Germany*, Bobbs-Merrill (Indianapolis), 1967.

Gordon, Harold J., *Hitler and the Beer Hall Putsch*, Princeton University Press (Princeton, NJ), 1972.

Harris, Nathaniel, *Hitler*, Trafalgar (North Pomfret, VT), 1989.

Hauner, Milan, *Hitler: A Chronology of His Life and Time*, St. Martin's Press (New York), 1983.

Heyes, Eileen, *Adolf Hitler*, Millbrook Press (Brookfield, CT), 1993.

Hitler, Adolf, *Mein Kampf*, translated by Ralph Manheim, Houghton Mifflin (Boston), 1971.

Johnson, Eric A., *Nazi Terror: The Gestapo, Jews, and Ordinary Germans*, Basic Books (New York), 2000.

Kershaw, Ian, *The "Hitler Myth": Image and Reality in the Third Reich*, Oxford University Press (New York), 1987.

Klemperer, Victor, *I Will Bear Witness 1941–1945: A Diary of the Nazi Years,* Volume 2, Random House (New York), 1998.

Langer, Walter C., *The Mind of Adolf Hitler: The Secret Wartime Report,* Basic Books (New York), 1972.

Manvell, Roger, *SS and the Gestapo,* Ballantine Books (New York), 1969.

Massaquoi, Hans J., *Destined to Witness: Growing Up Black in Nazi Germany,* W. Morrow (New York), 1999.

Merkl, Peter H., *The Making of a Stormtrooper,* Princeton University Press (Princeton, NJ), 1980.

Nevelle, Peter, *Life in the Third Reich: World War II,* Batsford (North Pomfret, VT), 1992.

Pulzer, Peter G., *The Rise of Political Anti-Semitism in Germany and Austria: 1867–1918,* John Wiley (New York), 1964.

Rich, Norman, *Hitler's War Aims,* W. W. Norton (New York), 1973.

Seaton, Albert, *The Russo-German War, 1941–1945,* Frederick A. Praeger (New York), 1970.

Shirer, William L., *Berlin Diary,* Knopf (New York), 1941.

Shirer, William L., *Twentieth Century Journey: A Memoir of a Life and the Times,* Volume 2, *The Nightmare Years, 1930–1940,* Bantam Books (New York), 1984.

Speer, Albert, *Inside the Third Reich,* Galahad Books (New York), 1995.

Spence, William, *Germany Then and Now,* Franklin Watts (New York), 1994.

Stein, R. Conrad, *Hitler Youth,* Children's Press (Chicago), 1985.

Stern, Fritz, *Dreams and Delusions: The Drama of German History,* Yale University Press (New Haven, CT), 1999.

Steward, Gail B., *Hitler's Reich,* Lucent Books (San Diego), 1994.

Tames, Richard, *Nazi Germany,* Batsford (North Pomfret, VT), 1992.

Toland, John, *Adolf Hitler,* Anchor Books (New York), 1992.

Wepman, Dennis, *Adolf Hitler,* Chelsea House (New York), 1989.

Williamson, David, *The Third Reich,* Bookwright Press (New York), 1989.

Italy and Fascism:

Chrisp, Peter, *The Rise of Fascism,* Bookwright Press (New York), 1991.

Hartenian, Lawrence R., *Benito Mussolini,* Chelsea House (New York), 1988.

Knox, MacGregor, *Mussolini Unleashed, 1939–1941: Politics and Strategy in Fascist Italy's Last War,* Cambridge University Press (New York), 1986.

Leeds, Christopher, *Italy under Mussolini,* Putnam (New York), 1972.

Lyttle, Richard, *Il Duce: The Rise and Fall of Benito Mussolini,* Atheneum (New York), 1987.

Moseley, Ray, *Mussolini's Shadow: The Double Life of Count Galeazzo Ciano,* Yale University Press, (New Haven, CT) 2000.

Stille, Alexander, *Benevolence and Betrayal: Five Italian Jewish Families Under Fascism,* Summit Books (New York), 1991.

Wiskemann, Elizabeth, *The Rome-Berlin Axis: A History of the Relations Between Hitler and Mussolini,* Oxford University Press (London), 1949.

Japan:

Barker, Rodney, *The Hiroshima Maidens: A Story of Courage, Compassion, and Survival,* Penguin Books (New York), 1985.

Behr, Edward, *Hirohito: Beyond the Myth,* Villard Books (New York), 1989.

Black, Wallace B., and Jean F. Blashfield, *Hiroshima and the Atomic Bomb,* Crestwood House (New York), 1993.

Butow, Robert J. C., *Tojo and the Coming of the War,* Stanford University Press (Stanford, CA), 1969.

Grant, R. G., *Hiroshima and Nagasaki,* Raintree, Steck-Vaughn (Austin, TX), 1988.

Hersey, John, *Hiroshima,* Vintage Books (New York), 1989.

Hogan, Michael J., editor, *Hiroshima in History and Memory,* Cambridge University Press (New York), 1996.

Hoobler, Dorothy, and Thomas Hoobler, *Showa: The Age of Hirohito,* Walker (New York), 1990.

Maruki, Toshi, *Hiroshima No Pika*, Lothrop, Lee & Shepard (New York), 1982.

Oe, Kenzaburo, *Hiroshima Notes*, Grove Press (New York), 1996.

Sekimori, Gaynor, *Hibakusha: Survivors of Hiroshima and Nagasaki*, Kosei (Tokyo), 1986.

Selden, Kyoko, and Mark Selden, editors, *The Atomic Bomb: Voices from Hiroshima and Nagasaki*, M.E. Sharpe (Armonk, NJ), 1989.

Severns, Karen, *Hirohito*, Chelsea House (New York), 1988.

Sherrow, Victoria, *Hiroshima*, New Discovery Books (New York), 1994.

Sherwin, Martin J., *A World Destroyed: Hiroshima and the Origins of the Arms Race*, Stanford University Press (Stanford, CA), 2000.

Stein, R. Conrad, *Hiroshima*, Children's Press (Chicago), 1982.

Japanese War Crimes:

Askin, Kelly Dawn, *War Crimes Against Women: Prosecution in International War Crimes Tribunals*, Martinus Nijhoff (The Hague), 1997.

Brackman, Arnold C., *The Other Nuremberg: The Untold Story of the Tokyo War Crimes Trials*, Morrow (New York), 1987.

Ginn, John L., *Sugamo Prison, Tokyo: An Account of the Trial and Sentencing of Japanese War Criminals in 1948, by a U.S. Participant*, McFarland (Jefferson, NC), 1992.

Hosoya, Chihiro, et. al., *The Tokyo War Crimes Trial: An International Symposium*, Kodansha (Tokyo), 1986.

International Military Tribunal for the Far East, *The Tokyo Major War Crimes Trial: The Records of the International Military Tribunal for the Far East: With an Authoritative Commentary and Comprehensive Guide*, edited by R. John Pritchard, published for the Robert M.W. Kempner Collegium by Edwin Mellen Press (Lewiston, NY), 1998.

Minear, Richard H., *Victor's Justice: The Tokyo War Crimes Trial*, Princeton University Press (Princeton, NJ), 1971.

Piccigallo, Philip, *The Japanese on Trial: Allied War Crimes Operations in the East, 1945–1951*, University of Texas Press (Austin, TX), 1979.

Röling, Bernard Victor Aloysius, *The Tokyo Trial and Beyond: Reflections of a Peacemonger*, Polity Press (Cambridge, England), 1993.

Tanaka, Toshiyuki, *Hidden Horrors: Japanese War Crimes in World War II*, Westview Press (Boulder, CO), 1996.

The United States:

Ambrose, Stephen E., *Band of Brothers: E Company, 506th Regiment, 101st Airborne from Normandy to Hitler's Eagle Nest*, Simon and Schuster (New York), 1992.

Ambrose, Stephen E., *The Victors: Eisenhower and His Boys: The Men of World War II*, Simon and Schuster (New York), 1998.

Bernstein, Alison R., *American Indians and World War II: Toward a New Era in Indian Affairs*, University of Oklahoma Press (Norman, OK), 1999.

Brimner, Larry Dane, *Voices from the Camps*, Franklin Watts (New York), 1994.

Brokaw, Tom, *The Greatest Generation*, Random House (New York), 1998.

Brokaw, Tom, *The Greatest Generation Speaks: Letters and Reflections*, Random House (New York), 1999.

Burns, James M., *Roosevelt: The Soldier of Freedom*, Harvest/Harcourt (New York), 1973.

Cannon, Marian, *Dwight David Eisenhower: War Hero and President*, Franklin Watts (New York), 1990.

Cohen, Stan, *V for Victory: America's Home Front During World War II*, Pictorial Histories Publishing (Missoula, MT), 1991.

Darby, Jean, *Douglas MacArthur*, Lerner (Minneapolis, MN), 1989.

Davis, Kenneth S., *FDR: The New Deal Years, 1933–1937*, Random House (New York), 1979.

Davis, Kenneth S., *FDR: The New York Years, 1928–1933*, Random House (New York), 1979.

Devaney, John, *Franklin Delano Roosevelt, President*, Walker (New York), 1987.

Divine, Robert A., *The Reluctant Belligerent: American Entry into World War II*, John Wiley and Sons (New York), 1965.

Dolan, Edward F., *America in World War II: 1942*, Millbrook Press (Brookfield, CT), 1991.

Dolan, Edward F., *America in World War II: 1943*, Millbrook Press (Brookfield, CT), 1992.

Donovan, Robert J., *PT 109: John F. Kennedy in World War II*, McGraw-Hill (New York), 1961.

Duden, Jane, *1940s*, Crestwood (New York), 1989.

Francis, Charles E., *The Tuskegee Airmen: The Men Who Changed a Nation*, Branden Publishing (Boston), 1993.

Freedman, Russell, *Franklin Delano Roosevelt*, Franklin Watts (New York), 1983.

Fremon, David K., *Japanese American Internment in American History*, Enslow Publishers (Springfield, NJ), 1966.

Gilbo, Patrick F., *The American Red Cross: The First Century*, Harper and Row, Publishers (New York), 1981.

Goodwin, Doris Kearns, *No Ordinary Time, Franklin and Eleanor Roosevelt: The Home Front in World War II*, Simon and Schuster (New York), 1994.

Graham, Otis L., Jr., and Meghan Robinson Wander, editors, *Franklin D. Roosevelt, His Life and Times: An Encyclopedic View*, G. K. Hall (Boston), 1985.

Hacker, Jeffrey H., *Franklin D. Roosevelt*, Franklin Watts (New York), 1983.

Harris, Jacqueline L., *The Tuskegee Airmen: Black Heroes of World War II*, Dillon Press (Parsippany, NJ), 1995.

Harris, Mark Jonathan, Franklin Mitchell, and Steven Schechter, editors, *The Homefront: America during World War II*, G. P. Putnam's Sons (New York), 1984.

Holway, John B., *Red Tail Black Wings: The Men of America's Black Air Force*, Yucca Tree (Las Cruces, NM), 1997.

Homan, Lynn M., and Thomas Reilly, *Tuskegee Airmen*, Arcadia Tempus Publishing Group (Charleston, SC), 1998.

Langer, William L., and S. Everett Gleason, *The Undeclared War, 1940–1941*, P. Smith (Gloucester, MA), 1968.

Lawson, Ted W., *Thirty Seconds Over Tokyo*, Buccaneer Books, 1999.

Levine, Ellen, *A Fence Away from Freedom*, G. P. Putnam (New York), 1995.

Mauldin, Bill, *Back Home*, William Sloane Associates (New York), 1947.

Mauldin, Bill, *The Brass Ring*, W. W. Norton (New York), 1971.

McKissack, Patricia, and Frederick McKissack, *Red-Tail Angels: The Story of the Tuskegee Airmen of World War II*, Walker (New York), 1995.

Miller, Nathan, *FDR: An Intimate History*, originally published in 1983, reprinted, Madison Books/University Press of America (Lanham, MD), 1991.

Morgan, Ted, *FDR: A Biography*, Simon and Schuster (New York), 1985.

Murphy, Audie, *To Hell and Back*, Holt (New York), 1949.

O'Connor, Barbara, *The Soldiers' Voice: The Story of Ernie Pyle*, Carolrhoda Books (Minneapolis, MN), 1996.

Olesky, Walter, *Military Leaders of World War II*, Facts on File (New York), 1994.

Perkins, Frances, *The Roosevelt I Knew*, Viking (New York), 1946.

Pfeifer, Kathryn Browne, *The 761st Tank Battalion*, Henry Holt (New York), 1994.

Pyle, Ernie, *Brave Men*, Henry Holt (New York), 1944.

Rubenstein, Harry R., and William L. Bird, *Design for Victory: World War II Posters on the American Home Front*, Princeton Architectural Press (New York), 1998.

Spies, Karen Bornemann, *Franklin D. Roosevelt*, Enslow (Springfield, NJ), 1999.

Stanley, Jerry, *I Am an American: A True Story of Japanese Internment*, Crown (New York), 1994.

Stein, R. Conrad, *The Home Front*, Children's Press (Chicago), 1986.

Stein, R. Conrad, *Nisei Regiment*, Children's Press (Chicago), 1985.

Sweeney, James B., *Famous Aviators of World War II*, Franklin Watts (New York), 1987.

Uchida, Yoshika, *Desert Exile: The Uprooting of a Japanese-American Family*, University of Washington Press (Seattle), 1982.

Whitman, Sylvia, *Uncle Sam Wants You: Military Men and Women in World War II*, Lerner (Minneapolis, MN), 1993.

Whitman, Sylvia, *V Is for Victory*, Lerner (Minneapolis, MN), 1993.

Woodrow, Martin, *The World War II GI*, Franklin Watts (New York), 1986.

Wrynn, V. Dennis, *Detroit Goes to War: The American Automobile Industry in World War II*, Motorbooks International (Osceola, WI), 1993.

Women and the War:

Bowman, Constance, *Slacks and Calluses: Our Summer in a Bomber Factory*, illustrated by Clara Marie Allen, Smithsonian Institution Press (Washington, DC), 1999.

Carl, Ann B., *A Wasp Among Eagles: A Woman Military Test Pilot in World War II*, Smithsonian Institution Press (Washington, DC), 1999.

Cole, Jean Hascall, *Women Pilots of World War II*, University of Utah Press (Salt Lake City, UT), 1992.

Colijn, Helen, *Song of Survival: Women Interned*, White Cloud Press (Ashland, OR), 1995.

Colman, Penny, *Rosie the Riveter: Women Working on the Home Front in World War II*, Crown (New York), 1995.

Danner, Dorothy Still, *What a Way to Spend a War: Navy Nurse POWs in the Philippines*, Naval Institute Press (Annapolis, MD), 1995.

Fessler, Diane Burke, *No Time for Fear: Voices of American Military Nurses in World War II*, Michigan State University Press (East Lansing, MI), 1996.

Frank, Miriam, Marilyn Ziebarth, and Connie Field, *The Life and Times of Rosie the Riveter: The Story of Three Million Working Women during World War II*, Clarity Educational Productions (Emeryville, CA), 1982.

Green, Anne Bosanko, and D'Ann Campbell, *One Woman's War: Letters Home from the Women's Army Corps, 1944–1946*, Minnesota Historical Society (St. Paul, MN), 1989.

Gruhzit-Hoyt, Olga, *They Also Served: American Women in World War II*, Birch Lane Press (Secaucus, NJ), 1995.

Gunter, Helen Clifford, *Navy WAVE: Memories of World War II*, Cypress House (Fort Bragg, CA), 1994.

Hicks, George L., *The Comfort Women: Japan's Brutal Regime of Enforced Prostitution in the Second World War*, W.W. Norton & Company (New York), 1995.

Holm, Jeanne, and Judith Bellafaire, editors, *In Defense of a Nation: Servicewomen in World War II*, Vandamere Press (Arlington, VA), 1998.

Honey, Maureen, editor, *Bitter Fruit: African American Women in World War II*, University of Missouri Press (Columbia, MO), 1999.

Howard, Keith, editor, *True Stories of the Korean Comfort Women*, Cassell (London), 1995.

Jopling, Lucy Wilson, *Warrior in White*, Watercress Press (San Antonio, TX), 1990.

Kaminski, Theresa, *Prisoners in Paradise: American Women in the Wartime South Pacific*, University Press of Kansas (Lawrence, KS), 2000.

Keith, Agnes Newton, *Three Came Home*, Little, Brown (Boston, MA), 1947.

Kelsey, Marion, *Victory Harvest: Diary of a Canadian in the Women's Land Army, 1940–1944*, McGill-Queens University Press (Toronto), 1997.

Lucas, Celia, *Prisoners of Santo Tomas: A True Account of Women POWs Under Japanese Control*, Cooper (London), 1975.

Monahan, Evelyn M., and Rosemary Neidel-Greenlee, *All This Hell: U.S. Nurses Imprisoned by the Japanese*, University of Kentucky Press (Lexington, KY), 2000.

Noggle, Anne, and Dora Dougherty Strother, *For God, Country, and the Thrill of It: Women Airforce Pilots in World War II*, Texas A&M University Press (College Station, TX), 1990.

Norman, Elizabeth M., *We Band of Angels: The Untold Story of American Nurses Trapped on Bataan by the Japanese*, Random House (New York), 1999.

Nova, Lily, and Iven Lourie, editors, *Interrupted Lives: Four Women's Stories of Internment During World War II in the Philippines*, Artemis Books (Nevada City, CA), 1995.

Reynoldson, Floria, *Women and War*, Thomson Learning (New York), 1993.

Scharr, Adela Riek, *Sisters in the Sky, Volume 1: The WAFS*, Patrice Press (St. Louis, MO), 1986.

Scharr, Adela Riek, *Sisters in the Sky, Volume 2: The WASP*, Patrice Press (St. Louis, MO), 1988.

Sinott, Susan, *Doing Our Part: American Women on the Home Front during World War II*, Franklin Watts (New York), 1995.

Tomblin, Barbara Brooks, *G. I. Nightingales: The Army Nurse Corps in World War II,* University Press of Kentucky (Lexington, KY), 1996.

Treadwell, Mattie E., *United States Army in World War II: Special Studies: The Women's Army Corps,* Office of the Chief of Military History, Department of the Army (Washington, DC), 1954.

Weatherford, Doris, *American Women and World War II,* Facts on File (New York), 1992.

Weitz, Margaret Collins, *Sisters in the Resistance: How Women Fought to Free France, 1940–1945,* John Wiley and Sons (New York), 1998.

Williams, Vera S., *WACs: Women's Army Corps,* Motorbooks International Publishers, 1997.

Williams, Vera S., *Women Airforce Service Pilots of World War II,* Motorbooks International Publishers (Osceola, WI), 1994.

Wise, Nancy Baker, and Christy Wise, *A Mouthful of Rivets: Women at Work in World War II,* Jossey-Bass (San Francisco, CA), 1994.

Zeinert, Karen, *Those Incredible Women of World War II,* Millbrook Press (Brookfield, CT), 1994.

Children in the War:

Bertini, Tullio Bruno, *Trapped in Tuscany, Liberated by the Buffalo Soldiers: The True World War II Story of Tullio Bruno Bertini,* Dante University Press (Boston), 1998.

Besson, Jean-Louis, *October 45: Childhood Memories of the War,* Creative Editions (Mankato, MN), 1995.

Butterworth, Emma Macalik, *As the Waltz Was Ending,* Four Winds (New York), 1982.

Chapman, Fern Schumer, *Motherland: A Daughter's Journey to Reclaim the Past,* Viking (New York), 2000.

Cross, Robin, *Children and War,* Thomson Learning (New York), 1994.

Drucker, Olga Levy, *Kindertransport,* Henry Holt (New York), 1992.

Emmerich, Elsbeth, *My Childhood in Nazi Germany,* Bookwright Press (New York), 1991.

Foreman, Michael, *War Boy: A Country Childhood,* Arcade (New York), 1990.

Heyes, Eileen, *Children of the Swastika: The Hitler Youth,* Millbrook Press (Brookfield, CT), 1993.

Holliday, Laurel, *Children in the Holocaust and World War II,* Pocket Books (New York), 1995.

Isaacman, Clara, *Clara's Story,* Jewish Publication Society (Philadelphia), 1984.

Kuper, Jack, *Child of the Holocaust,* Berkley Books (New York), 1993.

Loy, Rosetta, *First Words: A Childhood in Fascist Italy,* Metropolitan Books/Henry Holt (New York) 2000.

Lukas, Richard C., *Did the Children Cry?: Hitler's War Against Jewish and Polish Children, 1939–1945,* Hippocrene Books (New York), 1994.

Marx, Trish, *Echoes of World War II,* Lerner (Minneapolis, MN), 1994.

Nicholson, Dorinda Makanaonalani Stagner, *Pearl Harbor Child: A Child's View of Pearl Harbor— From Attack to Peace,* Arizona Memorial Museum Association (Honolulu), 1993.

Silwowska, Wiktoria, editor, *The Last Eyewitnesses: Children of the Holocaust Speak,* Northwestern University Press (Evanston, IL), 1998.

Stalcup, Ann, *On the Home Front: Growing up in Wartime England,* Linnet Books (North Haven, CT), 1998.

Toll, Nelly S., *Behind the Secret Window: A Memoir of a Hidden Childhood During World War II,* Dial Books (New York), 1993.

Tunnell, Michael O., and George W. Chilcoat, *The Children of Topaz,* Holiday House (New York), 1996.

Ungerer, Tomi, *A Childhood under the Nazis,* Tomic (Niwot, CO), 1998.

Wassiljewa, Tatjana, *Hostage to War,* Scholastic Press (New York), 1997.

Wilkomirski, Binjamin, *Fragments: Memories of a Wartime Childhood,* Schocken Books (New York), 1997.

Wojciechowska, Maia, *Till the Break of Day,* Harcourt, Brace, Jovanovich (New York), 1972.

Events in Europe, 1944 and Later:

Alperovitz, Gar, *Atomic Diplomacy: Hiroshima and Potsdam,* Simon and Schuster (New York), 1965.

Ambrose, Stephen E., *Citizen Soldiers: The U.S. Army from the Normandy Beaches to the Bulge to the Surrender of Germany,* Simon & Schuster (New York), 1997.

Balkoski, Joseph, *Beyond the Beachhead: The 29th Infantry Division in Normandy,* Stackpole Books (Mechanicsburg, PA), 1999.

Banfield, Susan, *Charles de Gaulle,* Chelsea House (New York), 1985.

Black, Wallace B., *Battle of the Bulge,* Crestwood House (New York), 1993.

Bliven, Bruce, *The Story of D-Day: June 6, 1944,* Random House (New York), 1956.

Bourke-White, Margaret, *"Dear Fatherland, Rest Quietly": A Report on the Collapse of Hitler's "Thousand Years,"* Simon and Schuster (New York), 1946.

Collins, Larry, and Dominique Lapierre, *Is Paris Burning?,* Castle, 2000.

Conot, Robert E., *Justice at Nuremberg,* Harper (New York), 1983.

Dolan, Edward F., *The Fall of Hitler's Germany,* Franklin Watts (New York), 1988.

Evans, Richard J., *In Hitler's Shadow: West German Historians and the Attempt to Escape from the Nazi Past,* Pantheon (New York), 1989.

Feis, Herbert, *Between War and Peace: The Potsdam Conference,* Princeton University Press (Princeton, NJ), 1960.

Goldstein, Donald M., Katherine V. Dillon, and J. Michael Wenger, *Nuts! The Battle of the Bulge: The Story and Photographs,* Brassey's (Washington, DC), 1994.

Hine, Al, *D-Day: The Invasion of Europe,* American Heritage Publishing Company (New York), 1962.

Keegan, John, *Six Armies in Normandy: From D-Day to the Liberation of Paris,* Penguin (New York), 1994.

Lamb, Richard, *War in Italy 1943–1945: A Brutal Story,* Da Capo Press (New York), 1996.

MacDonald, Charles B., *The Mighty Endeavor: American Armed Forces in the European Theater in World War II,* Da Capo Press (New York), 1992.

MacDonald, Charles B., *A Time for Trumpets: The Untold Story of the Battle of the Bulge,* Bantam Books (New York), 1985.

Marrin, Albert, *Overlord: D-Day and the Invasion of Europe,* Atheneum (New York), 1982.

Morin, Isobel V., *Days of Judgment,* Millbrook Press (Brookfield, CT), 1995.

Posner, Gerald L., *Hitler's Children: Sons and Daughters of the Third Reich Talk about Their Fathers and Themselves,* Random House (New York), 1991.

Rice, Earl, *The Nuremberg Trials,* Lucent Books (San Diego), 1997.

Ryan, Cornelius, *The Last Battle,* Simon & Schuster (New York), 1966.

Ryan, Cornelius, *The Longest Day: June 6, 1944,* Simon and Schuster (New York), 1994.

Sheehan, Fred, and Martin Blumenson, *Anzio, Epic of Bravery,* University of Oklahoma Press (Norman, OK), 1994.

Skipper, G. C., *Death of Hitler,* Children's Press (Chicago), 1980.

Skipper, G. C., *Mussolini: A Dictator Dies,* Children's Press (Chicago), 1981.

Stein, R. Conrad, *World War II in Europe: America Goes to War,* Enslow Press (Hillside, NJ), 1984.

Toland, John, *The Last 100 Days,* Random House (New York), 1966.

United States Department of State, *The Conferences at Malta and Yalta, 1945,* Greenwood Press (Westport, CT), 1976.

Whitelaw, Nancy, *A Biography of General Charles de Gaulle,* Dillon Press (New York), 1991.

Secret Codes and Weapons, Spies, and Sabotage:

Aldrich, Richard J., *Intelligence and the War Against Japan: Britain, America and the Politics of Secret Service,* Cambridge University Press (New York), 2000.

Alvarez, David J., editor, *Allied and Axis Signals Intelligence in World War II,* Frank Cass (Portland, OR), 1999.

Alvarez, David J., *Secret Messages: Codebreaking and American Diplomacy, 1930–1945,* University of Kansas Press (Lawrence, KS), 2000.

Ambrose, Stephen E., and Richard H. Immerman, *Ike's Spies: Eisenhower and the Espionage Establishment,* University Press of Mississippi (Jackson, MS), 1999.

Andryszewski, Tricia, *The Amazing Life of Moe Berg: Catcher, Scholar, Spy,* Millbrook Press (Brookfield, CT), 1996.

Bixler, Margaret T., *Winds of Freedom: The Story of the Navajo Code Talkers of World War II,* Two Bytes (Darien, CT), 1992.

Breuer, William B., *MacArthur's Undercover War: Spies, Saboteurs, Guerillas, and Secret Missions,* John Wiley and Sons (New York), 1995.

Daily, Robert, *The Code Talkers,* Franklin Watts (New York), 1995.

Durrett, Deanne, *Unsung Heroes of World War II: The Story of the Navajo Code Talkers,* Facts on File (New York), 1998.

Gardner, W. J. R., *Decoding History: The Battle of the Atlantic and Ultra,* United States Naval Institute (Annapolis, MD), 2000.

Goldston, Robert C., *Sinister Touches: The Secret War Against Hitler,* Dial Press (New York), 1992.

Halter, Jon C., *Top Secret Projects of World War II,* J. Messner (New York), 1978.

Harper, Stephen, *Capturing Enigma: How HMS Petard Seized the German Naval Codes,* Sutton Publishing, 2000.

Hinsley, Francis H., *British Intelligence in the Second World War,* Cambridge University Press (New York), 1993.

Hodgson, Lynn-Philip, *Inside—Camp X,* Blake Books, 1999.

Hohne, Heinz, *Canaris: Hitler's Master Spy,* Cooper Square Press (New York), 1999.

Holmes, W. J., *Double-Edged Secrets: U.S. Naval Intelligence Operations in the Pacific During World War II,* United States Naval Institute (Annapolis, MD), 1998.

Jakub, Jay, *Spies and Saboteurs: Anglo-American Collaboration and Rivalry in Human Intelligence Collection and Special Operations,* St. Martin's Press (New York), 1999.

Johnson, David Allen, *Germany's Spies and Saboteurs,* Motorbooks International (Osceola, WI), 1998.

Jones, Catherine, *Navajo Code Talkers: Native American Heroes,* Tudor Publications (Greensboro, NC), 1997.

Kahn, David A., *Hitler's Spies: German Military Intelligence in World War II,* Da Capo Press (Cambridge, MA), 2000.

Kilzer, Louis, *Hitler's Traitor: Martin Bormann and the Defeat of the Reich,* Presidio Press (Novato, CA), 2000.

Kiyosaki, Wayne S., and Daniel K. Akaka, *A Spy in Their Midst: The World War II Struggle of a Japanese-American Hero,* Madison Books (Lanham, MD), 1995.

Lawson, Don, *The Secret World War II,* Franklin Watts (New York), 1978.

MacDonnell, Francis, *Insidious Foes: The Axis Fifth Column and the American Home Front,* Oxford University Press (New York), 1995.

Marks, Leo, *Between Silk and Cyanide: A Codemaker's War 1941–1945,* Free Press (New York), 1999.

Marrin, Albert, *The Secret Armies,* Atheneum (New York), 1985.

McIntosh, Elizabeth P., *Sisterhood of Spies: The Women of the OSS,* GK Hall (Thorndike, ME), 2000.

Moon, Tom, *This Grim and Savage Game: The OSS and the Beginning of U.S. Covert Operations in World War II,* Da Capo Press (Cambridge, MA), 2000.

Paul, Doris A., *The Navajo Code Talkers,* Dorrance (Philadelphia, PA), 1973.

Paz Salinas, Maria Emilia, *Strategy, Security, and Spies: Mexico and the U.S. as Allies in World War II,* Pennsylvania State University Press (University Park, PA), 1997.

Rogers, James T., *The Secret War: Espionage in World War II,* Facts on File (New York), 1991.

Showell, Jak P. Mallman, *Enigma U-Boats: Breaking the Code—The True Story,* Naval Institute Press (Annapolis, MD), 2000.

Stevenson, William, *A Man Called Intrepid: The Secret War,* Harcourt, Brace (New York), 1976.

Sutherland, David, *He Who Dares: Recollections of Service in the SAS, SBS, and MI5,* United States Naval Institute (Annapolis, MD), 1999.

Tarrant, V. E., *The Red Orchestra,* John Wiley and Sons (New York), 1996.

Tickell, Jerrard, *Odette: The Story of a British Agent,* Chapman & Hall (London), 1949.

Warriors: Navajo Code Talkers, photographs by Kenji Kawano, Northland (Flagstaff, AZ), 1990.

Wires, Richard, *The Cicero Spy Affair: German Access to British Secrets in World War II,* Praeger (Westport, CT), 1999.

Holocaust and World War II Fiction:

Aaron, David, *Crossing by Night,* Thorndike Press (Thorndike, ME), 1993.

Abbott, Margot, *The Last Innocent Hour: A Novel*, St. Martin's Press (New York), 1991.

Allbeury, Ted, *A Time Without Shadows*, Mysterious Press (New York), 1991.

Allington, Maynard, *The Fox in the Field: A WWII Novel of India*, Brassey's (Washington, DC), 1994.

Amis, Martin, *Time's Arrow*, Harmony Books (New York), 1991.

Appelfeld, Aharon, *The Age of Wonders*, D. R. Godine (Boston), 1981.

Appelfeld, Aharon, *Badenheim 1939*, D. R. Godine (Boston), 1980.

Appelfeld, Aharon, *For Every Sin*, Weidenfeld & Nicolson (New York), 1989.

Appelfeld, Aharon, *Immortal Bartfuss*, Weidenfeld & Nicolson (New York), 1988.

Ballard, J. G., *Empire of the Sun*, V. Gollancz (London), 1984.

Bassani, Giorgio, *The Garden of the Finzi-Continis*, MJF Books (New York), 1996.

Bassett, James, *Cmdr. Prince, USN: A Novel of the Pacific War*, Simon and Schuster (New York), 1971.

Beach, Edward, *Run Silent, Run Deep*, Holt (New York), 1955.

Begley, Louis, *Wartime Lies*, Knopf (New York), 1991.

Bellow, Saul, *The Bellarosa Connection*, Penguin (New York), 1989.

Benchley, Nathaniel, *Bright Candles: A Novel of the Danish Resistance*, Harper and Row (New York), 1974.

Benchley, Nathaniel, *A Necessary End: A Novel of World War II*, Harper and Row (New York), 1976.

Boll, Heinrich, *Billiards at Half-Past Nine*, Weidenfeld and Nicholson (London), 1961.

Booth, Martin, *Hiroshima Joe*, Penguin (New York), 1987.

Boraks-Nemetz, Lillian, *The Old Brown Suitcase: A Teenager's Story of War and Peace*, Ben-Simon Publications (Port Angeles, WA), 1994.

Borowski, Tadeusz, *This Way For the Gas, Ladies and Gentlemen*, Penguin (New York), 1976.

Boulle, Pierre, *The Bridge over the River Kwai*, translated by Xan Fielding, Gramercy Books (New York), 2000.

Boyne, Walter J., *Eagles at War*, Crown (New York), 1991.

Callison, Brian, *A Flock of Ships*, Putnam (New York), 1970.

Clavell, James, *King Rat*, Little, Brown (Boston), 1962.

Dailey, Janet, *Silver Wings, Santiago Blue*, G. K. Hall (Boston), 1984.

De Hartog, Jan, *The Captain*, Atheneum (New York), 1966.

Deighton, Len, *City of Gold*, Thorndike Press (Thorndike, ME), 1992.

Deighton, Len, *Goodbye, Mickey Mouse*, Knopf (New York), 1982.

Deighton, Len, *XPD*, Thorndike Press, Thorndike, ME, 1981.

Demetz, Hanna, *The House on Prague Street*, St. Martin's Press (New York), 1980.

Dickey, James, *To the White Sea*, Houghton Mifflin (Boston), 1993.

Drucker, Malka, and Michael Halperin, *Jacob's Rescue*, Delacorte Press, (New York), 1996.

Drury, Allen, *Toward What Bright Glory?: A Novel*, Morrow (New York), 1990.

Earl, Maureen, *Boat of Stone*, Permanent Press (Sag Harbor, NY), 1993.

Epstein, Leslie, *King of the Jews*, Coward, McCann & Geoghegan (New York), 1979.

Fink, Ida, *The Journey*, Plume (New York), 1993.

Fleming, Thomas, *Loyalties: A Novel of World War II*, HarperCollins (New York), 1994.

Follett, Ken, *Churchill's Gold*, Houghton Mifflin (Boston), 1981.

Follett, Ken, *Eye of the Needle*, G. K. Hall (Boston), 1978.

Follett, Ken, *Night over Water*, Morrow (New York), 1991.

Forester, C. S., *The Good Shepherd*, Little, Brown (Boston), 1955.

Forsyth, Frederick, *The Odessa File*, Viking (New York), 1972.

Garfield, Brian, *The Paladin: A Novel Based on Fact*, Simon and Schuster (New York), 1979.

Gifford, Thomas, *Praetorian,* Bantam (New York), 1993.

Green, Gerald, *Holocaust,* Bantam (New York), 1978.

Greene, Graham, *The Tenth Man,* Simon and Schuster (New York), 1985.

Griffin, W. E. B., *The Corps,* Putnam (New York), 1990.

Griffin, W. E. B., *Honor Bound,* Putnam (New York), 1993.

Griffin, W. E. B., *Line of Fire,* Putnam (New York), 1992.

Harel, Isser, *The House on Garibaldi Street,* Viking Press (New York), 1975.

Harris, Robert, *Enigma,* Random House (New York), 1995.

Harris, Robert, *Fatherland,* Random House (New York), 1992.

Heller, Joseph, *Catch-22,* Dell (New York), 1961.

Hersey, John, *A Bell for Adano,* Knopf (New York), 1944.

Hersey, John, *The Wall,* Knopf (New York), 1950.

Hersey, John, *War Lover,* Knopf (New York), 1959.

Higgins, Jack, *Cold Harbour,* Simon and Schuster (New York), 1990.

Higgins, Jack, *The Eagle Has Flown,* Simon and Schuster (New York), 1991.

Higgins, Jack, *The Eagle Has Landed,* Holt (New York), 1975.

Hill, Grace Livingston, *All Through the Night,* J. B. Lippincott (New York), 1945.

Hunter, Stephen, *The Master Sniper,* Morrow (New York), 1980.

Iles, Greg, *Black Cross,* Dutton (New York), 1995.

Iles, Greg, *Spandau Phoenix,* Dutton (New York), 1993.

Isaacs, Susan, *Shining Through,* G. K. Hall (Boston), 1990.

Jones, James, *From Here to Eternity,* Scribner (New York), 1951.

Jones, James *The Thin Red Line,* Scribner (New York), 1962.

Katkov, Norman, *The Judas Kiss,* Dutton (New York), 1991.

Keneally, Thomas, *Schindler's List,* Simon and Schuster (New York), 1982.

Kerr, M. E., *Gentlehands,* Harper & Row (New York), 1978.

Kis, Danilo, *Hourglass,* translated by Ralph Manheim, Farrar, Straus (New York), 1990.

Klein, Edward, *The Parachutists,* Doubleday (Garden City, NY), 1981.

Korda, Michael, *Worldly Goods,* Random House (New York), 1982.

Kosinski, Jerzy, *The Painted Bird,* Modern Library (New York), 1970.

Kuznetsov, Anatoly, *Babi Yar,* Farrar, Straus and Giroux (New York), 1970.

Lanham, Edwin, *The Clock at 8:16,* Doubleday (Garden City, NY), 1970.

Lay, Beirne, Jr., and Sy Bartlett, *Twelve O'Clock High,* Harper (New York), 1948.

Leboucher, Fernande, *Incredible Mission,* Doubleday (New York), 1969.

Levitin, Sonia, *Annie's Promise,* Atheneum (New York), 1993.

Litewka, Albert, *Warsaw: A Novel of Resistance,* Sheridan Square Press (New York), 1989.

Lowry, Lois, *Number the Stars,* Houghton Mifflin (New York), 1989.

Ludlum, Robert, *The Holcroft Covenant,* R. Marek Publishers (New York), 1978.

MacInnes, Helen, *Above Suspicion,* Little, Brown (Boston), 1941.

MacInnes, Helen, *Assignment in Brittany,* Little, Brown (Boston), 1942.

MacInnes, Helen, *While Still We Live,* Harcourt Brace (New York), 1989.

MacLean, Alistair, *Force 10 from Navarone,* Doubleday (Garden City, NY), 1968.

MacLean, Alistair, *The Guns of Navarone,* Doubleday (Garden City, NY), 1957.

MacLean, Alistair, *H.M.S. Ulysses,* Collins (London), 1955.

MacLean, Alistair, *Where Eagles Dare,* Collins (London), 1967.

Mailer, Norman, *The Naked and the Dead,* Rinehart (New York), 1948.

Marvin, Isabel R., *Bridge to Freedom,* Jewish Publication Society (Philadelphia), 1991.

Matas, Carol, *After the War,* Simon & Schuster (New York), 1996.

Matas, Carol, *Daniel's Story,* Scholastic (New York), 1993.

Matas, Carol, *Lisa's War,* Scholastic (New York), 1987.

Michener, James, *Tales of the South Pacific,* Macmillan (New York), 1947.

Monsarrat, Nicholas, *The Cruel Sea,* Burford Books (Short Hills, NJ), 2000.

Morris, M. E., *The Last Kamikaze,* Random House (New York), 1990.

Nathanson, E. M., *The Dirty Dozen,* Random House (New York), 1955.

Ondaatje, Michael, *The English Patient,* Knopf (New York), 1992.

Orlev, Uri, *The Man from the Other Side,* translated from the Hebrew by Hillel Halkin, Houghton Mifflin (New York), 1989.

Ozick, Cynthia, *The Messiah of Stockholm: A Novel,* Knopf (New York), 1987.

Ozick, Cynthia, *The Shawl,* Knopf (New York), 1989.

Piercy, Marge, *Gone to Soldiers,* Summit Books (New York), 1987.

Provost, Gary, and Gail Levine-Provost, *David and Max,* Jewish Publication Society (Philadelphia), 1988.

Reeman, Douglas, *The Destroyers,* Putnam (New York), 1974.

Remarque, Erich Maria, *Arch of Triumph,* translated by Walter Sorrell and Denver Lindley, Ballantine (New York), 1998.

Remarque, Erich Maria, *The Night in Lisbon,* Harcourt, Brace & World (New York), 1964.

Remarque, Erich Maria, *A Time to Love and a Time to Die,* Harcourt Brace (New York), 1954.

Shaw, Irvin, *Young Lions,* Random House (New York), 1948.

Silman, Roberta, *Beginning the World Again,* Viking (New York), 1990.

Singer, Isaac Bashevis, *Enemies, a Love Story,* Noonday Press (New York), 1989.

Starbird, Kaye, *The Lion in the Lei Shop,* Harcourt, Brace (New York), 1970.

Steinbeck, John, *The Moon Is Down,* Viking (New York), 1942.

Struther, Jan, *Mrs. Miniver,* Harcourt, Brace (New York), 1940.

Taylor, Theodore, *To Kill the Leopard,* Harcourt Brace (New York), 1993.

Thayer, James, *S-Day: A Memoir of the Invasion of England,* St. Martin's Press (New York), 1990.

Thomas, Harlan, *A Yank in the RAF,* Random House (New York), 1941.

Trotter, William R., *Winter Fire,* Dutton (New York), 1993.

Tuccille, Jerome, and Philip Sayetta, *The Mission: A Novel about the Flight of Rudolf Hess,* D. I. Fine (New York), 1991.

Uris, Leon, *Battle Cry,* Putnam (New York), 1953.

Uris, Leon, *Exodus,* Doubleday (Garden City, NY), 1958.

Uris, Leon, *Mila 18,* Doubleday (Garden City, NY), 1961.

Uris, Leon, *QB VII,* Doubleday (Garden City, NY), 1970.

Vonnegut, Kurt, Jr., *Mother Night,* Delacorte Press (New York), 1966.

Vonnegut, Kurt, Jr., *Slaughterhouse-Five, or, The Children's Crusade: A Duty-Dance with Death,* Dell (New York), 1968.

Vos, Ida, *Anna Is Still Here,* Houghton Mifflin (Boston), 1993.

Vos, Ida, *Hide and Seek,* translated by Terese Edelstein and Inez Smidt, Houghton Mifflin (New York), 1981.

Welt, Elly, *Berlin Wild: A Novel,* Viking (New York), 1986.

Westheimer, David, *Von Ryan's Express,* Doubleday (Garden City, NY), 1964.

Westheimer, David, *Von Ryan's Return,* Coward McCann & Geoghegan (New York), 1980.

White, Theodore, *Mountain Road,* W. Sloan (New York), 1958.

Wiesel, Elie, *The Forgotten,* Summit Books (New York), 1992.

Wiesel, Elie, *Night,* Bantam (New York), 1960.

Wiesel, Elie, *The Town Beyond the Wall: A Novel,* Schocken Books (New York), 1995.

Wilder, Billy, *Stalag 17,* University of California Press (Berkeley, CA), 1999.

Wolff, Virginia Euwer, *The Mozart Season,* Henry Holt (New York), 1991.

Wouk, Herman, *The Caine Mutiny,* Doubleday (Garden City, NY), 1951.

Wouk, Herman, *War and Remembrance,* Little, Brown (Boston), 1978.

Wouk, Herman, *The Winds of War,* Little, Brown (Boston), 1971.

Yolen, Jane, *Devil's Arithmetic,* Viking Penguin (New York), 1988.

Index

Note: This is a cumulative index for volumes 1, 2 and 3. Volumes are paginated individually. Each volume number appears in boldface italics, followed by a colon. Page numbers appearing in italic type refer to pages containing illustrations: *m* indicates a map; *c* indicates a chart; and *t* indicates a table.

Brotherhood of Sleeping Car
Porters, *2:* 105-106, 130
See also: African Americans
and World War II
Brown, Willa, *3:* 490
See also: Tuskegee Airmen
Brownshirts. *See:* Sturmabteilung
Broz, Josip *See:* Tito, Josip Broz
Bruch, Kurt aus dem, *2:* 443
Brüggeman, Max, *2:* 437
Brükner, Heinz, *2:* 438
Brundage, Avery, *1:* 59
See also: Olympic Games
Bruns, Richard Wilhelm, *2:* 428
Bruttel, Emil, *2:* 443
Brylcreem Boys, The, 2: 463
Buchenwald, *3:* 265
After *Kristallnacht, 1:* 104
"Beast of Buchenwald," *2:* 238;
3: 264, 268
Bettelheim (Bruno) experi-
ence, *3:* 23
Liberation, *1: 377; 2:* 209,
229-238, *231, 233*
Prisoners, *1: 90, 328*
Under the Kochs (Karl and
Ilse), *3:* 265
Wiesenthal (Simon) experi-
ence, *2:* 339-345
See also: Koch, Ilse; Koch, Karl
Buck Privates, 2: 460
Bühler, Josef, *2:* 429
Bulgaria, *1:* 216, 296; *2:* 204-205
Bulge (battle). *See:* Battle of the
Bulge
Bülow, Friedrich von, *2:* 440
Bund Deutscher Mädel (BDM).
See: League of German Girls
Bundestag, *2:* 422
Bundles for Britain, *2:* 25
Bunker, The, 2: 466
Bunker Hill (USS), *2:* 284
Bunuel, Lucien, *3:* 30
Bureau of Motion Pictures, *2:* 456
Bürgin, Ernst, *2:* 437
Burgraf, Medislaw, *2:* 442
Burkart, Odilo, *2:* 436
Burma, *1:* 282-283
Burma Road, *2:* 250
Bush, Vannevar, *3:* 197
See also: Atom bombs; Man-
hattan Project; Science and
technology in World War II
"Butcher of Lyon." *See:* Barbie, Klaus
Bütefisch, Heinrich, *2:* 437
Buttcher, Herbert, *2:* 429
Buzz bombs, *2:* 82-83
See also: V-1 and V-2 bombs
Bye Bye Blues, 2: 460

C

Cabanatuan, *1:* 277
"Cage, The" (torture device), *2:* 262
Cage, The (book), *1:* 379-386
Calesson, Otto, *2:* 442
California (USS), *1:* 270, 298
Camp O'Donnell, *1:* 277, 278, 279
Campbell, Captain Abbie N., *3:* 242
Canadian troops, *2:* 48-49, *49,* 51,
55-58, *58m, 63,* 64-66
Canaris, Wilhelm, *2:* 76; *3:* 28-29, *29*
Capa, Robert, *3:* 40
See also: War correspondents
Capra, Frank, *2:* 161, 456; *3: 53,* 53-
58
See also: Propaganda
Carl, Ann B., *3:* 59-64
See also: WASPs
Cartoons, *2: 184, 186; 3: 299, 302*
Casablanca (conference), *1:* 287-
288, *288; 2:* 292
Casablanca (film), *2: 162,* 459
Cassidy, Edward Idris, *1:* 92
See also: Catholic church
Cassino, *1:* 314, *315*
Catch-22, 2: 460
Catholic church, *1:* 92; *2:* 353, 356-
357
Censorship, *2:* 161
Ceylon (Sri Lanka), *2:* 254
Chamberlain, Houston Stewart, *1:*
15, 17
Chamberlain, Neville, *1: 109,* 109-
110, 138; *3: 65,* 65-67
Chambers, Norah, *2:* 264
Chan, Won-loy, *3:* 90
Chelmno (*Kulmhof*), *1:* 160-162,
173, 329-330; *2:* 428
Chetniks, *2:* 10, 11
Chiang Kai-Shek, *1: 116; 3: 68,* 68-
74, *73*
Chiang Kai-Shek, Madame, *3:* 70-
71, *71*
Child money (*Kindergeld*), *1:* 83
China, *1:* 110-118, *114, 115; 2:* 398-
399, 400
Chirac, Jacques, *1:* 445; *2:* 352
Choltitz, Dietrich von, *2:* 61, 63, 64
Christian X (King of Denmark), *1:*
401
Christmann, Kurt, *2:* 408
Chuikov, Vasili, *1:* 318
Churchill, Peter, *3:* 206-207
See also: Intelligence in World
War II
Churchill, Winston, *1: 138,* 142, *240,*
295; *3: 75,* 75-79, *77, 402*

Achievements before and after
World War II, *3:* 75
Atlantic Charter, *1:* 222-224,
285, 291
"Be Ye Men of Valour," *1:* 139,
141, 143
"Blood, Toil, Tears and Sweat,"
1: 138-141
Childhood and education, *3:*
75-76
Coiner of term "Iron Curtain,"
3: 79
On Dunkirk evacuation, *1:*
130
Early days as prime minister, *1:*
138-139, *138; 3:* 78
On importance of Battle of the
Atlantic, *1:* 233
Newfoundland Conference, *1:*
208
On Palestine, *2:* 390
Personal relationship with
Roosevelt, *1:* 286
Postwar prime minister of
Great Britain, *3:* 79
Potsdam Conference, *2:* 89,
293
Prewar political and military
career, *3:* 76
On RAF pilots saving Britain,
1: 137
With Royal Canadian Air
Force, *1:* 240
"Their Finest Hour," *1:* 139,
143, 145
"V-for-victory" sign, *1:* 139,
143; 2: 158
Voted out of office, *3:* 78
War in southeastern Europe, *2:*
45
War in the Mediterranean, *2:*
45
Wartime statesman, *3: 75,* 78
Citizen Soldiers, 2: 219-224
See also: Battle of the Bulge
Civil Air Patrol (CAP), *2:* 103-105
Civilian Defense Corps, *2: 102*
Civilian Pilots Training Program, *3:*
60
Clark, Mark, *3:* 317
Clauberg, Carl, *1:* 367, 369
Claus, Gustav, *2:* 444
Clinton, Bill, *2:* 344, *366; 3: 277*
Clock, The, 2: 460
Coast Guard auxiliary (SPARS), *3:*
406
Cochran, Jacqueline, *2: 116; 3:* 59,
60, *80,* 80-86, *81*
Cochran, Woody, *3: 336*

S

Tomara, Sonia, *2:* 168
  See also: War correspondents
Topography of Terror, *2:* 362
Topp, Erich, *1:* 239
Tora! Tora! Tora!, 2: 457
Tory, Avraham, *1:* 259-263
Touvier, Paul, *2:* 328
Town Like Alice, A, 2: 463
Train, The, 2: 464
Transition Agreement, *2:* 420
Treason law (Nazi Germany), *3:* 421
Treaty of Versailles, *1:* 10-11, *11m,*
  21, 34
Treblinka
  As death camp, *1:* 329, 332
  Demjanjuk, John, *2:* 329, 407;
    3: 119-124
  Description, *1:* 335, 337-338,
    340
  "Ivan the Terrible," *2:* 329; *3:*
    120-123
  Kaplan, Chaim A., *1:* 192
  Korczak (Janusz) and orphans,
    1: 177
  "Permanent" prisoners, *1:*
    340-341
  Stangl, Franz, *3:* 447-448
  Uprising, *1:* 341
  Willenberg rescue òf Boehm, *1:*
    340
Trinity (nuclear test site), *2:* 85
Tripartite Pact, *1:* 145, 227, *267*
Triumph of the Will, 2: 159, 455; *3:*
  381, 382
Truman Doctrine, *2:* 91
Truman, Harry S, *2: 87,* 91; *3: 482,*
  482-487, *486*
  Atom bomb decision, *2: 87,*
    87-93; *3:* 484
  Childhood and political career,
    3: 482-487
  Conflict with MacArthur, *3:*
    291
  On German surrender, *2:* 212
  Memoirs, 2: 87-93
  Potsdam Conference, *2:* 88-89,
    90, 91, *293*
  Second presidential term, *3:*
    486-487
  On surrender of Japan, *2:* 305-
    311
  Truman Doctrine, *2:* 91
  as vice president, *3:* 483
Tschentscher, Erwin, *2:* 435
Tuskegee Airmen, *2:* 107, 140; *3:*
  104-107, 488-493, *489, 490, 491*
  Action in Italy, *3: 491*
  and racial integration, *3:* 107
  Training, *3: 490*

Tuskegee Airmen, The (film), *2:* 468
Twelve O'Clock High, 2: 459

U

U-boats, *1:* 124, 209, 211-212, 233,
  233-241, *238*
U-571, 2: 455, *456*
Ukraine, *1:* 217-218
Ultra (British intelligence
  organization), *2:* 80-81
    See also: Intelligence in World
      War II
Umezu, Yoshijiro, *2:* 452
Unconditional surrender (as Allied
  war goal), *1:* 288
Union of Soviet Socialist Republics.
  See: Soviet Union
United Nations, *1: 223, 2:* 329, 390,
  396, 396-397
United Nations Charter, *2:* 411
United Nations Conference on
  International Organization, *2:*
  397
United Nations Genocide
  Convention, *2:* 411, 424
United Nations Relief and
  Rehabilitation Agency (UNRRA),
  2: 384
United Nations War Crimes
  Commission, *2:* 408
United Service Organizations
  (USO), *2: 165,* 165-167, *166; 3:*
  310, *311*
United States Army Air Corps, *2:* 23
United States Holocaust Memorial
  Museum (USHMM), *1:* 386, 460,
  2: 361, *362, 366*
UNRRA (United Nations Relief and
  Rehabilitation Agency), *2:* 384
Unterseeboots. See: U-boats
Up Front, 2: 183-187, *184, 186; 3:*
  299, 300, *302*
Uranium, *2:* 84-85, 87
Uris, Leon, *1:* 369, *2:* 358
USHMM (United States Holocaust
  Memorial Museum), *1:* 386, 460,
  2: 361, *362, 366*
USO (United Service
  Organizations), *2: 165,* 165-167,
  166; 3: 310, *311*
USS *Arizona, 1:* 270, *297, 298*
USS *Bunker Hill, 2:* 284
USS *California, 1:* 270, 298
USS *Enterprise, 1:* 284, *286*
USS *Hornet, 1:* 284
USS *Indianapolis, 2:* 288-289
USS *Lexington, 1:* 284, *285*
USS *Missouri, 2:* 298, *307*

USS *Oklahoma, 1:* 270, 298
USS *Shaw, 1: 270*
USS *Texas, 2:* 48
USS *West Virginia, 1:* 269, 270, 298,
  299
USS *Yorktown, 1:* 284
USSR. *See:* Soviet Union
Ustaše, *2:* 10, 11
Utah Beach. *See under:* Allied
  invasion of Europe

V

V-E (Victory in Europe) Day. *See:*
  Victory in Europe (V-E) Day.
"V-for-victory," *1:* 139, *143; 2:* 158
V-J (Victory over Japan) Day. *See:*
  Victory over Japan (V-J) Day.
V-Mail (Victory Mail), *2:* 126, *128*
V-1 and V-2 bombs, *2: 82,* 82-83, *83,*
  90
Va'ada, *1:* 451
Vallon, Suzanne, *3:* 117
Vatican defense of Pope Pius XXII,
  3: 364
Vatican Holocaust Declaration, *1:*
  92; *2:* 356
Vautrin, Wilhelmina "Minnie," *1:*
  117
Veesenmayer, Edmund, *2:* 419, 440
Velodrome d'Hiver (Vel' d'Hiv'), *1:*
  438, *2:* 239
Vernay, Denise, *3:* 117
Versailles Treaty. *See:* Treaty of
  Versailles
Vichy. *See under:* France
Victor Emmanuel III (King of
  Italy), *1:* 309
"Victory gardens," *2:* 98, *99,* 122
Victory in Europe (V-E) Day, *2: 211,*
  212-213, *213*
Victory over Japan (V-J) Day, *2:*
  296, 308, 309
Viermetz, Inge, *2:* 438
"Vinegar Joe." *See:* Stilwell, Joseph
  Warren
Visconti, Luchino, *2:* 360
Voelkisch, 1: 15-16
    See also: Volk
Vogt, Josef, *2:* 435
Voices of D-Day, 2: 64-71
Volk, 1: 4
    See also: Anti-Semitism
Volk, Leo, *2:* 436
Volkenrath, Elisabeth, *2:* 416, 422
von Ribbentrop, Joachim, *1:* 120; *2:*
  317, 433; *3:* 494, *494-498, 495*
Von Ryan's Express, 2: 463

W

WAAC (Women's Army Auxiliary Corps), *2: 20,* 114, *115; 3:* 240-245, 406

WAC (Women's Army Corps), *2:* 114; *3: 240,* 240-245, *242, 243, 244,* 406

Waffen-SS. See: Schutzstaffel

WAFS (Women's Auxiliary Ferrying Service), *3:* 59, 60, 82-83, 406

Wainwright, Jonathan M., *1:* 275, 276, 277, *2: 307*

Wakasa, James H., *2:* 141

Wake Island, *1:* 273

Wall, The, 2: 358

Wallenberg, Raoul Gustav, *1:* 452-460, *453, 456; 3:* 499, *499-503, 500*

Walter, Frieda, *2:* 443

Wannsee Conference, *1:* 255-257, *256, 257c,* 327, *2:* 425

War: 1939-1945, The (diary), *1:* 324-325

    See also: Rommel, Erwin

War and Remembrance, 2: 467

War bonds, *2:* 96, *97*

War correspondents, *2: 167, 168,* 168-187, *170, 177, 182m, 184, 186*

    See also: names of individual correspondents

War crimes, *2:* 313-345, 424-444

    See also: Nuremberg Trials; Tokyo Trials

War crimes trials. *See:* Nuremberg Trials; war crimes trials in European countries by name; Tokyo Trials

War crimes trials conducted by Britain. *See:* British war crimes trials

War crimes trials in European countries other than Germany, *2:* 323-324

War crimes trials in Hungary, *2:* 425-426

    See also: individual defendant names

War crimes trials in Japan. *See:* Tokyo Trials

War crimes trials in the Netherlands, *2:* 426-427

    See also: individual defendant names

War crimes trials in Norway, *2:* 427-428

    See also: individual defendant names

War crimes trials in Poland, *2:* 428-429

    See also: individual defendant names

War crimes trials in Romania, *2:* 430-431

    See also: individual defendant names

War in the Pacific. *See:* Pacific War

War Refugee Board, *1:* 456, *2:* 375, 387

    See also: American War Refugee Board

Ward, Harold, *2:* 286-287

Warlimont, Walter, *2:* 441

Warsaw ghetto, *1:* 169-204, *171, 172, 174, 178, 179, 181, 183, 184, 185, 193, 194, 195, 196, 197, 198, 199*

    "Bloody Night" massacre, *1:* 174-175

    Construction, *1:* 169

    Deportation from, *1:* 174-176

    January *Aktion, 1:* 182-183

    Jewish anti-Nazi underground, *1:* 172-175, 177-186, *202*

    Jewish Combat Organization, *1:* 201, 202

    Jewish Fighting Organization, *1:* 177-186

    Jewish Military Association, *1:* 201

    Jewish National Committee, *1:* 202

    Judenrat official, *1: 191*

    Nazi soldiers, *1: 181, 183, 184, 185*

    Oneg Shabbat Archives, *1:* 174

    Polish anti-Nazi underground, *1: 172-173,* 179-183

    Scarcity of food, *1: 172*

    Secret tunnels and smuggling, *1: 170,* 172-173

    Street scene, *1: 199*

    Stroop, Jürgen, and the SS, *1: 181*

    Uprising, *1:* 182-186, *183, 184, 185, 202*

    Wall, *1: 171, 178*

    Warsaw Ghetto: A Christian's Testimony, 1: 198-203

    ZOB, *1:* 177-186

    See also: Judenräte

Warsaw Ghetto: A Christian's Testimony, 1: 198-203

Warsaw Home Army uprising, *1:* 185; *2:* 193-194

Wartheland, *1:* 149-150

WAS (Women's Voluntary Service), *2:* 117

Wasilewska, Wanda, *2: 193*

WASP Among Eagles, A, 3: 61, 63

WASPs (Women's Airforce Service Pilots), *2:* 116; *3: 61-63, 83, 85,* 406

    Memorial, *3:* 63

    Symbol, *3: 85*

Watch on the Rhine, 2: 459

WAVES (Women Accepted for Volunteer Emergency Service), *3:* 406

We Remember: A Reflection on the Shoah, 1: 92, *2:* 356

Webb, William F., *2:* 445, 447

Weglyn, Michiko Nishiura, *3: 504,* 504-508

    See also: Internment of Japanese Americans; Nisei

Wehrmacht (German armed forces), *1:* 86

Weichs, Maximilian von, *2:* 437

Weimar Coalition, *1:* 10

Weimar Republic, *1:* 10, 28

Weinbacher, Karl, *2:* 416, 417

Weingartner, Peter, *2:* 441

Weiss, Bernhard, *2:* 436

Weizsäcker, Ernst von, *2:* 419, 440

Weizsäcker, Richard von, *2:* 349

We'll Meet Again, 2: 468

Wels, Otto, *1:* 43

Werner, Herbert A., *1:* 233-241

West Germany, *2:* 347-350, *392m,* 392-393

    Adoption of United Nations Genocide Convention, *2:* 424

    Allied Control Council, *2:* 420-421

    Allied occupation strategy, *2:* 230, *292m*

    Allied occupation zones, *2: 392m,* 392-393

    Bundestag, *2:* 422

    Dilemma of condemning Nazi "desk criminals," *2:* 424

    Federal Republic of Germany, *2:* 421

    Ludwigsburger Zentralstelle, 2: 422-423

    Neo-Nazis, *2:* 350

    Silence about the Holocaust, *2:* 347-349

    Social Democratic party, *2:* 422

    War crimes prosecution, *2:* 422-423, 425

    See also: Cold War; German Democratic Republic

West Virginia (USS), *1: 269,* 270, 298, *299*